Lecture Notes in Computer Science 12210

More information about this series at http://www.springer.com/series/7409

Abbas Moallem (Ed.)

HCI for Cybersecurity, Privacy and Trust

Second International Conference, HCI-CPT 2020
Held as Part of the 22nd HCI International Conference, HCII 2020
Copenhagen, Denmark, July 19–24, 2020
Proceedings

 Springer

Editor
Abbas Moallem
San Jose State University
San Jose, CA, USA

ISSN 0302-9743   ISSN 1611-3349   (electronic)
Lecture Notes in Computer Science
ISBN 978-3-030-50308-6   ISBN 978-3-030-50309-3   (eBook)
https://doi.org/10.1007/978-3-030-50309-3

LNCS Sublibrary: SL3 – Information Systems and Applications, incl. Internet/Web, and HCI

This Springer imprint is published by the registered company Springer Nature Switzerland AG
The registered company address is: Gewerbestrasse 11, 6330 Cham, Switzerland

Foreword

The 22nd International Conference on Human-Computer Interaction, HCI International 2020 (HCII 2020), was planned to be held at the AC Bella Sky Hotel and Bella Center, Copenhagen, Denmark, during July 19–24, 2020. Due to the COVID-19 coronavirus pandemic and the resolution of the Danish government not to allow events larger than 500 people to be hosted until September 1, 2020, HCII 2020 had to be held virtually. It incorporated the 21 thematic areas and affiliated conferences listed on the following page.

A total of 6,326 individuals from academia, research institutes, industry, and governmental agencies from 97 countries submitted contributions, and 1,439 papers and 238 posters were included in the conference proceedings. These contributions address the latest research and development efforts and highlight the human aspects of design and use of computing systems. The contributions thoroughly cover the entire field of human-computer interaction, addressing major advances in knowledge and effective use of computers in a variety of application areas. The volumes constituting the full set of the conference proceedings are listed in the following pages.

The HCI International (HCII) conference also offers the option of "late-breaking work" which applies both for papers and posters and the corresponding volume(s) of the proceedings will be published just after the conference. Full papers will be included in the "HCII 2020 - Late Breaking Papers" volume of the proceedings to be published in the Springer LNCS series, while poster extended abstracts will be included as short papers in the "HCII 2020 - Late Breaking Posters" volume to be published in the Springer CCIS series.

I would like to thank the program board chairs and the members of the program boards of all thematic areas and affiliated conferences for their contribution to the highest scientific quality and the overall success of the HCI International 2020 conference.

This conference would not have been possible without the continuous and unwavering support and advice of the founder, Conference General Chair Emeritus and Conference Scientific Advisor Prof. Gavriel Salvendy. For his outstanding efforts, I would like to express my appreciation to the communications chair and editor of HCI International News, Dr. Abbas Moallem.

July 2020   Constantine Stephanidis

HCI International 2020 Thematic Areas
and Affiliated Conferences

Thematic areas:

- HCI 2020: Human-Computer Interaction
- HIMI 2020: Human Interface and the Management of Information

Affiliated conferences:

- EPCE: 17th International Conference on Engineering Psychology and Cognitive Ergonomics
- UAHCI: 14th International Conference on Universal Access in Human-Computer Interaction
- VAMR: 12th International Conference on Virtual, Augmented and Mixed Reality
- CCD: 12th International Conference on Cross-Cultural Design
- SCSM: 12th International Conference on Social Computing and Social Media
- AC: 14th International Conference on Augmented Cognition
- DHM: 11th International Conference on Digital Human Modeling and Applications in Health, Safety, Ergonomics and Risk Management
- DUXU: 9th International Conference on Design, User Experience and Usability
- DAPI: 8th International Conference on Distributed, Ambient and Pervasive Interactions
- HCIBGO: 7th International Conference on HCI in Business, Government and Organizations
- LCT: 7th International Conference on Learning and Collaboration Technologies
- ITAP: 6th International Conference on Human Aspects of IT for the Aged Population
- HCI-CPT: Second International Conference on HCI for Cybersecurity, Privacy and Trust
- HCI-Games: Second International Conference on HCI in Games
- MobiTAS: Second International Conference on HCI in Mobility, Transport and Automotive Systems
- AIS: Second International Conference on Adaptive Instructional Systems
- C&C: 8th International Conference on Culture and Computing
- MOBILE: First International Conference on Design, Operation and Evaluation of Mobile Communications
- AI-HCI: First International Conference on Artificial Intelligence in HCI

Conference Proceedings Volumes Full List

1. LNCS 12181, Human-Computer Interaction: Design and User Experience (Part I), edited by Masaaki Kurosu
2. LNCS 12182, Human-Computer Interaction: Multimodal and Natural Interaction (Part II), edited by Masaaki Kurosu
3. LNCS 12183, Human-Computer Interaction: Human Values and Quality of Life (Part III), edited by Masaaki Kurosu
4. LNCS 12184, Human Interface and the Management of Information: Designing Information (Part I), edited by Sakae Yamamoto and Hirohiko Mori
5. LNCS 12185, Human Interface and the Management of Information: Interacting with Information (Part II), edited by Sakae Yamamoto and Hirohiko Mori
6. LNAI 12186, Engineering Psychology and Cognitive Ergonomics: Mental Workload, Human Physiology, and Human Energy (Part I), edited by Don Harris and Wen-Chin Li
7. LNAI 12187, Engineering Psychology and Cognitive Ergonomics: Cognition and Design (Part II), edited by Don Harris and Wen-Chin Li
8. LNCS 12188, Universal Access in Human-Computer Interaction: Design Approaches and Supporting Technologies (Part I), edited by Margherita Antona and Constantine Stephanidis
9. LNCS 12189, Universal Access in Human-Computer Interaction: Applications and Practice (Part II), edited by Margherita Antona and Constantine Stephanidis
10. LNCS 12190, Virtual, Augmented and Mixed Reality: Design and Interaction (Part I), edited by Jessie Y. C. Chen and Gino Fragomeni
11. LNCS 12191, Virtual, Augmented and Mixed Reality: Industrial and Everyday Life Applications (Part II), edited by Jessie Y. C. Chen and Gino Fragomeni
12. LNCS 12192, Cross-Cultural Design: User Experience of Products, Services, and Intelligent Environments (Part I), edited by P. L. Patrick Rau
13. LNCS 12193, Cross-Cultural Design: Applications in Health, Learning, Communication, and Creativity (Part II), edited by P. L. Patrick Rau
14. LNCS 12194, Social Computing and Social Media: Design, Ethics, User Behavior, and Social Network Analysis (Part I), edited by Gabriele Meiselwitz
15. LNCS 12195, Social Computing and Social Media: Participation, User Experience, Consumer Experience, and Applications of Social Computing (Part II), edited by Gabriele Meiselwitz
16. LNAI 12196, Augmented Cognition: Theoretical and Technological Approaches (Part I), edited by Dylan D. Schmorrow and Cali M. Fidopiastis
17. LNAI 12197, Augmented Cognition: Human Cognition and Behaviour (Part II), edited by Dylan D. Schmorrow and Cali M. Fidopiastis

http://2020.hci.international/proceedings

Second International Conference on HCI for Cybersecurity, Privacy and Trust (HCI-CPT 2020)

Program Board Chair: **Abbas Moallem, San Jose State University, USA**

- Mohd Anwar, USA
- Xavier Bellekens, UK
- Jorge Bernal Bernabe, Spain
- Ulku Clark, USA
- Francisco Corella, USA
- Steven Furnell, UK
- Sebastian Korfmacher, Germany
- Nathan Lau, USA
- Karen Lewison, USA
- Phillip L. Morgan, UK

- Jason Nurse, UK
- Henrich C. Pöhls, Germany
- Sascha Preibisch, Canada
- Kazue Sako, Japan
- Hossein Sarrafzadeh, USA
- David Schuster, USA
- Ralf C. Staudemeyer, Germany
- Adam Wójtowicz, Poland
- Sherali Zeadally, USA

The full list with the Program Board Chairs and the members of the Program Boards of all thematic areas and affiliated conferences is available online at:

http://www.hci.international/board-members-2020.php

HCI International 2021

The 23rd International Conference on Human-Computer Interaction, HCI International 2021 (HCII 2021), will be held jointly with the affiliated conferences in Washington DC, USA, at the Washington Hilton Hotel, July 24–29, 2021. It will cover a broad spectrum of themes related to Human-Computer Interaction (HCI), including theoretical issues, methods, tools, processes, and case studies in HCI design, as well as novel interaction techniques, interfaces, and applications. The proceedings will be published by Springer. More information will be available on the conference website: http://2021.hci.international/.

General Chair
Prof. Constantine Stephanidis
University of Crete and ICS-FORTH
Heraklion, Crete, Greece
Email: general_chair@hcii2021.org

http://2021.hci.international/

Contents

Privacy and Trust

Usable Security Approaches

Human Factors in Cybersecurity

Awareness and Working Knowledge of Secure Design Principles: A User Study

May Almousa[1], Mahsa Keshavarz[2], and Mohd Anwar[1(✉)]

[1] North Carolina A&T State University, Greensboro, NC 27401, USA
manwar@ncat.edu
[2] Northern Arizona University, Flagstaff, AZ 86011, USA

Abstract. Software systems are everywhere, and therefore, software security breaches impact every enterprise system. Although the software engineers and system developers are provided with various secure software development guidelines and processes, attacks exploiting software vulnerabilities are on the rise. The prevalence of software vulnerabilities and the increasing number of hacked enterprise systems underline the need for guidance in the design and implementation of secure software. If the software engineers and system developers consider applying and implementing the Secure Design Principles (SDPs), the enterprise systems would be secured against many types of attacks. In this research, we conducted a survey study among participants who have experience in designing and/or developing software (such as native application, browser application, or mobile application) to test their familiarity and working knowledge of SDPs. We also explored if the demographic variables (age, gender, experience, education) are associated with their knowledge of SDPs. We also discovered misconception of secure design principles and gathered participants' opinions on the ways to implement SDPs.

Keywords: Secure software engineering · Secure design principles · Survey · Software developers

1 Introduction

Nowadays, IT systems and software are predominantly used to conduct many types of critical and important business and operational tasks. In many industries, such as healthcare, banking, finance, government, and e-commerce, the information stored and communicated using IT systems is of confidential nature [8]. The confidential nature of such information requires adoption of well-designed security mechanisms in systems and software tools to keep the private and confidential data of individuals and organizations protected from malicious attacks, and unauthorized access.

In the software and system development field, security refers to the process of implementing special purpose mechanisms that ensure confidentiality, availability, and integrity of the system and information objects. Information security is a

© Springer Nature Switzerland AG 2020
A. Moallem (Ed.): HCII 2020, LNCS 12210, pp. 3–15, 2020.
https://doi.org/10.1007/978-3-030-50309-3_1

continuous process in a system that aims to maintain availability, confidentiality, and integrity of the data stored or communicated by the system. With security mechanisms, system developers target three key components of security:

- **Integrity:** Ensuring that information is protected from being modified by unauthorized users.
- **Confidentiality:** Concealment of system's resources, information, and process against unauthorized access. It mainly refers to access control mechanisms, which depend on policies of allowing or not allowing system access requests.
- **Availability:** Availability requires a system to be accessible for the authorized users.

In the field of software development, standardization of security mechanism exists in different forms such as certification, encryption strength, authentication metrics, etc. Together with the security standards, the software engineers and system developers are expected to follow some secure design principles that recommend best practices in implementation of security measures in a system.

In this research, we conducted a survey to examine the familiarity and understanding of secure design principles among participants who have experience in designing and/or developing software.

Our contribution in this paper is to discover whether the software engineers and developers are aware of and have working knowledge of the Secure Design Principles. Also, our study investigates correlation between the knowledge gap (e.g., examine the association and the demographic variables such as age, gender, experience, education and the lack of knowledge of Secure Design Principles).

This paper is organized as follows. Section 2 provides background information on secure design principles. Section 3 contains a discussion of related work, and in Sect. 4, we discuss our approach on the study. In Sect. 5 we present our results, and lastly, Sect. 6 concludes with a recommendation for future work.

2   Background Information

In the field of information systems, principles of secure design (also known as secure design principles) operate as fundamental concepts that define the ways various security mechanisms should be designed and implemented. The scope of principles of secure design is not limited to just the technological aspects, rather it also accounts for the human factor aspects of the system mechanism. Many of the commonly adopted principles of secure design are derived from factors of non-technical aspect of the system, such as the principle of least privilege. Each of the security design principle establishes some level of restriction in allocating privileges on basis of specific criterions or attempts to minimize the level of complexity in security mechanism to reduce probability of failure in the security mechanism [10]. According to [11], the secure design principles (SDPs) are as follows:

- Principle of Least Privilege: In accordance with the secure design principle of least privilege, a user should always be allocated only the access privileges that are absolutely needed by the user to complete the assigned tasks. The first line of defense of in security is applying principle of least privilege to access controls.
- Principle of Fail-Safe Defaults: According to this secure design principle, as a default system behavior, the system should deny a user access to an object unless a user is explicitly provided access to that object. In addition, principle of fail-safe defaults assures the ability of a user to rollback. For example, if a user tries to complete a transaction and the system fails, the system should be able to rollback.
- Principle of Economy of Mechanism: This security design principle states that design of a security mechanism implemented in a system should always strive to remain as simple as possible.
- Principle of Complete Mediation: The security mechanism implemented by this principle requires that system must verify every access request to every object before allowing access. In another words, every access request should be mediated by the system.
- Principle of Open Design (Security by Obscurity): This principle stipulates that the level of security achieved by a mechanism should not depend on the secrecy of its design or deployment method.
- Principle of Separation of Privilege: As per this principle of secure design, in design of a system, access to an object should not be granted on the basis of a single access criterion getting satisfied.
- Principle of Least Common Mechanism: This principle of secure design requires that the mechanisms that are used to access resources should not be shared.
- Principle of Psychological Acceptability: This principle argues that human interface needs to be designed for ease of use so that users routinely and correctly apply the protection mechanisms.

The prevalence of software vulnerabilities and the increasing number of hacked systems show the high demand to improve the development of secure software. If the software engineers and system developers consider applying and implementing these SDPs, their systems would be secured against many types of attacks.

3   Related Work

Secure Design Principles provide a general guideline to the system developers in designing of security mechanisms, which are applicable for a wide variety of software, web-tool, system, and application development processes [2]. The Secure Design Principles exist as an abstract concept rather than a specific requirement, allowing flexible and convenient adoption of the principles of secure design.

The secure design principles are also applicable on the networking and communication protocols. The versatility of secure design principles is useful for deployment of security mechanisms in interconnected world of Internet of Things (IoT) [7]. The use of design principles enables networking protocols to achieve security while being lightweight and less burdensome on utilization of resources.

The secure design principles also emphasize practicality of the secure systems. It is the theme of secure design principles that targets simplicity and thoroughness in security mechanisms [1]. In this manner, the secure design principles require security mechanisms to not com-promise with usability or performance of a system.

The US Department of Defense (DoD) widely uses secure design principles for computer security. Some of the security experts like [11] list secure design principles as a set of precisely worded statements. Others refer to these principles as a collection of fundamental concepts. Since the first release of secure design principles, more principles have been added such as easiest penetration, weakest link, effectiveness, and adequate protection, which demonstrates a wider scope of security thinking. However, Smith (2012) [13] believes that in modern information security, some of these principles such as economy of mechanism, complete mediation and psychological acceptability do not play a central role. Economy of mechanism has been left far behind in both the profit-oriented and free software communities. Due to the distributed nature of modern net-work security, complete mediation has become impractical. Higher cost is a likely trade-off when deciding to adopt the security measures that has "psychological acceptability," which has more importance now.

Understanding the secure design principles is a big challenge. Reference [6] observes that access control, which is related to principle complete mediation, is a big challenge in organizations. Developing a shared understanding of policy between different stakeholders is a daunting task. The reason is that those who make policies are not the same as those who implement these policies. In [6] 12 semi-structured interviews with security practitioners were conducted using a new interface named AuthzMap to realize how people make sense, review access of users, and to identify the challenges in reviewing implemented access policies. The other challenge is expressing policies in role-based access control (RBAC) for resource owners. Authors of [5] discussed about this issue and used natural language to solve this problem. For understanding effective access policy in case of conflicting access rules, [9] proposed a new UI named "expandable grid". Expandable grid helps end-users of commodity Operating Systems to understand the access policy and solved the issue of conflicting access rules that happened in Windows file system.

Researchers [15,16] describe principles for secure systems design with an emphasis on groupware and believe that a reason for this concern is a lack of principles of secure information system designs that may be used when selecting or creating control measures. Most security experts agree that security by secrecy is a flawed tactic as there is a chance of threats going undetected [4]. Sistla et al. (2008) [12], designed a verification technique to check for the satisfaction of complete mediation property directly on code from Java standard libraries.

Issues such as lack of knowledge and not paying attention to principles will cause security violations. For example, [3] studied on design flows of SmartApps. They discovered that although SmartApps implements a separation of privilege, principle of least privilege is not considered, and this causes design flaws. The results estimate that over 55% of SmartApps in the store are over-privileged.

Syverson (1996) [14] discusses the limitations of design principles for cryptographic protocols. The paper illustrates the limitations by examining principles involving the encryption of signed data or signing of encrypted data. This paper concluded that it is better to use design principles at the beginning for guiding the preliminary design, in the middle by looking at the motivation for applying the principle to see if the motivation best served by following the principle or not, and at the end of designing a protocol to check that there is no possibility for violating the design.

4   Study Design

Nowadays, there are significant increase in the number of flaws and security vulnerabilities in different software and systems. Software developers spend years releasing patches and updates to fix the design flaws in an ongoing basis.

A reason behind high number of flaws and security issues being present in software is attributed to extensively complex software structure. Another reason is the lack of information or awareness of best practices such as secure design principles, which contributed significantly to the flaws and security issues in systems.

Our research study attempts to assess whether software developers or designers lack awareness and knowledge of the secure design principles. To test this argument, a questionnaire-based survey method was utilized with the objective of identifying the level of familiarity with principles of secure design among software engineering students and software developers. Analysis of answers provided by the survey participants will reveal whether or not secure design principles are applied by software developers.

4.1   Survey Design

To achieve the goal of this study, we only recruited people who have experience in software engineering and development. The survey started with informed consent, where our participants can agree or disagree to participate in the survey. The first set of survey questions are related to the participants' demographic information such as age, gender, experience, and education. The main part of the survey included 30 questions designed to gain insights into knowledge, familiarity, and use of the secure design principles among participants. To gain most accurate information from the participants, questions will be asked in different forms, including open-ended questions, and rating scale based questions (on 1–5 Likert scale items - strongly agree, agree, undecided, disagree, and strongly degree). These are some samples Likert items of the survey:

- By default, the user should have full access rights (e.g., Read-Write-Delete).
- Applying more security mechanisms will help your system to be more secure
- The simplicity in design and implementation of software is helpful for decreasing the possibilities of system errors.
- A security mechanism depends on secrecy of its design or implementation.
- Unless a user has explicitly been given access to an object, it should be denied access to that object.
- If a user has been verified in the system once, the users should be treated as a valid user for subsequent requests without the need for further verification.
- A secure design principle restricts a user from reassigning or sharing privilege with another user.
- A secure software system should have a minimum number of mechanisms.

4.2 Survey Sample

To avoid any kind of bias in the data collection process, participants were selected belonging to different age and education levels. Also, we used random selection to reduce skewness. The objective of the survey is to get insights into knowledge of principles of secure design among software engineers with experience of software designing, therefore, only participants over the age of 19 were accepted as participants. In the survey, all the participants are located in the USA and they included 18 computer science graduate students and 33 software developers and engineers working in the industry. The students were recruited through flyers that were distributed among the computer science graduate students at North Carolina A&T State University. The inclusion criteria were that the students should have experience in software engineering and development. The students experience in software development and security, and their knowledge of design principles can be gained from the courses that they took during their studies in graduate and undergraduate levels. The flyer is also posted in the Amazon Mechanical Turk (MTurk) website.

For a research study to get accurate results from a sample population, it is very important avoid selection bias. Keeping this into consideration, 33 participants got selected in an automated random manner by hiring services of Amazon Mechanical Turk. This platform has millions of users ready to take a survey. However, we put premium qualifications for the Amazon Mechanical Turk workers. So, only workers with the chosen qualifications can access the survey link.

4.3 Survey Distribution

The survey was distributed among all volunteers who met the inclusion (software engineers/software developers or graduate level software engineering students) and exclusion criteria (English speaking participants only). To make the survey more convenient for the participants, we used a popular digital survey platform "Survey-Monkey". We collected 51 responses form the participants. All the participants – students and MTurk workers received $5.00 gift card after completing the survey.

5   Results

The 51 participants in this research survey covered a wide range of demographics. The most popular age category was 25 to 34 (42%), but 18 to 24 and 35 to 44 were also strongly represented at 18% and 28% respectively (as shown in Fig. 1 below). The remaining 12% was split evenly between 45–54 and 55–64. Both females and males were represented at 30% and 70%, respectively.

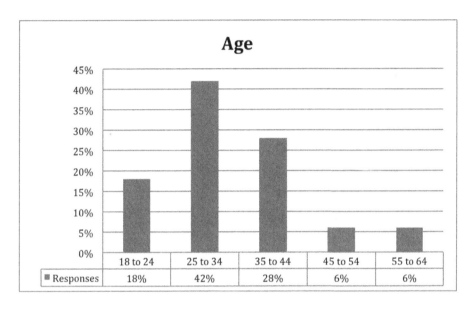

Fig. 1. Distribution of participants' age groups

Education was predominantly at a bachelor's degree level (59%); 22% were at master's degree Level and 12% at PhD degree level. Those below a bachelor's degree reported being at an associate degree level (8%) (as shown in Fig. 2 below).

The self-described level of experience in developing software was mostly Intermediate (57%) with a slight skew to Advanced (27%) over Low (16%). Quantitatively, reported years of experience in software design and development showed a similar distribution with the highest reported category being 1–3 years (35%), and high levels of representation all the way to 10% in 10+ years. Only 15% of respondents had less than one year of experience.

The results from this survey highlighted many areas where there is currently a misunderstanding of secure design principles. For the 28 multiple-choice questions, only 23% of respondents were both correct and confident. Another 31% were correct but not quite confident (e.g. "Agree" instead of "Strongly Agree"). Consequently, the remaining 46% of responses were either uncertain or incorrect. The "easiest" question in the set still only had 51% of respondents answering

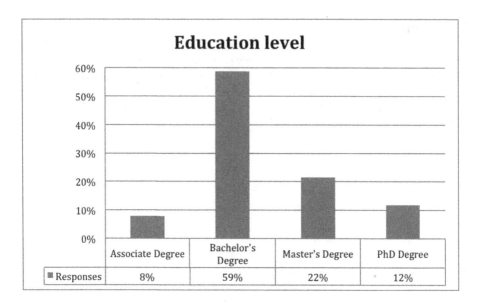

Fig. 2. Distribution of participants' education level

correctly; the "most difficult" question saw no respondent answering correctly. Figure 3 below demonstrates the participant's performance in a box-whisker plot.

It can be tested whether respondent performance depends upon education level. First, to investigate if there is any performance difference between respondents with Associate and bachelor's degrees, we conducted a t-test where the null hypothesis is that there is no significant performance difference between these two groups; the alternative hypothesis is that there is significant performance differences between the respondents of two education levels. Using the mean performances of Associate (56%) and Bachelor's (53%) degrees, we computed a t-value magnitude of 0.36. Since the critical magnitude for a two-sided test with 95% confidence is 2.04, the null hypothesis cannot be rejected; the performance of Associate and Bachelor's degrees are not discernibly different.

A similar analysis can be conducted to test if Master/PhD degrees perform better than that of Bachelor's degrees. The null hypothesis is that average performances are equal; the alternative hypothesis is that master/PhD degrees outperform Bachelor degrees. Comparing the mean performances of Bachelor's (53%) and Master/PhD (55%), the associated t-value is 0.80. The critical magnitude for a one-sided test with 95% confidence is 1.68. Therefore, the null hypothesis cannot be rejected; the data does not suggest Master/PhD degrees perform better than Bachelor's degrees.

An ANOVA was used to test if any of the levels of experience influences performance. The null hypothesis is that all levels of experience perform equally well; the alternative hypothesis is that at least one of the categories performs differently than the rest. Starting with the less than 1 year experience category

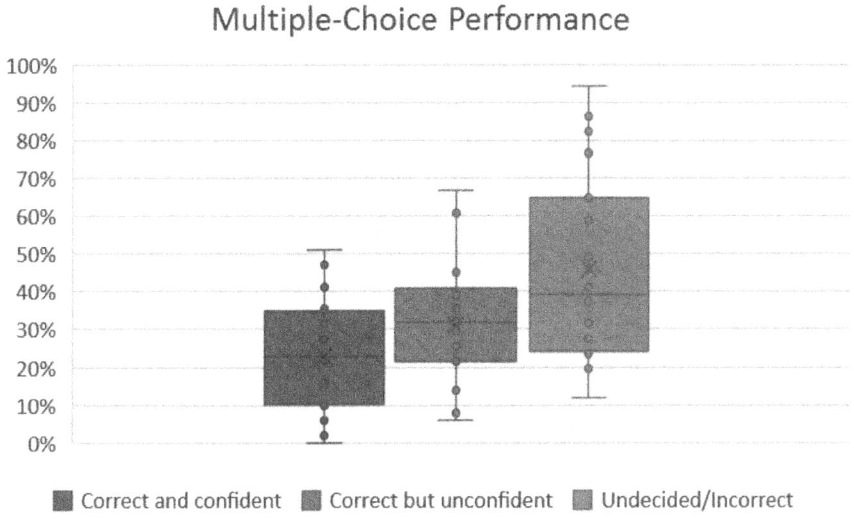

Multiple-Choice Performance

Fig. 3. The participants' performance on the Likert scale questionnaire

and progressing to 10+ years, the mean performances are 52%, 54%, 55%, 56%, and 51%. The computed F-value is 0.17, less than the F-critical of 2.57. Therefore, the null hypothesis cannot be rejected; no level of experience is discernibly different in terms of the knowledge of secure design principles than the rest.

On the matching question on the definition of some secure design principles, there was only 50% correctness on three of the five assignments, though, the most popular answer for each assignment was correct. This is again only marginally better than random selection.

The most troubling multiple-choice question on the knowledge of least privilege principle was "Access rights of users should be assigned based on their roles (higher role, more access rights)". Here 53% of respondents agreed and a further 35% strongly agreed, opposed to the correct answer (only access rights should be assigned that are required for assigned tasks): strongly disagree (0%), suggesting that there is an overemphasis on the importance of user roles in the granting of access rights.

Three other questions were also widely mistaken and showed a common theme of knowledge gap:

- A complex security model ensures a secure software;
- More security mechanisms will always help a system to be more secure;
- A secure software system should have a minimum number of mechanisms.

For these questions only 6% (age group: 25–34), 2% (age group: 25–34), and 6% (age group: 25–34) of responses were fully correct, significantly outweighed by the 78–88% undecided or incorrect. It appears there is an enormous gap in understanding the primary design components of a secure mechanism and how that is best carried out in practice.

The question most correctly answered by respondents (51%) was a disagreement to the following statement: by default, the user should have full access rights (e.g., Read-Write-Delete); still, 27% of respondents were either uncertain or incorrect.

No other question received more than 50% correctness, but following pattern emerged when looking at the next best-answered questions:

- It's better to grant a user a range of access rights (e.g., Read-Write-Delete), even if the user does not need all;
- Unless a user has explicitly been given access to an object, it should be denied access to that object;
- A secure design principle restricts a user from reassigning or sharing privilege with another user.
- Respondents were best able to recognize that permissions should be granted carefully and only for specific reason.

Grouping the questions by principle and analyzing performance, the Principles of Psychological Acceptability and Separation of Privilege were the two most frequently correct answers at 60.8%. The most incorrectly answered questions covered the Principles of Least Common Mechanism and Economy of Mechanism, with only 46.8% and 44.1% correct responses. The other four principles fell in the middle, between 54% and 60% (as shown in Fig. 4).

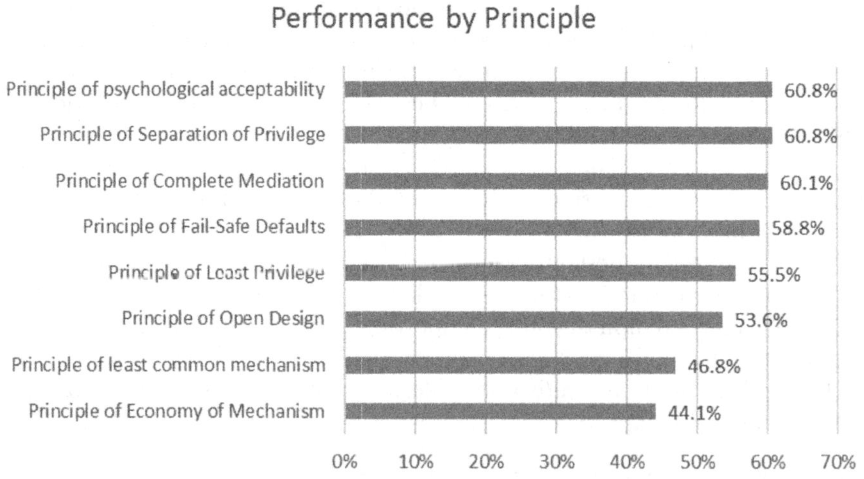

Performance by Principle

Fig. 4. The participants' performance for each principle

Of the five questions where a design principle to be matched with their appropriate description, economy of mechanism was most correct (73%). In subsequent order of recognition were: least privilege (60%), complete mediation (59%), separation of privilege (35%), and fail-safe defaults (32%).

Statistically, the results are better than random chance, but what these results seem to highlight most is how unique and recognizable the names of the principles are, rather than any previous knowledge of the principles. In the multiple-choice questions, a prevalent and erroneous view was that secure systems would have greater quantity and more complex mechanisms in place than that of non-secure systems. This reveals the inability of respondents to correctly identify the economy of mechanism, the most correct choice of the five principles by far.

One possible metric of respondents' interests in the secure design principles perhaps is the length of responses to the essay question. The question asked was, "what should be done to ensure that secure design principles are applied in developing software?" We received a response from 46 of the 51 participants. Of those who responded, only 19 provided a substantial answer with more than 100 characters; 15 were between 30 and 100 characters, and 12 were fewer than 30 characters (as shown in Fig. 5).

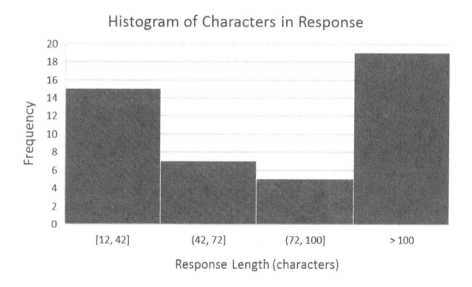

Fig. 5. The number of characters per response

The quality of the answers was comparable with the results from the previous sections. It evidenced the misunderstanding of secure design principles and the absence of knowledge on the topic seen in short, generic statements without mention of underlying fundamentals. Some of the meaningful/concrete suggestions from participants were:

– A balance of usability and security in needed since programmers lean on usability too much thus throwing security out of the window.

- Software development companies need security experts that are available to do testing, and make sure that resources are being used accurately, and safely to prevent risks to user's data.
- Companies with software developers should have a training program held every 1 to 2 years for its employees.
- Use of agile software development model help the developers to design, test, implement, and review to achieve better security.
- Computer security is a continuous process dealing with confidentiality, integrity, and availability on multiple layers of a system.
- Financial penalties for those who don't do follow the secure design principles will force them to follow all the principles carefully.

6 Conclusion and Future Work

In conclusion, security of software systems has a huge impact on our life. That is why it is important for software developers and engineers to apply best practices such as secure design principles and understand all principles of secure design. In this paper we conducted a survey study to gauge if the software developers are aware of or have working knowledge of the important secure design principles. This study is very important, because there are many attackers who exploit software vulnerabilities due to lack of knowledge of software developers. In this paper, we gathered participants of different age, gender, education levels, and levels of experience in developing software. Our participants include 18 computer science students and 33 software engineers recruited from MTurk.

In this study various questions were asked to measure the participants' knowledge. By analyzing the results of this survey, we conclude that there is a knowledge gap in secure design principles. It is shown that software developers are not familiar with the concept of secure design principles or they do not know how to apply and follow them in system design phase. We need to work more on the problem of how we can improve the software engineers' knowledge to prevent security violations in the systems. Also, we need to make sure that there is enough training, having knowledge about these principles is not enough. This is a first step to understand the level of awareness of these principles, and further studies are needed to understand more and find the ways to improve knowledge.

In the future, we plan to conduct a large-scale study and re-evaluate the current survey instrument as well as test different hypotheses on the contributing factors to the observed knowledge gaps. We will also consider the experience levels of the participants in terms of different types of software development environments as well as the types of software developed.

References

1. Benzel, T.V., Irvine, C.E., Levin, T.E., Bhaskara, G., Nguyen, T.D., Clark, P.C.: Design principles for security. Technical report, Naval Postgraduate School Monterey CA Department Of Computer Science (2005)

2. Bishop, M.: Computer Security: Art and Science. Addison Wesley Professional, Westford (2003)
3. Fernandes, E., Jung, J., Prakash, A.: Security analysis of emerging smart home applications. In: 2016 IEEE Symposium on Security and Privacy (SP), pp. 636–654. IEEE (2016)
4. Hole, K.J., Moen, V., Tjostheim, T.: Case study: online banking security. IEEE Secur. Priv. **4**(2), 14–20 (2006)
5. Inglesant, P., Sasse, M.A., Chadwick, D., Shi, L.L.: Expressions of expertness: the virtuous circle of natural language for access control policy specification. In: Proceedings of the 4th symposium on Usable privacy and security, pp. 77–88 (2008)
6. Jaferian, P., Rashtian, H., Beznosov, K.: To authorize or not authorize: helping users review access policies in organizations. In: 10th Symposium on Usable Privacy and Security ({SOUPS} 2014), pp. 301–320 (2014)
7. McGraw, G.: Software Security: Building Security In, 1st edn. Addison-Wesley Professional, Westford (2006). (Paperback) (Addison-Wesley Professional)
8. Medvidovic, N., Taylor, R.N.: Software architecture: foundations, theory, and practice. In: 2010 ACM/IEEE 32nd International Conference on Software Engineering, vol. 2, pp. 471–472. IEEE (2010)
9. Reeder, R.W., et al.: Expandable grids for visualizing and authoring computer security policies. In: Proceedings of the SIGCHI Conference on Human Factors in Computing Systems, pp. 1473–1482 (2008)
10. Saltzer, J., et al.: On the naming and binding of network destinations. In: Local Computer Networks, pp. 311–317 (1993)
11. Saltzer, J.H., Schroeder, M.D.: The protection of information in computer systems. Proc. IEEE **63**(9), 1278–1308 (1975)
12. Sistla, A.P., Venkatakrishnan, V., Zhou, M., Branske, H.: CMV: automatic verification of complete mediation for java virtual machines. In: Proceedings of the 2008 ACM Symposium on Information, Computer and Communications Security, pp. 100–111 (2008)
13. Smith, R.E.: A contemporary look at Saltzer and Schroeder's 1975 design principles. IEEE Secur. Priv. **10**(6), 20–25 (2012)
14. Syverson, P.: Limitations on design principles for public key protocols. In: Proceedings 1996 IEEE Symposium on Security and Privacy, pp. 62–72. IEEE (1996)
15. Wood, C.C.: Principles of secure information systems design. Comput. Secur. **9**(1), 13–24 (1990)
16. Wood, C.C.: Principles of secure information systems design with groupware examples. Comput. Secur. **12**(7), 663–678 (1993)

The Impact of Gamification Factor in the Acceptance of Cybersecurity Awareness Augmented Reality Game (CybAR)

Hamed Alqahtani[1]([✉]), Manolya Kavakli-Thorne[1], and Majed Alrowaily[2]

[1] Macquarie University, Sydney, Australia
hsqahtani@kku.edu.sa
[2] Tabuk University, Tabuk, Saudi Arabia

Abstract. Human behavior is considered to be the weakest link in the field of cybersecurity. Despite the development of a wide range of Augmented Reality (AR) applications in various domains, no AR application is available to educate users and increase their awareness of cybersecurity issues. Thus, we developed a game based on AR techniques as an Android app called CybAR. Since there have been few acceptance studies in the field of AR, it was particularly important to identify the factors that affect user acceptance of AR technology. This paper aims to identify whether gamification features influence users' acceptance of the CybAR app and increase their cybersecurity awareness. The predictors of CybAR app usage were derived from the extended unified theory of acceptance and usage of technology (UTAUT2) with the addition of the gamification factor. In this paper, we present the preliminary results of a study addressing the impact of gamification features on acceptance of the CybAR game. The theoretical model was tested in a quantitative study using structural equation modelling, conducted in Australia, with 95 Macquarie University students. The findings indicate that there is a significant relationship between gamification factors and behavioural intention to use the CybAR app and actual use of the CybAR app.

Keywords: Cybersecurity · Gamification · Behavioural analysis

1 Introduction

While digital technology has enabled innovation, economic growth and productivity, it has also led to a dramatic increase in the number of cyber-attacks. Several recent incidents of cyber-attack resulted in substantial financial losses to a number of organizations [32]. Security professionals and researchers are therefore expending considerable effort to identify effective methods of increasing cybersecurity awareness [14]. In this context, gamification is seen as a promising technology that can be integrated with cybersecurity awareness training to tackle cybersecurity threats. Gamification can be defined as the application of game design principles in non-gaming contexts [35]. The current project was

© Springer Nature Switzerland AG 2020
A. Moallem (Ed.): HCII 2020, LNCS 12210, pp. 16–31, 2020.
https://doi.org/10.1007/978-3-030-50309-3_2

motivated by the lack of research into the use of gamification through mobile augmented reality (AR) techniques as an educational tool about cybersecurity threats, with the aim of raising overall cybersecurity awareness. For this purpose, an AR based game, CybAR, was developed for the Android platform to build cybersecurity awareness. The main features of our AR game are its interactivity and its graphic presentation of the negative consequences of careless cybersecurity behavior. Previous research on AR acceptance factors is scarce, leaving an almost unexplored area of research. The UTAUT2 model was selected for use in the present study since it incorporates the gamification feature construct, thus providing opportunity for new insights into factors affecting the acceptance of new technology. UTAUT2 is an extension of UTAUT, which had been identified as the most comprehensive and predictive technology acceptance model [41, 42]. Therefore, UTAUT2, with the addition of gamification factors, provided the theoretical framework for this investigation of AR application acceptance. Our study follows the authors' recommendation in [6] that the UTAUT2 model with gamification impact factor needs to be explored. Thus, in this study, gamification was introduced as an independent variable in the conceptual framework (see Fig. 1) to assess its relationship with the intention and use behaviour of the AR app. The data were collected from 95 Macquarie University students in Australia. Using PLS 3.0-SEM, the results showed that the gamification factor had a positive association with behavioral intentions and use behaviour of the CybAR app. Gamification can help to make cybersecurity awareness training more enjoyable and increase users' perceptions of the acceptance of a technology [42]. To the best of our knowledge, the present study is the first to combine UTAUT2 factors and gamification feature constructs in work on acceptance of an AR app, using data from Australia. Hence it enriches the existing literature on AR app acceptance and provides new insights into how game techniques influence individual behaviour toward risky cybersecurity practices.

2 Theoretical Background

2.1 Cybersecurity and Augmented Reality

The United States Army defines cybersecurity as a combination of the underlying hardware, communication nodes, and a social layer of human and cognitive elements [17]. Dhamija et al. [18] reported that hackers could effectively target users due to the public's general lack of awareness about cybersecurity. Therefore, education is vital to protect users against cyber-attacks. Many organizations provide materials for preventing cyber-attacks, such as email bulletins or educational websites. However, Kumaraguru et al. [25] found that these materials only work if people continue to pay attention to them. Recently, gamification has emerged as a promising technique to improve cybersecurity awareness and increase the effectiveness of cybersecurity measures [22]. Several cybersecurity games have been developed for this purpose to better engage users and change user behavior to avoid cyber-attacks. The majority of these games are browser-based apps, but it may be more effective to employ mobile phone game apps [43]. AR is a recently developed technology that enhances users' experience by overlaying computational information on to their reality [1,3]. In spite of the popularity of widespread AR applications, there exists no AR based application that can be used to educate users about cybersecurity attacks and help to raise their cybersecurity awareness. Azuma [5] defined AR as a type of interactive, reality-based display environment that takes the capabilities of computer-generated display, sound, text and effects to enhance the user's real-world experience. AR combines real and computer-based scenes and images to deliver a unified but enhanced view of the world. AR systems have been used in different fields, such as education, marketing, medicine, and tourism [4,26]. However, their application in the context of education about a safe cybersecurity behavior has been less explored. Accordingly, we developed an AR game, CybAR, whose purpose is to demonstrate the negative consequences of risky cybersecurity behaviour and the value of safe cybersecurity behavior. Our aim in this study is to identify the role of gamification factor on affecting users' acceptance of CybAR.

2.2   Unified Theory of Acceptance and Use of Technology (UTAUT)

Previous research in psychology and sociology has generated various theoretical frameworks to explain the relationship between technology acceptance and usage. One of these is the unified theory of acceptance and use of technology (UTAUT). UTAUT [41] was developed through a review and consolidation of the constructs of eight well-known theories that previous researchers had employed to investigate information systems' usage behavior: the theory of reasoned action (TRA), the technology acceptance model (TAM), the motivational model (MM) [16], the theory of planned behavior (TPB), the PC utilization model (MPCU) [40], innovation diffusion theory (IDT), social cognitive theory (SCT) [29], and an integrated model of technology acceptance and planned behaviour (TAM-TPB) [38]. The model identifies four factors [42]: performance expectancy, effort expectancy, social influence, and facilitating conditions. Since its appearance, the UTAUT model has been widely used to explore user acceptance of mobile technologies [4], and has been tested and applied to several technologies [2,13]. Even though UTAUT provides a very detailed model, it has some limitations [33]. Therefore, the authors in [42] developed UTAUT2 in 2012, extending and adapting the theory to the consumer context. UTAUT2 now has seven factors: performance expectancy, effort expectancy, social influence, facilitating conditions, hedonic motivation, price value, and habit. Of the three new factors, hedonic motivation was added due to its importance as a key predictor in much earlier research [41], price because in a consumer context users must be able to afford the costs associated with the service use, and habit, because previous studies reported it to be a critical factor in the context of technology use [28]. In this model, the moderating variables are age, gender, and experience; voluntariness from the previous UTAUT is excluded. In our study, we dropped the moderating variables (age, gender, and experience) and the price construct because they were not relevant in our study, and substituted them with gamification impact as a construct variable.

2.3   Gamification

Mobile games are played by millions of adolescents and adults around the world [9]. They are highly diverse in relation to their purposes, interactivity and technology. Quality mobile games have been shown to improve concentration, enhance retention of information, and bring about behavioural change [34]. Over recent decades, mobile games - both serious games and gamification - have been designed for serious purposes: to educate, motivate, and persuade users in health, educational and other settings [11]. Serious games use gaming as the primary medium, whereas gamification involves the addition of game elements to non-game contexts as an innovative technique of influencing the motivation or engagement of people to solve real problems [15], and driving behaviours and producing the desired effect and results [11]. The potential for employing serious games and gamification to educate users about cybersecurity has been under-researched.

A small number of games to promote cyberattack awareness have been developed to better engage learners and change user behavior [22]. It has been claimed that well-designed games for user education can effectively mitigate cyber threats [43]. Examples of such games include CyberCIEGE [39] and anti-phishing gaming tools [31,37]. Most of these games, however, are technically oriented and, more importantly, are limited to web-based games. Although evaluations of these games have demonstrated an improvement in players' ability to identify phishing websites, their designs are not particularly effective at teaching players how to detect other forms of cybersecurity threat such as identity theft, ransomware and phishing through social media networks. Accordingly, we incorporated in our game all potential cyberattack techniques and which provides a more engaging experience for the acquisition of practical and conceptual knowledge. In this study, we show the potential effect of employing game mechanics and game design techniques to influence users' acceptance of an AR app using the UTAUT2 model.

3   Proposed Methodology

The research model proposed in this study is shown in Fig. 1. The theoretical framework is based on a combination of factors derived from the unified theory of acceptance and use of technology (UTAUT). The UTAUT factors are performance expectancy, effort expectancy, social influence, hedonic motivation, facilitating conditions and habit as predictors of behavioral intention. Behavioral intention is also a predictor of use behaviour. The model also identifies gamification factor as independent variable affecting behavioral intention and use behavior.

3.1   UTAUT

UTAUT was considered to be the most complete model for predicting information technology acceptance [30] until the development of UTAUT2

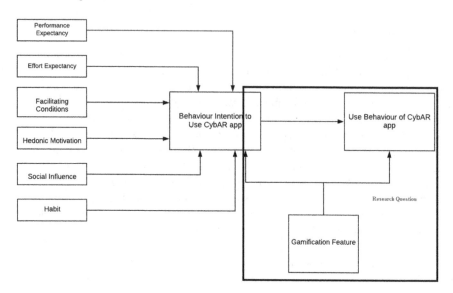

Fig. 1. Research model.

(see Table 1). Compared to its predecessor, UTAUT2 shows significant improvement in explained variance in studies of behavioral intention and technology use [42]. It is therefore employed in the present study, which show the relationship between independent variables (performance expectancy, effort expectancy, social influence, hedonic motivation, facilitating conditions and habit) and dependent variables, namely, behavior intention and initial use (adoption behavior), in relation to an AR app.

Based on the results of previous studies, performance expectancy, effort expectancy, social influence, hedonic motivation, facilitating conditions and habit are expected to be the most important factors that directly influence the intention of using the app [42]. Also, previous technology adoption studies mainly focused on behavioral intent without actually assessing initial use. However, recent findings have questioned the strength of the relationship between behavioral intent and use behavior in various contexts [24]. In relation to the gamification factor, technology acceptance has attracted considerable attention in different areas but few studies have applied UTAUT2 with gamification factor included in the model in the context of Augmented Reality and cybersecurity awareness. Thus, the goal of this study was to determine the impact of gamification as a predictor of behaviour intention and use behaviour of the CybAR app. It is our belief that the use of game techniques in a non-game context such as cybersecurity awareness will have a strong impact, increasing the rate of users' acceptance [6]. Therefore, the more entertainment value the AR app can provide, the greater will be the acceptance intention of users. Therefore, we hypothesised the following:

- Gamification impact will positively affect behavioural intention and use behaviour of the CybAR app.

Table 1. Comparison between UTAUT and UTAUT2

Constructs	UTAUT definitions	UTAUT2 definitions
Performance expectancy	The degree to which an individual that using the system will help him or her gains in job performance	The degree to which technology will provide benefits to consumers in performing some activities
Effort expectancy	The degree of ease associated with the use of the system	The degree of ease associated with the use of technology
Social influence	The degree to which an individual perceives important others believe that he or she should use new system	The consumers perceives that important others should use new technology
Facilitating conditions	The degree to which an individual believes that an organizational and technical infrastructure exists to support use of the system	Consumers' perceptions of the resource and support available to perform a behavior
Hednise motivation	Not considered	The fun and pleasure derived from using technology
Price value	Not considered	Consumers' cognitive tradeoffs between perceived benefits of the applications and monetary cost of using them
Habit	Not considered	The extent to which people tend to perform behaviors automatically because of learning

3.2 Cybersecurity Awareness Game Using Augmented Reality (CybAR)

There are some shortcomings in existing gamified approaches to education about cybersecurity challenges. Thus, our goal was to replace training programs that typically focus on reading about cybersecurity with a serious Augmented Reality game that mimics the actual forms of cybersecurity attacks. One of the main aims of CybAR was to provide more comprehensive education about cybersecurity attacks and to do so in a way that closely matches how they occur in the real world. Another goal of CybAR was to educate a less technically sophisticated audience to increase their awareness of the potential for cybersecurity attacks in their day-to-day online behaviour, rather than to teach specific technical or management skills. Cybersecurity Awareness using Augmented Reality

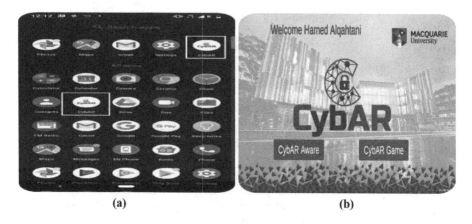

Fig. 2. (a) CybAR app. (b) CybAR main page.

Fig. 3. (a) Example of CybAR Task 1. (b) Example of CybAR Task 2.

(CybAR) is an AR mobile application game that not only teaches cybersecurity concepts but also demonstrates the consequences of actual cybersecurity attacks through immediate feedback. The CybAR application was developed using a Unity and Vuforia platform (see Fig. 2) and incorporates a commercial AR technique developed for the Android platform. The main characteristics of the AR game are interactivity and the display of the shocking consequences of careless cybersecurity habits. Before players begin a CybAR game, they should download and access an electronic booklet that contains all 20 tasks.

They can see the AR content for each task by moving the camera on the SCAN ME QR code next to each task to view the answers (see Fig. 3).

Each task requires players to choose the right option for the given scenario. This helps users to increase their cybersecurity awareness. CybAR includes important game elements such as scores, progress, levels and a leaderboard.

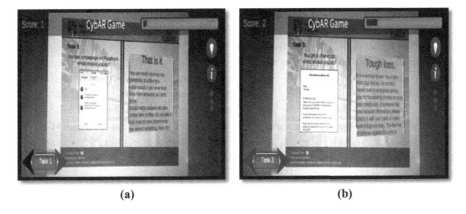

(a)   (b)

Fig. 4. (a) Correct answer feedback. (b) Wrong answer feedback.

Our goal was to replace traditional training programs that typically emphasise reading about cybersecurity with an AR game that simulates the actual methods of cybersecurity attacks. For each completed task, we developed responses inspired by protection motivation theory (PMT) [36] to trigger more secure behaviour among users.

- If the user has implemented the task correctly, a coping message appears, stating that it is easy to minimise the risk of cyberattack by making the right decision fir the task (see Fig. 4(a)).
- If the user has implemented the task incorrectly, a fear appeal message warns that their behaviour could leave them vulnerable to cyberattacks (see Fig. 4(b)).

4 Data Collection

A total of 95 students played the CybAR game and then completed an online questionnaire hosted on the Qualtrics platform. The study criteria required all participants to be 18 years of age or older with experience using IT assets in a professional capacity. Also, participants need an Android tablet or Android phone. Invitations to participate were distributed to students at Macquarie University via email, social media (Facebook and Twitter) and flyers posted in different locations on campus. All participants received information about the purpose of the game and the nature of the study and gave informed consent.

4.1 Measurements

The questionnaire items have been derived from different literature. The questionnaire contains three parts: UTAUT2 data constructs, gamification questions and general information and demographic characteristics. The items and scales for the UTAUT2 constructs were adapted from [41,42], the use behaviour from [16] and gamification impact from [6]. In relation to the UTAUT model, the items for each of the constructs (performance expectancy, effort expectancy, facilitating conditions, hedonic motivation, social influence, habit, behavioral intentions and use behavior constructs) were 5, 6, 4, 5, 3, 4, 3, and 2 items for each construct, respectively. There are 3 adapted items for gamification factor. Thus a total of 35 items are used to measure the 9 constructs of our proposed theoretical model (See Table 2). In both UTAUT components and gamification motivation factor, a five-point Likert scale ranging from "extremely disagree" = 1 to "extremely agree" = 5, is used to measure all the items.

5   Analysis and Preliminary Results

Two software tools were employed in data analysis. First, the survey data were recorded by Qualtrics and imported to SPSS. SPSS software is readily available and can be used to generate descriptive statistics and support the process of data analysis. Various analyses were performed using SPSS. Descriptive statistics were used to analyse each variable separately and to summarise the demographic characteristics of participants. Second, SmartPLS Version 3.0 was used for analytics. The Partial Least Squares (PLS) was used in this study as it is a rigorous technique for structural equation modeling (SEM). Before any analyses were conducted, data normality for each measured item was tested for skewness. The skewness values for the constructs were between −3 and +3. This indicated that the items were almost normally distributed, so further calculations were performed, as elaborated below.

5.1   Characteristics of Participants

We received far fewer responses than we had expected. Although the questionnaire link and invitation letter were sent to 300 respondents, and they were asked to pass it on to their friends, only 124 questionnaires were received. After filtering, 29 of these were found to be incomplete. There was a fairly equal distribution of males (56%) and females (44%). Regarding the age groups, the largest group of respondents (39%) was aged 25–34, followed by those aged 35–44 (22%), 18–24 (28%) and 45–54 (8%). Only 3% of participants belonged to the 55+ category. Most respondents were highly educated; 62% were undergraduate university students; 17% were postgraduate students; 16% were enrolled in a 2-year college degree; and 5% were high school students.

5.2   Model Validation

This section describes the assessment and testing of the proposed model using SEM. Because PLS does not provide goodness-of-fit criteria, the procedure for testing PLS was performed in two stages: assessing the reliability and validity of the measurement model; and testing the hypotheses in the structural model.

Table 2. UTAUT items.

Constructs	Items
Performance expectancy	Using CybAR application would enhance my effectiveness in applying cybersecurity threat prevention behaviour
	Using CybAR application would improve my cybersecurity threat prevention behaviour performance
	Using CybAR application would increase my productivity in cybersecurity threat prevention behaviour
	I found CybAR application useful
	Overall, using CybAR application is advantageous
Effort expectancy	I found CybAR application Mobile App easy to use
	Learning to use CybAR application was easy for me
	The CybAR application is easy to navigate
	My interaction with CybAR application was clear and understandable
	It was easy for me to find information at CybAR application
	It would be easy for me to become more skillful and experienced with CybAR application
Facilitating conditions	I have the resources/Knowledge necessary to use CybAR application
	Detail instructions about CybAR application use is available to me
	An assistant is available for help with using CybAR application
	A specified person is available in case of difficulty with CybAR application
Hedonic motivation	Using CybAR application is enjoyable
	Using CybAR application is fun
	The CybAR application is quite visually appealing
	Using CybAR application is entertaining
	Using CybAR application is pleasant
Social influence	People who influence me would think that I should use CybAR application to be aware of cybersecurity attacks
	People who are important to me would think that I should use the CybAR application to protect my devices from cybersecurity attacks
	People whose opinions are valued to me would prefer that I should use CybAR application to be knowledgeable about cybersecurity attacks
Habit	The use of mobile games has become habit for me
	I am addicted to use mobile games daily
	I must use mobile games for my daily routine
	Using mobile games daily has become natural to me
Gamification	If CybAR app is more fun/enjoyable I probably use it more often
	If using CybAR would give me great benefits, I probably use it more often
	If CybAR is more fun I probably advise others to use it
Behavioral intentions	I intend to use CybAR application
	I will use CybAR application for adapting cybersecurity threat prevention behavior whenever appropriate
	I predict I will reuse the CybAR application frequently
Use behavior	I will continue using CybAR application frequently
	I will use CybAR application to avoid cybersecurity attacks

Measurement Model: The measurement model is evaluated by estimating the internal consistency reliability. The internal consistency reliability is assessed using the values for Cronbach's alpha, composite reliability and average variance extracted (AVE) [10]. Cronbach's alpha is a measure of internal consistency that measures the correlation between items in a scale. The Cronbach's alpha for each construct had to be greater than 0.7 [27]. Composite reliability is similar to Cronbach's alpha. It measures the actual factor loadings rather than assuming that each item is equally weighted. The standardised path loading of each item should be statistically significant. In addition, the loadings should, ideally, be at least greater than 0.7. AVE indicates the amount of variance in a measure that is due to the hypothesised underlying latent variable. The average variance extracted (AVE) for each construct has to exceed 0.5. Values greater than 0.50 are considered satisfactory. They indicate that at least 50% of the variance in the answers to the items is due to the hypothesised underlying latent variable.

All scales reached a composite reliability value of at least 0.78 (ranging from 0.783 to 0.917). Thus, they exceeded the 0.70 threshold for composite reliability. In addition, the scales exhibited high internal consistency; the lowest Cronbach's alpha was 0.76, which is well above the 0.70 threshold for confirmatory research. The AVE for each construct was greater than 0.5 (ranging from 0.693 to 0.861). Therefore, the internal consistency reliability for the constructs was confirmed.

Construct validity consists of convergent validity and discriminate validity. Convergent validity is achieved when each measurement item correlates strongly with its proposed theoretical construct. It is checked by testing the factor loadings of the outer model. The outer model loadings for all items are all above 0.50. Therefore, convergent validity was established [19]. Discriminant validity is achieved when each measurement item correlates weakly with all other proposed constructs than the one to which it is theoretically associated. The discriminant validity of the measurement model is tested using two criteria suggested by Gefen and Straub [20]: (1) item loading to construct correlations is larger than its loading on any other constructs; and (2) the square root of the AVE for each latent construct should be greater than the correlations between that construct and other constructs in the model. The lowest acceptable value is 0.50. All items showed substantially higher loading than other factors except 2 items failed the test and were excluded, and the square root of the AVE for each construct exceeded the correlations between that construct and the other constructs. Therefore, discriminant validity was established. Table 3 shows the Discriminant Validity that all the scales used in the survey satisfy the requirements. The square roots of the AVE-s are shown in bold. Off diagonal elements are correlation between constructs. The AVE form the constructs should be greater than the AVE shared between the item and other items in the proposed model.

Structural Model: The structural model was also analyzed using SmartPLS version 3.0 as mentioned above. This proposed model presents 9 hypotheses that were used to examine the relationships between the latent variables. The structural model was assessed by evaluating the path coefficients and coefficient of determination. Path coefficients are explained with the t-statistics computed using bootstrapping 500 samples. The tests point to positive or negative relationships between exogenous constructs and endogenous variables and the strength of these relationships. Path coefficients should be directionally consistent with the hypothesis. Coefficient of determination as R2 values. R2 provides the amount of variance of dependent variables explained by the independent variables.

Table 3. Discriminant validity.

	PE	EE	FC	HM	SF	H	GM	BI	UB
Performance expectancy (PE)	0.848								
Effort expectancy (EE)	0.749	0.862							
Facilitating conditions (FC)	0.713	0.748	0.839						
Hedonic motivation (HM)	0.749	0.768	0.715	0.810					
Social influence (SF)	0.760	0.782	0.698	0.736	0.829				
Habit (H)	0.724	0.753	0.694	0.783	0.719	0.855			
Gamification (GM)	0.747	0.760	0.738	0.756	0.722	0.788	0.896		
Behavioral intentions (BI)	0.754	0.722	0.717	0.699	0.658	0.695	0.741	0.871	
Use behavior (UB)	0.719	0.759	0.773	0.705	0.763	0.686	0.777	0.738	0.813

In our analysis, the R2 coefficient of determination indicates the predictive power of the model for each dependent construct. According to [12], an R2 value of 0.67 in the PLS path model is considered substantial. Therefore, our model has the ability to explain the endogenous constructs. The UTAUT model explains 73.6% of variation in behavioural intention and 59.8% in use behaviour. According to the path coefficients and t-test values, we found adequate evidence for each hypothesis. The SEM results revealed that most of the proposed external variables have significant effect on avoidance motivation. Avoidance behaviour has significant influence on avoidance behaviour.

Due to space limitations, this paper only presents the preliminary results of the study, highlighting the gamification factor's impact on users' acceptance of the CybAR app. Comprehensive results, including all constructs and their correlations with use behaviour factors, and a summary of the hypothesis testing results will be presented in future work. The gamification was were found to be statistically significant in affecting behavioural intention to use the CybAR app and use behaviour of the CybAR app.

- Consistent with the hypothesis, the gamification factor had a positive influence on students' behavioural intention to use AR systems, with path coefficient $= 0.5$ and $t = 3.7$ ($p < 0.01$, 1-tail).
- Similarly, use behaviour of the CybAR app was positively influenced by the gamification factor, with path coefficient $= 0.41$ and $t = 2$ ($p < 0.05$, 1-tail), thus supporting the hypothesis.

6   Discussion and Implications

To the best of our knowledge, this is the first time that UTAUT2 and a gamification construct have been combined in a study of cybersecurity awareness application acceptance. The results indicated that gamification techniques such as points, progress, feedback and leaderboard positively affect the acceptance of the CybAR app. In other words, the results confirm a strong statistical relationship between gamification and behavioural intention as well as between gamification and use behaviour of the CybAR application. These findings are consistent with some previous research [6], but are not supported by others [8].

This study and its results have theoretical and practical implications. Theoretically, this research adds significantly to the existing literature on UTAUT2 and gamification. This study empirical validated and tested the UTAUT2 model and highlighted the importance of gamification constructs to understand behavioural intentions to use the CybAR app and actual use of the CybAR application in a cybersecurity awareness context. In doing so, we have presented theoretical evidence that the gamification factor is a significant predictor of technology acceptance in the cybersecurity awareness context, and this enhances the explanatory power of UTAUT2 For researchers, this study provides a basis for further work on acceptance and gamification in augmented reality applications. Practically, understanding the significant constructs in the design and implementation of cybersecurity awareness applications helps practitioners to achieve high user acceptance. The results of our study clearly indicate that cybersecurity awareness campaigns should incorporate gamification techniques in their design and implementation.

7   Conclusion, Limitations and Future Work

The careful application of gamification in cybersecurity awareness training can help increase individuals' cybersecurity knowledge about cyber-attacks in an interesting and enjoyable way, in turn increasing user acceptance, engagement and satisfaction. Using the CybAR application, the research extends the unified theory of acceptance and use of technology (UTAUT2) and prior research to include the gamification factor. The theoretical model was tested in a quantitative study using structural equation modelling, conducted in Australia, with 95 Macquarie University students. The findings indicate that there is a significant relationship between the gamification factor and behavioural intention to use the CybAR app and actual use of the CybAR app. The gamification factor positively influenced behavioural intention and use behaviour of the CybAR app, confirming the potential of games techniques to raise cybersecurity awareness. The research model in our study explained 73.6% of variation in behavioural intention and 59.8% in use behaviour.

Several limitations of this research should be noted. First, the study employed a cross-sectional research design. Longitudinal data will enhance our understanding of what constructs affect individuals' acceptance of using the CybAR app and enable to have more accurate findings from a specific group. Second, only quantitative data were collected in our study. Qualitative data generated from interviews or focus groups could yield insight into other factors that affect individuals' behavioural intention and use behaviour of CybAR app. Third, interpretation of the results was limited by the small sample size (95). A larger sample would have improved the ability to generalise the findings to a wider population. It should be noted, however, that the use of SmartPLS as a data analysis tool overcomes this limitation since it can generalise results with a very small sample size. Forth, the study was conducted in one university Macquarie University so the results may not be applicable to all Australian universities, even if the education system and culture are the same. Fifth, this study examined by using a marker-based AR application that applicable only for Android devices. Similar application should be developed for iOS users. Finally, not all factors related to the higher education institution were taken into consideration. AR usage in such institutions will be better understood if other factors, such as cultural dimensions and personality traits, are taken into account.

Several scholars have emphasized the importance of integrating cultural dimensions into technology adoption models [7]. Therefore, our future work should apply UTAUT2 with different cultural backgrounds [21]. Also, in information systems research, personality factors have been used in various disciplines [23]. Hence the incorporation of personality traits into models such as UTAUT can reveal how personality influences individuals' technology acceptance. Thus, in our future work to identify the personality traits that affect users' acceptance of CybAR and increase their cybersecurity awareness.

References

1. Alqahtani, H., Kavakli, M.: iMAP-CampUS (an intelligent mobile augmented reality program on campus as a ubiquitous system): a theoretical framework to measure user's behavioural intention. In: Proceedings of the 9th International Conference on Computer and Automation Engineering, pp. 36–43. ACM (2017)
2. Alqahtani, H., Kavakli, M.: A theoretical model to measure user's behavioural intention to use iMAP-CampUs app. In: 2017 12th IEEE Conference on Industrial Electronics and Applications (ICIEA), pp. 681–686. IEEE (2017)
3. Alqahtani, H., Kavakli, M., Sheikh, N.U.: Analysis of the technology acceptance theoretical model in examining users behavioural intention to use an augmented reality app (iMAP-CampUS). Int. J. Eng. Manage. Res. (IJEMR) **8**(5), 37–49 (2018)
4. Arth, C., Grasset, R., Gruber, L., Langlotz, T., Mulloni, A., Wagner, D.: The history of mobile augmented reality. arXiv preprint arXiv:1505.01319 (2015)
5. Azuma, R.T.: A survey of augmented reality. Presence Teleop. Virt. Environ. **6**(4), 355–385 (1997)
6. Baptista, G., Oliveira, T.: Understanding mobile banking: the unified theory of acceptance and use of technology combined with cultural moderators. Comput. Hum. Behav. **50**, 418–430 (2015)
7. Baptista, G., Oliveira, T.: Why so serious? Gamification impact in the acceptance of mobile banking services. Internet Res. **27**, 118–139 (2017)
8. Bogost, I.: Exploitationware. In: Colby, R., Johnson, M.S.S., Colby R.S. (eds.) Rhetoric/Composition/Play through Video Games. Palgrave Macmillan's Digital Education and Learning, pp. 139–147. Springer, New York (2013). https://doi.org/10.1057/9781137307675_11
9. Brooks, F.M., Chester, K.L., Smeeton, N.C., Spencer, N.H.: Video gaming in adolescence: factors associated with leisure time use. J. Youth Stud. **19**(1), 36–54 (2016)
10. Bryman, A., Cramer, D.: Quantitative Data Analysis with SPSS 12 and 13: A Guide for Social Scientists. Routledge, Abingdon (2004)
11. Burke, J.W., McNeill, M., Charles, D.K., Morrow, P.J., Crosbie, J.H., McDonough, S.M.: Optimising engagement for stroke rehabilitation using serious games. Vis. Comput. **25**(12), 1085 (2009). https://doi.org/10.1007/s00371-009-0387-4

12. Chin, W.W.: Commentary: issues and opinion on structural equation modeling. MIS Q. **22**, 7–16 (1998)
13. Chou, T.L., ChanLin, L.J.: Augmented reality smartphone environment orientation application: a case study of the fu-jen university mobile campus touring system. Procedia Soc. Behav. Sci. **46**, 410–416 (2012)
14. Ciampa, M.: Security Awareness: Applying Practical Security in Your World. Cengage Learning, Boston (2013)
15. Connolly, T.M., Boyle, E.A., MacArthur, E., Hainey, T., Boyle, J.M.: A systematic literature review of empirical evidence on computer games and serious games. Comput. Educ. **59**(2), 661–686 (2012)
16. Davis, F.D.: Perceived usefulness, perceived ease of use, and user acceptance of information technology. MIS Q. **13**, 319–340 (1989)
17. Dawson, J., Thomson, R.: The future cybersecurity workforce: going beyond technical skills for successful cyber performance. Front. Psychol. **9**, 744 (2018)
18. Dhamija, R., Tygar, J.D., Hearst, M.: Why phishing works. In: Proceedings of the SIGCHI Conference on Human Factors in Computing Systems, pp. 581–590. ACM (2006)
19. Fornell, C., Larcker, D.F.: Evaluating structural equation models with unobservable variables and measurement error. J. Mark. Res. **18**(1), 39–50 (1981)
20. Gefen, D., Straub, D., Boudreau, M.C.: Structural equation modeling and regression: Guidelines for research practice. Commun. Assoc. Inf. Syst. **4**(1), 7 (2000)
21. Hofstede, G.: Culture and organizations. Int. Stud. Manage. Organ. **10**(4), 15–41 (1980)
22. Jin, G., Tu, M., Kim, T.H., Heffron, J., White, J.: Game based cybersecurity training for high school students. In: Proceedings of the 49th ACM Technical Symposium on Computer Science Education, pp. 68–73. ACM (2018)
23. Kajzer, M., D'Arcy, J., Crowell, C.R., Striegel, A., Van Bruggen, D.: An exploratory investigation of message-person congruence in information security awareness campaigns. Comput. Secur. **43**, 64–76 (2014)
24. Khan, I.U., Hameed, Z., Khan, S.U.: Understanding online banking adoption in a developing country: UTAUT2 with cultural moderators. J. Glob. Inf. Manag. (JGIM) **25**(1), 43–65 (2017)
25. Kumaraguru, P., Sheng, S., Acquisti, A., Cranor, L.F., Hong, J.: Teaching johnny not to fall for phish. ACM Trans. Internet Technol. (TOIT) **10**(2), 7 (2010)
26. Lee, G.A., Dunser, A., Kim, S., Billinghurst, M.: CityViewAR: a mobile outdoor AR application for city visualization. In: 2012 IEEE International Symposium on Mixed and Augmented Reality-Arts, Media, and Humanities (ISMAR-AMH), pp. 57–64. IEEE (2012)
27. Li, C.Y., Ku, Y.C.: The effects of persuasive messages on system acceptance. In: PACIS, p. 110. Citeseer (2011)
28. Limayem, M., Hirt, S.G., Cheung, C.M.: How habit limits the predictive power of intention: the case of information systems continuance. MIS Q. **31**(4), 705–737 (2007)
29. Locke, E.A.: Social foundations of thought and action: a social-cognitive view. Acad. Manage. Rev. **12**, 169–171 (1987)
30. Martins, C., Oliveira, T., Popovič, A.: Understanding the internet banking adoption: a unified theory of acceptance and use of technology and perceived risk application. Int. J. Inf. Manage. **34**(1), 1–13 (2014)
31. Misra, G., Arachchilage, N.A.G., Berkovsky, S.: Phish phinder: a game design approach to enhance user confidence in mitigating phishing attacks. arXiv preprint arXiv:1710.06064 (2017)

32. Moallem, A.: Cybersecurity Awareness Among Students and Faculty. CRC Press, Boca Raton (2019)
33. Negahban, A., Chung, C.H.: Discovering determinants of users perception of mobile device functionality fit. Comput. Hum. Behav. **35**, 75–84 (2014)
34. Read, J.L., Shortell, S.M.: Interactive games to promote behavior change in prevention and treatment. Jama **305**(16), 1704–1705 (2011)
35. Robson, K., Plangger, K., Kietzmann, J.H., McCarthy, I., Pitt, L.: Is it all a game? Understanding the principles of gamification. Bus. Horiz. **58**(4), 411–420 (2015)
36. Rogers, R.W.: A protection motivation theory of fear appeals and attitude change1. J. Psychol. **91**(1), 93–114 (1975)
37. Sheng, S., et al.: Anti-phishing phil: the design and evaluation of a game that teaches people not to fall for phish. In: Proceedings of the 3rd Symposium on Usable Privacy and Security, pp. 88–99. ACM (2007)
38. Taylor, S., Todd, P.: Assessing IT usage: the role of prior experience. MIS Q. **19**, 561–570 (1995)
39. Thompson, M.F., Irvine, C.E.: CyberCIEGE scenario design and implementation. In: 2014 {USENIX} Summit on Gaming, Games, and Gamification in Security Education (3GSE 2014) (2014)
40. Thompson, R.L., Higgins, C.A., Howell, J.M.: Personal computing: toward a conceptual model of utilization. MIS Q. **15**, 125–143 (1991)
41. Venkatesh, V., Morris, M.G., Davis, G.B., Davis, F.D.: User acceptance of information technology: toward a unified view. MIS Q. **27**, 425–478 (2003)
42. Venkatesh, V., Thong, J.Y., Xu, X.: Consumer acceptance and use of information technology: extending the unified theory of acceptance and use of technology. MIS Q. **36**(1), 157–178 (2012)
43. Wen, Z.A., Lin, Z., Chen, R., Andersen, E.: What. hack: engaging anti-phishing training through a role-playing phishing simulation game. In: Proceedings of the 2019 CHI Conference on Human Factors in Computing Systems, p. 108. ACM (2019)

Does Decision-Making Style Predict Individuals' Cybersecurity Avoidance Behaviour?

Hamed Alqahtani[✉] and Manolya Kavakli-Thorne

Macquarie University, Sydney, Australia
hsqahtani@kku.edu.sa, manolya.kavakli@mq.edu.au

Abstract. In the field of cybersecurity, human behaviour is considered as the weakest link. We applied gamification techniques to the development of an Augmented Reality game, CybAR, which was designed to educate users about cybersecurity in an effective and entertaining way. This research incorporates decision-making style into Technology Threat Avoidance Theory (TTAT) of CybAR game use. This paper particularly focuses on the role of decision-making style in avoidance of risky cybersecurity behaviour based on factors derived from Technology Threat Avoidance Theory (TTAT). A cross-sectional survey was conducted among 95 students at Macquarie University to assess the effect of individual differences, namely, decision-making style, as a moderator variable between motivation behaviour and cybersecurity avoidance behaviour factors. The findings indicated that the moderating effect of decision-making style had a significant effect on avoidance behaviour. In particular, rational decision-making was a strongly significant moderator of avoidance behaviour and cybersecurity avoidance behaviour, while dependent and avoidant styles were less significant moderators of avoidance behaviour and cybersecurity avoidance behaviour.

Keywords: Cyber security awareness · Decision making style · Gamification

1 Introduction

Digital technology has facilitated innovation, economic growth and productivity. However, it has also led to a dramatic increase in the number of cyberattacks, which can be responsible for substantial financial losses. A recent incident in Australia, for instance, involved the loss of sensitive personal information worth tens of millions of dollars. According to a 2016 report on IT security from the SANS Institute, large organisations spend approximately 35% of their annual security budget on end-user training and awareness [15].

Security professionals and researchers are devoting considerable effort to addressing human behaviour as the weakest link in cybersecurity operations, but research on the human factors in cybersecurity is still in its infancy [19]. Recently,

© Springer Nature Switzerland AG 2020
A. Moallem (Ed.): HCII 2020, LNCS 12210, pp. 32–50, 2020.
https://doi.org/10.1007/978-3-030-50309-3_3

the focus has shifted towards a more human-centred perspective on cybersecurity, since it is not always practical to implement educational campaigns and warning messages intended to increase users' awareness of cybersecurity risks. Gamification, which refers to the application of game design principles in non-gaming contexts, is an emerging technology that shows promise in addressing these gaps. It can be integrated with cybersecurity awareness training programs to tackle cybersecurity threats [29, 34]. Our study was motivated by the lack of research on the use of mobile augmented reality techniques to educate people about cybersecurity threats and raise overall cybersecurity awareness. To address this gap, we developed an AR based game, CybAR, for the Android platform. Key elements of the CybAR game interface were selected based on Technology Threat Avoidance Theory (TTAT) [27] in order to enhance user interaction and to measure the effect of the game on coping appraisal factors, threat appraisal factors, avoidance motivation and risky online avoidance behaviour, as shown in Fig. 1.

Past TTAT studies focused more on the factors of coping and threat appraisal. Threat appraisal is identified by perceived vulnerability and susceptibility to risks, as well as rewards associated with unsafe behaviours. Coping appraisal is determined by coping response efficacy, self-efficacy and response costs associated with safe or adaptive behaviors [3].

Yet this warrants further investigation, especially since the role of individual decision-making styles in this behaviour has not been fully explored. Previous research found evidence of decision-making style differences in relation to behavioural intentions around cybersecurity [14, 18]. Decision-making style is the response style exhibited by an individual in a decision-making moment [35]. Decision-making styles are classified into five groups: rational, avoidant, dependent, intuitive, and spontaneous. This paper uses the TTAT model to identify the impact of individuals' decision-making style on risky online avoidance behaviour based on results from a survey of 95 students from Macquarie University. The findings are expected to help researchers and security practitioners to identify users who are more susceptible to potentially dangerous security behaviours. Although this has been studied in other disciplines [24], it has just started to be examined in the cybersecurity field. For the present study, the participants were shown an Augmented Reality app called CybAR that can provide useful information regarding security awareness. Using the CybAR app, our goal was to investigate the decision-making style factors influencing cybersecurity avoidance behaviour using structural equation modeling (SEM) and partial least squares (PLS). The results indicate that rational, dependent and avoidant styles were significant moderators of avoidance behaviour and cybersecurity avoidance behaviour.

2   Theoretical Background

2.1   Gamification in Cybersecurity Awareness

There is no widely accepted definition of cybersecurity [38]. Kassicieh et al. [22] define cybersecurity as a set of approaches that protect data, systems and networks from cyberattacks. The United States Army defines cybersecurity as a combination of the underlying hardware, communication nodes, and a social layer of human and cognitive elements. According to Dhamija et al. [12], the general public's lack of awareness of cybersecurity means that hackers can efficiently and effectively target users. Therefore, user education is vital to protect against cyberattacks. Cybersecurity awareness involves assessing users' vulnerabilities while providing knowledge about how to detect and avoid cyberattacks. Materials widely used for cybersecurity training include notes, videos and email bulletins. However, these materials are often not very engaging and separate the learning material from the context in which users routinely apply the information [25]. Automated tools have largely failed to mitigate cybersecurity attacks; even the best anti-phishing tools have been found to miss more than 20% of phishing attempts [36]. This situation is exacerbated by the fact that most systems depend on humans to make sensitive trust decisions during their online activities [3]. Accordingly, there has been a shift in thinking about the best ways of combating cybercrime to emphasise creating awareness and encouraging individuals to adopt better cybersecurity practices [23], including gamified approaches to educate users and improve their threat avoidance behaviour. Gamification shows promise as a technique to enhance the effectiveness of cybersecurity awareness programs, and several cybersecurity games have been developed to better engage users and change their behaviour to avoid cyberattacks [42].

Gamification emerged as a concept of interest in the field around 2010 [21]. Several researchers have demonstrated multiple benefits from cybersecurity games such as Control-Alt-Hack, Protection Poker, CyberCIEGE, Anti-Phishing Phil and What.Hack [40]. A few games have been designed to teach cybersecurity concepts. For example, Control-Alt-Hack [11] is a board game that teaches players about high-level security concepts such as phishing and social engineering. Although this does help to increase awareness and understanding of cybersecurity issues as a whole, it is not sufficiently specific to imitate the low-level decisions required for anti-phishing strategies in practical contexts. Protection Poker is a software security game designed to help software development teams estimate risks and prevent most damaging attacks [41]. CyberCIEGE presents a virtual world interface that mimics the role of a network manager in safeguarding the network with a limited budget [39]. Capture-The-Flag (CTF) is a game-based computer security competition for students to practise the skills necessary to defend against hackers [28]. In general, board games in information security do not teach hands-on security skills, such as how to define cybersecurity attacks, which are the main purpose of our game. Recently, new designs for anti-phishing games [29, 36] have drawn inspiration from the popular framework for anti-phishing training to teach users how to prevent computer system and network settings from being compromised. The Anti-Phishing Phil and What.Hack online games were developed to challenge players to recognise real-life phishing URLs and emails in an entertaining way.

The effectiveness of these games suggests that a mobile-based application focused on raising cybersecurity awareness would be a useful tool. Thus, we develop an effective augmented reality (AR) game that designed to increase cybersecurity awareness and knowledge in an active and entertaining way. The Cybersecurity Awareness using Augmented Reality (CybAR) game is an AR mobile application that not only teaches cybersecurity concepts but also demonstrates the consequences of actual cybersecurity attacks through feedback. Augmented Reality (AR) has recently emerged as a technology that can enhance users' experience by overlaying computational information onto their reality. Azuma [5] defined augmented reality as "an interactive experience of a real-world environment where the objects that reside in the real world are enhanced by computer-generated perceptual information, sometimes across multiple sensory modalities, including visual, auditory, haptic, somatosensory and olfactory." Despite the popularity of AR applications in various fields, such as education, marketing, medicine and tourism [1], no previous AR-based application has been developed to educate users about cybersecurity attacks and raise their cybersecurity awareness.

2.2   Technology Threat Avoidance Theory

In the literature, Health Belief Model (HBM) theory [33] and Protection Motivation Theory (PMT) [32] have been used widely to explain users' intention to behave securely in a cybersecurity context, and how and when users adopt adaptive or maladaptive behaviours when they are informed of a threatening security incident. HBM defines a conceptual model for describing non participation health behaviour of people in different components. The components of HBM include perceived severity, perceived susceptibility, perceived barriers, perceived benefits, and cues to action. PMT is an extension of HBM that considers intention to protect oneself as the determinant of health behaviour, and the aim is dependent on perceived severity, perceived susceptibility, self-efficacy, and response-efficacy. As a motivation of HBM and PMT, Mohamed et al. [30] conducted an empirical study of cybersecurity filed and found that perceived severity, perceived susceptibility, perceived benefits, and self-efficacy are correlated with security practices. In 2009, Liang et al. [27] extended the PMT by adding and refining multiple factors, and expanding/renaming the attitude change PMT outcome area to adopt different coping behaviours in TTAT. Noxiousness and probability PMT factors were combined into a new aggregate TTAT factor named perceived threat, consisted of two sub-factors: perceived susceptibility and perceived severity. The efficacy PMT factor was also further refined as an aggregate factor called perceived avoidability, comprised of three sub-factors: a) perceived effectiveness, b) perceived cost, and c) self-efficacy of a coping response. Self-efficacy reflects confidence in one's ability to apply avoidance behaviour. Finally, TTAT coping behaviours are further refined to differentiate between emotion-focused coping to not administer an avoidance behaviour, and problem focused coping to avoid, mitigate, or nullify a threat by applying avoidance behaviour. Risky cybersecurity behaviour happens when users do not exercise avoidance behaviour in circumstances where it is warranted. This poses a notable risk to institutions and organizations. Factors which motivate protective action are vital in affecting cybersecurity user decision-making. The role and impact of TTAT factors as predictors of avoidance risky Cybersecurity behaviours is needed to grow. The specific purpose of the TTAT factors is to identify the constructs that should be integrated into AR game to help users avoid insecure practices. Based on the literature, we find the relationship between TTAT factors (perceived threat, safeguard effectiveness, safeguard cost, self-efficacy, perceived severity, perceived susceptibility) and (avoidance motivation and avoidance behaviour) play the role to raise users' cybersecurity awareness. Multiple researchers have investigated associations between TTAT factors and avoidance behaviours initially described by Atkinson et al. [4]. Avoidance behaviours described here were typically comprised of activity to protect IT assets from cyber threats. The body of knowledge currently lacks research which examines the impact of individual differences on avoidance behaviour. Individual differences can contain a wide range of variables that vary between people [14]. Understanding the variability between individuals is essential to understand the underlying psychological mechanisms which may impact user awareness with regard to cybersecurity behaviour. This paper determines the role of individual differences namely decision-making style on users' cybersecurity behaviour. The body of knowledge expands to adequately address the range of action described by addressing the major categories of General Decision-Making Style including rational, avoidant, dependent, intuitive, and spontaneous.

2.3   Decision-Making Style

It is important to consider the possible impact of decision-making style on cybersecurity avoidance behaviour. The IS literature has started to use decision-making style assessment to understand users' behaviour. One of the most widely used decision-making style tests is the general decision-making style (GDMS) test [18]. Decision-making style is defined as "a habitual pattern used by individuals when making decisions" [35]. Some studies refer to decision-making styles as personality traits, whereas in [35], decision-making style is not seen as a personality trait but as "the learned, habitual response pattern exhibited by an individual when confronted with a decision situation". Scott and Bruce in [35] identify five categories of decision-making styles. The rational style is characterised by a "comprehensive search for information, inventory of alternatives and logical evaluation of alternatives"; the intuitive style by "attention to details in the flow of information rather than systematic search for and processing of information and a tendency to rely on premonitions and feelings"; the dependent style by "a search for advice and guidance from others before making important decisions"; the avoidant style by "attempts to avoid decision-making whenever possible"; and the spontaneous style by "a feeling of immediacy and a desire to come through the decision-making process as quickly as possible". Of these, the rational style has been found to be consistently related to intentions and behaviours [14,18] and is, thus, the most important decision-making style in relation to behaviours [18]. Rational decision-makers are thought to use logic when making decisions and are less likely to use escape-avoidance strategies. Peer (2015) found both dependent decision-making and impulsive decision-making to be inversely correlated with good security behaviours [14]. Information security executives with an avoidant decision-making style tend to react more cautiously to a given situation as addressed in [18]. Similarly, an individual with an intuitive decision-making style has been found to have significant concern for information security and privacy [14,18].

3   Methodology

The constructs of TTAT have been widely adopted as antecedents of online safety behaviour. Very rare studies, however, have investigated the role of individual differences namely decision-making style between cybersecurity avoidance motivation and avoidance of risky cybersecurity behaviour. The research model for this study is depicted in Fig. 1. It examines also the relationship among a number of TTAT factors, namely: fear, safeguard effectiveness, safeguard cost, self-efficacy, perceived severity and perceived susceptibility, as predictors of avoidance motivation. Avoidance motivation is also a predictor of avoidance behaviour. We used the word fear instead of perceived threat as suggested by [6]. The model employs individual's decision-making as a moderator variable between cybersecurity avoidance motivation and avoidance of risky cybersecurity practices. Users' cybersecurity threat avoidance behaviour is determined by avoidance motivation, which is affected by perceived threat. Fear is influenced by the interaction of perceived severity and susceptibility. Users' avoidance motivation is also determined by three constructs-safeguard effectiveness, safeguard cost

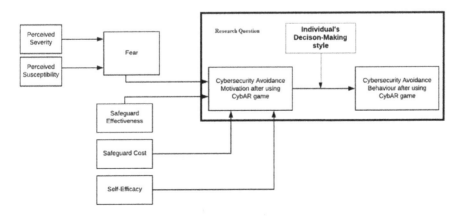

Fig. 1. Research model.

and self-efficacy, consistent with TTAT [27]. Safeguard effectiveness is defined as the individual assessment of the efficacy of a measure to avoid a cybersecurity threat. For example, the individual evaluation regarding application of CybAR can be applied to prevent cyberattacks. Safeguard cost is payback for safeguard effectiveness. This refers to the physical and cognitive costs in time, money and inconvenience required to adopt the safeguard measure. Self-efficacy is defined as an individual's confidence in adopting the safeguard measure. Ng et al. [31] reported that individuals are more motivated to perform IT security-related behaviours as their level of self-efficacy increases.

Although intentions are commonly used to predict behavioural outcomes, dispositional factors such as decision-making style may account for even more variance. Decision-making style has been theorised to significantly impact the relationship between avoidance motivation and avoidance behaviours, although few studies have yielded conclusive evidence [14,18]. Therefore, this research investigated the role of decision-making style as a moderator of the relationship between motivation behaviour and avoidance behaviour. Multiple studies have also investigated the connection between decision-making style and phishing susceptibility [14]. Jeske et al. [20] evaluated the influence of impulsive decision-making on mobile security practices. Therefore, we tested the following hypothesis:

- Users' decision-making style significantly moderates their security motivation and avoidance behaviour.

4   Data Collection

A total of 95 students played the CybAR game and then completed an online questionnaire hosted on the Qualtrics platform. The study criteria required all participants to be 18 years of age or older with experience using IT assets in a professional capacity. Also, participants need an Android tablet or Android phone. Invitations to participate were distributed to students at Macquarie University via email, social media (Facebook and Twitter) and flyers posted in different locations on campus. All participants received information about the purpose of the game and the nature of the study and gave informed consent.

4.1   Cybersecurity Awareness Game Using Augmented Reality (CybAR)

There are some shortcomings in existing gamified approaches to education about cybersecurity challenges. Thus, our goal was to replace training programs that typically focus on reading about cybersecurity with a serious Augmented Reality game that mimics the actual forms of cybersecurity attacks. One of the main aims of CybAR was to provide more comprehensive education about cybersecurity attacks and to do so in a way that closely matches how they occur in the real world. Second, their design fails to incorporate design elements from

Fig. 2. (a) CybAR app. (b) CybAR main page.

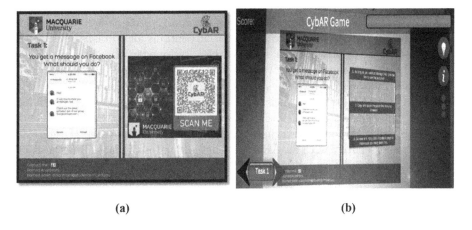

Fig. 3. (a) Example of CybAR Task 1. (b) Example of CybAR Task 2.

well-known information system theories. In contrast, CybAR's design includes safeguard effectiveness, perceived susceptibility and other elements derived from Technology Threat Avoidance Theory (TTAT), as shown in Fig. 1. Another goal of CybAR was to educate a less technically sophisticated audience to increase their awareness of the potential for cybersecurity attacks in their day-to-day online behaviour based on these elements from TTAT, rather than to teach specific technical or management skills. Cybersecurity Awareness using Augmented Reality (CybAR) is an AR mobile application game that not only teaches cybersecurity concepts but also demonstrates the consequences of actual cybersecurity attacks through immediate feedback. The CybAR application was developed using a Unity and Vuforia platform (see Fig. 2) and incorporates a commercial AR technique developed for the Android platform. The main characteristics of the AR game are interactivity and the display of the shocking consequences of

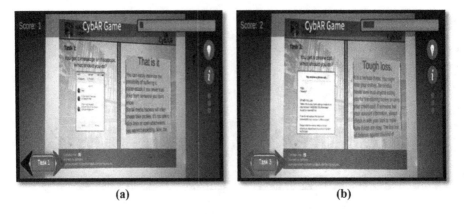

Fig. 4. (a) Correct answer feedback. (b) Wrong answer feedback.

careless cybersecurity habits. Before players begin a CybAR game, they should download and access an electronic booklet that contains all 20 tasks.

They can see the AR content for each task by moving the camera on the SCAN ME QR code next to each task to view the answers (see Fig. 3).

Each task requires players to choose the right option for the given scenario. This helps users to increase their cybersecurity awareness. CybAR includes important game elements such as scores, progress, levels and a leaderboard. Our goal was to replace traditional training programs that typically emphasise reading about cybersecurity with an AR game that simulates the actual methods of cybersecurity attacks. For each completed task, we developed responses inspired by protection motivation theory (PMT) to trigger more secure behaviour among users.

- If the user has implemented the task correctly, a coping message appears, stating that it is easy to minimise the risk of cyberattack by making the right decision fir the task (see Fig. 4(a)).
- If the user has implemented the task incorrectly, a fear appeal message warns that their behaviour could leave them vulnerable to cyberattacks (see Fig. 4(b)).

4.2 Measurements

The proposed model constructs were operationalised using validated items from previous related research. Some changes in wording were made to reflect the purpose of the study (see Table 1) [27]. For the TTAT model, the items for each of the factors depend on Liang and Xue's theoretical model and relevant research literature as shown in Table 1. Fear, perceived susceptibility and perceived severity is measured by the number of items based on the privacy literature in IS [37] and practitioner research that report the negative impact of cyberattacks. The elements of safeguard effectiveness, safeguard cost and Self-efficacy are developed based on relevant health behaviour research [13]. The number of items for avoidance motivation grows based on the behavioural intention measures from technology adoption research [10], with a focus on threat avoidance rather than IT adoption. Finally, threat avoidance behaviour was measured with six self-developed items and three adapted from [10]. There are 35 items were used to measure the 8 constructs of Liang and Xue's theoretical model. The study questionnaire contained four items for fear, four items for perceived severity, three items for perceived susceptibility, three items for safeguard effectiveness, three items for safeguard cost, five items for self-efficacy, four items for avoidance motivation, and nine items for threat avoidance behaviour. The items in the online questionnaire were kept simple and easy to follow to encourage completion. The responses were constructed on a 5-point Likert scale from "strongly disagree" (1) to "strongly agree" (5). All of the questionnaire items were close-ended to facilitate analysis.

Additionally, the TTAT survey asked users to self-report on decision-making styles. To measure decision-making styles, we use the General Decision-Making Style (GDMS) questionnaire [35] to assess rational, intuitive, dependent, avoidant, and Spontaneous decision-making styles. GDMS is widely used [2] to determine how individuals approach decision-making situations and contain a 25-item scale (See Table 2). A panel review was conducted by academic experts to assess the original instrument. Amendments were made to clarify items.

5   Analysis and Preliminary Results

Two software tools were employed in data analysis. First, the survey data were recorded by Qualtrics and imported to SPSS. SPSS software is readily available and can be used to generate descriptive statistics and support the process of data analysis. Various analyses were performed using SPSS. Descriptive statistics were used to analyse each variable separately and to summarise the demographic characteristics of participants. Second, SmartPLS Version 3.0 was used for analytics. The Partial Least Squares (PLS) was used in this study as it is a rigorous technique for structural equation modeling (SEM). Before any analyses were conducted, data normality for each measured item was tested for skewness. The skewness values for the constructs were between -3 and $+3$. This indicated that the items were almost normally distributed, so further calculations were performed, as elaborated below.

5.1   Characteristics of Participants

We received far fewer responses than we had expected. Although the questionnaire link and invitation letter were sent to 300 respondents, and they were asked to pass it on to their friends, only 124 questionnaires were received. After filtering, 29 of these were found to be incomplete. There was a fairly equal distribution of males (56%) and females (44%). Regarding the age groups, the largest group

Table 1. Technology threat avoidance theory items.

Constructs	Items
Perceived severity	It is extremely likely that my devices will be infected by a cybersecurity attacks in the future
	My chances of getting cybersecurity attacks are great
	I feel cybersecurity threats will infect my computer in the future
	It is extremely likely that cybersecurity threats will infect my computer
Perceived susceptibility	Having my devices hacked by cybersecurity attacks is a serious problem for me
	Cybersecurity attacks would steal my personal information from my computer without my knowledge
	Cybersecurity attacks would invade my privacy
Fear	My personal information collected by Cybersecurity attacks could subject to unauthorized secondary use
	Cybersecurity attacks pose a threat to me
	Cybersecurity attacks is a danger to my computer
	It is dreadful to use my computer if it being attacked by cybersecurity attacks
Safeguard effectiveness	CybAR application would be useful for detecting cybersecurity attacks
	CybAR application would increase my performance in protecting my computer from cybersecurity attacks
	CybAR application would enable me to detect cybersecurity attacks on my computer faster
Safeguard cost	It will take very less time to gain awareness about cybersecurity attacks through CybAR application
	It will take less cost to gain awareness about cybersecurity attacks through CybAR application
	Using CybAR application for detecting cybersecurity attacks is convenient for me
Self-efficacy	I would be able to use CybAR application efficiently for applying cybersecurity threats prevention behavior
	In case of being infected by cybersecurity attacks, I can react effectively in a timely manner
	I have the necessary skills to deal with cybersecurity attacks
	I am confident of recognizing cybersecurity attacks
	I could successfully gain anti-cyber threats behavior if someone taught me how to do it first
Avoidance motivation	I would say positive things about the CybAR application
	I intend to obtain CybAR application to avoid cybersecurity attacks
	I predict I would use CybAR application to avoid cybersecurity attacks
	I plan to use CybAR application to avoid cybersecurity attacks
Avoidance behaviour	I used CybAR application during the experiment
	I will continue using CybAR application frequently
	I will use CybAR application to avoid cybersecurity attacks
	I update my anti-cyber threats knowledge frequently through CybAR application
	CybAR app encourages me to have strong and multiple passwords for my different accounts
	CybAR app promotes me to change and review my privacy/security settings on all my accounts
	CybAR app induces me to keep all applications and anti-virus software on my devices up-to date
	CybAR app encourages me to not open or click attachments from people whom I don't know
	CybAR app promotes me to back up important files on my devices

Table 2. General decision-making styles (GDMS).

Sr No.	Items
1	When I make decisions, I tend to rely on my intuition
2	When I make a decision, it is more important for me to feel the decision is right than to have a rational reason for it
3	When making a decision, I trust my inner feelings and reactions
4	When making decisions, I rely upon my instincts
5	I generally make decisions that feel right to me
6	I rarely make important decisions without consulting other people
7	I use the advice of other people in making my important decisions
8	I like to have someone steer me in the right direction when I am faced with important decisions
9	I often need the assistance of other people when making important decisions
10	If I have the support of others, it is easier for me to make important decisions
11	I put off making decisions because thinking about them makes me uneasy
12	I avoid making important decisions until the pressure is on
13	I postpone decision-making whenever possible
14	I generally make important decisions at the last minute
15	I often put off making important decisions
16	I make decisions in a logical and systematic way
17	I double check my information sources to be sure I have the right facts before making decisions
18	My decision-making requires careful thought
19	When making a decision, I consider various options in terms of a specified goal
20	I explore all of my options before making a decision
21	When making decisions I do what feels natural at the moment
22	I generally make snap decisions
23	I often make impulsive decisions
24	I often make decisions on the spur of the moment
25	I make quick decisions

of respondents (39%) was aged 25–34, followed by those aged 35–44 (22%), 18–24 (28%) and 45–54 (8%). Only 3% of participants belonged to the 55+ category. Only two options for nationality were available - Australian and non-Australian. The majority (70%) reported that they were non-Australian. Most respondents were highly educated; 62% were undergraduate university students; 17% were postgraduate students; 16% were enrolled in a 2-year college degree; and 5% were high school students.

5.2 Model Validation

This section describes the assessment and testing of the proposed model using SEM. Because PLS does not provide goodness-of-fit criteria, the procedure for testing PLS was performed in two stages: assessing the reliability and validity of the measurement model; and testing the hypotheses in the structural model.

Measurement Model. The measurement model is evaluated by estimating the internal consistency reliability. The internal consistency reliability is assessed using the values for Cronbach's alpha, composite reliability and average variance extracted (AVE) [7]. Cronbach's alpha is a measure of internal consistency that measures the correlation between items in a scale. The Cronbach's alpha for each construct had to be greater than 0.7 [26]. Composite reliability is similar to Cronbach's alpha. It measures the actual factor loadings rather than assuming that each item is equally weighted. The standardised path loading of each item should be statistically significant. In addition, the loadings should, ideally, be at least greater than 0.7. AVE indicates the amount of variance in a measure that is due to the hypothesised underlying latent variable. The average variance extracted (AVE) for each construct has to exceed 0.5. Values greater than 0.50 are considered satisfactory. They indicate that at least 50% of the variance in the answers to the items is due to the hypothesised underlying latent variable.

All scales reached a composite reliability value of at least 0.71 (ranging from 0.715 to 0.887). Thus, they exceeded the 0.70 threshold for composite reliability. In addition, the scales exhibited high internal consistency; the lowest Cronbach's alpha was 0.79, which is well above the 0.70 threshold for confirmatory research. The AVE for each construct was greater than 0.5 (ranging from 0.613 to 0.724)

Table 3. Construct reliability and validity.

	Cronbach's alpha	Composite reliability	Average variance extracted (AVE)
Avoidance behaviour	0.891	0.765	0.662
Avoidance motivation	0.837	0.785	0.636
Fear	0.798	0.791	0.724
Safeguard effectiveness	0.850	0.859	0.628
Safeguard cost	0.821	0.715	0.652
Self-efficacy	0.843	0.865	0.710
Perceived severity	0.851	0.887	0.613
Perceived susceptibility	0.869	0.853	0.711

as shown in Tables 3. Therefore, the internal consistency reliability for the constructs was confirmed.

Construct validity consists of convergent validity and discriminate validity. Convergent validity is achieved when each measurement item correlates strongly with its proposed theoretical construct. It is checked by testing the factor loadings of the outer model. The outer model loadings for all items are all above 0.50. Therefore, convergent validity was established [16]. Discriminant validity is achieved when each measurement item correlates weakly with all other proposed constructs than the one to which it is theoretically associated. The discriminant validity of the measurement model is tested using two criteria suggested by Gefen and Straub [17]: (1) item loading to construct correlations is larger than its loading on any other constructs; and (2) the square root of the AVE for each latent construct should be greater than the correlations between that construct and other constructs in the model. The lowest acceptable value is 0.50. All items showed substantially higher loading than other factors, and the square root of the AVE for each construct exceeded the correlations between that construct and the other constructs. Therefore, discriminant validity was established.

Structural Model. The structural model was also analyzed using SmartPLS version 3.0. This proposed model presents 8 hypotheses that were used to examine the relationships between the latent variables. The structural model was assessed by evaluating the path coefficients and coefficient of determination. Path coefficients are explained with the t-statistics computed using bootstrapping 500 samples. The tests point to positive or negative relationships between exogenous constructs and endogenous variables and the strength of these relationships. Path coefficients should be directionally consistent with the hypothesis. Coefficient of determination as R2 values. R2 provides the amount of variance of dependent variables explained by the independent variables. In our analysis, the R2 coefficient of determination indicates the predictive power of the model for each dependent construct. According to [8], an R2 value of 0.67 in the PLS path model is considered substantial. Therefore, our model has the ability to explain the endogenous constructs. Our research model is able to explain 64.2% of the variance in fear, 61.5% of the variance in Avoidance Motivation and around 66.1% of the variance in Avoidance Behaviour. According to the path coefficients and t-test values, we found adequate evidence for each hypothesis. The SEM results revealed that most of the proposed external variables have significant effect on avoidance motivation. Avoidance behaviour has significant influence on avoidance behaviour.

The goal of this study was to determine the decision-making styles that are predictive of good security behaviours. Due to space limitations, this paper only presents the preliminary results of the study in relation to the effect of decision-making style on avoidance behaviour. Comprehensive results, including all constructs and their correlations with avoidance behaviour factors, and a summary of the hypothesis testing results will be presented in future work. The moderating effect of decision-making style was then tested. The R2 values between the main and interaction effects were compared and Cohen's f2 was calculated based on [8]. Interaction effect sizes were considered small if 0.02, medium if 0.15, and large if 0.3 [9]. The results of this analysis support the role of decision-making style as a moderator of the relationship between avoidance motivation and avoidance behaviour. Rational decision-making style had a medium sized moderating effect; avoidant and dependent decision-making styles had a small/medium effect. Other decision-making styles had a small effect on avoidance behaviour, as shown in Table 4.

Table 4. Decision-making style as moderators.

Interaction term	Cohen's f^2	Effect size
Rational × Avoidance motivation on avoidance behaviour	0.19	Medium
Avoidant × Avoidance motivation on avoidance behaviour	0.11	Small/Med
Dependent × Avoidance motivation on avoidance behaviour	0.09	Small/Med
Intuitive × Avoidance motivation on avoidance behaviour	0.02	Small
Spontaneous × Avoidance motivation on avoidance behaviour	0.04	Small

6   Discussion and Implications

The purpose of this study was to examine the effect of individual differences, namely, decision-making style, as a moderator variable between motivation behaviour and cybersecurity avoidance behaviours. Only rational, avoidant and dependent decision-making styles were found to be significant moderators of avoidance motivation and behaviour. Rational decision-making style had a medium-sized moderating effect; avoidant and dependent decision-making styles had a small/medium effect. Our results are consistent with previous research which found rational and avoidant decision-making to be significant moderators of safe online practice [14, 18]. However, they contradict other previous studies reporting that the dependent style was not an important factor in avoidance behaviour. Additionally, in our study, there was no observed impact of intuitive and spontaneous decision-making styles on avoidance behaviour consistent with the correlation found in [14, 18].

This result proposes that people who exhibit strong safe online practices may do so because they have rationally evaluated the risks of unsafe behaviour when online. Also, our results suggest that it is a safe practice for people to ask their peers or friends before making a decision that might lead them to risky online behaviour. Furthermore, our study suggests that people with avoidant decision-making style are more likely to avoid unsafe cybersecurity behaviour.

Our study has practical and theoretical implications for academics and information security managers. Practically, the current study furthers our understanding of how individuals seek to protect themselves online. The results can be employed by governments and individuals to encourage online safety. Our results can help security practitioners to prioritise their training efforts towards on end users who exhibit decision-making styles that are significant predictors of poor security behaviour avoidance.

Theoretically, the combination of concepts drawn from previous online safety research within the extended TTAT paradigm proposed here provides additional insights for future research. This study also tested the link between avoidance motivation and avoidance behaviour when adding decision-making styles as moderators, which has not previously been examined in the context of secure user behaviours. Finally, this project explored the role of individual differences, namely, decision-making style as a moderator of avoidance motivation and avoidance behaviour and identified important relationships. These results can also help researchers to analyse the influence of other individual differences, including the five big factor traits (personality) and risk-taking preferences, on safe cybersecurity habits.

7   Conclusion and Limitations

Understanding the influence of individual differences such as decision-making style on cyber security behaviour study extends the limited work on online safety. A cross-sectional survey was conducted among 95 students at Macquarie University to assess the effect of individual differences, namely, decision-making style, as a moderator variable between motivation behaviour and cybersecurity avoidance behaviour. The findings indicated that rational, avoidant and dependent decision-making moderate the relationship between avoidance motivation and avoidance behaviour, supporting the hypothesis. These results can inform the design and deployment of more effective cyber security, including technological protections and user education.

Several limitations of this research should be noted. First, the study employed a cross-sectional research design. Longitudinal data will enhance our understanding of what constructs affect individuals' avoidance behaviour by using the CybAR app. In our study, only quantitative data were collected. Qualitative data generated from interviews or focus groups could yield insight into other factors that affect individuals' avoidance behaviour and avoidance motivation. Second, interpretation of the results was limited by the small sample size (95). A larger sample would have improved the ability to generalise the findings to a wider population. It should be noted, however, that the use of SmartPLS as a data analysis tool overcomes this limitation since it can generalise results with a very small sample size. Third, the study was conducted in one university Macquarie University so the results may not be applicable to all Australian universities, even if the education system and culture are the same. Fourth, this study examined by using a marker-based AR application that applicable only for Android devices. Similar application should be developed for iOS users. Finally, not all factors related to the higher education institution were taken into consideration. AR usage in such institutions will be better understood if other factors, such as cultural motivation and cybersecurity knowledge, are taken into account.

References

1. Alqahtani, H., Kavakli, M., Sheikh, N.U.: Analysis of the technology acceptance theoretical model in examining users behavioural intention to use an augmented reality app (imap-campus). Int. J. Eng. Manag. Res. (IJEMR) **8**(5), 37–49 (2018)
2. Appelt, K.C., Milch, K.F., Handgraaf, M.J., Weber, E.U.: The decision making individual differences inventory and guidelines for the study of individual differences in judgment and decision-making research. Judgm. Decis. Mak. **6**, 252–262 (2011)
3. Arachchilage, N.A.G., Love, S., Beznosov, K.: Phishing threat avoidance behaviour: an empirical investigation. Comput. Hum. Behav. **60**, 185–197 (2016)
4. Atkinson, J.W.: Motivational determinants of risk-taking behavior. Psychol. Rev. **64**(6p1), 359 (1957)
5. Azuma, R.T.: A survey of augmented reality. Presence Teleop. Virt. Environ. **6**(4), 355–385 (1997)
6. Boss, S., Galletta, D., Lowry, P.B., Moody, G.D., Polak, P.: What do systems users have to fear? Using fear appeals to engender threats and fear that motivate protective security behaviors. MIS Q. (MISQ) **39**(4), 837–864 (2015)
7. Bryman, A., Cramer, D.: Quantitative Data Analysis with SPSS 12 and 13: A Guide for Social Scientists. Routledge, London (2004)
8. Chin, W.W.: Commentary: Issues and opinion on structural equation modeling (1998)
9. Cohen, J.: Statistical power analysis. Curr. Dir. Psychol. Sci. **1**(3), 98–101 (1992)
10. Davis, F.D.: Perceived usefulness, perceived ease of use, and user acceptance of information technology. MIS Q. **13**, 319–340 (1989)
11. Denning, T., Lerner, A., Shostack, A., Kohno, T.: Control-Alt-Hack: the design and evaluation of a card game for computer security awareness and education. In: Proceedings of the 2013 ACM SIGSAC Conference on Computer & Communications Security, pp. 915–928. ACM (2013)
12. Dhamija, R., Tygar, J.D., Hearst, M.: Why phishing works. In: Proceedings of the SIGCHI Conference on Human Factors in Computing Systems, pp. 581–590. ACM (2006)
13. Downs, J.S., Holbrook, M., Cranor, L.F.: Behavioral response to phishing risk. In: Proceedings of the Anti-phishing Working Groups 2nd Annual eCrime Researchers Summit, pp. 37–44 (2007)
14. Egelman, S., Peer, E.: Scaling the security wall: developing a security behavior intentions scale (SeBIS). In: Proceedings of the 33rd Annual ACM Conference on Human Factors in Computing Systems, pp. 2873–2882 (2015)
15. Filkins, B., Hardy, G.: It security spending trends. SANS (2016). https://www.sans.org/reading-room/whitepapers/analyst/security-spending-trends-36697
16. Fornell, C., Larcker, D.F.: Evaluating structural equation models with unobservable variables and measurement error. J. Mark. Res. **18**(1), 39–50 (1981)

17. Gefen, D., Straub, D., Boudreau, M.C.: Structural equation modeling and regression: guidelines for research practice. Commun. Assoc. Inf. Syst. **4**(1), 7 (2000)
18. Gratian, M., Bandi, S., Cukier, M., Dykstra, J., Ginther, A.: Correlating human traits and cyber security behavior intentions. Comput. Secur. **73**, 345–358 (2018)
19. Howard, D., Prince, K.: Security 2020: Reduce security Risks This Decade. Wiley Publishing, Indianapolis (2010)
20. Jeske, D., Briggs, P., Coventry, L.: Exploring the relationship between impulsivity and decision-making on mobile devices. Pers. Ubiquit. Comput. **20**(4), 545–557 (2016). https://doi.org/10.1007/s00779-016-0938-4
21. Jin, G., Tu, M., Kim, T.H., Heffron, J., White, J.: Game based cybersecurity training for high school students. In: Proceedings of the 49th ACM Technical Symposium on Computer Science Education, pp. 68–73. ACM (2018)
22. Kassicieh, S., Lipinski, V., Seazzu, A.F.: Human centric cyber security: what are the new trends in data protection? In: 2015 Portland International Conference on Management of Engineering and Technology (PICMET), pp. 1321–1338. IEEE (2015)
23. Kirlappos, I., Sasse, M.A.: Security education against phishing: a modest proposal for a major rethink. IEEE Secur. Priv. **10**(2), 24–32 (2011)
24. Krasniqi, B.A., Berisha, G., Pula, J.S.: Does decision-making style predict managers' entrepreneurial intentions? J. Glob. Entrepr. Res. **9**(1), 1–15 (2019)
25. Kumaraguru, P., Sheng, S., Acquisti, A., Cranor, L.F., Hong, J.: Teaching johnny not to fall for phish. ACM Trans. Internet Technol. (TOIT) **10**(2), 7 (2010)
26. Li, C.Y., Ku, Y.C.: The effects of persuasive messages on system acceptance. In: PACIS, p. 110. Citeseer (2011)
27. Liang, H., Xue, Y.: Avoidance of information technology threats: a theoretical perspective. MIS Q. **33**, 71–90 (2009)
28. Mirkovic, J., Peterson, P.A.: Class capture-the-flag exercises. In: 2014 USENIX Summit on Gaming, Games, and Gamification in Security Education (3GSE 2014) (2014)
29. Misra, G., Arachchilage, N.A.G., Berkovsky, S.: Phish phinder: a game design approach to enhance user confidence in mitigating phishing attacks. arXiv preprint arXiv:1710.06064 (2017)
30. Mohamed, N., Ahmad, I.H.: Information privacy concerns, antecedents and privacy measure use in social networking sites: evidence from Malaysia. Comput. Hum. Behav. **28**(6), 2366–2375 (2012)
31. Ng, B.Y., Xu, Y.: Studying users' computer security behavior using the health belief model. In: PACIS 2007 Proceedings, p. 45 (2007)
32. Rogers, R.W.: A protection motivation theory of fear appeals and attitude change1. J. Psychol. **91**(1), 93–114 (1975)
33. Rosenstock, I.M.: Historical origins of the health belief model. Health Educ. Monogr. **2**(4), 328–335 (1974)
34. Scholefield, S., Shepherd, L.A.: Gamification techniques for raising cyber security awareness. arXiv preprint arXiv:1903.08454 (2019)
35. Scott, S.G., Bruce, R.A.: Decision-making style: the development and assessment of a new measure. Educ. Psychol. Meas. **55**(5), 818–831 (1995)
36. Sheng, S., et al.: Anti-phishing phil: the design and evaluation of a game that teaches people not to fall for phish. In: Proceedings of the 3rd symposium on Usable Privacy and Security, pp. 88–99. ACM (2007)
37. Smith, H.J., Milberg, S.J., Burke, S.J.: Information privacy: measuring individuals' concerns about organizational practices. MIS Q. **20**, 167–196 (1996)

38. Stevens, T.: Global cybersecurity: new directions in theory and methods. Politics Gov. **6**(2), 1–4 (2018)
39. Thompson, M.F., Irvine, C.E.: CyberCIEGE scenario design and implementation. In: 2014 USENIX Summit on Gaming, Games, and Gamification in Security Education (3GSE 2014) (2014)
40. Wen, Z.A., Lin, Z., Chen, R., Andersen, E.: What.Hack: engaging anti-phishing training through a role-playing phishing simulation game. In: Proceedings of the 2019 CHI Conference on Human Factors in Computing Systems, p. 108. ACM (2019)
41. Williams, L., Meneely, A., Shipley, G.: Protection poker: the new software security game. IEEE Secur. Priv. **8**(3), 14–20 (2010)
42. Yasin, A., Liu, L., Li, T., Wang, J., Zowghi, D.: Design and preliminary evaluation of a cyber security requirements education game (SREG). Inf. Softw. Technol. **95**, 179–200 (2018)

Examining Human Individual Differences in Cyber Security and Possible Implications for Human-Machine Interface Design

Laura M. Bishop[1,2] , Phillip L. Morgan[1,2(✉)] , Phoebe M. Asquith[1,2] , George Raywood-Burke[1,2], Adam Wedgbury[1] , and Kevin Jones[1]

[1] Airbus, The Quadrant, Celtic Springs Business Park, Newport NP10 8FZ, UK
{phillip.morgan.external,phoebe.p.asquith.external,
adam.wedgbury,kevin.jones}@airbus.com
[2] Human Factors Excellence Research Group, School of Psychology, Cardiff University,
Tower Building, 70 Park Place, Cardiff CF10 3AT, UK
{bishoplm2,morganphil,asquithpm,raywood-burkeg}@cardiff.ac.uk

Abstract. With society now heavily invested in cyber-technology and most cyber-attacks due to human error, it has never been more vital to focus research on human-centric interventions. Whilst some studies have previously investigated the importance of end-user individual differences (gender, age, education, risk-taking preferences, decision-making style, personality and impulsivity) the current study extended the research to also include acceptance of the internet and the constructs used to explain behavior within the Theory of Planned Behavior (TPB) and Protection Motivation Theory (PMT). Seventy-one participants completed a battery of questionnaires on personality, risk-taking preferences, decision-making style, personality, impulsivity, acceptance of the internet, the combined PMT and TPB questionnaire, as well as an online cyber-security behaviors questionnaire. Gender, age and education did not relate to any cyber-security behaviors, however a number of individual differences were associated. These behaviors include financial risk-taking, avoidant decision-making plus ease of use, facilitating conditions, and trust in the internet. It was also found that safer cyber-security behaviors are seen in those who appraise threat as high, perceive themselves to have the required skills to protect themselves, see value in this protection and understand their place in the cyber-security chain. These findings emphasize the importance of understanding how individual differences relate to cyber-security behaviors in order to create more tailored human-centric interventions such as computer-based decision support systems and other human-machine interface solutions.

Keywords: Human factors · Cyber-security behavior · Individual differences

1 Introduction

With society now heavily invested in computer systems and internet connectivity, never has it been more vital to identify ways in which to safeguard cyberspace [1]. In 2019,

© Springer Nature Switzerland AG 2020
A. Moallem (Ed.): HCII 2020, LNCS 12210, pp. 51–66, 2020.
https://doi.org/10.1007/978-3-030-50309-3_4

over 41,686 security incidents were reported to have taken place across the globe with a data breach confirmed in around 2,000 of these incidents [2]. Of these incidents, 71% were financially motivated, with 56% of breaches taking months or longer to uncover. In the UK alone, the National Cyber Security Centre (NCSC) defends around 12 cyber-attacks on UK organizations each week, including critical national infrastructure, where a breach of security has the potential to cause the UK severe and widespread disruption [3]. Whilst cyber-technology can offer great benefits to communication, productivity and information sourcing, attacks towards online data and system integrity are continuing to evolve in both number and level of intelligence.

The majority of cyber-attacks are made possible through intentional or unintentional human behavior. Despite this, research in the area of cyber-security has largely focused on technical system interventions, with a dearth of research relating to sociotechnical and human-centered aspects. A common example of unintentional human error is in cases involving social engineering: where an attacker employs psychological manipulation to encourage humans to click on malicious links, download malicious attachments or reveal personal information [4]. Social engineering is largely utilized in phishing emails, which appeared as the top threat action responsible for cyber-security breaches in 2019 [2]. Such emails (influence techniques) provided the point of entry for malware in 94% of cases [2]. It is therefore crucial for more research that focuses on investigating the role the human plays in the protection of technology, in order to create interventions (including human-machine interface/HMI solutions) that complement the technical tools currently available.

Human behavior in cyber-security is complex, influenced by the individual characteristics of the end-user, as well as environmental and situational factors [5]. Despite this, interventions within organizations currently tend to employ a one-size-fits-all approach that rarely results in positive behavioral change [6, 7]. However, in order to better tailor interventions, it is important to determine which specific factors render an end-user as more susceptible to a cyber-attack, and to use these insights to create interventions that are more targeted in nature and flexible in their approach to different users.

The aim of the current study is to build upon the limited research currently available and determine which specific individual differences influence cyber-security behaviors in order to create tailored interventions that can be used within businesses to mitigate human susceptibility to cyber threats.

2 Background

To date, the field of cyber-security has largely focused its research on technically-oriented interventions, such as analysis of aggregated logs and system monitoring. However, these interventions are reactive, and less attention is given to addressing end-user vulnerabilities to develop preventative and human-centered security solutions. Despite most organizations utilizing technical interventions, cyber offenders are finding increasingly sophisticated ways of bypassing such efforts, leaving attack outcomes firmly in the hands of the end-users. By better understanding what makes a human more vulnerable to a cyber-attack, tailored human-centric interventions can be devised to compliment the technical tools currently available.

2.1 Human Strength and Vulnerability Within Cyber-Security

Although research has begun to explore this crucial area, more work is needed to identify key individual differences that influence human cyber-security strengths and vulnerabilities, to develop effective tailored human-centered interventions. A number of human characteristics that relate to cyber-security behaviors have been identified, including risk-taking attitude, decision-making strategy and level of impulsivity [8]. Less desirable cyber-security behaviors were found in those more impulsive, as well as those more likely to take health/safety risks (e.g., drive under the influence of alcohol), and procrastinate or rely upon others when making a decision. Gratian et al. [5] built on these findings by investigating risk-taking attitude and decision making style within an educational setting, as well as how gender and personality also relate to cyber-security behaviors. Gender in particular was found to be an important predictor, with men more likely to generate strong passwords, proactively search for contextual clues to cyber risk, and, more regularly update their systems. Some personality traits were also predictive of cyber-security behavior with extroverts more likely to secure their devices and those more conscientious creating strong passwords and allowing system updates. In regards to decision-making, a more rational processing style was linked to more positive behaviors and a spontaneous style more negative. Finally, risk-taking attitude was also found to be a good predictor of cyber-security behavior with those less likely to take a financial risk generating stronger passwords and those more likely to take a health/safety risk weaker passwords. One aim of the current study is to look to validate findings from these previous studies and expand upon them examining at the relationship between cyber-security behavior and both acceptance of the internet and the Theory of Planned Behavior.

2.2 Cyber-Security and Acceptance of the Internet

The Unified Theory of Acceptance and Use of Technology model (UTAUT) [8] is a theory, and associated questionnaire, designed to examine a user's behavioral intentions specifically around the use of technology. Its four core constructs (performance expectancy, effort expectancy, social influence and facilitating conditions) are used to explain the likelihood that a person will accept the technology and how they intend to use it. There are a number of additional external constructs that are regularly included within the model to further explain acceptance including trust, perceived risk, anxiety, hedonic motivation, price value and habit [9, 10]. The UTAUT questionnaire has been previously used to determine factors that influence the acceptance of technology such as mobile banking, mobile internet and internet services with very good reliability, $\alpha = .7$ to $.9$ across studies [11, 12, 13]. Thus, a key aim of the current study is to extend research on individual differences by investigating which specific constructs within the UTAUT model of acceptance may further account for cyber-security behaviors.

2.3 Protection Motivation Theory and the Theory of Planned Behavior

A number of theories have been highlighted in the literature as useful in understanding and modelling cyber-security perceptions and behaviors, although largely independently. One of the main theories applied to cyber threat assessment is Protection Motivation

Theory (PMT), a framework originating within the health domain. PMT suggests two appraisal systems take place when assessing threat: threat appraisal whereby the probability and severity of the threat is considered, and coping appraisal whereby judgements are made in relation to response efficacy, self-efficacy and response costs [14]. The outcome of these appraisals influence how motivated a person is to protect themselves against the threat. Should both threat appraisal and coping appraisal be high – e.g. if a severe threat is expected and the person feels a response will be effective – they will be motivated to act [15]. Research to date suggests response efficacy to have a larger influence on motivation to act than threat severity [16].

Another leading theory is the Theory of Planned Behavior (TPB) consisting of three constructs said to influence behavioral intention; attitude, subjective norms and perceived behavioral control (TPB) [17]. Information security awareness, organizational policy and experience and involvement in IS security have been found to influence these constructs in turn impacting information security behavior [18]. Some attempt has been made to bring both PMT and TPB together into a combined model, with findings suggesting attitude and subjective norms in TBP and threat appraisal and self-efficacy in PMT to be the most important factors when looking to combine the models [19, 18]. The current study involved using the combined model presented by Safa et al. [18] to investigate relationships between the factors within PMT and TPB and cyber-security behaviors, as well as a range of other scales and measures reported in this paper.

2.4 The SeBIS Online Security Behaviors Questionnaire

Whilst the combined PMT and TPB behavior questionnaire has its own behavior construct, both the research by Egelman and Peer [8] and by Gratain et al. [5] utilized the SeBIS online security behaviors questionnaire to examine behavior. The SeBIS was devised by Egelman and Peer [8] to compensate for the lack of a standard measurement tool for cyber-security behaviors. The questionnaire comprises of 16 items split across four sub-scales: password generation; updating; device securement; and proactive awareness. Password generation focuses largely on the creation of passwords and whether they are shared across accounts with updating more focused on the updating of programs, anti-virus software and so on. Device securement targets the locking of computer devices before being away from them, whether passwords are utilized, and proactive awareness the proactive search for contextual clues such as the checking of websites and links for legitimacy. By including the SeBIS in this study we can not only compare our research with that of Egelman and Peer [8] and Gratian et al. [5] but also the behavior construct within PMT and TPB behavior questionnaire.

To conclude, threats to cyber-security are increasing in both number and severity, with human behavior one of the main reasons for successful infiltration of systems. This is most evident within industry and critical national infrastructure sectors, where high numbers of employees as well as challenges such as different roles and different levels of expertise with and knowledge of cyber-security. There is therefore an urgent need to identify the key individual differences that relate to cyber-security behaviors within the workplace. Once these factors are identified, they can be regularly assessed and interventions developed that are more optimally tailored to an individual's strengths and vulnerabilities rather than the often assumed vulnerabilities of humans per se.

3   Method

3.1   Participants

Seventy-one participants were recruited from Cardiff University (staff and PhD students: 48% of the sample) and via the Prolific online marketing tool (52% of the sample). Of these participants, 31% were male, 68% female and 1% of a different identity. Participants were aged between 18 and 65 with 70% between 24–44 years of age. The sample was well educated (UK GCSEs to Doctorate level) with 80% of participants in holding at least an undergraduate degree. Cardiff University staff and students were not rewarded for taking part. Prolific pays an hourly rate to its users for completion of questionnaires, so participants were paid accordingly.

3.2   Study Design and Procedure

This study employed a between-subjects and correlational design to investigate how user characteristics (gender, age, education, personality, risk-taking preferences, decision-making preferences, impulsivity, acceptance of the internet) and factors within both PMT and the TPB relate to cyber-security behaviors.

Participants accessed the study via Qualtrics©, an online survey platform, on PCs and tablets. Before completing the survey participants were presented with a brief introduction sheet, request for consent and a demographics form including age, gender and level of education. Participants were then asked to complete the IPIP personality traits measure [20] where they were presented with 50 statements (10 questions for each sub-scale including extroversion, openness to experience, neuroticism, conscientiousness and agreeableness) and asked to which extent each statement applied to themselves, rated from 1 (very inaccurate) to 5 (very accurate). Risk-taking preferences were then measured using the DOSPERT risk-taking preferences questionnaire [21] whereby participants were asked to rate how likely they were to engage in 30 risky behaviors from 1 (extremely unlikely) to 7 (extremely likely). The 30 questions covered five different forms of risk taking (social, recreational, financial, health/safety, ethical) with six questions per factor.

Participants then completed the GDMS decision-making style questionnaire [22] indicating to which extent they agree or disagree with 25 statements with five overarching decision-making styles (intuitive, dependent, avoidant, rational, spontaneous) ranging from 1 (strongly disagree) to 5 (strongly agree). Next, participants completed the Barratt Impulsiveness Scale (BIS-11) [23] indicating how regularly they had experienced a list of 30 statements ranging from 1 (rarely/never) to 5 (always). Participants then completed the TPB and PMT questionnaire [18] rating 42 statements, from nine sub-scales e.g. threat appraisal, from 1 (strongly disagree) to 7 (strongly agree). Following this the participants were asked to complete the UTAUT acceptance of the internet questionnaire [10] containing 30 statements (with 9 subscales including performance expectancy, effort expectancy, social influence, trust, facilitating conditions, hedonic motivation, price value, habit and behavioral intention) rated from 1 (strongly disagree) to 7 (strongly agree) Finally, participants completed the SeBIS online security behaviors questionnaire containing 16 statements (with 4 overarching constructs of updating, device securement, password generation and proactive awareness), rating how often they undertake each behavior from 1 (never) to 5 (always). After completion of all questionnaires participants were provided with a study debrief.

4 Results

This study was designed to investigate the relationships between end-user individual differences and cyber-security behaviors (see Subsects. 4.1, 4.2, 4.3 and 4.4 below and Table 1 for a combined summary) as well as differences between individuals based on e.g., demographic factors such as age, gender, and educational level. The individual differences analyzed included gender, age, education, personality, risk-taking preferences, decision-making style and level of impulsivity. Also analyzed were factors from the acceptance of the internet questionnaire and constructs found within PMT and the TPB. A test of internal consistency was applied to all measures used in the study with Cronbach's Alpha reaching high reliability within the SeBIS online security behaviors questionnaire ($\alpha = .83$), TPB and PMT questionnaire ($\alpha = .95$), Barratt Impulsivity questionnaire ($\alpha = .87$), GDMS decision-making style ($\alpha = .80$), DOSPERT risk-taking preferences questionnaire ($\alpha = .84$), and IPIP Personality Traits questionnaire ($\alpha = .75$). The key assumptions for parametric testing were not met due to the use of ordinal data, and therefore non-parametric statistical tests were utilized.

4.1 SeBIS Device Securement

The independent-samples Kruskal-Wallis test was used to investigate potential differences between end-user demographics and device securement as measured by the SeBIS online security behaviors questionnaire, with no significant differences found in gender, age or level of education. Spearman's rank correlation was then used to analyze relationships between personality and SeBIS device securement. Again, no significant relationships were found. In reference to risk-taking preference a significant negative relationship was found between device securement and self-reported financial risk-taking ($r = -0.25, n = 71, p = .04$). No significant relationships were found between the SeBIS online security behaviors questionnaire and decision-making style or impulsivity.

Analyses were then carried out to examine whether there were significant relationships between device securement and acceptance of the internet. A significant positive relationship was found between device securement and effort expectancy ($r = 0.24, n = 71, p = .04$), with those finding the internet easier to use also reporting better device securement. No other significant relationships between these factors were found.

Further analyses investigated device securement and the PMT and TPB behavior questionnaire responses. A significant positive relationship was found between device securement and value of information security organization policy ($r = 0.27, n = 71, p = .02$). A significant positive relationship was also found between device securement and the attitude construct ($r = 0.33, n = 71, p < .01$), with those having a more positive view on information security also more likely to secure their device. Finally, threat level appraisal was found to have a significant and positive relationship with device securement ($r = 0.47, n = 71, p < .01$).

4.2 SeBIS Proactive Awareness

A test of differences was performed between end-user demographics and proactive awareness. No significant differences were found across age, gender or education. Correlation analyses also found no significant relationships between proactive awareness and personality, risk-taking preference, decision-making style or impulsivity.

Further analyses investigated relationships between proactive awareness and acceptance of the internet questionnaire. A significant positive relationship was found between proactive awareness and effort expectancy ($r = 0.25, n = 71, p = .04$), with those finding the internet easier to use also reporting more proactive awareness. A significant negative relationship was found between proactive awareness and trust in internet reporting ($r = -0.29, n = 71, p = .02$).

Correlation analyses were also conducted between proactive awareness and the PMT and the TPB questionnaire responses. A range of significant relationships found. There was a significant positive relationship between information security risk awareness and proactive awareness ($r = 0.43, n = 71, p < .01$). A significant positive relationship was found between proactive awareness and information security organization policy ($r = 0.31, n = 71, p = .01$), with those seeing more value in organization policy reporting themselves as more proactively aware. Information security experience and involvement was significantly positively related to proactive awareness ($r = 0.41, n = 71, p < .01$). Attitude and proactive awareness were significantly and positively correlated ($r = 0.29, n = 71, p = .02$), with those viewing information security conscious care as necessary also reporting more proactive awareness. Proactive awareness significantly and positively correlated with both perceived behavioral control ($r = 0.39, n = 71, p = .01$) and security self-efficacy ($r = 0.30, n = 71, p = .01$). Threat level appraisal also significantly and positively correlated with proactive awareness ($r = 0.44, n = 71, p < .01$). Finally, proactive awareness significantly and positively correlated with the behavior construct within the TPB ($r = 0.60, n = 71, p < .01$).

4.3 SeBIS Updating

A test of differences was performed between end-user demographics and updating, with no significant differences found for age, gender or education. Correlation analyses also revealed no significant relationships between updating and personality, risk-taking preference, decision-making style or impulsivity. Analyses were then carried out to detect for any relationships between updating and acceptance of the internet. A significant positive relationship was found between updating and hedonic motivation ($r = 0.32, n = 71, p < .01$). This suggests those finding the internet more enjoyable to use also report evidence of better updating practices.

Additional analyses were performed between updating and the PMT and TPB questionnaire responses, with a number of significant relationships found. A significant positive relationship was found between information security awareness and updating ($r = 0.41, n = 71, p < .01$), with those who are aware of potential threat are also more likely to report updating behaviors. A significant positive relationship was found between updating and an individual's value in the information security organization policy ($r = 0.30, n = 71, p = .01$). Information security experience and involvement significantly and positively related to updating ($r = 0.38, n = 71, p < .01$). Attitude and updating also significantly and positively correlated ($r = 0.28, n = 71, p = .02$), with those viewing information security conscious care as necessary also reporting updating their system more regularly. Updating also significantly and positively correlated with security self-efficacy ($r = 0.31, n = 71, p = .01$). Threat appraisal also significantly and positively correlated with updating ($r = 0.31, n = 71, p = .01$), with those appraising threat as higher also reporting more updating. Finally, updating significantly and positively correlated with the behavior construct within the theory of planned behavior ($r = 0.36, n = 71, p < .01$).

4.4 SeBIS Password Generation

A test of differences was performed between end-user demographics and password generation, with no significant differences found for age, gender or education. Correlation analyses also found no significant relationships between proactive awareness and personality, risk-taking preference or impulsivity. A significant negative relationship was however found between strong password generation and an avoidant decision-making style ($r = 0.24, n = 71, p < .04$).

Analyses were then carried out to examine for any relationships between password generation and acceptance of the internet. A significant positive relationship was found between password generation and effort expectancy ($r = 0.25, n = 71, p = .04$), with those finding the internet easier to use also reporting more positive password related behaviors. A significant positive correlation was also found between password generation and facilitating conditions ($r = 0.24, n = 71, p = .04$), with those feeling they have the skills and resources available to use the internet reporting more positive password related behaviors.

Analyses were also conducted between password generation and the PMT and TPB behavior questionnaire responses, with a number of significant relationships found. There was a significant positive relationship between information security awareness and password generation ($r = 0.35, n = 71, p < .01$) with those more likely to search for contextual clues such as suspicious links or websites more likely to report themselves as proactively aware. Attitudes and password generation also significantly and positively correlated ($r = 0.25, n = 71, p = .03$), with those viewing information security conscious care as necessary also reporting more proactive awareness. Password generation significantly and positively correlated with perceived behavioral control ($r = 0.36, n = 71, p = .01$), with those perceiving information security conscious care behavior as achievable also reporting better password generation behaviors. Threat level appraisal also significantly and positively correlated ($r = 0.26, n = 71, p = .03$) with password generation. Finally, password generation significantly and positively correlated with the behavior construct within the TPB ($r = 0.42, n = 71, p < .01$).

5   Discussion

This study investigated a number of individual differences and how they relate to cyber-security behaviors. Previous research had indicated a number of characteristics that did associate with cyber-security behaviors; this study extended these characteristics to also include the acceptance of the internet questionnaire and the combined PMT and TBP questionnaire. Findings from the current study suggest end-users should remain aware of the high probability of an attack, as well as receiving interventions for specific and more general internet skills to protect themselves with subsequent improvements to cyber-security behavior(s). It also appears important for both cyber-security and its policies to be viewed as beneficial by employees and that they are aware of their significance within the cyber-security chain. These findings highlight the importance of a better understanding of the human-centric qualities associated with cyber-security behaviors, in order to inform new and effective interventions.

Table 1. Findings from correlational analyses. *Note.* – represents no significant relationship.

Individual difference	Device securement	Proactive awareness	Updating	Password generation
Demographics	–	–	–	–
Personality	–	–	–	–
Decision-making		–	–	Self-reported avoidant
Risk-taking	Financial	–	–	–
Impulsivity	–	–	–	–
Acceptance	Effort expectancy	Effort expectancy Trust	Hedonic motivation	Effort expectancy Facilitating conditions
PMT & TPB	ISOP ATT Threat appraisal	ISA ISOP ISEI ATT PBC Threat appraisal ISSE Behavior	ISA ISOP ISEI ATT Threat appraisal ISSE Behavior	ISA ATT PBC Threat appraisal Behavior

Note. ISA = Information Security Awareness, ISOP = Information Security Organization policy, ISEI = Information Security Experience and Involvement, ATT = Attitude, PBC = Perceived Behavioral Control, ISSE = Information Security Self-efficacy

5.1 Individual Differences and Device Securement

In order to determine which individual differences relate to cyber-security behavior, this study first analyzed whether gender, age or education significantly correlated with device securement, with no significant correlations anticipated. As found in Gratian et al. [5], no significant effects were found in relation to any of these demographic factors. We also investigated whether significant relationships existed between the five personality traits and device securement. The study by Gratian et al. [5] found extroversion to be a unique predictor of cyber-security behavior; however, no such relationship between extroversion, or any of the personality sub-scales, and device securement was found in the current study.

Both studies by Gratian et al. [5] and Egelman and Peer [8] found device securement related to decision-making style with the former finding a rational decision-making style to be a predictor of device securement, and the latter a relationship between device securement and avoidant decision-making. This was not replicated within this study. However, the finding by Egelman and Peer [8] that impulsivity was not related to device securement, was replicated. The current findings also established that those more likely to take financial risk, report themselves as less likely to secure their device. This finding appears credible, as not securing your device can potentially leave you open to financial risk.

As acceptance of the internet had not previously been examined within the cyber-security domain, relationships with device securement could not be anticipated. However previous research around acceptance and technology did suggest it worth investigating. Findings from the current study indicated a significant relationship between the effort expectancy construct and device securement, suggesting those finding the internet more difficult to use are also less likely to secure their device. This may possibly be due to a lack of technical knowledge preventing our participants from utilising passwords and auto-lock functions.

Also analyzed were the relationships between the combined PMT and TPB questionnaire and device securement, with the aim of determining whether any constructs within the questionnaires can potentially be used to explain this behavior. A significant positive relationship was found between information security organization policy and device securement implying that end-users that better value IS policy are also more likely to lock their device. As correlational analysis was utilized, causation cannot be assumed. However, it is possible that should an organization continue to highlight the value of policy employees may be more likely to benefit from their advice around device securement. It was also found that those who see the benefit in conscious cyber-security behavior will also be more likely to engage in device securement. Again, by highlighting the benefits of cyber-security to an organization, end-users will be more likely to adopt its policies and improve device securement within the business. Further research will however need to be undertaken to confirm this. Finally, threat appraisal was found to relate to device securement with those appraising the probability and severity of threat as high more likely to secure their device. It may therefore be of importance to keep employees aware of any threat that takes place both within and outside of the business, in order for them to be able to assess threat appropriately.

In respect of device securement, significant relationships were found between this construct and those more likely to take a financial risk as well as those finding the internet harder to use. It was also found that those who see an attack as likely and value the importance of cyber-security will be more likely to secure their device. This suggests that organizations should keep employees informed of the true risk of an attack and therefore the importance of following policy to protect from this risk.

5.2 Individual Differences and Proactive Awareness

Remaining proactively aware of potential threat is an important step towards protection. Those that report not fully investigating links and websites before utilizing them, as well as those that report leaving security issues to be fixed by others, are at higher risk of a security breach. It is therefore important to understand relationships between individual differences and proactive awareness, to create interventions that can target these differences. Analyzed first were the relationships between proactive awareness and gender, age and education. A relationship was anticipated between gender and proactive awareness as found within the Gratian et al. [5] study, however this study found no relationships between any of the demographics and proactive awareness. No relationships were also found between proactive awareness and personality, risk-taking preference, decision-making style or impulsivity.

Correlational analyses were then undertaken to determine any relationships between the acceptance of the internet questionnaire and proactive awareness. As found with updating, proactive awareness correlated with effort expectancy with those finding the internet harder to use being less likely to check links and emails before utilizing them. A relationship was also found between proactive awareness and trust with those less trusting of the internet remaining more proactively aware of potential threat. It is therefore important that whilst organizations ensure their employees become confident in use of the internet, this confidence does not increase trust.

Analyses were conducted on proactive awareness and the PMT and TPB behavior questionnaire responses to investigate whether constructs within the combined model relate to people remaining proactively aware. Proactive awareness was significantly related with information security awareness, suggesting those who are more proactively aware are also more likely to be aware of potential cyber-security risks. Higher proactive awareness was also found in those more likely to see the value in both IS organizational policy, as well as cyber-security more generally. As with updating, it is therefore important that organizations inform employees of the benefits of IS policy and the value in its recommendations. Proactive awareness was also significantly related to how experienced and involved participants felt they were in cyber-security, suggesting a need for all employees to feel more involved in the domain be clear of where they sit within the cyber-security chain. A positive relationship was also found between proactive awareness and participants who felt they had the skills to protect themselves and that protection was achievable. It is therefore important to increase security self-efficacy in the workplace as should employees feel unable to protect the business; else the they simply might not try. Threat appraisal was also found to relate to proactive awareness with those perceiving threat as both unlikely and less severe not taking the time to be conscious of the risks. As mentioned previously, providing employees with updates on incidents both within and outside of the company may positively influence this appraisal. Finally, proactive awareness correlated with the behavior construct within the protection motivation theory and theory of planned behavior questionnaire suggesting proactive awareness to be an indicator of cyber-security behavior more generally.

Those more proactively aware were therefore found to be more technologically literate and in full understanding of potential risk. These findings also suggest it important to advise employees of the benefits of remaining up to date on cyber-security policy and making clear that they are firmly positioned inside the cyber-security chain.

5.3 Individual Differences and Updating

We also wanted to better understand which individual differences relate to updating behaviors, such as the updating of software and anti-virus programs. Whilst in larger organizations this is less likely to be a concern (as such updates are often automatically rolled-out), it is still important to remain aware in order to advice should something appear out of date. We anticipated differences in updating behavior within gender, age and education as was the case in the Gratian et al. study [5]. This was however not supported. Also, there were no significant relationships between updating and personality, risk-taking preference, decision-making style or impulsivity as anticipated by the literature.

Also examined were relationships between the constructs found within the acceptance of the internet questionnaire and updating behavior. Analyses revealed that those rating the internet as more enjoyable to also report more evidence of updating. It is unclear whether those finding the internet more fun to use are also more willing to protect the system they enjoy using or whether by making regular updates the internet remains fun. It is also possible that those that do regularly update are more capable when it comes to cyber-technology and will therefore find it more fun and enjoyable to use generally.

A number of significant relationships were found between updating and the protection motivation theory and the theory of planned behavior questionnaire. Those more likely to update their computers reported having a better understanding of the risks around cyber-technology and were clearer on how to remain up to date to avoid these risks. They were also more likely to place a higher value on IS policy and cyber-security more generally as well as feel more involved in the process. As with proactive awareness, better updating behaviors were also associated with higher security self-efficacy and higher threat appraisal. Therefore, if employees do not see an attack as a true threat and do not feel they have the skills to stop it they are unlikely to protect themselves and the organization. Finally, updating was found to correlate with the behavior construct within the protection motivation theory and theory of planned behavior questionnaire suggesting it a good indicator of cyber-security behavior more generally.

These findings again suggest the importance of employees perceiving risk as high and having the skills to be able to keep their system up-to-date. As mentioned previously, it is important for employees to remain clear on the benefits of cyber-security policy and that they are aware of the importance of their role in the cyber-security chain.

5.4 Individual Differences and Password Generation

Finally, we set out to better understand individual differences in relation to secure password generation. There were no significant differences in updating behavior based on gender, age and education, again in contrast to findings reported by Gratian et al. [5]. Correlation analyses were undertaken and revealed that those more likely to avoid making decisions were less likely to create strong and separate passwords. This may be due to avoiding the effort of choosing stronger passwords or avoiding changing passwords already created. No relationships were found between password generation and personality, risk-taking preference or impulsivity. We also investigated the possible relationship between the constructs found within the acceptance of the internet questionnaire and password generation, and again found better password generation behaviors in those who find the internet easier to use. This highlights the potential importance of providing employees with general computer skills training and not just training related directly to cyber-security. A relationship was also found between password generation and the facilitating conditions construct suggesting those who feel they have the skills and resources available to use the internet will generate better passwords. Often when creating passwords advice is not provided leaving those who do not regularly use the internet or lack in skill at risk.

As with the other behavioral constructs a number of relationships were found between the PMT and TPB questionnaire responses and password generation. Again, those more likely to generate strong passwords reported having a better understanding of the risks around cyber-technology. Better password generation was also found in those who viewed information security conscious care as beneficial. It was also found that those creating stronger passwords also appraised the threat of an attack as high and felt protecting themselves from it achievable. Again, this potentially highlights the importance of communicating incidents as well as ensuring employees perceive themselves as holding the skills to protect themselves.

Password generation is a key concern both within the workplace and within the general public. This study has found that those creating weak passwords also report low cyber-security skills, as well as low internet skills more generally. They were also found to appraise threat as low, suggesting it key to consider ways in which to communicate effectively to employees the true risk of not creating stronger passwords across multiple accounts and why security conscious care is critical.

6 Limitations

Limitations in this study include the use of surveys only and not all responses may truly represent participant individual differences and cyber-security behaviors. That is, some participants may subjectively rate themselves incorrectly in relation to their actual individual differences and behaviors due to, e.g., response bias, not fully understanding questions, and so on. Also, the study involved a large number of scales and measures and there may have been fatigue and/or boredom effects. However, the order in which the scales and measures were presented to participants was randomized.

Correlational analyses were mainly used due to the exploratory nature of the study meaning that in most cases (apart from analyses of demographic factors) causation cannot be determined – e.g., does individual difference factor x cause behaviour y? Regression analysis could be considered for such data in the future, as well as employing methods to split data (e.g., median split method) to examine whether there are differences between e.g., low and high scorers on measures. However, the sample-size ($N = 71$) within the current study is likely to be too small to detect differences if they exist, especially for cases where effect sizes may be small or even small to medium. The sample was also well educated with over half of the sample university staff and PhD students, therefore the findings may not represent the general population.

Finally, despite most participants taking part in the study being in paid employment (noting most PhD students were in receipt of a stipend and some also worked part-time), and mostly working in jobs/roles/sectors where cyber-security is or at least should be important, future studies should look to include samples or subsamples of employees who have background education and job roles in areas more related to IT. Employees with roles such as cyber-security specialists and computer scientists would provide important comparisons between groups of individuals with different levels of IT and security expertise. Non-incentives, self-selecting samples could also be prioritized to increase the likelihood of engaged participation.

7 Conclusions, HCI Recommendations and Future Research

With society now heavily invested in cyber-technology and the majority of cyber-attacks due to human error, it has never been more vital to create interventions that are human-centric. This study investigated how a number of individual differences relate to cyber-security behaviors in order to better tailor interventions to the end-user. A number of factors were found to relate to cyber-security behavior more generally such as the need for end-users to appraise risk as high and perceive themselves to be skilled in protection. Should an end-user not anticipate threat and feel indefensible effort will be at a minimum. It also appears important that end-users understand the value of cyber-security and its policies as well as are aware of how to remain up to date. Another key factor is end-users understanding where they sit in the cyber-security chain and that their commitment to it is key. This suggests that organizations will benefit from communicating true threat probability and severity to their employees and that interventions focus on both general internet skills as well as skills in how to prevent an attack.

There were also a number of factors that related specifically to one of the cyber-security behaviors. In respect of device securement those who are more likely to take financial risk are less likely to secure their device. Whilst this may be difficult to tackle within the workplace, providing standardized securement processes, perhaps as HMI hard constraints, may help negate this issue. Those with an avoidant decision-making style were also found to be less likely to create strong separate passwords. People with less trust in the internet also reported more proactive awareness again highlighting the importance in communicating incidents both within and outside of the business. Those reporting incidents of updating rated the internet as more enjoyable, and stronger password generation was found in those who felt they had the right skills and resources to use the internet. Again these support the finding that providing general internet skills to end-users may improve cyber-security behaviors. HMI design and HCI solutions could be developed (such as decision support systems and reminders) to support individuals to make better cyber safe decisions.

Future research should continue to investigate relationships between individual differences and cyber-security behaviors increasing both the number of characteristics included as well as behaviors analyzed. Once there is better understanding around the characteristics involved research can focus on understanding which individual differences are the highest predictors of cyber-security behaviors. These can then be used to assess cyber strengths and vulnerabilities of employees entering a workplace and to directly target interventions (such as adaptable and adaptive decision support systems) to these individuals and then reassess post-intervention to gauge success. Overall, the current research highlights the importance of better understanding how human-centric individual differences relate to cyber-security behaviors in order to provide more targeted interventions.

Acknowledgements. The research was supported by a fully funded PhD studentship awarded to the first author (Laura Bishop) from the School of Psychology at Cardiff University. Other support was provided by Airbus where the PhD student is a member of the Airbus Accelerator in Human-Centric Cyber Security team, under the Technical Leadership of the second author (Dr Phillip Morgan) who is also Laura Bishop's PhD Lead Supervisor.

References

1. Asquith, P.M., Morgan, P.L.: Representing a human-centric cyberspace. In: 11 International Conference on Applied Human Factors and Ergonomics (2020, in press)
2. Verizon. 2019 Data Breach Investigations Report (2019). https://enterprise.verizon.com/res ources/reports/2019-data-breach-investigations-report-emea.pdf
3. National Cyber Security Centre. The Annual Review 2019 (2019). https://www.ncsc.gov.uk/news/annual-review-2019
4. Ghafir, I., et al.: Security threats to critical infrastructure: the human factor. J. Supercomput **74**, 4986–5002 (2018). https://doi.org/10.1007/s11227-018-2337-2
5. Gratian, M., Bandi, S., Cukier, M., Dykstra, J., Ginther, A.: Correlating human traits and cyber security behavior intentions. Comput. Secur. **73**, 345–358 (2018)
6. Scholl, M.C., Fuhrmann, F., Scholl, L.R.: Scientific knowledge of the human side of information security as a basis for sustainable trainings in organizational practices. In: Proceedings of the 51st Hawaii International Conference on System Sciences, pp. 2235–2244 (2018)
7. Bada, M., Sasse, A.M., Nurse, J.R.: Cyber security awareness campaigns: why do they fail to change behaviour? arXiv preprint arXiv:1901.02672 (2019)
8. Egelman, S., Peer, E.: Scaling the security wall: developing a security behavior intentions scale (SeBIS). In: Proceedings of the 33rd Annual ACM Conference on Human Factors in Computing Systems, pp. 2873–2882. ACM (2015)
9. Dwivedi, K., Rana, N.P., Chen, H., Williams, M.D.: A meta-analysis of the unified theory of acceptance and use of technology (UTAUT). In: Nüttgens, M., Gadatsch, A., Kautz, K., Schirmer, I., Blinn, N. (eds.) TDIT 2011. IAICT, vol. 366, pp. 155–170. Springer, Heidelberg (2011). https://doi.org/10.1007/978-3-642-24148-2_10
10. Venkatesh, V., Thong, J.Y., Xu, X.: Consumer acceptance and use of information technology: extending the unified theory of acceptance and use of technology. MIS Q. **36**, 157–178 (2012)
11. Oh, J.C., Yoon, S.J.: Predicting the use of online information services based on a modified UTAUT model. Behav. Inf. Technol. **33**(7), 716–729 (2014)
12. Wang, H.Y., Wang, S.H.: User acceptance of mobile internet based on the unified theory of acceptance and use of technology: investigating the determinants and gender differences. Soc. Behav. Pers. Int. J. **38**(3), 415–426 (2010)
13. Yu, C.S.: Factors affecting individuals to adopt mobile banking: empirical evidence from the UTAUT model. J. Electron. Commer. Res. **13**(2), 104 (2012)
14. McGill, T., Thompson, N.: Old risks, new challenges: exploring differences in security between home computer and mobile device use. Behav. Inf. Technol. **36**(11), 1111–1124 (2017)

15. van Bavel, R., Rodríguez-Priego, N., Vila, J., Briggs, P.: Using protection motivation theory in the design of nudges to improve online security behavior. Int. J. Hum. Comput. Stud. **123**, 29–39 (2019)
16. Posey, C., Roberts, T.L., Lowry, P.B.: The impact of organizational commitment on insiders' motivation to protect organizational information assets. J. Manag. Inf. Syst. **32**(4), 179–214 (2015)
17. Ajzen, I.: The theory of planned behaviour: reactions and reflections. Psychol. Health **26**(9), 1103–1127 (2011)
18. Safa, N.S., Sookhak, M., Von Solms, R., Furnell, S., Ghani, N.A., Herawan, T.: Information security conscious care behaviour formation in organizations. Comput. Secur. **53**, 65–78 (2015)
19. Sommestad, T., Karlzén, H., Hallberg, J.: The sufficiency of the theory of planned behavior for explaining information security policy compliance. Inf. Comput. Secur. **23**(2), 200–217 (2015)
20. Goldberg, L.R., et al.: The international personality item pool and the future of public-domain personality measures. J. Res. Pers. **40**(1), 84–96 (2006)
21. Blais, A.R., Weber, E.U.: A domain-specific risk-taking (DOSPERT) scale for adult populations. Judg. Decis. Mak. **1**, 33–47 (2006)
22. Scott, S.G., Bruce, R.A.: Decision-making style: the development and assessment of a new measure. Educ. Psychol. Measur. **55**(5), 818–831 (1995)
23. Patton, J.H., Stanford, M.S., Barratt, E.S.: Factor structure of the Barratt impulsiveness scale. J. Clin. Psychol. **51**(6), 768–774 (1995)

Building Connections for a Secure User Experience

David Blank[1]([✉]) and Ravi Kanth Kosuru[2]([✉])

[1] Institute for Industrial Engineering, Fraunhofer IAO, Nobelstr. 12, 70569 Stuttgart, Germany
`david.blank@iao.fraunhofer.de`
[2] Institute of Human Factors and Technology Management IAT, University of Stuttgart,
Stuttgart, Germany
`ravi-kanth.kosuru@iat.uni-stuttgart.de`

Abstract. The focus on design areas that motivate users, enhance user experience instead of just making it usable has made security with respect to data privacy an important topic. There is also a general lack of easily comprehensible information and awareness when it comes to new regulations like the General Data Protection Regulation (GDPR) [1]. Changes in processes or requirements that involve the use of certain data are avoided without studying the finer details of dependencies and connections. This hinders projects with design ideas that might otherwise enhance user-experience. We introduce a method to enable innovative design for human-machine interfaces in compliance with data protection and security regulation that is based on our extensive experience with industrial projects. The paper will provide examples of design concepts that address the security concerns raised while conforming to the main topics of ISO 9241.

Keywords: Security · Method · User experience · Usability

1 Introduction

The ISO 9241 outlines the most important factors for usability. They are: suitability for the task, suitability for learning, suitability for individualization, conformity with user expectations, self-descriptiveness, controllability, and error tolerance [2]. This, combined with the Human-Centered Design-Process [3] and its definition of user experience (UX), forms the base for every good HMI-Design. It ensures the project focus always lies on the user.

The UX and need-based models show the importance of security for UX. It can be described as «the absence of danger and the independence of outer circumstances» [4]. This means that the users must feel comfortable while using the system. Failing which, the system either becomes unusable or results in a bad UX. On the other hand, positive user experience gets limited while focusing on the security aspects and might, even at times, be annoying for the user. A good interface ensures such aspects remain in the background while ensuring the user feels secure and comfortable. Better usability should not be at the expense of security, which in turn has a negative impact on UX. The user should be able to find any security-related information for clarification on demand.

Our method was conceived and developed during a project (here on referred to in the rest of the paper) where we created a system that provides instructions for shop floor machine maintenance. The goal of the system was to tap into the rich experience and knowledge of the workers, and make it shareable. This however, led to concerns with data privacy and security from the project teams, which included production management, and development teams. This was the major motivation for developing the method to build and visualize the various connections, to understand the concerns and find possible solutions.

2   Related Work

2.1   Methods

Although there is not much work that explicitly tries to solve user experience problems caused due to data security concerns, there is quite a bit of research and tools for understanding risk [5], for example to help SMEs to comply to the GDPR [6]. The concerns regarding gathering personal data and the benefits of using such data for personalization of interfaces are also an active area of research. Information about individuals is an important pre-requisite for personalization. It has been observed that designing personalization systems that also provide the best privacy-related user experience need a human-centered perspective. The relation between the intention of people to disclose certain personal data and the corresponding benefits promised by personalization have been studied [7].

2.2   Inspiration

Most procedural police dramas, detective, and spy thrillers have protagonists trying to trace connections between various scenarios and characters. One of the most common plot points is the pin board where various character photos and clues are placed and interconnected with colorful yarns. This serves as a useful tool to guide the viewer through the thought process of the protagonist as well the plot. It also provides opportunities to ask the right questions that help propel the story forward. This was a major inspiration for the method that is outlined in this paper. We saw in such a system, the advantage of providing a visual canvas that helps one begin with asking the right questions and communicate their ideas effectively.

3   Method

The need for the method was driven by the necessity to provide effective answers for concerns raised using the discussion with the workers council in the project. One concern was that, users would not share their knowledge as they did not have any incentive and feel insecure, as their skills might not be unique anymore. A preliminary user test with a prototype of the user interface showed that the concern was unfounded. They saw the overarching benefit of a shared information pool for their own work and the company. The second concern was about data privacy. The system would store information generated from the users and consist of user actions, communication between users, etc. and combined with gamified design elements like points and ranking. There was a fear among the team that such proposals would be met with objections from the workers council. There were extensive discussions and meetings between various stakeholders, which did not lead to any conclusion. We then formulated a method to visualize the most important aspects of the projects that showed the relevant dependencies and benefits.

3.1 Core Concept

The core concept lies in formulating the major aspects as a triangle with each side representing a major category. One side (Side A) represents possible data types such as usernames, sensor data with a description. The second side (Side B) designates relevant roles and responsibilities, or users and their interests. The third side (Side C) lists benefits or aspects, which would lead to innovative design. These, can be then connected to each other, showing the relevant needs and dependencies (see Fig. 1. Methodical Triangle).

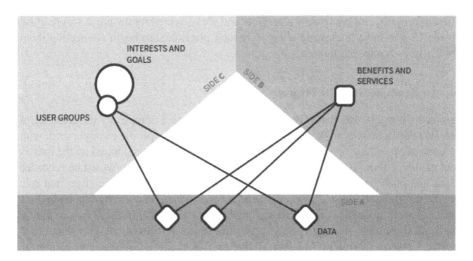

Fig. 1. Methodical Triangle that displays the core concept

3.2 Tools

We designed cards that would represent the necessary information for the different sides. The data cards used on Side A contained a name for the data group, the data contained, space for comments, and indication of information level, what can be learned from the data, and estimated security level. The cards for Side B described the idea or service. In addition, everyone could define if they are the provider of such a solution or the user (see Fig. 2. Cards). In our implementation, every project team had his own representative pin color. They were also provided with threads that would be used for connecting the different pins.

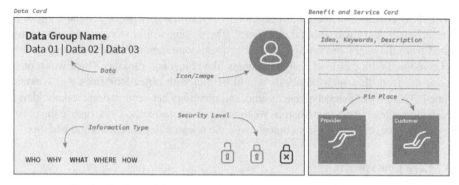

Fig. 2. Cards used for representing the relevant information and ideas

3.3 Process

We prefilled Side A on a pin Board with different types of data relevant for the project. We used the «UXellence®» Methods [8, 9] to identify the stakeholders and their interests for side B. This is important to be able to empathize with the relevant stakeholders. The different benefits, sub-components, services and ideas created for the project were listed on side C. The most interesting ideas were then prioritized to begin connecting them physically with pins and threads.

3.4 An Example from the Project

One of the insights was that every user has the focus on a completely different set of data, which can be seen in the lines starting from side C. A specific example dealt with the issue of providing an adaptive information screen that changed based on the user in front of the system. This however, meant specific user information would be recorded which had push back from the project teams. Connecting the feature "user and role specific information display" (top of side B) it became clear that linked data (side A) is interesting for the quality of the feature, however not all of it is mandatory (see Fig. 3. Application example from the project). For example, pseudonymous user data could be used instead of explicitly mentioning the user. A manual switchover is also quite effective and offers sufficient advantages. These solutions did not surface readily in the initial meetings. After this first success, further compromises were made in a very short time.

3.5 Key Elements

The focus on building connections from the perspective of benefits had a major contribution in finding solutions to the data privacy concerns.

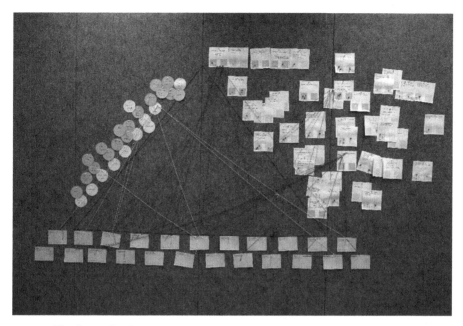

Fig. 3. Application example from the project that shows the interconnections

Visualization

Visualization made aspects of the project that could not be communicated during the discussions, effectively graspable. Interestingly, it was found certain issues were unfounded in the first place. The visualization showed that certain information was not necessary to be saved in the end or had no effect on certain components.

Visualizing something, i.e. pinning it to the wall or writing it down, gives the participants a chance to think about it, to comment on it, to suggest or make changes to it and the results are seen in real-time and serve as a live protocol.

The second effect is that facts become clearer. The moment the link becomes visible on the wall, a connection becomes tangible and other possible complex connections become apparent.

Physical Activity

The physical act of pinning the relevant components and connecting them stimulated the decision-making. Similar to Design Thinking, active participation is a core part of the approach. The physical activity is an important aspect, that juggles the mind, aids focus, and creates awareness and undoing it means effort. Similar activating elements are seen in education where learning content is distributed with a classroom [10, 11].

4   Implications on Design

There are quite a few examples of applications that force users to create accounts with no apparent relevance. They are explicitly just used for gathering data and the services are not directly dependent on the user profile. Such practices limit the confidence of users and sow doubts in users in general. For example, the Application "NVIDIA GeForce Experience" requires one to create an account for driver updates and settings. This is especially explicit in smartphone apps where certain applications ask for access to resources that they might not need. For example, a compass asking for access to the images or the Internet connection. Due to the many misuse reports and infringements [12], trust declines or turns into general rejection.

The issue of data protection has gained prominence in recent years. The introduction of the basic data protection regulation (GDPR), has brought in sweeping changes, especially with regard to collection and storage of personal data.

In the field of user experience and interaction design, we are increasingly confronted with situations where there are advantages to storing and analyzing context and user data. In discussions with the works council, for example, the data and conclusions that could be drawn about an employee were the conflict point. Objections were raised on the explicit need for such data or which data if at all. As described in the specific example (see Sect. 3.4) we used our method to find a fitting solution.

Our method has implications for conflicts that may arise during certain design decisions for systems as outlined in the following examples from the project. We also mention the factors for usability, as given in the ISO norm (see Sect. 1) that the design examples address.

4.1   Example 1: Collecting and Sharing Knowledge

Positive Effect on Error Tolerance
Man is an excellent *sensor*. Workers over time learn to understand their machines and get an intuitive feel for possible errors and optimization potentials. The main goal of the project was to make this knowledge available to other employees. We wanted users to be able to, quickly and easily, document any errors and their solutions on the job. This creates an increasing corpus of instructions and learning materials. These need to be well structured and designed to reduce the cognitive load on the learner [13, 14]. People can comprehend multi-modal information that combines text and images easier, compared to pure textual descriptions [15].

Machine manufacturers, whose machines are in use by multiple customers, could also take advantage of the sharing concept. They could pool general error information and user-generated instructions centrally to disseminate to other customers, as well use it to improve their products and services. However, there is an ever-present concern of a customer's critical information being passed to a competitor. The use of cameras on the shop floor is very often prohibited due to these concerns.

Giving Feedback
Collection of direct feedback, evaluation, and asking necessary questions contribute extensively to the design of user interfaces. Microsoft's insider program is an excellent example of such a system. A broader group of people and changes could be continuously addressed in addition to improving learning material or instructions.

4.2   Example 2: Highly Adaptive and Responsive UIs

Positive Effect on Suitability for Individualization, Suitability for the Task, Conformity with User Expectations
Adaptive and responsive UIs offer better usability and user experience if implemented effectively. They could be realized in multiple ways that have different implications on data security.

Customizing Based on User Data
The ability to manually change or optimize a user interface such as font size or contrast helps create solutions that work in multiple scenarios. [16, 17]. For a single user system, only one set of settings need to be saved. However, for multi-user systems, settings need to be linked to the users. Settings can be synchronized for users active on multiple systems. The generic profile information that is stored for an user could be used by a ticket vending machine for improving services. However, doubts arise on where such a profile is stored and what conclusions can be drawn from it. The relationship between the promised benefit and the data perceived by the user must be considered when personalizing a process. Trust is best achieved by giving the user full control over the data and the possibility to hide everything without any major disadvantage [7].

Data- and Sensor-Based Adaptation
User adaption can also be based on sensor data and offer even greater value. Our smartphones already use sensor data to adapt the user interface. For example rotating between landscape and portrait, or brightness based on ambient light. A motion sensor could be used to increase the line spacing of text when the user moves, to improve readability. If a user leans forward to read something, an inference might be small font size. The system could recognize this and offer to enlarge the font [18].

The position, viewing direction, and movement direction of an user on the shop-floor can be used to display content on a production machine [19]. If he is standing further away, he probably wants general information about the overall machine, if he approaches a specific part, the interface can automatically switch to a detailed view.

4.3   Example 3: Gamified Design

Positive Effect on Suitability for Learning
In companies where usability has been integral for a while, the focus has moved into employee motivation and learning. Gamification elements such as high scores, scores or levels, have become useful tools. These are used to strengthen the communication in the company, give incentives that go beyond the monetary aspect, give feedback, encourage learning, and document progress. These ensure progress is visible and make decisions inevitable. For other employees, it is also interesting to see who is an expert and who to contact if problems arise. Learning opportunities also help overcome boredom due to mundane tasks. Competition stimulates and can be designed in such a way that it does not demotivate. Collecting points and badges as well as reaching levels can help formulate goals. User tests in our projects have shown that this has positive effects on the entire system. The potential of such methods is underlined by the high level of interest in the industry.

5 Conclusion and Outlook

The core message of our method and this paper is to show the importance of visualization to address design issues that hinder user experience due to concerns of data security. The method outlined in the previous sections is a triangle with the three arms serving as the key components of a system: stakeholders, data, and functionality. The visualization of the relevant concepts of a project and the ability to show the interconnections physically allows one to understand the influencing factors. It also allows one to ask the right questions to fill missing gaps and communicate the information across the table. Data security should not compromise on user experience nor should the latter be at the expense of a trustworthy and reliable system. Collecting usage data over a longer period of time helps optimize processes, identify workarounds and build on them. Functions and elements that are seldom or not used at all can be identified and then either made more accessible or removed. The security problem lies in the possibility of maintaining usage statistics that links to specific users.

There are increasingly new forms of technologies that are set to take over the work place of the future. One of the cutting edge research areas is capturing and understanding the flow state [20] of an individual. A user in a state of flow needs to be kept away from distractions such as telephone calls or annoying messages from e-mail applications or chats. Any information or messages can then be relayed once the user is out of the flow state.

Depending on the workload of the user, different modalities could be selected to communicate critical information such as warnings [21].

Novel technologies such as Brain-Computer Interfaces (BCIs) enable a precise analysis of workload and performance to an unprecedented degree. For those who have to do a lot of cognitive work, the advantages however outweigh the disadvantages [22, 23]. Using the visualization method as described in this paper will be an indispensable tool for future discussions with relevant stakeholders.

References

1. Verordnung (EU) 2016/679 des Europäischen Parlaments und des Rates vom 27. April 2016 zum Schutz natürlicher Personen bei der Verarbeitung personenbezogener Daten, zum freien Datenverkehr und zur Aufhebung der Richtlinie 95/46/EG. DSGVO (2016)
2. DIN EN ISO 9241-110:2019-09, Ergonomie der Mensch-System-Interaktion_- Teil_110: Interaktionsprinzipien (ISO/DIS_9241-110:2019); Deutsche und Englische Fassung prEN_ISO_9241-110:2019. Beuth Verlag GmbH, Berlin
3. DIN EN ISO 9241-210:2019-05, Ergonomie der Mensch-System-Interaktion_- Teil_210: Prozess zur Gestaltung gebrauchstauglicher interaktiver Systeme (ISO/FDIS_9241-210:2019); Deutsche und Englische Fassung prEN_ISO_9241-210:2019. Beuth Verlag GmbH, Berlin
4. Fronemann, N., Peissner, M.: User experience concept exploration. User needs as a source for innovation. In: Roto, V. (ed.) Proceedings of the 8th Nordic Conference on Human-Computer Interaction: Fun, Fast, Foundational, Helsinki, Finland, 26–30 October 2014, pp. 727–736. ACM, New York (2014)

5. DIN EN ISO 13849-1:2016-06, Sicherheit von Maschinen_- Sicherheitsbezogene Teile von Steuerungen_- Teil_1: Allgemeine Gestaltungsleitsätze (ISO_13849-1:2015); Deutsche Fassung EN_ISO_13849-1:2015. Beuth Verlag GmbH, Berlin
6. Fähnrich, N., Kubach, M.: Enabling SMEs to comply with the complex new EU data protection regulation. In: Open Identity Summit 2019. Lecture Notes in Informatics (2019)
7. Wadle, L.-M., Martin, N., Ziegler, D.: Privacy and personalization. The trade-off between data disclosure and personalization benefit. In: Papadopoulos, G.A., Samaras, G., Weibelzahl, S., Jannach, D., Santos, O.C. (eds.) Adjunct Publication of the 27th Conference on User Modeling, Adaptation and Personalization – UMAP 2019 Adjunct, pp. 319–324. ACM Press, New York (2019)
8. Krüger, A.E., Fronemann, N., Peissner, M.: Das kreative Potential der Ingenieure. menschzentrierte Ingenieurskunst. In: Binz, H., Bertsche, B., Bauer, W., Roth, D. (eds.) Stuttgarter Symposium für Produktentwicklung (SSP). Entwicklung smarter Produkte für die Zukunft, Stuttgart, p. 40 (2015)
9. Krüger, A.E., Peissner, M., Fronemann, N., Pollmann, K.: Building ideas. In: Björk, S., Eriksson, E. (eds.) Proceedings of the 9th Nordic Conference on Human-Computer Interaction, pp. 1–6. ACM, New York (2016)
10. Krebs, H., Faust-Siehl, G.: Lernzirkel im Unterricht der Grundschule. Mit zahlreichen praktischen Beispielen verschiedener Autoren. Reformpädag.-Verl. Jörg Potthoff, Freiburg (1997)
11. Potthoff, W., Hepp, R.: Lernen und üben mit allen Sinnen. Lernzirkel in der Sekundarstufe. Reformpädag. Verl. Potthoff, Freiburg (1996)
12. Wu, L.: Various Google Play 'Beauty Camera' Apps Send Users Pornographic Content, Redirect Them to Phishing Websites and Collect Their Pictures. https://blog.trendmicro.com/trendlabs-security-intelligence/various-google-play-beauty-camera-apps-sends-users-pornographic-content-redirects-them-to-phishing-websites-and-collects-their-pictures/
13. Sweller, J.: Cognitive load during problem solving: effects on learning. Cogn. Sci. **12**, 257–285 (1988)
14. Sweller, J.: Cognitive technology: some procedures for facilitating learning and problem solving in mathematics and science. J. Educ. Psychol. **81**, 457–466 (1989)
15. Fletcher, J.D., Tobias, S.: The multimedia principle (2005)
16. Peissner, M., Edlin-White, R.: User control in adaptive user interfaces for accessibility. In: Kotzé, P., Marsden, G., Lindgaard, G., Wesson, J., Winckler, M. (eds.) INTERACT 2013. LNCS, vol. 8117, pp. 623–640. Springer, Heidelberg (2013). https://doi.org/10.1007/978-3-642-40483-2_44
17. Ziegler, D., Pollmann, K., Fronemann, N., Tagalidou, N.: HCD4Personalization – Menschzentrierte Interaktionsgestaltung anhand individueller Eigenschaften der Nutzenden. In: Mensch und Computer 2019 - Workshopband, Bonn, Germany, pp. 524–528 (2019)
18. Zimmermann, G., Strobbe, C., Ziegler, D.: Inclusive responsiveness – why responsive web design is not enough and what we can do about this. In: Di Bucchianico, G. (ed.) AHFE 2018. AISC, vol. 776, pp. 203–215. Springer, Cham (2019). https://doi.org/10.1007/978-3-319-94622-1_20
19. Peissner, M.: Entwurfsmusterbasierter Ansatz für adaptive Benutzungsschnittstellen zur Überwindung von Nutzungsbarrieren (2014, Unpublished)
20. Csikszentmihalyi, M.: Flow - der Weg zum Glück. Der Entdecker des Flow-Prinzips erklärt seine Lebensphilosophie. Herder, Freiburg, Basel, Wien (2016)
21. Mayer, R.E., Moreno, R.: Nine ways to reduce cognitive load in multimedia learning. Educ. Psychol. **38**, 43–52 (2003)
22. Cinel, C., Valeriani, D., Poli, R.: Neurotechnologies for human cognitive augmentation: current state of the art and future prospects. Front. Hum. Neurosci. **13**, 13 (2019)
23. Blankertz, B., et al.: The Berlin brain-computer interface: progress beyond communication and control. Front. Neurosci. **10**, 530 (2016)

Human Cyber Risk Management by Security Awareness Professionals: Carrots or Sticks to Drive Behaviour Change?

John M. Blythe[1]([⊠]), Alan Gray[1], and Emily Collins[2,3]

[1] CybSafe, London E14 5AB, UK
john@cybsafe.com
[2] School of Psychology, Cardiff University, Cardiff CF10 3AT, UK
[3] School of Management, University of Bath, Bath BA2 7AY, UK

Abstract. Cyber crime is rising at an unprecedented rate. Organisations are spending more than ever combating the human element through training and other interventions, such as simulated phishing. Organisations employ "carrots" (rewards) and "sticks" (sanctions) to reduce risky behaviour. Sanctions (such as locking computers and informing one's line manager) are problematic as they lead to unintended consequences towards employee trust and productivity. This study explored how organisations use rewards and sanctions both in their campaigns and specifically following simulated phishing. We also assessed what factors (such as control over rewards, tendency to blame users) influenced security awareness professionals' use of rewards and sanctions. The findings revealed that organisations use a variety of rewards and sanctions within their campaigns, with sanctions being used across 90% of the organisations. We did not find any factors that influence security awareness professionals' usage of rewards and sanctions. Our findings suggest the need for a greater consideration of the human element of cyber security. In particular, campaigns should take a more informed approach to use of behaviour change strategies that consider the organisational structure in which they are implemented and the role (and influence) of security awareness professionals within that structure.

Keywords: Security awareness professionals · Cyber security culture · Behaviour change · Reward and punishment

1 Introduction

Cyber security has been a tier 1 priority for the UK Government since 2011 [1]. Since then, cyber threats have massively increased: we have seen ransomware impact on our health services and data breaches become more and more common. Organisations, small and large, continue to struggle with managing cyber security risks.

The threat is very real. Cybercrime accounts for 50% of all crime in England and Wales [2], and with the introduction of GDPR, companies can now be fined up to twenty million pounds for inadequate data protection. Employees are known to be a major

© Springer Nature Switzerland AG 2020
A. Moallem (Ed.): HCII 2020, LNCS 12210, pp. 76–91, 2020.
https://doi.org/10.1007/978-3-030-50309-3_6

contributing factor to security breaches in organisations [3]. It's unsurprising, then, that measures are being taken (and millions being spent) to manage human cyber risk. But some of these measures used by organisations are sparking concern - heavy monitoring and the use of metrics to target, and punish, 'at risk' employees [4–8]. Indeed, more companies in the UK are beginning to adopt a culture of blame when it comes to their employees and cyber security [9]. Some security professionals, for instance, commonly endorse a belief in the employee as the "weakest link" and tend to place the responsibility of a breach upon individual users, rather than the organisation's culture, the quality of available training, or the design of security policies and procedures themselves [10–13].

When it comes to managing human cyber risk, security-awareness professionals rely on metrics. Metrics serve an important function for decision makers in organisations: helping to assess risk over time and to aid strategic investment in cyber security resources–particularly if they focus on targeting the three key pillars of human cyber risk: Awareness, Behaviour and Culture [14]. Most commonly, organisations gather metrics on training completion and click-rates on simulated phishing tests. However, there has been a trend towards using such metrics to exclude, constrain and control staff [13]. Some organisations use metrics gathered from simulated phishing to identify 'weak links' and punish them into online security: docking pay and locking computers until awareness programs have been completed and the user in question has been remedied and strengthened [6, 15]. Whilst simulated phishing does have benefits for enacting behaviour change through "just-in-time" training [16–18], it is the use of metrics derived from simulated phishing that raises concerns over its potential unintended consequences.

1.1 Related Work

Punishment is an increasingly prevalent means by which organisations attempt to facilitate knowledge transfer and behaviour change. By this view, known as the Rational Choice Model (RCM), people are rational entities who commit a crime or wrongdoing only if the perceived benefits outweigh the costs [20, 21]. Preventing bad behaviour (i.e. risky security behaviour), then, according to the RCM, is as simple as appealing to reason: i.e. making the costs, through punishment, outweigh the benefits [22]. From this perspective, risky security behaviours are deterred as certainty and severity of punishment increases [23].

Penalties like locking computers and informing line managers of "repeat clickers", along with other more minor retributions, are likely to have a negative impact on employees and their productivity. Staff may also become irritable if they can't work because they are locked out of systems, making it harder for professionals to implement further policies.

Not only is employee morale likely to drop, but so too might an employee's trust in the firm and respect for management [6, 7]; this in turn may make implementing cyber security policies even more troublesome, given that awareness professionals already struggle with gaining the legitimacy necessary to broadcast their message, and see this as a key barrier to cyber awareness (cf. [9]).

Moreover, this culture of blame may actively encourage employees to be less productive. Rather than use their own initiative, employees, under such conditions, may be more inclined to 'play it safe,' seeing their role as circumscribed and demarcated and ignoring whatever lies beyond its stipulated scope [19]. A particularly damaging outcome for sectors, such as healthcare and medicine, where cyber security is not just an important 'add on' but an integral part of the job.

The use of rewards is considered a more positive strategy. Rewards include financial, non-financial and psychological benefits provided to employees in return for their efforts [24] and can be extrinsic (such as pay and benefits) or intrinsic (such as job fulfilment). Research has shown that reward strategies serve as a reliable mechanism for improving behaviour [25], workplace trust [26] and work engagement [27], even when the rewards are non-material (e.g. through gamification). However, the use of rewards employed within an organisational context for changing security behaviour has received little investigation.

The use of rewards and sanctions in organisations will also depend upon the personal and organisational resources available to security professionals [9]. While security professionals have traditionally realised their security aims by taking an authoritarian stance [28], the flattening of organisational structures has increased the need for security professionals to persuade, rather than coerce, employees toward secure behaviour [9]. To be successful here, within these new organisational structures, research in the field of management studies has suggested that an organisational "change agent" must possess expertise, credibility, political access to senior management and control of rewards and sanctions in order to be effective [29].

These resources are necessary because any given change strategy can face resistance within the organisation from staff across all levels [29]. Unless an employee's experiences converge entirely with the strategist's, without adequate power (expertise, reward and sanction control), strategic initiatives will encounter disagreements and fail to be successfully executed by awareness professionals. Employees, after all, may agree on one end, but disagree on the means by which it may be achieved [30]. The awareness professionals' expertise and control of rewards and sanctions may therefore be key to managing human cyber risk but whether security professionals perceive themselves as possessing these resources and this sort of power, however, also remains unknown.

Viewing employees as part of the "problem" [13] in cyber security may also influence the degree of usage of rewards and sanctions. Employees in cyber security are commonly referred to as the "weakest link" [31]. As such, recent calls have focussed on viewing employees as part of the "solution" [13] - where we recognise that human errors do happen and that we not demonise employees but instead recognise that people are part of the system and their ability can have a positive role in cyber security. Whilst most research has looked at this mindset in security professionals [9], there is little research on these influences on their use of rewards and sanctions.

1.2   Aims and Research Questions

Based on the existing work focusing on the impact of punishment on employee behaviour, particularly in the context of simulated phishing. The primary aim of this study was to explore how organisations use behavioural strategies of rewards and sanctions, as part of their cyber security awareness campaigns and how they deal with "repeat-clickers' as identified in phishing simulations. The second aim of this paper was to assess whether use of rewards and sanctions is influenced by security professionals' perceived control of rewards and sanctions, tendency to blame the user and their perceived impact of simulated phishing.

Using a cross-sectional online survey, the present study addressed the following research questions:

1. *What is the prevalence of reward and sanction use within organisations?*
2. *How do organisations approach the treatment of those who repeatedly click upon simulated phishing links?*
3. *What factors influence security professionals' use of rewards and sanctions?*

2 Method

2.1 Participant Recruitment and Characteristics

Data was collected via Qualtrics between October 9th and November 29th, 2019. Security awareness professionals were recruited using social networking sites (LinkedIn, Twitter), and through the lead author's institution's customers, partners and contacts. Recruitment focused on those with responsibility for the '*Human Element of Cyber Security*' such as Information Security Awareness Managers, Cyber Security Education and Awareness Officers, and Cyber Security Education and Awareness Leads.

93 participants responded to the advert and clicked to participate in the study. 48 cases were excluded due to incomplete or missing data (of which 38 had completed the consent form but nothing else). The final dataset included 45 participants (19 male, 16 female, 1 prefer to self-describe, 2 prefer not to say, 7 missing; age range: under 25 = 4, 25–34 = 3, 35–44 = 11, 44–54 = 13, over 55 = 4, prefer not to say = 3, missing = 15), and was comprised of security awareness professionals working in either the public (12), private (23) or charity (1) sectors (prefer not to say = 2, missing = 7), from a range of organisation sizes (small < 50 staff = 3, Medium between 50 and 249 staff = 4, large > 250 staff = 28, prefer not to say = 3, missing = 7). 71% of participants used simulated phishing in their organisation.

To be included in the study, all participants were required to be aged 18 and have responsibility for security awareness within their organisation. To participate in the second part of the study on simulated phishing, all participants were required to use the tool in their organisation.

2.2 Measures

Behaviour Change Strategies
We developed a list of 11 potential strategies covering rewards and sanctions (see Appendix A), derived from security blogs advising on behaviour change and the Behaviour Change Technique Taxonomy [32]. Respondents answered whether their organisation had used any of the methods within the last 12 months when it comes to managing human cyber risk and resilience. Answers were permitted via three mutually exclusive tick-boxes (Yes, No, I Don't Know). Managerial incentives are defined as those practices employed to encourage a particular behaviour and encompassed both material

and social rewards (e.g. gifts and public recognition). Sanctions, on the other hand, were aimed at discouraging an action, and again were understood in material and non-material terms (e.g. disciplinary warning, restriction of privileged access). We chose not to refer to these as "incentives" and "sanctions" to reduce social desirability bias within responses. It is important to note that many sanctions within cyber security are not considered as such, but rather as further training devices, even if they may result in trouble with one's line manager and pay deductions. With this in mind, sanctions were understood to be practices which sought to prevent a behaviour, either by direct punishment (material or otherwise) or by incurring mandatory effort beyond one's typical work role (e.g. locking computer until training is complete, enforced training resits etc.).

Treatment of Repeat Clickers

To assess how organisations dealt with "repeat-clickers" in simulated phishing exercises, we asked the following open-ended question: *"Your organisation discovers that an employee is repeatedly clicking on simulated phishing emails. What would your company currently do (if anything) and why?"*

Reward and Coercive Power

Reward and coercive power were measured by subscales adapted from the Rahim Leader Power Inventory (RLPI) [33]. Participants were asked to consider the extent to which they agreed with a series of eleven statements on a seven-point scale, ranging from "strongly agree" to "strongly disagree". While the RLPI addressed perceived leader power from a subordinate employee's perspective (i.e. the perceived power of their line-manager), the present study measured a supervisor's own perceptions of power. Both reward and coercive power scales demonstrated high reliability: $\alpha = .852$ and $.879$ respectively.

Attitudes Towards User and Perceived Consequences of Simulated Phishing

The 'attitudes towards users' scale targeted the tendency to blame the users for clicking on a malicious link. This self-devised scale was composed of three items (e.g. *"It is the responsibility of individual employees to avoid clicking on phishing links"*). The scale showed low internal reliability: $\alpha = .622$ (though c.f [34], who suggests alpha values as low as .5 provide sufficient evidence of reliability).

The measure of perceived consequences of simulated phishing was a five-item scale, targeting the perceived consequences security professionals may associate with their organisation's use of simulated phishing ($\alpha = .912$). The scale addresses some potential side effects that have been hypothesized to result from simulated phishing [6–8]. These side effects include employee frustration, resentment towards security staff, loss of trust, and harm to employee morale. Example items include *"Our simulated phishing policy is damaging to employee morale"* and *"My organisation's simulated phishing policy harms the relationship between our company and its employees"*. See Appendix B for full scales.

2.3 Procedure

Before beginning the study, full ethical approval was granted by CREST's and the School of Management at the University of Bath's ethics committee. All participants accessed the study via a link, recruited via email or social media platforms (e.g. LinkedIn, Facebook, Twitter). All those who clicked the link were first redirected to an information page, covering the study's rationale, what it required of participants, and how their data may be used in future, and consent was granted from participants wishing to take part. Following consent, participants were then asked a series of closed questions on the metrics their organisation recorded and the measures they took to encourage 'good' and reduce 'bad' cyber security behaviour. This was followed by questions on their perceived ability to control employee rewards and sanctions (i.e. coercive and reward power).

Participants were only taken to the second part of the study which focuses solely on phishing, and phishing simulations, if they indicated that their organisation uses simulated phishing metrics. They were first asked an open question regarding how they responded to repeat clickers. This was supplemented with a series of questions concerning the individual's perceptions of simulated phishing. The questionnaire ended with a series of demographic questions. Participants were debriefed on completion of the survey and informed of the overall aims of the project. They were reminded of their ability to withdraw their data at any time, and without need for explanation.

3   Results

We conducted separate analyses for each research question. First, we explore the usage of behaviour change strategies and treatment of repeat clickers. We then explore which factors predict use of rewards and sanctions

3.1   Use of Behaviour Change Strategies

The reporting frequency (%) of each behavioural change measure was assessed and the results of which can be seen in Fig. 1.

Figure 1 shows that public recognition was the most common form of reward given to those demonstrating security behaviour (66% vs 63% certificates and 49% gift). The mean number of rewards was 4 (SD = 2) and the mean number of punishments was 1 (SD = 1). Overall, most respondents appeared to offer some form of reward: only 15% did not offer a single reward from the list, with 22% offering at least one of the listed rewards and 29.3% selecting all three. The most common form of punishment practiced from the list was informing an employee's line manager of risky behaviour (61%). The rarest, on the other hand, was naming and shaming an employee for risky behaviour (15%) and locking an employee's workstation until awareness training is complete (17%). Overall, most respondents appeared to offer some form of punishment: only 10% did not administer a single punishment from the list, with 20% administering at least one of the listed punishments and 24% selecting five or more.

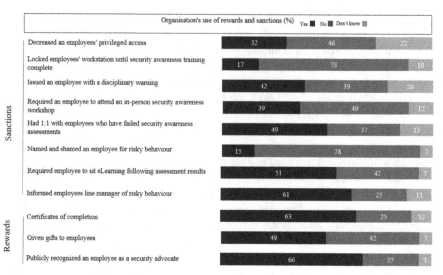

Fig. 1. Reporting frequency (%) of rewards and sanctions

3.2 Treatment of "Repeat-Clickers"

The open-ended responses were analysed using thematic analysis, following guidelines by [35]. Three key themes were drawn: '*Grading the response*', '*Tailoring the training*' and '*Non-punitive emphasis*'.

Grading the Response: Many reported a stepped-response to repeat clickers (27%), with clickers being regularly re-phished and allocated further, more intensive training (or punishment) with each additional failing. For example,

> "*We assign additional awareness training as the first step. Then there is a sit down meeting with a regional information security officer as the next step…. limiting of a person's access to email, web, etc. as possible next consequences.*"

Training often begins via the learning management system (LMS) and progresses, with repeat offences, to 1:1 meetings and consultations (with security officers, managers, and CISOs). This is frequently accompanied, in the later stages, with an invitation to discuss the problem with their line-manager, where disciplinary action may be taken; one respondent even mentioned the possibility of discharge.

Tailoring the Training: Many respondents mention various attempts to tailor training to the individual (36%). This seems to be achieved by either focusing the training topic around the type of phishing email or the role served by the employee within the company. Interestingly, within those who tailor training, there seems to be an attempt to understand clicking by looking to factors beyond the individual. Meetings and discussions are used to formulate a potential cause for the error (e.g. phishing type; role vulnerability)—and these are used to design targeted treatments (e.g. role-specific training to detect where current awareness instruction is failing). For example,

"Each click comes with point in time education, repeat offenders must take retraining. We feel that repeat clicking is indicative of lack of knowledge needed to identify phishing emails, so we try to equip them to do better. If after meeting with a specific individual or group it seems like there is something about their specific role that makes them more susceptible to clicking, we try to work with them to design role specific training."

Non-punitive Emphasis: Several respondents emphasised taking a "non-punitive" approach to remediating clickers (36%). Perhaps based on the view that "clicking is indicative of a lack of knowledge"—and therefore potentially a difficulty at a 'macro', rather than individual level—respondents recognised the importance of being "nice about it". An "open culture" was understood as necessary for preventing 'people hiding or covering up issues', as well as for creating a context for "long-term change". For example,

"Talk to them as an education and training intervention, rather than a punitive one."

"Show them the error and how they were caught out. Show them the way to avoid it in the future and be nice about it. Everyone makes mistakes and an open culture is required to prevent people from hiding or covering issues us because they have made a mistake."

3.3   Predicting Use of Rewards and Sanctions

Descriptive Statistics. The means and standard deviations for the control of rewards and sanctions' measures and participants' perceptions of the perceived consequences of simulated phishing and tendency to blame users are presented in Table 1. In order to obtain a more easily interpreted percentage value, reward and punishment rates were calculated for each respondent according to the following two formulae:

- Reward Rate = *(total number of rewards used ÷ total number of rewards listed) x 100)*.
- Punishment Rate = *(total number of punishing behaviours used ÷ total number of punishing behaviours listed) x 100)*.

Correlations Among the Scales. Correlations between the five scales were then calculated. A significant positive correlation was found between reward power and coercive power ($r = .784$, $p < 0.01$ [$n = 39$]), suggesting that as perceived reward power increased so too did perceived coercive power. There was also a significant positive correlation between reward rate and punishment rate ($r = .314$, $p < 0.05$ [$n = 41$]), suggesting that as reward rate increased so too did punishment rate. No further significant correlations were found among the five scales (e.g. tendency to blame the user, perceived consequences of simulated phishing etc.).

A multiple linear regression was then conducted to predict 'Punishment Rate' from 'Perceived Consequences of Simulated Phishing', 'Tendency to Blame the User',

Table 1. Means and Standard deviations for total scores on leader power (reward and coercive), tendency to blame the user, perceived consequences of simulated phishing, and reward and punishment rates.

Variable	Mean	SD	N=
Reward power (1–7)	4.24	1.44	39
Coercive power (1–7)	3.31	1.54	39
Tendency to blame the user (1–7)	3.57	1.13	32
Perceived consequences of simulated phishing	2.99	1.45	32
Reward rate (1–100)	59.35	34.57	41
Punishment rate (1–100)	38.11	26.36	41

'Reward Rate', 'Reward Power', and 'Coercive Power'. A non-significant regression equation was found (F5,25 = .335.898, p > .005, R2 = .092).

An additional multiple linear regression was then calculated to predict 'Reward Rate' from 'Perceived Consequences of Simulated Phishing', 'Tendency to Blame the User', 'Punishment Rate', 'Reward Power', and 'Coercive Power'. Again, this was non-significant ($F_{5,25} = 727.013$, $p > .005$, $R^2 = .109$.).

4   Discussion

In this paper we aimed to explore how organisations use rewards and sanctions as part of their cyber security awareness campaigns, and how they deal with "repeat-clickers' as identified in phishing simulations. We also assessed whether the use of rewards and sanctions is influenced by security professional's perceived control of rewards and sanctions, tendency to blame the user and their perceived impact of simulated phishing. We capture our interpretation of the findings in more detail in the next section, before moving on to a discussion of the work's limitations, implications, and conclusion.

4.1   Behaviour Change Strategies

Managerial incentives and sanctions were readily reported among our respondents, with all organisations using at least one of the strategies listed and many employing the full range. These findings demonstrate that organisations use a combination of strategies to deliver behaviour change, with variability in the types of sanctions employed by organisations. As acknowledged in the introduction, such strategies, at least as far as punishment is concerned, may prove counterproductive: decreasing an employee's morale, organisational trust, and even willingness to engage in cyber security behaviour [6–8].

While less concern has been expressed about rewards in cyber security management, there is also reason to believe that they too could pose a negative impact: replacing intrinsic motivation with its inferior extrinsic counterpart [36, 37] and removing security behaviours that aren't rewarded or monitored in some way. Furthermore, rewarding what should be 'normal security behaviour' might make employees see it as exceptionally good behaviour, and something that is not generally achieved. This said, however, claims regarding the efficacy of reward and punishment in cyber security remain largely hypothetical and untested [e.g. 37–39]. Future research should focus on an experimental assessment of the effects of incentives and sanctions on employee morale, organisational trust, and cyber security practice.

The present study also uncovered substantial variation in the prevalence of individual reward and punishment strategies. Public recognition was the most common form of reward given to those demonstrating strong cyber security behaviour—with newsletter mentions and certificates being appreciably more likely than material gifts. While the efficacy of varying reward types remains to be tested (Cf. [40, 41]), it is likely that the value of public recognition in this context depends strongly on an organisation's cyber security culture, and the individual's internalisation of those values [42].

Similarly, the most common form of punishment was informing an employee's line manager of risky behaviour. Again, this strategy will rely on the cyber security culture within which it is executed, and the line manager's understanding and respect for cyber security in general. It is hard, for instance, to imagine such reporting leading to much change if the line managers themselves are ignorant of the value of cyber security, or consider it a frustration and mere bureaucracy.

Many who employ punishment techniques, to be clear, do not understand them as such: preferring to understand these methods within the rubric of 'training,' rather than sanctions per se [4]; and while all effort was made to couch questions with this in mind, several practices may have been dismissed because of injudicious lapses in language sensitivity. The rarest sanction, for example, was 'naming and shaming an employee for risky behaviour', with just 15% of respondents reporting its use.

4.2 Treatment of Repeat Offenders

Considering the treatment of repeat clickers, re: simulated phishing, thematic analysis revealed three key themes: "grading the response", "tailoring the training", and "non-punitive emphasis".

Training was the most common recourse—though what form that training took was varied (e.g. LMS, 1:1, educational videos) and often graded (in severity) for repeat clickers, with clear efforts to tailor the treatment and a frequent emphasis on non-punitive methods. This attempt at acknowledging the needs of the individual, rather than unrolling blanket policy when it comes to at-risk employees, demonstrates that organisations are tailoring their approaches. Many participants used a graded response to dealing with repeat clickers—with the severity of the sanction increasing as click rate increased.

Most organisations used simulated phishing as a means to deliver more tailored training to their staff. Simulated phishing allows organisations to identify "high-risk" employees, giving them more targeted training that may be specific to the role or individual needs.

Although organisations did employ a range of sanctions, 36% of participants emphasized a "non-punitive" approach to remediating clickers, with few participants acknowledging the need for an open culture around cyber security risks. These findings suggest that whilst organisations are employing sanctions, there is a trend towards security awareness professionals understanding the need for a more humanistic approach.

4.3 Predicting Use of Rewards and Sanctions

Correlational analysis revealed two significant positive correlations: the first between perceived reward and perceived coercive power, the second between reported reward rate and reported punishment. This suggests that rewarding good cyber security behaviour within an organisation is often paired with punishing bad behaviour. In other words, control over carrots is often paired with control over sticks, both in terms of the awareness professional's perceived power to execute rewards and punishments, and in their use by the company as a whole.

The role of punishment in cyber security is routinely cautioned [6, 15]. It has been suggested that its value as a tool for behaviour change may fluctuate depending on whether or not the sanctions are seen as 'just' and 'procedurally fair' within the workplace [43]. Punishment is counterproductive in security. It leads to under reporting, resentment towards IT staff and impacts on trust and productivity [4]. A common mistake with simulated phishing is that it is used to play "gotcha" with employees – acting as means to entrap employees into security [44]. The current study supports the assumption that organisations do use punishment measures as means to change behaviour. Previous research has been largely anecdotal [4, 6], and the current study highlights the prevalence of punishment use in organisations.

Contrary to the Hardy model, resource factors hypothesized to be critical in the production of an effective change agent [29] did not predict the use of behaviour change strategies. Reward and coercive powers failed to predict either reward or punishment rates, suggesting that control over these resources may not guarantee their use, and that mere resource disposal may be necessary but not sufficient in the creation of an effective change agent. On the other hand, the role of the "security awareness professional" encompasses different types of job roles and levels of seniority. As the cyber security sector continues to mature and become more professionalised [45], this diversity is expected to continue. This may mean that there is variability in awareness's professionals' control of rewards and sanctions due to their position in the company and level of seniority. For example, whilst awareness professionals themselves may not believe in the use of punishment, the use of such policies may be dictated by senior management and the board of directors (who themselves have their own mental models around human cyber risk [46]). Research in management studies has shown that political access to senior management is important for "change agents" in organisations [29]. Future research should therefore look at this access to senior management and also explore variability in the security awareness professional role and how their control of rewards and sanctions may be constrained by organisational structures and senior management influence.

4.4 Limitations and Future Directions

It should be mentioned that the practice of punishing employees is sufficiently stigmatised to raise concerns over the reliability of the present data. While all participants were repeatedly informed of their anonymity, and no explicit mention of 'punishment' was made to reduce social desirability bias, professionals may have shied away from specifying the particulars of their sanctioning strategies for fear of litigation, or indicting their organisations.

The present study limits its scope to the perceptions and practices of professionals and ignores the effect of these practices on the employees themselves. It would, however, be interesting to expand this study to include the perceptions of the on-the-ground workers themselves. While much literature has assumed that simulated phishing practices are detrimental to employee morale and organisational trust, there is currently no work addressing this assumption beyond various small case-studies [47].

Another key concern for future research is understanding how professionals decide on a particular security campaign. The present work addresses the conclusions of professionals, in terms of their recording and managerial strategies, but not how they arrived at those decisions—ignoring the rationale at play, and the pressures potentially imposed by senior management.

Finally, we looked at the prevalence of behaviour change strategies as they pertained to rewards and sanctions. For behaviour change strategies to be effective, however, they need to target the drivers and barriers to security behaviour [48]. Different strategies are more or less effective depending on whether it is a lack of capability, motivation and/or opportunity preventing the security behaviour [48]. For effective behaviour change, the choice of strategies should therefore be guided by evidence and behaviour change frameworks [48]. However, a "behavioural science" informed approach will depend on the capability of the security awareness professionals. Future work should explore the extent to which organisations' behaviour change interventions are based on behavioural science.

5 Summary and Conclusions

This study is the first to show that organisations vary widely in the "carrot" and "sticks" deployed. It highlights the need for a greater consideration of the human element of cyber security and demonstrates that punishment is widely used to manage human cyber risk. The use of rewards and punishments to promote cyber security is practiced to bridge the 'knowing-doing gap' in cyber security awareness, wherein knowledge of best practice is seldom met with adherence and actual security. Unfortunately, managerial incentives and sanctions remain untested as behavioural change tools in cyber security and may even incur numerous unintended consequences [4].

Contrary to the 'user as the weakest link' view, users do wish to protect their organisations and are often hindered from doing so by unusable security measures and policies [4]. This forms what research has described as a 'cycle of bad security' [5]: starting with a negative view of the user that is ultimately vindicated by excluding them from security policy design and by failing to consider their everyday experience.

Security awareness professionals play an important role in managing human cyber risk. We found diversity in professionals' views and use of "punishment" as a tool but changing awareness professionals' beliefs about the human element and utility of behaviour change strategies will be key in addressing human cyber risk [13]. We found that some professionals do recognise the need for a "non-punitive" approach but further guidance and recognition of this within industry standards and frameworks should be considered.

Developing "Just and Fair" cultures in organisations [15] which focus on security accountability between leaders and staff and drops notions of blame are also needed. Researchers refer to this as a paradigm shift in cyber security towards focusing on "humans as a solution" [13]. This paradigm acknowledges the complexity and interconnectedness of cyber security within the workplace and views humans as contributors to the success of cyber security. This paradigm shift extends beyond the professional to the organisation more broadly, with a focus on the "tone at the top" and the role of boards and senior management in organisational cyber resilience.

Acknowledgements. This work was funded by the Centre for Research and Evidence on Security Threats (ESRC Award: ES/N009614/1).

Appendix A

Behaviour Change Strategies Scale
To the best of your knowledge, has your organisation used any of the following within the last 12 months when it comes to managing human cyber risk and resilience? (*Yes/No/I Don't know*)

- Publicly recognised an employee as a security advocate (e.g. in an organisational newsletter, email etc.)
- Given gifts to employees (e.g. prize draw, vouchers, time off)
- Informed an employee's line manager of risky behaviour (e.g. non-course completion, failing a phishing test)
- Certificates of completion (e.g. awareness course completion)
- Required an employee to sit/resit e-learning following assessment results
- Named and shamed an employee for risky behaviour
- Had a 1:1 with employees who have failed security awareness assessments
- Required an employee to attend an in-person security awareness workshop
- Issued an employee with a disciplinary warning
- Locked an employee's work station until security awareness training is complete
- Decreased an employee's privileged access
- Other (please specify): _____

Appendix B

Attitudes Towards Users' Scale
Please indicate the extent to which you agree with the following statements (Strongly Agree - Strongly Disagree)

- It is the responsibility of individual employees to avoid clicking on phishing links
- Employees who click on simulated phishing links should be punished
- It is wrong to blame employees who click on simulated phishing links

Perceived Consequences of Simulated Phishing
Please indicate the extent to which you agree with the following statements (Strongly Agree - Strongly Disagree)

- Our simulated phishing policy is damaging to employee morale
- My organisation's simulated phishing policy harms the relationship between our company and its employees
- Employee satisfaction suffers because of my organisation's simulated phishing policies
- Employees feel 'tricked' when our organisation sends them simulated phishing emails
- Our simulated phishing policy is damaging to employee productivity

References

1. HM Government. National Cyber Security Strategy 2016–2021 (2016)
2. Office for National Statistics. Crime in England and Wales: year ending March 2018 (2018)
3. Blythe, J.M., Coventry, L.: Costly but effective: comparing the factors that influence employee anti-malware behaviours. Comput. Hum. Behav. **87**, 87–97 (2018)
4. Sasse, A.: Scaring and bullying people into security won't work. IEEE Secur. Priv. **13**(3), 80–83 (2015)
5. Reinfelder, L., Landwirth, R., Benenson, Z.: Security managers are not the enemy either. In: Proceedings of the 2019 CHI Conference on Human Factors in Computing Systems, p. 433. ACM (2019)
6. Murdoch, S.J., Sasse, M.A.: Should you really phish your own employees?. https://tech.new statesman.com/business/phishing-employees. (2017)
7. Caputo, D.D., Pfleeger, S.L., Freeman, J.D., Johnson, M.E.: Going spear phishing: exploring embedded training and awareness. IEEE Secur. Priv. **12**(1), 28–38 (2014)
8. Kirlappos, I., Sasse, M.A.: Fixing security together: leveraging trust relationships to improve security in organizations. Proceedings of the NDSS Symposium 2015, no. 1, pp, 1–10 (2015)
9. Ashenden, D., Sasse, A.: CISOs and organisational culture: their own worst enemy? Comput. Secur. **39**, 396–405 (2013)
10. Adams, A., Sasse, A.: Users are not the enemy. Commun. ACM **42**(12), 40–46 (1999)
11. Inglesant, P., Sasse, M.: The true cost of unusable password policies: password use in the wild. In: Proceedings of the SIGCHI Conference on Human Factors in Computing Systems, pp. 383–392. (2010)

12. Parkin, S., van Moorsel, A., Inglesant, P., Sasse, M.: A stealth approach to usable security: helping IT security managers to identify workable security solutions. In: Proceedings of the 2010 Workshop on New Security Paradigms, pp. 33–49. (2010)

13. Zimmermann, V., Renaud, K.: Moving from a 'human-as-problem" to a 'human-as-solution" cybersecurity mindset. Int. J. Hum Comput Stud. 131, 169–187 (2019)

14. Coventry, L., Briggs, P., Blythe, J., Tran, M.: Using behavioural insights to improve the public's use of cyber security best practices. Gov. UK report (2014)

15. NCSC. The trouble with phishing (2018). https://www.ncsc.gov.uk/blog-post/trouble-phishing

16. Kumaraguru, P., Rhee, Y., Acquisti, A., Cranor, L. F., Hong, J., Nunge, E.: Protecting people from phishing: the design and evaluation of an embedded training email system. In: Proceedings of ACM CHI 2007 Conference on Human Factors in Computing Systems, vol. 1, pp. 905–914. (2017)

17. Kumaraguru, P., Sheng, S., Acquisti, A., Cranor, L.F., Hong, J.: Teaching Johnny not to fall for phish. ACM Trans. Internet Technol. 10(2), 1–31 (2010)

18. Siadati, H., Palka, S., Siegel, A., McCoy, D.: Measuring the effectiveness of embedded phishing exercises. In: 10th USENIX Workshop on Cyber Security Experimentation and Test (2017)

19. Rezaei, A., Allameh, S.M., Ansari, R.: Effect of organisational culture and organisational learning on organisational innovation: an empirical investigation. Int. J. Prod. Quality Manag. 23(3), 307–327 (2018)

20. McCarthy, B.: New economics of sociological criminology. Ann. Rev. Sociol. 28, 417–442 (2002)

21. Becker, G.: Crime and punishment: an economic approach. J. Polit. Econ. 76(2), 169–217 (1968)

22. Bankston, W., Cramer, J.: Toward a macro-sociological interpretation of general deterrence. Criminol. Interdiscip. J. 12(3), 251–280 (1974)

23. Herath, T., Rao, H.R.: Protection motivation and deterrence: a framework for security policy compliance in organizations. Eur. J. Inf. Syst. 18(2), 106–125 (2009)

24. Bratton, J., Gold, J.: Human Resource Management: Theory and Practice. Palgrave, London (2017)

25. Ajmal, A., Bashir, M., Abrar, M., Khan, M.M., Saqib, S.: The effects of intrinsic and extrinsic rewards on employee attitudes; mediating role of perceived organizational support. J. Serv. Sci. Manag. 8(04), 461 (2015)

26. Burke, W.W.: Organization Change: Theory and Practice. Sage publications, Thousand Oaks (2017)

27. Jacobs, S., Renard, M., Snelgar, R.J.: Intrinsic rewards and work engagement in the South African retail industry. SA J. Ind. Psychol. 40(2), 1–13 (2014)

28. Dhillon, G., Backhouse, J.: Current directions in IS security research: towards sociotechnical perspectives. Inf. Syst. J. Blackwell 11(2), 127–153 (2001)

29. Hardy, C.: Understanding power: 'Bringing about strategic change'. Br. J. Manag. (Special Issue) 17, S3–S16 (1996)

30. Walsh, C.: Power and advantage in organizations. Organ. Stud. 2(2), 131–152 (1981)

31. Sasse, M.A., Brostoff, S., Weirich, D.: Transforming the 'weakest link'—a human/computer interaction approach to usable and effective security. BT Technol. J. 19(3), 122–131 (2001)

32. Michie, S., et al.: The behavior change technique taxonomy (v1) of 93 hierarchically clustered techniques: building an international consensus for the reporting of behavior change interventions. Ann. Behav. Med. 46(1), 81–95 (2013)

33. Rahim, A.M.: Relationships of leader power to compliance and satisfaction with supervision: evidence from a national sample of managers. J. Manag. 12(4), 545–556 (1989)

34. Nunnally, J.C.: Psychometric Theory, 2nd edn. McGraw-Hill, New York (1978)
35. Braun, V., Clarke, V.: Using thematic analysis in psychology. Qual. Res. Psychol. **3**(2), 77–101 (2006)
36. Boss, S.R., Kirsch, L.J., Angermeier, I., Shingler, R.A., Boss, R.W.: If someone is watching, I'll do what I'm asked: Mandatoriness, control, and information security. Eur. J. Inf. Syst. **18**, 151–164 (2009)
37. Patterson, K., Grenny, J., Maxfield, D., McMillan, R., Switzler, A.: Influencer: the Power to Change Anything. McGraw-Hill, New York, NY (2008)
38. Siponen, M., Willison, R., Baskerville, R.: Power and practice in information systems security research." In: Proceedings of the International Conference on Information Systems, pp. 1–12. Association for Information Systems, Paris (2008)
39. Warkentin, M., Willison, R.: Behavioral and policy issues in information systems security: the insider threat. Eur. J. Inf. Syst. **18**(2), 101–105 (2009)
40. Harris, M., Furnell, S.: Routes to security compliance: be good or be shamed? Comput. Fraud Secur. **12**, 12–20 (2012)
41. Aurigemma, S., Mattson, T.: Deterrence and punishment experience impacts on ISP compliance attitudes. Inf. Comput. Secur. **25**(4), 421–436 (2017)
42. Han, J., Kim, Y.J., Kim, H.: An integrative model of information security policy compliance with psychological contract: examining a bilateral perspective. Comput. Secur. **66**, 52–65 (2017)
43. Kim, B., Lee, D., Kim, B.: Deterrent effects of punishment and training on insider security threats: a field experiment on phishing attacks. Behav. Inf. Technol. 1–20 (2019)
44. Krebs, B.: Should failing phishing tests be a fireable offense? (2019). https://krebsonsecurity.com/2019/05/should-failing-phish-tests-be-a-fireable-offense
45. UK Government.: Developing the UK cyber security profession (2019). https://www.gov.uk/government/consultations/developing-the-uk-cyber-security-profession
46. Hinna, A., De Nito, E., Mangia, G., Scarozza, D., Tomo, A.: Advancing public governance research: individual and collective dynamics in and around the boardroom. Stud. Public Non-Profit Govern. **2**, 3–39 (2014)
47. Baldwin, T.T., Ford, J.K., Blume, B.D.: The state of transfer of training research: moving toward more consumer-centric inquiry. Hum. Resour. Dev. Q. **28**(1), 17–28 (2017)
48. Michie, S., Van Stralen, M.M., West, R.: The behaviour change wheel: a new method for characterising and designing behaviour change interventions. Implement. Sci. **6**(1), 42 (2011)

Analyzing Cybersecurity Understanding Using a Brain Computer Interface

Kingberli Capellan, Manuel Condado, Isabel Morais, and Patricia Morreale$^{(\boxtimes)}$

School of Computer Science and Technology, Kean University, Union, NJ, USA
{capellak,condadom,moraisis,pmorreal}@kean.edu

Abstract. Widespread internet device use is simultaneously increasing individual cybersecurity risk. Individual awareness of cybersecurity risk must begin early, in high school and with a curriculum that engages the student's interest in a highly technical topic. The research project presented here explores the best way to teach cybersecurity to high school students to accomplish these goals. Researchers developed and delivered cybersecurity lectures to the students weekly, observing that each lecture and activity caused a different reaction and interest level depending on the way the topic was approached. Results from this research show the best way to engage students in cybersecurity education topics, as measured by assessment using a brain computer interface (BCI). A curriculum with eight topics was prepared, with selected subjects providing an entry point for different learning styles. Active learning activities and student outcomes show the validity of this approach, as do pre- and post-survey assessments. The results from this work can be used to further develop appropriate engaging cybersecurity education, while reducing student stress.

Keywords: Cybersecurity · Brain computer interface · Human computer interaction

1 Introduction

The research presented measures the effectiveness of a cybersecurity curriculum provided to high school students. The objective of the offered curriculum was to increase student awareness of the types of cyberattacks that take place and the related security issues that may occur because of a cyberattack. High school students were selected to receive several weeks of cybersecurity education, with pre- and post-surveys administered before and after the cybersecurity education, with a goal of determining which lessons were most useful in raising the awareness of students regarding cybersecurity threats.

In order to measure student engagement, a brain computer interface (BCI) was used. A BCI is a collaboration between a brain and a device that enables signals from the brain to direct some external activity, such as control of a prosthetic limb or mouse cursor. For this research project, a BCI headset was used to examine the brain waves a person emits when the user is focused, stressed, relaxed, excited, and engaged. The Emotiv Insight

© Springer Nature Switzerland AG 2020
A. Moallem (Ed.): HCII 2020, LNCS 12210, pp. 92–104, 2020.
https://doi.org/10.1007/978-3-030-50309-3_7

headset (see Fig. 1) was used throughout the project [1]. The BCI headset is noninvasive and goes directly on the student's head. The headset allowed researchers to record the participants' emotions, allowing evaluation of how the students feel about each pre and post-survey question and how they were taught.

Fig. 1. Emotiv Insight headset

Thirty high school students were selected to participate, providing a representative sample population. This study was conducted during a semester and the students returned weekly for lessons and testing.

2 Related Work

According to Daniel Mason, the education of professionals in cybersecurity is closely related to the training of a doctor, a pilot or an athlete. Time spent learning and doing tasks is imperative for success [2]. Hence the need for a curriculum where students have the opportunities to test their skills and share their learning experiences. The success of these curriculums greatly depends on how the technical thinking abilities of the students is regarded. Prior work on teaching found that it is more effective when using "representational forms" and building interconnections within the concepts [3]. This research also hypothesizes that if the traditional methods of school education are changed to methods where active learning experiences are made available, the mindset of these students towards cybersecurity will change.

Cybersecurity education is also found in places where individuals do not have access to new technologies for educational purposes. For example, in some rural communities of Hawaii, a program called "Developing Career and Technical Education (CTE)" was designed especially for women and high school students to be exposed to a higher education in cybersecurity and be able to obtain a certificate upon completion [4]. For students to benefit from these programs, they must be challenged in a way that is appealing to them.

Students, particularly high school students, seem to be more interested when topics presented to them are relevant to their daily lives. They do not tend to picture themselves as adults in need for cybersecurity to keep their information and interests safe, but rather they seemed curious in knowing how it applies them now and how they can integrate their friends and family into that picture [5]. Previous research has shown that when these factors are taken into consideration, students tend to make an "extra effort" in their learning experience. Practical challenges that include competitions, independent thinking, and the opportunity to apply the concepts they learned to their routine [6]. In this study, we introduced high school students without any technical background to cyber-security concepts and related news in ways that include written activities, PowerPoint presentations and interactive videos. Students were able to interact with one and share their ideas and learning experiences.

Being aware of one's own emotions can sometimes be difficult for people. When shown visual stimuli, people can be unsure of what they are supposed to feel [6]. With the help of a BCI, people are able to see their emotional state and take control of their emotions [7]. Within a video game, participants were put in a dark room and, using their emotions, controlled how much light was present. Not only could individuals change an in-game environment by monitoring emotions, but they could also use emotions to only see advertisements that they want [8]. A study was done having users watch multiple advertisements while wearing a BCI, and if the BCI read too many negative emotions within ten seconds, then the advertisement was switched. Additionally, BCIs have been used with gaze tracking [9], showing that control can be achieved with little training. Understanding emotions and using a BCI with ease are important, especially in a study that focused on recognizing the emotional state of students with a mental disorder or mood disruption problems [10].

A brain computer interface is an external device that sends the brain's electrical activity from a user to a computer [11]. The BCI displays electroencephalography (EEG) signals that detects instantaneous excitement and negative feelings [12]. These are all a part of the BCI's performance metrics [13], which measure the four basic emotional states: excitement, boredom/engagement, frustration (anger), and meditation. When comparing BCIs, a Neurosky Mindwave headset is preferred by users for its wearability while the Emotiv Epoc showed greater accuracy when determining a user's mental state [14]. Noninvasive BCIs usually require multiple wires with electrode caps to gather the EEG data, which in turn is uncomfortable for users to wear [15]. With an EmotivBCI, the wires are nonexistent and the headset is very portable, and simple to set up. The lower, affordable price point of EmotivBCIs is also ideal research on a small scale. The BCI can also be used to control objects. For instance, when using a BCI to control a robot versus a keyboard, the keyboard is far superior [16]. This is attributed to people being more comfortable with using a keyboard than a BCI due to the years of experience with a keyboard, compared to less experience with the BCI.

3 Methodology

Participants selected were ninth and tenth grade high school students. As they were minor children, written permission from parents was obtained for them to participate in this study. Thirty students returned their forms signed (seven ninth grades and twenty-three tenth graders), permitting them to participate in the study. Students in this research were assigned to one of two groups based on their class ranking. Freshmen students were assigned to the *non-technical* group, and sophomore students were assigned to the *technical* group (shown in Fig. 2). Instructional delivery was different for the two groups. The non-technical group was based on traditional classroom and the use of PowerPoint slides. Students are limited to listening the instructor and trying to understand the concepts being taught, with some time allowed for questions. Students in the technical group participated in a more hands-on approach, which included an activity to reinforce the material that was taught on that given day.

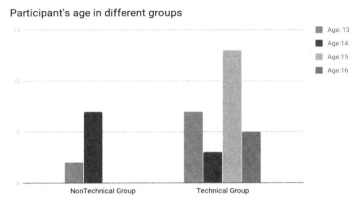

Fig. 2. Participants by ages and groups

Before the cybersecurity classes began, students were told what they were going to be learning throughout the week and given a pre-assessment. The pre-assessment collected demographic information, social media use & the amount spent online. Students were tested on their knowledge on topics in the field of cybersecurity and whether their school offered cyber security classes. It was expected that students would not have prior knowledge on any of cyber security topics. A post-assessment was given after the lesson to test for effectiveness of the approach used.

Selected students were tested with the BCI, as shown in Table 1 below. These students were randomly selected to take the pre and post assessment, which included questions about cyber security so that it could be determined how much the students learned during the cyber security classes. The research team made sure to convey the importance of coming to every class, especially when taking the pre and post assessments so the study could have consistency.

Table 1. Students who used the BCI during the pre and post-assessments

Grade	Assessment	No BCI	BCI	Total students
9th	Pre-assessment	3	4	7
	Post-assessment	3	3	6
10th	Pre-assessment	15	6	21
	Post-assessment	10	5	15

Of the seven ninth graders who agreed to participate, only four students were tested with the BCI. The research team pre-tested the four students using BCI in one day, while the other students took the paper pre-test in another room. One by one, the four students took the assessment with the BCI, which was placed on their head by one of the researchers. From the twenty-one tenth graders, six students were tested with the BCI. Again, the students were chosen at random to participate in the assessments with the BCI. The students taking the test with the BCI were put in a separate room to take their test while the rest of the students took the assessment in their classroom.

To understand the results of the assessment, the classes and the assessment questions must be explained. First, the classes were split up by grade, having each grade taught by a different teaching style. The ninth graders, dubbed the non-technical group, were taught using traditional methods, such as lectures from a PowerPoint presentation. The tenth graders, dubbed the technical group, were taught using activities and videos along with the PowerPoint presentation. Both classes were taught the same topics relating to cyber security. These topics included cybersecurity ethics, encryption/decryption, phishing, cybercrime, virtual private networks (VPNs) and cyber privacy, swatting, and cryptocurrency.

The pre-assessment was made up of twenty-six questions, including both multiple choice and open-ended questions. The first half of the test included demographics questions and questions to determine if the students knew anything about cyber security and if they thought it was serious or not. The second half of the assessment included questions on the topics we would be teaching in the following weeks. Students were not expected to know the answers and were told to try their best. The post assessment took place at the end of the semester and included sixteen questions, all related to the topics discussed during previous classes. The questions consisted of multiple choice, true or false, and open-ended questions. Students were instructed not to skip any questions and to give their best guess if they did not know the answer.

The BCI was used with the students and shows the student's focus, stress, excitement, engagement, relaxation, and interest levels. A number from zero to one hundred, zero meaning the lowest score for that emotion and one hundred meaning the student strongly feels that emotion denotes each emotion. Each student was tested separately and in their own room, so there would be no distractions for the student and to give space for the researchers to set up the equipment. Instead of having the student put the headset on themselves, a researcher was responsible for putting the headset on the student. The Emotiv Insight headset has five sensors, which all need to touch the skin on the head in order to obtain accurate readings. Researchers made sure that the students were comfortable with the headset, as moving their hair and trying to get the sensors as close to the skin as possible could be slightly uncomfortable. Though this did not happen, at any point during the assessments, students were able to stop the test because they were uncomfortable with the headset or any other reason.

4 Pre and Post Assessments with Cybersecurity Curriculum

4.1 Pre-assessment

Twenty-eight participants took part in the overall pre-assessment, seven of whom were part of the non-technical group and 21 participants belonged to the technical group. Those in the non-technical group were dominantly, 14 years of age, with one individual being 13 years old. In the technical group majority of participants were 15 years of age, followed by five participants being 16 years age and lastly three participants were 14 years age. Based on the findings in the pre-assessment, schools are working to narrow the demand for cybersecurity professionals. As shown in Table 2, 2 out of 7 students from the non-technical group reported their school having some type of cybersecurity courses whereas 20 out of 21 students from the technical group reported their school offering cybersecurity courses.

Table 2. Does your school offer cybersecurity related courses?

		Responses		Total
		No	Yes	
Group	Non-technical	5	2	7
	Technical	1	20	21
Total		6	22	28

One explanation for the discrepancy between the non-technical (freshmen) group and technical (sophomores) is at the time of pre-assessment freshmen students may not be familiar with the courses their school has to offer. The pre-assessment failed to question whether the student was enrolled in one of the cybersecurity related courses their school has to offer, although one open-ended question in the pre-assessment asked if the student has some knowledge in cybersecurity (shown in Table 3).

Table 3. Do you know anything about cybersecurity?

		Response		Total
		No	Yes	
Group	Non-technical	4	3	7
	Technical	12	9	21
Total		16	12	28

Mixed responses were received, with 3 out of 7 students in the non-technical group and 9 out of 21 reported some knowledge on cybersecurity. A follow-up open-ended question was asked to those that reported having some knowledge asking if they could explain briefly what they knew. Students were also asked about their preferred instructional method (shown in Table 4) with the majority of students interested in activity-based learning.

4.2 Cybersecurity Curriculum

A cybersecurity curriculum was developed for use with this research, which included videos, slides, and activities. The curriculum (Table 5) is designed to expose the students to a range of topics.

Table 4. Do you prefer to learn new things through activities or lectures?

		Responses				Total
		Activities	Lecture	N/A	Other	
Group	Non-technical	5	0	1	1	7
	Technical	20	1	0	0	21
Total		25	1	1	1	28

Table 5. Overview of the cybersecurity curriculum

Week	Cybersecurity curriculum topics
0	**Introduction of cybersecurity curriculum**; distribution of consent and assent forms
1	**Cybersecurity and Ethics** *(Pre-assessment):* Students taught how to use internet-connected devices in a way that is safe for them and others
2	**Encryption & Decryption**: After exposure to different encryption algorithms and their usage, students were given an encrypted sentence using Caesar cipher (shifting the letters two positions to the right in this case) and asked to find the hidden message. Then, they were encouraged to create their own
3	**Phishing:** Students were asked to identify fake versus real emails from well-known retail companies and banks, by spotting the most common strategist that are used when performing phishing attacks. Videos and news were shown, making them aware of what type of information is at risk and how easy it is stolen
4	**Cybercrime and legal consequences**: In spite of the need for cybersecurity professionals, the cyber skills can also be used to cause harm. Students learned the legal consequences that their actions might have and shown some of the most famous cyber criminals' punishment for their actions
5	**Virtual Private Networks (VPNs) and Cyber Privacy**: Introduced the need for maintaining privacy when using the internet. How VPNs work, why they are used
6	**Swatting** *(Day 1 of post-assessment):* Swatting involves fake calls to law enforcement to report a crime that does not exist. Students learned about incidents that were reported on the news and videos with recorded calls to 911. Explanations were provide on how the law enforcement deals with these situations
7	**Transition from High School to College** *(Day 2 of post-assessment):* Students learned about opportunities (conferences, scholarships and career paths) to continue their education in Cybersecurity
8	**Cryptocurrency (Last day):** Cryptocurrency was presented and how this relates to cybersecurity. Students learned in simple terms how the transactions are made, how organization and clarity is kept, and how people obtain the currency. Videos were shown on the topic, including the owners of the most cryptocurrency nowadays

The researchers noticed that the videos and active lessons were particularly well received.

4.3 Post-assessment

Students in both the technical group and non-technical group were informed approximately two weeks ahead of time about the post-assessment. The post-assessment was used to test the student's knowledge in the areas of cybersecurity that were taught in the curriculum. Examining the post-assessments took two Saturdays for both groups. Due to absences and some parents who did not want their child participating in the post-assessment, despite signing a consent and assent form and having the child participate in the pre-assessment, 21 students took the post-assessment. Six of the students belonged to the non-technical group (freshmen) and 15 students belonged to the technical group (sophomore), compared to the 28 students that participated in the pre-assessment.

The first question in the post-assessment evaluated students on the risks associated with public Wi-Fi. Responses were similar between both groups. Students used phrases such as "you can get hacked (S1)," "someone can see in your information (S23)", "private information can be obtained" (S24), "your device can be hacked (F1)" or "a person can access your information if they have a middleman access (F5)". The association between public Wi-Fi and hacking information is high and the word hacking or hacker is used three times once by each participant in the non-technical group (freshmen) out of five.

Encryption and decryption are a topic in which students had difficulty grasping. This assumption is based on the feedback received during the lecture and results of the post-assessment. For the most part, it was the area on private keys and public keys, and symmetric/asymmetric encryption. In the encryption and decryption lecture it was demonstrated how Caesar cipher works by encrypting a simple sentence and afterwards decrypting it afterwards. All this material was being taught within a 45 time period and was being presented as the second lecture in the curriculum.

Question 2 in the post assessment tested the participant's knowledge on the problems with current encryption algorithms. Two out of the five participants in the non-technical group (freshmen) and six out of fifteen in the technical group (sophomore) did not give any response and ignored the question. Responses varied greatly such as "someone can decrypt it" or "hackers can figure out the encryption". In addition, question 6, further tested the participant's knowledge in the area of encryption and decryption (shown in Table 6).

Table 6. Q6: a network requires a secure method of sharing encryption algorithms over a public network. Which of the following is the BEST choice?

		Responses			Total
		Bcrypt	Steganography	Symmetric encryption	
Group	Non-technical	2	1	3	6
	Technical	3	1	11	15
Total		5	2	14	21

The question asked for the best method of sharing encryption keys over a public network. Four choices were given, Bcrypt, symmetric encryption, steganography and

Diffie-Hellman. No respondent in either group answered the question correctly. Lastly, question 7 evaluated the area of public and private keys. Only one person in each group provided the correct answer. Zero participants proved the correct answer in the pre-assessment.

Table 7. Q4: a user's personal files are encrypted. The user is unable to access this data unless they pay the criminals to decrypt the files. What is this cybercrime called?

		Responses					Total
		Botnet	Ransomware	Spam	Trojan	N/A	
Group	Non-technical	1	1	1	2	1	6
	Technical	1	5	9	0	0	15
Total		2	6	10	2	1	21

The next area the post-assessment tested was on phishing and cybercrimes, with four possible choices for question 4 (shown in Table 7). Answers varied in both groups. In non-technical group Trojan was the picked by two students, followed spam, ransomware and botnet being picked once. Whereas ransomware being the correct answer, it was chosen five out fifteen times in the technical group (sophomore). This was followed by spam being chosen nine out of 15 by the technical group (sophomore). One possible explanation is the way the lecture was presented. Ransomware was listed as being one of many malware attacks that can originate from an email and the technical group presentation relied more on visual aids.

Finally, the post-assessment tested the student's knowledge in Virtual Private Networks (VPN). VPNs were the fifth lecture in the curriculum. VPN use was discussed and how countries like China block websites as a way to regulate the internet, censoring the internet. One method to circumvent China's censorship is using a VPN. The VPN works by connecting the user to a remote user and encrypting the user's data. Question 5 asked participants what risks could be minimized using VPNs. Responses were similar such as "They cannot take your personal information and you can be more secure", "maintain your information securely". Freshmen responses were "your network can be secure and your location" and "it would be difficult for someone to steal your information".

5   Results

The results of the pre and post assessments are presented by grade, with 9th graders designated as Freshman (F) and 10th graders designated as Sophomores (S). This allowed researchers to be able to distinguish between the different teaching methods used in the classes. For anonymity, students were given identification numbers.

Pre-assessment, Ninth Graders: Having the students fill out the demographic questions first allowed researchers to obtain a baseline reading when the students are answering simple questions about themselves. As soon as the students began taking the assessment, the engagement levels for the students spiked. Focus levels for the students during the demographic questions stayed consistent around thirty. Students F2 and F4 each had a focus score of thirty-one and thirty respectively. Meanwhile, students F1 and F3 had high focus level throughout the assessment. The only outlier being F3's focus level towards the end when it dropped to seven before ending at thirty. When the assessment turned from demographic questions to cyber security questions is where the students' emotion levels started to change. Student F1's interest level jumped to eighty when answering the first questions regarding the risks of using public Wi-Fi. Student F2's engagement and stress both spiked when answering the Wi-Fi question, implying that the student was ready to answer the question, but possibly scared to get the answer wrong. Student F3's engagement level was at ninety-three, focus was around fourteen, and interest level spiked to ninety-seven. From F3's emotion levels, it can be assumed that the student was felt positive about the topics, but the focus level could indicate that the student was not thinking too hard about the answers. From the answers to the questions student F3 gave, they seemed to be the first response that came to mind. It is interesting to note that F3 did have the longest pre-test time with the BCI of the ninth graders. Finally, student F4 is the only student whose emotion levels during the cyber security questions were around 50–60 for a majority of categories. From F4's data, it is assumed that F4 did not feel too positive or negative throughout the assessment, but instead felt at ease.

Pre-assessment, Tenth Graders: On the final demographic question, student S1's engagement, interest, and excitement levels were all in the fifties and sixties. This changed when S1 began the cyber security questions, which is when engagement made a jump immediately to seventy. The only outlier from S1's pre-assessment emotion levels seems to be the focus levels, which stayed low the entire time. Student S2's engagement level stayed around sixty and the excitement level peaked at seventy-one near the end of the test. Student S3 started the assessment with a low stress level of seventeen but jumped to fifty-seven as the demographics questions continued and ended the section with a stress level of seventy-nine. When student S3 started the cyber security questions, focus jumped to a high of ninety-two, which corresponds to all of the questions answered being correct. Student S3 was one of the more engaged students throughout the cyber security classes. Student S4's results were interesting with regard to excitement, interest, and stress levels. Excitement and interest levels were low all around, with the stress level staying around a steady thirty. However, at the end of the assessment S4's excitement dropped to fourteen and stress levels stayed the same when the researcher stated that time was running out. This was interesting because, out of every student who used the BCI, S4 was the only one with low scores but understood a majority of the topics. With student S5, the longer the assessment was taking to complete the higher S5's engagement and interest levels became. Finally, S6 maintained a steady level of 30–50 for relaxation, stress, and focus throughout the entire exam. On the other hand, S6's excitement level never passed thirty and interest peaked during the questions regarding cybercrime and safety on the internet.

Post-assessment, Ninth Graders: Student F1 did not return to take the post assessment with the BCI, so there isn't any data to determine if F1's stress levels decreased after knowing the topics. Student F2's results show moderate interest and engagement when answering encryption, phishing, and hacking questions, all with levels around fifty. Alternatively, the stress levels for those topics never went over forty. When comparing F2's pre-test stress and engagement levels on the topic of Wi-Fi, student F2 had a stress level around forty-two and an engagement level of fifty-four, which is an improvement from the spike that occurred in the pre-assessment. From student F3's post-assessment it is possible to see the drop in focus levels. The pre-assessment started off well, with student F3 having a moderate focus level, which increased to around eighty-eight when answering a question on phishing. However, similar to the pre-test, the end of the assessment saw focus levels drop to around twenty. Additionally, F3's stress level stayed around forty throughout the exam, which was not seen in the pre-assessment. This could be attributed by the excitement that came from the pre-test that encouraged student F3 to feel better. When it came time to take the post-test, student F3 possibly felt more pressure to perform well. Finally, student F4's post-assessment emotion levels did not have significant change from the pre-assessment. The only change in emotion levels occurred when answering questions on virtual private networks (VPNs). Engagement and interest levels both jumped to eighty-one and eighty, respectively, during these questions. However, even though this is where the student was most engaged and interested, the student did not have the correct answer for one of the questions. From this, researchers concluded that the student was passionate about the topic but did not retain the class information. The researchers plan to improve future class lessons on VPNs.

Post-assessment Results, Tenth Grade Students: Student S1 had low to moderate interest, engagement, and focus levels throughout the post-assessment. When answering questions on phishing the student seemed to keep his emotions in check. This is concluded by seeing emotion levels during other questions jump around, but on questions related to phishing the emotion levels stay calm. Student S1's stress levels also stayed around fifty for the majority of the assessment, which leads the researchers to conclude that student S1 did not feel confident in his knowledge of the subject. This means that both the activities and lessons taught in class did not provide the student with adequate knowledge or the student did not understand the lessons. Student S2 felt relaxed and engaged throughout the post assessment, with relaxation levels ranging from forty to fifty and engagement levels around 50–60. It should be noted that student S2 did not answer a majority of the questions correctly and, when asked if the technical teaching approach was effective, the student responded with a no, stating that they prefer to learn other ways. Student S3 had extremely high emotion levels when taking the post-assessment, with interest, excitement, and engagement levels reaching the high eighties. These high emotion levels came from questions regarding Wi-Fi, encryption, phishing, and VPNs. However, like S2, student S3 did not answer the questions correctly, which leads the researchers to believe that the student liked the topics but did not have a clear understanding of it. Student S4 had stress levels ranging from 50–80 throughout the assessment; however, the majority of questions were answered correctly. It can be concluded that student S4 was not confident in their own answers, which is explained by the high stress and correct answers. Like student F1 who did not show for the post-assessment, student S5 did not show up for the final test, therefore, there is no further data. Student S6 had moderate to high emotion levels all around, except for stress, which stayed around forty. Student S6 saw peeks during questions about Wi-Fi, Encryption, VPNs, and hacking.

6 Conclusions

Examining student emotions with a BCI while taking an assessment is simple, yet analyzing their emotions is difficult. With the BCI, researchers were able to see when students were interested and engaged with the topic. It was possible to observe students really focus on questions and see when a question is stressing them out. It is difficult to figure out why the students felt this way. It was concluded that students felt positive emotions when the student liked the topic, but they did not necessarily get the correct answer. This is attributed to the student not paying attention in their class, the teaching style being ineffective, and/or the information on the topic not being presented correctly. Researchers found that students felt more stressed when taking an assessment on topics they were previously taught, even if they knew the correct answer. High stress levels can have negative effects on one's confidence, leading to uncertainty during test taking. Further research should be done to identify why students feel stressed when they know the answers on an exam. Using a BCI, researchers could use it during classes to identify if students feel stressed during the lessons.

7 Future Work

This study was both a learning opportunity for the students involved and the researchers. Time was a signification constraint on the classes. More time would be helpful during testing and classes. In the future, researchers will expand on topics discussed in class, providing more information for the students to learn. Additionally, researchers will allow more time for setting up the BCI with each student. Moderate readings were obtained from the students, but with more time, a higher accuracy from the BCI could be obtained. Additionally, the Emotiv Insight headset must be placed very close to the skin and it was difficult to move the headset around on the student's head without issues arising. Better communication with the students will lead to being able to place the headset on correctly, which will increase the accuracy. Future work should include longer study and class times for the students.

The results presented here included a cybersecurity curriculum outline, which can be used in any introductory cybersecurity classroom, particularly 9th and 10th grade high school. Encryption and decryption, topics introduced in week two originally, should be exchanged with swatting, a topic from week six, as the swatting topic was observed to be engaging for students. Encryption and decryption, with the associated complexity, should be shared later, or deferred for a later course.

References

1. EMOTIV Insight 5 Channel Mobile EEG - Emotiv, Emotiv (2018). https://www.emotiv.com/product/emotiv-insight-5-channel-mobile-eeg/. Accessed 18 May 2018
2. Manson, D., Pike, R.: The case for depth in cybersecurity education. ACM Inroads (2015). https://dl.acm.org/citation.cfm?id=2568212. Accessed Mar 2019
3. Dark, M.: Thinking about cybersecurity. IEEE J. Mag. (2015). https://ieeexplore.ieee.org/abstract/document/7031840. Accessed Mar 2019

4. Nakama, D., Paullet, K.: The urgency for cybersecurity education: the impact of early college innovation in Hawaii rural communities, August 2018. https://files.eric.ed.gov/fulltext/EJ1 188021.pdf

5. Cheung, R.S.Y., Cohen, J.P.: Challenge based learning in cybersecurity education. Semant. Scholar, 01 Jan 2011. https://www.semanticscholar.org/paper/Challenge-Based-Learning-in-Cybersecurity-Education-Cheung-Cohen/1906647d669e659a6cc465367069d27a5853 c820#citing-papers. Accessed 02 Apr 2019

6. Deja, J., Cabredo, R.: Using EEG emotion models in viewer experience design: an exploratory study. In: Proceedings of the 4th International Conference on Human-Computer Interaction and User Experience in Indonesia, CHIuXiD 2018 (2018). https://doi.org/10.1145/3205946. 3205958. Accessed 1 Mar 2019

7. Bernays, R., et al.: Lost in the dark: emotion Adaption. In: Adjunct Proceedings of the 25th Annual ACM Symposium on User Interface Software and Technology - UIST Adjunct Proceedings 2012 (2012). https://doi.org/10.1145/2380296.2380331. Accessed 1 Mar 2019

8. Rajamani, K., Ramalingam, A., Bavisetti, S., Abujelala, M.: CBREN: computer brain entertainment system using neural feedback cognitive enhancement. In: Proceedings of the 10th International Conference on Pervasive Technologies Related to Assistive Environments - PETRA 2017 (2017). https://doi.org/10.1145/3056540.3064971. Accessed 1 Mar 2019

9. Brennan, C., McCullagh, P., Lightbody, G., Galway, L.: The BCI as a pervasive technology - a research plan. In: Proceedings of the 8th International Conference on Pervasive Computing Technologies for Healthcare (2014). https://doi.org/10.4108/icst.pervasivehealth.2014. 255755 Accessed 1 Mar 2019

10. Mehmood, R., Lee, H.: Towards building a computer aided education system for special students using wearable sensor technologies. Sensors 17(2), 317 (2017). https://doi.org/10. 3390/s17020317

11. Rebolledo-Mendez, G., Freitas, S.: Attention modeling using inputs from a brain computer interface and user-generated data in second life. In: Proceedings of the Workshop of Affective Interaction in Natural Environments (AFFINE) (2008). Accessed 1 Mar 2019

12. Fouad, I., Labib, F.: Using Emotiv EPOC neuroheadset to acquire data in brain-computer interface. Int. J. Adv. Res. 3(11), 1012–1017 (2015). Accessed 1 Mar 2019

13. Mavridou, I.: Gestures - emotions interaction: e-Viographima application for visual artistic synthesis. In: Proceedings of the 3rd International Symposium on Movement and Computing - MOCO 2016 (2016). https://doi.org/10.1145/2948910.2948953. Accessed 1 Mar 2019

14. Folgieri, R., Zampolini, R.: BCI promises in emotional involvement in music and games. Comput. Entertain. 11(4), 1–10 (2015). https://doi.org/10.1145/2582193.2633447. Accessed 1 Mar 2019

15. Pinto, R., Ferreira, H.: Development of a non-invasive brain computer interface for neurorehabilitation. In: Proceedings of the 3rd 2015 Workshop on ICTs for improving Patients Rehabilitation Research Techniques - REHAB 2015 (2015). https://doi.org/10.1145/2838944. 2838975. Accessed 1 Mar 2019

16. Dollman, G., De Wet, L., Beelders, T.: Effectiveness with EEG BCIs: exposure to traditional input methods as a factor of performance. In: Proceedings of the South African Institute for Computer Scientists and Information Technologists Conference on - SAICSIT 2013 (2013). https://doi.org/10.1145/2513456.2513476. Accessed 1 Mar 2019

Cyber-Risk in Healthcare: Exploring Facilitators and Barriers to Secure Behaviour

Lynne Coventry[1](✉) (iD), Dawn Branley-Bell[1] (iD), Elizabeth Sillence[1] (iD),
Sabina Magalini[2] (iD), Pasquale Mari[2] (iD), Aimilia Magkanaraki[3] (iD),
and Kalliopi Anastasopoulou[3] (iD)

[1] Northumbria University, Newcastle upon Tyne NE1 8ST, UK
{lynne.coventry,dawn.branley-bell,
elizabeth.sillence}@northumbria.ac.uk
[2] Fondazione Policlinico Universitario Agostino Gemelli, Rome, Italy
Sabina.Magalini@unicatt.it, Pasquale.mari3@gmail.com
[3] 7th HealthCare Region of Crete, 3rd klm of National Road Heraklion-Moires,
71500 Heraklion, Crete, Greece
{amagkanaraki,kanastasopoulou}@hc-crete.gr

Abstract. There are increasing concerns relating to cybersecurity of healthcare data and medical devices. Cybersecurity in this sector is particularly important given the criticality of healthcare systems, the impacts of a breach or cyberattack (including in the worst instance, potential physical harm to patients) and the value of healthcare data to criminals. Technology design is important for cybersecurity, but it is also necessary to understand the insecure behaviours prevalent within healthcare. It is vital to identify the drivers behind these behaviours, i.e., why staff may engage in insecure behaviour including their goals and motivations and/or perceived barriers preventing secure behaviour. To achieve this, in-depth interviews with 50 staff were conducted at three healthcare sites, across three countries (Ireland, Italy and Greece). A range of seven insecure behaviours were reported: Poor computer and user account security; Unsafe e-mail use; Use of USBs and personal devices; Remote access and home working; Lack of encryption, backups and updates; Use of connected medical devices; and poor physical security. Thematic analysis revealed four key facilitators of insecure behaviour: Lack of awareness and experience, Shadow working processes, Behaviour prioritisation and Environmental appropriateness. The findings suggest three key barriers to security: i) Security perceived as a barrier to productivity and/or patient care; ii) Poor awareness of consequences of behaviour; and iii) a lack of policies and reinforcement of secure behaviour. Implications for future research are presented.

Keywords: Cybersecurity · Health · Healthcare · Cyberthreat · Behaviour change

A. Moallem (Ed.): HCII 2020, LNCS 12210, pp. 105–122, 2020.
https://doi.org/10.1007/978-3-030-50309-3_8

1 Introduction

Cybersecurity in healthcare is of increasing concern. New technological interventions continue to improve the treatment of a wide range of medical issues, and undoubtedly, healthcare technology has potential to save, and enhance, human life [1–3]. Many hospitals now operate using a complex interconnected network of IT systems and devices. This includes connected health devices and administration systems storing electronic health patient records (EHRs). Hospitals and clinics also rely upon remote working and/or the transfer of test results and other sensitive data via electronic channels [4]. Unfortunately, an increase in new technology and interconnectivity also introduces new security vulnerabilities and challenges [5, 6]. This is not purely a technical problem, but a complex sociotechnical one that will only be solved by understanding ways in which technology and humans can interact to create the strongest defences; as well as the way that this interaction can create vulnerabilities.

Healthcare is an attractive target for cybercrime for two fundamental reasons: it is a rich source of valuable data [4] and its defenses are weak [6]. The mass media highlights that vulnerabilities within healthcare are being exploited [7, 8], and the sector urgently needs to increase its resilience against cyberattacks and breaches [6, 8]. Breaches can reduce patient trust, cripple health systems and threaten human life [9]. The WannaCry attack in 2017 is a key example of the type of consequences that cyberattacks can have within the healthcare sector [10]. WannaCry was a ransomware attack which affected computers in more than 100 countries. The National Health Service (NHS) England was amongst those affected. with 80 (34%) NHS trusts, 603 primary care organisations and 595 GP practices infected by the ransomware. This resulted in the cancellation of over 19,000 patient appointments, and a substantial financial cost to the NHS [11]. Around the world, ransomware attacks are still being experienced, disrupting services, and even forcing some practitioners to quit the healthcare sector [12].

Although technological protection such as strong firewalls and antivirus can go some way towards protecting against cyberthreat; strong cybersecurity also relies upon secure staff behaviour, which has largely been ignored [6]. Cybersecurity is not just a technical problem, but a complex sociotechnical problem [13]. Staff behaviour has been shown to be one of the major contributors to cybersecurity vulnerability [4] and humans have often been described as cybersecurity's 'weakest link' [14]. However, it is important to recognise that staff can also be one of the strongest links in cybersecurity, when secure employee behaviour acts – in effect – as a 'human firewall' [6].

Whilst in some instances, staff misbehaviour is deliberate, i.e., deliberate insider threat. A significant proportion of cyberattacks and breaches are unintentional consequences of staff behaviours that introduce vulnerability without malicious intent [4]. Healthcare represents a unique environment, one where staff prioritise effective and efficient patient care. Understandably, cybersecurity may not be the primary focus during their day-to-day working lives. Staff working within this sector also report being overworked, fatigued and stressed [15–18]. This creates psychosocial risks for cybersecurity [19]. It is important that research identifies key vulnerabilities in staff behaviour and investigates how to address these in a manner that does not burden staff and/or negatively impact upon patient care. In order to do this, it is necessary to identify the driving factors behind staffs' insecure behaviour, for example is this behaviour driven by a need to save time? Due to a lack of awareness? Or some other factor(s)? Previous research shows a range of factors which can influence secure or insecure behaviour, including for example self-efficacy, attitudes, external influences, coping and threat evaluation [20]. Many insecure behaviours have been found to be instrumental, reasoned and conducted as a means to an end, e.g., to save time [4]. Therefore, effective interventions can only be designed following the identification of drivers behind insecure behaviour [4]. This study addresses this gap in the current literature through a series of in-depth focus groups and interviews with healthcare staff across three sites, and three countries (Ireland, Italy and Greece); enabling the exploration and identification of key barriers to cybersecurity in the healthcare environment.

To summarise the main contributions of this study are:

- Identification of insecure behaviour(s) by healthcare staff
- Identification of the key factors facilitating insecure behaviour(s) and/or providing barriers to more secure behaviour
- Preliminary discussion of the implications of these findings for the design of interventions and the role of HCI in facilitating secure behaviour.

2 Methodology

Three focus group sessions took place across three sites: Gemelli hospital in Rome, the 7th Health Region of Crete, and the HSE SSW Hospital Group, Ireland. These sessions were conducted face-to-face at the hospital location or remotely via Skype. Each session lasted between 45–60 min, and included between 2–9 staff members. A total of 50 staff took part. A range of healthcare staff were included from administration staff, doctors, nurses, IT staff, etc. (Table 1).

During the focus group, the facilitators asked opened ended questions focusing upon the following areas:

- Awareness of any previous incidents at the hospital they would describe as cyber-related
- Type of cybersecurity risks that staff felt were of most concern within the hospital
- The type of data and technology that staff interact with on a daily basis and the perceived security of this technology
- Security of staff behaviour and any risky behaviours that they were aware of
- General awareness of potential cyber-risk and vulnerability to attack.

For those interviewees that could not attend the focus groups (for example, due to unforeseen patient emergencies), we collected additional survey-based responses to these questions. The results were analysed using thematic analysis [21] to identify key themes. Ethical approval was granted by Northumbria University ethics committee before commencing.

Table 1. Job Roles

Location	Job Role
Gemelli Hospital, Rome	Lab Technicians
	Administration Staff
	IT Team
7th Health Region of Crete (7HRC)	IT Teams across 2 different hospitals
	Biomedical Engineers
	Health Centre Staff (nurses, GPs, health workers)
	Managers
The HSE SSW Hospital Group, Ireland	Lab Technicians
	Administration Staff
	Medical Consultants
	Finance Staff
	Emergency staff including paramedics and ambulance staff
	Nurses
	Doctors

3 Results

This section describes the five themes that developed in the analysis. The first details the type of insecure cybersecurity behaviours occurring across the healthcare sites. The remaining four themes explain key facilitators underpinning these behaviours: Lack of awareness and experience; Shadow working processes; Behaviour prioritization and Environmental appropriateness.

3.1 Insecure Cybersecurity Behaviours

Within this theme, seven types of insecure cybersecurity behaviours were identified that would pose a risk to healthcare institutions: *Poor computer and user account security; Unsafe e-mail use; Use of USBs and personal devices; Remote access and home working; Lack of encryption, backups and updates; Use of connected medical devices; and poor physical security.* These were identified as risk behaviours as they have been linked to increased cybersecurity risk in the literature [22].

Poor Computer and User Account Security
Concerns around the security of login credentials and computer access were prevalent across all three sites. Two major concerns were noted: *Open workstations* within the hospital and *poor password security.*

Many participants reported that computers within the healthcare environment are often used/shared by many different users. To save time logging in and out of their individual accounts, staff report leaving workstations logged into a single staff user account. Because of this, it is common to find *open workstations* throughout the hospital. Users were particularly likely to leave a computer logged into a single staff members account within the labs – where it was perceived that only known individuals would have physical access to the computer. This suggests that trust amongst colleagues plays a role in this behaviour.

Password security was a subject over which both the medical staff and the IT staff expressed frustration. IT staff described *poor password security* as a "single point of [security] failure". We identified three key areas of concern: *repetition of passwords, writing passwords down,* and *use of automatic login/remember me* options on the workstations. Within the hospital, systems are in place that require employees to change their work passwords periodically (usually around every 2–3 months). The system does not allow staff to use the previous 2–3 passwords, however some staff report simply using the same 3–4 passwords on a rotating cycle to get around this, and to help them remember their passwords. Staff report frustration that it is "not possible to remember 20 different passwords" – so users use the same passwords across multiple systems as often as possible (often the same password they use for personal computer and internet use). As aforementioned, junior and admin staff often use senior staff login credentials; due to this they tend to be the first to receive the notice that the current password is about to expire. Consequently, junior and admin staff often change doctors and directors' passwords. This could result in passwords that may be difficult for the senior staff to remember (due to a lack of personal salience).

Systems generally generate specific password requirements (e.g., the password must be more than a specified number of letters, contain a number or symbol, etc.). This is designed to support secure password choices; however, staff report that these rules vary across the different platforms that they use and this can lead to frustration. All of the factors (number of passwords required, regular need to update passwords, staff member changing others' passwords, and differing password requirements) can contribute to difficulty in password memorability. Consequently, many staff report that passwords are written down - often on sticky labels attached to computer monitors, visible by everyone. Many computer systems also ask staff if they would like the computer to automatically remember their login credentials, e.g., by ticking "remember me" or "save password". This is not a recommended security behaviour, particularly on shared devices, however, staff often accept this option to save time and forgotten passwords. Staff do not generally use a secure password manager to remember passwords (e.g., KeyPass), with the exception of some IT staff. While 'remember me' may improve usability it has an unintended consequence for security.

Phishing

Staff use e-mail on a daily basis, and we identified concerns around dealing with *phishing emails* which may lead to stolen credentials or introduction of malware into the system. Staff reported *phishing e-*mails as a regular, ever increasing occurrence, and IT staff described it as a key cause for concern. Although spam filters are in place, these often fail to keep up with ever-evolving phishing approaches and do not always correctly identify e-mails as spam. Conversely, important e-mails can also be incorrectly diverted to the spam folder – providing a potential barrier to staff productivity. Furthermore, reliance upon spam filters could provide staff with a false sense of security and the inaccurate assumption that those e-mails which reach their inbox must be 'safe'. Therefore, training and staff awareness is important.

At *some* of the hospitals, IT staff send regular internal e-mails warning staff not to open attachments. However, staff perceive this advice as unfeasible as they often need to open email attachments to do their job. Medical reports and assessments are often sent as email attachments by patients, patients' friends/family, and by other clinics and medical facilities (e.g., clinics across the region). Due to staff not knowing who will be e-mailing the document(s), they cannot rely upon recognising the e-mail address to identify if this is a genuine/safe e-mail. Instead, staff rely upon recognising (or searching for) the patient's name in the email subject box. This introduces significant vulnerability to exploitation. In addition to being unfeasible, advice from IT to not open attachments was perceived as contradictory, as genuine internal e-mails from IT and management often include links or attachments.

Use of USBs and Personal Devices

Staff reported regular use of USB sticks to save and transfer data at work. USBs are typically their own personal devices, not supplied by their employer nor used exclusively for work. All levels of staff reported using USBs, including junior and admin (e.g., to pass files to senior staff and directors), doctors, nurses, hospital residents (i.e., students) and IT staff. Perhaps even more concerning, external visitors and patients often bring their records on USB sticks to the hospital (e.g., reports from other clinics). These USBs are plugged straight into the hospital workstations without any prior safety procedures. These workstations are connected to the hospital network and not isolated machines. Sites differed in regards to whether an antivirus automatically scans USB devices when they are inserted into a computer; however even if this is activated it may not stop malware spreading. To try to minimise risk, some IT teams have closed the USB ports on specific workstations (e.g., computers within the radiology department) but this is not generally the norm across most machines.

Staff generally perceived no danger related to USB use, with the exception of the IT and technical teams who expressed concern but also regarded USB usage as necessary, and therefore unavoidable. Indeed, in some roles, USBs actually form part of the compulsory method for staff to confirm their identity by electronic signature.

In addition to USB sticks, staff bring other *personal devices* to work – such as laptops and smartphones (with many staff accessing work e-mail via their personal smartphone). Most staff reported that personal devices are only permitted to connect to the free public WiFi and not to the main hospital network. However, IT and technical staff described struggling to monitor and prevent staff from plugging their devices directly into the hospital network using Ethernet cables. This can be prevented by having ports paired with devices, however this is limiting when equipment is being regularly moved around the environment. In some limited circumstances, personal laptops can be connected to the hospital network with prior permission from IT. For those sites in remote, rural areas or small practices, it is more common for staff members to use their own devices for work. In these circumstances there are not always restrictions on connecting these devices to the hospital systems. Lost or stolen devices pose a significant security concern, as IT do not install software to enable them to remotely wipe the device.

For some IT staff, the lack of a clear policy against bringing your own device to work is seen as a big problem. Unfortunately, any changes would have to be enforced by the governance board, who were generally described as lacking a "security mind-set" and being reactive rather than proactive (i.e., waiting until something happens before acting rather than putting preventative measures in place).

Lack of Encryption, Backups and Updates

Alarmingly, no staff reported regularly encrypting data before transmitting it within - or particularly outside - of the hospital. This means that data being shared (and accessed on personal devices) represents an even greater vulnerability. Staff reported never being instructed – or taught – to encrypt files. A minority of the sites require staff to use SSL to send e-mails, and some departments (e.g., accounting) use digital signatures to exchange files, but this was in the minority.

Staff demonstrated a significant lack of awareness in relation to data backups, with most simply 'assuming' that backups took place automatically. Staff perceived backups as something that would be managed by IT or the department head – but they were not sure whether this was actually the case. In most cases this is correct, although staff should be made more aware what is and is not backed up from different devices. For instance, staff described how one senior manager's workstation could not be re-established after a ransomware attack as the manager had switched off the automatic backup software. Staff also reported a reluctance to install software updates on the workstations as they perceived these as problematic, e.g., "every update breaks one of the systems". Installation problems can result in time away from their job to solve the problem – often involving liaising with IT and/or external businesses responsible for the software or system. Therefore, although systems often alert staff when updates are required, these alerts are often dismissed by repeated use of the "remind me later" button. Additionally, staff often do not have time to shut down the system for upgrades, for example transplant personnel work 24/7 and do not perceive there to be a suitable time to shut down the workstations for updating.

Use of Connected Medical Devices

Some sites use a range of *connected medical devices* (i.e., devices connected to the internet) such as monographs, CT scanners, and MRI scanners. In general, staff perceived connected devices to be introducing new challenges and threats – that many did not feel prepared nor trained for.

For some of these devices, remote access is not possible – i.e., these cannot be controlled or accessed from outside of the hospital. This is typically achieved by the devices being on a separate internal network. However, for other devices, remote access is required by the device suppliers (e.g., to adjust device settings). This again raises security issues. These issues can be complex to address as some responsibility for connected medical devices lies with the biomedical engineers, rather than IT – and IT staff describe the biomedical engineers as being "focused upon usability rather than security".

IT staff also described the software used for medical devices as typically outdated and unsupported. This is concerning as it makes updating and patching impossible.

Poor Physical Security
In addition to more traditional cybersecurity risks, insecure physical access to healthcare facilities was also a concern for some sites. Facilities were often reported as being easy to enter with a lack of substantial physical barriers to prevent unauthorised access. Staff described unauthorised people frequently entering 'staff only' areas. This is particularly problematic in large hospitals where staff are unable to identify or recognise all of their colleagues. Furthermore, although offices may be locked, there are certain areas such as nurses and doctors' workstations which are always accessible. Security cameras have been installed in some locations to improve security, but the lack of additional physical security measures remains an issue.

3.2 Lack of Awareness and Experience

This theme explores participants lack of personal awareness of cyberattacks in their workplace and the potential consequences of their actions.

While awareness of cyberthreats and data breaches in general is high, previous experience of cyber breaches or attacks was low across all three sites. Although staff displayed some awareness of cyberbreaches that have occurred in healthcare more generally, the sites themselves have experienced very few incidents. Those incidents that have occurred were described as minor, e.g., ransomware that had been successfully addressed (without payment) due to backups of the data. No critical incidents had been experienced, with some staff members describing the hospitals as having "been lucky so far". This lack of learned experience may facilitate insecure behaviours. For example, some staff members reflected upon the lack of negative effects they have personally experienced despite using the internet and technology on a daily basis ("well nothing bad has happened so far!"). This could lead staff to underestimate the prevalence of cyberbreaches and/or lead them to feel that their current behaviour must be 'safe' thus reinforcing the behaviour, even if this is not accurate.

Risk Awareness and Lack of Cybersecurity Training
Although many staff were aware that they are expected to behave securely, most demonstrated a lack of understanding why certain behaviours were important. Often, they did not identify potential risks associated with their behaviour. For example, we asked whether staff thought it possible that their own workstation use could affect medical equipment and medical devices in the wider hospital. Generally, staff did not think this was possible nor likely. They did not recognise that they could potentially introduce malware into the wider hospital system. Interestingly, those staff members who *did* identify that it was possible for some workstation use to impact upon medical devices within the hospital, regarded this as more of an issue for those working in close physical proximity to the medical equipment:

"This is more of a risk for those working near the instruments, e.g., in the surgery"

"[We are] too peripheral to influence things like that. [As we are] so far removed from the medical system"

One staff member explained that they previously acted more securely (e.g., always using their own computer login) when they worked in a department that was more "central to the hospital" as they perceived this to be more vulnerable.

In addition to physical proximity, *type* of computer usage was also perceived to affect risk:

"I only read and see things when I use the computers, I do not input data – therefore I do not see this as a danger [to the system or the hospital]"

This lack of awareness is troubling, and one that should be addressed through staff training and education. A *lack of cybersecurity training* was one of the issues raised by the majority of staff, with many feeling underprepared and unaware of how to use technology securely. Some staff reported receiving no formal computer or cybersecurity teaching and described being self-taught and/or relying on learning by observing their colleagues. In particular, admin staff expressed frustration with their lack of training stating that they felt "out of the loop" and "always the last staff members to be trained (if at all)". One admin staff member described being most likely to be "forgotten about, despite having everyone's' passwords". They felt that they are "not considered important for security" and that this is due to others in their employment not understanding what tasks they actually do (as per our previous discussion on shadow working).

Even some IT staff reported not receiving cybersecurity training and reported using their own initiative to communicate with other colleagues by email to warn about risks they have informally learned about. Therefore, ad-hoc communication – as a result of staff initiative - occurs in some organisations but there is a lack of formal training. Some of the hospital staff did report that new training is being developed and that this is beginning to be rolled out, which will likely include some cybersecurity content.

3.3 Shadow Working Processes

This theme refers to behaviours which are occurring within healthcare institutions to enable efficient working practices, but which are clearly going against policy and in some cases even against country laws such as staff members *sharing login credentials, bypassing official communication channels and remote working*. The staff enact these behaviours in good faith believing they enable their job without a risk to cybersecurity. In some instances, senior management and IT are well aware of these behaviours, but are at a loss as to how these behaviours can be changed.

Sharing Login Credentials

Sharing of personal login credentials was prevalent. Staff regard sharing logins as a necessity in order to complete their daily duties. Unauthorised use of login credentials can actually be classified as a criminal behaviour [23], although it is possible that staff are not aware of this. A major driver behind the sharing of login credentials is an inconsistency between staff system access levels and the tasks that they are expected to perform by their immediate managers. Administration and junior doctors are restricted in regards to system access privileges, therefore they cannot do a lot of the tasks that senior staff expect of them. However, senior staff do not always have time to do the more administrative elements of their job due to a high workload, time pressure and a focus upon delivering efficient patient care. As one participant states "Surgeons could not do surgery if they spent all their time making appointments". Therefore, to enable them to focus their time more efficiently, senior staff delegate tasks such as prescribing, making appointments, and entering written notes into the system to more junior members of staff. To work around junior staff access restrictions, senior staff members share their own login credentials. In addition to cybersecurity and legal concerns, this behaviour also raises safety concerns. For example, non-medical staff are reportedly entering information from medical notes (including diagnoses) onto hospital systems. Handwritten notes can leave a degree of interpretation, and the staff member inputting the information often has to decide which categories and options they select on the computer system to accurately reflect the patient's condition and treatment. Mistakes could have significant consequences, despite this workaround being driven by staff motivation to improve patient care.

This is a problem that is not easily solved by technology alone, clear governance and workload reduction is required. We must ensure that the true way that hospitals work is recognized, and changes to policy are in place to facilitate effective patient care without putting safety at risk Literature suggests that system design is adding to staff burden through poor usability of all devices and software e.g., electronic health records [24].

Bypassing Official Communication Channels

We found evidence of staff bypassing official communication channels and emailing sensitive patient information in an insecure manner. Some medical staff reported e-mailing sensitive patient information (including detailed descriptions of a patient's condition and/or treatment) to a large group of their colleagues. This ensures that all of their colleagues are updated and that all key information about the patient and their current condition is easily accessible and summarised in one place. This raises concerns over the security and privacy of the e-mailed data (e.g., staff indicated that there is a lack of discrimination as to which colleagues are copied into the e-mails, and as aforementioned the data is not encrypted). Furthermore, if information is being sent via e-mail, it is possible that this is not being updated on the central system and therefore vital information may be missed from the patient's electronic health record. Staff also report e-mailing sensitive information to their personal home e-mail to enable them to work from home.

Interestingly, staff at one site described using the smartphone messenger application, WhatsApp, to communicate with their work colleagues. This included using the app to send patient details, test results and/or photos of the patient to one another, in order to ask their opinion. Staff perceive WhatsApp as a quicker, more convenient method to quickly share information/photos, compared to using the official systems. WhatsApp can reduce staff burden, enabling them to focus on patient care (e.g., allowing them to stay by the patient's bed whilst gathering second opinions rather than leaving to use a workstation). Although this behaviour was only reported at one of the three sites within this sample, previous studies have identified WhatsApp usage at other healthcare sites [25] suggesting this is not an isolated occurrence. Although this method of communication may be quick, convenient and effective – it can also pose security risks when patient data is being sent via a third-party application; particularly one that is often sent and/or received on personal mobile devices and while WhatsApp is encrypted the images may also reside on the phone.

Remote Access and Home Working

Remote access to the hospital network and home working was not the norm, for most staff in our sample. Home working was not an official policy for most sites. However, it is possible for certain members of staff if required – and if authorisation to do so is provided by the IT team. For example, staff responsible for the allocation of organ transplants use remote access to enable them to quickly allocate a donor as soon as an organ becomes available, without first needing to travel to the hospital. For some sites, as a security measure, every remote access connection has to be approved by someone within the hospital (e.g., by calling the hospital and asking another member of staff to press a button to approve the remote access). The IT team at some of the sites are also able to restrict the parts of the system that can be accessed remotely.

In comparison to remote access, saving hospital files onto personal devices to allow home working was reported more frequently. Interestingly some staff commented that even "the chiefs do it" – as social learning theory would predict [Akers, R. L., and Jensen, G. F. (Eds.). (2011). Social learning theory and the explanation of crime (Vol. 1). Transaction Publishers.] the behavior of others is influencing and/or reinforcing this behaviour. Staff report using personal devices on public WiFi networks, for example whilst travelling. Although staff are aware that this could pose some risk, they are also keen to be actively working – and contactable - whilst outside of the hospital; providing another example of a situation where staff feel conflicted between acting securely and productivity.

3.4 Behaviour Prioritisation

Staff demonstrated an awareness that their behaviour differs from that which is expected or advised (shadow behaviours) It is necessary to understand the underlying reasons for this behavior. This theme acknowledges that cybersecurity is often perceived as having low priority compared to other activities required at work. Participants prioritise (i) *productivity and seeing patients,* (ii) *medical expenditure over cybersecurity* and that these priorities are reinforced by (iii) *not enforcing cybersecurity policies.*

Productivity

Cybersecurity measures were often described by staff as counterproductive and time consuming. This is particularly undesirable in a healthcare setting, where patient care is understandably prioritised, and staff are overworked and under severe time pressure [26]. Anything that is seen as increasing staff burden will be negatively regarded by staff. For example, senior management may restrict staff computer access rights (e.g., to prevent computer settings being changed and new software being installed without an admin login). However, this is often perceived as a barrier to work through preventing installation of required software.

Some staff also felt that security measures may be more focused upon monitoring or restricting staff, rather than improving security for staff and patients. This could potentially affect their motivation to comply. Security measures will also be rejected if quicker workarounds are available, and/or if the measures are not perceived as effective. Due to these negative perceptions of security, particularly as a barrier to productivity and patient-care, senior management and IT technicians described cybersecurity as being a cultural issue – rather than a technical issue; One which requires a "culture change" and a shift in attitudes towards cybersecurity.

Medical Spending Prioritised over Cybersecurity
IT staff acknowledge that the healthcare environment is unique in that priorities must lie with patient care and saving lives – therefore it is not always easy to impose security requirements. They also report a lack of resources and/or budget for cybersecurity. For example, managers were perceived as not allocating adequate budget for cybersecurity, because they want to use this money to purchase something tangible, i.e., "something they can see" such as a hospital bed, or a new medical device. Due to budget constraints, cybersecurity tends to get missed from the business priorities. It was felt that governmental changes may help to prioritise, enforce and regulate cybersecurity.

Lack of Policy and Reinforcement of Safe Behaviour
Staff reported a lack of cybersecurity policies at work, or a lack of reinforcement for any policies that do exist. Staff feel that there is a lack of structural, clear guidance and clarification regarding (un)desirable behaviours. When policies do exist, staff feel that this is unfortunately, never enforced – and conversely good behaviour is never rewarded. Some work places require staff to sign a document to say they will abide by a security policy; however, IT staff feel that new staff often sign this document without actually reading it. IT staff described feeling hopeful that the introduction of the new EU Cybersecurity Act may help to address some of these problems around security policy and reinforcement. The new law imposes that the government identifies 'critical structures' and these structures will have to adopt extra security measures in an allocated period of time. Hospitals are likely to be identified as critical structures. As the law only got approved on the 18th May 2019, IT staff are still in the stage of establishing how to implement the requirements. Therefore, time will tell what impact this will have upon cybersecurity in healthcare.

Staff reported feeling that cybersecurity only becomes a concern if there is a major incident and the employer and/or employees face legal action. For example, one site described how a previous court case found that a patient's surgical report had been rewritten 8 times. This resulted in a new procedure being introduced to monitor and limit amendments to patient data, including the requirement for a clear audit trial. Other behaviours reported by the staff in our sample could potentially lead to legal action, e.g., sharing of login credentials [23], but this may not be widely enforced.

Interestingly, reinforcement of secure behaviour may also come from unexpected sources. For example, some staff reported acting more securely depending upon the department that they are working in. One employee described only using their own login credentials when they worked in a department that used login times to record employees working hours. Therefore, using logins to record working hours had an unexpected secondary benefit of increasing more secure behaviour through discouraging use of shared login credentials.

3.5 Environmental Appropriateness

This theme explains the ways that the work and systems fail to provide appropriate, flexible, mobile, efficient ways of working that the staff desire, in ways that are deemed secure. There is tension between official secure procedures and what staff see as essential within their work environment and current work culture. One example of this is system readiness. Staff raised concerns about the availability of equipment which led to them being apprehensive about automatic timeout of systems, switching users, and software updates.

No-delay Availability
Automatic log-out after a period of inactivity, might improve cybersecurity but it is not implemented across all of the workstations. Auto log-out is not feasible on all computers such as those on the ward, where it could potentially interfere with delivery of patient-care (e.g., if a doctor forgets their login credentials, or logging in and out is perceived to take too much time). For other workstations, even if implemented, auto log-out is ineffectual as the workstation is in constant use (e.g., by different staff).

Current Culture and Need for Change
There was a perception that awareness of cybersecurity issues within the healthcare organisations was low, and needed to be improved. IT staff reported feeling that behaviour is slowly improving due to staff gaining some understanding of cybersecurity issues, but that there is a long way to go before behavior would change. Many staff expressed dissat-isfaction at not being kept well informed, nor receiving adequate training. Staff expressed a desire to be "kept in the loop" and in particular to be provided with explanations why – and how - certain behaviours are important for security. They expressed that in order to facilitate behaviour change, it is important that security measures are not just imposed upon staff but that staff are involved in the reasoning behind the changes. Some staff felt that being provided with relatable stories and/or real-life events could help illustrate importance and relevance – particularly as many of the staff have not experienced any adverse effects to suggest that change in their behaviour is necessary. Others felt that new regulations (e.g., GDPR) and policy could help influence behaviour. Staff (include those from IT) also identified that cybersecurity procedures need to be easier to read and more user-friendly, to encourage staff to read them and to aid comprehension. One staff member suggested that it would be beneficial to have a clear contact within the organisation, such as an easily accessible helpline or cybersecurity champion, who they could approach for more information about cybersecurity issues.

The majority of staff described their place of work as "understaffed and overworked" and for many, being too busy and under major time-constraints was seen as a key driver for unsafe behaviour. Security measures need to be realistic for the healthcare environment, user friendly, and time efficient. Current security measures can often be seen as burdensome, for example multiple login screens can be repetitive, frustrating and time consuming. Staff suggested that it would be beneficial if these systems were more cohe-sive; for example, if there was an easy way to update passwords (and other information) across all systems without logging into each system individually.

For IT staff, cybersecurity was perceived as a cultural issue. They perceived technical solutions to be available to deal with many cyberthreats, but felt that a culture shift in staff attitudes was needed in order to adequately improve cybersecurity. IT described cyberse-curity as an "everyday battle to keep things safe" and often described the elder members of staff – with a lot of experience and numerous years spent working in the healthcare environment – as one of the main groups acting insecurely. Interestingly, they also perceived the youngest and/or newest employees to be acting insecurely, and suggested that there may be different factors influencing each group (e.g., elder staff not liking change or not being familiar with technology and younger staff being inexperienced at work and/or overconfident in their own ability to use technology).

As aforementioned, reinforcement of secure (or insecure) behaviour can sometimes come from unexpected sources. For example, some staff described access to their own personal information as a key motivator to prevent sharing of login credentials. Previously, some hospital systems allowed users to access their personal portal (including salary information) using their main staff login credentials. Staff did not like this as it meant users using their shared login information could see their private details. As a consequence, the system was changed so that personal salary information is now held on a separate system, requiring a separate login. Unknowingly, this change likely removed one of main drivers preventing the sharing of login credentials. This provides food for thought when designing future systems.

In addition to addressing staff behaviour and governmental regulation, staff feel that it would be beneficial for systems to be in place that enable risk assessment of cyberthreat vulnerabilities, in the same manner that organisations can assess other security risks (e.g., physical risks). At the moment they feel that overall cybersecurity is weak as there are no method(s) to assess vulnerabilities. However, all staff described computer systems in healthcare as paramount to their everyday jobs – showing that raising cybersecurity levels is critical.

4   Recommendations for Change

This section pulls together recommendations for change to address the issues raised by staff.

Standardisation

- Password security options have evolved from the traditional view of secure passwords, to three random words which can be easier to remember (https://www.cyberessentials online.co.uk/the-latest-password-guidance-from-the-ncsc/). The medical community should agree a format (similar to how the finance industry consolidated on PIN format) and ensure all medical equipment universally follow that guideline.

Research
Research is needed in the following areas:

- Securing legacy devices is a non-optional priority. Guidance on security, pre and post market, for medical devices is relatively new (e.g. MDCG 2019-16 in Europe) and must be fully implemented into the development and post-market monitoring environment.

- To identify a different policy for managing passwords. Changing passwords should not just be based on time elapsed (i.e., requiring periodic change). The hospital must also ensure they passwords are properly encrypted and that staff have a separate and strong password for email, which if hacked can be used to launch a phishing attack.
- As technology improves and less phishing emails are getting through to staff, paradoxically it is harder for people to detect a phishing email in a low signal environment [27]. If 100% elimination cannot be guaranteed, more research is required to establish an optimal level of fake phishing emails. This level can be maintained through phishing simulation training, to optimise human detection.
- More work is need to establish how to effectively manage updates in relation to two key issues. Firstly, how to effectively schedule updates in 24/7 environments. Secondly, how to accurately predict downtime and ensure it is easy to recover if an update disrupts a system.
- Research is required to explore how best to provide feedback to staff regarding the constant threat their establishment is under and the effectiveness of their behaviour, without creating an environment of constant fear that leads to dysfunctional coping and stress. This should be mindful of findings relating to Protection Motivation Theory [28] and the need to emphasise coping behaviours alongside threat information [29].

Technology Improvements

- Allow the local administrator to manage 'remember me' function and similar functions which impact security. This will enable the removal of options such as remember me if this does not comply with local policies.
- Explore means of enabling automatic change of user when staff physically move away from a device. More ethnographic research is required to establish how to maintain context (e.g., current patient record), when login changes between staff working on the same patient case.
- An alternative, mobile, secure channel must be provided to support data transfer between people and locations. This is required for activities such as working from home, bringing in research and presentations to supervisors, and patients bringing in medical records.
- A secure app, running on a smartphone which is approved by the medical industry and links directly to the electronic health records is needed to ensure central information is up-to-date, easy to share between staff, and does not disrupt working at the patient bedside.
- Encryption tools must be readily available and easy to use. Staff should be trained how to use these tools and made aware of the importance of encryption.
- HCI must ensure that the design of all software is optimised to reduce the burden on staff. Usability, and consistency across device interfaces is key to reduce burden on staff, as well as for any security components.

Ultimately, all tools must be easy to use and not add to the psychosocial stress of the healthcare staff.

5 Conclusion

Our overall findings suggest that insecure behaviours are commonplace across healthcare organisations, on an international scale; and awareness of the breadth of risks associated with these behaviours is generally low. Staff are aware of the external threats but not necessarily how their behaviours facilitate these threats. Awareness training is required to ensure that staff are more aware of the potential implications of their behaviour in the workplace. Staff within healthcare work within a very fast-paced and potentially stressful environment, with a lot of time pressures and responsibilities that do not always facilitate secure behaviour. Current behaviours are engrained habits which coexist with a practical rationalisation that they are required to facilitate efficient patient care. Without awareness of what constitutes unsafe/risky behaviour and the potential consequences (including a lack of learned experience), it is not realistic to expect staff to behave securely. It is vital that they are clearly informed by their employer of what is expected of them, and *why*; and who to approach if they require any further information or guidance.

The administrators and junior medics in our interviews reported feeling as if their roles were not recognised or were regarded as unimportant. In addition to being demoralising for staff, this can also result in staff members not receiving adequate training. This is driven by shadow working, i.e., a discrepancy between the responsibilities covered in their official written job description, and the tasks that they *actually* conduct on a daily basis. These shadow work processes create a security weakness, in addition to potentially having a negative impact on staff wellbeing through a lack of recognition. We see this as a key area for improvement that requires further understanding of the organisational culture which has led to the existence of these shadow behaviours. Such recognition could be made in different ways, from the introduction of the role of medical scribes to acknowledged responsibility for junior medics and remove the burden from senior medics.

Due to the unique working environment within healthcare, there are limitations on the type of technological interventions which can be introduced. For example, it is not feasible to impose auto log-off on workstations where emergency access is required, nor to require staff to take several steps to access one system. It is vital that any interventions are user-friendly, time-efficient and non-burdensome; otherwise they will – at best, be ineffective (e.g., promoting staff to find 'workarounds') – or at worst, negatively impact upon patient care and/or wellbeing. This need for quick, convenient systems is seen in the workarounds that staff have created, e.g., use of WhatsApp.

Some issues may be more straightforward to, at least partially, address from a technological perspective, such as the use of USB devices and sharing of attachments. For example, screening USB devices on machines that are isolated from the main hospital network. However, it is still important that staff are kept informed of the importance and rationale behind these interventions. This will help to help facilitate their adoption and continued use, and minimise perceptions of security as simply a barrier to productivity and another "hoop to jump through" for no perceived reason or reward.

In conclusion, the findings from this study highlight a range of insecure behaviours currently occurring within healthcare environments. No technology is a silver bullet ready to reduce cybersecurity risks. Rather, this complex socio-technical will be solved by understanding the underlying reasons for behavior, implementation of appropriate processes and appropriate design of technology.

These findings have implications for the design of both behaviour change interventions aiming to promote secure behavior and the design of technology itself to ensure that the secure use of technology is as easy as the insecure and not adding to the psychosocial stress of the users. Further research should focus upon potential intervention techniques, including gathering feedback from healthcare staff around perceived appropriateness, feasibility and acceptance. Engagement of the clinical leadership to shift cybersecurity conversations from technical to one linked to patient safety and organizational resilience is needed. This means presenting cybersecurity data in terms of clinical and business outcomes.

References

1. Kotz, D., Gunter, C.A., Kumar, S., Weiner, J.P.: Privacy and security in mobile health: a research agenda. Computer (Long Beach Calif) **49**, 22–30 (2016). https://doi.org/10.1109/MC.2016.185
2. Burns, A.J., Johnson, M.E., Honeyman, P.: A brief chronology of medical device security. Commun. ACM **59**, 66–72 (2016). https://doi.org/10.1145/2890488
3. Coulter, A., Roberts, S., Dixon, A.: Delivering Better Services for People with Long-Term Conditions. Building the House of Care (2013)
4. Hedström, K., Karlsson, F., Kolkowska, E.: Social action theory for understanding information security non-compliance in hospitals the importance of user rationale. Inf. Manag. Comput. Secur. (2013). https://doi.org/10.1108/IMCS-08-2012-0043
5. Shenoy, A., Appel, J.M.: Safeguarding confidentiality in electronic health records. Camb. Q. Healthc. Ethics **26**, 337–341 (2017). https://doi.org/10.1017/S0963180116000931
6. Coventry, L., Branley, D.: Cybersecurity in healthcare: a narrative review of trends, threats and ways forward. Maturitas **113**, 48–52 (2018). https://doi.org/10.1016/j.maturitas.2018.04.008
7. Systems shut down in Victorian hospitals after suspected cyber attack (2019). https://www.theguardian.com/australia-news/2019/oct/01/systems-shut-down-in-victorian-hospitals-after-suspected-cyber-attack
8. Albert, M: Why do we need to wait for people to be hurt?. Medical cyber attacks soar 1400%. In: SFGate (2019). https://www.sfgate.com/healthredesign/article/medical-cyber-attacks-terrorism-hospital-health-13853912.php. Accessed 11 Oct 2019
9. Kam, R.: The human risk factor of a healthcare data breach - Community Blog. In: Heal. IT Exch (2015). https://searchhealthit.techtarget.com/healthitexchange/CommunityBlog/the-human-risk-factor-of-a-healthcare-data-breach/. Accessed 10 Apr 2018
10. Scott, M., Wingfield, N.: Hacking attack has security experts scrambling to contain fallout (2017). https://www.nytimes.com/2017/05/13/world/asia/cyberattacks-online-security-.html
11. National Audit Office: Investigation: WannaCry cyber attack and the NHS (2018)
12. Sussman, B.: Doctors Quitting Due to Ransomware Attacks. In: SecureWorld (2019). https://www.secureworldexpo.com/industry-news/are-doctors-quitting-after-ransomware-attacks. Accessed 30 Jan 2020
13. Zimmermann, V., Renaud, K.: Moving from a "human-as-problem" to a "human-as-solution" cybersecurity mindset. Int. J. Hum Comput Stud. **131**, 169–187 (2019). https://doi.org/10.1016/j.ijhcs.2019.05.005
14. Boyce, M.W., Duma, K.M., Hettinger, L.J., et al.: Human performance in cybersecurity: a research agenda. In: Proceedings of the Human Factors and Ergonomics Society 55th Annual Meeting, pp 1115–1119 (2011)

15. Hall, L.H., Johnson, J., Watt, I., et al.: Healthcare staff wellbeing, burnout, and patient safety: a systematic review. PLoS One **11**, e0159015 (2016). https://doi.org/10.1371/journal.pone.0159015
16. Hall, L.H., Johnson, J., Heyhoe, J., et al.: Exploring the impact of primary care physician burnout and well-being on patient care. J. Patient Saf. **1** (2017). https://doi.org/10.1097/PTS.0000000000000438
17. Johnson, J., Hall, L.H., Berzins, K., et al.: Mental healthcare staff well-being and burnout: a narrative review of trends, causes, implications, and recommendations for future interventions. Int. J. Ment. Health Nurs. **27**, 20–32 (2018). https://doi.org/10.1111/inm.12416
18. Bridgeman, P.J., Bridgeman, M.B., Barone, J.: Burnout syndrome among healthcare professionals. Am. J. Heal. Pharm. **75**, 147–152 (2018). https://doi.org/10.2146/ajhp170460
19. Zaccaro, S.J., Dalal, R.S., Tetrick, L.E., et al.: The psychosocial dynamics of cyber security: an overview. In: Psychosocial Dynamics of Cyber Security. Routledge, pp 31–42 (2016)
20. Blythe, J.M.: Cyber security in the workplace: understanding and promoting behaviour change. In: Proceedings of CHI 2013 Doctoral Consortium (2013)
21. Vossler, A., Moller, N., Braun, V., et al.: How to use thematic analysis with interview data. In: The Counselling and Psychotherapy Research Handbook (2017)
22. Williams, B.: The dangers of password sharing at work. In: TechRadar (2019). https://www.techradar.com/news/the-dangers-of-password-sharing-at-work. Accessed 14 Oct 2019
23. Caldwell, F.: Why Sharing Passwords Is Now Illegal And What This Means for Employers And Digital Businesses (2016)
24. Zahabi, M., Kaber, D.B., Swangnetr, M.: Usability and safety in electronic medical records interface design: a review of recent literature and guideline formulation. Hum. Factors **57**, 805–834 (2015). https://doi.org/10.1177/0018720815576827
25. Johnston, M.J., King, D., Arora, S., et al.: Smartphones let surgeons know WhatsApp: An analysis of communication in emergency surgical teams. Am. J. Surg. (2015). https://doi.org/10.1016/j.amjsurg.2014.08.030
26. Coventry, L., Branley-Bell, D., Magalini, S., et al.: Cyber-risk in healthcare: exploring facilitators and barriers to secure behaviour (2020)
27. Sawyer, B.D., Hancock, P.A.: Hacking the human: the prevalence paradox in cybersecurity. Hum. Factors **60**, 597–609 (2018). https://doi.org/10.1177/0018720818780472
28. Briggs, P., Jeske, D., Coventry, L.: Behavior change interventions for cybersecurity. In: Behavior Change Research and Theory: Psychological and Technological Perspectives, pp 115–136. Academic Press (2017)
29. Witte, K., Allen, M.: A meta-analysis of fear appeals: Implications for effective public health campaigns. Heal Educ. Behav. **27**, 591–615 (2000). https://doi.org/10.1177/109019810002700506

Another Week at the Office (AWATO) – An Interactive Serious Game for Threat Modeling Human Factors

Lauren S. Ferro$^{(\boxtimes)}$ and Francesco Sapio$^{(\boxtimes)}$

Sapienza University of Rome, Rome, Italy
{lsferro,sapio}@diag.uniroma1.it

Abstract. Another Week at the Office (AWATO) is serious game aimed to educate users about threat modeling to help them and/or security analysts identify human factor related threats. AWATO offers an interactive experience where players assume the role of a security analyst where they must observe characters within an office, monitor their emails and phone calls, and identify concerning behavior (e.g. writing passwords on post-it notes).

Keywords: Videogame · Threat modeling · Human factors · Edutainment

1 Introduction

By now, it is evident that the use and purpose of video games has evolved far beyond entertainment purposes. Over the last decade, the use of video games and other similar forms of interactive media has provided ways to not only adapt existing methods of teaching and education towards more modern approaches. In addition, it has also, and more importantly, allowed users to obtain instantaneous feedback. In this way, interactive training and educational tools have allowed users to then learn from their mistakes in a more efficient and instantaneous manner. As a result, it is highly relevant that with a digital modernity and the rise of digital natives, other domains are also following a similar path in terms of providing their content in a way that aligns with how users currently obtain, create, and produce it such as via applications or interactive training.

One area where the adaption of training and educational material has occurred is within the field of cybersecurity. For example, considering that the everyday user can be a target of an attack, scholars as well as companies themselves have tried different approaches towards ensuring that the knowledge and practices of both workers and users are up to date. However, even when the right practices are in place and users know what to do and the consequences if they do not practice safe cyber behavior, problems can still exist. For example, if we consider normal human behavior, there are many factors that can influence it, both in a private and home environment and within a public and/or

© Springer Nature Switzerland AG 2020
A. Moallem (Ed.): HCII 2020, LNCS 12210, pp. 123–142, 2020.
https://doi.org/10.1007/978-3-030-50309-3_9

work environment. For example, social norms can play a large factor in whether cybersecurity protocols are followed and even enforced in work environments where employees readily share passwords among each other. Therefore, we must also consider how such Human Factors can potentially impact a users behavior and in-turn how that can potentially impact the overall security of a system and user's data.

There are several approaches to understanding behavior that can ultimately leave a system vulnerable to attacks and breaches. Some of them can occur from the outside, where an attack comes from someone trying to gain access to sensitive data, such as a hacker trying to access account records. On the contrary, attacks can also happen from the inside out, whether deliberate or not. For example, people within a company communicating sensitive information to the wrong people, or allowing it to be authorized by those who should not. Therefore, to address these types of threats, security analysts can apply a procedure known as threat modeling to identify potential threats and vulnerabilities, the absence of appropriate safeguards or workplace policies, so that they can be enumerated, mitigated, and potentially avoided. However, until now, threat modeling does not focus on human behavior as being a threat to a system. For example, while a threat model may focus on a safeguard to protect unauthorized access to a database, it negates the concept of a user sharing login credentials or leaving their computer unattended during work hours. As a result, a threat model can only be as useful as much as it considers a users behavior; where if the model does not take into account Human Factors such as a users *Lack of Knowledge* or workplace *Norms*, then it overlooks more fundamental vulnerabilities that could impact the overall security of a system and its data.

2   Background

Cyberattacks can be the *"coup de grâce"* to an unsuspecting and unprepared business often resulting in financial lost, a tarnished reputation, or a complete closure of a company. Cyberattacks and efforts towards protecting and defending systems are often focused on implementing strategies that rely on AI and/or machine learning algorithms to automatically detect or deter intruders. However, even with the most elaborated, complex, and well-designed algorithm or software, human error is still the cause of 95% of cyber incidents [16]. In fact, malicious cyber attacker target users via the following methods of attacks (Verizon, 2019)[1]:

- 29% of breaches resulted from weak or stolen passwords
- 52% of breaches stemmed from hacking
- 32% of breaches involved phishing
- 28% of breaches involved malware
- 33% of breaches were social attacks

---

[1] https://enterprise.verizon.com/resources/reports/dbir/.

In addition, of these breaches, 43% of breaches involved small business victims where 71% of breaches were financially motivated, which targets a fundamental resource of most companies. However, the concerning issue regarding these attacks is that 56% of breaches took months or longer to discover, meaning that if they were detected earlier, it is likely that the damage could have been significantly reduced. However, it is possible that in many cases people are not aware or even considers themselves a target for cyber attacks. Moreover, victims may also be unaware of how their actions may ultimately leave them vulnerable even if they have taken precautions towards protecting themselves.

2.1 Threat Modeling

In general, a threat refers to any unauthorized method that gains access to sensitive information, networks, and applications. These are a few common threats that can be addressed by using threat modeling such as dealing with Malware, Phishing, Denial of Service (DoS/DDoS), Hacking, Insider Threats, etc. One way to approach to understand how to improve the cybersecurity of a system from threats is via threat modeling. Here are many different types of threat modeling approaches, frameworks, techniques [10], models, and theories that all work towards identifying threats and approaches to address them. Each of these have their own context in mind such as preventing attackers from breaching a system, finding weak points within a systems architecture, develop strategies to mitigate potential attacks, and so forth. Therefore, to illustrate these differences, we discuss several distinct types of approaches and how they address the concept of threat modeling. For example, one of the most popular models is STRIDE, which is a methodology that was introduced by Praerit Garg and Loren Kohnfelder at Microsoft [20]. The methodology is used to classify vulnerabilities. Others include, DREAD (Damage + Reproducibility + Exploitability + Affected Users + Discoverability) [9], which is used to rate, compare, and prioritize the severity of risk presented by each threat that is classified using STRIDE. In addition, others such as P.A.S.T.A (Process for Attack Simulation and Threat Analysis) [22], Trike [19], OCTAVE (Operationally Critical Threat, Asset, and Vulnerability Evaluation) [1, 21] all have various approaches to assessing and planning for attacks from different approaches (i.e. risk or context centered). Lastly, one other method to consider are Attack Trees [10, 21], which are diagrams that depict attacks on a system in tree form. In these cases, the *"root"* of the tree is the goal for the attack, and the "leaves" are different ways to achieve that goal.

If we consider all the above attacks and techniques, the central element is human interaction – albeit causing it or allowing an attack to happen whether intentionally or not. Therefore, it makes sense to consider the human, their behavior, weaknesses, and strengths both as individuals and as part of a collective society (within the workplace and within a public domain) as part of a threat model.

2.2   Human Factors

While the domain of Human Factors is user centered, it also considers the tools (e.g. PC, Mobiles, etc.), tasks (e.g. browsing the web), and environment (e.g. home or office), and even culture of the user. To this end, the information about these aspects can help designers and researchers to improve the design and solutions to addressing issues and threats.

To understand the Human Factors associated within a context of cybersecurity, we must look at the user as an individual, part of a (online) team, culture, and ultimately the system that they are interacting with [17]. However, even if in recent times, publications on Human Factors within cybersecurity are gaining momentum, a major gap exists to understand the domain and the current state of which Human Factors is centered within cybersecurity. Moreover, of the research that does exist, its scope is often limited [24] or ambiguous and varied, or only acknowledges the concept of Human Factors in passing [23]. For example, research on cybersecurity within the context of Human Factors has presented several perspectives. In addition, Young et al. [24] considers cybersecurity as a state of a system where the system change is brought on by a user's behavior. Whereas Mancuso et al. [12] (among others) offer frameworks, which aim to maintain interactions between the components of a cyber-attack while offering a further abstraction useful to future Human Factors research; and others that look at the frame a user's online behavior via a (national) cultural perspective [7].

It is evident here that the extent of variation among definitions, it makes it difficult for the concept of Human Factors in cybersecurity to advance in a more concentrated way. Especially considering that Human Factors and cybersecurity (HFCS) draws on multi-disciplinary areas such as psychology (e.g. social engineering, deception), engineering, and computer science (machine learning and artificial intelligence) to improve techniques and approaches towards cyberattacks.

2.3   Human Factors and Threat Modeling

Up until now, Human Factors research and Threat Modeling research has been considered within their own domains. However, their use together has the innovative potential to add an additional layer or considerations towards improving the security of a system and the integrity of data. For example, Ferro [4], propose an adaption to the popular STRIDE model – STRIDE-HF (Spoofing, Tampering, Repudiation, Information disclosure, Denial of service, Escalation of privileges - Human Factors) that considers the twelve Human Factors outlined by Dunpont [3]:

- **Lack of Communication**: people not communicating with each other within a working and/or online environment.
- **Complacency**: a feeling of self-satisfaction that can lead to a lack of awareness of potential dangers.

- **Lack of Knowledge**: not having enough experience and specific knowledge that can lead to poor decisions.
- **Distraction**: when a user's attention has been taken away from the task that they are required to do.
- **Lack of Teamwork**: not providing enough support towards a group of people, co-workers, etc., who rely on your support.
- **Fatigue**: is a physiological reaction resulting from prolonged periods of work and stress.
- **Lack of Resources**: not having enough resources (e.g. time, tools, people, etc.) to complete a task.
- **Pressure**: pressure to meet a deadline interferes with our ability to complete tasks correctly, then it has become too much.
- **Lack of Assertiveness**: not being able or allowed to express concerns or ideas.
- **Stress**: acute and chronic stress from working for long periods of time or other demanding issues such as family or financial problems.
- **Lack of Awareness**: working in isolation and only considering one's own responsibilities, often leading to a disconnect from what others are doing.
- **Norms**: workplace practices that develop over time, which can then influence others behaviors.

In addition, it aligns these twelve Human Factors to the STRIDE threat model and in doing so, it provides a way for us to consider the types of human behavior that can result in a STRIDE element to occur. For example, if someone shares their password with a colleague as a result of workplace *Norms*, then it can result in an *Elevation of Privilege*. Therefore, to this end, such considerations could be use as preventative measures for addressing cyber related issues. Furthermore, the rationale behind selecting the STRIDE model as a foundation to expand upon is for several reasons. For example, STRIDE in comparison to Attack trees offers a more dynamic approach to identifying threats – more so because STRIDE is aimed to help uses find attacks in a simple way based on categorization rather than an explicit and logical approach. For example, if we are to include Human Factors as part of an Attack Tree, it could become over-complicated if we are to define every kind of behavior that could take place with regards to each type of threat. Moreover, the development of a Human Factor Attack Tree would need to consider the behaviors of users and then the issues that each of those behaviors leads to in an explicit methodological way. One might even consider Attack Trees for individual users that capture the behaviors that they demonstrate and what they are likely to result in (e.g. threats to a system). As a result, a Human Factor Attack Tree can become incredibly large quite fast and is not an ideal approach, at least not manually. There is the possibility, in the future where data logs can be used to developed Attack Trees automatically, in a similar way that [13] have achieved via the use of declarative specification of interaction models that exploit logs for identifying exactly what has gone wrong during a user's interaction. However, this is outside the scope of this paper.

Development of STRIDE-HF. Extending upon the description by Ferro [4], the development of the (theoretical model) of STRIDE-HF considers existing literature on Human Factors (and or related concepts) within the domain of cybersecurity and specifically phishing to align with the focus of doctoral research. The first step was to explore literature based on threat modeling. The intention during this step was to study literature surrounding "human behavior centered" threat models and frameworks that are or can be could consider human error as part of the threat analysis process. Several models and ideologies existed where human behavior was at the focus. For example, Reason's [18] models present generic error-modeling systems, and more specific approaches towards identifying areas where humans behavior is likely to be problematic and the kind of behaviors to pay attention to. On the other hand Cranor [2] presents a human-in-the-loop approach to identify and mitigate threats. In other schools of thought, there are considerations to take a psychological perspective and apply them towards understanding the user, such as cognitive or behaviorist approaches. In addition, other concepts such as state machines and ceremonies are used to map out human behavior to identify problematic areas. However, many of these concepts have only been used as a lens to see threat modeling through or they do not consider behavior outside of specific security scenarios. For example, such threat models lack the consideration of how workplace cultural norms influence the sharing of passwords or elevation of privilege to achieve a task to save time. In addition, the impact that a Lack of Awareness, Knowledge, or Resources has on protecting a system. In many cases humans are often not provided with learning material, or the material that they are provided with is overwhelming with technical jargon and therefore being useless. This is a concept briefly touched on in a digital sense in terms of discussing *"wicked"* and *"kind"* environments [8] in the context of cybersecurity where environments should be clear and understandable (e.g. simple UI, more complex options hidden from users, and roles and rules for users are explicit). As a result, models and frameworks consider specific parts of user behavior whether it is placed within the context of cybersecurity or as a subset of security issues (e.g. software design). Therefore, it is still clear that threat modeling with Human Factors/human behavior at its core is still relatively in its infancy. Hence, for the purpose of this project, a choice was made to use a more established model to build upon where Human Factors could be integrated as part of the model's structure. Consequently, STRIDE was chosen as an appropriate foundation to extend upon.

The second step was to consider the STRIDE model in the context of human error and how human error is related with each of the STRIDE elements. To this end, STRIDE and its variations (e.g. STRIDE-per-element and STRIDE-per-interaction) were researched to properly understand how Human Factors could be incorporated. However, the core model was deemed most appropriate to extend upon.

The third step was to envision the STRIDE-HF model as a functional model that security professionals could use and how it could be envisioned to address threats. This model is outlined in Table 1 which describes the STRIDE-HF model in the context of human behavior that can allow a threat to occur.

Table 1. STRIDE - HF

Threat	Human Factor(s)	Behavior (examples)	Response (examples)
Spoofing	Lack of Awareness, Lack of Knowledge, Lack of Resources	Downloading files online or via email attachment	Educate users about what to look for when accessing links within emails
Tampering	Distraction, Lack of Awareness, Stress, Pressure, Fatigue	Modifying files to backdate them. Unblocking blocked ports to get access	Implement a platform where documents must be uploaded (logs date, time, user, etc.)
Repudiation	Accidentally/on purpose deleting files	Not submitting files on time/to the right location	Change how files are managed and are monitored
Information Disclosure	Complacency, Distraction, Norms, Stress, Pressure, Lack of Assertiveness	Sharing passwords among colleagues for a time trade-off	Enforce stronger punishments for password sharing
Denial of Service	Distraction, Lack of Awareness, Stress, Pressure	Unplugging hardware for other purposes (e.g. additional charging space)	Clearly label exposed cables to indicate their use
Elevation of Privilege	Lack of Assertiveness	Giving access to a file because someone with authority asked for it	Create a more accessible way to report bad behavior of superiors

* More likely to be responsible for the STRIDE element over other Human Factors.

Addressing Threats. To address threats using the STRIDE-HF model, users of the model must understand the workplace culture and/or how employees interact with each other and the system. In addressing the workplace culture, the security analyst would need to understand several things to predict the kinds of and the severity of human behavior related security risks. For example, if workplace culture is relaxed and people often share files carelessly, then it raises the likelihood that certain behaviors will have a higher chance as being used as attack vectors. For example, if an employee passes on a malicious file to another co-worker that then gets uploaded on to a server. Therefore, to this end, security policies need to be adaptive and regularly monitored and enforced. However, this is two-fold where understanding the behavior is not alone to address human factor related issues. For example, if a workplace environment has a high risk of receiving phishing emails, but does not have an anti-virus installed or a policy for downloaded content, then the system allows for certain behaviors to occur (e.g. downloading potentially unsafe files and opening them without scanning them). As a result, the system is unnecessarily exposed. An additional consideration is to take into account the work environment. With open-plan office spaces becoming popular, the likelihood of threats such as Information Disclosure, Repudiation, and Denial of Service – even if unintentionally, is increased. This is due to the ease at which conversations can be overheard, the frequency that computers are left unattended and in cases unlocked, and rate of sensitive data being displayed on-screen with the potential for anyone to observe it.

2.4   Gaming

The area of game design and development has certainly seen an increased interest outside the domain of entertainment. Many areas such as military, medicine, and education are adopting the medium and adapting it to serve many different purposes - that varies from training and simulation to education. For example, many games (academic and commercial) exist, which that have been summarized by [6] that focus on cybersecurity and/or their related issues (e.g. hacking). For example, CyberCIEGE [11] is a serious game intended to educate users about network security concepts and is used as a training tool by agencies of the U.S. government, universities, and community colleges. It involves the player having to configure parts of the system as well as responding to multiple choice questions. In a similar way, CyberNEXS [15] aims to prepare security professionals, network administrators, system administrators, and students with the tools and skills they need to effectively protect and defend IT systems against today's real-world threats. Lastly, in a more direct way, *The Weakest Link: A User Security Game*[2] consists of a series of multiple-choice questions based on a scenario that is given to you. You play as a new employee who "practice" correct safe behavior must, which is represented by your response to the questions. Each time a question is answered incorrectly, the reason for it being incorrect is given along with more information. At the end of the game, the player is given a score based on their response and whether they are the "weakest link" when it comes to security practices.

However, what is equally as important to note in conjunction with academic or industry developed games, are commercial games. It is relevant to note these given the tangential learning [5,14] that can occur whilst playing them. For example, in the game Orwell[3], players investigate a series of attacks via communication streams such as social media and conversations to gather evidence to uncover who is responsible behind the attacks. While not explicit, the player can begin to understand the level of ease that it is to develop a "profile" of someone online based on the kind of information that is available and how it can be used to achieve various tasks. In a similar way, the Hacker Duality[4] allows the players to interact on the backend of an attack by assuming the role of a "hacker" and

---

[2] "*The Weakest Link*", n.d., https://www.isdecisions.com/user-security-awareness-game/.

[3] Osmotic Studios, 2016, https://store.steampowered.com/app/491950/.

[4] Exosyphen studios, 2011, https://store.steampowered.com/app/70120/Hacker_Evolution_Duality/.

using various techniques to meet in-game goals albeit to disable access or to compete against other hackers.

It is important to note that many of these games, including others listed by [6] that discuss relevant and popular types of cyberattacks, many which are outlined by Verizon (2019)[5]. However, given the breadth of all these games across various contexts, not one single game at the time this paper exists that specifically aims to address various cybersecurity related topics and how to address them with the intention to improve them in the context of user behavior. As a result, it has provided the motion for this research. To this end, it is clear that games have clearly contributed to modern approaches to educate users about cyber related topics.

3   Development of AWATO

Another Week at the Office (AWATO) is serious game aimed to educate users about threat modeling to help them and/or security analysts identify human factor related threats. It has been developed in Unreal Engine 4[6] over several months using an iterative design process.

3.1   Idea Development

The idea for this project was to create a multipurpose tool with several overall intentions. The first was to create an engaging interactive experience that is accessible to everyone, meaning that no prior experience was required by the end user to use it. The second intention was to provide an serious game to promote awareness of threat modeling and Human Factors by using STRIDE-HF. The third intention was to raise awareness of potential human factor related issues relating to cybersecurity breaches that the user could relate to. For example, if workers are *Stressed*, they are more likely to forgo scanning a downloaded document with anti-virus software in favor of efficiency.

Aesthetics. The focus on this game was not weighted on the appearance, but rather the content. However, at the same time, we wanted to create an serious game that aligned with contemporary graphics; and to a certain extent provide an (visual) improvement on what currently exists. Therefore, in the creation of AWATO we utilized the asset pack: POLYGON - City Pack[7] and POLYGON - Office Pack[8] created by Synty Studios, Lowpoly Stylized Office Pack by Park JongMyung[9], and custom 3D assets (created in Autodesk Maya) that

---

[5] https://enterprise.verizon.com/resources/reports/dbir/.

[6] www.unrealengine.com.

[7] https://syntystore.com/products/polygon-city-pack.

[8] https://syntystore.com/products/polygon-office-pack.

[9] https://www.unrealengine.com/marketplace/en-US/product/lowpoly-stylized-office-pack.

were modeled by the authors. The user interface and additional graphic elements were created by the authors in Adobe Illustrator. Lastly, the game itself is created inside of the Unreal Engine and the interaction was created using both Blueprints and C++.

Selection of Cybersecurity Issues. We selected cybersecurity related issues that could align well with the Human Factors and that could be easily represented in a meaningful way within the game's environment. It is acknowledged by the authors that this is not a complete representation of all the types of cybersecurity related issues that exist or that do align with the chosen Human Factors and it is something intended for future work. However, it should also be considered that the choices thus far have been made to establish a foundation upon which more complicated threats will be implemented. The process for choosing the cybersecurity issues were also influenced by the key issues raised in the Verizon report (2019)[10].

3.2   Game Development

Another Week at the Office (AWATO) is a serious game where you play the role of a recently hired security analyst who must identify cybersecurity issues caused by human error within AWATO Corp, aptly titled after the game's name. The company office is the central location for the game. It is a typical office space where employees are currently working towards the launch of a new and innovative product set for unveiling at the end of the week. Therefore, it is your job to ensure that there are no breaches within the office and to ensure the integrity of the data since AWATO Corp have many high-profiled investors and stakeholders. To ensure the integrity and authenticity of the data and a successful product launch, it is your job to identify threats and classify them within the STRIDE-HF (Spoofing, Tampering, Repudiation, Information Disclosure, Denial of Service, Elevation of Privilege - Human Factors) model. Therefore, it is your job to identify which behavior has led to which threat and to identify them as soon as possible within the STRIDE-HF framework. The more threats that you identify the more likely that your product launch with go off without a hitch.

Characters. In total, there are 10 characters. The types of characters and their role within the company that we chose were intended to reflect individuals that you would typically find within a work space. We acknowledge that this is only a general representation, and the types of employees do vary between companies.

Locations. Like the characters, we wanted to include rooms that are also typically found within a workplace. In total, there are 9 playable rooms (Reception, CEO office, Manager Office, Security Office, Server Room, General Work Space, Kitchen, Janitor Closet, and Car park. Like the characters, the rooms are only a general representation of reality with core components.

---

[10] https://enterprise.verizon.com/resources/reports/dbir/.

- *Reception*: The reception features your typical assets (computer, printer, documents, etc). The reception is managed by one character.
- *Office Spaces*: The general and manager office spaces, shown in Fig. 3, consist of 5 employees. These employees' range in terms of the job title, therefore, it is important for the player to pay attention to this while playing the game. You can see an example in Fig. 1.
- *Bathroom*: While the player does not go "into" the bathroom, the bathroom exists for the two reasons. The first being that it is an essential part of an office space; and secondly, because while users travel to and from the bathroom, it is likely that they may drop notes, forget to lock their computer, etc.
- *Kitchen*: The kitchen, is accessible by the player and was included for the same reasons as the bathroom because it is a space where employees converse, and an easy distraction (e.g. while making a coffee to forget a notebook). As a result, it was included in the game environment.
- *Security Room*: The security room is not typically found in all office spaces, particularly smaller businesses. However, it is an essential area since it contains many aspects associated with maintaining the integrity of data.
- *Server Room*: The server room was included to illustrate the importance within the technological ecosystem to ensure that the integrity, authenticity, and accessibility of data is kept.
- *Janitors Room*: The Janitors rooms features standard supplies and trash. The reason to include it is because sometimes sensitive documents are not disposed of correctly and therefore, can end up in the wrong hands if thrown away in waste bins.

Fig. 1. An example of the work space within AWATO

Work Terminals. Each character has their own PC (including the player), which has all the basic applications that you would find on an office PC (e.g. word processing, email, anti-virus software, etc.). In addition, the desktop of each PC has several files (e.g. images, pdf and document files). This is the central hub that connects a player to most of the gameplay. Here, the player can access each of the characters PC and observe their interaction with files (whether they have been scanning files that they download), their emails (e.g. if they have been engaging in phishing scams, or sharing sensitive information), and lastly to see if anti-virus software is installed or updated. Throughout the game, NPCs will receive emails[11]. You can see an example of the emails in-game in Fig. 2 of three types.

- **General Communication (positive):** in these instances, emails between users are not dangerous and often follow general everyday conversations.
- **General Communication (negative):** these types of emails also follow general everyday conversations; however, they reveal sensitive information (e.g. passwords, account details, privileged information).
- **Spam Emails:** contain your typical phishing scams where people are asking for details from a user.

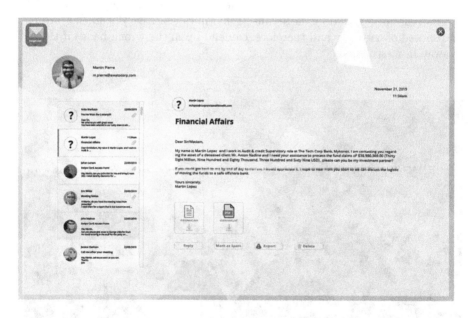

Fig. 2. An example of emails in AWATO.

---

[11] The emails were created within an excel spreadsheet and implemented into the game via Blueprint scripts in the Unreal Engine.

3.3   Incorporation of STRIDE-HF

The innovative part of this game is the relationship between threat modeling and the Human Factors that have likely caused it. In AWATO, Human Factors have been incorporated by aligning the Human Factors with the STRIDE framework. In this way, we can focus on errors that are more likely to occur, and how they will occur because of their relevant factor.

One of the main objectives for the player to do in AWATO is to identify bad behavior of users and understand what caused it. For example, if an NPC is constantly responding to spam emails then it is up to the player to find why. For example, are they constantly being distracted? Perhaps they are practicing unsafe behavior by sharing passwords with colleagues. It is up to the player to identify the cause by analyzing what the NPC is doing and enter it into the STRIDE-HF Matrix in Fig. 3. In order to provide the users with some context about what the STRIDE-HF elements are, the user can access a document on their "Desktop" within the game that provides them with a brief explanation about the topics.

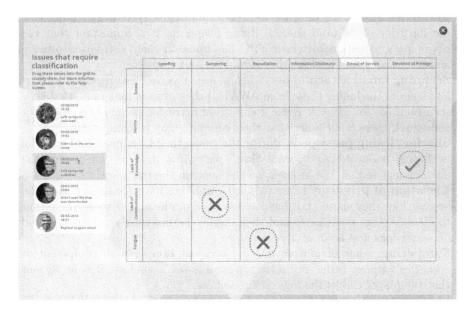

Fig. 3. An example of the STRIDE-HF Matrix in AWATO

The matrix provides a feedback loop to the player, by displaying the wrong selected answers to the player. As a result, it allows the player to choose an additional STRIDE-HF element until they select the correct one. In addition, a wrong or right choice is also indicated by audio feedback that further assists the player to identify the correct STRIDE-HF element for the issue. Lastly, once a player has correctly classified an issue using the STRIDE-HF table, they can then review these issues later to reflect upon previous judgments before classifying the next issue.

Security Issues and In-Game Events. The game's threats also focus on issues that are related to Human Factors. For example, where traditional STRIDE issues occurred, we considered the possibility for the same "intentional" issue occurring by accident. For example, someone "tampering" with wires to get something to work but unknowingly causing the servers to disconnect.

- **Phishing Scams**: One of the biggest issues in-game is phishing scams. This is because some NPCs will send replies to phishing emails, which then exposes the system to vulnerabilities. Therefore, it is important that the player identifies these early on.
- **Locked devices**: During the game, the NPCs will take breaks to go to the bathroom, eat, and grab a coffee. In these periods, an NPC will leave his or her workstation unattended, which will be sometimes locked with a password and others not leading to unauthorized access.
- **Updating (patches, anti-virus)**: Downloading and sharing files brings with it the risk of an infected file contaminating a system and impacting the integrity of its (and shared) data. Therefore, it is important that the player pays attention to which NPC has updated their anti-virus software and uses it to scan files that they download and transfer.
- **Scanning email attachments**: when players receive files in-game from various sources (including those from AWATO) they need to make sure that they scan each file for viruses. Even if it is from a trusted source (e.g. friend or colleague), there is a chance that their compute may be compromised.
- **Sharing/losing passwords**: during the game, the player must find out who is sharing passwords and locate "lost" passwords that are left around the environment (e.g. in the kitchen, on the floor, in the trash, etc.).
- **Elevation of privilege**: refers to when employees have access to part of the system/files they should not have access to. From here, it is up to the player to identify trust boundaries and then modify permissions accordingly based on server logs and account access.
- **Tampering**: some employees may by accident tamper with equipment or even files without being aware that it is an issue. Therefore, it is important that the player checks the logs on the servers.
- **Sharing sensitive information**: during email conversations, NPCs may by accident reveal sensitive content to others because they may be feeling stressed or because they are unaware that the content is restricted (e.g. because of a Lack of Communication) therefore, the player must identify where and when this occurs and identify why it is occurring.

4   Testing

AWATO was validated using a paired t-test to see if participants could identify threats and relate them to their respective Human Factor.

4.1 Testing Procedure

Overall, the testing process followed the following procedure:

1. A pre-test questionnaire to establish a baseline regarding the level of knowledge that users had about threat modeling, cybersecurity topics, and demographic information.
2. Users were then asked to complete a Scenario Questionnaire. In this questionnaire, participants read through a list of scenarios and asked to identify three things. The first is the error that occurred, the second is the Human Factor responsible, and the third is the STRIDE element that the error aligns with.
3. The third step required that users then played the game AWATO and were required to observe the same if not similar situations that also featured within the scenarios and then identify them according to the Human Factor and STRIDE element that they felt aligned with the error.
4. Lastly, users were then asked to complete a post-study questionnaire similar to the Scenario Questionnaire, where they had to identify Human Factors responsible for the errors within the scenarios and the STRIDE element that they aligned with. In addition, this questionnaire also contained some general questions related to the design of AWATO to see if any extraneous variables (e.g. glitches in the game, navigational issues, etc.) existed that may have impact on the final results.

Below, is an example of one of the scenario based questions:

Scenario #3 - Susan and the cat pictures *Susan is a lover of all animals. During her break she spends her free time surfing the internet for funny or cute pictures of animals, mainly cats, which she then shares online via social media. Recently, she has been receiving emails from a new online website "Funny Cats Online" with cute pictures attached to emails. She downloads them and sometimes forwards the emails to other colleges who also enjoy a funny cat picture or two.*

From here, the participant is required to identify the errors that have occurred from a list of several (by selecting check boxes). For example, in relation to the above scenario, the participant is asked to identify the errors Susan made from the options below:

Please select the areas where cybersecurity has been breached.

- Surfing the internet for cat pictures
- Registering for Funny Cats Online
- Not scanning the email attachments for viruses
- Not checking the validity of the email sending her cat pictures
- etc.

Following this part of the questionnaire, the participant is asked to identify the most appropriate STRIDE element, and lastly the most relevant Human Factor(s).

4.2   Test Design

Each question was tested using the paired t-test (with a confidence level set to 95%), which determines whether the mean difference between two sets of observations is zero. In the context of this experiment, this is the difference between a participant's knowledge of threat modeling and aligning threats to a relevant Human Factor before the game/scenarios and after. In particular, we have used the following Hypothesis:

- **Null-Hypothesis** (H_0): there is no improvement in understanding the STRIDE-HF model by playing AWATO.
- **Experimental Hypothesis** (H_1): playing AWATO increases the understanding of the STRIDE-HF model.

In order to perform the paired t-test, we needed to assign a score to our questionnaire (excluding demographic questions). In particular, we awarded up to a maximum of 10 points for each scenario, using the following criteria:

- *Up to 2 **Points***: identification of the issue.
- *Up to 3 **Points***: identification of the STRIDE element involved in the scenario.
- *Up to 3 **Points***: identification of the Human Factor related to the scenario
- *Up to 2 **Points***: identification of the consequences of the scenarios.

4.3   Test Results

We had a total of $N = 15$ participants who performed all four stages of the test.

In Table 2 we present the resulting p-values for each scenario. *The Null-Hypothesis (H_0) is rejected for all scenarios, consequently, the Experimental Hypothesis (H_1) is supported.*

Table 2. p-values for each scenarios resulted from the paired t-test.

Scenario	p-value
S1	0.03397
S2	0.02445
S3	0.00543
S4	0.00281
S5	0.00257
S6	0.00224

As it can be observed in Table 2, the p-values gets lower as the scenarios get harder. This is likely due to the fact that easy scenarios are easier to identify the STRIDE and Human Factor that is related to the scenario; even without playing

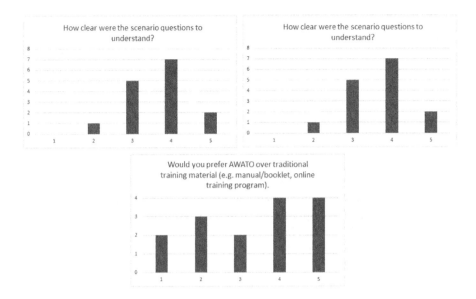

Fig. 4. Overview of the results (five-point Likert scale) for the questions related to the use of AWATO as an educational tool

AWATO. On the other hand, more complex scenarios require some knowledge about the STRIDE-HF framework, and playing AWATO becomes more crucial to classify the scenario.

The questions related to the use of AWATO as an educational tool were evaluated on a five-point Likert scale, and the results are presented in Fig. 4.

60% of the users found the scenarios very clear, leaving only 6.6% of the users slightly unsure about the scenario questions. Of the 15 participants, 40% agreed that AWATO could be used as a training tool, where 26.6% did not feel as though it could be. As a result, the remaining participants felt neutral about it. Finally, when asked if AWATO could replace traditional tools/materials, the answers were more distributed. One third of participants disagreed that AWATO could be used to replace traditional tools/materials (33.3%), but more than half (53%) were enthusiastic towards accepting AWATO as a potentially new way of learning. However, from verbal feedback of the participants, several felt that to use AWATO as a training tool, the game needs to improve and be iterated upon.

5 Discussion

The purpose of AWATO was two-fold. The first was to test STRIDE-HF and see if it could be used as a way to threat model users behavior to reduce unsafe cyber practices. Secondly, AWATO was used to determine whether a serious game could be developed to educate users about cybersecurity related issues and show how to threat model these issues based on Human Factors. Initial results show that

AWATO shows potential to achieve these goals. More importantly, AWATO, is the first type of a cybersecurity (related) game, which allows users to consider the behavior of users rather than just the threats. It is also important to note that while there is a gap in terms of software and/or training tools available for IT professionals or manages [6], by targeting the everyday user, we can begin to develop stronger foundations and open up a common dialogue among the workplace.

5.1   Limitations

The main limitation of AWATO is that it requires further empirical testing determine the effectiveness of the serious game as an educational tool and in term resource to educate employees beyond what we have analyzed. The results presented here in this paper indicate that there is potential, but we believe that for AWATO we be developed into a more robust tool, further developments will require expert input (i.e. from threat modelers and security analysts). In addition, given that STRIDE-HF is mainly a theoretical model that is based on existing literature there is a need to conduct a more specific analysis of the STRIDE-HF framework to incorporate into AWATO to ensure that the STRIDE-HF matrix accurately reflects the STRIDE *and* the corresponding HF elements. In this way, with a more empirically based STRIDE-HF framework we can then implement more specific behaviors within the game for the player to identify. As a result, we can then begin testing the game within additional work environments. Lastly, we also anticipate the integration of a more solid learning element where players are informed about wrong decisions in terms of why their classification is wrong or right so that the user can understand in a more informative way the impact of their decisions.

6   Conclusion

Overall, we can conclude that AWATO has demonstrated that there is potential to educate users and while providing a tool to assist users in understanding the process of threat modeling. It is clear that users respond well to the use of an interactive educational tool and in some cases prefer it to traditional material. Future directions include developing AWATO to contain customizable features allowing people to use it and modify it so that is can be used as part of a training situation in a way that reflects the work environment of where the serious game is being played. It is anticipated that ultimately, AWATO can serve as a way to inform users about human error related issues and their impact on a work environment with the intention to influence a user's real life behavior and/or open up a dialogue between employees about practicing safe cybersecurity and improving circumstances within the workplace to accommodate it.

References

1. Alberts, C.J., Behrens, S.G., Pethia, R.D., Wilson, W.R.: Operationally critical threat, asset, and vulnerability evaluation (octave) framework, version 1.0. Technical report, Carnegie-Mellon Univ Pittsburgh PA Software Engineering Inst (1999)
2. Cranor, L.F.: A framework for reasoning about the human in the loop (2008)
3. Dupont, G.: The dirty dozen errors in maintenance. In: The 11th Symposium on Human Factors in Maintenance and Inspection: Human Error in Aviation Maintenance (1997)
4. Ferro, L.S.: Keep your attackers close, but your users closer (2019)
5. Floyd, D., Portnow, J.: Tangential learning: How games can teach us while we play. Extra Credits (2008)
6. Hendrix, M., Al-Sherbaz, A., Bloom, V.: Game based cyber security training: are serious games suitable for cyber security training? Int. J. Serious Games **3**(1) (2016)
7. Henshel, D., Sample, C., Cains, M., Hoffman, B.: Integrating cultural factors into human factors framework and ontology for cyber attackers. In: Nicholson, D. (ed.) Advances in Human Factors in Cybersecurity. Advances in Intelligent Systems and Computing, vol. 501, pp. 123–137. Springer, Cham (2016). https://doi.org/10.1007/978-3-319-41932-9_11
8. Hogarth, R.M., Lejarraga, T., Soyer, E.: The two settings of kind and wicked learning environments. Curr. Dir. Psychol. Sci. **24**(5), 379–385 (2015)
9. Howard, M., LeBlanc, D.: Writing Secure Code. Pearson Education, London (2003)
10. Hussain, S., Kamal, A., Ahmad, S., Rasool, G., Iqbal, S.: Threat modelling methodologies: a survey. Sci. Int. (Lahore) **26**(4), 1607–1609 (2014)
11. Irvine, C.E., Thompson, M.F., Allen, K.: CyberCIEGE: gaming for information assurance. IEEE Secur. Priv. **3**(3), 61–64 (2005)
12. Mancuso, V.F., Strang, A.J., Funke, G.J., Finomore, V.S.: Human factors of cyber attacks: a framework for human-centered research. In: Proceedings of the Human Factors and Ergonomics Society Annual Meeting, vol. 58, pp. 437–441. SAGE Publications, Los Angeles (2014)
13. Marrella, A., Ferro, L.S., Catarci, T.: An approach to identifying what has gone wrong in a user interaction. In: Lamas, D., Loizides, F., Nacke, L., Petrie, H., Winckler, M., Zaphiris, P. (eds.) INTERACT 2019. LNCS, vol. 11748, pp. 361–370. Springer, Cham (2019). https://doi.org/10.1007/978-3-030-29387-1_20
14. Mozelius, P., Fagerström, A., Söderquist, M.: Motivating factors and tangential learning for knowledge acquisition in educational games. Electron. J. e-Learn. **15**(4), 343–354 (2017)
15. Nagarajan, V., Huang, D.: Secure web referral service. In: The International Conference on Information Network 2012, pp. 53–58. IEEE (2012)
16. Nobles, C.: Botching human factors in cybersecurity in business organizations. HOLISTICA J. Bus. Public Admin. **9**(3), 71–88 (2018)
17. Parsons, K., McCormac, A., Butavicius, M., Ferguson, L.: Human factors and information security: individual, culture and security environment. Technical report, Defence Science and Technology Organisation Edinburgh (Australia) Command... (2010)
18. Reason, J.: The Human Contribution: Unsafe Acts, Accidents and Heroic Recoveries. CRC Press, Boca Raton (2017)
19. Saitta, P., Larcom, B., Eddington, M.: Trike v1 methodology document. Draft, work in progress (2005)
20. Shostack, A.: Threat Modeling: Designing for Security. Wiley, Hoboken (2014)

21. Sosonkin, M.: Octave: operationally critical threat, asset and vulnerability evaluation. Polytechnic University, April 2005
22. UcedaVelez, T., Morana, M.M.: Risk Centric Threat Modeling. Wiley Online Library, Hoboken (2015)
23. Vieane, A., Funke, G., Gutzwiller, R., Mancuso, V., Sawyer, B., Wickens, C.: Addressing human factors gaps in cyber defense. In: Proceedings of the Human Factors and Ergonomics Society Annual Meeting, vol. 60, pp. 770–773. SAGE Publications, Los Angeles (2016)
24. Young, H., van Vliet, T., van de Ven, J., Jol, S., Broekman, C.: Understanding human factors in cyber security as a dynamic system. In: Nicholson, D. (ed.) AHFE 2017. AISC, vol. 593, pp. 244–254. Springer, Cham (2018). https://doi.org/10. 1007/978-3-319-60585-2_23

Not Annoying the User for Better Password Choice: Effect of Incidental Anger Emotion on Password Choice

Laheem Khan, Kovila P. L. Coopamootoo$^{(\boxtimes)}$, and Magdalene Ng

Newcastle University, Newcastle upon Tyne, UK
{kovila.coopamootoo,magdalene.ng}@newcastle.ac.uk

Abstract. Literature often reports users' experience of frustration, irritation [52], annoyance [42] with respect to security. With regards to password choice, annoyance due to complexity has been linked with weaker passwords [42].

We investigate the influence of incidental anger versus neutral emotion stimulus on password choice.

We design a between-subject controlled lab experiment with N = 56 participants, with a GMail registration scenario. We employ standard video clips as mood induction protocol [59]. We measure password strength via zxcvbn and emotion via IBM's Tone Analyzer and PANAS-X.

We find that participants in the anger stimulus condition created significantly weaker passwords than those in the neutral stimulus condition, t(54) = 2.901, p = .005, with a near large effect size, g = .77.

This study provides the empirical evidence of the effect of incidental anger emotion on password choice. Our findings are consequential for security because they suggest that if users feel frustration (which may arise from various sources including requirements for security compliance, human-computer interaction design, or any incidental life situation), the impact is likely a weaker security choice, that is, a risk-seeking rather than a risk-avoiding choice.

Keywords: Password · Security · Use · Choice · Emotion · Anger

1 Introduction

Users often perceive security as a barrier that interferes with their productivity [21]. They experience weariness or reluctance towards security or frustration, denial, complacency or overwhelm [52]. User discontent have been observed when forced to adhere to password policies [27,30], and annoyance by the shift in stricter password policies [42,49].

Few recent research have begun to measure and investigate the impact of users' current state of cognition and emotion during security and privacy decision-making [10]. These include the effects of cognitive depletion [24], fear and stress [19] and prior effortful security task [14] on password choice, fear

© Springer Nature Switzerland AG 2020
A. Moallem (Ed.): HCII 2020, LNCS 12210, pp. 143–161, 2020.
https://doi.org/10.1007/978-3-030-50309-3_10

with respect to privacy evaluations, and happiness with respect to wilful self-disclosure or sharing [13]. However, cyber security and privacy research has yet to investigate the influence of anger in decision-making. As a consequence, this paper reports on a study aiming to address this gap.

Although there has been demonstrated user and research preference for not having the burden of a portfolio of passwords [18,51], passwords are still the cheapest and most common method of authentication. They are unlikely to disappear in the near future and password choice research present a typical scenario where users make security decisions as a secondary task. The results of such user studies can further inform the landscape of usable security research. In addition, since password research has benefitted from much effort, research synthesis can be conducted across investigations.

1.1 Contributions

In this paper we reproduced methods already employed in the context of user-password research, such as those in [10,14,19]. The paper provides empirical evidence of the effects of incidental anger emotion on password choice. It demonstrates risk-seeking choices in a security context, as a direct consequence of an external source of anger, in a lab study. It also compares effects of anger from this study, and fear and Captcha stimulus, from previous studies with similar measurements, on password strength.

1.2 Outline

After the introduction, we provide background research in the area of emotion influences and password research. We then provide the aim and methodology of our study including ethics. We follow with the results and discussion before completing with the conclusion.

2 Background

2.1 Influence of Emotion

While affect (as expressed emotion) are thought to impact judgment and decision-making [47,57], research intentions on affect influences in cyber security [19] and privacy [9,13] are relatively new. Fear and anger emotions are particularly important because of their influence on threat appraisal, on risk perception [35], and on coping strategies influencing behaviour [4,61] and their likely mis-attribution [57].

Fear vs. Anger. Although both negative emotions, fear and anger differ in the appraisal themes of certainty and control, and have opposing effects on risk perception [35]. Anger produced in one situation carries over to a wide range of other situations, increasing both optimistic expectations for one's future and the likelihood of making risk-seeking choices. Fear, on the other hand, leads to more pessimistic expectations and more risk-avoidant choices [33,37]. Fear also decreases the human's perceived ability to exercise control whereas anger increases one's perceived ability.

Frustration is a precursor to anger [4,5,7] and anger produced in one situation carries over to a wide range of other situations, increasing both optimistic expectations for one's future and the likelihood of making risk-seeking choices [35].

Incidental vs. Integral Emotion. While emotions are often an outcome of a situation [38], human judgment and decisions can also be based on fleeting incidental emotion that become the basis for future decisions and hence outlive the original cause for the behaviour [34].

We distinguish between emotional experiences that are either (1) normatively relevant to present judgments and choices [34], defined from a consequentialist perspective [26], or experienced feelings about a stimulus [44], that is *integral affect*, or (2) normatively unrelated to the decision at hand [26,34,46] or independent of a stimulus [44], but can be mis-attributed to it and influence decision processes [48] that is *incidental affect*. The impact of incidental emotions on decision-making is well established [57] and have been shown to influence how much people eat [25], help [39], trust [15], procrastinate [53], or choose price different products [36].

Duration of Emotion. Emotions are processes that unfold over time and unlike a mood, an emotional experience is elicited by a certain event and has a clear onset point [6]. The duration of an emotional episode can be defined as the amount of time between this onset point and the first moment the emotional experience is no longer felt [55]. Research has empirically shown that emotions generally last from a couple of seconds up to several hours. In addition, it is thought that the duration of an emotional response is positively related to the duration of the eliciting event [20].

2.2   Text Passwords

Although text passwords are the cheapest and most commonly used method of computer authentication, a large proportion of users are frustrated when forced to comply to password policies such as monthly reset [29]. Users may therefore develop habits to cope with the situation, for example via password re-use [22] writing passwords down, incrementing the number in the password at each reset [1], storing passwords in electronic files and reusing or recycling old passwords [29].

On average, the user has 6.5 passwords, each shared across 3.9 different sites and that each user has 25 accounts requiring passwords and type 8 passwords per day [17].

3 Aim

We investigate the main RQ *"How does anger emotion influence password choice?"*

3.1 Impact on Password Strength

While security has been described as being 'irritating', 'annoying', and 'frustrating', together with being cumbersome, and overwhelming [52], annoyance has also been associated with a shift to stricter password policies [42], with a result of more guessable password choices for the latter.

Frustration, irritation, annoyance are expressions of anger [4, 5, 7] where anger is one of the measurable emotions.

We investigate incidental anger that can be induced from requirements for security compliance, human-computer interaction design, or any incidental life situation.

Question 1 (RQ-P). How does incidental anger emotion influence password strength?

$H_{P,0}$: There is no difference in password strength between users induced with incidental anger emotion and those with neutral emotion.

$H_{P,1}$: There is a significant difference in password strength between users induced with incidental anger emotion and those with neutral emotion.

3.2 Emotion Induced

Mood Induction Protocol [40, 59] is a process for inducing emotions during user studies. The common methods are film stimuli [45], autobiographical recall [40] or music and guided imagery together [31, 59]. Film/video stimuli produce the largest effect sizes (magnitude of the impact) [23, 45, 59].

Question 2 (RQ-E). How does [anger/neutral] video stimulus impact reported anger?

$H_{E,0}$: There is no difference in reported anger between users induced with incidental anger emotion and those with neutral emotion.

$H_{E,1}$: There is a significant difference in reported anger between users induced with incidental anger emotion and those with neutral emotion.

3.3 Password Reuse and Strategy

We investigate whether there is any difference behind password choices across the two conditions.

Question 3 (RQ-R). How does password reuse and password strategy differ across the two conditions?

3.4   Treatment Comparison

We evaluate how the effects of anger in the current study compare with that of previous studies with fear stimulus [19] and Captcha stimulus [14].

Question 4 (RQ-C). How does the effect of anger stimulus on password strength compare with other treatments?

4   Methodology

We designed a between-subject lab experiment with $N = 56$. We follow the good practice guidelines for empirical research in security and privacy [11,12, 41,43], founded on scientific hallmarks. We used standard questionnaires and methods, as well as reproduced methods employed before [14,24]. We define research questions and hypotheses at the fore and discuss limitations. We follow the standard APA Guidelines [3] to report statistical analyses, and we report on effect sizes, assumptions and test constraints.

4.1   Participants

Participants were recruited from the Newcastle University student population, via departmental email and flyers. With the study lasting on average 20 min, participants were remunerated £10 for their time.

The $N = 56$ participants consisted of 21 female, 34 male and 1 identified as other gender. The mean age $= 26.95$, $sd = 9.345$. 55.4% of the participants had an undergraduate education level, 17.9% postgraduate, 17.9% further education (PhD), 7.1% secondary school while 1.8% did not choose. 30% of the participants reported a computer science related education background.

We employed a randomised block sample design, similar to previous lab experiment in the same context [14]. While we an expected equal number of participants in each condition, at analysis we removed 3 participants who showed signs of not going through the experiment protocol. We consequently ended up with 27 participants in the control group and 29 in the experimental group.

4.2   Procedure

The procedure consisted of (1) pre-task questionnaires for demographics and emotion, (2) a manipulation to induce anger emotion versus a neutral state, (3) a password entry for a mock-up GMail registration, (4) a manipulation check on emotion induced, and (5) a debriefing. Figure 1 depicts the experiment design.

We designed the GMail registration task to mimic Google Email registration online. Similar to the real online policy, we suggested passwords of at least 8 characters long, including digits, uppercase letters and symbols.

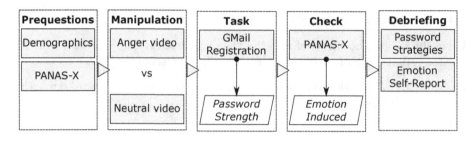

Fig. 1. Experiment design.

4.3   Manipulation

We employed a *Mood Induction Protocol* (MIP) [40,59] via standard film stimuli to either induce emotion of anger or to induce a neutral emotional state [23,45]. Video stimulus are one of the most effective methods of inducing emotions in lab studies [8,59], with Ray [45] and Hewig et al. [28] providing validated lists of such stimulus.

Apparatus. The duration of an emotion is influenced by the emotion-eliciting event characteristics such as the event duration, characteristics of the emotion itself and characteristics of the person experiencing the emotion [54]. Because the length of the chosen video clip influences how long the emotion will last during the study, we chose two clips of similar length. We chose a clip from the movie *Witness* lasting for 91 s for the anger stimulus and a clip from *Hannah and her sisters* lasting for 92 s for the neutral stimulus, both from a database of standard video clips for MIP [28,45].

Manipulation Check. We employ emotion elicitation methods as manipulation check to verify whether the manipulation was successful. In the debriefing questionnaire, we queried participants on the video. We asked for freeform text to "After watching the video, what emotions did you feel?" In addition to qualitatively looking into the emotions reported, we use the IBM's Tone Analyzer as a tool to compute participants' emotional tone from their self-reports. IBM's Tone Analyzer service uses linguistic analysis to detect joy, fear, sadness, anger, analytical, confident and tentative tones found in text.

We also administered a standard questionnaire, the *Positive and Negative Affect Schedule* (PANAS-X) [58], both at the beginning of the study and after manipulation and GMail registration to enable evaluation of difference in affect state caused by the stimulus. We chose to administer the second one after the GMail registration, since we used a 60-item questionnaire which can be long enough to dilute the stimulus effect on the password strength. We set the time boundary of the elicitation to "How do you feel right now?" and used the full

60-item PANAS-X scale based on a 5-point Likert items anchored on 1 - "very slightly or not at all", 2 - "a little", 3 - "moderately", 4 - "quite a bit" and 5 - "extremely".

4.4   Measurement

We measured the dependent variable (DV) password strength via $\log_{10}$ number of password guesses and an ordinal value from 0 to 4 of password strength via zxcvbn [60]. This is similar to the previous studies [14, 19].

4.5   Ethics

The study received ethics approval from the institution and followed its ethics guidelines. The laboratory setting ensured a face-to-face environment where participants could ask questions or cease the experiment should they feel any discomfort. They received an informed consent form and could withdraw from the experiment at any time.

Participants were exposed to mild anger emotion, not more than daily life. In particular, we chose not use the strongest standard stimulus for anger emotion. Our choice of stimulus also comes from a database of mood induction protocol stimulus that have been validated in affective psychology research and found appropriate for use in experiments [28, 45].

Although participants were asked to create a new GMail account during the experiment, at debriefing they were told that it was only for the purpose of the study.

We computed password strength via zxcvbn offline and anonymised and stored participant data on an encrypted hard disk.

5   Results

All inferential statistics are computed at a significance level α of 5%. We estimate population parameters, such as standardized effect sizes of differences between conditions with 95% confidence intervals.

5.1   Emotion Manipulation Check

As verification of the influence of the video stimulus, we investigate RQ-E "How does [anger/neutral] video stimulus impact reported anger?" via $H_{E,0}$ that "There is no difference in reported anger between users induced with incidental anger emotion and those with neutral emotion".

Self-report. We look into participants' freeform responses to "After watching the video, what emotions did you feel?" in the debriefing questionnaire. We find a large number of participants reporting frustration, anger or disgust in the anger stimulus condition compared to only one.

For the anger stimulus condition, we find that 69% of participants responded with angered, irritated, frustrated or disgusted, for example P31 reported "disgust at the teenager bullying the amish", P33 "Frustration on behalf of the amish being unable to defend themselves against those that were hassling them" and P51 "annoyed and wronged like something should've been done about it." There was also a mix of anger and feeling sorry, such as P39 "angry at the bullies. Sorry for the others" and P46 "I felt sorry for the family, I thought the bully was a jerk. I wanted to see the end and see the other guy smack him one!"

The other 31% of participants in this condition reported excitement, intrigue or curiosity such as P56 "Excited; [sic] want to watch the complete film", P55 "Intrigued, excited, saddened, amused" and P38 "Empathy, confusion, wonder, curiosity".

For the neutral stimulus condition, participants reported a mix of emotions including (a) inspiration such as P3 "Inspired because of the conversation" and P6 "Inspired by the woman chasing her dream", (b) happiness such as P7 "happier" and P9 "Slightly happier", (c) boredom such as P8 "Bored. I was expecting something to happen during the video", (d) sadness/anger such as P13 "sad for her, emphatic" and P23 "Felt sad/pity for the women who mentioned her audition [sic] Angry at her friend for not supporting her" or (e) mixed emotions such as P19 "Mixed emotions, inquisitive, happy, concerned, interested".

Emotional Tone. In addition, we use IBM's Tone Analyzer to compute participants' emotional tone from their self-reports. We compute an independent samples t-test on anger emotional tone (TA_anger) across the two conditions. There was a statistically significant difference in TA_anger between the two conditions, with $t(54) = -3.021$, $p = .004$, CI$[-.450, -.090]$, with a large effect size Hedges $g = 1.38$, power statistics $1 - \beta = .91$. Figure 2 shows the impact of the two stimulus on TA_Anger, showing a clear distinction between the two conditions.

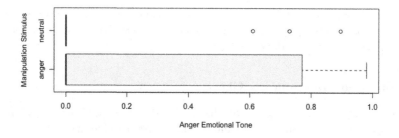

Fig. 2. IBM Tone Analyzer anger tone by condition.

PANAS-X Affect Score. PANAS-X 'hostility' score is the sum of the individual "angry", "hostile", "irritable", "scornful", "disgusted" and "loathing" PANAS-X scores. We compute diff-hostility as the difference in hostility score between reports after the manipulation check and GMail registration and reports at the beginning of the study. We then run an independent samples t-test on diff-hostility across the two conditions. Although we do not observe a significant difference between the two conditions, with $t(54) = -1.782$, $p = .081$, CI$[-3.295, .197]$, we the magnitude of difference between the two conditions is Hedges $g = .46$, which refers to a near medium effect size. Figure 3 shows the impact of the two stimulus on diff-hostility, showing a clear distinction between the two conditions.

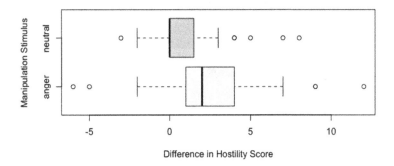

Fig. 3. Change in hostility after manipulation.

5.2   Password Descriptives

We describe the password characteristics and composition across the two conditions in Tables 1. We detail password length, the number of digits, lowercase letters, uppercase letters and symbols.

Table 1. Password characteristic descriptives

Characteristics	Overall			Neutral condition			Anger condition		
	(N = 56)			(N = 27)			(N = 29)		
	Mean	Median	Sd	Mean	Median	Sd	Mean	Median	Sd
Length	10.36	10	2.786	10.52	10	2.578	10.21	9	3.005
# digits	2.38	2	1.987	2.96	3	2.328	1.83	2	1.441
# lwrcase	6.55	6	3.865	5.74	6	3.938	7.31	6	3.685
# uprcase	1.14	1	1.600	1.52	1	2.082	0.79	1	0.861
# symbols	0.29	0	0.653	0.30	0	0.724	0.28	0	0.591

5.3   Password Re-use

We asked participants whether they registered the GMail account via a password they currently use for any services. In general, of the $N = 56$ participants, 42% answered "Yes" to the question "Is it a password that you use for any other services?" From the neutral stimulus condition, 33% reused an existing password, whereas from the anger stimulus condition 51.7% reused an existing password.

We then asked participants to select the services they use the password for and the last time they used it. Figure 4 depicts the reuse context from the 24 participants who responded "Yes" to having reused an existing password.

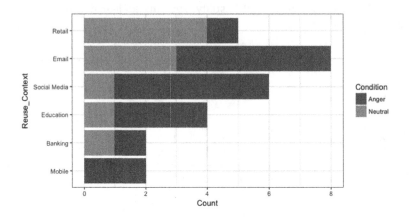

Fig. 4. Password reuse context by condition.

For the question "When was the last time you used this password?", in the neutral condition, 4 participants responded "past week" and 1 "today" whereas in the anger condition, 1 participant responded "past week" and 5 "today".

5.4   Password Strength

We investigate RQ-P "How does incidental anger emotion influence password strength?" via $H_{P,0}$ that "There is no difference in password strength between users induced with incidental anger emotion and those with neutral emotion".

The distribution of the zxcvbn $\log_{10}$ guesses is measured on interval level and is not significantly different from a normal distribution for each condition. Saphiro-Wilk for (a)neutral: $D(27) = .969$, $p = .576 > .05$, (b) anger: $D(29) = .944,\ p = .132 > .05$. We also compute Levene's test for the homogeneity of variances. For the zxcvbn $\log_{10}$, the variances were not significantly unequal across conditions, $F(1, 54) = .027$, $p = .871 > .05$. We provide the descriptive statistics in Table 2.

All Participants. We compute an independent samples t-test with the zxcvbn $\log_{10}$ guesses as dependent variable. There was a statistically significant difference in password strength for neutral ($M = 8.346$, $SD = 2.502$) and anger ($M = 6.425$, $SD = 2.452$) conditions, $t(54) = 2.901$, $p = .005$, CI[.593, 3.249], effect size Hedges $g = .765$, power statistics $1 - \beta = .81$.

In addition, we compute a Mann-Whitney test on the ordinal values of zxcvbn password strength score across the two conditions. There was a statistically significant difference in password strength score, where participants in the anger stimulus condition chose weaker password strength ($Mdn = 1$) than participants in the neutral stimulus condition ($Mdn = 3$), $U = 218$, $z = -2.965$, $p = .003$.

Table 2. Descriptive statistics of password strength via zxcvbn $\log_{10}$ guesses by condition.

Condition	N	Mean	Std. dev.	Std. error	95% CI		Min	Max
					LL	UL		
Neutral	27	8.346	2.502	0.481	7.356	9.336	2.837	12.241
Anger	29	6.425	2.452	0.455	5.492	7.358	2.403	13.122
Total	56	7.351	2.638	0.352	6.645	8.057	2.403	13.122

Non-Password-ReUse Participants. Since 42% of participants reused an existing password, we compute the mean difference between the anger and neutral group for those participants who did not reuse a password, $N = 32$, [18 neutral, 14 anger].

We compute an independent samples t-test with the zxcvbn $\log_{10}$ guesses as dependent variable. There was a statistically significant difference in password strength for neutral ($M = 8.715$, $SD = 2.563$) and anger ($M = 5.899$, $SD = 2.074$) conditions, $t(54) = 3.342$, $p = .002$, CI$[1.095, 4.536]$, effect size Hedges $g = 1.196$, power statistics $1 - \beta = .87$.

In addition, we compute a Mann-Whitney test on the ordinal values of zxcvbn password strength score across the two conditions. There was a statistically significant difference in password strength score, where participants in the anger stimulus condition chose weaker password strength ($Mdn = 1$) than participants in the neutral stimulus condition ($Mdn = 3$), $U = 56.5$, $z = -2.763$, $p = .006$.

Therefore, for all participants as well as those who did not reuse a password, for both zxcvbn $\log_{10}$ guesses and the ordinal zxcvbn password strength score, we reject the null hypothesis $H_{P,0}$.

5.5 Password Strategy

We code participants' password strategies across the following six categories, with qualitative details below and a summary in Fig. 5.

Random. 19.6% [3 neutral, 8 anger] of the participants did not have a strategy, or created a one-time password or something they would not use again, for example P27 described "made a new password that was explicitly not a real or particularly strong", P48 "used a random word with a combination of random numbers" and P38 "something easy to remember and pertaining to this task as I didn't think I'd be using it for anything else".

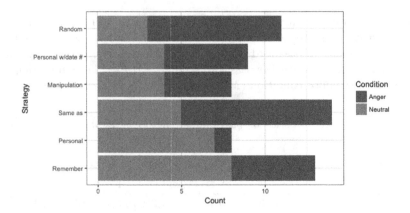

Fig. 5. Password strategy by condition.

Personal. 30.3% [11 neutral, 6 anger] of the participants chose a password related to their preference or something personal to them, with 14.3% [7 neutral, 1 anger] not adding a date or number such as P9 "I chose a personal part of my life as no one else will be able to guess it" or P22 "The names of my children mixed".

Personal with Date or Number. While overall 30.3% [4 neutral, 5 anger] of the participants chose a password related to their preference, 16.1% [4 neutral, 5 anger] combined the personal data with numbers or dates, for example P1 "I came up with something new for this experiment so I used my Mum's nickname for me with my year of birth" and P47 "picked something personal to me and added some numerics".

Manipulation. We found that 14.3% [4 neutral, 4 anger] participants had a strategy involving complexity combinations, changing characters to numbers or the equivalent in another language, for example as expressed by P14 "I thought of a word/series of words relating to the video and substituted letters for numbers" and P51 "Make sure it's long enough, has an upper case letter and number in it. Also one that I could actually remember".

Same As. 25% [5 neutral, 9 anger] participants reported a re-use strategy, for example as expressed by P3 "This is the password I use for every site", P35 "normal password", P17 "I have selected one of the passwords I have been using since being a child. This time I selected a seldom used one which is not associated with any other important accounts", P42 "my usual original password I use for each account I make for the first time" and P52 "a strong password I already use".

Easy to Remember. 23.2% [8 neutral, 5 anger] participants reported that they created an easy to remember password, for example as expressed by P11 "One that I could remember, but that I didn't use for anything else and was not easily guessable by other people" or P13 "in this case just [sic] used sentence that I might not to [sic] forget afterwards" and P56 "None, I used the most convenient strategy that would be easy to remember".

5.6   Treatment Comparison Across Studies

We investigate RQ-C, that is, "How does the effect of anger stimulus on password strength compare with other treatments?"

We conduct a meta-analysis, which is a statistical methodology for combining quantitative evidence from studies and is key for research synthesis. It helps to distinguish one-time results from consistent findings, as well as to compare treatments across studies. The meta-analysis was computed with the R packages meta and metafor [56]. We provide a graphical display via a forest plot of the estimated meta-analysis results from the studies with (1) the anger and neutral treatments of the current study, with (2) the fear and stress treatments of Fordyce et al.'s study [19], and (3) the captcha treatments of Coopamootoo et al.'s study [14]. We note that the three studies employed the same password creation scenario via a mockup GMail account and measured password strength via zxcvbn.

We provide the forest plot in Fig. 6. Each treatment is represented by a point-effect estimate (the mid-point of the box, or the best guess of the true effect in the population) and a horizontal line for the confidence interval. The area of the box represents the weight given to the treatment. The diamond represents the overall effect. The width of the diamond depicts the confidence interval for the overall effect.

Figure 6 shows the overall treatment effect and comparison across treatments with the anger emotion and the Captcha treatments demonstrating more negative effects in password strength, that is weaker password choices than the fear and stress treatments.

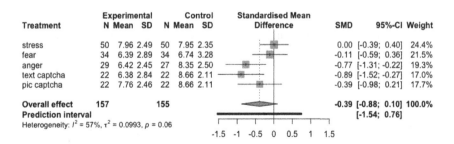

Fig. 6. Forest plot of treatment effects.

6   Discussion

We induced anger emotion via a source external to the GMail registration and password creation scenario and find a significant effect of the anger stimulus condition in resulting in weaker password choice, with a near large effect size $g = .765$.

6.1   Effect on Password Strength

Our findings support the observation from affect psychology research of more risk-seeking choices with anger emotion [35]. Given the impact of incidental anger emotion, we postulate requirements for human-interaction designs to support users in avoiding frustrated states. However, similar to Mazurek et al. [42] who reported participants' annoyance due to a change to stricter password policy, we also observed an effect from anger emotion induced by an external source. We do not yet know the emotional aspects of password creation itself.

6.2   Password Reuse

We observed that overall, a larger number of participants reused an existing password in the anger group than in the neutral group, with social media passwords showing the most distinct appearance in the anger group and retail passwords in the neutral group, while email password reuse is somewhat balanced in both groups. This percentage of reported password reuse is not surprising when compared to previous reports of password reuse by a student population (100%) [2] and in general (34.6 to 82%) [2,32].

We did not find a significant effect of the experiment condition on password reuse given our sample size. However further investigation on the effects of emotion on reuse and reuse contexts with a larger sample size will provide a deeper understanding.

6.3   Password Strategy

For reported password strategy, we observed a higher number of participants choosing a random [3 neutral, 8 anger] and "same as" [5 neutral, 9 anger] password in the anger group than in the neutral group. This may be an indication of less thoughtful choices, yet this can only be confirmed via further research investigations.

In addition the neutral group had a larger number of passwords that can be remembered [8 neutral, 5 anger] or that used a personal strategy [11 neutral, 6 anger] than the anger group.

While these observations are informative, we cannot make conclusive remarks due to the small numbers per strategy or reuse context. However, future research specifically on the effects of emotion on password memorability and password strategies, will likely provide finer and more conclusive details of the impact of emotion.

6.4   Treatment Impact

The meta-analysis across studies enabled a comparison of the impact of different treatments on password strength. This is a first research synthesis of emotion research in the area of cyber security that compares fear with anger treatments. Research and comparison of these two negative valence emotions are particularly important because of their differing threat appraisal tendencies and risk-avoiding versus risk-seeking choices. From the meta-analysis, we can visualise the impact of feeling anger during security tasks relative to feeling fear or a more neutral affect tone.

In addition, the meta-analysis demonstrates the effect of solving a Captcha as stimulus versus watching a medium effect anger video, where it is likely that frustration was involved in the previous Captcha study (evidenced by the number of attempts at solving the Captcha).

6.5   Ecological Validity

Previous password studies fall into two main categories: (1) those using real-world password datasets from security leaks, or (2) those generating passwords within controlled lab studies and Amazon Mechanical Turk online studies; where passwords collected from user studies are thought to be comparable to and a reasonable approximation of real passwords [16, 42]. Our study was designed as a controlled lab experiment, employing a GMail registration task with its password policy suggesting passwords of at least 8 characters long, including digits, uppercase letters and symbols.

In addition, we compare Table 1 with the large-scale study conducted at CMU [42] in 2013 and from that leaked data sets in 2016 [50]. Our mean password length of 10.36 CI[9.61,11.10] is not far from that of Mazurek et al.'s CMU dataset of 10.7 [42] and Shen et al.'s of 9.46 [50]. Our passwords had a mean of 2.38 digits, 1.14 uppercase letters and 0.29 symbols while Mazurek et al.'s CMU dataset had a mean of 2.8 digits, 1.5 uppercase letters and 1.2 symbols.

6.6   Limitations

Our sample was drawn from a University student and academic population, 55.4% at an undergraduate level and 35.8% at a post-graduate level, with 30% reporting to have a Computer Science background. Since students and IT professionals are thought to exhibit nuanced behaviour from students [2], it is possible that a representative sample drawn from the country population may show different password characteristics.

Although we observe a near to large effect size on password strength and power statistics of .81, our sample is not large. A larger sample size would have provided clearer indications for password reuse and strategy.

7   Conclusion

This paper provides a first study with empirical evidence of the effects of anger emotion, induced via a film stimulus video with no connection with cyber security, on password choice. It demonstrates risk-seeking choices in a security context, while describing a study that induced and measured anger emotion. The paper compares the effects of anger, fear and Captcha stimuli on password strength. Our findings show the impact of emotion on a security choice, where the emotion may be induced from the environment or any incidental situation.

References

1. Adams, A., Sasse, M.A.: Users are not the enemy. Commun. ACM **42**(12), 40–46 (1999)
2. Alomari, R., Thorpe, J.: On password behaviours and attitudes in different populations. J. Inf. Secur. Appl. **45**, 79–89 (2019)
3. American Psychological Association (APA): Publication manual, 6th revised edn. American Psychological Association (2009)
4. Averill, J.R.: Studies on anger and aggression: implications for theories of emotion. Am. Psychol. **38**(11), 1145 (1983)
5. Averill, J.R.: Anger and Aggression: An Essay on Emotion. Springer, New York (2012). https://doi.org/10.1007/978-1-4612-5743-1
6. Beedie, C., Terry, P., Lane, A.: Distinctions between emotion and mood. Cognit. Emotion **19**(6), 847–878 (2005)
7. Berkowitz, L., Harmon-Jones, E.: Toward an understanding of the determinants of anger. Emotion **4**(2), 107 (2004)
8. Coan, J.A., Allen, J.J.: Handbook of emotion elicitation and assessment. Oxford University Press, Oxford (2007)
9. Coopamootoo, K.P.: Work in progress: Fearful users' privacy intentions: an empirical investigation. In: Proceedings of the 7th Workshop on Socio-Technical Aspects in Security and Trust, pp. 82–89. ACM (2018)
10. Coopamootoo, K.P.L., Groß, T.: Mental models for usable privacy: a position paper. In: Tryfonas, T., Askoxylakis, I (eds.) HAS 2014. LNCS, vol. 8533, pp. 410–421. Springer, Cham (2014). https://doi.org/10.1007/978-3-319-07620-1_36
11. Coopamootoo, K.P.L., Groß, T.: Evidence-based methods for privacy and identity management. In: Lehmann, A., Whitehouse, D., Fischer-Hübner, S., Fritsch, L., Raab, C. (eds.) Privacy and Identity 2016. IAICT, vol. 498, pp. 105–121. Springer, Cham (2016). https://doi.org/10.1007/978-3-319-55783-0_9
12. Coopamootoo, K.P.L., Groß, T.: Cyber Security and Privacy Experiments: A Design and Reporting Toolkit. In: Hansen, M., Kosta, E., Nai-Fovino, I., Fischer-Hübner, S. (eds.) Privacy and Identity 2017. IAICT, vol. 526, pp. 243–262. Springer, Cham (2018). https://doi.org/10.1007/978-3-319-92925-5_17
13. Coopamootoo, K.P., Groß, T.: Why privacy is all but forgotten - an empirical study of privacy and sharing attitude. Proc. Priv. Enhancing Technol. **4**, 39–60 (2017)
14. Coopamootoo, K.P., Groß, T., Pratama, M.: An empirical investigation of security fatigue - the case of password choice after solving a captcha. In: The LASER Workshop: Learning from Authoritative Security Experiment Results (LASER 2017). USENIX Association (2017)

15. Dunn, J.R., Schweitzer, M.E.: Feeling and believing: the influence of emotion on trust. J. Pers. Soc. Psychol. **88**(5), 736 (2005)
16. Fahl, S., Harbach, M., Acar, Y., Smith, M.: On the ecological validity of a password study. In: Proceedings of the Ninth Symposium on Usable Privacy and Security, p. 13. ACM (2013)
17. Florencio, D., Herley, C.: A large-scale study of web password habits. In: Proceedings of the 16th international conference on World Wide Web, pp. 657–666. ACM (2007)
18. Florêncio, D., Herley, C., Van Oorschot, P.C.: Password portfolios and the finite-effort user: Sustainably managing large numbers of accounts. In: Usenix Security, pp. 575–590 (2014)
19. Fordyce, T., Green, S., Groß, T.: Investigation of the effect of fear and stress on password choice. In: Proceedings of the 7th Workshop on Socio-Technical Aspects in Security and Trust, pp. 3–15. ACM (2018)
20. Frijda, N.H.: The Laws of Emotion. Psychology Press, London (2017)
21. Furnell, S., Thomson, K.L.: Recognising and addressing 'security fatigue'. Comput. Fraud Secur. **2009**(11), 7–11 (2009)
22. Gaw, S., Felten, E.W.: Password management strategies for online accounts. In: Proceedings of the Second Symposium on Usable Privacy and Security, pp. 44–55. ACM (2006)
23. Gross, J.J., Levenson, R.W.: Emotion elicitation using films. Cogniti. emotion **9**(1), 87–108 (1995)
24. Groß, T., Coopamootoo, K., Al-Jabri, A.: Effect of cognitive depletion on password choice. In: The LASER Workshop: Learning from Authoritative Security Experiment Results (LASER 2016), pp. 55–66. USENIX Association (2016)
25. Grunberg, N.E., Straub, R.O.: The role of gender and taste class in the effects of stress on eating. Health Psychol. **11**(2), 97 (1992)
26. Han, S., Lerner, J.S., Keltner, D.: Feelings and consumer decision making: the appraisal-tendency framework. J. Consum. Psychol. **17**(3), 158–168 (2007)
27. Herley, C.: So long, and no thanks for the externalities: the rational rejection of security advice by users. In: Proceedings of the 2009 Workshop on New Security Paradigms Workshop, pp. 133–144. ACM (2009)
28. Hewig, J., Hagemann, D., Seifert, J., Gollwitzer, M., Naumann, E., Bartussek, D.: A revised film set for the induction of basic emotions. Cogn. Emot. **19**(7), 1095 (2005)
29. Hoonakker, P., Bornoe, N., Carayon, P.: Password authentication from a human factors perspective. In: Proc. Human Factors and Ergonomics Society Annual Meeting, vol. 53, pp. 459–463. SAGE Publications (2009)
30. Inglesant, P.G., Sasse, M.A.: The true cost of unusable password policies: password use in the wild. In: Proceedings of the SIGCHI Conference on Human Factors in Computing Systems, pp. 383–392. ACM (2010)
31. Jallais, C., Gilet, A.L.: Inducing changes in arousal and valence: comparison of two mood induction procedures. Behav. Res. methods **42**(1), 318–325 (2010)
32. Komanduri, S., et al.: Of passwords and people: measuring the effect of password-composition policies. In: Proceedings of the SIGCHI Conference on Human Factors in Computing Systems, pp. 2595–2604. ACM (2011)
33. Lerner, J.S., Gonzalez, R.M., Small, D.A., Fischhoff, B.: Effects of fear and anger on perceived risks of terrorism: a national field experiment. Psychol. Sci. **14**(2), 144–150 (2003)
34. Lerner, J.S., Keltner, D.: Beyond valence: toward a model of emotion-specific influences on judgement and choice. Cognit. Emotion **14**(4), 473–493 (2000)

35. Lerner, J.S., Keltner, D.: Fear, anger, and risk. J. Pers. Soc. Psychol. **81**(1), 146 (2001)
36. Lerner, J.S., Small, D.A., Loewenstein, G.: Heart strings and purse strings: carry-over effects of emotions on economic decisions. Psychol. Sci. **15**(5), 337–341 (2004)
37. Lerner, J., Keltner, D.: How much risk can you handle? testing the appraisal tendency hypothesis with fearful, angry, and happy people. Manuscript submitted for publication (1999)
38. Loewenstein, G., Lerner, J.S.: The role of affect in decision making. In: Handbook of Affective Science, vol. 619, no. 642, p. 3 (2003)
39. Manucia, G.K., Baumann, D.J., Cialdini, R.B.: Mood influences on helping: direct effects or side effects? J. Pers. Soc. Psychol. **46**(2), 357 (1984)
40. Martin, M.: On the induction of mood. Clin. Psychol. Rev. **10**(6), 669–697 (1990)
41. Maxion, R.: Making experiments dependable. Dependable and Historic Computing, pp. 344–357 (2011)
42. Mazurek, M.L., et al.: Measuring password guessability for an entire university. In: Proceedings of the 2013 ACM SIGSAC Conference on Computer & Communications Security, pp. 173–186. ACM (2013)
43. Peisert, S., Bishop, M.: How to design computer security experiments. In: Futcher, L., Dodge, R. (eds.) WISE 2007. IAICT, vol. 237, pp. 141–148. Springer, New York (2007). https://doi.org/10.1007/978-0-387-73269-5_19
44. Peters, E., Vastfjall, D., Garling, T., Slovic, P.: Affect and decision making: a "hot" topic. J. Behav. Decis. Making **19**(2), 79 (2006)
45. Ray, R.D.: Emotion elicitation using films. In: Handbook of Emotion Elicitation and Assessment, pp. 9–28 (2007)
46. Schwarz, N.: Feelings as Information: Informational and Motivational Functions of Affective States. Guilford Press, New York (1990)
47. Schwarz, N.: Emotion, cognition, and decision making. Cogn. Emotion **14**(4), 433–440 (2000)
48. Schwarz, N., Clore, G.L.: Mood, misattribution, and judgments of well-being: informative and directive functions of affective states. J. Pers. Soc. Psychol. **45**(3), 513 (1983)
49. Shay, R., et al.: Encountering stronger password requirements: user attitudes and behaviors. In: Proceedings of the Sixth Symposium on Usable Privacy and Security, p. 2. ACM (2010)
50. Shen, C., Yu, T., Xu, H., Yang, G., Guan, X.: User practice in password security: an empirical study of real-life passwords in the wild. Comput. Secur. **61**, 130–141 (2016)
51. Stajano, F.: Pico: no more passwords!. In: Christianson, B., Crispo, B., Malcolm, J., Stajano, F. (eds.) Security Protocols 2011. LNCS, vol. 7114, pp. 49–81. Springer, Heidelberg (2011). https://doi.org/10.1007/978-3-642-25867-1_6
52. Stanton, B., Theofanos, M.F., Prettyman, S.S., Furman, S.: Security fatigue. IT Professional **18**(5), 26–32 (2016)
53. Tice, D.M., Bratslavsky, E., Baumeister, R.F.: Emotional distress regulation takes precedence over impulse control: if you feel bad, do it!. J. Pers. Soc. Psychol. **80**(1), 53 (2001)
54. Verduyn, P., Delaveau, P., Rotgé, J.Y., Fossati, P., Van Mechelen, I.: Determinants of emotion duration and underlying psychological and neural mechanisms. Emot. Rev. **7**(4), 330–335 (2015)
55. Verduyn, P., Delvaux, E., Van Coillie, H., Tuerlinckx, F., Van Mechelen, I.: Predicting the duration of emotional experience: two experience sampling studies. Emotion **9**(1), 83 (2009)

56. Viechtbauer, W., et al.: Conducting meta-analyses in R with the metafor package. J. Stat. Softw. **36**(3), 1–48 (2010)
57. Vohs, K.D., Baumeister, R.F., Loewenstein, G.: Do Emotions Help or Hurt Decisionmaking?: A Hedgefoxian Perspective. Russell Sage Foundation (2007)
58. Watson, D., Clark, L.A., Tellegen, A.: Development and validation of brief measures of positive and negative affect: the panas scales. J. Pers. Soc. Psychol. **54**(6), 1063 (1988)
59. Westermann, R., Spies, K., Stahl, G., Hesse, F.W.: Relative effectiveness and validity of mood induction procedures: a meta-analysis. Eur. J. Soc. Psychol. **26**(4), 557–580 (1996)
60. Wheeler, D.L.: zxcvbn: low-budget password strength estimation. In: Proceedings USENIX Security (2016)
61. Witte, K.: Putting the fear back into fear appeals: the extended parallel process model. Commun. Monogr. **59**(4), 329–349 (1992)

Development of a Test Battery for Cyber Soldiers

Patrik Lif$^{(\boxtimes)}$, Jacob Löfvenberg$^{(\boxtimes)}$, Per Wikberg$^{(\boxtimes)}$, and Ove Jansson$^{(\boxtimes)}$

Swedish Defence Research Agency, Linköping, Sweden
{patrik.lif,jacob.lofvenberg,per.wikberg,ove.jansson}@foi.se

Abstract. There is a great need for people with specialist knowledge about cyber-security in both the civil and military sector. The Swedish Armed Forces has decided that a basic education for conscript cyber soldiers shall be established. The work presented in this paper describes the development of an aptitude test for use in the selection process of conscript cyber soldiers, including a work analysis, test development, and initial validation. Based on the results from the work analysis and a literature review on other cyber tests, the test battery CyberTest Future Soldiers (CTFS) was developed. The cyber test (CTFS) consists of one skill test (with six subareas), one abilities test (with four subareas), and one survey regarding the test taker's interests. The results from the initial validation show that the different test sections (skill and ability) measure different aspects important for performance. This lack of correlation makes it possible to select highly skilled people as well as people on a lower skill level, but who should perform well during the education due to their high level of abilities.

Keywords: Cyber test · Abilities · Skills · Validation

1 Background

The Swedish society is undergoing a large-scale digitization process. A few years ago, programmer and system developer became the most common professions in Stockholm, Sweden [1], and there is still a great need for people with specialist knowledge about cybersecurity. In both the short and long term, the demand for engineering graduates in the cyber area will be significantly higher than the supply [2]. The Swedish Armed Forces face the challenge of meeting a growing cyber threat, which requires recruitment of qualified people. The need for personnel applies to both civil and military positions, and personnel will need to perform jobs ranging from simpler technical tasks (e.g. connecting hardware), to highly advanced tasks (e.g. detecting and diverting cyber-attacks). Experience from other countries suggests that cyber personnel must be present, available, and part of the military hierarchy. At the same time, recruiting and hiring qualified cyber personnel such as officers, soldiers, and civilian employees, has proven to be a challenge. Traditional recruitment and staffing processes are complex and slow, which leads to problems in providing the organization with individuals who meet the set requirements at a reasonable cost. As in other professions, there are great individual differences between people with expertise in the digital domain. According to Freedberg [3], the

© Springer Nature Switzerland AG 2020
A. Moallem (Ed.): HCII 2020, LNCS 12210, pp. 162–174, 2020.
https://doi.org/10.1007/978-3-030-50309-3_11

best programmers perform 50–100 times better than their colleagues. Supplying orga-nizations with the best cyber personnel is thus a challenge, and therefore it is necessary to spend resources on the selection process [4]. There are at least two important aspects to consider:

- In many organizations, more knowledge is needed regarding the skills and individual characteristics that are relevant for cyber operator roles.
- Useful selection tests need to be designed to measure these skills and individual characteristics.

The Swedish Armed Forces has decided that a basic education for conscript cyber soldiers shall be established. Their vision is to develop an education with high status and a high civil merit value, which, in turn attracts qualified applicants. To achieve this vision, the selection process needs to be adapted to the education so that it is possible to select the best candidates available and filter out those with insufficient knowledge. This will probably mean selection criteria based on the background data submitted via the recruitment authority's website, regular assessment tests, and any recently developed complementary cyber test.

This paper describes a work in progress focusing on the development of an aptitude test for use in the selection process of conscript cyber soldiers.

2 Introduction to Test Procedures

There is no clear definition of intelligence, and intelligence tests have received much criticism over the years. Still, there is a consensus within the research society that estab-lished tests measure general intelligence [5]. Even though there is a lack of definition, intelligence is usually divided into different types [6], which has consequences for the interpretation of test results. For example, if a test contains a large number of verbal items, verbal intelligence is measured; if there is a large number of items with symbols and figures, spatial ability is measured instead. Schmidt and Hunter [7, 8] showed that a combination of general mental ability, work samples, structured interviews, and integrity tests is the best known method for predicting job performance.

Aptitude refers to an inherent or innate orientation that favors the development of a certain ability. This is different from acquired abilities, which is the result of training. In terms of mental ability, aptitude is closely related to intelligence. Intelligence tests and aptitude tests differ in the sense that intelligence tests intend to measure general mental ability, whereas aptitude tests are intended to measure the capacity or potential to acquire education or training [9]. Examples of such abilities include learning a new language, producing music, and being able to concentrate [10]. Two Swedish examples of aptitude tests are The Enrolment Test (swe. I-prov 2000) [11], and the Military Academy Test (swe. MHS-prov) [12]. The I-prov 2000 consists of ten sections: two non-verbal problem solving sections, three verbal sections, four spatial sections, and a section for technical understanding. The MHS-prov is used for certain special military selections, for instance, the selection process for combat pilots [13]. The MHS-prov contains twelve test sections: three logical/inductive sections, four spatial sections, and five verbal sections.

2.1 Personality

Perhaps the most common theoretical reference frame when it comes to personality is the five-factor model that defines five basic personality variables [14, 15]:

- openness – the degree to which an individual is open to novel experiences
- conscientiousness – the degree to which an individual is organized, dependable and carefully plans his or her actions
- extraversion – the degree to which an individual is sociable, energetic and seeks the company of others
- agreeableness – the degree to which an individual is empathic, compassionate and cooperative
- neuroticism – the degree to which an individual has a tendency for anger, depression and vulnerability.

The five personality variables have been shown to correlate with work performance in certain job categories [16, 17], such as leadership-related professions [18] and sales-related professions [19]. Even though personality tests can be used for selecting people for some work roles, there is a substantial amount of criticism against them [20, 21]. The correlation between measures of personality and measures of work performance is weak, and personality tests should most likely not be used for predicting work performance since there are better alternatives. From a historic perspective, it is interesting that personality tests during 1960–1980 largely disappeared from the list of best practice. However, in the 1990s, there was a surge in the usage of personality tests and today this type of tests are very popular, despite low validity in predicting work performance [22].

The most common way of measuring personality is objective methods, often by using multiple choice items. The tests are usually self-assessment tests, which means that the answers are based on the individual's own subjective assessment. There are also projective personality tests, where the individual's response to ambiguous stimuli is interpreted, usually by a psychologist. A classic example is the Rorschach test [23], where the individual describes what they see when shown a series of inkblots.

Below is a description of related work focusing on the cyber profession and existing aptitude tests for conscript cyber soldiers. The analysis and description of selected roles within the cyber profession are necessary for the selection process. The analysis of existing aptitude tests adds relevant knowledge and inspires our continued work.

2.2 The Cyber Profession

Development of aptitude tests for the selection of conscript cyber soldiers requires expertise in psychology and cyber security, as well as a good understanding of the cyber soldier profession. A major challenge lies in describing the tasks and roles of cyber soldiers with sufficient accuracy. The profession requires both technical expertise and understanding of human behavior [23]. The National Initiative for Cyber Security Education (NICE) is the most well-known framework for describing work roles in cybersecurity [24]. The framework describes categories, specialty areas, work roles, tasks, knowledge, skills and abilities (Table 1).

Table 1. Description of framework content.

Categories	Specialty areas
Analyse	All sources intelligence, Exploitation analysis, Targets, Threat analysis
Collect & operate	Collection operations, Cyber operations, Cyber operations planning
Investigate	Digital forensics, Investigation
Operate & maintain	Customer service and technical support, Data administration, Knowledge management, Network services, System administration, Systems security analysis
Oversight & development	Cybersecurity, Leadership, Legal education and training, Information system security operations, Legal advice and advocacy, Security program management, Strategic planning and policy development
Protect & defend	Computer network defence analysis, Computer network defence infrastructure support, Incident response, Vulnerability assessment and management
Secure provision	Information assurance compliance, Software assurance and security engineering, Systems development, Systems requirements planning, Systems security architecture, Technology research and development, Test and evaluation
Analyse	All sources intelligence, Exploitation analysis, Targets, Threat analysis

In order to show the scope of NICE, incident management is described in this paper. Incident management corresponds to the role of Cyber Defence Incident Responder, which includes seventeen tasks, thirty areas of knowledge, eight skills, and two abilities. Tasks include gathering information about intrusions in the form of source code, malware, and using the information to assess whether an organization has suffered similar attacks before. Another example is producing a technical compilation of information in accordance with predetermined procedures. For a complete description of the knowledge areas, skills and abilities, see the NICE framework [24, 25]. There are also complete descriptions of knowledge, skills and abilities for the other 32 specialty areas in the framework.

The Department of Homeland Security [26] describes critical tasks for a number of work roles as well as potential consequences if the tasks are not performed correctly. Although this description is much less detailed, it provides some guidance on roles that are of interest. The roles listed are:

- System and Network Penetration Tester
- Application Penetration Tester
- Security Monitoring and Event Analysis
- Incident Responder In-Depth

- Threat Analyst/Counter-Intelligence Analyst
- Risk Assessment Engineers
- Advanced Forensics Analysts for Law Enforcement
- Secure Coders and Code Reviewers
- Security Engineers-Operations
- Security Engineers/Architects for Building Security In.

The information on work tasks and work roles provides an understanding of what requirements should be set when selecting conscript cyber soldiers. In our work, the aptitude tests for conscript cyber soldiers is based on analyses of tasks, areas of knowledge, and skills and abilities related to the profession.

2.3 Existing Cyber Aptitude Tests

Below is a description of three currently used tests for selecting cyber soldiers. However, as the tests are not available for analysis, the descriptions are general and lack details of the actual content. The purpose of the descriptions is to provide the reader with an overview of the content.

The Defence Cyber Aptitude Test (DCAT) was developed in collaboration between the International Business Machines Corporation (IBM) and the British Ministry of Defence [27]. The purpose of the test is to evaluate whether soldiers within the British Armed Forces have abilities relevant to the cyber area. Such soldiers can then be educated and retrained to become cyber soldiers. The test contains several different parts measuring behavior and cognitive abilities. However, technical knowledge is not measured.

Cyber Aptitude and Talent Assessment (CATA) is a framework and a process for developing tests. It was developed in collaboration between the Center for Advanced Language (CASL) at the University of Maryland, USA, and the US Air Force [28]. The test is based on the second generation of Defence Language Aptitude Battery (DLAB). To develop a test battery, Cambell et al. [28] suggested that multiple tests should be used to measure overall and specific abilities. The test is designed to measure cyber aptitude and not just general intelligence.

The Armed Services Vocational Aptitude Battery (ASVAB) is used by the US Armed Forces to select soldiers [29, 30]. The ASVAB consists of several subtests, combined in different ways and given different weight depending on the profession to be recruited. For example, the requirements for the role of Cryptologic Technician: Networks is to achieve a minimum score based on the formula AR (arithmetic reasoning) + 2 × MK (mathematics knowledge) + GS (general science), where AR, MK and GS yield different subtest scores [28]. As there was concerns about ASVAB being outdated and insufficient for selecting cyber soldiers, the new subtest Information/Communication Technology Literacy (ICTL), now known as the Cyber Test (CT), was designed. The CT is a cognitive ASVAB subtest and is expected to have a strong relationship with cyber-related tasks or course grades. Among other things, the CT is expected to measure interest, motivation, and skill [30]. The development of the new test included a review of existing taxonomies in cybersecurity and interviews with cyber experts.

An analysis of the overall content of DCAT, CATA, and ICTL showed that the contents of the three tests are only partially the same, see Table 2. Verbal ability, spatial ability, and error identification and ability to locate details are part of all three tests. Mathematical ability is part of DCAT and ASVAB/CT, while CATA does not contain this ability as an individual item, even though it is probably indirectly included in rule induction and complex problem solving. Creativity is part of CATA and ASVAB/CT, and it is reasonable to consider it an important ability in many cyber roles. The remaining abilities are included in only one of the tests.

Table 2. Abilities included in DCAT, CATA, and ASVAB/CT.

Ability	DCAT	CATA	ASVAB/CT
Mathematical ability	×		×
Verbal ability	×	×	×
Spatial ability	×	×	×
Error identification and ability to locate details	×	×	×
Attention		×	
Vigilance		×	
Creativity		×	×
Practical problem solving	×		
Information ordering			×
Rule induction & complex problem solving		×	
Need for closure and tolerance for risk		×	

3 Development of CyberTest Future Soldiers

The development of a cyber test battery for the Swedish Armed Forces included development of many different subtests, e.g., intelligence tests and personality tests supplemented with various cyber tests. The test battery was named CyberTest Future Soldiers (CTFS).

The development of CTFS included a work analysis, test development, and a validation process. The work was carried out in an interdisciplinary team of researchers with expertise in psychology, IT, cybersecurity, and cognition, respectively. Multiple civil and military organizations also contributed to the work, and interviews with subject matter experts were conducted. A simplified description of the development process is shown in Fig. 1. The work included analyses of selected work roles, analyses of existing tests, selection of abilities to be measured, and development of items and subtests into a test battery. Finally, an initial validation of items, subtests, and the test battery was conducted.

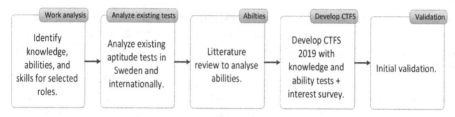

Fig. 1. Development process of the cyber aptitude test.

3.1 Work Analysis

The work analysis started with a hierarchical task analysis [31]. A cybersecurity expert observed professional log analysts during a realistic exercise [32], which resulted in an overall structure of activities conducted by the team leader, the scout and the analyst, as illustrated in Fig. 2.

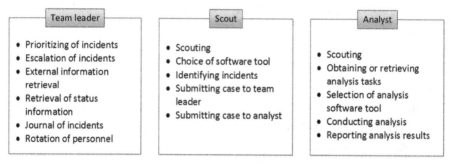

Fig. 2. Hierarchical task analysis for log analysts.

This was only the initial step in the analysis of the log analysts' work role. Work analyses were conducted for other work roles, but these will not be further described in this paper. The next step involved a more detailed description, including all tasks performed by different roles. It was also important to describe knowledge, skills and abilities by using, e.g. the NICE framework [25]. The framework provides a good description of, amongst other things, log analysts, but it is still necessary to analyze whether this description is applicable to the Swedish Armed Forces. The NICE framework contains seven categories, each consisting of two to seven specialty areas [24]. The NICE framework shows what knowledge, skills and abilities are required to perform each task. In addition, capacity indicators are described. These are a combination of education, certification, training, experience and attributes that can indicate a greater likelihood for the individual to successfully perform a certain work role [24, 25]. The NICE framework is comprehensive and provides a good overall view of what tasks and roles are included in the cybersecurity area.

In the NICE framework [24], abilities differ significantly between roles. For example, log analysts need the ability to design incident response for cloud service models and the ability to apply techniques for determining intrusions. System administrators, on the other hand, need abilities such as defining incidents, problems and events in the ticketing system, as well as applying organizational goals and objectives to their development process. However, even if these abilities together with skills and knowledge constructs in NICE provide a good understanding of different roles, they do not match the cognitive abilities that are typically used in aptitude tests. Matching role description abilities with aptitude test abilities still remains. The abilities to be included in the present aptitude test have not yet been decided upon. As this aptitude test should complement existing tests, which abilities add the most value to test validity must be considered.

3.2   CTFS Test Development and Overall Content

The test development was conducted on the basis that the new cyber test (CTFS) should complement the existing Swedish enrolment test. The selection of future cyber soldiers will be based on several tests (e.g. I-prov) and assessments (e.g. psychological evaluation), and CTFS will act as a complement focusing on questions relating to the cyber domain. Based on the work analysis and the content of existing tests, an analysis was conducted regarding the abilities and skills needed by cyber soldiers. These abilities were then investigated through a literature review. Based on the results of this work, three parts were included in the CTFS test battery: a skill test, an abilities test, and a survey for measurement of interests (Fig. 3).

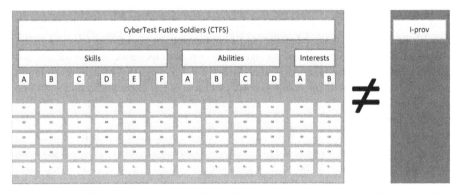

Fig. 3. The CTFS includes subtests for skills, abilities and a survey for interests. Selected abilities were explicitly chosen so as not to correlate with the I-prov that is also used in the selection process.

The skill test contains six subareas of cybersecurity that were considered significant, based on previous analyses. The ability test contains four subareas that were considered to be particularly important. The choice of subareas was also made on the basis of the work analysis and the contents of international cyber tests.

The interest survey complements the skill and ability test, but is not considered a test in itself. During the interviews with subject matter experts, it was revealed that many current employees working with cybersecurity have a private interest in computers and information technology. It is therefore valuable to explore if applicants have interests that match relevant areas. For legal reasons a more detailed description of CTFS cannot be presented.

3.3 Validation Process and Results

Initial work has been carried out to validate CTFS. A large number of items were formulated and validated against several test groups matching the target audience, as well as against audiences with a higher level of education and experience than expected from future test takers. Using the data collected from the test groups, an item analysis [33–35] was performed with the intention to evaluate the quality and difficulty of CTFS. During the item analysis, each question and each response alternative were analyzed. At an early stage, the difficulty level of every item was analyzed in order to be able to select items with varying degrees of difficulty for further evaluation in the next test iteration. The distribution of incorrect responses was also analyzed to aid in the identification of poorly formulated questions and response options. The groups with a higher level of education were used for face validity [35, 36], where subject matter experts took the test and gave feedback on content relevance, difficulty, deficiencies, and errors.

An analysis of the test battery was conducted with 24 participants with similar backgrounds as those of future applicants. Since the test was designed to measure both skill and abilities, it was of interest to investigate whether there was a correlation between the skill test and the abilities test. It was also of interest to investigate if there were any correlations between the different parts of the skill tests to ensure that the same ability is not measured in the respective subtests. First, the data were found not to fulfill all the assumptions of parametric data (due to the small sample size, the variables were not approximately normally distributed), as shown by the Shapiro-Wilk test [36] ($p < .05$). Based on this result, in conjunction with the small sample size, the non-parametric test Kendall's Tau [37] was selected as the statistical measure of choice.

Second, Kendall's Tau showed no significant correlations between the skill test and the ability test (summarized score of all abilities), $\tau = .25, p > .05$. Third, the correlation between the different skill tests (A-F) shows that most of the correlations had a p-value greater than .5. Correlations with $p < .5$ were found between test A and E/F, B and D, and between E and F. Although the correlations were statistically significant, only smaller correlations were found ($.30 < \tau < .35$). Fourth, the correlation between the different ability tests (A-D) shows significant correlations between D and A/B/C, and between A and B, with correlations $.50 < \tau < .53$, and in one case $\tau = .39$. This indicates a moderate correlation, where the different subtests partly measure the same ability. However, it should be noted that this result cannot, and should not, be generalized due to the small sample size (n = 24).

The process for test validation has only begun and is a longitudinal work that will take several years to conduct. Since CTFS is intended to predict future job performance, measurements of predictive validity is top priority. In this longitudinal study, the intention is to conduct several statistical analyses comparing test scores with grades during education, grades after graduation, teachers' student evaluations, and work performance after graduation. Basic military education normally consists of a number of stages where various skill and performance tests can be carried out. The results from these tests should be analyzed together with the results of CTFS to investigate how CTFS can explain variance in educational performance. At some point after the military education, the cyber aptitude test is to be validated against future job performance in different roles. One goal of the CTFS is for it to act as a complement to other existing tests [11]. Thus, it is important to analyze CTFS together with the results of all other tests to investigate if more variance in work performance can be explained by adding CTFS.

4 Discussion

The Swedish society is in a large-scale digitization process, where programmer and system developer are currently the most common professions in Stockholm. There is a great need for programmers and people with specialist cyber knowledge, and both civilian companies and the military sector in Sweden and other countries search for skilled personnel. The demand for software developers in the United States is expected to grow by 24 percent between 2016 and 2022, which is much faster than the average profession [38]. Within this context, the Swedish Armed Forces needs to recruit cybersecurity personnel that can fill positions ranging from basic technical positions to positions that require advanced technical skills. Therefore, a test battery for selecting conscripts has been developed.

The work presented in this paper describes a test developed by the Swedish Defence Research Agency, which is to be used to select the top cyber soldier candidates for the Swedish Armed Forces. The cyber test (CTFS) consists of one skill test (with six subareas), one abilities test (with four subareas), and one survey regarding the test takers' interests. The test was developed through a work analysis, literature review, target group validation, and expert group validation. The skill test measures the applicants' initial knowledge in a number of selected areas. The applicants will be 18–20 years old and are expected to have a certain level of skill in information technology. Applicants with no or low prior skills will probably not complete the advanced training that cyber soldiers will undergo. In contrast to measuring skill, the ability test measures the applicants' potential. Potential here refers to the participants' capability to develop a number of selected abilities. The combination of measuring existing information technology skills and potential will hopefully facilitate the selection process.

Four different ability tests were included in CTFS, but during the work analysis other possible abilities were identified albeit not implemented due to time constraints. In future work, these abilities will be further analyzed and possibly included in test versions. To validate the test battery the test result should be compared to an overall assessment conducted when the conscript cyber soldiers have completed their education. This will provide an important basis for further development and tuning of the test battery.

During the validation processes, it was discovered that there was no significant or large correlation between the skill and abilities test. This result indicates that the test sections (skill and ability) measure different aspects important for performance. This lack of correlation makes it possible to select highly skilled people, as well as people on a lower skill level, but who should perform well during education due to their high level of abilities.

An identified weakness in test development in general (including CTFS) concerns ecological validity of the test. Most tests are developed to be used in the context of a laboratory or a classroom, which often does not match the setting in which the abilities are meant to be used. In future work, the test will be validated in relation to job performance and also include more elements from real-life problems.

In addition, future work should also include an in-depth analysis of the different roles, for example, analysis of abilities required by a certain role, which can reveal how the results of the different subareas should be weighted. There are different approaches for work analyses, but the result is typically information regarding what tasks and sub-tasks are linked to a role, as well as what knowledge and which skills that are required. To some extent, the result of a work analysis can be regarded as an elaborate job description. In addition, a work analysis provides substantial information about work processes and experts' cognitive thinking in a given situation. These work analyses are preferably carried out by a team of individuals with knowledge in different areas, such as technological solutions, tactical application, training of conscript cyber soldiers, psychology, selection testing, and so on. The in-depth work analysis will be used to further develop current subtests, but also to identify new possible subtests.

It is also of interest to study existing tests in more detail, as they can provide valuable information. Examples of such tests are DCAT, CATA and ICTL. These tests include measures of mathematical ability, verbal ability, spatial ability, and the ability to detect errors and find details in large information sets. These four abilities are considered valuable for many of the relevant roles. There are also courses that can provide information about what topics are central to different cyber roles. Cyber tests and courses for different types of certifications and SANS programs [39] should be studied further.

Development of a test battery for conscript cyber soldiers is a long-term undertaking. This paper presents an overview of the initial stages. The work is interdisciplinary, drawing on competence in cybersecurity, psychology, and psychological testing. Continued work will be deepened and broadened through work analyses, and a practical skills test that will be developed and used for selection of future cyber soldiers. There are also ideas to complement CTFS with a practical test where applicants' craftsmanship within the cyber domain can be tested. The practical tests could be performed at the Swedish Defence Research Agency in Linköping, Sweden, which is host to the cyber laboratory CRATE [40] where cyberattacks can be carried out with in-house tools [41] to train or test personnel.

References

1. Stockholms Handelskammare: Programmerare - vanligaste yrket i Stockholmsregionen, Stockholm (2014)
2. SCB: Trender och Prognoser 2017 (2017)
3. Freedberg, S.: Do young humans + artificial intelligence = cybersecurity? Intel Cyber Strategy Policy (2017). https://breakingdefense.com/2017/11/do-young-humans-artificial-int elligence-cybersecurity/
4. Construx: Productivity Variations Among Software Developers and Teams The Origin of 10x | Construx. Construx (2019)
5. Johnson, W., te Nijenhuis, J., Bouchard, T.J.: Still just 1 g: consistent results from five test batteries. Intelligence **36**(1), 81–95 (2008)
6. Gardner, H.: Frames of Mind: The Theory of Multiple Intelligences. Basic Books, New York (2011)
7. Schmidt, F.L., Hunter, J.E.: The validity and utility of selection methods in personnel psychology: practical and theoretical implications of 85 years of research findings. Psychol. Bull. **124**(2), 262 (1998)

8. Schmidt, F.L., Oh, I.-S., Shaffer, J.A.: the validity and utility of selection methods in personnel psychology: practical and theoretical implications of 100 years. Working Paper (2016)
9. McClelland, D.C.: Testing for Competence rather than for 'intelligence'. Am. Psychol. **28**(1), 1 (1973)
10. Bennett, G., Seashore, H.G., Wesman, A.G.: Administrators' Handbook for the Differential Aptitude Test (Forms V and W). Psychological Corp, New York (1982)
11. Carlstedt, B.: Begåvning, utbildningsval och utbildningsresultat | Pedagogisk Forskning i Sverige. Pedagog. Forsk. i Sverige **7**(3), 168 (2002)
12. Annell, S.: Vilka sökande antas till och påbörjar polisutbildningen? Karlstad (2014)
13. Lantz, J., Wolgers, G.: Psykologiska tester och testanvändning i samband med psykologiskt urval av flygförare i Försvarsmakten 1944–2013: en sammanfattande historik och testöversikt (2013)
14. Goldberg, L.R.: The structure of phenotypic personality traits. Am. Psychol. **48**(1), 26–34 (1993)
15. John, O.P., Srivastava, S.: The big five trait taxonomy: history, measurement, and theoretical perspectives. In: Handbook of Personality: Theory and Research, pp. 102–138 (1999)
16. Barrick, M.R., Mount, M.K., Judge, T.A.: Personality and performance at the beginning of the new millennium: what do we know and where do we go next? Pers. Perform. **9**(1/2), 9–30 (2001)
17. Salgado, J.F.: The five factor model of personality and job performance in the European community. J. Appl. Psychol. **82**(1), 30–43 (1997)
18. Sparks, C.P.: Testing for management potential. In: Clark, K.E., Clark, M.B. (eds.) Measures of Leadership, pp. 103–112. Center for Creative Leadership, Greensboro (1990)
19. Sitser, T., van der Linden, D., Born, M.P.: Predicting sales performance criteria with personality measures: the use of the general factor of personality, the big five and narrow traits. Hum. Perform. **26**(2), 126–149 (2013)
20. Morgeson, F., Campion, M., Dipboye, R., Hollenbeck, J., Murphy, K., Schmitt, N.: Are we getting fooled again? Coming to terms with limitations in the use of personality tests for personnel selection. Pers. Psychol. **60**(4), 1029–1049 (2007)
21. Morgeson, F.P., Campion, M.A., Dipboye, R.L., Hollenbeck, J.R., Murphy, K., Schmitt, N.: Reconsidering the use of personality tests in personnel selection contexts (2007)
22. ChallyGroup: The Trouble with Personality Tests, Larkspur, CA (2011)
23. Saner, L.D., Campbell, S., Bradley, P., Michael, E., Pandza, N., Bunting, M.: Assessing aptitude and talent for cyber operations. In: Nicholson, D. (ed.) Advances in Human Factors in Cybersecurity. Advances in Intelligent Systems and Computing, vol. 501, pp. 431–437. Springer, Cham (2016). https://doi.org/10.1007/978-3-319-41932-9_35
24. Newhouse, B., Keith, S., Scribner, B., Witte, G.: National Initiative for Cybersecurity Eduction (NICE) cybersecurity workforce framework, Gaithersburg, MD, USA (2017)
25. National Initiative for Cybersecurity Careers and Studies: NICE Cybersecurity Workforce Framework | National Initiative for Cybersecurity Careers and Studies. Department of Homeland Security (2018)
26. Napolitano, J.: Homeland security advisory council cyberskills task force report (2012)
27. IBM: Defense Cyber Aptitude Test (DCAT). IBM (2018)
28. Cambell, S., O'Rourke, P., Bunting, M.: Identifying dimensions of cyber aptitude: the design of the cyber aptitude and talent assessment. In: Human Factors and Egonomics Society 59th Annual Meeting, pp. 721–725 (2015)
29. ArmedForces: Navy Rating ASVAB Score Requirements. U.S. Armed Forces (2018)
30. Morris, J., Waage, F.: Cyber aptitude assessment-finding the next generation of enlisted cyber soldiers (2015)
31. Stanton, N.A., Salmon, P.R., Walker, G.B., Jenkins, D.: Human Factors Methods: A Practical Guide for Engineering and Design. Ashgate Publishing Limited, Surrey (2013)

32. Lif, P., Granasen, M., Sommestad, T.: Development and validation of technique to measure cyber situation awareness. In: 2017 International Conference On Cyber Situational Awareness, Data Analytics And Assessment (Cyber SA), pp. 1–8 (2017)

33. Moses, T.: A Review of developments and applications in item analysis. In: Bennett, R., von Davier, M. (eds.) Advancing Human Assessment. Methodology of Educational Measurement and Assessment, pp. 19–46. Springer, Cham (2017). https://doi.org/10.1007/978-3-319-586 89-2_2

34. Understanding Item Analyses | Office of Educational Assessment. https://www.washington. edu/assessment/scanning-scoring/scoring/reports/item-analysis/. Accessed 07 Oct 2019

35. Kehoe, J.: Basic item analysis for multiple-choice tests. Pract. Assess. Res. Eval. 4(10) (1995)

36. Shapiro, S.S., Wilk, M.B.: An analysis of variance test for normality (complete samples). Biometrika 52(3/4), 591 (1965)

37. Field, A., Miles, J., Field, Z.: Discovering Statistics Using R. Sage Publications Inc., London (2012)

38. Bureau of Labor Statistics: Software Developers : Occupational Outlook Handbook: U.S. Bureau of Labor Statistics. United States Department of Labor (2019)

39. SANS: SANS Cyber Security Certifications & Research. SANS (2018). https://www. sans.org/. Accessed 23 Nov 2018

40. Sommestad, T.: STO-MP-IST-133 Experimentation on operational cyber security in CRATE (2015)

41. Holm, H., Sommestad, T.: SVED: scanning, vulnerabilities, exploits and detection. In: MILCOM 2016 - 2016 IEEE Military Communications Conference, pp. 976–981 (2016)

"Trust Me, You Will Need It": Cybersecurity as Extracurricular Subject at Estonian Schools

Birgy Lorenz(✉) and Kaido Kikkas

Tallinn University of Technology, Tallinn, Estonia
{Birgy.lorenz,Kaido.Kikkas}@taltech.ee

Abstract. Discovering new talents in IT and cybersecurity is increasingly vital in the information society. The traditional approach has been to start professional profiling when the youth reach grade 10 (age 16–17) – many young people find a topic to focus on in the secondary school and finally form a profession with the 3rd-level studies (trade school or university). Yet, this may be an outdated way, as the leaders of tomorrow will need competencies in more than one field, cyber skills being likely one of them. The initial results of the Estonian best-practice: Competition CyberCracker School round for 7–12th graders suggests that the method works in several aspects. First, the number of talented youth is quite large in comparison with population numbers - the mass screening in the first rounds allows find also those who would not enter any competitions (for various reasons). Second, while the gender gap still exists (interviews with the participants reveal that the number of girls seeing themselves as future cybersecurity specialists is still small compared to boys), the 2/2 quota does not reflect 'equality on paper only' - the actual enthusiasm does not differ (once the latter have actually reached the final round). Overall, the positive trend is clearly visible - just in a year (2018/2019), the number of participants went up from 1000 to 2344 and the number of participating schools from 47 to 65.

Keywords: Cybersecurity · User awareness of privacy threats · Competition · Gamification · Training · Hackers

1 Introduction

Many countries focus their education increasingly on the STEAM disciplines. The skillset for the future would include both creative problem-solving as well as critical thinking [2, 9]. Hardly anyone would deny that ICT will permeate most other areas, too [8]. Yet the new possibilities come with new risks. In earlier times, a starting enterprise had to face risks that were mostly internal and local, whereas the information society of today has to face additional global risks stemming from various malicious activities in cyberspace. The numbers and damages of cybercrime have seen a 72% increase during the last five years [10] and it would be unrealistic to hope that one remains unaffected in the years to come. Instead, one should plan and find qualified and interested parties to protect one's services and infrastructure.

© Springer Nature Switzerland AG 2020
A. Moallem (Ed.): HCII 2020, LNCS 12210, pp. 175–188, 2020.
https://doi.org/10.1007/978-3-030-50309-3_12

Cybersecurity stands apart from some other areas of IT in that 'ordinary', education-derived knowledge and skills do not suffice – an additional ingredient is needed which has been labeled as 'hacker mindset' [4] or 'security culture' [14] to help the management to improve overall security [14].

However, it seems that many scholars and governments have not reached this point yet, as a common discussion topic is still whether Informatics/CS should be compulsory and what should it contain (Informatics Education in Europe: Are We All In The Same Boat? [5]). This leaves the impression that if a child is able to click a mouse and join social media, he/she should be ready for the information society as explained at The Digital Competence Framework 2.0 [15]. At the same time, children are often 'injected' with a false sense of confidence suggesting that they can handle their digital safety. Sadly, reality differs – their skills are lacking both in handling 'normal' online life and technologies and more so in situations where something bad has actually happened in the digital realm.

Practitioners in enterprise and military have found a way to get youth interested in higher-order cybersecurity skills – namely various Capture the Flag (CTF) [1] competitions. At these, they identify young talents who are about to enter the labor market (they thus have both time and skills). Examples include the Cyber Patriot in the U.S. and European Cyber Security Challenge in Europe – virtually every region of the world has got it's own smaller or larger competitions targeting already skilled young specialists. But what is still largely missing today is the understanding and roadmap about how an ordinary student becomes a cyber-talent - can it be learned at all, why some get there and others won't, is it just for boys etc.

1.1   A Snapshot: Estonia

The current situation (as such) is not bad – the discussions about making digital safety, a younger brother of cybersecurity compulsory at schools are underway, the curriculum and the official textbook have been developed [12, 13], so is the CyberSecurity Strategy that stresses finding and educating young talents [7] and the CyberOlympics program launched by the Ministry of Defence at 2015 (explained below). However, many of the suggested measures are defined as complementary, 'nice to have' ones that are envisioned to be funded by the private sector. As the curricula do present cybersecurity-related activities as mandatory, the teachers are divided into two camps – one considers children much more knowledgeable than adults in ICT matters, the others (mostly ICT teachers) doubt that the agile clicking displayed by students actually translates into real ICT skills [6].

The main shortcomings are evident: not all children receive necessary support and training, as teaching digital competencies, as a separate subject is not mandatory and the schools lack harmonized programs [3, 11]. In turn, this creates an uneven foundation for both further studies and 'digital survival' in the information society. The current choice of options available for schools is extremely broad, ranging from culture to language to STEAM subjects. On the one hand, Estonia has set IT as a priority, taking actual steps towards schools participating in software development and programming within its curricula. On the other hand, the lack of people able to defend the budding infrastructure may become a serious obstacle (relying on external security services is not reasonable in the end). Cybersecurity as an extracurricular subject is still widely treated as an enthusiast's hobby in secondary education - at the same time, the related curricula at universities tend to already assume solid knowledge of (or at least serious interest in) the area from prospective students.

1.2 The CyberOlympics Programme in Estonia

The CyberOlympics project strives to find cybersecurity talent in Estonia (see Table 1). The goals of the CyberOlympics program have been formulated as a. identifying young talents in cyber defense; b. implementing proper training programs for young talents in the field; c. educating the wider audience to raise citizen awareness about crime prevention and possibilities to get educated; d. promoting cybersecurity education and career possibilities in Estonia; e. analyzing possible shortcomings and shortcuts in cybersecurity awareness and training programs; and f. proposing scientific solutions such as competency analysis.

The program has several sub-competitions: CyberSpike for higher-level young talents ages of 14–24; CyberCracker testing for 4–9 graders; CyberCracker school round for 7–12th graders to detect young talents; CyberPin for 1–6 graders. In this study we are explaining the CyberCracker school round that is held for Grades 7–12, sending the top two girls and two boys to the final round. This allows teachers and parents to discover those students who can think systematically when solving logic and crypto puzzles, read code, and (perhaps most importantly) enjoy thinking 'out of the box' – something that is not really favored at today's schools. One of the crucial issues is finding suitable exercises - this involves various parties (youth already active in the field, university staff, entrepreneurs and teachers with related skills/interest). Of the similar initiatives elsewhere, the most comparable ones are held in the Czech Republic (Cyber-Security High School Challenge) and in the UK.

In this paper, we will have a closer look at the CyberCracker school round, which aims to find new talents who can be sent on to larger national and international competitions. We note that on this level, all activities are voluntary – meaning that any regular planning is hardly possible.

2 Methods

Cybersecurity as an extracurricular subject has 'sneaked' into schools via the CyberOlympics program, especially the CyberCracker (see above). Members of research and security communities have volunteered to develop and test materials, create puzzles and provide training. Schools were contacted via their general contact channels (twice) but also through various social media communities where they participate. The tasks were developed by teams involving cybersecurity researchers, IT experts and also participants of the older-level CyberSpike competition (see Table 2).

Both the preliminary and final round actually presented the participants with more tasks that were realistically possible to solve – thus posing an additional challenge in task choosing (whether to solve many easy ones or focus on the harder ones giving more points).

Table 1. CyberOlympic annual tasks

Name	For whom/level	Time	Content
CyberPin - competition	7–12-year-old, mainstream to beginner talent	February	Logic, crypto and IT problem-solving challenges
CyberCracker - survey	10–15-year-old, mainstream	October	Awareness study on digital safety
CyberCracker school round - competition	12–18-year-old, beginner talent	October-December	Olympics-like competition - school and national rounds
CyberSpike - competition	14–24-year-old talent	March, June	Higher-level hacking competition and training program sending students to participate in the European Cyber Security Challenge and many other hacking challenges all over the world
Participation foreign competitions - competition	16–24-year-old talent, beginner talents	March, October-November	Magic CTF (USA) European Cyber Security Challenge (EU) CyberPatriot (USA)
Seminars/conferences	Teachers, parents	February, October, June, December	Sharing best practices between researchers and practitioners. Community development
Curriculum and material development	Students starting from primary, teachers	All year	Gamified cybersecurity education makes it more practical through providing interesting exercises that also help develop thinking skills

2.1 Preliminary Round

In 2018 it consisted of 22 questions and was presented as a fill-out document form. Grading was work-intensive, as all submissions had to be graded individually. The questions had various weights and the time limit was either 45 or 90 min (decided by the school). The questions were in Estonian only.

The 2019 version had 28 questions and grading was partially automated. Each school was generated its own test and data table, questions were weighted and the time limit was 90 min. This time, the questions were also available in Russian.

Table 2. CyberCracker school round timetable

Timeline	Organizational	CyberCracker school round 2018	CyberCracker school round 2019
September	Develop a test for the preliminary round	Gathering students information	Gathering students information
1. October – 15. November	Pretesting support	47 schools participated (620 students)	65 schools participated(2344 students),
November	Develop exercises for the final round	Preparing students for the final round	Preparing students for the final round
December	Final round	22 in the final round (102 students)	50 in the final round (188 students)

2.2 Final Round

According to the reglement, each school could send 2 girls and 2 boys who had not participated in a cybersecurity contest before – the aim was to reach new participants every year (earlier participants were allowed to act as mentors). The gender balance rule directed the schools towards finding and training also female talents who had been somewhat neglected in STEAM education.

The general rules were: duration 2 h, 2 laptops and any number of smart devices with Internet connection allowed, 'peeking' on other participants were allowed while outside help was not, the exercises had 4 levels of difficulty with corresponding weights, the languages used were Estonian and English.

- In 2018, 33 exercises were used. The solutions were submitted to the jury on paper and immediate feedback was given. The exercises were weighted, hints were given during the competition and they did not carry penalties. The overall topic was to catch the crackers who had taken over the contest environment. In every 15 min, hints and overall standings were displayed on a screen;
- The 2019 version with 41 exercises used a web-based CTF (Capture the Flag) environment making following the contest more convenient. The exercises were weighted with easier exercises having dynamic weights (the more contestants got them right, the fewer points were given) and hints carried penalties (using them deduced points). 4 exercises had to be done physically outside the competition premises. The overall topic was an escape room, or 'Escape from a Movie' - one had to break out of the movie world by passing through different rooms and solving puzzles. Every 15 min, various videos, trailers and slides were displayed on several screens to create a suitable atmosphere.

As the participants differed greatly in background and age, they were distributed into categories to make evaluation more equal: basic school (Grades 7–9), secondary schools (gymnasiums; Grades 10–12), and combined schools (Grades 1–12), vocational schools, also overall Top 3 were nominated. The three best participants from each category received various educational prizes like visits to IT and cybersecurity companies or participation in different training events.

3 Exercise Development

Perhaps the greatest challenge in education related to digital safety and cybersecurity is the gap between one's self-image and actual skills. In most cases, students imagine themselves to be smart and skillful as they manage at most everyday tasks. This is sometimes corroborated by training materials and tests that aim to provide the students with successful experience at the cost of knowledge. While this is somewhat acceptable in the beginning, digital safety level (aiming not to frighten children off the topic), an inflated self-image becomes a problem on the higher levels. As the CyberCracker had the aim of talent-finding rather than universal awareness-raising, the exercises were deliberately designed to be harder than what their previous education would suggest.

While many participants had previous experience with earlier competitions in Informatics that featured puzzles and programming tasks, the tasks in the CyberCracker preliminary round focused on ingenuity and the ability to notice potential weaknesses and analyze them based on real-life challenges. This continued in the final round where the participants had to display deeper knowledge in a quite realistic environment (the first symptoms point to one thing, the actual problem lies at another and the root cause is yet another) – they had to cope in a fuzzy environment where solutions are usually found by thinking 'out of the box' and making higher-order connections between concepts.

Some examples of the exercises are given below.

Preliminary Round Examples:

- You sit in a computer lab. The computer seems to be really slow. Also, occasionally the cursor seems to move around on its own. What would you do?
- The school's IT manager uses the CamScanner app for Android to scan documents. Find out if it is safe to use or should it be removed immediately.
- Your e-mail to a teacher and receive an error message in return. The message contains an error code, #4.2.2 SMTP. Find out what does it stand for.
- Someone had created accounts with your name and pictures on Facebook and WhatsApp. Find out what law applies to this kind of activity. Explain what to do to remove the accounts.
- Your computer announces the IP address conflict – someone else is already using the address and you cannot get online. You learn that the conflicting address is 192.168.1.4. How can this happen? What steps can you take to get connected?
- Your trainer has sent you an e-mail containing a file with .exe extension. You remember that file hashes can be looked up from the Web to determine whether it is malware. The hash is SHA-256: 24d004a104d4d54034dbcffc2a4b19a11f39008 a575aa614ea04703480b1022c. Find out what it is.
- Your friend hid a password into an image file. Find the password! (See Fig. 1)

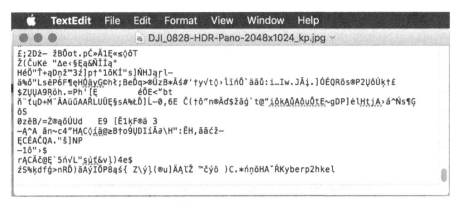

Fig. 1. Picture hack

- Your friend's computer runs a Multicraft server that is managed by the Apache web-server. If someone uses the service, it will create a log entry as seen from the picture below. What can we learn from the picture? (See Fig. 2)

```
root@srini:/var/log/apache2# cat access.log.1 | grep "../.../.../etc/passwd"
127.0.0.1 - - [27/Oct/2014:04:00:48 -0400] "GET /../.../.../.../.../.../.../.../etc/pa
sswd HTTP/1.1" 400 506 "-" "Mozilla/4.0 (compatible; MSIE 8.0; Windows NT 5.1; Trident/4.0)

127.0.0.1 - - [27/Oct/2014:04:00:48 -0400] "GET /../.../.../.../.../.../.../.../etc/pas
swd HTTP/1.1" 400 506 "-" "Mozilla/4.0 (compatible; MSIE 8.0; Windows NT 5.1; Trident/4.0)"
127.0.0.1 - - [27/Oct/2014:04:00:48 -0400] "GET //../.../.../.../.../.../.../.../etc/p
asswd HTTP/1.1" 400 506 "-" "Mozilla/4.0 (compatible; MSIE 8.0; Windows NT 5.1; Trident/4.0
)"
127.0.0.1 - - [27/Oct/2014:04:00:48 -0400] "GET /../.../.../.../.../.../.../.../etc/passwd HTTP
/1.1" 400 506 "-" "Mozilla/4.0 (compatible; MSIE 8.0; Windows NT 5.1; Trident/4.0)"
127.0.0.1 - - [27/Oct/2014:04:00:48 -0400] "GET /scripts/fake.cgi?arg=/dir/../.../.../.
./etc/passwd HTTP/1.1" 404 529 "-" "Mozilla/4.0 (compatible; MSIE 8.0; Windows NT 5.1; Trid
ent/4.0)"
127.0.0.1 - - [27/Oct/2014:04:01:08 -0400] "GET /cgi-bin/pdesk.cgi?lang=../.../.../.../.
./../etc/passwd%00 HTTP/1.1" 404 530 "-" "Mozilla/4.0 (compatible; MSIE 8.0; Windows NT 5.1
; Trident/4.0)"
127.0.0.1 - - [27/Oct/2014:04:02:04 -0400] "GET /search?NS-query-pat=../.../.../.../.../.
./../etc/passwd HTTP/1.1" 404 519 "-" "Mozilla/4.0 (compatible; MSIE 8.0; Windows NT 5.1; T
rident/4.0)"
127.0.0.1 - - [27/Oct/2014:04:02:09 -0400] "GET /ifx/?LO=../.../.../.../.../etc/passwd HTTP/1.1
" 404 517 "-" "Mozilla/4.0 (compatible; MSIE 8.0; Windows NT 5.1; Trident/4.0)"
root@srini:/var/log/apache2#
```

Fig. 2. Multicraft server log

Final Round Examples:
Easier exercises had prescribed one-time activities like "post the picture and introduction of the team into social media", "find the missing word from the title", "find out if the statement is true or false", "find out which messages contain phishing" etc.

Intermediate exercises introduced puzzles and analytical tasks: "analyze the main security concerns among young people in the 2018 survey", "decrypt the message using the book", "fix the mess in the cable board – connect every cable to the corresponding port".

Difficult and very difficult exercises were supported by hints and demanded creative thinking and problem-solving skills: "find the password from the encrypted file", "analyze the network log and answer the question", "find the text and Morse code from the picture" etc.

- Kevin is home alone again. He went to stroll on the Internet and got lost. Help him to find the way home.
- Which command should be entered into the terminal to get the result below? (See Fig. 3)

```
Default Server:   server.kehtna.mtk
Address:   192.168.0.2
```

Fig. 3. Linux server command hunt

- What is written here? (See Fig. 4)

Fig. 4. Cracked QR-Code

- Little Katherine from Grade 1 wrote the numbers 1, 2, 3, 6 and 7 on paper and asked her Mother to continue the sequence. She thought a bit and found the solution. What numbers did she write on the positions of 11, 12 and 13? Note: the 20th number is 36. List three numbers.

More examples are available (in Estonian) at https://ylesanded.targaltinternetis.ee/.

4 Results

4.1 Preliminary Round

The feedback from teachers shows that the official digital competencies are based on studying rather than problem-solving that was central in the CyberCracker. According to our survey, 75.2% of students take part in regular Informatics lessons, and 20% had participated in Robotics classes or clubs. Interest in IT seems to grow by age: in the basic school, it was 30% and in the secondary, 50%. Problem-solving is more common among older students – 70% of the Grade 12 students claim to be able to solve their digital problems with the help of the Internet. The ability to solve cybersecurity-related problems was claimed by 50% of secondary school students and 35% of the basic school ones. 25% of the basic school students and 45–50% of the secondary ones are willing to help others to solve their IT-related problems.

The analysis of success rates in the preliminary round showed that about 17% of the participants formed the talent group who managed to solve 3/4 of the tasks (the rest typically managed just 1/4). Nature and difficulty level of the exercises proved to be very fitting for the goal. The feedback was mostly positive even if the success rate was lower – many participants mentioned learning what does the word 'effort' means. It was also mentioned that the participation was already an 'act of courage' as this type of exercises were unknown to them before. Still, only 46% of the schools that organized the preliminary round actually took part in the finals. However, the new rules applied in the next year (one-time participation only, gender balance) helped to raise the percentage – 77% of the schools holding the preliminary round reached the finals, too.

The percentages of solving the challenges were the following:

- 85% of the participants solved the easy tasks, showing that the common level of knowledge only allows solving the problems that are clearly predefined (especially with multiple choice answers).
- Intermediate tasks were attempted by 61% of the participants.
- Difficult tasks were attempted only by 32%. At the same time, the talents of Top 1–2% were able to solve most of the problems even without resorting to hints.

The analysis of the preliminary round results showed that in 2018, less skilled participants did not dare to skip exercises or use hints when facing difficulties. This is probably due to the practice in many other competitions were solving problems in the sequence is demanded – but in cybersecurity, the ability to adapt according to circumstances and one's skills is important. For example, harder problems were worth tackling because of the hints offered – thus one had to calculate the 'cost' of hints and use them if it was worthwhile. For conventional good students, this was likely too risky – but cybersecurity talents tend not to be conventional good students bogged down by rules and traditions. In the following year, the rules of the competition stated in several places that exercise skipping were allowed.

Most respondents found the exercises realistic which one of the goals was. At the same time, they were more of interest to older students. When asked about a possible rematch, the answer seemed to be related to success – 61% claimed that they were unable to reach their full potential due to lack of time and/or skills.

Notably, the feedback from teachers accented the difficulty of finding suitable female participants for the competition. A widespread stereotype among girls was that IT and cybersecurity is 'not their business' and it took considerable effort from the teachers to overcome it. Nevertheless, as seen below, they actually proved very capable team members in the final round.

4.2 Final Round

In the final round, clearly defined exercises involving Internet search were considered easy, e.g. "find the missing word", "determine if the statement is true or false" etc. On the other hand, analytical and problem-solving ones like "decrypt the cipher using the book" were considered difficult.

Comparing the success rates of different groups reveals differences between them. The groups in the table below are basic schools (BS; Grades 1–9), combined schools (CS; Grades 1–12), gymnasiums (G; secondary schools or Grades 10–12) and vocational schools (VS) (see Table 3).

Table 3. Success rates for different age groups in CyberCracker school round

Success rates	BS	CS	G	VS
Easy tasks	53%	46%	62%	57%
Intermediate tasks	21%	28%	34%	12%
Difficult and very difficult tasks	14%	33%	38%	5%

As seen from the table, gymnasiums were the most and basic schools the least successful. At the same time, the difficulties within the group were consistent, or the most difficult tasks were the same for older and younger participants – but the older Grades had more skills and creativity to cope better. So the strategies differed: basic and vocational schools focused more on easy tasks, the others on more difficult ones (yielding more points).

As mentioned, the final round demanded teams be balanced by gender. The prejudice that girls' skill and motivation level does not compete with boys proved groundless. Besides working on problems, female participants were notably good at promoting teamwork, discussing various issues with organizers and interpreting hints given. As the 4-member teams were allowed only two computers, girls and boys were notably equally represented at operating them.

5 Discussion

Today's Estonian cybersecurity talent has a 'male face', as IT and competition motivate more young men than women. Looking at girls' results in the preliminary rounds we see that while their numbers are small, their results are not much different from boys if they would have similar experiences and backgrounds. As the 2019 final round had equal numbers, the observed behavior did not differ either (there were team members more 'in control' who actually entered the answers, while the others helped to find them). Some teachers suggested that boys prefer the tasks which have one definite solution (that can be checked automatically) while girls tend to favor the ones which do not follow strict logic and contain analytical/social component. However, this suggestion lacks empirical proof so far and should be studied further in future research. Comparing skills we noticed that girls tend to lack certain technical skills and often compensate it by picking easier tasks and doing things in order (not skipping the tasks).

We found the share of potential cybersecurity talents to be around 17% - these students a. answered most questions correctly, and b. responded more in detail and also offered critical feedback to the organizers. So both skills and attitude played a role. Yet another factor was time – in the competition, success needs both creativity and speed of thinking; in real life slower speed is often acceptable if the problem-solving skills are adequate.

The CyberCracker is thus well-suited for discovering talents but is not enough to develop them. There is a community to share materials, exercises and recommendations, but again this is a voluntary effort. While many teachers are willing to learn and pass the knowledge on, this area is scarcely covered in lessons. There are no established materials, training or competitions for teachers.

The growing interest towards cybersecurity is thus left on students themselves, as the communities suitable for students are few and far away. This has led to a situation that one's interest in the topic is sometimes hidden from others – also because 'hacking' is associated with criminals and malicious activities due to media misusing the term. The experts belong to another generation, and they are active in different channels like national newspapers and portals that are not used by the youth, so the latter lack both information and role models. The problem has been somewhat alleviated by the rise of social media that has brought younger and older enthusiasts together (Facebook communities, the Craigslist portal forums, various foreign channels) and now competitions.

The talents come from various levels of success at school (from excellent to poor), making discovering them more difficult for schools. Parents can rarely help, as their knowledge of the area is typically inadequate. More aware parents may direct their children towards activities like programming or robotics that are a good springboard into cybersecurity due to similar attitudes and skillsets developed. Therefore, most cyber-talents are discovered 'on the road' when incidents happen and they get a chance to use their skills.

The number of national cybersecurity competitions is still small. The first one was organized in 2015 by the Ministry of Defence and HITSA, continuing typically on yearly basis (in 2017, TalTech and the Estonian Internet Foundation joined the initiative). Only from 2018 onwards, new initiatives have addressed various target groups – but many of them have been open competitions unrelated to schools, so only those interested will participate (sometimes, students are afraid of participating alone, or are even prohibited by parents due to the negative connotations mentioned above).

The CyberCracker is the first one directly connected to schools and organized with active participation by them. The competitions have had professional backing, so schools are not left alone to organize them – the main challenge for schools has been to find enough participants and provide adequate training for teachers and mentors. It is very important that the veterans of higher-levels competitions return to their schools as mentors to train younger hackers from their schools and community – they know the relevant paths in education, have contact in the hacker community and also are aware of the legal background. They should be supported in developing their communicative and mentoring skills and analytical abilities.

Recommendations for Estonia

Teaching cybersecurity should get national-level backing by organizing national advanced-level competitions. It should also be promoted more among local authorities – local youth should be backed to take part in not only the national Song Festival but also cybersecurity competitions.

Additional efforts are needed to promote IT-related careers among girls. Both gender-specific (clubs etc.) and mixed-gender activities are needed - the latter should provide diverse tasks that also include more social components.

Teachers need help – there is an urgent need for relevant textbooks and study aids, especially concerning the discovery of talented students. Teachers have asked for both beginner and advanced level materials, and measurable learning outcomes.

Finally, some financial aid is needed for schools to cover the costs of training and competitions to push the talent hunt at a higher level.

A Recommended Yearly Plan of Activities for Schools

- Autumn – the CyberCracker preliminary round for Grades 7–12. Identify the group of cybersecurity talents to be trained separately, form the official school team.
- Winter – the school team participates in the CyberCracker final round. The exercises should be brought back to school and introduced to other students. Some of the talents should go to other competitions like CyberSpike or Magic CTF.
- Spring – lessons of Informatics should make use of the acquired exercises. The discovered talents and competition veterans should be included in the teaching activities, as well as directed towards creating new materials and exercises.

Organizing the Competition

The preliminary round should last at least 90 min if the aim is also to test strategic thinking in choosing exercises. Otherwise, it should last longer (around 3 h) to allow for deeper-level answers.

The strategy should be discussed with students. Under the current rules, it is more advantageous to focus on intermediate and difficult tasks, as the reward is higher (even considering the risks).

It is important to develop the competition environment and automated grading to allow easier feedback and make it easier for the teachers. Right now, schools lack the ability to house their own CTF solutions that are used by the final round organizers, due to the difficulty of set it up themselves. A somewhat working solution is to use Google Forms for the preliminary round and a dedicated CTF environment for the finals.

In the final round, tasks should be more dynamic with hints costing less in penalties – it allows for better feedback about the tasks and participants. An important decision is whether time counts or not – in the former case, the first team to submit a solution gets more points (it helps in deciding the winner as draws are not possible).

6 Conclusion

While school curricula should be further developed regarding cybersecurity, competitions like the CyberCracker play an important role in finding and developing future experts of cybersecurity. What is currently lacking is the follow-up mechanism for continuing training/education for the discovered talent pool – the related programs and curricula in established universities cannot accommodate all of them. Another thing to focus on in the future is the development process of study materials and exercises which should be based on a different mindset than the mainstream ones currently used at school (creative, inventive 'hacker' thinking). Inclusion of female students should be more a priority, especially on the motivational and awareness level – they should realize that they are in fact viable candidates (the main problem is not discrimination but attitudes and self-image concerning the field).

References

1. Atan: What is CTF and how to get started! Dev.to (2019). https://dev.to/atan/what-is-ctf-and-how-to-get-started-3f04
2. Beckford, A.: The skills you need to succeed in 2020, Forbes (2018). https://www.forbes.com/sites/ellevate/2018/08/06/the-skills-you-need-to-succeed-in-2020/
3. Center for Applied Anthropology/Rakendusliku Antropoloogia keskus: Tuleviku tegija teekond startup ökosüsteemi (2018). https://media.voog.com/0000/0037/5345/files/Raport%2015.11.18.pdf
4. Esteves, J., Ramalho, E., De Haro, G.: To improve cybersecurity, think like a hacker. MIT Sloan Manag. Rev. **58**(3), 71 (2017)
5. Informatics Education in Europe: Are We All In The Same Boat? Informatics Europe (2017). http://www.informatics-europe.org/component/phocadownload/category/10-reports.html?download=60:cece-report
6. Lorenz, B.: TalTechi küberkaitseteadlane Birgy Lorenz: Eesti kooli digipädevuste hamletlik dilemma - kas arendame või klikime? Edasi.org (2019). https://edasi.org/50385/taltechi-kuberkaitseteadlane-birgy-lorenz-eesti-kooli-digipadevuste-hamletlik-dilemma-kas-arendame-voi-klikime/
7. Ministry of Economy and Communication: The Strategy of Cybersecurity 2019–2022/Majandus-ja Kommunikatsiooniministeerium. Küberjulgeoleku strateegia 2019–2022 (2019). https://www.mkm.ee/sites/default/files/kuberturvalisuse_strateegia_2019-2022.pdf
8. OECD: Computers and the Future of Skill Demand (2017). http://www.oecd.org/publications/computers-and-the-future-of-skill-demand-9789264284395-en.htm
9. OECD: The Future of Education and skills. Education 2030 (2018). http://www.oecd.org/education/2030/E2030%20Position%20Paper%20(05.04.2018).pdf
10. Ponemon: Ther Cost of CyberCrime, Accenture (2019). https://www.accenture.com/_acnmedia/pdf-96/accenture-2019-cost-of-cybercrime-study-final.pdf

11. Praxis: IKT haridus Eesti üldhariduskoolides ja lasteaedades (2017). http://www.praxis.ee/2017/05/eesti-koolid-vajavad-digihariduse-susteemsemat-korraldust/
12. The Cybersecurity Textbook for Gymnasiums 2019/Gümnaasiumi küberkaitse õpik (2019). https://web.htk.tlu.ee/digitaru/kyberkaitse/
13. The Gymnasium Curricula for CyberSecurity: Estonian Atlantic Treaty Association (EATA) Valikõppeaine "Küberkaitse". Eesti NATO Ühing (2017). https://1drv.ms/w/s!AuRLzcD9F Vl7ywlqPX-J4ewoLgIy
14. Van Niekerk, J.F., Von Solms, R.: Information security culture: a management perspective. Comput. Secur. **29**(4), 476–486 (2010)
15. Vuorikari, R., Punie, Y., Gomez, S.C., Van Den Brande, G.: DigComp 2.0: the digital competence framework for citizens. Update phase 1: The conceptual reference model (No. JRC101254). Joint Research Centre (Seville site) (2016)

Security Matters … Until Something Else Matters More: Security Notifications on Different Form Factors

Heather Molyneaux[1][✉], Elizabeth Stobert[2], Irina Kondratova[1], and Manon Gaudet[1]

[1] National Research Council Canada, 42 Dineen Drive, Fredericton, NB E3B 9W4, Canada
heather.molyneaux@nrc-cnrc.gc.ca
[2] Carleton University, 1125 Colonel by Drive, Ottawa, ON K1S 5B6, Canada

Abstract. With differing form factors and the rise of IOT devices, the nature of life and work is changing. How will these changes affect how people view their own privacy and security? Will people react differently depending on the type of device and the size of the screens on which warnings are displayed? In this study we conduct a task based scenario followed by a survey in order to gauge what young adults notice when browsing online, how they react to security warnings and cookies notifications within the task scenario and their own daily life, as well as gather other information on their usual browsing habits on different devices, and their thoughts about online security.

Keywords: Human computer interaction · Privacy · Security · Trust · Browser warnings

1 Introduction

User interfaces are changing. Screen sizes and form factors are, for the most part, shrinking. How do these changes affect how warnings are presented to users? Do these warnings change how users view their own privacy and security? Do people react differently to the same warnings depending on the type of device and the size of the screens on which warnings are displayed?

Relatively little attention has been devoted to studying the effect of screen size and the device form factor on users' responses to security warnings. In this study we were particularly interested in how young adults perceive differences in security and privacy on different form factors and their awareness of passive browser messages or warnings on different devices. Young people are a group of particular interest because they are the future workers – their beliefs and habits have direct impact on the future of workplace privacy and security systems designs.

Security and privacy are topics of interest to both computer security experts and novice computer users alike [1]. However, even though many users are interested in protecting their own privacy and security online, users still have difficulty making decisions when faced with browser warnings, app permissions, and software update notifications.

© Springer Nature Switzerland AG 2020
A. Moallem (Ed.): HCII 2020, LNCS 12210, pp. 189–205, 2020.
https://doi.org/10.1007/978-3-030-50309-3_13

We draw upon the current research on user reactions to browser warnings and security messages on mobile and desktop computers to inform our own research. Our study design combines both observations in a simple user task as well as a self-reported survey asking the same participants to reflect on their mobile vs. desktop and laptop browsing habits and their attitudes towards security and privacy on those devices.

2 Background

Even though many users are interested in protecting their own privacy and security online, users still have difficulty making decisions when faced with browser warnings, app permissions, and software update notifications. Molyneaux, Kondratova and Stobert [2] describe four factors that affect users' online decision-making: the role of browser warning messages and alert design; habituation; awareness; and screen size and form factor.

2.1 Browser Warning Messages and Alert Design

What messages say and how they say it has an influence on how people react. Design is one factor to consider when examining why users ignore browser warnings. In a 2015 study Fagan et al. found that annoyance and confusion over update messages lead users towards noncompliance – even participants who self-reported caring about security and privacy were still hesitant to apply software updates [3]. What the message says can affect the user. Carpenter et al. [4] found that the term "hazard" rather than "warning" or "caution" was the most effective wording of a warning message. Timing is also an important factor in privacy notices and user recall. Participants who were shown a privacy notice while using an app were more likely to recall the content of that notice [5].

2.2 Habituation

Once people see a certain type of message its effectiveness may decline; habituation occurs after only a few exposures to a type of warning, and warnings become "seen" but no longer perceived [6]. Studies show that participants faced with familiar looking messages, such as those resembling an End User License Agreement (EULA) automatically click on "accept" during interruptions typical of EULA – a finding that has repercussions not just with EULAs but also online safety and privacy [7].

2.3 Awareness

Users may not even be aware of some currently employed security measures [8]. Likewise users may not be able to identify phishing attempts even when primed to identify them [9], leading to most people having a high risk of succumbing to phishing attacks.[10]. Greater awareness of phishing threats, through training, or education on things like the necessity of stronger passwords could, in conjunction with other methods, such as detection tools, build user resilience to security and privacy threats [11, 12].

2.4   Screen Size and Form Factor

Awareness of security risks on smaller devices such as smartphones, is a growing concern for cybersecurity researchers. Security awareness on personal computers (PC) in user studies was higher than mobile platform awareness levels. Researchers note that mobile users require a different set of security awareness skills than those needed for PC [13]. At the same time, users on mobile devices are three times more vulnerable to phishing attacks [14] and a high percentage of mobile browsers do not consistently show security warnings. When warnings are shown visibility is often reduced because of limited screen size compared to desktop or laptop computers [15, 16]. Such indicators or warnings may not show at all, or might be distorted in mobile browsers because the edges of pop-ups sometimes extend beyond the side of the display, or buttons can overlap text.

In our study we examine the effect of screen size and the device form factor on users' responses to security warnings. In particular we are interested in how young adults perceive differences in security and privacy on different form factors and their awareness of passive browser messages or warnings on different devices by conducting a task based scenario followed by a survey to gather other information on their usual browsing habits on different devices, and their thoughts about online security.

3   Methodology

In order to study the effect of form factor on user attention, we devised a user study based on a browsing task over two different devices. We were interested in seeing if users would notice cookie notifications, and if so, how they would interact with the notification, as they are a type of online notification that is ubiquitous. The study consisted of a think aloud method followed by a survey, approved by the National Research Council's Research Ethics Board.

Users were asked to look up movie reviews on an iPhone (4" screen, Safari) and a laptop (14" screen, Chrome). Tasks for the two conditions were framed as common scenarios in order to ground them within a real-life experience. Since factors such as habituation are magnified by the fact that security is often a users' secondary task [17], we were careful to choose a scenario that would frame the security warnings as a secondary task to avoid priming the participants, even though that studies have shown that priming and warnings do not influence the degree to which participants give out information such as personal data [18]. Users were given scenarios that involved friends asking their opinion on going to see a movie, requiring them to look up movie reviews on a particular movie review website. The users were asked to follow the think aloud protocol, whereby they were instructed to "talk while you are completed the task, say whatever you are looking at, thinking, doing, and feeling." Also participants were asked to read the tasks out loud before performing them and the think aloud protocol, in order for them to get used to talking out loud for the study.

The website www.moviereviews.com was chosen for this task because at the time of the study the site displayed a cookie notification on both mobile and laptop/desktop sites. We were interested in seeing if the participants noticed the notification while doing the task and how they would react to it. On the laptop/desktop interface the website also displayed a "not secure" TLS warning indicator to the left of the URL search bar in the Chrome browser.

Participants were divided into 2 groups – one group who completed the iPhone task first, and the other group who started with the laptop task. This was done to account for any order effects that might occur. They were asked to follow the think aloud method whereby participants were instructed to talk out loud while completing the task, and to verbalized what they are seeing, thinking, doing and feeling. A researcher took observational notes, capturing the participants' search path and verbalization.

We coupled the task with the survey to find out users usual online behaviours on cellphones and laptops/desktops and investigate how they react to (or are habituated to ignore) different notices on websites in their everyday browsing. The user study was immediately followed by the survey which captured demographic information, as well as baseline information on the frequency with which users performed certain tasks on their phone and laptops, followed by questions pertaining to the cookie notification displayed on the website during the task, and participants' regular online behaviors when they encounter browsers warnings during searching tasks.

In particular, for the user study, we were interested in seeing if the participants noticed the cookie notification banner at the top of the laptop website page as well as the cookie notification banner on the phone. We were also interested in whether there were any differences depending on task order, computer literacy levels, education level, gender etc.

We were also interested in seeing the differences in everyday online browsing tasks with different devices (if participants used the different devices for different tasks), and the study participants' explanations for those differences, in particular, if the rational for the differences related to privacy, security and trust. We also used questions in the survey as a way to validate the data gathered during the task and observation, and as an additional means to gather information on the participants' usual reactions to online warnings, and any additional privacy and security issues they wanted to discuss in the text response portions of the survey.

Participants were recruited from a local university campus. This was done to focus on young people's habits and beliefs in order to reflect on how these habits and beliefs have impact on future design for privacy, security and trust. Users were recruited through posters which were displayed on bulletin boards in common areas on the campus. Participants were all between the ages of 19-29, and all participants were students. The study included undergraduates, graduate students and recent graduates. The study took place over a 5 week period with a total of 40 participants.

Quantitative responses were calculated for percentages (single response answers) and frequencies (multiple responses). Qualitative responses were coded through a process of inductive coding whereby the researchers grouped comments in the task and written comments in the survey corresponding with noticed cookie notifications on the laptop, on the phone and noticing the TLS warning message on the laptop. The participants' responses to a question about their usual reaction to pop-ups was also coded to show the frequency of different reactions according to device (smartphone or laptop).

4   Findings

This section of the paper first reports on the participants demographics from the survey followed by the responses on the frequency of various types of online tasks users report doing on their own smartphones and laptops or desktops. This data is discussed then contextualized using responses to a open text follow up question asking participants to discuss differences in their online behaviors on the two types of devices, and responses related to security and privacy are discussed. Next the findings from the task scenario are discussed, including the user path, their response to the cookies notification on both forms and if they notices the TLS warning on the laptop condition. Responses to questions in the survey gauging differences in the task and real life scenarios are also reported and discussed. Finally we will discuss the five main considerations emerging from the task and survey concerning browsing online with the two form factors: Convenience, context, privacy, security, and trust.

4.1   Demographics

Participants were asked how they self-identify as well as about their current work situation, and the highest level of institutional education that they have completed. A slim majority of participants identified as female (55%), with 43% identifying as male, and one as transgendered. Most of the participants noted they are currently students 80% with many noting that they also work (15 part time and 11 full time). Everyone in the study reported having a high school diploma or above, with most of the participants in the study (53%) reported have completed some post-secondary courses, with 18% noting they had a post-secondary degree and 10% having a graduate degree. We also had the participants self-evaluate their technical literacy skills at the end of the survey. Everyone assessed themselves as average or above, with 30% assessing themselves as average, 48% as experienced and 22% as experts.

4.2   Frequency of Browsing and Other Online Tasks

Participants were also asked about the frequency with which they browsed the internet with a laptop or desktop. Most of the participants (68%) reported browsing the internet with a laptop or a desktop frequently – on a daily basis. When asked how frequently they used a smartphone to browse the internet even more (85%) reported daily use.

In addition to general questions about frequency of browsing, we also asked participants to report the frequency with which they completed certain tasks on each device according to a 5 point Likert scale with responses: Never, Rarely- once a month or less, Sometimes- once a week, Often – several times a week and Frequently-daily. Participants reported completing tasks more frequently on phones rather than on laptops or desktops in all categories including searching online (68%, 58%), SMS (83%, 30%), email (68%, 45%) IM (83%, 28%), banking (10%, 3%), shopping (0%, 0%), watching videos (60%, 38%) and buying tickets for movies or concerts (0%, 0%). (For all values see Figs. 1 and 2).

When asked about any differences in their normal browsing behaviors on the different types of devices the participants mentioned security and privacy issues surrounding the

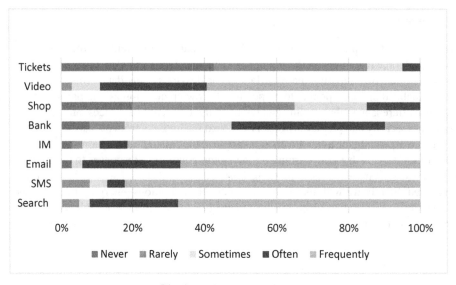

Fig. 1. Tasks on smartphone

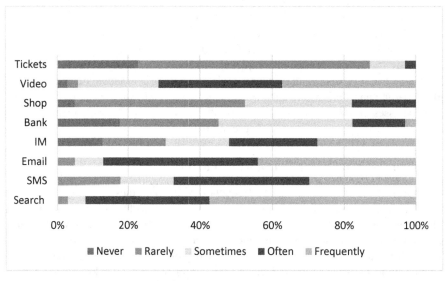

Fig. 2. Tasks on laptop/desktop

nature of the task, or described the affordances of the form factor itself. Some reported differences due to convenience of apps and quick response time on phone over the larger form factor.

Half of participants (50%) reported differences in tasks because of the availability, accessibility and convenience of using the phones, with quicker start up times and user friendly apps that make social media, banking and other tasks easy.

- "Sometimes I watch videos on my phone more because it's more mobile, banking on my phone is more convenient, can't text with my laptop, social media apps are better/more convenient." (P10)
- "My smartphone is more accessible. There are apps that take me straight to my social media. Also, start-up time is instantaneous" (P15)
- "For banking and buying movie tickets, it would be easier to use the mobile app as the UI is easier to locate and you don't need to type any detail until you get to personal data. I am using fingerprint to banking app so I don't need to type the IDs and the password for it." (P32)

A quarter of the participants (25%) mentioned privacy, security and trust issues as the reason for reported differences in tasks.

- "I do not trust banking as much on my smartphone as I do on my laptop. Due to the smartphones portability it is much easier to lose/steal which makes me anxious." (P5)
- "I find it easier to do banking on my laptop, I have my credit card and bank card numbers saved in a virtual keychain and I don't have it memorized, I don't have those card numbers saved on my phone." (P19)

Others spoke about issues of security when using the different devices, although these commons varied amongst the participants. Thoughts about security and privacy on the different devices also varied according to context.

- "On smartphones some tasks like banking, checking emails and instant messaging are easier and accessible faster than by laptop. However, online shopping I do more on laptop because it seems more 'secure'" (P35)
- "I normally use my computer to study or work on so I don't really open my social media accounts on it. I pretty much only text on my phone, mainly because the computer screen is too big and I don't like imagining people reading my texts. I also never open my bank account on my computer for privacy. Since I use more my phone I open videos less often on my computer." (P36A)

Some participants indicated a preference towards the user of smaller screens for online searches in public. Although smaller devices are more vulnerable to loss, they indicated that they would be preferable to larger screens in order to avoid potential shoulder surfing.

Participants' attitudes toward convenience and privacy, security and trust were varied. Mobile devices were used more frequently for more than social media, searching and IM tasks. A large number of participants indicated that they use their mobile devices for activities requiring credit card information, such as banking, shopping and buying movie and concert tickets.

4.3 User Task

The task scenarios presented the participants with situations which could realistically occur – a friend texts on the phone asking the participant's thoughts on a movie; or, in the laptop or desktop scenario, a friend sends the participant a message over Facebook while they are finishing up a term paper. Participants were asked to find a movie review on a particular website, chosen because both the desktop and mobile versions of the site contain the same cookie notification. The cookie notifications were passive notifications in that the participant could scroll down the page and read information without interacting with the notification. In addition to the cookies notification, in the laptop condition the website URL bar presents the user with a TLS warning.

Participants would read the task, open the website and either not notice the cookie notifications or they would read the text and not take action, instead scrolling down to complete the task. A few participants (5%) did agree to the cookie notification even though they did not know what they were agreeing to. Only one participant opened the privacy statement by clicking on the "more info" button, and this was due to the difficulty they faced in looking up the movie review – they clicked more info looking for more information on the website itself, and then quickly closed the window when they realized it was the privacy policy (P26).

The user task path of participants in the different conditions was similar (Figs. 3, 4), even though we initially thought that those with the iphone task first would be more likely to notice the cookies message on the laptop, since the cookies notification is more prominent in the iPhone condition and those completing the iPhone task first might be primed to see the notification on the laptop.

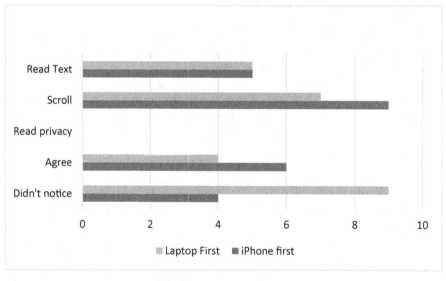

Fig. 3. User path on iPhone

4.4 Noticing Cookies

Overall more people noticed the cookie notification on the iPhone (65%) than the laptop (47.5%), and participants were much more likely to click "agree" on the iPhone (22.5%);

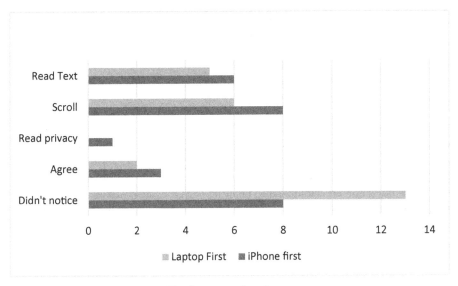

Fig. 4. User path on laptop

although a few participants did click agree on the laptop (12.5%). A Chi-square test of independence was performed to examine the relationship between seeing the cookies notification and the order in which the tasks were performed. The relationship between these variable was not statistically significant in either the phone first task $X = .32$, p > .01 or the laptop first task $X = .21$, p > .01. Task order did not seem to have much effect on the user path, with a few minor exceptions noted by the participants in the qualitative survey responses.

- "I didn't read or agree the warning on the phone because I had already done it on the laptop. However, I almost never read or agree with those when using my devices." (P29)

More people reported not noticing the cookie notification on the laptop (53%) than on the iPhone (35%). The small size of the screen on the smartphone made it easier to notice the notification even though not all users in the study reported noticing it on the smartphone.

In our study we found that majority of participants either ignored the notification, or did not even notice it.

- "I am so used to cookie and browsing terms popping up that they barely register anymore." (P3)
- "Cookies policy is always everywhere now which is annoying but I generally just ignore it." (P21)

A smaller group of participants saw the notification and clicked on the accept button without knowing what they were accepting.

- "just because... to get it out of the way" (P2)
- "asking if I accept any terms – every time I always accept I don't even read which is probably odd but I do it anyway" (P36)

When the browser message design resembles something the users are familiar with they seem to make automatic decisions based on their previous experiences with similar messages. The high prevalence of ignoring the message or not even seeing the message speaks to the fact that these cookie notifications are everywhere online and most of the users in our study are habituated to ignoring such messages – either automatically scrolling immediately after seeing them or not even seeing them in the first place. A small number of participants were habituated to agreeing to the terms of the cookies notification without reading. Screen size seemed to play a small role, as more of the participants agreed to cookies on the iPhone than on the laptop.

4.5 Noticing the TLS Warning

	Didn't notice	Noticed
Female	19	3
Male	11	6
Other	1	0
High school	7	1
Some post-secondary	15	6
Post-secondary degree	6	1
Graduate degree	3	1
Average computer skills	9	3
Experienced computer skills	14	2
Expert computer skills	8	1

Fig. 5. Noticing laptop "Not Secure" message in relation to gender, education and level of computer expertise

Only nine of the study participants noticed the insecure browser warning in the laptop condition. Six of the nine participants who noticed the TLS warning expressed concern over the notice, one just read it without comment (P35), one sarcastically said "that's always fun" (P33), and another read the not secure message but decided not to worry about it (P15) (Fig. 5).

Of those who expressed concern over the TLS warning, one noted that they would not enter sensitive information on the website, another said they would have to be careful if they were to order anything for the website. Others felt there might be some "bad stuff" (P21) on the site or that the site was "iffy." (P27) One participant stated that they would avoid a website like this unless they really needed to go visit the site, which indicated that they would use a potentially harmful website even if they were suspicious of the site.

- Searches for the movie in search bar says "not secure. Wonderful" and "don't put anything sensitive in" (P2)
- "I saw that the website was not secure on the laptop – I would generally avoid these websites unless 100% necessary" (P5)
- "not secure … I'm always a bit sketched out when it pops up unsecure." (P6)
- "this site is not secure so I will have to pay attention if I order anything from this site" (P18)
- "And now I'm realizing that the website is not secure for laptop. Might get some bad stuff." (P21)
- "is not a secure website, which is kind of iffy" (P27)

Men were more likely to notice the TLS warning message than women. Higher self-reported computer literacy levels did not lead to users being more prone to noticing the TLS warning message – in fact, those identifying as experts were slightly less likely to notice the security warning.

This group of participants, those who noticed the not secure message, were not more likely to notice the cookie notification – one participant didn't notice it on either device, another didn't notice it on the laptop, but did on the phone and 3 users in the subgroup didn't notice it on the phone but did notice it on the laptop. Only 2 of the 9 were from the group who did the smartphone task first – it could be that those who were in the laptop first condition were more conscious of the TLS warning message because of task order, but this observation comes from a small subsample.

4.6 Differences in Task and Real Life Behavior

Participants were asked "If there are any differences in how you reacted during the task and how you would normally react please let us know below." Researchers initially coded responses as no difference and then divided up the responses indicating that there was a difference in behavior according to themes.

27 participants (67.5%) indicated that there was no difference between how they reacted during the task and how they would normally behave. Of those 27 responses, 14 participants wrote down that they would react in the same way, and 13 participants left the text box blank, wrote "N/A" or "0". 13 participants noted specific differences in their reactions. Of the 13, 4 stated differences due to nature of the task (that they were unfamiliar with the specific website for movie reviews) and observation by the researcher – these factors were not related to the cookie notification itself, but rather the participants lamented slow task time due to unfamiliarity with the device, the website itself or because of nervousness attributable to being observed. 5 participants stated they would react to the cookie notification differently on their own device because of privacy, security and trust issues (for example, one person who noticed the not secure warning on the laptop stated they wouldn't have stayed on that site on their own device). However, 4 of the participants noted that they didn't agree to the cookie notification within the task but would have on their own device if the notification was bugging them, or in the way of completing their task.

These findings suggest that accepting cookies, potentially without reading terms, might also occur more frequently when users are browsing on their own devices. Users are more likely to accept cookies if it is a condition of completing their task - if the notice interrupts task at hand, by taking up too much of the screen or by impeding navigation altogether.

- "This is normally how I react to pop-ups like this, if I can browse with(out) interacting with it I will not touch it" (P7)

One participant noted two criteria for accepting cookies: if the notification gets in the way of the task and if the site looks reputable. This indicates that trust is an important part of the decision to accept cookies notifications on websites.

- "I will accept cookies without reading details if 1) I really want to read things and 2) the site looks legitimate (usually news sites only)" (P6)

4.7 Usual Reaction to Pop-Ups

Participants were also asked an open text question about how they usually react to pop-ups when they are browsing on their own mobile devices as well as a separate question asking how they normally act when browsing on their own laptop or desktop. Participants employed various strategies when faced with cookie notifications, pop-ups and other browser warnings while on their personal devices. We categorized these strategies as: Close or ignore; close or ignore unless there was no way to finish task; Read the pop-up and decide what to do based on the content of the message and the reputation of the website; leave the website and try to finish the task on another site; and accept the message (generally were referring to cookie notifications). A few participants mentioned using Ad Blocker on their personal laptops – this was also coded for our analysis.

Most of the participants reported that they would normally close or ignore the pop-up on their laptops and on their phones. When responses asking about how users normally deal with pop-ups on their own devices, 29 participants responded that they employed the same strategy for dealing with pop-ups on both their laptops and phones (mainly the close or ignore strategy).

Interestingly enough, more people (20%) reported being more likely to carefully read pop-ups on their laptops. This is perhaps due to the fact that many of the participants reported using their laptops or desktops as work devices, and therefore they are more cautious when on these devices.

Screen size also played a role in how the participants usually reacted to pop-ups and other notifications when on their own devices. When asked how they normally reacted to pop-ups while on their own phone participant 2 responded "Really depends on the site, I try to turn it off if possible, and when it comes to pop-ups related to cookies I'd usually accept if the pop-up takes too much space." (P22) When asked "how do you normally react to pop-ups when you are browsing on your own laptop or desktop computer" the same participant stated "I ignore it more cause the screen space on a laptop is larger" (P2)

4.8 Form Factor Considerations

The user task and survey revealed five main considerations accounting for the differences in their use of cell phones compared to laptops and desktops. These themes included convenience, context, privacy security and trust.

Convenience was an important consideration; for example, users reported differences in tasks on different devices due to differences in the ease of use of the devices and the types of tasks they are completing. Phones were reported more frequently used for most of the tasks because of the portability of the device and ease of access. Many tasks can be done through mobile applications which open quickly and are often well designed to ensure greater ease of user.

- "...simply because I use my phone more frequently, and it is more convenient to access the information on my phone." (P14)
- "Banking is more convenient on my phone. I may shop more on my laptop because I can open many tabs for many options, so it's more convenient. Searching for information is more convenient on phone cause I can open the device instantly" (P22)
- "I use my phone more for social media usage, etc. because it is more convenient" (P39)

One participant discussed differences in device usage depending on location, with a preference to "use my laptop to do my everyday tasks while I'm at home or in the library. Otherwise I use my phone to do tasks if it's necessary or sometimes it's more convenient to do tasks using the phone I use" (P3).

The *context* of device use is also important to consider. Twenty-six participants in the study reported working full or part time. In the comments section asking for more information on differences better tasks performed on the two types of devices some users described a division based larger on "work" and "play"

- "Smart phone is very handy and convenient to carry around. It is faster to start it. Use for quick checks. Laptop is bigger and easier to type so use for documents, work, watch movies with others" (P26)
- "My laptop is mostly for professional work such as assignments or answering emails whereas my phone is most for social media purpose and texting" (P11)

Responses about privacy in our survey were varied and do not necessarily line up with attitudes found in previous studies [19]. Some of the participants in our study considered the smaller screen size of the phone as offering increased privacy because of concerns about shoulder surfing, for example. These examples may indicate a shifting landscape of trust in devices.

- "I normally use my computer to study or work on so I don't really open my social media accounts on it. I pretty much only text on my phone, mainly because the computer screen is too big and I don't like imagining people reading my texts. I also never open my bank account on my computer for privacy. Since I use more my phone I open videos less often on my computer." (P36)

Security was also discussed by the users in our study as a determining factor in the types of online activities they engage in on various devices. While the participant mentioned issues of privacy as their rationale for using their cell phone for banking, others stated that they felt the smartphone is less secure than their laptop.

- "I try not to make online purchases or do any banking on my phone because it is less secure than on my laptop in my private home network." (P3)

While some mentioned not making online purchases on their phones for reasons Chin et al. mention [19], others preferred using the phone for information sensitive tasks like banking, but not for other tasks such as online shopping.

- "On smartphones some tasks like banking, checking emails and instant messaging are easier and accessible faster than by laptop. However, online shopping I do more on laptop because it seems more "secure" (P35)

Trust was another concept participants wrote about in the survey. Reeder et al. found that users relied on site reputation, which was a major factor in them proceeding through warnings on trusted sites [20]. This concept of trust in decision making holds true to the beliefs of the study participants, with some participants trusting the security of performing tasks on one device over another.

- "I do not trust banking as much on my smartphone as I do on my laptop. Due to the smartphones portability it is much easier to lose/steal which makes me anxious" (P5)

However, our findings indicate that more participants reported frequent banking on their smartphones over laptops and desktops – some citing convenience of banking applications for the phone. It is possible that they place trust in the security of the banking applications.

Users asked about their normal behavior when acting on a pop-up notification general reported ignoring such messages those who discussed the possibility of accepting messages were careful to note that they would only do so if they trusted the website.

- "Whether or not I would agree depends on the site typically -> e.g. if it's something a trust or regularly used. In this case I agreed to the mobile one because it was quite large and obtrusive" (P9)
- When answering the questions about normal responses to pop-ups from both own phone and own laptop, one participant noted "I close them or ignore them, unless they are from a website that I trust" (P30)

5   Discussion and Conclusions

Habituation was a major theme in many of the findings of research papers examining user responses to browser warnings, and it was also a theme in our study. Many users are accustomed to entering certain personal information on a daily basis for a variety of reasons, or are asked to consent to a variety of consent dialogs, such as end user license agreement (EULA) dialogues, or cookie notifications.

In our study we found that the majority of participants either did not even notice the cookies notification or that they ignored the notification entirely. Most of the participants did not notice the TLS warning warnings in the laptop task. Why is this an important issue? When prompted for information in a way that seems familiar to them users may fill in personal information and consent without knowing first what they are consenting to, and how their information is going to be used.

This was an in lab study – participants were not completing the tasks on their own equipment; as a result they might be more conscious of, and react differently to browser warning (not secure) on their own laptops, and might not be so quick to ignore or click accept on cookie notifications on their own machine. With these issues in mind we designed the task as a scenario where the participants are imagining they are at home on their own devices. We also included questions in the survey asking participants if they would behave differently on their own devices – for the most part people reported they would behave in the same or a similar manner.

We chose this approach because of the richness of the data it allowed us to collect, giving us deep insight into participants' choices and decision-making process. However, this approach limited the quantity of data we were able to collect. The small sample size meant an even smaller number noticed cookies and the TLS warning message. However, our analysis gave us insight into how users have been habituated to such notifications and have adopted different strategies, including ignoring all notifications unless action needs to be taken in order for them to meet their goals.

In the context of the simple task in this study, ignoring warnings or messages or accepting them without understanding the implications may not have such immediately understood consequences; however it does leave users open to attacks from malicious threat actors. And if these types of habituated behaviors extend to future tasks, such as a failure to read the terms and conditions on a standard agreement for travel in an autonomous car, this could lead to possibly life threatening conditions.

While some individuals would pay greater attention when the stakes are higher, previous articles have found that even when the user's own private information, such as banking information, is at stake there still seems to be a trend towards accepting terms even if warning pages are present [8].

While it is not currently feasible to examine habituation in user behavior in future technology scenarios – the novelty of something like a user agreement for rising in autonomous vehicles would be cause for participants to read something like that in detail and it would take time for users to become habituated to such messages - it is important to keep current studies of habituation in mind when designing end user license agreements for future technologies as well as designing alerts and notifications related to privacy and security.

Our study showed that there are differences in the tasks people do on different form factors as a result of five considerations: convenience, context, privacy, security and trust. These considerations have implications for technology design. For example, several study participants reported not wanting to do tasks they considered sensitive on their phones, demonstrating a belief that one type of device is more secure than the other.

These beliefs could carry over to future technological design, whereby users may place more trust on devices that have larger screens or devices that are in their home, which could have broader implications.

References

1. Jorgensen, Z., et al.: Dimensions of risk in mobile applications: a user study. In: CODASPY 2015, 2–4 March 2015, San Antonio, Texas, pp. 49–60 (2015)
2. Molyneaux, H., Kondratova, I., Stobert, E.: Understanding perceptions: user responses to browser warning messages. In: Moallem, A. (ed.) HCII 2019. LNCS, vol. 11594, pp. 164–175. Springer, Cham (2019). https://doi.org/10.1007/978-3-030-22351-9_11
3. Fagan, M., Khan, M., Buck, R.: A study of user's experiences and beliefs about software update messages. Comput. Hum. Behav. **51**, 504–519 (2015)
4. Carpenter, S., Zhu, F., Kolimi, S.: Reducing online identity disclosure using warnings. Appl. Ergon. **45**(5), 1337–1342 (2014)
5. Balebako, R., Schaub, F., Adjerid, I., Acquisti, A., Cranor, L.F.: The impact of timing on the Salience of smartphone app privacy notices. In: SPSM 2015, 12 October 2015, Denver, Colorado, pp. 63–74 (2015)
6. Anderson, B.B., Jenkins, J.L., Vance, A., Kirwan, C.B., Eargle, D.: Your memory is working against you: how eye tracking and memory explain habituation to security warnings. Decis. Support Syst. **92**, 3–13 (2016)
7. Böhme, R., Köpsell, S.: Trained to accept? a field experiment on consent dialogs. In: CHI 2010, 10–15 April, Atlanta, Georgia, pp. 2403–2406 (2010)
8. Schechter, S., Dhamija, R., Ozment, A., Fischer, I.: The emperor's new security indicators: an evaluation of website authentication and the effect of role playing on usability studies. In: IEE Symposium on Security (2007)
9. Alsharnouby, M., Alaca, F., Chiasson, S.: Why phishing still works: user strategies for combating phishing attacks. Int. J. Hum Comput Stud. **82**(10), 69–82 (2015)
10. Iuga, C., Nurse, Jason R.C., Erola, A.: Baiting the hook: factors impacting susceptibility to phishing attacks. Hum.-centric Comput. Inf. Sci. **6**(1), 1–20 (2016). https://doi.org/10.1186/s13673-016-0065-2
11. Purkait, S., Kumar De., S, Suar, D.: An empirical investigation of the factors that influence internet user's ability to correctly identify a phishing website. Inf. Manage. Comput. Secur. **22**(3), 194–234 (2014)
12. Mamonov, S., Renbunan-Fich, R.: The impact of information security threat awareness on privacy-protective behaviors. Comput. Hum. Behav. **83**, 32–44 (2018)
13. Bitton, R., Finkelshtein, A., Sidi, L., Puzis, R., Rokach, L.: Taxonomy of mobile users' security awareness. Comput. Secur. **73**, 266–293 (2018)
14. Goel, D., Jain, A.K.: Mobile phishing attacks and defense mechanisms: state of art and open research challenges. Comput. Secur. **73**, 519–544 (2018)
15. Shah, R., Patil, K.: Evaluating effectiveness of mobile browser security warnings. ICTACT J. Commun. Technol. **7**(3), 1373–1378 (2016)
16. Virvilis, N., Tsalis, N., Mylonas, A., Gritzalis, D.: Mobile devices: a phisher's paradise. In: 2014 11th International Conference on Security and Cryptography (SECRYPT), pp. 1–9. IEEE, August 2014
17. Whitten, A., Tygar, J.D.: Why johnny can't encrypt: a usability case study of PGP 5.0. In: Proceedings of the 8th USENIX Security Symposium, August 1999 (1999)
18. Junger, M., Montoya, L., Overink, F.-J.: Priming and warnings are not effective to prevent social engineering attacks. Comput.-Hum. Behav. **66**, 75–87 (2017)

19. Chin, E., Felt, A.P, Sekar, V., Wagner, D.: Measuring user confidence in smartphone security and privacy. In: Symposium on Usable Privacy and Security (SOUPS), 11–13 July, Washington DC, pp. 1–16 (2012)
20. Reeder, R., et al.: An experience sampling study of user reactions to browser warnings in the field. In: Proceedings of the 2018 CHI Conference on Human Factors in Computing Systems. ACM (2018)

A New Hope: Human-Centric Cybersecurity Research Embedded Within Organizations

Phillip L. Morgan[1,2](✉) ⓘ, Phoebe M. Asquith[1,2] ⓘ, Laura M. Bishop[1,2] ⓘ,
George Raywood-Burke[1,2] ⓘ, Adam Wedgbury[1] ⓘ, and Kevin Jones[1]

[1] Airbus, The Quadrant, Celtic Springs Business Park, Newport NP10 8FZ, UK
{phillip.morgan.external,phoebe.p.asquith.external,
adam.wedgbury,kevin.jones}@airbus.com
[2] Human Factors Excellence Research Group, School of Psychology, Cardiff University,
Tower Building, 70 Park Place, Cardiff CF10 3AT, UK
{morganphil,asquithpm,bishoplm2,raywood-burkeg}@cardiff.ac.uk

Abstract. Humans are and have been the weakest link in the cybersecurity chain
(e.g., [1–3]). Not all systems are adequately protected and even for those that are,
individuals can still fall prey to cyber-attack attempts (e.g., phishing, malware,
ransomware) that occasionally break through, and/or engage in other cyber risky
behaviors (e.g., not adequately securing devices) that put even the most secure systems at risk. Such susceptibility can be due to one or a number of factors, including
individual differences, environmental factors, maladaptive behaviors, and influence techniques. This is particularly concerning at an organizational level where
the costs of a successful cyber-attack can be colossal (e.g., financial, safety, rep-
utational). Cyber criminals' intent on infiltrating organization accounts/networks
to inflict damage, steal data, and/or make financial gains will continue to try and
exploit these human vulnerabilities unless we are able to act fast and do something about them. Is there any hope for human resistance? We argue that technological solutions alone rooted in software and hardware will not win this battle.
The 'human' element of any digital system is as important to its enduring security posture. More research is needed to better understand human cybersecurity
vulnerabilities within organizations. This will inform the development of methods (including those rooted in HCI) to decrease cyber risky and enhance cyber
safe decisions and behaviors: to fight back, showing how humans, with the right
support, can be the best line of cybersecurity defense.

In this paper, we assert that in order to achieve the highest positive impactful
benefits from such research efforts, more human-centric cybersecurity research
needs to be conducted with expert teams embedded within industrial organizations
driving forward the research. This cannot be an issue addressed through laboratory-
based research alone. Industrial organizations need to move towards more holistic
– human- and systems- centric – cybersecurity research and solutions that will
create safer and more secure employees and organizations; working in harmony
to better defend against cyber-attack attempts. One such example is the Airbus
Accelerator in Human-Centric Cyber Security (H2CS), which is discussed as a
case study example within the current paper.

Keywords: Cybersecurity · Cyber psychology · Human factors

© Springer Nature Switzerland AG 2020
A. Moallem (Ed.): HCII 2020, LNCS 12210, pp. 206–216, 2020.
https://doi.org/10.1007/978-3-030-50309-3_14

1 Why Are Humans Regarded as the Weakest Link in Cybersecurity?

1.1 Cybersecurity Incidents with Humans as a Cause

There is a proliferation and increasing sophistication of cyber-attack attempts targeted at individuals and many of these are designed to gain access to accounts and systems within the organizations they work for. In 2018, over 53,000 financial gain motivated cybersecurity incidents were reported across only 65 countries [4]. During the same year more than 990 million records were exposed due to human error [5], and phishing email rates increased 250%, representing slightly more than one out of every 200 emails received by users [6].

Login details and passwords were stolen from Sony Pictures in 2015, allowing fraudsters to hack-in. A key cause: employees clicking on fake links [7]. The Pentagon network breach, also in 2015, was in part caused by employees being lured by links within malevolent emails masquerading as genuine communications. Staff not accepting urgent updates and non-regular scans of websites were cited as a key cause for the personal data of 157, 000 TalkTalk customers being stolen in 2016. There are many other infamous examples, including breaches at LinkedIn [8], Marriott [9], Equifax [10], and Yahoo [11]. These are just some high-profile examples with human vulnerabilities often being exploited by cyber criminals' intent at infiltrating organizations to inflict damage, steal data, and/or make financial gains.

The extent of the problem paints a picture where, at first blush, it seems that cyber-attack methods targeted at humans have a much higher than acceptable chance of success, with potentially colossal implications for employees and the organizations they work for. This is in many cases despite positive steps taken by many organizations such as cybersecurity training and other awareness-based interventions aimed at informing and, in some cases, educating employees to be more cyber safe. However, these alone do not seem to be the solution to mitigating human susceptibility to scams and other malicious attempts to gain access to organization accounts and systems [12]. We suggest that a better understanding of underlying human vulnerabilities at the individual level is needed such that bespoke (not 'one-size-fits-all') interventions can be developed. And, that it is especially important to develop, test (and in some cases improve and retest) and implement these within the context of organizational settings *with* employees who are meant to benefit from them the most.

1.2 Why Are Humans Seemingly so Vulnerable to Cyber-Attack Attempts?

In order to understand why humans are, on occasion, vulnerable to cyber-attack attempts at work, we need to consider a range of factors that go beyond risk and risky decision making. These include *cognitive factors* such as awareness, perception, understanding, and knowledge, *environmental* (including organizational) *factors* such as security culture, and, factors that are likely to increase maladaptive behaviors such as work pressures and stresses (e.g., time constraints, high workload).

Some of these factors can be grouped into *perception of security risk*. Examples include: level of information and cybersecurity knowledge; psychological ownership of work devices; threat appraisal factors; and experience(s) of a previous cyber breach. The lower a person scores on such dimensions, the higher the risk they present to the cyber-security integrity of the organization. Incorrect or suboptimal perceptions can negatively influence cyber decisions and behavior [12–15]). Others are *security culture and awareness* factors and are related to attitudes that are formed within and about workplaces [16]. Attitudes are multidimensional, and influenced by, for example, actions and behaviors of others (e.g., 'we all do it so therefore it is okay', 'no-one does anything about it so therefore it must be fine'), ability (e.g., technical expertise or lack of, knowledge of social factors), and motivation (e.g., job satisfaction, desire to work within and/or excel in the same company). The more a person adheres to an organizational cultural that does not engender cyber-safe actions and behaviors, and the less motivated they are about their job and/or role in the organization, the more likely they are to engage in unsafe cyber behaviors.

Heuristics and biases in decision making are also likely to increase human vulnerability to succumbing to cyber-attack attempts, and people are far from immune to these when at work. Examples include: relying more on information that comes to mind easily (e.g., check email sender details) and missing other possibly very important information (e.g., a suspicious hyperlink) (*availability heuristic*); making decisions based on the way information is framed (e.g., the system is 95% safe – positive wording, versus the system is 5% unsafe – negative wording) (*framing effect*); continuing to invest into something that is unlikely to result in success in order to try and avoid failure or blame (*sunk-cost effect*); and making emotional decisions based upon fear, threat, or panic (e.g., 'we could lose the contract if I don't respond immediately') (*affect heuristic*). Another bias, very much rooted in human interaction with interface and computer mediated communications is the tendency to adopt a trustworthy (truthful) rather than suspicious stance when interacting with communications (*truth default*, e.g., [17, 18]. This is related to more automatic heuristic processing where, for example, influence cues within communications (e.g., urgency, compliance with authority, avoidance of loss: see [19]) are less likely to be noticed and processed than perhaps more obvious cues to malevolence such as authenticity cues (e.g., accurate email address). This is a major parameter of the Suspicion, Cognition, Automaticity Model/SCAM [18]), and a key challenge is to find ways to encourage humans interacting with computers at work to take a less trustworthy stance and process information to a deeper level using more cognitively intensive strategies.

Other factors can also increase human susceptibility to cyber-attack attempts and/or, in some cases, exacerbate the effects of other vulnerabilities such as using heuristics and biases in decision making. For example, human individual differences ([19, 20]) such as a high propensity to trust, low self-control/high impulsivity, low self-awareness, high risk taking, high self-deception, low expertise, and a high need for affiliation, can increase the likelihood of unsafe cyber behaviors. Williams, Beardmore, and Joinson [19] also stress the important role of individual contextual factors such as cognitive overload, financial need, and fatigue, as well as more deep rooted organizational factors such as hierarchical organizational, individualistic and relational cultural values.

As well as, and in some cases despite, low vulnerability to many/all of the above factors – maladaptive cybersecurity behaviors can occur as a result of other things that are largely out of one's control. For example, when working: under pressure, with high cognitive load (e.g., performing a complex task and/or needing to switch to and from more than one task), under stress, and in conditions where performance on a demanding task is interrupted [20]. Such *workload* related factors can reduce the ability to detect potential cues to malevolence and lead to cyber risky behaviors, and in some cases exacerbation of likelihood of falling prey to other vulnerabilities such as cognitive biases. We know that time pressure can have negative effects on the performance of tasks, and it is argued (despite little research evidence to date) that those involving human cybersecurity are not an exception [21]. Williams, Beardmore and Joinson [19] posit that when operating under high workload conditions (e.g., due to high cognitive load, time pressure, and so on) and even when suspicion is roused, people may feel that they do not have the resources (e.g., time) required to try and deal with them in a cyber safe manner, potentially disregarding or ignoring the possible risks in order to achieve what seems to be the most important goal, such as meeting a deadline.

Taken together, it really is of little surprise that many humans do and can fall foul of engaging in unsafe cybersecurity behaviours and that these will be displayed within workplaces as well as at other times (e.g., at home). Also, many cyber criminals are aware of at least some of these factors, and can and will exploit them to try and gain access to computer systems for malicious purposes. However, we – the defenders – are now more than ever aware of the human vulnerabilities, which in itself is a key step forward to tacking the issue. That is, if information about the vulnerabilities are communicated effectively to as many organizations and their employees as possible, such that socio-technical and not just technical cyber hygiene workplace practices can become the norm.

2 Humans as a Line of Defence in Cybersecurity: Human-Centric Cybersecurity Research Within an Industrial Organizational Setting

It is not enough to simply be aware of human cyber vulnerabilities; we also need to better understand them and how they manifest within organizations, and to develop solutions to alleviate their effects within *and* amongst employees working within organizations. In this section, we introduce how we are rising to the challenge within Airbus with a new *Accelerator in Human-Centric Cyber Security* (H2CS) The core team within the accelerator are psychologists with a plethora of research experience and methods, not only in cyber psychology, but also in areas such as human cognition (e.g., perception, attention, memory, decision making), neuroscience, neuroimaging, human-machine interface (HMI) design, human-computer interaction (HCI), artificial intelligence, automation, and human-robotic interaction. All are embedded within Airbus to best deliver the outcomes of the accelerator, including a range of research themes and developing industry-appropriate solutions to tackle and alleviate human cybersecurity vulnerabilities. Example Airbus H2CS research themes (discussed further in this section) include:

– Developing best-in-class tools to measure human cyber strengths, vulnerabilities and behaviors (Sect. 2.1);

- Exploring factors known to cause error-prone and/or risky behaviours in the context of cybersecurity within industrial organizational settings (Sect. 2.2);
- Developing understandable & trustworthy human-centric cybersecurity communications that meet the needs of the wider employee base (Sect. 2.3);
- Utilizing the research findings *and* other best existing human factors principles to inform the design and ensure the security from a human perspective of HMIs used within industry-based workplaces as well as HCI principles for using them (Sect. 2.4).

2.1 Developing Best-in-Class Tools to Measure Human Cyber Strengths, Vulnerabilities and Behaviors Within Industrial Organizational Settings

Most of the human cyber strengths, vulnerabilities and behaviors discussed in Sect. 1.2 are *known unknowns*; i.e., factors that individually or in combination could cause cyber risky behaviors amongst employees within organizational settings. However, these factors will be manifested by some individuals (not all), to different degrees, in different ways, and under different circumstances. It is therefore crucial to develop measures to identify vulnerabilities for use within industrial (and related) organizations. These measures need to speak to a range of questions. For example, are any of the human vulnerability factors so strong that they will be prevalent across most individuals and within most organizations? Are some of the factors an issue but not as powerful such that they are only apparent amongst certain personas and/or very large samples are required to detect them. Are some of the vulnerabilities different within different departments of the same organization, and if so, why (e.g., security criticality linked to hardware and/or software being used and/or developed, level of technical expertise, work cultures)? Are some of the vulnerabilities more (or less) apparent when individuals work away from their normal workplace environment? These and other questions need to be answered in order to identify human-centric cyber metrics to inform the development of solutions (e.g., interventions) that will be most effective for individuals (bespoke), departments (wider applicability) and organizations (generic) as a whole.

To begin the speak to these questions, the Airbus H2CS team have developed and are testing a range of tools to measure human-centric cyber vulnerabilities (as well as strengths) and risky cyber behaviours amongst people working within industry settings. For example, the Airbus Cyber Strengths and Vulnerabilities tool consists of a battery of established scales to measure the influence of demographic factors (e.g., age, gender), individual differences (e.g., impulsivity, risk taking, decision-making styles), contextual factors (e.g., job role, tools used), as well as aspects of organizational commitment and job satisfaction, protection motivation (e.g., role in cybersecurity), and knowledge, attitudes and behaviours (see [22]). The selection of some scales and measures within this tool have also been informed by well-established theories, such as the Theory of Planned Behavior [23] and Protection Motivation Theory [15]. Initial findings suggest that such a comprehensive tool is needed to identify not only factors that strongly predict cyber risky behavior(s), such as security self-efficacy and psychological ownership of devices, but also factors that seem to be weak predictors of such behaviors. Correlations between factors are also being identified and considered during the process of iteratively developing and streaming the tool. Findings from such tools are being developed into human-cyber vulnerability metrics and personas that we are using to develop interventions – bespoke and generic – to mitigate and alleviate vulnerabilities and therefore human risk of unsafe cybersecurity actions and behaviors.

2.2 Exploring Factors Known to Cause Error-Prone and/or Risky Behaviours in the Context of Cybersecurity Within Industrial Organizational Settings

When trying to map factors that are likely to increase human cybersecurity vulnerabilities, as well as *known unknowns*, there are *known knowns*. By this, we mean factors that almost universally have a negative effect on task performance, behavior(s) and sometimes well-being, such as when working: under time pressure [24]; with high levels of stress [25]; under cognitive resource depletion or high cognitive load [26]; and in situations where tasks are disrupted, for example due to interruption [27, 28]. Despite many thousands of research outputs on these topics, there has been a dearth of literature and research on their effects and possible mitigations in the context of cybersecurity. Chowdhury, Adam, and Skinner [21] recently conducted a systematic review examining time pressure effects on cybersecurity behaviour, and identified only 21 relevant articles. Of these, few used explicit manipulations of time pressure and fewer still included cybersecurity workers focusing instead on, e.g., student and home computer-user samples. There is much work to be done, and we are tacking this head-on through a number of cybersecurity themed experimental studies conducted within industrial work settings that are determining the effects (and boundary conditions) associated with these and other known knowns.

It is important to add that many of the factors are difficult to control, manage or indeed at an organizational and/or employee level. For example, companies cannot simply operate in a way that all staff never (or even rarely) work under time pressure and/or with high cognitive load, and things like interruptions (e.g., emails, drop-in visitors) and other types of distraction (e.g., having to switch between tasks, background sound/speech) are often part of the fabric of the jobs of many employees. Thus, solutions need to be researched and developed to (1) better manage them (e.g., technical solutions to better schedule when employees engage with computer-based communications such as non-urgent emails) and (2) help to mitigate their negative effects before, during, and/or after their occurrence (e.g., interface features that encourage making notes on or committing important information to memory before switching to another task).

2.3 Developing Understandable and Trustworthy Human-Centric Cybersecurity Communications that Meet the Needs of the Wider Employee Base

Asquith and Morgan [29] assert that as well as a need to better understand the cyber strengths, vulnerabilities and behaviours of humans when working with technology (within a 'human-centric cyber space'), of paramount importance in cybersecurity defence is the efficient and effective communication of cybersecurity information (including metrics derived from e.g., tools such as those discussed in Sect. 2.1) to the organizations and employees that they are developed for. Noting that solutions may very well need to be bespoke, for example they may differentiate between technical and less technical employees and adjust the terminology used, accordingly. As much as targeted cybersecurity communications may be effective at individual team levels, solutions need to be developed and implemented on a wider scale to instill and/or improve the cyber-security culture of the organization [30, 31], by for example, encouraging employees to engage more with each other about cybersecurity information.

The communications need to be up-to-date and clearly linked to the technologies and systems they represent. Those intended to benefit from the communications (i.e., employees) should be able to easily interpret and understand them to a meaningful level. To protect against a successful attack, those interacting with the communications (e.g., employees) need to understand the value of the system or data to potential attackers, vulnerabilities in the attack surface and the resources available to potential attackers to aid them in a successful breach [32]. This more tailored use of human-centric cybersecurity communications will be more likely to support decision making than is the case with many existing systems and methods, by developing a resistant defence rather than purely quantifying and displaying risk factors.

An approach we are adopting within H2CS, to develop effective human-centric cybersecurity communications is one of co-development with the people who are meant to benefit from them. For example, understanding the effectiveness of presenting risk information in improving security behaviour is only possible by measuring effect or through receiving feedback from staff members, themselves. This process will help to increase the feeling of job involvement and commitment [33], which has been shown to improve cybersecurity awareness and behavioral intentions [34, 35].

2.4 Drawing upon Research Findings and HCI Principles to Inform the Design of More Secure HMIs for Use by Employees Within Industry Settings

There will always be some human cyber vulnerabilities that cannot be mitigated by solutions informed by the key known unknowns and known knowns, discussed above, and/or with improved methods and content of communication to the wider employee base. For example, behaviours and habits that can be so hard to break (e.g., *Einstellung effects*, and so-called hard-grained task performance strategies that are difficult to break even when an alternative strategy is more beneficial) that hard constraints (i.e., changes to a task or process that prevent certain actions) need to be considered. By hard constraints here, we refer to HMI features that prevent people from doing certain things (e.g., replying to an email without verifying the credentials of the sender) in order to reduce risky actions and behaviors and encourage people to learn from the hard constraints and try to apply characteristics of them when performing other tasks. It could be beneficial to add a hard constraint(s) to some aspects/features of HMIs – e.g., to access HMI features that could be targeted by cyber criminals online and/or when working with sensitive data on a device that could be targeted.

Hard constraints such as information access costs (e.g., masking information with a small time and mouse/cursor cost to uncover it) and implementation costs (e.g., a time cost to implement an action(s) such as when trying to reply to an email from a non-verified sender), can lead to powerful shifts to cognitively effortful information processing strategies. This shift discourages automatic surface processing strategies that are known to lead to risky cyber behaviours [18]. Such HMI design principles are known to encourage more task-relevant, planned behaviour and more intensive memory-based processing that can, for example, protect against forgetting important information after a task is interrupted [28] and improve problem solving behaviours [36]. The benefits of such methods have been demonstrated multiple times using basic laboratory tasks ([28, 36–40]). What we aim to understand within our current studies is whether, and if so to what extent, such manipulations of HMI hard constraints can encourage more cognitively intensive strategies that will encourage humans to act and behave even more securely in HCI situations within workplace settings.

3 Conclusions

We do not dispute that humans possess a number of characteristics and limitations that increase vulnerability to cyber-attack methods. Statistics relating to humans being involved in successful cybersecurity breaches are staggering and very alarming. Within the current paper, we have presented and discussed a number of factors that can likely account for many of the human vulnerabilities that have resulted in such breaches within organizations, with the exception of more malicious insider threat factors that are beyond the scope of the current paper. Vulnerabilities such as: suboptimal perceptions of security risks; issues with security awareness and culture within some organizations; overreliance on flawed heuristics and decision making biases; individual differences in relation to factors such as risk tasking, impulsivity, trust, and self-awareness; and, maladaptive behaviors due to factors such as time pressure, high cognitive load, high stress, and working under conditions where interruptions and distractions are prevalent.

A number of these issues are receiving some research attention, but there is much work to do. Like us, other researchers are acknowledging that humans have the potential to be a solution and not a problem to a number of cybersecurity challenges [41]; in fact, some have been suggesting this for quite some time [1], although doubts have been raised. In a number of cases, some factors are being examined in relative isolation to others, such as work that often focuses on a subset of individual differences without considering others that might also explain risky cyber behaviours. Some research is perhaps too focused on human vulnerabilities without consideration of environmental or situational factors, and vice versa. Whilst not a criticism per se, far too much research involves studying population samples (e.g., university students) that are not representative of the sectors in which possible solutions to human-centric cybersecurity issues are intended to benefit, such as workplace organizations and the employees who work within them. We need to embrace the idea that humans can be a significant part of the solution to cyber-attack attempts as advocated by others [1, 41], and drive forward with cutting edge research that tackles the wider range of human cyber vulnerabilities discussed within the current paper.

Within the current paper we discuss a step-change involving human factors psychology research in the context of cybersecurity conducted for and within an industrial organization with potential wide-ranging benefits to other organizations and workplace settings. Airbus have established a first-in-class Accelerator in Human-Centric Cyber Security (H2CS) with a core team of psychologists driving forward and working with others on research to examine human cyber vulnerabilities within workplace settings and to develop interventions to alleviate and in many cases mitigate many of these vulnerabilities. The team are working on a number of research projects to develop and test industry-appropriate solutions to tackle and alleviate human cybersecurity vulnerabilities. These include: best-in-class tools to measure human cyber strengths, vulnerabilities and behaviors that also consider workplace environmental factors; investigating factors known to cause risky behaviours in the context of cybersecurity within workplace settings; development of understandable & trustworthy human-centric cybersecurity communications that meet the needs of the wider employee base (Sect. 2.3); and implementing and testing human factors HMI and HCI techniques that discourage sup-optimal and trusting information processing strategies and instead encourage more effortful cognitive strategies that encourage people to think deeper about the decisions they make and actions/behaviors they engage in. Within the paper, we have provided insights into these research projects to not only promote the work of the accelerator, but also to encourage others to be involved and to consider the value of human-centric cybersecurity research embedded within organizations.

Acknowledgements. The research and Airbus Accelerator in Human-Centric Cyber Security (H2CS) is further supported by Endeavr Wales and Cardiff University. The first author (Dr Phillip Morgan) as Technical Lead, the second author (Dr Phoebe Asquith) as a Cardiff University Research Associate, the fourth author (George Raywood-Burke) as a PhD student funded by the programme, and support in kind for the third author (Laura Bishop) who is funded via a PhD studentship from the School of Psychology at Cardiff University.

References

1. Sasse, M.A., Brostoff, S., Weirich, D.: Transforming the 'weakest link'–a human computer interaction approach to usable and effective security. BT Technol. J. **19**(3), 122–131 (2001). https://doi.org/10.1023/A:1011902718709
2. D'Arcy, J., Hovav, A., Galletta, D.: User awareness of security countermeasures and its impact on information systems misuse: a deterrence approach. Inf. Syst. Res. **20**(1), 79–98 (2009)
3. Stanton, J.M., Stam, K.R., Mastrangelo, P., Jolton, J.: Analysis of end user security behaviors. Comput. Secur. **24**(2), 124–133 (2005)
4. Verizon. 2018 data breach investigation report 1–8 (2018)
5. IBM. Cost of data breach report 2018 (2018)
6. Microsoft SIR 2018 (2018)
7. Perera, D.: Sony hackers used fake emails. Politico, 21 April 2015 (2015). https://www.politico.com/story/2015/04/sony-hackers-fake-emails-117200
8. Schuman, E.: LinkedIn's disturbing breach notice (2016). https://www.computerworld.com/article/3077478/security/linkedin-s-disturbing-breach-notice.htmlComputerworld
9. Forbes. Marriott breach: starwood hacker gains access to 500 million customer records (2018). https://www.forbes.com/sites/forrester/2018/11/30/marriot-breach-starwoods-hacker-tier-rewards-millions-of-customer-records/#3f90b0245703
10. Yurieff, K.: Equifax data breach: what you need to know (2017). http://money.cnn.com/2017/09/08/technology/equifax-hack-qa/index.html
11. Weise, E.: It's new and it's bad: Yahoo discloses 1B account breach (2016). https://www.usatoday.com/story/tech/news/2016/12/14/yahoo-discloses-likely-new-1-billion-account-breach/95443510
12. Bada, M., Sasse, A.M., Nurse, J.R.: Cyber security awareness campaigns: Why do they fail to change behaviour? arXiv preprint arXiv:1901.02672 (2019)

13. Pfleeger, S.L., Caputo, D.: Leveraging behavioral science to mitigate cyber security risk. Comput. Secur. **31**(4), 597–611 (2012)
14. Egelman, S., Peer, E.: Scaling the security wall: developing a security behavior intentions scale (sebis). In: Proceedings of the 33rd Annual ACM Conference on Human Factors in Computing Systems, pp. 2873–2882. ACM (2015)
15. McGill, T., Thompson, N.: Old risks, new challenges: exploring differences in security between home computer and mobile device use. Behav. Inf. Technol. **36**(11), 1111–1124 (2017)
16. Scholl, M.C., Fuhrmann, F., Scholl, L.R.: Scientific knowledge of the human side of information security as a basis for sustainable trainings in organizational practices. In: Proceedings of the 51st Hawaii International Conference on System Sciences, pp. 2235–2244 (2018)
17. Levine, T.R.: Truth default theory: a theory of human deception and deception detection. J. Lang. Soc. Psychol. **33**, 378–392 (2014)
18. Vishwanath, A., Harrison, B., Ng, Y.J.: Suspicion, cognition, and automaticity model of phishing susceptibility. Commun. Res. **45**, 1146–1166 (2016)
19. Williams, E.J., Beardmore, A., Joinson, A.: Individual differences in susceptibility to online influence: a theoretical review. Comput. Hum. Behav. **72**, 412–421 (2017)
20. Williams, E.J., Morgan, P.L., Joinson, A.J.: Press accept to update now: individual differences in susceptibility to malevolent interruptions. Decis. Support Syst. **96**, 119–129 (2017)
21. Chowdhury, N.H., Adam, N.T.P., Skinner, G.: The impact of time pressure on cybersecurity behaviour: a systematic review. Behav. Inf. Technol. **38**(12), 1290–1308 (2019)
22. Bishop, L., Morgan, P.L., Asquith, P.M., Burke, G-R., Wedgbury, A., Jones, K.: Examining human individual differences in cyber security and possible implications for human-machine interface design. In: Moallem, A. (ed.) Human-Computer International: 2nd International Conference on HCI for Cybersecurity, Privacy and Trust, LNCS 12210, pp. 1–17 (2020, in press). To appear
23. Ajzen, I.: The theory of planned behaviour: reactions and reflections. Psychol. Health **26**(9), 1103–1127 (2011)
24. Kelly, J.R., McGrath, J.E.: Effects of time limits and task types on task performance and interaction of four-person groups. J. Pers. Soc. Psychol. **49**(2), 395–407 (1985)
25. Henderson, R.K., Snyder, H.R., Gupta, T., Banich, M.T.: When does stress help or harm? the effects of stress controllability and subjective stress response on stroop performance. Front. Psychol. **3–179**, 1–15 (2012)
26. Paas, F., Renkl, A., Sweller, J.: Cognitive load theory and instructional design: recent developments. Educ. Psychol. **38**(1), 1–4 (2010)
27. Monk, C., Trafton, J.G., Boehm-Davis, D.A.: The effect of interruption duration and demand on resuming suspended goals. J. Exp. Psychol. Appl. **14**, 299–313 (2008)
28. Morgan, P.L., Patrick, J., Waldron, S., King, S., Patrick, T.: Improving memory after interruption: exploiting soft constraints and manipulating information access cost. J. Exp. Psychol. Appl. **15**, 291–306 (2009)
29. Asquith, P.M., Morgan, P.L.: Representing a human-centric cyberspace. In: 6th International Conference on Human Factors in Cybersecurity, 2020, 11th International Conference on Applied Human Factors and Ergonomics, San Diego, US, pp. 1–7 (2020)
30. Rathbun, D.: Gathering security metrics and reaping the rewards. SANS Institute, Information Security Reading Room (2009). https://www.sans.org/reading-room/whitepapers/leadership/gathering-security-metrics-reaping-rewards-33234
31. Herrmann, D.S.: Complete Guide to Security and Privacy Metrics: Measuring Regulatory Compliance, Operational Resilience, and ROI. Auerbach Publications, Boca Raton (2007)
32. Fleming, M.H., Goldstein, E.: Metrics for measuring the efficacy of critical-infrastructure-centric cybersecurity information sharing efforts. In: Homeland Security Studies and Analysis Institute Report RP: 11-01.02.02-01, pp. 1–57 (2012)

33. O'Driscoll, M.P., Randall, D.M.: Perceived organisational support, satisfaction with rewards, and employee job involvement and organisational commitment. Appl. Psychol. Int. Rev. **48**(2), 197–209 (1999)
34. Reeves, A., Parsons, K, Calic, D.: Securing mobile devices: evaluating the relationship between risk perception, organisational commitment and information security awareness. In: Proceedings of the 11th International Symposium on Human Aspects of Information Security and Assurance (HAISA), pp. 145–155 (2017)
35. Hearth, T., Rao, H.R.: Protection motivation and deterrence: a framework for security policy compliance in organisations. Eur. J. Inf. Syst. **18**, 106–125 (2009)
36. Morgan, P.L., Patrick, J.: Paying the price works: increasing goal access cost improves problem solving and mitigates the effect of interruption. Q. J. Exp. Psychol. **66**(1), 160–178 (2013)
37. Gray, W.D., Sims, C.R., Fu, W.-T., Schoelles, M.J.: The soft constraints hypothesis: a rational analysis approach to resource allocation for interactive behavior. Psychol. Rev. **113**(3), 461–482 (2006)
38. Morgan, P.L., Patrick, J.: Designing interfaces that encourage a more effortful cognitive strategy. In: Proceedings of the 54th Annual Meeting of the Human Factors and Ergonomics Society, Cognitive Engineering and Decision Making Section, San Francisco, California, USA, pp. 408–412 (2010)
39. Morgan, P.L., Patrick, J., Patrick, T.: Increasing information access costs to protect against interruption effects during problem solving. In: Proceedings of the 32nd Annual Meeting of the Cognitive Science Society, Portland, Oregon, USA, pp. 949–955 (2010)
40. Patrick, J., et al.: The influence of training and experience on memory strategy. Memory Cogn. **43**(5), 775–787 (2015)
41. Zimmermann, V., Renaud, K.: Moving from a 'human-as-problem" to a 'human-as-solution" cybersecurity mindset. Int. J. Hum Comput Stud. **131**, 169–187 (2019)

Sleeping with the Enemy: Does Depletion Cause Fatigue with Cybersecurity?

Andrew Reeves[1]([✉]) [iD], Dragana Calic[2] [iD], and Paul Delfabbro[1] [iD]

[1] School of Psychology, University of Adelaide, Adelaide, South Australia, Australia
{andrew.reeves,paul.delfabbro}@adelaide.edu.au
[2] Defence Science and Technology Group, Edinburgh, South Australia, Australia
dragana.calic@dst.defence.gov.au

Abstract. Cybersecurity training and awareness programs can act to exacerbate rather than improve the cybersecurity threat posed by naïve and non-malicious actions of employees [1, 2]. Employees report being unable to keep up with cybersecurity demands while also managing their core workload [1]. Cyber Fatigue is a weariness, aversion, or lack of motivation regarding cybersecurity [3]. It manifests due to overexposure to cybersecurity and a lack of available cognitive or workplace resources to cope with its demands. The current study examined the effect of non-attitudinal fatigue, which results from repetitive cybersecurity actions, on password-creation behaviour. Data collection involved an online experimental task and a set of standardised and adapted psychometric measures. Based on previous research [4, 5], cyber fatigue was induced in the two experimental conditions using a CAPTCHA task. The study was completed by 187 (97 male, 90 female) employed adult participants. However, we found no significant relationship between depletion and password creation behaviours. Our findings have important practical implications for interventions and provides insight for training aimed at improving employee behaviour.

Keywords: Cyber fatigue · Cybersecurity · Information security · Fatigue · Employee behaviour

1 Introduction

Employee behaviour continues to be a risk to workplace cybersecurity. In 2019, 47% of global cybersecurity decision makers reported insider threat to be the biggest risk to their organisation's security [6]. Moreover, the majority of these threats arise from naïve and accidental behavior [6, 7]. Businesses invest in security education, training, and awareness (SETA) programs to inform their employees and best equip them for the challenge of evolving cybersecurity threats but, despite this effort, employee behaviour remains a potential source of security breaches for organisations [6].

An important and somewhat paradoxical observation is that cybersecurity SETA programs can serve to exacerbate rather than improve employee behavior, particularly when they lead to fatigue and disengagement from cybersecurity concerns [2]. Why

© Springer Nature Switzerland AG 2020
A. Moallem (Ed.): HCII 2020, LNCS 12210, pp. 217–231, 2020.
https://doi.org/10.1007/978-3-030-50309-3_15

this occurs has been a focus of recent research, with Choi, Park [8] describing privacy fatigue as a state of detachment from privacy concerns arising from an over-supply of security information. A related term, breach fatigue has similarly been used to describe feelings of nihilism and inevitability regarding cyber incidents, where individuals start to believe nothing they can do can mitigate the threat [8]. Others attribute fatigue to a lack of awareness of threats [1]. These approaches largely focus what factors influence an employee's attitude, and how their attitude results in poor cybersecurity behaviours. This focus means they can miss the non-attitudinal instances of fatigue [3]. Such instances can occur when employees are cognitively or physiologically tired of performing the often repetitive actions required to maintain cybersecurity, without necessarily forming a poor attitude [3, 9]. To capture these non-attitudinal instances of fatigue alongside these more specific conceptualisations, Reeves, Calic [3] offer a more encompassing four-component model. This approach describes cyber fatigue as:

> A weariness, aversion, or apparent lack of motivation in regard to cybersecurity, which exists not solely as a result of individual predispositions, but primarily because of prior overexposure to cybersecurity or lack of available cognitive or workplace resources. [3, p. 6]

The following sections outline previous research in this area and the Four-Component Model of Cyber Fatigue to be empirically examined.

1.1 Non-attitudinal Cyber Fatigue

Many existing approaches to employee cybersecurity disengagement focus on the attitudinal factors that limit employee compliance, such as employee value-perception of cybersecurity [2], a lack of employee awareness [1], or appreciation of cybersecurity [10]. In these approaches poor employee behavior is commonly attributed to a lack of awareness or, especially, motivation [See 11–14]. In contrast, non-attitudinal approaches consider the work-related factors that contribute to employee non-compliance with cybersecurity demands [3]. Examples of this are based on workload models and include ego depletion and habituation. Respectively, these refer to the worsening of employee decision making due to an exhaustion of cognitive resources and the diminishing strength of orientation towards stimuli which are familiar [4, 15]. These non-attitudinal disengagements can result from cybersecurity demands, such as performing repetitive or intensive security processes [16]. It is possible that an employee can be fatigued by the constant effort required to maintain good cybersecurity (e.g., choosing new passwords, checking emails for authenticity), while simultaneously having good awareness and a positive attitude towards cybersecurity as a whole. Approaches that focus solely on attitude and motivation may miss these cases of employee disengagement.

Incorporating non-attitudinal factors of fatigue with existing approaches into a single model allows for an explanation of otherwise conflicting observations. For example, some authors have suggested that, due to the increased chance of people adopting technologies they have control over [see 17, 18], fatigue should be eased by granting *greater* agency to employees regarding their cybersecurity behaviours [19]. However, as this could be seen as increasing the decision-making load on the employee, others have suggested taking the decision-making ability *away* wherever possible [1]. These contradictory recommendations make the literature hard to apply by business and employees. The four-component model suggests that both recommendations can be appropriate depending on what is the cause of the fatigue [3]. If employee disengagement is due to a perceived intrusion of cybersecurity into their job role [19], the former recommendation would be appropriate. If it is instead due to an overload of cybersecurity responsibility [20], the latter would be appropriate. This approach highlights the importance of determining the cause of the behaviour and aligning interventions appropriately.

The four-component model was developed through literature review methods [21] and has yet to be examined empirically [3]. One of the key tenants of the model, that the non-attitudinal factors of poor employee behaviour such as ego depletion require greater research attention, is the focus of the current study.

1.2 Ego Depletion and Cybersecurity

The phenomenon of ego depletion and the concept of self-regulation continue to be topics of considerable discussion [9, 22–24]. Self-regulation tasks refer to "processes by which the self intentionally alters its own responses, including thoughts, emotions, impulses, performance, and behaviours" [9 p. 79]. The limited strength model holds that performing these tasks requires the use of a limited resource which, once depleted, impairs future self-regulation behaviours [9]. Specifically, the model focuses on *effortful* self-regulation (i.e., not autonomous). In this way, two processes can be identified as types of non-attitudinal cyber fatigue: ego depletion and habituation. Respectively, they can be considered the conscious and unconscious components of non-attitudinal cyber fatigue. The standard depletion effect is well replicated: exertion of effort on a task inhibits performance on subsequent tasks [9, 23–25]. While the reason for this effect was originally believed to be due to depleted cognitive resources, it is now believed that the brain is instead acting to conserve available resources as a result of unsustainably high resource consumption. Baumeister and Vohs [9] and Dang [24] present in-depth and up-to-date accounts of ego depletion.

While the mechanism underpinning depletion effects is still contested, the outcomes of a depleted state are well replicated. Depleted individuals perform more impulsive behaviours [26, 27], likely because their ability to control such impulses is inhibited [9]. They are also less likely to comply with social norms [9, 28], more likely to give up on difficult tasks [29], and to relay on shortcuts and biases in decision making [30].

There are limited studies available applying the limited strength model approach to a cybersecurity context. Groß, Coopamootoo [5] found individuals depleted by a Stroop task created weaker passwords than non-depleted individuals. Surprisingly, they also found a small amount of depletion resulted in slightly stronger passwords, which the authors attributed to a cognitive stimulation effect [16]. While Groß, Coopamootoo [5] used standard psychological methods in the form of a Stroop task to induce depletion, Coopamootoo, Groß [4] demonstrated this effect could be observed following a single CAPTCHA task, a task that is common in real-world password creation contexts. A recent extended report called for further studies examining the effect of depletion on cybersecurity behaviours [20]. As ego depletion has been identified as a type of non-attitudinal cyber fatigue, this led to the present study.

1.3 The Current Study

This study is the first empirical examination of elements included in the four-component model. We examine non-attitudinal fatigue, focusing on the effect of ego depletion on cybersecurity behaviours. The study replicates the design of Coopamootoo, Groß [4] in a more ecologically valid context: participants completed a password creation task they believed to be for a real account. The outcome cybersecurity behaviour is password creation. For assessment of password strength, many previous studies use only the complexity of the password itself to estimate its strength. However, other factors outside of the content of the password are critical to establishing its strength. Firstly, whether a password is the same as one used on another account will influence how 'strong' it is, especially if the other account is compromised. For example, a workplace password *W4gb-enamel@* achieves a perfect zxcvbn score of 4/4. However, if it is the same as a password used for a breached social media account, it cannot be considered 'strong'. Likewise, if the employee writes this password down it may also no longer be considered 'strong'. For specificity, *password entropy* are used to refer to the complexity of the content of the password, while *reuse* and *likelihood to record* are used to refer to the other factors of password strength.

As the outcomes of ego depletion include regression to the status quo and greater reliance on shortcuts [24], it is necessary to examine whether these outcomes of the depleted state manifest in a cybersecurity context as, respectively, a greater likelihood of a password being reused (status quo) or written down/recorded inappropriately (shortcuts). In addition to applying their design in a more ecologically valid context, the current study expands on Coopamootoo, Groß [4] by also examining these additional factors of password strength. Following the results of Coopamootoo, Groß [4], and the established outcomes of depletion [9, 20, 24], it is expected that:

H1) Greater non-attitudinal fatigue, in the form of depletion, will be associated with poorer cybersecurity behaviours. Specifically, greater levels of depletion will be associated with:

a) lesser password entropy,
b) greater likelihood of recording the password (e.g., writing it down), and,
c) greater likelihood of the password being a reuse of an existing password.

2 Method

2.1 Participants

A total of 187 participants were recruited via the online platform, Prolific. Participants were required to be employed in a role that requires the use of a computer and over the age of 18. Basic demographic data were gathered, including age group, gender, and nationality. In regard to gender, an option for "other/prefer not to say" was provided but was not selected by any participants. Ethical approval was provided by the University of Adelaide, School of Psychology, Human Research Ethics Subcommittee. Participants took an average of 27 min to complete the study, which included some additional tests for ongoing studies. As shown in Table 1, the demographic characteristics of the sample represent a broad spectrum of employees.

Table 1. Demographic characteristics of the sample.

Variable	Frequency	%
Gender		
Male	97	51.9
Female	90	48.1
Age		
19 or under	6	3.2
18–29	71	38.0
30–39	72	38.5
40–49	20	10.7
50–59	15	8.0
60 or over	3	1.6
Nationality		
Australian	9	4.8
United Kingdom	122	1.6
United States of America	53	65.2
New Zealand	3	28.3

2.2 Procedure

As shown in Fig. 1, participants were randomly allocated to one of three groups: experiment group A (n = 62), experiment group B (n = 65), and the control group (n = 60). Each group followed an identical procedure, save for a CAPTCHA task.

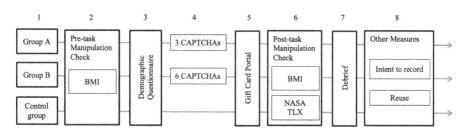

Fig. 1. Overview of experiment procedure

Participants in group A completed three picture CAPTCHA tasks in sequence, and those in group B completed six. Participants in the control group were not shown the CAPTCHA task and were taken directly to the portal following the demographic questionnaire. Following the post-task manipulation checks, the participants were provided a full debriefing, including an explanation of how the researcher is only able to see the strength rating of the chosen password and not the password itself. The debriefing explained that all participants would be automatically entered into the draw to win the gift card, regardless of what action they took at the portal. Despite what it said on the portal, participants are informed there was no need to log in at a later date. They were then given the choice to continue with the survey or withdraw. At the end of the study, participants were given the opportunity to provide feedback via an open-ended field, and these responses were analysed for any negative perceptions of the study design. No participants expressed issues with the process, with many saying they found the procedure engaging. Intent to record and reuse were measured via self-report items.

2.3   Materials

CAPTCHA Depletion Task

Following Coopamootoo, Groß [4], the depletion task consisted of a series of picture CAPTCHA tasks. Picture CAPTCHAs present users with a collection of 9 similar images. They are then asked to select all images that meet a certain condition. Picture CAPTCHA tasks were chosen over text CAPTCHAs as they were found to be more effective by Coopamootoo, Groß [4]. Picture CAPTCHAs are also more relevant to real-world contexts as text-CAPTCHAs are becoming increasingly rare [20].

Manipulation Check: Brief Moods Inventory and the NASA Task Load Index

The NASA Task Load Index (NASA TLX) [34], assesses workload via the dimensions of Mental Demand, Physical Demand, Temporal Demand, Performance, Effort and Frustration. These dimensions are rated using a visual analogue scale. The TLX is presented after the gift card portal, at point 6 on Fig. 1. Participants are therefore rating the workload of what they have completed at points 2–5 (refer to Fig. 1). As the CAPTCHA task is the only point of difference between the groups, the difference in TLX ratings can be used as a measure of the difference in workload placed on participants by the CAPTCHA tasks.

To examine the effect workload has on the mood of the participants, the Brief Moods Inventory (BMI) was used as a pre and post-task manipulation check. The BMI is a short-form of the Brief Moods Introspection Scale and asks participants to rate their mood in regard to keywords such as excited, tired, thoughtful, and happy [35].

Gift Card Portal

The portal presented an opportunity for participants to enter the draw to win one of three gift cards, each valued at $100AUD. The portal required the participant to create a password to register an account. Its function is threefold:

1. To provide a legitimate chance to enter the draw and continue with the survey;
2. To analyse the complexity of the password solely on the participants device; and,
3. To return the strength rating of the password to the survey system for later analysis.

To achieve point 1, the portal was hosted on its own domain name to differentiate it from the rest of the survey. SSL authentication was used to encourage participant trust in the site and to match real-world conditions. Furthermore, on choosing to take part in the study, participants were informed that the study includes a chance to win one of three gift-cards. This served to ensure participants were not surprised to see the portal appear and were not suspicious of it. The participant ID was prefilled for participants. Participants were reminded that this password is separate from the password they use on the survey platform, to avoid confusion. The password strength estimation tool, Zxcvbn [33], was used to facilitate point 2. Query strings were used to enable point 3.

The portal advised participants that they would need to log into it later to check if they had won the draw. This was to more closely match real-world conditions by adding a small amount of value to the account they create. Participants did not, in fact, need to log into the portal later, and this was fully explained in the debriefing. Instead, the winner of the gift-card draw was advised via a direct message over the survey recruitment platform, Prolific. An image of the portal is shown in Fig. 2.

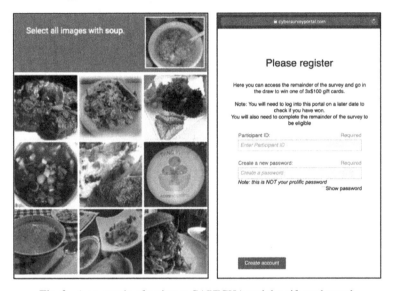

Fig. 2. An example of a picture CAPTCHA and the gift card portal.

To enable a client-side analysis of the chosen password, the website contained a copy of zxcvbn [33]. A *client-side analysis* is where the password analysis occurs on the participant's device and is never sent to the researcher's server. This ensures the researcher cannot access participants' passwords and serves to ethically facilitate the analysis of the passwords. Once the analysis completes (<1 s), the participant is taken back to the survey platform. The result of the analysis is sent to the survey system using a query string.

Password Strength Estimation and the Zxcvbn Password Strength Estimator
Multiple solutions for client-side analysis of participant passwords are available. The zxcvbn tool, developed by Wheeler and Dropbox Inc. [33], was chosen over a neural networks approach [e.g., 32] or Shannon Entropy [e.g., 31] as it has demonstrated similar

accuracy in workplace contexts as the former, while its ability to incorporate higher-level factors, such as dictionary words, overcomes the limitations of the latter. It achieves this while being fast, light, and easy to deploy in a web-application [33].

In the present study, zxcvbn produced the strength of the provided passwords as a log10 of the raw number of guesses it would take to guess the password, as used in Coopamootoo, Groß [4] and recommended by Groß, Coopamootoo [20]. Zxcvbn also expresses the log10 number of guesses as a number from 0 to 4, as a rating of password strength.

3 Results

Analysis began by checking assumptions for parametric testing. The majority of the variables were non-normal, resulting in non-parametric tests used in most cases. Summary of descriptive statistics are presented in Table 2. The largest group of participants created a password of strength 1 (out of 4). The majority of participants (56%) indicated they used a password that they use on another system, partially or completely. Approximately 30% indicated they intended to record the password they chose.

Table 2. Descriptive statistics for strength rating, reuse, and intent to record (N = 187)

Variable	Frequency	%
Password strength rating (0–4)		
0	14	7.5
1	76	40.6
2	45	24.1
3	40	21.4
4	12	6.4
Reuse		
Unique password	83	44.4
Partial reuse	44	23.5
Exact reuse	60	32.1
Intent to record		
No	132	70.6
Yes	55	29.4

3.1 Manipulation Check

The purpose of the CAPTCHA task was to induce depletion in the participants and observe the effect on password creation behaviours. To check the depletion was successful, NASA TLX and BMI scores were analysed across the experiment groups. As the NASA TLX distribution was non-normal, a Kruskal-Wallis test was performed. The shape of the distributions was compared across groups and found to be sufficiently similar to allow the analysis to proceed. Group membership significantly predicted scores on TLX dimensions Mental Demands, Effort, Frustration, Physical Demands, and total TLX score, but not Temporal Demands and Performance. Group membership predicted scores on the BMI happy, calm, and excited subscales. Participants in the CAPTCHA groups reported being less happy and calm following the task than before, while the control group reported a positive change in these mood states. Participants in the CAPTCHA groups reported expending greater effort, greater levels of frustration, and greater levels of mental and physical demands, than the control group, indicating the manipulation was successful. Unexpectedly, group membership did not significantly predict scores on the BMI tired or worn-out subscales. Table 3 presents the results of the manipulation check.

Table 3. Summary of Kruskal-Wallis tests of group membership predicting NASA TLX and BMI score

Manipulation check item	X^2	Group means^		
		Control	Group A (3 CAPTCHAs)	Group B (6 CAPTCHAs)
NASA TLX	7.35*	29.51	34.40	38.03
Effort	12.34**	35.68	56.07	75.90
Frustration	7.89*	27.80	57.02	94.86
Mental demands	7.08*	48.88	61.64	81.92
Physical demands	6.37*	10.37	2.82	13.20
Temporal demands	1.35	32.17	40.64	36.12
Performance	1.14	287.7	297.8	268.4
BMI				
Happy	10.49**	4.40	−5.51	−6.00
Excited	7.49*	.75	−4.29	2.37
Calm	6.29*	.10	−3.81	−9.03
Worn-out	5.01	−11.70	−5.68	−5.32
Thoughtful	5.01	6.82	−2.79	3.71
Angry	4.63	.22	−1.87	.69
Tired	1.90	−11.00	−6.03	−6.06
Sad	0.37	−5.68	−3.50	−2.82

* significant at the 0.05 level; ** significant at the .01 level ^BMI means are reported as the mean change in BMI rating after the task. Note: Degrees of freedom is 2 for all measures.

In regard to the TLX items, pairwise comparisons indicated that the control group and group B were significantly different on all TLX items, however group A was not significantly different from either for most TLX items. This was mostly due to the mean of group A being equidistant from the control group mean and the group B mean. An example of this is presented in Fig. 3. While this difference was not statistically significant, possibly due to smaller sample size, the relationship is consistent with the expectation that the conditions for group B would have more effect on mood than the control group, and group A would be somewhere in-between.

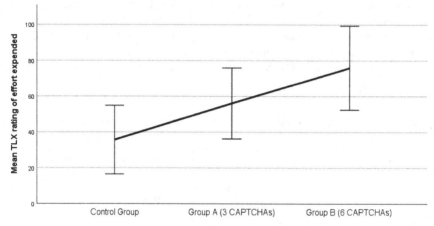

Fig. 3. Mean of effort expended in the task as reported by participants

In regard to the BMI subscales, pairwise comparisons indicated that the control group differed from group A and B, but group A and B did not differ from each other, for most of the subscales. An example of this is presented in Fig. 4.

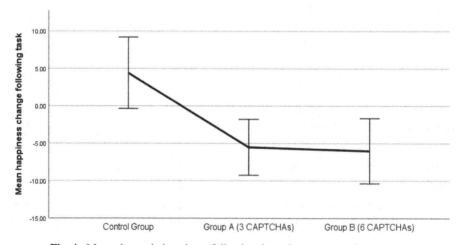

Fig. 4. Mean change in happiness following the task across experiment groups

3.2 Zxcvbn Password Score

A one-way ANOVA was performed to examine the effect of group membership on the entropy of chosen passwords (as measured by the log10 of the number of guesses needed). Group membership was not associated with a significant difference in password entropy, $F(2, 185) < 1$.

3.3 Password Reuse and Intent to Record

Chi-square tests of independence were performed to examine the relationship between group membership and the two robustness measures: password reuse and intent to record. Group membership was not associated with any difference in password reuse, $X^2(4) = 3.13, p = .536$, nor intent to record, $X^2(2) = 2.37, p = .306$.

4 Discussion

This study is the first to empirically examine the four-component model of cyber fatigue. Contrary to our hypothesis, no relationship was found between depletion level and password creation behaviours. The following sections outline possible explanations for this result, with implications for the four-component model, future study designs, and applied considerations.

4.1 Password Creation and Self-regulation

Self-regulation tasks require individuals to deliberately regulate themselves, such as overriding an impulsive behaviour or suppressing an emotion [36]. In particular, depletion effects occur primarily for *effortful* self-regulation tasks [9]. In the current study, and based on previous research [4, 20], a CAPTCHA task was used as the depleting task. The results of the NASA TLX in the current study support its use as a depletion task. Given previous research which noted that password creation is cognitively effortful and requires considerations of complexity, attack vectors, and use-cases, we hypothesised that the task would be hindered in a depleted state [5]. However, our findings suggest this may not always be the case. Password creation behaviours seemed unaffected by depletion, perhaps, indicating that the task did not require as much, or any, cognitive effort.

A potential explanation comes from the other type of action fatigue identified in the four-component model: habituation. As passwords have become commonplace in the daily lives of individuals, password creation behaviours may be highly habituated [37]. If this is the case, when individuals receive a password-creation prompt, they will perform a largely pre-determined behaviour. That is, they will either use the same password they always use, or create a password based on a habituated pattern (e.g., the same word with different numbers or symbols). For these individuals, password creation behaviours are not cognitively effortful self-regulation tasks. Instead, they are habituated, almost unconscious, behaviours. Similar results have been found in other domains of cybersecurity, where individuals unconsciously accepted or dismissed security warnings, having no memory, when asked later, of doing so [15].

4.2   Methodological Considerations: Participant-Aware Vs. Participant-Unaware Design

Password creation behaviours being the result of habituated, automatic processes may explain the lack of relationship between depletion level and outcome behaviours in the current study. However, the question remains as to why our findings do not match that of previous, similar studies. While research on ego depletion and password behaviour is limited, two recent studies found depleted individuals created significantly weaker passwords, where depletion was induced using validated psychometric tools [5] and later a CAPTCHA task [4], as used in the current study.

This inconsistency may be explained by methodological differences. Due to practical and ethical considerations, previous password creation studies task participants with creating a password in a context where they are *aware* that the password they created was viewed and assessed by the researcher [4, 5, 20]. These will be referred to as *participant-aware* designs. These designs are common due to the difficulty of deploying large-scale studies where the created password can be assessed automatically, without any action from the researcher [38]. However, recently new tools have been developed that enable the strength of passwords to be assessed, without the researcher needing to view the password, and indeed without the password ever having to leave the participant's device. The use of the zxcvbn tool allowed the current study to assess the created passwords completely client-side. This made it possible to run a study where participants were unaware that the password they were creating was to be assessed for its strength, or even that the password creation task was part of the study. Therefore, the current study utilised a *participant-unaware* design.

While the intent was to replicate the findings of previous studies using a more ecologically valid task, the change to a participant-unaware design may explain the difference between the current findings and previous research. In participant-aware designs, the act of creating a password may become a self-regulation task, simply due to participants being aware that they are being assessed. That is, when an individual is presented with a password-creation task, where they know their response is being recorded, some may be hesitant to provide a password they use in day-to-day life, as they wouldn't want this password to be known. Others may not be as concerned about giving away their passwords, but they may wish to do well at the task, and so provide a password that is stronger than one they would normally use. In both scenarios, the individuals are overriding their initial impulse to perform a habitual behaviour to perform a 'better' behaviour. In this way, the password-creation task becomes a self-regulation task. In a participant-unaware design no such overriding-of-habit is required, and participants fall back on their habituated behaviours. Therefore, in participant-unaware designs, password creation ceases to be a self-regulation task. This may explain the lack of a relationship between depletion level and password creation behaviours in the current study, and the significant relationship found in previous studies [4, 5, 20]. If this is the case, there are considerable implications for practitioners. Counter to intuition, employees may not create better passwords when they are less depleted. Instead, focus should be placed on altering habituated behaviours. As this was not the original purpose of the study, future studies should look to confirm this hypothesis.

4.3 Implications for SETA Programs and Future Research

While it is likely that participant habituation to password creation was behind the lack of depletion effects observed here, the effect may be moderated by how recently an employee has received cybersecurity training. That is, individuals who have recently completed a cybersecurity training program at their workplace, or elsewhere, may override their habitual behaviour when they are next presented with a password creation opportunity at work. While this is no doubt the aim of such programs, it also makes the task a self-regulation task, and therefore within range of depletion effects. Further research should look to examine the effect of depletion on password creation behaviours when a previous experience has forced cybersecurity to be salient, such as a recent training program or intervention.

4.4 Ego Depletion and Mood

Changes in participant mood as a result of depletion did not match expectations. Depleted individuals did not rate being more tired or worn-out following the task but did indicate they were less happy and less calm. In regard to feeling tired as a result of depletion, while some previous studies have detected an effect [4], others suggest that the effect of depletion on subjective mood is so small that it can only be detected in meta-analyses [9], such as Hagger, Wood [23]. While it may seem intuitive that the tired and worn-out subdimensions of the BMI would be sensitive to depletion effects, some authors have suggested that there is no clear subjective state that constitutes a signature feeling of depletion [9]. Depleted individuals are equally likely to feel greater positive emotions as negative ones [39], meaning mood scales such as the BMI may be unable to detect a consistent change in mood in depleted individuals. This appears to be the case in the current study, even though greater granularity was facilitated through the use of a visual analogue scale for the BMI items, as recommended by Groß, Coopamootoo [20]. The NASA TLX, being a measure of workload, avoids this issue, and appeared to be sensitive to depletion effects. The sensitivity of the NASA TLX to the manipulation, with inconsistent results on the mood scale, is consistent with recent arguments that depletion tasks deplete cognitive resources without necessarily resulting in a predictable, signature mood state [9].

5 Conclusion

This is the first study to empirically examine an aspect of the four-component model of cyber fatigue. The model holds that poor employee cybersecurity behaviour resulting from non-attitudinal factors are under researched in extant literature. Unexpectedly, cybersecurity behaviour (i.e., password creation) was not influenced by depletion level. This suggests some cybersecurity behaviours may not be performed as conscious, self-regulated tasks, but are instead highly habituated. This has implications for practice, as different interventions will be required to modify habituated behaviours. This also has implications for future research looking to examine depletion effects in a cybersecurity context. Future studies should consider whether the outcome behaviour of interest is truly a self-regulation task. Furthermore, the effect of recent employee cybersecurity experiences, such as training, could have the unintended effect where cybersecurity behaviours become acts of self-regulation, making them vulnerable to depletion effects.

References

1. Stanton, B., et al.: Security fatigue. IT Prof. **18**(5), 26–32 (2016)
2. Furnell, S., Thomson, K.-L.: Recognising and addressing 'security fatigue'. Comput. Fraud Secur. **2009**(11), 7–11 (2009)
3. Reeves, A., Calic, D., Delfabbro, P.: Encouraging employee engagement with cyber security: how to tackle cyber fatigue. SAGE Open: Special Collection on Organizational Cybersecurity (2020, submitted)
4. Coopamootoo, K.P.L., Groß, T., Pratama, M.F.R.: An empirical investigation of security fatigue: the case of password choice after solving a CAPTCHA. In: LASER 2017, Arlington, VA, USA, pp. 39–48 (2017)
5. Groß, T., Coopamootoo, K.P.L., Al-Jabri, A.: Effect of cognitive depletion on password choice. In: LASER 2016, San Jose, CA, p. 55–66 (2016)
6. Telstra Corporation: Telstra Security Report 2019 (2019). https://www.telstra.com.au/content/dam/shared-component-assets/tecom/campaigns/security-report/Summary-Report-2019-LR.pdf
7. Pattinson, M., Butavicius, M., Parsons, K., McCormac, A., Calic, D.: Factors that influence information security behavior: an Australian web-based study. In: Tryfonas, T., Askoxylakis, I. (eds.) HAS 2015. LNCS, vol. 9190, pp. 231–241. Springer, Cham (2015). https://doi.org/10.1007/978-3-319-20376-8_21
8. Choi, H., Park, J., Jung, Y.: The role of privacy fatigue in online privacy behavior. Comput. Hum. Behav. **81**, 42–51 (2018)
9. Baumeister, R.F., Vohs, K.D.: Chapter two - strength model of self-regulation as limited resource: assessment, controversies, update. In: Olson, J.M., Zanna, M.P. (eds.) Advances in Experimental Social Psychology, pp. 67–127. Academic Press, Cambridge (2016)
10. Liang, H., Xue, Y.: Avoidance of information technology threats: a theoretical perspective (technology threat avoidance theory) (Report). MIS Q. **33**(1), 71 (2009)
11. Abraham, S., Chengalur-Smith, I.: Evaluating the effectiveness of learner controlled information security training. Comput. Secur. **87**, 101586 (2019)
12. Ameen, N., et al.: Employees' behavioural intention to smartphone security: a gender-based, cross-national study. Comput. Hum. Behav. **104**, 106184 (2020)
13. Hina, S., Panneer Selvam, D.D.D., Lowry, P.B.: Institutional governance and protection motivation: theoretical insights into shaping employees' security compliance behavior in higher education institutions in the developing world. Comput. Secur. **87**, 101594 (2019)
14. Wall, J.D., Buche, M.W.: To fear or not to fear? A critical review and analysis of fear appeals in the information security context. Commun. Assoc. Inf. Syst. **41**, 277–300 (2017)
15. Amran, A., Zaaba, Z.F., Mahinderjit Singh, M.K.: Habituation effects in computer security warning, pp. 119–131. Taylor & Francis (2018)
16. Groß, T., Coopamootoo, K.P.L., Al-Jabri, A.: Effect of cognitive depletion on password choice. In: The {LASER} Workshop: Learning from Authoritative Security Experiment Results ({LASER} 2016), San Jose, CA (2016)
17. Kroenung, J., Eckhardt, A.: The attitude cube – a three-dimensional model of situational factors in IS adoption and their impact on the attitude-behavior relationship. Inf. Manag. **52**(6), 611 (2015)

18. Zolotov, M., Oliveira, T., Casteleyn, S.: E-participation adoption models research in the last 17 years: a weight and meta-analytical review. Comput. Hum. Behav. **81**, 350–365 (2018)
19. Lowry, P.B., Moody, G.D.: Proposing the control-reactance compliance model (CRCM) to explain opposing motivations to comply with organisational information security policies. Inf. Syst. J. **25**(5), 433–463 (2015)
20. Groß, T., Coopamootoo, K., Al-Jabri, A.: Effect of cognitive depletion on password choice extended technical report (2019)
21. Popay, J., et al.: Guidance on the conduct of narrative synthesis in systematic reviews. A product from the ESRC Methods Programme, version 1 (2006)
22. Danziger, S., Levav, J., Avnaim-Pesso, L.: Extraneous factors in judicial decisions. Proc. Natl. Acad. Sci. **108**(17), 6889–6892 (2011)
23. Hagger, M.S., et al.: Ego depletion and the strength model of self-control: a meta-analysis. Psychol. Bull. **136**(4), 495–525 (2010)
24. Dang, J.: An updated meta-analysis of the ego depletion effect. Psychol. Res. **82**(4), 645–651 (2017). https://doi.org/10.1007/s00426-017-0862-x
25. Abdullah, F., Ward, R.: Developing a general extended technology acceptance model for E-learning (GETAMEL) by analysing commonly used external factors. Comput. Hum. Behav. **56**(C), 238–256 (2016)
26. Vohs, K.D., Faber, R.J.: Spent resources: self-regulatory resource availability affects impulse buying. J. Consum. Res. **33**(4), 537–547 (2007)
27. Vohs, K.D., Heatherton, T.F.: Self-regulatory failure: a resource-depletion approach. Psychol. Sci. **11**(3), 249–254 (2000)
28. Gailliot, M.T., et al.: Breaking the rules: low trait or state self-control increases social norm violations. Psychology **3**(12), 1074 (2012)
29. DeWall, C.N., et al.: How leaders self-regulate their task performance: evidence that power promotes diligence, depletion, and disdain. In: Self-Regulation and Self-Control, Routledge, pp. 340–378 (2018)
30. Wang, J., et al.: Trade-offs and depletion in choice. J. Mark. Res. **47**(5), 910–919 (2010)
31. Mamonov, S., Benbunan-Fich, R.: The impact of information security threat awareness on privacy-protective behaviors. Comput. Hum. Behav. **83**(C), 32–44 (2018)
32. Melicher, W., et al.: Fast, lean, and accurate: modeling password guessability using neural networks. In: Proceedings of the 25th USENIX Conference on Security Symposium, pp. 175–191. USENIX Association, Austin (2016)
33. Wheeler, D.: zxcvbn: low-budget password strength estimation. In: 25th USENIX Security Symposium (USENIX Security 16), Austin, TX (2016)
34. Hart, S.G., Staveland, L.E.: Development of NASA-TLX (Task Load Index): results of empirical and theoretical research. In: Advances in Psychology, pp. 139–183. Elsevier (1988)
35. Mayer, J.D., Gaschke, Y.N.: The brief mood introspection scale (BMIS) (1988)
36. Baumeister, R.F., et al.: Ego depletion: is the active self a limited resource? J. Pers. Soc. Psychol. **74**(5), 1252–1265 (1998)
37. Malimage, K.: The role of habit in information security behaviors. In: Warkentin, M., et al. (eds.) ProQuest Dissertations Publishing (2013)
38. Komanduri, S., et al.: Of passwords and people: measuring the effect of password-composition policies. In: Proceedings of the SIGCHI Conference on Human Factors in Computing Systems, pp. 2595–2604. ACM, Vancouver (2011)
39. Vohs, K.D., et al.: Depletion enhances urges and feelings. (Unpublished manuscript). University of Minnesota, Minneapolis, MN (2014)

Whose Risk Is It Anyway: How Do Risk Perception and Organisational Commitment Affect Employee Information Security Awareness?

Andrew Reeves[1]($\boxtimes$) , Kathryn Parsons[2] , and Dragana Calic[2]

[1] University of Adelaide, Adelaide, SA, Australia
andrew.reeves@adelaide.edu.au
[2] Defence Science and Technology, Edinburgh, SA, Australia
{kathryn.parsons,dragana.calic}@dst.defence.gov.au

Abstract. Since information security (InfoSec) incidents often involve human error, businesses are investing greater resources into improving staff awareness and compliance with best-practice InfoSec behaviours. This research examined whether employees who feel that they may be personally affected by workplace InfoSec incidents are more likely to behave in accordance with those best-practice behaviours. To further understand this, we also examined organisational commitment and risk perception. Data collection involved an online questionnaire measuring these constructs in relation to three workplace cyber threats: phishing, malware, and mobile devices. The questionnaire was completed by 269 employed Australians. Participants who felt more personally affected by attacks associated with mobile devices were more likely to report following best-practice behaviours in that context at work. This was not the case for phishing and malware attacks. Other variables, including age, gender, employment level and InfoSec training, were also found to predict reported compliance with best-practice behaviours, and employees with more frequent training self-reported poorer compliance. Theoretical and practical implications are discussed.

Keywords: Risk perception · Organisational commitment · Information Security Awareness (ISA)

1 Introduction

Today's increasingly global organizations rely on robust and efficient processes, effective people, and importantly, secure technology. However, these systems are often threatened by cyber breaches or attacks. Traditionally, the focus of management on mitigating this threat has been to implement technological solutions to bolster information security (InfoSec). Despite these efforts, the number of InfoSec breaches continues to be significant. A 2019 Cyber Security Report indicated that 64% of European and 63% of Asia-Pacific businesses were interrupted by a security breach in the preceding year [1]. Employees have been found to be the most prevalent cause of InfoSec breaches [2, 3].

© Springer Nature Switzerland AG 2020
A. Moallem (Ed.): HCII 2020, LNCS 12210, pp. 232–249, 2020.
https://doi.org/10.1007/978-3-030-50309-3_16

This human involvement is rarely malicious, and is instead associated with naïve and accidental behaviours [4]. As a result, businesses are investing more resources into training programs designed to teach their staff how to identify and avoid these threats. To develop effective training programs, it is crucial to understand the factors that affect employee behavior in an InfoSec context. In particular, the extent to which an employee understands their role in ensuring their workplace's information security, and the extent to which they comply with best practice behaviours, will determine the level of human-aspects risk present in business [5, 6]. The extent to which an employee is aware-of and complies-with InfoSec best practice behaviours are together referred to as their Information Security Awareness (ISA) [6]. Previous studies have found employee perception and appreciation of InfoSec risks will influence their ISA and behavioral outcomes [7, 8]. The current study expands on this work by investigating the potentially related role of organisational commitment, examining employee perceptions of the relatively new InfoSec risk associated with the Internet of Things, and by investigating a currently under-studied type of risk perception – that of perceived personal risk. The following sections will introduce these constructs, with a discussion of previous scholarly work in the area, and where the current study builds upon previous research.

1.1 Information Security Awareness

ISA is defined by two key components: understanding and compliance. Understanding refers to "the degree or extent to which every employee understands the importance of information security, the levels of information security appropriate to the organization, [and] their individual security responsibilities" [6, p. 289]. Compliance is concerned with the level of commitment people have to these best-practice behaviours, exemplified by following an organization's InfoSec policies, rules, or guidelines [9]. Therefore, in line with the Knowledge, Attitude, and Behavior (KAB) model, ISA can be understood as the combination of a person's knowledge of, and attitude towards, best-practice InfoSec behaviours, as well as their compliance with these behaviours [10].

Previous research has looked to identify factors that may relate to better ISA in employees. McCormac, Zwaans [11] examined individual difference variables and found greater employee emotional stability, conscientiousness, and agreeableness were all related to greater ISA. In addition, employees with less propensity for taking risks had greater ISA [11]. While many relevant factors have been identified, there is a need to further assess the individual and other factors that may relate to ISA [5].

In addition, there is reason to expect that job role will affect ISA. Pattinson, Butavicius [9] found that bank employees had better ISA compared to the general public. They explain that this was likely due to their training and work environment, which had stringent InfoSec requirements. This leads us to question whether similar differences would be present between regular employees and management. Managers and team leaders may have more experience in their industry or organization, and may have received more InfoSec training than regular employees. They may also be more invested in the future of their organization. It is therefore expected that:

H1: Managers and team leaders will have greater ISA than regular employees.

1.2 Employee Perception of the Internet of Things

While many InfoSec risks are well established, such as phishing and mal-ware, the constantly-changing nature of the InfoSec landscape means new threats are emerging [2, 3]. For example, 66% of InfoSec professionals report they consider the risks associated with the Internet of Things (IoT) to be moderate to extreme [12]. IoT risks are unique, as they involve devices (e.g., mobile devices), that are often located outside of physically restricted areas (e.g., a restricted work building or production floor), but remain connected to the central work network [13]. Additionally, these devices are often designed without security in mind, resulting in potential vulnerabilities [14]. Each device therefore becomes a potential entry point for an attacker.

Being a relatively new threat, employee perceptions of IoT devices are critical to examining the level of risk they pose. Despite this, human aspects research on the topic remains limited, with only two previous papers available in extant literature. While not focusing on employees specifically, Williams, Nurse [15] found that despite indicating they care about their security and privacy, consumers continue to purchase IoT devices without checking that the expected security controls are in place. Similarly, Zheng, Apthorpe [16] found that the general public's perception of IoT is generally positive, however many expressed concern regarding privacy and security issues relating to the technology. For this reason, it may be expected that employees who are more concerned regarding the risks of IoT devices may be more vigilant, and therefore have greater Information Security Awareness (ISA). However, this has yet to be examined empirically.

1.3 Perceptions of Risk and the Psychometric Paradigm

People's perceptions of risk events have been studied in a variety of fields [17]. Risk is commonly defined as the probability of adverse effects and the magnitude of the consequences [18]. The Psychometric Paradigm, developed Paul Slovic and colleagues, is the most established and widely accepted framework to describe perception of risk [e.g., 17, 19–22]. It identifies eighteen risk perception constructs, which can be explained by two factors: *dread* and *familiarity*. *Dread* refers to the extent to which someone is scared, troubled, or generally retracts away from the risk, at the level of a gut reaction. Dread is often captured by measuring the extent to which someone feels they could stay calm if the risk event occurred [21, 22]. Familiarity refers to the extent to which someone feels they have knowledge of the risk, the extent to which they understand it, and how much control they have over it and its consequences [21–23]. The psychometric paradigm holds that people feel most threatened by risks that are highly dreaded and unfamiliar [21]. As a result, people may actively change their behavior to avoid risks that meet these criteria. In the case of InfoSec, threat avoidance behaviours align with good ISA behaviours (e.g., avoiding the threat of phishing may involve being careful with the links in emails, which is also a sign of good ISA). Following this theory, greater ISA can be an outcome of greater threat perception and can be used as a proxy for the level of threat an individual perceives from an InfoSec risk. It is therefore expected that individuals who feel more threatened by an InfoSec risk (i.e., perceive greater dread and unfamiliarity) will have greater ISA:

H2a: Individuals who report feeling less familiar with InfoSec risks will have greater ISA.

H2b: Individuals who perceive greater dread regarding these InfoSec risks will have greater ISA.

1.4 Information Security Risk Perceptions

Previous research has explored InfoSec risk perceptions at a high level of abstraction [e.g. 24] or has examined the employees' perception of risk *to the organization*, and used this to predict their InfoSec behaviours [8, 23, 25]. For example, employees who do not believe their organization is at risk of a cyber-attack are more likely to be complacent with InfoSec-related matters [25]. However, it has been suggested that perceived organisational risk is not the only risk perception factor that will influence an employee's behavior.

Pattinson and Jerram [8] investigated the InfoSec risk perceptions of 12 employees from a local government organization. Using the Repertory Grid Technique [26], they identified 11 items, categorized as 'Risk perceptions relating to me'. These items refer to the personal risks perceived by the respondents as a result of an InfoSec risk [8]. It may be expected that individuals who believe they will personally be affected by a cyber-attack in their organization will be more likely to act more securely. For instance, an individual who believes their own personal information may be leaked should their organization's data be compromised may be more likely to choose secure passwords and be vigilant against phishing attacks. Although Pattinson and Jerram [8] identified constructs relating to personal risk as important for InfoSec, they are yet to be studied in relation to ISA.

A similar study was conducted by Bulgurcu, Cavusoglu [25], in which 467 American employees completed a survey measuring various factors in regards to their intent to comply with their organization's InfoSec policy. The authors found that employees were more likely to comply with an InfoSec policy if they felt the cost of non-compliance was great, either because workplace sanctions were severe or because the information technology systems were highly vulnerable to attack. They also found that an employee's perception of the consequences of non-compliance are influenced by their ISA. While the results are valuable, their study was limited by the use of a brief, non-validated measure of ISA designed for the study. The measure also captured ISA at a high level of abstraction by asking respondents to rate their agreement with items such as: "Overall, I am aware of the potential security threats and their negative consequences" [25, p. 536]. These items rely on the respondent's beliefs regarding InfoSec risks, rather than capturing ISA in a more specific manner. These items are therefore susceptible to response biases such as the social-desirability bias [5, 27]. Therefore, further research needs to examine the relationship between personal risk perceptions and ISA with a more comprehensive measure of ISA that focuses on best-practice behaviours rather than policy compliance. From a theoretical perspective, based on the factors proposed by Pattinson and Jerram [8] and the results of Bulgurcu, Cavusoglu [25], it is expected that:

H3: Individuals who perceive more personal risk from organisational InfoSec threats will have greater ISA.

1.5   Organisational Commitment

It may be expected that perceived personal risk would be related to the level of commitment an employee has to the business. Organisational commitment refers to how attached an employee is to their place of work. An employee who is greatly attached and committed to their workplace should work harder, strive to make fewer mistakes, and follow organisational policy diligently [28]. Businesses therefore focus on enhancing organisational commitment to increase productivity and reduce risk and turnover [29–31]. Organisational commitment has also been associated with greater motivation to learn in workplace training [32], leading to more positive outcomes of training programs [33, 34]. In line with these findings, more committed employees may have more engagement with information-security related organisational training, as well as greater commitment to follow security policy, leading to greater ISA. However, there is limited literature exploring the relationship between organisational commitment and ISA

Meyer and Allen [35] developed a measure of organisational commitment, here referred to as the three-component conceptualization of organisational commitment questionnaire (3C-OCQ). The 3C-OCQ views organisational commitment as a combination of the affective, normative, and continuance factors that influence an employee's decision to remain in their organization. The affective component concerns the emotional aspects of commitment. The normative component refers to the extent to which an employee feels that remaining at one organization is expected by society or is morally right. Finally, the continuance component refers to the more pragmatic reasons an employee might wish to remain within an organization, such as the difficulty of finding new work and the cost of moving organizations.

The three-component conceptualization has been examined in relation to ISA only once. Stanton, Stam [36] studied the relationship between ISA and the 3C-OCQ. Although the authors reported a positive relationship between organisational commitment and ISA, to date, research has yet to examine the potentially differing relationships between the three components of organisational commitment and ISA.

Therefore, there is a need to re-examine the effects of the three components of organisational commitment on ISA using a validated, holistic ISA measure, such as the Human Aspects of InfoSec Questionnaire [HAIS-Q; 5]. Following Stanton, Stam [36], it is expected that:

H4a: Individuals with greater *affective* organisational commitment will have better ISA.
H4b: Individuals with greater *normative* organisational commitment will have better ISA.
H4c: Individuals with greater *continuance* organisational commitment will have better ISA.

1.6   The Present Study

Building on existing literature, it is expected that employees who feel more threatened by workplace InfoSec risks will be more likely to be in management positions, have greater perception of personal risk, perceive a greater risk of the InfoSec threats (i.e., greater dread and unfamiliarity), and be more committed to their organization. In each case, those who feel more threatened should be more likely to take action to avoid the threat, resulting in greater ISA. This research model and associated hypotheses is presented in Fig. 1. No study to our knowledge has yet empirically examined these relationships on a single cohort.

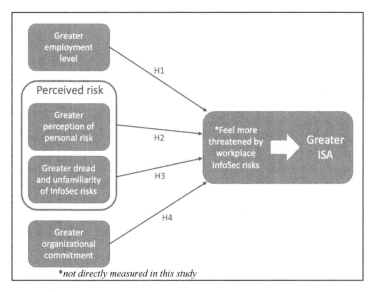

Fig. 1. Research model and hypotheses for the current study

Since previous research has demonstrated a relationship between ISA, demographic variables, and InfoSec training [37], these variables are also examined. To test this model, we used three threats, namely phishing, malware, and an Internet of Things (IoT) threat associated with mobile devices (in the current study, the theft of a laptop). These threats were selected as the focus of this study as phishing and malware are often identified as significant threats to organisational InfoSec [1], while the IoT has been identified as an under-researched threat of concern to many security professionals [12, 38]. It is expected that the hypotheses presented above will be consistent across the three threat areas.

2   Method

2.1 Participants

A total of 269 participants (54% males, 46% females) responded to an online questionnaire. Participants represented all age categories (31% between 18 and 29 years of age, 28% between 30 to 39, 17% between 40 to 49, 15% between 50 and 59, and 9% aged 60 and above), and most participants had completed a Bachelor's degree (26%) or a post-graduate degree (31%). Approximately 18% had not completed high school education. Participants were recruited through the researchers' Facebook pages, and a closed invitation-only panel recruitment method via Qualtrics. Data collection occurred in May 2017. Participants were required to be employed in Australia and be over the age of 18. Basic demographic and workplace data were gathered, including age, gender, self-reported knowledge of computers, education level, employment level, and workplace InfoSec training frequency. Approximately 45% of respondents self-identified as 'Staff/Individual Contributor' and 55% as 'Manager/Team Leader' (definitions were not provided).

2.2 Materials

The survey consisted of the following measures, each scored on a 5-point Likert scale (1 = strongly disagree to 5 = strongly agree).

The Human Aspects of InfoSec Questionnaire (HAIS-Q)
The Human Aspects of InfoSec Questionnaire (HAIS-Q) is a 63-item measure of ISA [5]. For the purposes of this study, 27 items were used, which relate to the three threat areas examined in this study, namely, Email-use, Information-handling, and Mobile-devices. These subsections of the HAIS-Q assess ISA in regard to phishing, malware, and IoT/mobile devices respectively. Previous studies have found Cronbach's alpha scores of .78 for the Email-use, .79 for the Information-handling, and .81 for the Mobile-devices subsections [5]. The Cronbach's alpha scores obtained in this study were .82, .82 and .81, respectively. Higher scores relate to better ISA.

Three-Component Organisational Commitment Questionnaire (3C-OCQ)
This scale, developed by Allen and John [39], contains 24 items and measures the affective, normative, and continuance components of commitment to an organization. Internal consistency for all three of these components is high, with previous studies finding Cronbach's alpha scores of .87 for the affective component, .79 for the normative component, and .75 for the continuance component [39]. The Cronbach's alpha scores in this study were .82, .73 and .71, respectively.

Perception of Personal-Risk for InfoSec Threats Scale (PPRITS)
The Perception of Personal-Risk for InfoSec Threats Scale (PPRITS) was developed for this study to measure how personally at-risk individuals feel in relation to organisational InfoSec threats, based on the *Risk perceptions relating to me* developed theme by Pattinson and Jerram [8]. The scale consists of 11 items adapted from the nine personal risk perceptions identified by Pattinson and Jerram [8]. Full scale items are presented in Table 1.

The scale was used to assess each of the three threats of interest: phishing, malware, and IoT/mobile devices. To assess each threat, a definition of the key term (i.e., phishing, malware, IoT/mobile devices) was provided, before asking respondents to rate their agreement with the 11 items relating to personal risk (shown in Table 1). Each item is measured based on perceived likelihood and severity. The product of the likelihood and severity ratings are summed to create a total Perception of Personal Risk score, where higher scores represent greater perceived risk. The definition of the mobile devices threat positioned the threat of a laptop as an IoT-related risk. Participants were asked to rate the perceived likelihood and severity of consequences for each of the 11 items. The

Table 1. Perception of Personal-Risk for InfoSec Threats Scale (PPRITS)

Phishing	Malware	IoT/mobile devices
Definition: Phishing emails are malicious emails which appear to have been sent by a known contact or organization. An attachment or link in phishing emails may install malware on your work network or direct you to a malicious website set up to trick you into divulging sensitive information, such as work passwords and account IDs.	*Definition: Malware refers to software which is specifically designed to disrupt, damage, or gain unauthorized access to a computer system or data. Removable media (USB) devices can often become infected with malware. When connected to a work computer, the infection can spread to the work network, where it can cause data loss or leakage of sensitive information.*	*Definition: The 'Internet of Things' (IoT) refers to a network of internet-connected devices, including laptops, smartphones, and smart-appliances. In organizations, IoT devices are often located outside of physically restricted areas, but remain connected to the organization's central network. Each IoT device therefore becomes a potential point of entry for an attacker, allowing them access to sensitive information on the organization's network.*
Instructions: *You unintentionally click on a link in a phishing email on a work device.* *Please rate the likelihood and severity of the following:* (5-pt Likert)	*Instructions:* *You unintentionally connect an infected USB to a work computer.* *Please rate the likelihood and severity of the following:* (5-pt Likert)	*Instructions: You leave a work-connected device (e.g., Laptop, tablet, smart phone) unattended in a public place, and it is stolen.* *Please rate the likelihood and severity of the following* (5-pt Likert):*

I am reprimanded	*I am demoted*
I am fired	*My personal information is damaged/destroyed/leaked*
I can't do my job properly	*It is an inconvenience/time-consuming/nuisance*
My professionalism/quality of my work is tarnished	*It causes me stress*
I am required to take action and fix the problem	*My workload will increase*
I lose confidence in the information or systems required for me to do my job	

Cronbach's alpha scores were .94 for phishing, .95 for malware and .95 for IoT/mobile devices.

Psychometric Paradigm of InfoSec Threats Scale (PPITS)

These items measure participants' perception of dread and novelty in relation to the three InfoSec threats (i.e., phishing, malware, and IoT/mobile devices). To limit excess respondent fatigue caused by long questionnaires, four items were used from the eighteen developed by Slovic, Fischhoff [22]. The items used for the dread factor were

"Dreaded" (how calm could an individual stay should the event occur) and "Control of Consequences" [22, p. 5]. For the familiarity factor, "Immediacy of Consequences" and "Well-Known" (aka. known to science) were used. As only four items were chosen for reasons of length, they were not collapsed beneath dread and novelty factors. Instead, they were treated as four separate items in the analyses. Table 2 details the exact wording of the items used.

Table 2. Psychometric Paradigm of InfoSec Threats Scale (PPITS) (5-pt Likert)

	Phishing	Malware	IoT/Mobile Devices
Well-known	*The threat posed by phishing is well-known.*	*The threat posed by malware is well-known.*	*The threat posed to cyber security by mobile computing is well known.*
Dread	*If I realized I had clicked on a phishing link, I would be able to consider the consequences calmly.*	*If I realized I had connected an infected USB to a work computer, I would be able to consider the consequences calmly.*	*If I left a work-connected device unattended in public, and it was stolen, I would be able to consider the consequences calmly.*
Control of Consequences	*If I realized I had clicked on a phishing link, the consequences would be outside of my control.*	*If I realized I had connected an infected USB to a work computer, the consequences would be outside of my control.*	*If I left a work-connected device unattended in public, and it was stolen, the consequences would be outside of my control.*
Immediacy of Consequences	*If I realized I had clicked on a phishing link, the consequences might not be immediately apparent.*	*If I realized I had connected an infected USB to a work computer, the consequences might not be immediately apparent.*	*If I left a work-connected device unattended in public, and it was stolen, the consequences might not be immediately apparent.*

3   Results

Preliminary testing was conducted to inspect the data for normality and no major violations were observed. Pearson bivariate correlations were examined between ISA and all measured variables. The correlations revealed that the significant relationships differed across the three threat areas. Therefore, three multiple regressions were conducted (i.e., one for each threat area) to determine which of the measured variables may predict participants' ISA. Each of the regressions consisted of a two-step hierarchical regression, in which age and gender were added in the first step. This was done to control for their effects, as age and gender are well established predictors of ISA [e.g., 5, 40]. Added in step 2 were the variables that significantly correlated with Email-use ISA, Information-handling ISA, and Mobile-device ISA, respectively. Variables that did not correlate with ISA in the respective threat area were not included in the regressions and are therefore not reported in the below tables.

3.1 Predicting Email-use ISA

Table 3 presents the results of a hierarchical multiple regression used to test the extent to which the measured variables predicted Email-use ISA. At step 1, the model explained approximately 15% of the variance in Email-use ISA, $F(2, 266) = 22.6$, $p < .001$. Email-use ISA was generally better for older employees, and females tended to outperform males. At step 2, the model explained approximately 33% of the variance, $F(9, 259) = 14.2$, $p < .001$. Unexpectedly, staff/individual contributors tended to outperform managers and team leaders. Affective organisational commitment also predicted ISA, as did one PPITS item: dreaded. Table 3 presents the predictors in order of importance, as determined by their respective standardized beta values.

Table 3. Summary of hierarchical regression for email-use ISA (N = 269)

Variable	β (standardized)	t
Stage 1 $F(2, 266) = 22.6$, $p < .001$; $R^2 = .145$		
Age	.33	5.77***
Gender (Female = 2)	.21	3.81***
Stage 2 $F(9, 259) = 14.2$, $p < .001$; $R^2 = .327$		
Employment level	−.26	−4.82***
Age	.24	4.30***
Affective org. commitment	.20	3.78***
Gender	.17	3.15**
Dreaded	−.13	−2.18*
Training frequency	−.11	−2.03*
Immediacy of consequences	−.11	−1.97
Education	.08	1.60
Well-known	.04	.64

* $p < .05$, ** $p < .01$, *** $p < .001$

3.2 Predicting Information-Handling ISA

As presented in Table 4, at step 1, both age and gender were significant, together explaining approximately 16% of the variance in Information-handling ISA, $F(2, 266) = 25.6$,

$p < .001$. At step 2, the model explained approximately 27% of the variance, $F(7, 261)$ $= 11.8, p < .001$. The significance of the predictors largely mirrored those found in the Email-use threat area. Unlike the Email-use threat area, age was a greater predictor of Information-handling ISA than employment level, and gender was a greater predictor than affective organisational commitment. Table 4 presents the predictors in order of importance.

Table 4. Summary of hierarchical regression for information-handling ISA (N = 269)

Variable	β (standardized)	t
Stage 1 $F(2, 266) = 25.6, p < .001; R^2 = .162$		
Age	.35	6.20***
Gender (Female = 2)	.22	3.97***
Stage 2 $F(7, 261) = 11.8, p < .001; R^2 = .278$		
Age	.26	4.53***
Employment level	−.24	−4.37***
Gender	.18	3.33**
Affective org. commitment	.16	3.06**
Dreaded	−.12	−1.98*
Well-known	.10	1.61
Training frequency	−.07	−1.24
Immediacy of consequences	−.04	−.73

$* p < .05, ** p < .01, *** p < .001$

3.3   Predicting Mobile-Devices ISA

For the case of Mobile-devices ISA, the same 2-step hierarchical regression was conducted. As shown in Table 5, the results mirror those of the previous two regressions at step 1, explaining 18% of the variance, $F(2,266) = 25.6, p < .001$. The model at step 2 explained approximately 36% of the variance, $F(9, 259) = 14.2, p < .001$. Unlike the previous two threat areas, perceived personal risk correlated significantly with Mobile-devices ISA and was therefore included in the regression, where it was the third greatest predictor behind age and employment level. Table 5 presents the predictors in order from greatest to least importance.

3.4   Summary Across the Threat Areas

Although the predictors that explained significant variance in ISA differed across the three threat areas, age and employment level were the most significant predictors for all threats. In addition to age and employment level, gender and affective organisational

Table 5. Summary of hierarchical regression for mobile-devices ISA (N = 269)

Variable	β (standardized)	t
Step 1 $F(2, 266) = 25.6, p < .001; R^2 = .182$		
Age	.39	6.97***
Gender (Female = 2)	.21	3.69***
Step 2 $F(9, 259) = 14.2, p < .001; R^2 = .363$		
Age	.29	5.37***
Employment level	−.22	−4.23***
Perceived personal risk	.19	3.42**
Affective org. commitment	.18	3.23**
Gender	.16	3.12**
Well-known	.16	2.65**
Training Frequency	−.09	−1.66
Education	.08	1.68
Normative org. commitment	.02	.29
Control of consequences	−.03	−.47

** $p < .01$, *** $p < .001$

commitment were the only consistent predictors across all three threats. In all cases, results suggest that females, older adults, those with higher affective organisational commitment, and those who are not in management positions have higher ISA. Table 6 presents an overview of all variables examined.

4 Discussion

This study examined the relationship between ISA, individual differences variables (organisational commitment and risk perceptions) and workplace variables (employment level and InfoSec training) using a single cohort. ISA was examined in relation to three InfoSec threats: phishing, malware, and the IoT/mobile devices. The following sections discuss the individual and workplace variables that predicted ISA, as these differed depending on the InfoSec risk being examined.

4.1 Relationships with ISA Consistent Across the Three Threat Areas

In keeping with previous literature [5, 9, 11], age and gender were significant predictors of ISA in this study, across all three InfoSec threats examined. Older participants had higher ISA scores, as did females. Managers were found to have significantly poorer ISA than regular staff members across all threat areas. While unexpected, this finding could suggest that managers, due to their increased responsibilities, may not feel they have adequate time to comply with best-practice behaviours [36]. There are also implications

Table 6. Summary of independent variables predicting ISA by threat area (N = 269)

Variable	Email-use	Information-handling	Mobile-devices
Age	✓(+)	✓(+)	✓(+)
Gender (Female = 2)	✓(+)	✓(+)	✓(+)
Education	✗	^	✗
Employment Level	✓(-)	✓(-)	✓(-)
Training Frequency	✓(-)	✗	✗
Knowledge of Computers	^	^	^
Affective Org. Commitment	✓(+)	✓(+)	✓(+)
Normative Org. Commitment	^	^	✗
Continuance Org. Commitment	^	^	^
Perceived Personal Risk	^	^	✓(+)
Dreaded	✓(-)	✓(-)	^
Immediacy of Consequences	✓(-)	✗	^
Well-known	✗	✗	✓(+)
Control of Consequences	^	^	✗
Total variance explained (%)	33	24	33

✓Explained significant variance. ✗ *Significant correlation with ISA but did not predict significant variance in the regression.* ^ *Did not correlate significantly with ISA and was not included in the regression. ( ) Direction of effect*

for organisational culture, as managers play a critical role in forming the culture of an organization [41]. If management have poor ISA, the ISA of the surrounding workforce could be inhibited, potentially making it more difficult to establish a strong security culture within the organization. This finding highlights the importance of organizations developing their security processes to work with manager's goals and to minimize the interruption to their job role caused by security processes. Gearing InfoSec training in such a way would act to avoid instilling complacency in the workforce. ·

Greater affective organisational commitment was also associated with greater ISA in all three threat areas. However, continuance and normative commitment were not. A potential explanation comes from work conducted by Eisenberger, Rockstuhl [42], who found that employees with high affective organisational commitment are more likely to perform extra-role activities (i.e., activities that are beneficial to the business but are not mandatory for their job role) than those high on continuance or normative commitment. The result found in the current study may indicate that employees perceive best-practice InfoSec behaviours to be extra-role. From an applied perspective, businesses looking to enhance the ISA of their staff may focus on adjusting their security processes to become in-role for a greater proportion of their workforce. Doing so would enable the existing continuance and normative commitment of the employees to drive greater ISA. Furthermore, this result highlights the importance of creating an environment where employees feel valued and satisfied with their work, as this is likely to increase their affective commitment [42], with flow-on effects to improve their cybersecurity behaviours.

4.2 Security Training Frequency

More frequent InfoSec training at work was associated with lower Email-use ISA. Previous research has found that employees who have undertaken formal InfoSec training may be overconfident and complacent, leading to poorer ISA [9]. Recent work has highlighted that the frequency of security training is less important than ensuring that the training style matches that of the individual employee's preferences [37], which was not captured in the current study.

Furthermore, it has been suggested that an overload of InfoSec training may result in negative behavioral outcomes, such as fatigue and intentional disobedience [43, 44]. As email-use is a well-established InfoSec risk [1, 12], this negative relationship could be the result of a previous overabundance of InfoSec training on the subject. Further work could look to determine the role of fatigue in mediating the relationship between more frequent InfoSec training and poor behavioral outcomes.

4.3 Perception of Personal Risk

In regard to phishing and malware attacks, there was no relationship between an employee's perception of being personally at-risk (e.g., of reprimand, data loss, reduced productivity) and their ISA. This was unexpected, as it was thought that people who felt personally at-risk would want to avoid the risk, and therefore have better ISA. However, a significant relationship between perceived personal risk and ISA was found for the mobile devices threat area. This inconsistent result may be due to the nature of phishing and malware risks which may not be immediately visible or tangible to individuals. In contrast, the IoT/mobile devices threat used in this study related to the theft of a laptop, which will have immediate tangible consequences. If an employee feels that such an event would impact them personally, it would be simple for them to change their behavior in order to ensure that event does not happen (e.g., by never leaving the laptop unattended). In the case of phishing and malware, it is not as straightforward for someone to determine what they should do to avoid the risk. That is, as the result of falling for a phishing or malware attack is often not immediately visible and there may be no immediate feedback for the individual to adjust their behavior. For example, an individual may discover that they have unwittingly given away important credentials or installed malware on their computer, but the action that caused this may have occurred weeks prior to being discovered.

4.4 The Psychometric Paradigm

Individuals who perceived the risk of IoT/mobile devices as well-known had greater ISA. However, this was not the case for phishing and malware. As with the perception of personal risk measure, this difference across the threat areas may be due to the more complex nature of phishing and malware. That is, it would make sense that people who are more familiar with the risk would be better at avoiding it, but only when the actions required to avoid the risk are explicit. When the risk-mitigation behaviours are less clear, specialized training is required [45]. This is likely the case for phishing and malware.

The extent to which participants were able to control the consequences associated with the risks was not significantly correlated with ISA in all three threat areas. This indicates that, regardless of how much an individual perceives the consequences of a phishing, malware, or IoT attack to be controllable, their ISA may not be affected. This unexpected result may relate to the separate skill sets required for risk-containment, as opposed to risk-mitigation [46]. Someone may be confident that they could handle the consequences of a phishing attack, but still not be sure how to avoid the attack. Furthermore, this result could indicate the discrepancy between people's perception of their own ability, and their real-world performance.

In regard to dread, individuals who were less scared of phishing or malware attacks had greater ISA. While this does not seem intuitive, this may indicate that ISA is influencing risk perceptions, rather than the other way around. Individuals with greater ISA may feel more confident they can avoid the risk, and therefore may not perceive it to be as scary. Interestingly, while this was found to be the case for the phishing and malware, no such relationship was found in regard to IoT/mobile devices. This may be because the theft of a laptop would be perceived as more of a personal risk compared to phishing or malware. While there may be some personal impact, the consequences of a phishing or malware attack in an organization will largely be business-related. In contrast, the consequences of a theft of a laptop is much more personal. Therefore, it may be expected that how scary someone finds the risk would be unaffected by their confidence in mitigating it. This is also consistent with the results of the perceived personal risk measure, which was only a significant predictor of IoT/mobile devices ISA, and not email use or information handling ISA.

Alternatively, this result may reflect an avoidance of cybersecurity training due to perceived dread. That is, if an employee is scared of the risks associated with phishing or malware, they may avoid any interaction with training that involves this topic, leading to poorer ISA than their colleagues.

4.5 Limitations and Future Directions

The relationships presented in this study are correlational. As this study has identified multiple meaningful relationships, and speculated regarding the causal nature of the effect, future work should look to confirm this. The variables examined in this study together predicted between 24% and 33% of the variance in ISA across the threat areas. While this result is significant, it also indicates that there are other predictors of ISA that have yet to be identified. For example, variables such as organisational culture will likely affect adherence to best-practice InfoSec behaviours [41, 47]. Future research could look to examine culture in relation to other constructs examined in the current study, such as risk perception.

The measure used to assess perception of personal risk was developed for this study. While the items used have been previously found to be important in understanding employee InfoSec risk perceptions [8], the use of this measure has not yet been empirically validated. That said, current findings support its use. A valid measure of perceived personal risk would be expected to correlate with organisational commitment, as more committed individuals should perceive a risk to the business as a risk to themselves. In keeping with this, the perceived personal risk measure correlated significantly with organisational commitment. Furthermore, a measure of perceived personal risk should relate to ISA, as people who feel more at-risk should actively avoid performing behaviours that lead to that risk. This, too, was the case in the present study, but only in the mobile devices threat area. These results partly support the measure's convergent validity. Further research should look at validating this measure with objective measures of behavior.

The inconsistent relationships found regarding the psychometric paradigm and ISA indicate further research is required. Due to length constraints, this study was only able to focus on four of the 17 psychometric paradigm items. Nonetheless, the current preliminary application of the psychometric paradigm to the InfoSec realm has demonstrated that different risk perception variables are important for different InfoSec threats. Future research should extend the current study by applying all items alongside a validated ISA measure, such as the HAIS-Q. Methods such as principle component analysis could then be used to determine which risk perception variables are most important for each InfoSec threat.

4.6 Conclusion

This study found that different InfoSec threats are perceived differently, with important implications for InfoSec training programs. Risk perception was found to be an important predictor of employee ISA, but only in certain contexts. Our results suggest that, in certain contexts, employees perceive a risk to the business to be a risk to themselves. This highlights the interconnectivity between work and private life and suggests that perceptions of InfoSec risks in both domains are important in informing employee InfoSec behaviours. Future research should look to further examine this, specifically by examining the way employee perception of personal risk interacts with their behavior regarding abstract threats, such as social engineering. Also, how emotionally-attached an employee is to their workplace influenced their ISA. Finally, training should be tailored to managers, who were found to have significantly poorer ISA than regular staff members. Since management play an integral role in organizational security culture, it is vital to ensure security processes are aligned with manager's goals and the strategic direction of the organization.

References

1. Telstra Corporation: Telstra Security Report 2019 (2019). https://www.telstra.com.au/content/dam/shared-component-assets/tecom/campaigns/security-report/Summary-Report-2019-LR.pdf
2. PricewaterhouseCoopers: Key findings from the global state of information security survey 2016. Turnaround and transformation in cyber security (2015)
3. Telstra Corporation: Telstra Cyber Security Report 2017: Managing risk in a digital world (2017)
4. Parsons, K., et al.: The influence of organizational information security culture on information security decision making. J. Cogn. Eng. Decis. Mak. **9**(2), 117–129 (2015)
5. Parsons, K., et al.: The human aspects of information security questionnaire (HAIS-Q): two further validation studies. Comput. Secur. **66**, 40–51 (2017)

6. Kruger, H.A., Kearney, W.D.: A prototype for assessing information security awareness. Comput. Secur. **25**(4), 289–296 (2006)
7. Williams, M., Nurse, J.R., Creese, S.: Privacy is the boring bit: user perceptions and behaviour in the internet-of-things. In: 2017 15th Annual Conference on Privacy, Security and Trust (PST) (2017)
8. Pattinson, M., Jerram, C.: A study of information security risk perceptions at a local government organisation. In: Australasian Conference on Information Systems, Melbourne, Australia (2013)
9. Pattinson, M., et al.: The information security awareness of bank employees. In: Clarke, N., Furnell, S. (eds.) Human Aspects of Information Security & Assurance (HAISA 2016) (2016)
10. Parsons, K., et al.: Determining employee awareness using the human aspects of information security questionnaire (HAIS-Q). Comput. Secur. **42**, 165–176 (2014)
11. McCormac, A., et al.: Individual differences and information security awareness. Comput. Hum. Behav. **69**, 151–156 (2017)
12. Marsh and McLennan Companies and Microsoft Corporation: 2019 Global Cyber Risk Perception Survey (2019)
13. Cisco: The Internet of Things: Reduce Security Risks with Automated Policies (2015)
14. Sharevski, F.: Experiential user-centered security in a classroom: secure design for IoT. IEEE Commun. Mag. **57**(11), 48–53 (2019)
15. Williams, M., Nurse, J.R.C., Creese, S.: Privacy is the boring bit: user perceptions and behaviour in the internet-of-things. In: Proceedings - 2017 15th Annual Conference on Privacy, Security and Trust, PST 2017 (2018)
16. Zheng, S., et al.: User perceptions of smart home IoT privacy. In: Proceedings of the ACM on Human-Computer Interaction, vol. 2, no. CSCW (2018)
17. Sjöberg, L., Moen, B.-E., Rundmo, T.: Explaining risk perception. An evaluation of the psychometric paradigm in risk perception research, Trondheim, Norway (2004)
18. Rayner, S., Cantor, R.: How fair is safe enough? The cultural approach to societal technology choice1. Risk Anal. **7**(1), 3–9 (1987)
19. Siegrist, M., Keller, C., Kiers, H.A.L.: A new look at the psychometric paradigm of perception of hazards. Risk Anal. **25**(1), 211–222 (2005)
20. Sjöberg, L.: The different dynamics of personal and general risk. Risk Manag. **5**(3), 19–34 (2003)
21. Slovic, P., Fischhoff, B., Lichtenstein, S.: Facts and fears: understanding perceived risk. In: Schwing, R.C., Albers, W.A. (eds.) Societal Risk Assessment: How Safe is Safe Enough?. General Motors Research Laboratories, pp. 181–216. Springer, Boston (1980). https://doi.org/10.1007/978-1-4899-0445-4_9
22. Slovic, P., Fischhoff, B., Lichtenstein, S.: Facts and fears: societal perception of risk. Adv. Consum. Res. **8**, 497 (1980)
23. Farahmand, F., et al.: Risk perceptions of information security: a measurement study. In: 2009 International Conference on Computational Science and Engineering (2009)
24. Huang, D.-L., Rau, P.-L.P., Salvendy, G.: Perception of information security. Behav. Inf. Technol. **29**(3), 221–232 (2010)
25. Bulgurcu, B., Cavusoglu, H., Benbasat, I.: Information security policy compliance: an empirical study of rationality-based beliefs and information security awareness. MIS Q. **34**(3), 523–548 (2010)
26. Fransella, F.: A Manual for Repertory Grid Technique. Academic Press, London (1977). Bannister, D. (ed.)
27. Edwards, A.: The relationship between the judged desirability of a trait and the probability that the trait will be endorsed. J. Appl. Psychol. **37**(2), 90–93 (1953)
28. Mowday, R.T., Steers, R.M., Porter, L.W.: The measurement of organizational commitment. J. Vocat. Behav. **14**(2), 224–247 (1979)

29. Cetin, S., Gürbüz, S., Sert, M.: A meta-analysis of the relationship between organizational commitment and organizational citizenship behavior: test of potential moderator variables. Empl. Responsib. Rights J. **27**(4), 281–303 (2015). https://doi.org/10.1007/s10672-015-9266-5

30. Cohen, A.: Organizational commitment and turnover: a meta-analysis. Acad. Manag. J. **36**(5), 1140–1157 (1993)

31. Suparjo: Job satisfaction as an antecedent of organizational commitment: a systematic review. Int. J. Civ. Eng. Technol. **8**(9), 832–843 (2017)

32. Kontoghiorghes, C.: Predicting motivation to learn and motivation to transfer learning back to the job in a service organization: a new systemic model for training effectiveness. Perform. Improve. Q. **15**(3), 114–129 (2002)

33. Bashir, N., Long, C.S.: The relationship between training and organizational commitment among academicians in Malaysia. J. Manag. Dev. **34**(10), 1227–1245 (2015)

34. Bulut, C., Çulha, O.: The effects of organizational training on organizational commitment. Int. J. Train. Dev. **14**, 309–322 (2010)

35. Meyer, J.P., Allen, N.J.: A three-component conceptualization of organizational commitment. Hum. Resour. Manag. Rev. **1**(1), 61–89 (1991)

36. Stanton, J.M., et al.: Examining the linkage between organizational commitment and information security. In: IEEE International Conference on Systems, Man and Cybernetics (2003)

37. Pattinson, M., et al.: Matching training to individual learning styles improves information security awareness. Inf. Comput. Secur. (2019, ahead-of-print)

38. ISACA: State of cybersecurity: implications for 2016. An ISACA and RSA conference survey (2016)

39. Allen, N.J., John, P.M.: The measurement and antecedents of affective, continuance and normative commitment to the organization. J. Occup. Psychol. **63**(1), 1–18 (1990)

40. Pattinson, M., Butavicius, M., Parsons, K., McCormac, A., Calic, D.: Factors that influence information security behavior: an australian web-based study. In: Tryfonas, T., Askoxylakis, I. (eds.) HAS 2015. LNCS, vol. 9190, pp. 231–241. Springer, Cham (2015). https://doi.org/10.1007/978-3-319-20376-8_21

41. Nel, F., Drevin, L.: Key elements of an information security culture in organisations. Inf. Comput. Secur. **27**(2), 146–164 (2019)

42. Eisenberger, R., et al.: Is the employee-organization relationship dying or thriving? A temporal meta-analysis. J. Appl. Psychol. **104**(8), 1036–1057 (2019)

43. Reeves, A., Calic, D., Delfabbro, P.: Encouraging employee engagement with cyber security: how to tackle cyber fatigue. SAGE Open: Special Collection on Organizational Cybersecurity (2020, submitted)

44. Lowry, P.B., Moody, G.D.: Proposing the control-reactance compliance model (CRCM) to explain opposing motivations to comply with organisational information security policies. Inf. Syst. J. **25**(5), 433–463 (2015)

45. Caputo, D.D., et al.: Going spear phishing: exploring embedded training and awareness. IEEE Secur. Priv. **12**(1), 28–38 (2014)

46. Supakkul, S., et al.: Goal-oriented security threat mitigation patterns. In: ACM International Conference Proceeding Series (2010)

47. Wiley, A., McCormac, A., Calic, D.: More than the individual: examining the relationship between culture and information security awareness. Comput. Secur. **88**, 101640 (2020)

The Man in the Besieged Castle: Heuristic Evaluation of Home Security Systems

Luis Martín Sánchez-Adame[1]![ORCID], Sonia Mendoza[1(✉)]![ORCID],
Beatriz A. González-Beltrán[2]![ORCID], Amilcar Meneses-Viveros[1]![ORCID],
and José Rodríguez[1]![ORCID]

[1] Computer Science Department, CINVESTAV-IPN, Mexico City, Mexico
luismartin.sanchez@cinvestav.mx,
{smendoza,ameneses,rodriguez}@cs.cinvestav.mx
[2] Systems Department, UAM-Azcapotzalco, Mexico City, Mexico
bgonzalez@azc.uam.mx

Abstract. Home security systems are increasingly popular and affordable. Whether DIY solutions with various accessories or simpler proposals, they are a tool that many consider essential for their home. However, these systems are not without problems. An important one is the anxiety and the sensation of siege that can cause, i.e., that users feel insecure inside their own homes. We propose five design guides focused on consistency, through these and with the help of five experts we perform a heuristic evaluation of three popular solutions in the market to try to find the causes that lead to the harmful effects of security systems. Our results reveal that the leading cause of the false siege is the excess of notifications.

Keywords: Heuristic evaluation · Consistency · Home security systems · Design guidelines

1 Introduction

Artificial Intelligence (AI), and Internet of Things (IoT) are very discussed topics today, although they are not new in Computer Science. Phenomena such as cheaper technology [16], and industrial automation [1], have caused many questions and problems to arise in both areas.

A particular branch of IoT with a significant growth is that of home security systems. This type of systems generally consists of a camera that streams video over the Internet, microphones, speakers, and a cloud platform from which users can remotely monitor their homes. With the promise of increasing quality of life, and improving the security of their properties, many users have adopted these systems [2]. However, they are controversial, since much has been investigated from the perspective of information security [6], privacy [4], and social psychology [11].

© Springer Nature Switzerland AG 2020
A. Moallem (Ed.): HCII 2020, LNCS 12210, pp. 250–260, 2020.
https://doi.org/10.1007/978-3-030-50309-3_17

A significant problem that is particularly emerging in IoT home surveillance systems is that users feel besieged in their own home [10]. By integrating AI algorithms (e.g., detection of human forms) this type of systems sends alerts to the users' mobile devices, every time a movement is detected, creating a false sense of insecurity. Although crime levels in the USA have gone down [7], the perception of citizens does not match that data [8]. Thus, users do not have clear information about when it is an actual alert, and when it is an error or a situation that does not require any measure. This lack of consistency can lead to situations of stress, anxiety, and unnecessary vigil [9].

All of the above poses a challenge for HCI researchers because the privacy notifications and settings of these systems must be exceptionally clear and convenient if they are to be used in real life [22]. To improve the design of these technologies, and thus try to mitigate the feeling of siege and insecurity, we evaluate three popular security systems in the market: Ring Doorbell, Nest Hello, and Eufy Doorbell, with the help of the consistency design guidelines for multi-device systems that we had previously developed [17]. The purpose of our guidelines is to preserve the consistency property of multi-device systems, i.e., that users can obtain similar functionality, and a positive UX (User eXperience) regardless of the devices that they could use. In this particular case, consistency can help keep the user truly informed, know the status of each device, offer useful alternatives before the various notifications, and provide non-invasive controls and configurations.

The organisation of this article is as follows. First, we analyse the works related to our study topic (see Sect. 2). Next, we describe the research methodology that we use in the elaboration of our proposal (see Sect. 3). Next, we explain our consistency design guidelines (see Sect. 4). Then we detail our case studies, i.e., the heuristic analysis of the three home security systems (see Sect. 5). Finally, we close with the conclusions and some ideas for future work (see Sect. 6).

2   Related Work

In this section, we present various related works that support the problem we pose, and they are an overview of state of the art.

Alshamari [3] explored the differences between usability factors and aspects related to security and privacy. He developed some basic guidelines for reducing the gap between usability and security, as well as frameworks and some models for the same objective. However, his study is theoretical, and no tests of any kind were made.

Mäkinen [13] examined why and how home surveillance systems are used and what the meanings and implications of these systems are to the residents. Through a series of interviews, she discovered that being under surveillance, especially in the privacy of one's own home, can evoke positive and negative feelings simultaneously. This is an exploratory study where possible solutions to the problems raised are not provided.

Shehan and Edwards [18] discussed a range of usability issues with home networking, as well as the sources of many of these issues. They contend that these problems will not disappear over time as the networking industry matures, but rather are due to structural usability flaws inherent in the design of existing network infrastructure, devices, and protocols. While this study does not address security systems, it is a vision of what HCI can bring to DIY systems.

Urquhart and Rodden [19] presented a series of critical challenges to consider for the regulation of domestic IoT. They argue that novel regulatory strategies can emerge through a better understanding of the relationships and interactions between designers, end-users and technology. This is a discussion/position paper with no experiments.

Zeng et al. [20] conducted semi-structured interviews with fifteen people living in smart homes to learn about how they use their smart homes, and to understand their security and privacy-related attitudes, expectations, and actions. Although their interviews provide guidelines for future work, they are only general aspects of those that recommend a thorough investigation.

All these works demonstrate the importance of our field of study, and at the same time, they are a sample of the gap we try to fill with our research.

3   Research Methodology

The research methodology for the development of our proposal is based on the Design Science Research Methodology (DSRM) process model proposed by Peffers et al. [14] (see Fig. 1).

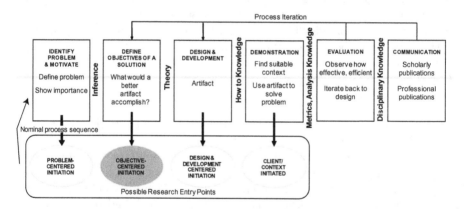

Fig. 1. We started from an *Objective-Centred Initiation* (coloured in orange) in the DSRM process model [14]. (Color figure online)

An *Objective-Centred Initiation* has been chosen as a research entry point because our goal is to improve the design of home security systems. As for *Identification & Motivation*, we have already described the problem of false siege feeling, and the role of GUI consistency in that matter. The *Objective of a Solution*, the second step of the process, is to implement our set of design guidelines to help developers to create consistent applications to improve UX. The third step *Design & Development* is the description of our guidelines for GUI consistency (see Sect. 4). *Demonstration* and *Evaluation* are described in our case study (see Sect. 5). This is the first iteration of the process. Subsequent iterations will begin in the *Design & Development* stage, in order to improve said guidelines.

4   Consistency Guidelines

As we have already mentioned, our design guidelines were initially created to improve the consistency of multi-device applications [17]. Now we decided to use them to evaluate the consistency in home security systems, and this has two objectives. The former one is to test the flexibility of our guidelines in a different environment (although we believe it is still related) for which they were designed. The latter one is that through consistency, we intend to eliminate the feeling of false siege that users of such systems may experience.

Below we list the five design guidelines we created:

- **Honesty:** Interaction widgets have to do what they say and behave expectedly. An honest GUI has the purpose of reinforcing the user's decision to use the system. When the widgets are confusing, misleading, or even suspicious, users' confidence will begin to wane.
- **Functional Cores:** These are indivisible sets of widgets. The elements that constitute a Functional Core form a semantic field, out of their field they lose meaning. The granularity level of interaction for a Functional Core depends on the utility of a particular set of widgets.
- **Multimodality:** Capability of multi-device systems to use different means of interaction whenever the execution context changes. In general, it is desirable that regardless of the input and output modalities, the user can achieve the same result.
- **Usability Limitations:** When multimodality scenarios exist, it is possible that situations of limited usability could be reached. When the interaction environment changes and its context is transformed, the environment can restrict the user's interaction with the system.
- **Traceability:** It denotes the situation in which users can observe and, in some cases, modify the evolution of the GUI over time.

5   Case Study

The evaluation has been worked out with the help of five UX experts (1 woman and 4 men, between 30 and 50 years old). We chose the experts for their experience applying usability and UX tests, and because they are familiar with the topics of our research. All the experts are university professors and have postgraduate studies; Two of them belong to our university. Their experience comes from both work in industry and research centres (between 5 and 25 years). It should be noted that none is related to this work in addition to their participation in the evaluation.

The methodology we use for heuristic evaluation comes from works such as Chuan et al. [5], and Kumar et al. [12]. An important point that we wanted to adopt is that proposed by Quiñones and Rusu [15], i.e., to contrast the results of the evaluation using our heuristics with the results of using another set of similar heuristics. Nevertheless, we could not find such work.

We chose three home security systems: *Ring Video Doorbell 1*, *Nest Hello*, and *Eufy Doorbell* because of their popularity in the market. The three systems are similar to each other; All three are video intercom systems that have WiFi connectivity, video streaming, two-way audio, motion alerts, and they are integrated into their proprietary security system that is controlled from a mobile app.

Before starting the evaluation, we gathered and explained to the experts each of our design guidelines, their purpose, and discussed some examples so that everyone had a similar starting point. Afterwards, the experts took the systems home and tested each one for a week. We ask them to keep a diary of their experiences, noting, among other things, the problems they encountered, the characteristics they liked, and the possible failures they might experience. They were always taking into account our design guidelines.

Once all the experts had tested all the systems, each of them drafted a list of problems and violations of the guidelines that we propose. Once the evaluators have identified potential consistency problems, the individual lists have been consolidated into a single master list. The master list was then given back to the evaluators who independently have assessed the severity of each violation. The ratings from the individual evaluators are then averaged, and we present the results in Table 1. For the rating, we adapted the severity classification proposed by Zhang et al. [21]:

0 - Not a consistency problem at all.
1 - Cosmetic problem only. No need to be fixed unless extra time is available.
2 - Minor consistency problem. Fixing this, should be given a low priority.
3 - Major consistency problem. Important to fix, should be given a high priority.
4 - Consistency catastrophe. Imperative to fix this before the product can be released.

Evaluators found a total of 15 consistency problems using our guidelines (a mean of 3 problems per evaluator). The severity rating of problems had an average of 2.42 (3.1 for Ring, 1.7 for Nest, and 2.5 for Eufy). For the master list, a total of 10 problems were evaluated and guidelines were violated 24 times. Honesty and Traceability were the two most frequently violated guidelines, 10 and 6 times, respectively. In contrast, the guideline with less detected problems was Functional Cores with 1 violation (see Fig. 2a).

Table 1. Consistency problems and its rating.

System	Problem	Guidelines[†]	Severity
Ring	It does not fulfil its doorbell function at all; As the sound comes from the device itself, it can only be heard outside, and sometimes notifications to my phone arrived long after the person had ringed (up to 10 min later)	H, M, T	4
	The system never alerted me that the batteries were running out. I only knew it when in a long time, I did not receive any notification and went to check	H, U, T	4
	No matter how you set the sensitivity of the camera to start recording, it began to do so only when a person was very close to the door, or when they were leaving	H, T	3.2
Nest	Possibly it has the most sensitive sensor of the three systems, although I put it to a minimum, notifications of movement were too many, reaching the point of being exasperating	H, U	2.2
	Facial recognition can be a useful feature, but it was wrong a couple of times since it identified a stranger as if he were a relative	H, T	1.4
	On several occasions I could watch the video stream from my phone without any problem, however, when consulting that clip stored in the cloud, people appeared and disappeared suddenly, it was clear that the video was cut, I could not know what the problem was	H, M	2.2
Eufy	When you get a notification that there is activity and you tap on the notification it takes you to the live view instead of what it recorded	H, M, U	2.6
	I installed the application on my phone and also on my husband's. Only one person can log in to the service at the same time, i.e., we can both watch video streaming, but only one of us receives notifications when someone rings	H, F, M, T	3
	Sometimes the applications notified me of motion alerts, especially at night, but the video stream showed nothing. This happened even if I deactivated said movement alerts	H, T	3.4
All	Interactions with people who ring the doorbell can become awkward (and potentially dangerous), as one is speaking as if one were at home when it might not be so. As the person who rang now knows that the house is alone	H	1

† Honesty (H), Functional Cores (F), Multimodality (M), Usability Limitations (U), Traceability (T).

With respect to the severity of the problems detected, we can see in Fig. 2b that severity level 1 - "Cosmetic problem only" was the most frequent with 30%. On the contrary, we can notice that the lowest classification 0 - "Not a consistency problem at all" got 0%.

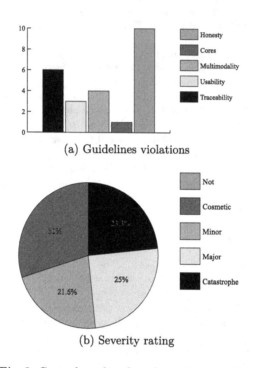

(a) Guidelines violations

(b) Severity rating

Fig. 2. General results of our heuristic evaluation.

For the individual evaluations of the systems, it is notorious that the heuristic in which more problems were consistently found was Honesty, while Functional Cores was only violated once in the case of Eufy (see Fig. 3). Interestingly, severity ratings vary diametrically in all systems. For example, the most severe "catastrophe" rating occupies 60% in the case of Ring, while in Nest nothing was rated in that range, and Eufy only obtained 10% (see Fig. 4).

In general, we can say that the worst-rated application was Ring since it was the one that obtained a good part of its ratings in the most severe range. On the contrary, Nest obtained the best marks, since 50% of its problems were classified as minor.

It is no coincidence that the guideline with the highest number of violations was Honesty, as it relates to the problem that afflicted all our evaluators in all systems, false alarms and the excessive amount of notifications. This is a

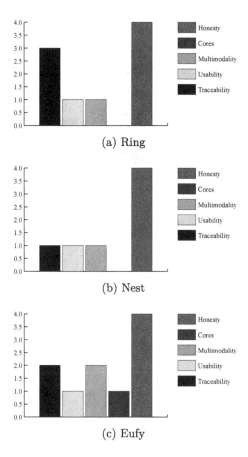

Fig. 3. Guidelines violations in Ring 3a, Nest 3b, and Eufy 3c.

severe problem because according to our evaluators, it was the leading cause that sometimes they felt anxious, and the sensation of the siege came. The systems tried to mitigate this by configuring the sensors and recognising faces, but none of these measures was helpful.

It is a complex challenge. A good part of the solution lies in improving the AI of these types of systems, but it is not the only thing that could be done. Improving the design of the doorbells by themselves as well as the way to install them could help people living in a particularly busy street, this could lead to more effective handling of notifications. More transparent controls and configurations would also be of great help so that users could choose the settings that best fit their environment and thus obtain a positive UX.

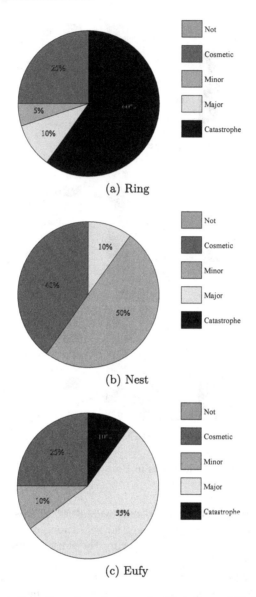

Fig. 4. Severity ratings in Ring 4a, Nest 4b, and Eufy 4c.

6   Conclusion and Future Work

In this paper, we analyse some of the most popular home security systems in the market and the possible siege effect that users may experience. We perform a heuristic evaluation with the help of five UX experts using our five consistency guidelines.

Our results revealed that the main reason that users felt besieged and anxious in their homes was the excess of notifications, as well as false alarms. Security systems made them believe that someone had knocked on their door or that there was movement near the entrance of their homes when, in reality, this was not the case.

Our evaluators were satisfied with the heuristics, allowing them to focus their evaluation and identify problems more quickly. However, they suggested that heuristics must be refined so that they can be understood and applied more efficiently.

With the problematic scenarios that our evaluators identified, as well as the UX journals they wrote, we plan to propose more focused solutions to solve the sense of siege in security systems, but without getting users to feel false security.

References

1. Acemoglu, D., Restrepo, P.: Automation and new tasks: How technology displaces and reinstates labor. Technical report, National Bureau of Economic Research, March 2019. https://doi.org/10.3386/w25684, http://www.nber.org/papers/w25684

2. AlHammadi, A., AlZaabi, A., AlMarzooqi, B., AlNeyadi, S., AlHashmi, Z., Shatnawi, M.: Survey of IoT-based smart home approaches. In: 2019 Advances in Science and Engineering Technology International Conferences (ASET), pp. 1–6, March 2019. https://doi.org/10.1109/ICASET.2019.8714572

3. Alshamari, M.: A review of gaps between usability and security/privacy. Int. J. Commun. Netw. Syst. Sci. **9**(10), 413–429 (2016)

4. Bastos, D.: Internet of things: a survey of technologies and security risks in smart home and city environments. In: IET Conference Proceedings, pp. 30–37, January 2018. https://doi.org/10.1049/cp.2018.0030

5. Chuan, N.K., Sivaji, A., Ahmad, W.F.W.: Usability heuristics for heuristic evaluation of gestural interaction in HCI. In: Marcus, A. (ed.) DUXU 2015. LNCS, vol. 9186, pp. 138–148. Springer, Cham (2015). https://doi.org/10.1007/978-3-319-20886-2_14

6. Dey, S., Hossain, A.: Session-key establishment and authentication in a smart home network using public key cryptography. IEEE Sensors Lett. **3**(4), 1–4 (2019). https://doi.org/10.1109/LSENS.2019.2905020

7. FBI: 2017 crime statistics released, September 2018. Accessed September 2019. https://www.fbi.gov/news/stories/2017-crime-statistics-released-092418

8. Gramlich, J.: 5 facts about crime in the U.S., January 2019. Accessed September 2019. https://www.pewresearch.org/fact-tank/2019/01/03/5-facts-about-crime-in-the-u-s/

9. Guariglia, M.: Amazon's ring is a perfect storm of privacy threats, August 2019. Accessed September 2019. https://www.eff.org/deeplinks/2019/08/amazons-ring-perfect-storm-privacy-threats

10. Guariglia, M.: Five concerns about amazon ring's deals with police, August 2019. Accessed September 2019. https://www.eff.org/deeplinks/2019/08/five-concerns-about-amazon-rings-deals-police

11. Klobas, J.E., McGill, T., Wang, X.: How perceived security risk affects intention to use smart home devices: a reasoned action explanation. Comput. Secur. **87**, 101571 (2019). https://doi.org/10.1016/j.cose.2019.101571. http://www.sciencedirect.com/science/article/pii/S0167404819301348
12. Kumar, B.A., Goundar, M.S., Chand, S.S.: A framework for heuristic evaluation of mobile learning applications. Educ. Inf. Technol. (2020). https://doi.org/10.1007/s10639-020-10112-8, https://doi.org/10.1007/s10639-020-10112-8
13. Mäkinen, L.A.: Surveillance on/off: Examining home surveillance systems from the user's perspective. Surveill. Soc. **14**(1), 59–77 (2016)
14. Peffers, K., Tuunanen, T., Rothenberger, M., Chatterjee, S.: A design science research methodology for information systems research. J. Manage. Inf. Syst. **24**(3), 45–77 (2007)
15. Quiñones, D., Rusu, C.: How to develop usability heuristics: a systematic literature review. Comput. Stand. Interfaces **53**, 89–122 (2017). https://doi.org/10.1016/j.csi.2017.03.009. http://www.sciencedirect.com/science/article/pii/S09205 48917301058
16. Rosoff, M.: Why is tech getting cheaper?, October 2015. Accessed September 2019. https://www.weforum.org/agenda/2015/10/why-is-tech-getting-cheaper/
17. Sánchez-Adame, L.M., Mendoza, S., Meneses Viveros, A., Rodríguez, J.: Towards a set of design guidelines for multi-device experience. In: Kurosu, M. (ed.) HCII 2019. LNCS, vol. 11566, pp. 210–223. Springer, Cham (2019). https://doi.org/10.1007/978-3-030-22646-6_15
18. Shehan, E., Edwards, W.K.: Home networking and hci: What hath god wrought? In: Proceedings of the SIGCHI Conference on Human Factors in Computing Systems, CHI 2007, pp. 547–556. Association for Computing Machinery, San Jose, California, USA (2007). https://doi.org/10.1145/1240624.1240712
19. Urquhart, L., Rodden, T.: New directions in information technology law: learning from human-computer interaction. Int. Rev. Law Comput. Technol. **31**(2), 150–169 (2017). https://doi.org/10.1080/13600869.2017.1298501
20. Zeng, E., Mare, S., Roesner, F.: End user security and privacy concerns with smart homes. In: Thirteenth Symposium on Usable Privacy and Security (SOUPS 2017), pp. 65–80. USENIX Association, Santa Clara, CA, July 2017. https://www.usenix.org/conference/soups2017/technical-sessions/presentation/zeng
21. Zhang, J., Johnson, T.R., Patel, V.L., Paige, D.L., Kubose, T.: Using usability heuristics to evaluate patient safety of medical devices. J. Biomed. Inform. **36**(1), 23–30 (2003)
22. Zheng, S., Apthorpe, N., Chetty, M., Feamster, N.: User perceptions of smart home IoT privacy. Proc. ACM Hum. Comput. Interact. **2**(CSCW), 200:1–200:20 (2018). https://doi.org/10.1145/3274469

Natural vs. Technical Language Preference and Their Impact on Firewall Configuration

Artem Voronkov and Leonardo A. Martucci[✉]

Karlstad University, Karlstad, Sweden
{artem.voronkov,leonardo.martucci}@kau.se

Abstract. Firewalls are network security components designed to regulate incoming and outgoing traffic to protect computers and networks. The behavior of firewalls is dictated by its configuration file, which is a written sequence of rules expressed by a set of keys and parameters. In this paper, we investigate whether certain representations of firewall rule sets can affect understandability. To collect data for our investigation, we designed an online survey for an audience who are familiar with firewalls, in which we aimed to compare two different rule set representations: `iptables` and English. We collected data from 56 participants. Our results show that participants' perception of a certain rule set representation depends on their firewall expertise. Participants with basic or intermediate knowledge of firewalls consider rule sets expressed in English to be 40% easier to understand, whereas advanced or expert firewall users deemed it to be 27% more difficult. We will discuss the reasons for these results and describe their possible implications.

Keywords: Firewalls · Human-computer interaction · User study · Rule set representation · Survey

1 Introduction

Firewalls are network security components designed to regulate incoming and outgoing traffic to protect computers and networks. To ensure that firewalls properly perform their assigned tasks, they must be correctly configured. However, people responsible for managing firewalls (administrators) often make mistakes [19], which may result in security vulnerabilities. The behavior of a firewall depends on its configuration file, which is a written sequence of rules expressed by a set of keys and parameters. The syntax is usually technical and specific to the firewall or operating system. Learning the syntax and extracting the semantics of a set of rules can be a large task for those who configure firewalls [14].

In this paper, we examine how people read and understand firewall rule sets. The goal of our study is to investigate whether representing firewall rules in a certain way can make them easier for to understand. We selected two different syntaxes that are used to describe firewall policies:

© Springer Nature Switzerland AG 2020
A. Moallem (Ed.): HCII 2020, LNCS 12210, pp. 261–270, 2020.
https://doi.org/10.1007/978-3-030-50309-3_18

- English, and
- `iptables`—a well-known Linux kernel firewall with its own policy description syntax.

To achieve our goal, we surveyed 56 people who are familiar with firewalls and collected their responses regarding understandability of the rule set representations.

Our results show a significant difference in understandability of the same rule sets expressed in `iptables` and English. That difference is dependent on the level of firewall expertise of the participant. The rule sets presented in English are 40% easier to understand, according to our participants with basic and intermediate knowledge of firewalls. Those more experienced in firewalls considered English rule sets to be 27% more difficult.

The rest of the paper presents a review of work related to our study in Sect. 2. Our research methodology is described in Sect. 3. The results of our survey, discussion of our findings, and limitations of our study are presented in Sect. 4. Finally, the concluding remarks are given in Sect. 5.

2   Related Work

An excessive complexity of firewall languages is a well-known issue that has been studied in literature. For this reason, firewall configuration files are often of low quality as shown by Wool, who studied 84 Check Point Firewall-1 and Cisco PIX rule sets and discovered critical errors in most of them [19].

Different methods to approach this problem were suggested in scientific papers. For example, a range of higher-level firewall languages was proposed [1,8,20]. These languages are designed to help system administrators avoid mistakes while configuring firewalls. However, IT professionals are often reluctant to learn and utilize new languages, as Wong pointed out [18].

Others proposed different graphical user interfaces (GUI) for firewalls to improve their usability (see [13] for a survey on firewall GUIs). However, most of the proposed visualization schemes lack proper evaluation in terms of usability testing and/or user studies, as noted in [13].

In parallel to this work, we looked into usability metrics for improving firewall rule sets [15], which provide formal mathematical models to improve rule sets based on qualitative studies with IT professionals. However, such a solution was designed and tested using a single syntax (`iptables`).

In the field of software engineering, different programming languages were compared in terms of understandability [4,7,16]. Furthermore, there were some attempts to compare human and programming languages [3]. To the best of our knowledge, there has not been any research comparing different firewall languages with each other or with human languages.

3   Methodology

In this section, we present our research methodology, including the details of our survey, the recruitment strategy and participants, and ethical considerations.

3.1 Survey Details

We collected the data through an online survey from September to December 2019.[1] The survey used *skip logic* and therefore had a non-fixed number of questions. The participants were asked from a minimum of 12 to a maximum of 16 questions, of which four to eight were open ended. All questions were required to be answered; therefore, we added the option "not sure" in some open-ended questions, so a participant could skip them in case of uncertainty about the correctness of his or her answers.

The survey consisted of two parts: (1) we asked the participants demographic-related questions, including age, gender, and expertise; (2) the participants were shown two firewall rule sets expressed with different syntaxes (English and `iptables`, in no particular order) and were asked to evaluate their understandability.

We started with two rule sets $\{a_1, b_1\}$ that were originally written using `iptables` syntax, one of the most common software firewalls syntaxes, and found in a public repository of real-world firewall rule sets.[2] The two selected rule sets were approximately of the same complexity level, according our metrics [15]. We translated the `iptables` rule sets into English and obtained two new rule sets $\{a_2, b_2\}$. Each participant was shown a pair of rule sets—either $\{a_1, b_2\}$, or $\{a_2, b_1\}$, which were presented sequentially, i.e. one after the other.

To decide which pair of rule sets is to be shown, we used the following approach. We randomly selected a pair of rule sets for the first participant and stored that information together with his or her number of years of experience with configuring firewalls. When the next participant with the same experience took part in the survey, he or she was shown the other pair of rule sets. Thus, we alternated which rule set representation the participants saw first: `iptables` or English.

After displaying each rule set, we asked one to three open-ended questions (see an example in Fig. 1) to the participants. These open-ended questions aimed to verify if they completely understood the given rule set and its functionality.

```
Does the policy allow an (every) incoming TCP packet on interface eth0
to port 80? Select Yes/No and specify the position of the rule
(for default policy write ''0'') that makes the decision.
```

Fig. 1. An example of a question that tests whether a participant understood the given firewall rule set.

The number of questions asked to a participant depends on the correctness of his or her answers. As soon as a participant provided a correct answer, the remaining (one or two questions) were skipped. Since the questions were open ended, we considered the probability of accidental right answers (right guess) to be low.

---

[1] The survey is available at https://survey.cs.kau.se/rulesets_comparison/.

[2] https://github.com/diekmann/net-network.

In the last question, we asked the participants to evaluate how easy or difficult, in their opinion, to understand each of the rule sets using a 7-point Likert scale.

The survey took an average of 660 s ($M = 579$, $SD = 311$, $Q1 = 400$, and $Q3 = 864$) of the participants' time to be completed.

The survey was pre-tested with five subjects before its dissemination. Although no significant changes were necessary to be implemented to the original design, the received feedback helped us eliminate some ambiguity in the wording and slightly improve the design of the study.

3.2   Recruitment and Participants

Reddit[3] has been demonstrated to be a good source to recruit participants, especially when people with a highly tailored knowledge are required [14]. We adopted the recruitment strategy from [14] and used the following channels for finding participants:

1. System administrators' subreddit. The *Sysadmin* subreddit[4], which is known to be one of the largest communities of system administrators (ca. 400k members), yielded a significant part of our participant recruitment.
2. Other subreddits. For this study, we needed participants with varying firewall expertise. Moreover, we knew that our study would be much more time consuming, which meant that the completion rate would be significantly lower. Therefore, we reached out for three other subreddits: *Networking*[5], *Netsec*[6], and *Linux*[7], which have members who have firewall knowledge.
3. Professional networks. We contacted several colleagues from our professional networks and asked them to distribute our survey to our target group, i.e. professionals with firewall knowledge.

The participants of our study were volunteers and received no financial compensation for taking part in the survey. Among the 516 participants who started the survey, 82 completed it (ca. 16% completion rate).

As aforementioned, we used up to three control questions to check whether a participant completely understood the given rule sets. The participants who did not give at least one correct answer for each of the two rule sets were excluded from the survey's data. Thus, 25 participants (ca. 30% of those who finished the survey) did not meet this requirement and hence their data were discarded. Additionally, one participant was removed as he or she filled out nonsensical answers.

---

[3] https://www.reddit.com/.
[4] https://www.reddit.com/r/sysadmin/.
[5] https://www.reddit.com/r/networking.
[6] https://www.reddit.com/r/netsec.
[7] https://www.reddit.com/r/linux.

Table 1. Participant demographics ($N = 56$).

	Metric	Participants
Age	18–24	8 (14.3%)
	25–34	27 (48.2%)
	35–44	13 (23.2%)
	45–54	4 (7.1%)
	55–64	2 (3.6%)
	Prefer not to answer	2 (3.6%)
Gender	Female	6 (10.7%)
	Male	43 (76.8%)
	Prefer not to answer	6 (12.5%)
Experience with configuring firewalls	<1 year	7 (12.5%)
	1–3 years	13 (23.2%)
	4–6 years	9 (16.1%)
	7–9 years	5 (9.0%)
	10+ years	22 (39.2%)
Proficiency with firewalls	Basic knowledge	11 (19.6%)
	Intermediate	13 (23.2%)
	Advanced	19 (33.9%)
	Expert	13 (23.2%)

Table 1 summarizes the demographics of the remaining 56 participants. Our sample is skewed age- and gender-wise with 63% of participants being younger than 35 years and with only 11% of participants being female, due to the specificity of the target audience and recruitment approach. We recruited the majority of our participants via Reddit since its users are known to be younger than the general population [10]. Moreover, the percentage of female users in the selected subreddits is low, e.g. only 7.5% and 5.0% for the *Sysadmin* and *Networking* subreddits [2], respectively, which explains the skewness of our data sample.

As expected, the completion rate of our survey is considerably lower than that in our previous study [14] with (mainly) Reddit users—59% and 16%, respectively. There are two main reasons for such a significant difference. First, this survey consumed an average of 660 s, while our past study needed only an average of 177 s to be completed. Since all our participants are volunteers, a significant number of participants dropped out from our survey. Second, the control questions in the survey, which tested the participants' understanding of the given firewall rule sets, significantly increased the dropout rate, as we could evaluate in our results. Such control questions were not included in our past study [14].

3.3 Ethical Considerations

The survey was conducted in accordance with the Swedish Ethical Review Act [11] and the Good Research Practice guidelines from the Swedish Research Council [12]. Prior to data collection, this study was approved by our institutional ethics review board (IRB). The following precautions were considered to ensure that the participants were treated ethically and with respect:

- The participants completed an IRB-approved consent form before starting the survey. The purpose of the study, its approximate duration, our commitment to confidentiality, and their rights as participants, including the right to withdraw from the study at any point in time, were stated in the form.
- The minimum amount of personal data (see Table 1) was collected.
- No sensitive personal data were collected.

4   Results and Discussion

From each participant, we obtained two difficulty scores: one for the rule set expressed using `iptables` and one for the rule set expressed in English. Since our samples are dependent, the data were analyzed using the Wilcoxon signed-rank test [17] to compare the average scores of these samples and assess them for significant differences. The Wilcoxon signed-rank test is a non-parametric equivalent to the paired sample t-test that does not carry assumptions of normality of data distribution and can be applied to ordinal data [6].

The Wilcoxon test did not yield significant results when all data points were considered. ($p = 0.843$). However, a deeper look at the data shows that the data records differ significantly depending on the participant's firewall expertise. We then divided our data set into two parts:

1. 24 participants who have basic or intermediate knowledge on firewalls
2. 32 participants who are advanced or expert firewall users

For each of these two data subsets, we displayed some descriptive statistics and ran the Wilcoxon signed-rank test (see Tables 2, 3, 4 and 5).

From Tables 2 and 4, we see that mean scores for `iptables` and English rule sets differ: 2.92 and 4.08 for less-experienced participants and 4.66 and 3.66 for proficient participants. The Wilcoxon signed-rank test indicated that the difficulty score of the rule sets expressed in English was statistically significant higher than the score of the same rule sets when presented as `iptables` ($z = 2.823$, $p = 0.005$) for the subset with a limited firewall knowledge; i.e. the rule sets in English were more easily understood by the participants with basic or intermediate knowledge on firewalls. On the contrary, advanced and expert firewall users considered the `iptables` rule sets to be significantly easier than the corresponding English ones ($z = 2.350$, $p = 0.019$).

Table 2. Descriptive statistics for the subset of participants with basic or intermediate firewall knowledge.

	N	Mean	Std. Deviation	Minimum	Maximum
Iptables_Score	24	2.92	1.248	1	5
English_Score	24	4.08	1.381	1	7

Table 3. The Wilcoxon signed-rank test for the subset of participants with basic or intermediate firewall knowledge.

		N	Mean rank	Sum of ranks
English_Score -	Negative ranks	5ᵃ	6.20	31.00
Iptables_Score	Positive ranks	15ᵇ	11.93	179.00
	Ties	4ᶜ		
	Total	24		

a. English_Score < Iptables_Score
b. English_Score > Iptables_Score
a. English_Score = Iptables_Score

Additionally, we measured the effect size of the Wilcoxon test for both of the data subsets. We calculated Pearson's correlation coefficient, r, as the following [9]:

$$r = \frac{z}{\sqrt{N}}$$ where N corresponds to the total number of participants.

For the first and second subsets, r equals to 0.47 and 0.42, respectively. Both r lie between 0.3 and 0.5, which corresponds to moderate effect [5].

4.1   Discussion

A possible explanation for why our participants prefer a certain representation of rule sets depending on their firewall expertise is that learning the syntax of iptables requires a significant effort.

Inexperienced system administrators and other users with basic or intermediate knowledge on firewalls considered iptables rule sets difficult to understand, since they are usually not extensively familiar with its syntax. Therefore, the rule sets that are expressed in English {a2, b2} were easier for them. In contrast, the participants with extensive experience on firewalls are more familiar with the iptables syntax, which is more concise than English and therefore preferred by them.

Different representations can be used to show firewall rule sets to different categories of people. In general, system administrators have many other responsibilities apart from configuring firewalls [14], and they do not usually have time to learn multiple and complex firewall syntaxes. Moreover, inexperienced users

Table 4. Descriptive statistics for the subset of participants with advanced or expert firewall knowledge.

	N	Mean	Std. Deviation	Minimum	Maximum
Iptables_Score	32	4.66	1.638	1	7
English_Score	32	3.66	1.734	1	7

Table 5. The Wilcoxon signed-rank test for the subset of participants with advanced or expert firewall knowledge.

		N	Mean rank	Sum of ranks
English_Score -	Negative ranks	20[a]	15.25	305.00
Iptables_Score	Positive ranks	8[b]	12.63	101.00
	Ties	4[c]		
	Total	32		

a. English_Score < Iptables_Score
b. English_Score > Iptables_Score
a. English_Score = Iptables_Score

can be trained using a language that does not require a significant time investment to be learned. In particular, rule sets expressed in English are suitable, since there is no additional learning of syntax involved. Furthermore, if several people with different firewall expertise work on the same rule set, a translation tool that can convert it from one representation to another would be extremely valuable.

4.2   Limitations

One of the limitations of our survey is that most of the participants were recruited through Reddit, an online platform. Since the study participants were volunteers, there is a self-selection bias that leads to the sample not being fully representative. Moreover, since they did not receive any financial compensation, and the survey consumed more than 10 min of their time on average to be answered, its completion rate was rather low, which in turn significantly reduced the sample size of our survey.

The study was conducted online and hence we could not observe the participants answering the questions. Although we included (up to three) control questions to improve the quality of the survey by selecting only participants with some experience in dealing with firewall rule sets, the answers to some questions, e.g. demographic related, might still be untrue. There is also the possibility of misinterpreted or misunderstood questions by the participants. We mitigated this limitation by carefully considering the design of the survey and pretesting our survey with five people.

The syntax of `iptables` is not very expressive while being considerably verbose. It was recommended by some Reddit users to utilize Cisco Adaptive Security Appliance (ASA) configuration files that are familiar to a wider audience and thereby increase the number of potential participants. [8] The translation of firewall rule sets into English might also be improved and eventually automated.

5 Conclusion

In this paper, we presented an online study for an audience who are familiar with firewalls, in which we compared two different rule set representations. The survey was successfully completed by 56 participants and their data were analyzed using the Wilcoxon signed-rank test.

Our results show that a rule set expressed in English received on average a 40% higher difficulty score (easier to understand) from inexperienced users (with basic and intermediate knowledge on firewalls) when compared to the corresponding `iptables` rule set.

Among the participants who are advanced or expert firewall users, we observed the opposite. The rule sets presented in the form of `iptables` were 27% easier to read and understand when compared to the corresponding ones in English.

Our work demonstrates that users might prefer different rule set representations depending on their firewall expertise. The theoretical significance of this work is that we showed the need for multiple rule set representations, so both inexperienced users and experts could efficiently use the firewall. This finding presents opportunities for future research. For example, manufacturers of firewalls might need to compare several rule set representations to determine their strengths and be able to create a better firewall interface.

As a part of our future work, we plan to increase the number of rule set representations tested as well as to recruit more participants for future surveys.

Acknowledgments. We are very grateful to everyone who participated in our survey. We would also like to thank the moderators of the *Sysadmin* (`r/sysadmin`), *Networking* (`r/networking`), *Netsec* (`r/netsec`), *Linux* (`r/linux`) subreddits for allowing us to reach out to their community.

This work was supported by the Knowledge Foundation of Sweden HITS project and by the Swedish Foundation for Strategic Research SURPRISE project.

References

1. Bodei, C., Degano, P., Galletta, L., Focardi, R., Tempesta, M., Veronese, L.: Language-independent synthesis of firewall policies. In: 2018 IEEE European Symposium on Security and Privacy (EuroS&P), pp. 92–106. IEEE (2018)

---

[8] https://www.cisco.com/c/en/us/products/security/adaptive-security-appliance-asa-software/index.html.

2. Burkhart, B.: Subreddit gender ratios (2017). http://bburky.com/subredditgenderratios/
3. Connolly, J.H.: Context in the study of human languages and computer programming languages: a comparison. In: Akman, V., Bouquet, P., Thomason, R., Young, R. (eds.) CONTEXT 2001. LNCS, vol. 2116, pp. 116–128. Springer, Heidelberg (2001). https://doi.org/10.1007/3-540-44607-9_9
4. Crosby, M.E., Scholtz, J., Wiedenbeck, S.: The roles beacons play in comprehension for novice and expert programmers. In: PPIG, p. 5 (2002)
5. Field, A.: Discovering Statistics Using IBM SPSS Statistics. Sage, Thousand Oaks (2013)
6. Meek, G.E., Ozgur, C., Dunning, K.: Comparison of the t vs. Wilcoxon signed-rank test for Likert scale data and small samples. J. Mod. Appl. Stat. Methods **6**(1), 10 (2007)
7. Nanz, S., Torshizi, F., Pedroni, M., Meyer, B.: Design of an empirical study for comparing the usability of concurrent programming languages. Inf. Softw. Technol. **55**(7), 1304–1315 (2013)
8. Pozo, S., Varela-Vaca, A., Gasca, R.: AFPL2, an abstract language for firewall ACLs with NAT support. In: 2009 Second International Conference on Dependability, pp. 52–59. IEEE (2009)
9. Rosenthal, R., Cooper, H., Hedges, L.: Parametric measures of effect size. Handb. Res. Synthesis **621**, 231–244 (1994)
10. Sattelberg, W.: The demographics of reddit: who uses the site? (2018). https://www.techjunkie.com/demographics-reddit/
11. Svensk Författningssamling (SFS): Lag (2003:460) om etikprövning av forskning som avser människor [The Act concerning the Ethical Review of Research Involving Humans]. Utbildningsdepartementet, Stockholm, Sweden (2003)
12. Swedish Research Council (VR): Conducting ethical research (2018). https://www.vr.se/. Accessed 12 Dec 2019
13. Voronkov, A., Iwaya, L.H., Martucci, L.A., Lindskog, S.: Systematic literature review on usability of firewall configuration. ACM Comput. Surv. **50**(6), 1–35 (2017). https://doi.org/10.1145/3130876
14. Voronkov, A., Martucci, L.A., Lindskog, S.: System administrators prefer command line interfaces, don't they? An exploratory study of firewall interfaces. In: Fifteenth Symposium on Usable Privacy and Security (SOUPS 2019) (2019)
15. Voronkov, A., Martucci, L.A., Lindskog, S.: Measuring the usability of firewall rule sets. IEEE Access **8**, 27106–27121 (2020). https://doi.org/10.1109/ACCESS.2020.2971093
16. Wiedenbeck, S., Ramalingam, V., Sarasamma, S., Corritore, C.L.: A comparison of the comprehension of object-oriented and procedural programs by novice programmers. Interact. Comput. **11**(3), 255–282 (1999)
17. Wilcoxon, F.: Individual comparisons by ranking methods. Biometr. Bull. **1**(6), 80–83 (1945). http://www.jstor.org/stable/3001968
18. Wong, T.: On the usability of firewall configuration. In: Symposium on Usable Privacy and Security (2008)
19. Wool, A.: Trends in firewall configuration errors: measuring the holes in swiss cheese. IEEE Internet Comput. **14**(4), 58–65 (2010)
20. Zhang, B., Al-Shaer, E., Jagadeesan, R., Riely, J., Pitcher, C.: Specifications of a high-level conflict-free firewall policy language for multi-domain networks. In: Proceedings of the 12th ACM Symposium on Access Control Models and Technologies, pp. 185–194. ACM (2007)

Analysis of Factors Improving Accuracy of Passive User Identification with Streams of Face Images for Ubiquitous Commerce

Adam Wójtowicz$^{(\boxtimes)}$ ⓘ and Jacek Chmielewski ⓘ

Department of Information Technology, Poznań University of Economics and Business, al. Niepodległości 10, 61-875 Poznań, Poland
awojtow@kti.ue.poznan.pl

Abstract. Ubiquitous commerce services set new requirements for access control methods, e.g. to enable full payment automation it is necessary to passively perform initial customer identification at point of sale. Face biometrics seems to be promising in these scenarios since it does not require user to continuously carry relevant object nor to actively participate. In theory, the accuracy of customer identification should improve with the number of face images, however additional low-quality face images that are included in the recognition stream actually can degrade identification accuracy. Therefore, in this work various criteria of filtering image stream are analyzed to improve accuracy of final identification decision: user attention (face rotation), user mimics, or user height different from the template. The analysis is performed for various lightning conditions, various recognition algorithms, various sensor types, and various recognition distances in the environment simulating real point of sale. In this paper we report on new systematic experiments performed on our earlier context-aware passive payment authorization system. Results have been obtained as an effect of data mining and statistical analysis of log sets.

Keywords: User identification · Passive identification · Face recognition · Ubiquitous commerce · Context-aware authorization · Payment authorization

1 Introduction

With the constant development of ICT in the areas of mobility, connectivity, interoperability, cloud technologies, and data analysis techniques, new interrelated computing paradigms emerge, such as ubiquitous and pervasive computing, Internet of Things (IoT), and recently Internet of Everything (IoE). As opposed to IoT, IoE is not limited only to things, but "brings together people, process, data, and things to make networked connections more relevant and valuable". This paradigm constitutes a platform for new categories of ubiquitous services and applications, such as smart homes/spaces/environments/cities, but also increases the need for new categories of access control mechanisms: "without cyber security the Internet of Everything is nothing". Ubiquitous services are accessed by end users which requires adequate user identification and authentication (passive, biometric or multi-device), then users interact

© Springer Nature Switzerland AG 2020
A. Moallem (Ed.): HCII 2020, LNCS 12210, pp. 271–284, 2020.
https://doi.org/10.1007/978-3-030-50309-3_19

with services which require authorization of their actions (in a manner that is context-aware, adaptive, or collaborative), and finally, after service usage, the service provider analyses historical and/or real-time usage data which requires proper audit controls (that are privacy-preserving by design). In our research, we address these requirements for new access control methods that correspond to ubiquitous service specificity. Particularly, multimodal system based on context-aware payment authorization model deployed and evaluated at a physical PoS has been developed [1]. It performs risk and trust assessment for dynamic selection of payment authorization method (biometrics-, knowledge-, possession-based methods are involved). Multiple devices (mobile and stationary, client's and seller's) are used contextually. Consequently, the payment process is simplified as much as possible, up to being fully passive, while maintaining controlled security-convenience balance. The simplification of the payment process concerns reducing the execution time of the process and minimizing the number of operations required to be performed by the client.

To enable full payment automation in architectures such as the one described in our earlier article [1], it is necessary to use passive initial customer identification based on detection of the presence of a particular person at a particular location. Identification method which seems to be one of the most promising in ubiquitous computing scenarios is face biometrics, since it does not require user to continuously carry relevant object or sensor and can be utilized effectively without the active participation of the user. It can be assumed that there is a short but continuous time period in which a user prepares to the transaction which produces several dozens of face images and this is the timespan for the initial passive identification. A rule-based heuristic algorithm has been developed [2] in which final identification decision is a result of a number of face matchings calculated within given time period. The evaluation of the proposed approach has been based on an experiment performed in existing PoS with a group of its regular customers who usually conduct routine transactions. The evaluation has confirmed that automatic passive transactions provide users with higher convenience level and similar duration as compared to traditional transactions and that applying context-based authorization method selection based on trust, risk and convenience criteria results in gradually decreasing transaction duration [2]. However, it also demonstrated approximately 82% accuracy of face recognition, which still can be improved.

In theory, the accuracy of user identification should improve with the number of captured face images. However, additional low-quality face images (e.g. wrong orientation, poses, mimics, distance, or lightning) that are included in the recognition stream actually degrade identification accuracy, and because of the passivity requirement it is undesirable to force a customer to wait too long to collect a number of high-quality images. Therefore, in this work various criteria of filtering image stream are analyzed to improve quality of image stream: user attention (rotated faces are uncertain), user mimics (images too different from neutral-mimics templates), or user height different from the template. The analysis is performed for various lightning conditions, various recognition algorithms, various sensor types, and various recognition distances. Also the effect of using pre-recognizer trained to recognize attribute such as user body height that pre-segment the template database before final matching is analyzed. These criteria are expected to improve not only accuracy but also scalability of the solution, due to reduction of computational power requirements (lower number of recognitions) and reduction of communication effort. In this paper we report on our new experiments with above mentioned modifications of a passive payment system. Results have been obtained as an effect of data mining and statistical analysis of log sets and have been confronted with formulated research hypotheses.

2 Background

Human face recognition is a biometrics commonly used for user identification. It is applied, for example, in commercial and law enforcement sectors. Various use cases impose various constraints and technical challenges. These challenges have been investigated by researchers for more than 40 years [3, 4], but still in many areas there is no perfect solution. For example, the Handbook of Face Recognition [5] highlights most important technology challenges and face recognition evaluation publications, such as Face Recognition Technology (FERET) [6] and Face Recognition Vendor Test (FRVT) [7, 8], show that the performance of many existing face recognition solutions deteriorates with changes in lighting, pose, and other factors [9, 10]. In [11] Beveridge and others measured the effects of covariates such as gender, age, expression, image resolution and focus on three face recognition algorithms. Their main conclusions are that covariates matter but almost no covariates affect all algorithms in the same way and to the same degree. In [12] Lui and others presented a meta-analysis for covariates that affect performance of face recognition algorithms, with results drawn from 25 studies conducted over the past 12 years. Apart from comments on the influence of age, gender, and race, they state that "there is universal agreement that changing expression hurts recognition performance". In [13] Erdogmus and Dugelay propose to address the issue of expressions by enhancing the enrollment sample with a number of synthetic face images with different expressions. With this approach they managed to achieve significant improvements in face recognition accuracies for each tested database and algorithm. These issues persist for both single-image recognition and video recognition solutions [14]. Additionally to facial expressions, also pose and illumination are deteriorating recognition performance [15]. The impact of pose is similar to the one of expressions, while the illumination-related issue adds another layer of complexity. The illumination-related topics have been analyzed [16], modeled [17], and avoided. The last approach seems to be the most promising. Usually, in real-life scenarios, users of face recognition systems have little to none control over face lighting conditions, so supporting the face recognition with multispectral [18, 19] or 3D information [20] may help maintaining a satisfactory face recognition quality. The 3D face pattern expressed as depth images gives interesting results when processed with the use of Convolutional Neural Networks. As Lee and others present in [21] a face recognition system using this approach provides very accurate face recognition results and it is robust against variations in head rotation and environmental illumination.

In face recognition systems that operate in identification, not verification scenario (1-to-many, matching a specific face to one of a vast database of faces) there is an additional layer of technical challenges related to the size of the database [22]. As the

FRVT NIST report shows [8], recognition performance degrades with database size: "Search durations scale approximately as a power of the database size. The exponents are dependent on the algorithm". The problem may be reduced by segmenting or filtering the database, thus limiting the face recognition process to a subset of the full database [23]. This reduction may be based on information contained in biometric data (e.g. anatomical Bertillion features), on additional non-biometric data such as the age of the subject, height, gender or on external information. An interesting example of the last approach is Zero-Effort Payments system proposed by Microsoft Researchers in [24]. It assumes the subject is carrying a Bluetooth Low Energy (BLE) device, which enables fast and passive device identification, thus enabling some sort of subject pre-identification. In crowded locations, the BLE-based device identification is not conclusive, because each reading would result in multiple identifiers, but it is enough to significantly reduce the number of database records used by the face recognition process.

3 Passive User Identification in Ubiquitous Commerce

Payment systems, usually linked with banking systems, handle money transfers for their users, making the payment process convenient. Payment systems have three main requirements: to identify the buyer, to identify the seller, and to avoid or minimize the risk of fraudulent money transfer orders. These requirements are handled by popular payment systems based on smart cards, where the buyer uses a personal smart card and the seller uses a physical device connected to a payment system – a payment terminal. The terminal identifies the seller and enables two-way communication with a payment system, while the buyer's card is read by the terminal and identifies the buyer. The terminal is used also to authorize the transaction – by requesting the buyer to confirm her identity by providing a secret (PIN). It all works in practice but requires the buyer and the seller also to handle manual activities related to the transaction. So, the convenience of the process could be improved further to fulfil the requirements of ubiquitous commerce. However, in most cases increasing convenience reduces the security and the risk of misuse arises.

A different approach to these requirements is considered in physical shops without a human seller, such as "Amazon Go" [25] and "Take & Go" [26]. In these solutions, the human seller is replaced by a system composed of a mobile application and some form of in-store tracking technology. Each potential buyer has to install a dedicated application linked to a payment card on her smartphone. After registration procedure, a buyer is allowed to enter a seller-less shop presenting her smartphone at the entrance. This manual action is a necessary identification step. It can also be used to authorize access of a buyer to a given shop. While in a shop, a buyer collects products on her own and heads to the checkout section. The in-store tracking technology automatically builds a summary of collected products for every buyer and enables checkout automation. The buyer only needs to confirm the list of products and may leave the shop. The system automatically charges the payment card selected in the smartphone application. Depending on the tracking technology used it is possible to completely automate the checkout step. The "Take & Go" uses RFID as product tags and does not actively track each buyer, so the checkout includes manual buyer identification and checkout confirmation actions. However, the "Amazon Go" employs active product and buyer tracking based on a combination of machine learning, computer vision and data pulled from multiple sensors to automatically compile a list of collected products for each buyer. This approach enables fully automated checkout and payment. Buyers just leave the store, so the only manual action they have to take is related to the first requirement – the identification of a buyer. Moreover, the shop physical access control assures that the transaction risk is usually acceptable for automatic or confirmed checkout – which addresses the third, security-related, requirement without a need of any additional payment authorization methods.

The requirements related to user identification convenience and payment security are also addressed in the context-aware passive payment authorization system (denoted in this work as CAPPA), which we have presented in [1] and [2]. Our goal was to reach a scenario in which the seller simply places an order, receives the goods and leaves the store, without any manual action related to the payment while still maintaining a required security level of the transaction. To make it possible CAPPA system uses passive face-based buyer identification and a specialized algorithm for dynamic selection of authorization methods. The face-based buyer identification is used in a passive manner, which means that the buyer is not forced to present her face in any particular way. CAPPA system exploits the fact that buyers spend a while in front of a seller while placing an order, so there is a time window in which the system can capture a sequence of face images and complete the identification process. When the buyer is identified and order is placed CAPPA algorithm evaluates the risk of a given transaction and selects payment authorization method/methods that guarantee the risk is below a given threshold, including the "auto" authorization method, which does not require any manual action from the buyer.

The design of CAPPA system differs in several ways from a typical card-based payment system. The system has to maintain a database of buyer biometric profiles instead of card numbers. This requires a specialized enrollment process in which images of buyer's face are recorded according to a predefined protocol, processed into a biometric profile and stored in a database. The enrollment and database are handled by an operator of CAPPA system, which may act as a payment operator (PO) for multiple sellers. Instead of enrolling with every seller separately, it requires only one-time enrollment for buyers. At the same time, it appears that this variant is easier to deploy in practice because of the higher level of trust that buyers have in POs – because the PO acts as a "trusted third party" in the buyer-seller relation.

Once collected, the biometric profile is then used in the passive buyer identification process. A Point of Sale (PoS) is equipped with a specialized system that tracks user's skeleton, detects face images, recognizes face images as belonging to a given user, and based on the stream of such recognitions makes identification decisions in real time, no later than when a seller decides that an order is complete and it is time to initiate the payment process. Instead of a single face image, a stream of images is being processed while the buyer places an order, making it possible to use a rule-based heuristic algorithm in which final identification decision is a result of many, possibly contradictory, face matchings calculated within a given time period. Therefore, even some number of false matchings does not impact the final identification decision in the negative way. The details of this approach are presented in [2]. The new experiments on filtering the stream of face images in order to improve recognition accuracy are described below in Sect. 4 and Sect. 5.

In practice, the risk of a transaction is different for each buyer-seller pair, may change over time, depends on the amount and order type (product/service). The parameters collected by CAPPA system are used to calculate the risk of a particular transaction and decide which authorization methods should be allowed, to make sure the required security level is maintained. The mechanism considers various trust/risk requirements for biometric-based, possession-based and knowledge-based authorization methods, for active and passive methods, for methods based on buyer and seller infrastructure, and various convenience levels of the particular authorization methods. The technical details are described in [1].

Our previous experiments [2] confirm that CAPPA system makes it possible to maintain the right balance between convenience and security, thus maximizing the convenience without sacrificing security. Considering parameters of a particular order and a history of buyer-seller relations it is possible to select the most convenient authorization method even in an environment limited to a subset of possible authorization methods. Including automatic, passive payment authorizations for trusted buyer-seller pairs, which constitutes an enabler for ubiquitous commerce. The controlled balance between security and convenience reduces security concerns and convenience constraints for all sides and may attract newcomers, allowing the payment operator to quickly grow its userbase and reach the "network effect". The fact that the buyer is identified before paying can be a key advantage for the seller, as this information may be used to introduce significant improvements in the customer service process, including full personalization of service and automation of loyalty procedures.

On the other hand, issues related to user privacy cannot be omitted when developing such approaches: there is a number of serious risk to end-user privacy resulting from the use of biometric systems, particularly face biometrics [27]. Perhaps, some level of personal privacy is the price user pays for having both security and convenience on the optimal level. However, in the proposed approach those risk are minimized by the architecture employing single trusted and regulated payment operator processing sensitive biometric data for many sellers. And if a trusted seller-buyer relationship also exists, the buyer orders products, receives the merchandise and leaves without having to search for any attribute necessary to authorize the payment, so it can be assumed that the convenience of the process is maximized for every transaction. All that is still open for improvement is the efficiency of the process itself, particularly, the accuracy of the passive user identification.

4 Experiment Design

4.1 Experiment Setup

The initial goal of this work is to create an evaluation environment that allows for conducting series of experiments on customer face recognition algorithms and factors that impact their accuracy. The evaluation environment and evaluation procedures have been designed to meet two requirements that seemingly are mutually exclusive. The first one is to take into account a number and a variance of conditions that are present in real-world ubiquitous commerce, such as variable distance, lighting, sensor type, customer look, mimics or attention. Such variance of conditions has been observed during earlier experiments employing real customers at real PoS conducted in a long period of time. However, in those unstructured experiments detailed impact of a single condition was impossible to extract and analyze. Thus, the second requirement for the presented evaluation environment has been formulated: to minimize random factor and mutual interference and provide experiment structure allowing objective quantitative analysis for various conditions/factors/algorithms/parameters.

Experiment setup contains the following components:

1. Changeable outdoor/indoor light sources
2. Physical barriers, floor and wall markers
3. Video capture system employing eye vision and infrared vision sensors, user skeleton tracking and face detection systems (based on the one described in [1, 2])
4. User registration and identification systems (based on the one described in [1, 2]). For the experiments the identification system works in off-line mode, i.e. recognizes users on images and identifies users on streams of recognitions based on pre-recorded video sequences.
5. Data acquisitions and data analysis modules.

The experiment procedure applied for the presented work contains all elements of typical customer behavior in PoS. According to the procedure each test customer:

1. Goes out from behind a wall curtain that is situated 4 m away from the sensor.
2. Approaches the first stop situated 2.5 m away from the sensor (following the floor marker), stops there.

    a. While talking (talking mimics) looks left, right, center following the wall markers (exposes rotated face)
    b. While not talking (no mimics) looks left, right, center following the wall markers (exposes rotated face)
    c. Looks directly up to the camera

3. Approaches the second stop situated 1 m away from the sensor (following the floor marker), stops there

    a. While talking (talking mimics) looks left, right, center following the wall markers (exposes rotated face)
    b. While not talking (no mimics) looks left, right, center following the wall markers (exposes rotated face)
    c. Looks directly up to the camera.

With presented procedure the "difficulty" of the recognition gradually decreases: the distance decreases, talking mimics is followed by neutral mimics, rotated face images are followed by straight face images.

4.2 Collected Data and Measures Used

18 test customers have been participating in the experiments. For each participant 3 video sequences in various lighting conditions have been recorded:

– sequence in Strong Indoor Lighting conditions (SIL-1);
– sequence in Weak Outdoor Lighting conditions (WOL);
– sequence in Strong Indoor Lighting conditions (SIL-2).

Thus, in total 54 sequences have been recorded. Each sequence contains both eye vision (EV) and infrared vision (IV) video data.

SIL-1 is used to extract 8 eV and 8 IV still images for each person: far horizontal with mimics, far horizontal no mimics, far up-to-camera with mimics, far up-to-camera no mimics, close horizontal with mimics, close horizontal no mimics, close up-to-camera with mimics, close up-to-camera no mimics. Recognizers based on EV and IR data and based on Eigenfaces (EF)/Fisherfaces (FF) face recognition algorithms are trained to identify participants with these images. Therefore, 4 recognizes are trained (EF-EV, EF-IV, FF-EV, FF-IV), each with 144 images (8 positions * 18 participants). For each training image, automatically measured participant body height is also acquired and stored. WOL and SIL-2 are not used to extract any training images.

Recognition experiment takes place continuously during the whole sequence to simulate real-time recognition in ubiquitous commerce scenarios, cf. Sect. 1 and article [2]. Recognition takes place for all three sequences corresponding to different lighting conditions: SIL-1 (from which training images are acquired), WOL, and SIL-2 (the same conditions as in case of SIL-1, but fully independent from the training set). For each type of sequence, 5 recognition tests are performed for each customer:

– no filtering of face image stream, raw stream (denoted F-N)
– filtering out rotated faces (pitch < 0.45; yaw < 0.35; roll < 0.3) (denoted F-R)
– filtering out faces with mimics (attribute jawopen < 0.5) (denoted F-M)
– filtering out faces of customers for whom difference between measured body height and registered body height is more than 10 cm (denoted F-H)
– filtering out all face images F-R combined with F-M and F-H

In total: 5 test types * 3 sequence types * 18 customers = 270 recognition sessions have been performed. For each recognition session, following 20 recognition measures have been calculated:

– Shortest Time to the First Correct Recognition (STFCR) in a given video: for All vision types and algorithms (STFCR-A), for Eye Vision and Eigenfaces algorithm (STFCR-EV-EF), for Eye Vision and Fisherfaces algorithm (STFCR-EV-FF), for Infrared Vision and Eigenfaces algorithm (STFCR-IV-EF), for Infrared Vision and Fisherfaces algorithm (STFCR-IV-FF),
– Distance of Farthest Correct Recognition (DFCR) in a given video: for Eye Vision and Eigenfaces algorithm (DFCR-EV-EF), for Infrared Vision and Eigenfaces algorithm (DFCR-IV-EF), for Eye Vision and Fisherfaces algorithm (DFCR-EV-FF), for Infrared Vision and Fisherfaces algorithm (DFCR-IV-FF)

– Number of Correct/Incorrect Recognitions (NCR/NIR) in a given video: for Eye Vision and Eigenfaces algorithm (NCR-EV-EF/NIR-EV-EF), for Infrared vision and Eigenfaces algorithm (NCR-IV-EF/NIR-IV-EF), for Eye Vision and Fisherfaces algorithm (NCR-EV-FF/NIR-EV-FF), for Infrared Vision and Fisherfaces algorithm (NCR-IV-FF/NIR-IV-FF), for All algorithms and vision types (NCR-A/NIR-A), Number of Incorrect Recognitions Before First Correct (NIRBFC).

Based on data of simple measures listed above, the following 7 aggregated measures have been calculated:

– B-STFCR: Cumulated number of times a given recognizer (EV-EF, EV-FF, IV-EF, IV-FF) gives the Best STFCR, summed up for all participants. Presented separately for various filtering methods (F-R, F-M, F-H) and for various types of sequences (SIL-1, WOL, SIL-2)
– I-STFCR: Cumulated number of times a given filtering method (F-R, F-M, F-H) gives STFCR Improvement comparing to F-N, summed up for all participants. Presented separately for various algorithms (EV-EF, EV-FF, IV-EF, IV-FF) and for various types of sequences (SIL-1, WOL, SIL-2). "Positive" I-STFCR is defined as number of cases in which identification duration is faster than for F-N, added to number of "enabling" cases for which time difference cannot be calculated. "Negative" I-STFCR is defined as number of cases in which identification duration is slower than for F-N, added to number of "disabling" cases for which time difference cannot be calculated. "Enabling" case is defined as one in which for given video sequence applying given filtering method enables correct identification: correct identification occurs with this filtering method, and does not occur at any time without this filtering method. Correspondingly "disabling" case is defined as one in which for given video sequence, applying given filtering method disables correct identification: correct identification does not occur at any time with this filtering method, but occurs without this filtering method.
– B-DFCR: Cumulated number of times a given recognizer (EV-EF, EV-FF, IV-EF, IV-FF) gives the Best DFCR, summed up for all participants. Presented separately for various filtering methods (F-R, F-M, F-H) and for various types of sequences (SIL-1, WOL, SIL-2)
– I-DFCR: Cumulated number of times a given filtering method (F-R, F-M, F-H) gives DFCR Improvement comparing to F-N, summed up for all participants. Presented separately for various algorithms (EV-EF, EV-FF, IV-EF, IV-FF) and for various types of sequences (SIL-1, WOL, SIL-2)
– A-RA: Recognition Accuracy (NCR/(NCR + NIR)) Averaged for all participants, for different recognizers (EV-EF, EV-FF, IV-EF, IV-FF). Presented separately for various filtering methods (F-R, F-M, F-H) and for various types of sequences (SIL-1, WOL, SIL-2)
– I-RA: Cumulated number of times a given filtering method (F-R, F-M, F-H) gives RA Improvement comparing to F-N, summed up for all participants. Presented separately for various algorithms (EV-EF, EV-FF, IV-EF, IV-FF) and for various types of sequences (SIL-1, WOL, SIL-2)

– I-NIRBFC: Cumulated number of times a given filtering method (F-R, F-M, F-H) gives NIRBFC improvement comparing to F-N, summed up for all participants. Presented separately for various algorithms (EV-EF, EV-FF, IV-EF, IV-FF) and for various types of sequences (SIL-1, WOL, SIL-2)

Those 7 measures are used for the final data analysis.

5   Results

5.1   Filtering Out Rotated Faces (F-R)

Experimental results have not confirmed the hypothesis that filtering out images containing rotated faces (F-R, c.f. Sect. 4.1) from the recognition stream improves B-STFCR, I-STFCR, B-DFCR, I-DFCR, A-RA, I-RA, I-NIRBFC for all conditions:

– Applying F-R improves significantly B-STFCR, I-STFCR and B-DFCR only for SIL-1 recordings (that is only in case of the testing set similar to the training set).
– Applying F-R improves significantly I-DFCR for WOL and SIL-2 recordings in case of IV recognizers.
– Applying F-R has ambiguous impact on A-RA, I-RA, I-NIRBFC.

The reasons for that are twofold. First, slightly rotated faces can be still recognized correctly despite the rotation (c.f. construction of the training set described in Sect. 4.1). Second, if the faces are too much rotated, they are not recognized at all (false negative error may appear), but also they are not misrecognized as belonging to another user, since they are too different from the pattern of any correct face. Thus, they do not introduce false positives, and false positives have much higher negative impact on final identification decision than false negatives.

5.2   Filtering Out Faces with Mimics (F-M)

Experimental results have confirmed the hypothesis that filtering out images containing face with mimics (F-M, c.f. Sect. 4.1) from the recognition stream improves B-STFCR and I-STFCR. Applying F-M improves significantly B-STFCR for SIL-1 recordings in all cases, for WOL recordings in case of IV vision and for SIL-2 recordings in case of EV (cf. Fig. 1).

Data presented in Fig. 1 illustrate that for testing in difficult light conditions F-M combined with IV produces better results, and for testing in similar (to the training video sequence) light conditions F-M combined with EV produces better results. It can be easily explained by higher independence of infrared imaging from lighting conditions. Choice of the algorithm (EF/FF) does not matter here. The improvement is also confirmed by I-STFCR results (cf. Fig. 2) for IV recognizers. Especially in difficult light conditions F-M produces a higher number of "positive" I-STFCR than number of "negative" I-STFCR (for definitions see Sect. 4.2).

In turn, F-M has not introduced significant improvement to distance-focused measures (B-DFCR, I-DFCR). It can be simply explained by the fact that face details (mimics)

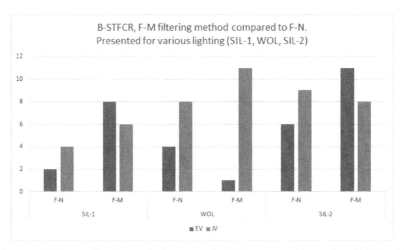

Fig. 1. B-STFCR, F-M filtering method compared to F-N. Presented for various lighting (SIL-1, WOL, SIL-2)

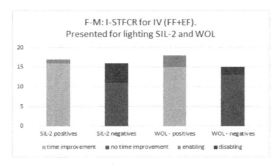

Fig. 2. F-M: I-STFCR for IV (FF + EF). Presented for SIL-2 and WOL lighting

have lower impact on longer distance recognition, because of the low quality of images captured from longer distances.

5.3 Filtering Out Faces of Customers for Whom There Is Difference Between Measured and Registered Body Height (F-H)

Experimental results have confirmed the hypothesis that filtering out from the recognition stream faces of customers for whom there is a difference between measured and registered body height (F-H, c.f. Sect. 4.1) improves distance-focused measures such as I-DFCR (cf. Fig. 3). It can be observed that DFCR improvement takes place in difficult lighting conditions, which can be easily explained: when it is hard to recognize or even detect faces, the impact of other factors (height) on identification decision increases. Also, height measurement quality is not as much dependent on distance as face image. Actually in some cases the dependence is opposite: close shot may disallow precise height measurement, thus F-H performs well for longer distance recognition.

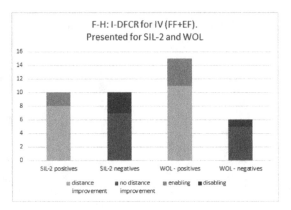

Fig. 3. F-H: I-DFCR for IV (FF + EF). Presented for SIL-2 and WOL lighting

Also accuracy-focused measures, such as A-RA (cf. Fig. 4) and I-RA, show improvement when F-H filtering is applied. In case of good lighting (SIL-2), F-H gives the best A-RA and I-RA from all analyzed approaches for both EV and IV, and in case of more difficult lighting (WOL), F-H gives the best A-RA and I-RA for IV vision.

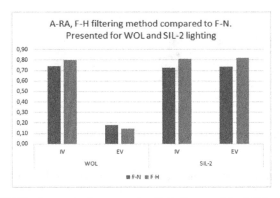

Fig. 4. A-RA, F-H filtering method compared to F-N. Presented for WOL and SIL-2 lighting

6   Conclusions

One of the most significant technical requirements for mass adoption of ubiquitous commerce is related to effective passive customer identification. Face biometrics is promising in this area, but it requires improvements in quality of recognition process in terms of final identification duration at PoS, distance, or accuracy. Presented experimental results obtained within experiment environment have confirmed that in case of high-level user identification algorithms based on face image streams, pre-filtering the image stream can effectively improve the accuracy of the subsequent identification process. Filtering decision criteria have been based on face rotation, user mimics or body height; to remove possible bias the experiments have been conducted in various lightning conditions, for two different algorithms, and for eye and infrared vision.

The general conclusion is that using in the identification stream as many face images as detected does not produce optimal identification decisions since low-quality recognitions disrupt final identification decision. However, at the same time, filtering out too many low-quality face images also does not produce optimal identification decisions, since the decisions are frequently false if based on too few recognitions. The pre-filtering criteria should not be permissive nor restrictive ones. The results of this work can help to properly choose and optimize them and consequently, to construct effective next generation ubiquitous commerce systems based on face biometrics.

References

1. Wójtowicz, A., Chmielewski, J.: Technical feasibility of context-aware passive payment authorization for physical points of sale. Pers. Ubiquit. Comput. **21**(6), 1113–1125 (2017). https://doi.org/10.1007/s00779-017-1035-z
2. Wójtowicz, A., Chmielewski, J.: Payment authorization in smart environments: security-convenience balance. In: Hammoudi, S., Śmiałek, M., Camp, O., Filipe, J. (eds.) ICEIS 2018. LNBIP, vol. 363, pp. 58–81. Springer, Cham (2019). https://doi.org/10.1007/978-3-030-261 69-6_4
3. Arya, S., Pratap, N., Bhatia, K.: Future of face recognition: a review. Procedia Comput. Sci. **58**(2), 578–585 (2015). https://doi.org/10.1016/j.procs.2015.08.076
4. Solanki, K., Pittalia, P.: Review of face recognition techniques. Int. J. Comput. Appl. **133**(12), 20–24 (2016)
5. Li, S.Z., Jain, A.K.: Handbook of Face Recognition. Springer, Heidelberg (2011). https://doi.org/10.1007/978-0-85729-932-1
6. Phillips, P.J., Moon, H., Rizvi, S.A., Rauss, P.J.: The FERET evaluation methodology for face-recognition algorithms. IEEE Trans. Pattern Anal. Mach. Intell. **22**(10), 1090–1104 (2000). https://doi.org/10.1109/34.879790
7. NIST: Face Recognition Vendor Tests (FRVT). https://www.nist.gov/programs-projects/face-recognition-vendor-test-frvt-ongoing
8. Grother, P.J. Ngan, M.L.: Face recognition vendor test (FRVT) performance of face identification algorithms NIST IR 8009 (2014)
9. Valentin, D., Abdi, H., O'Toole, A.J., Cottrell, G.W.: Connectionist models of face processing: a survey. Pattern Recognit. **27**(9), 1209–1230 (1994)
10. Zhao, W., Chellappa, R., Phillips, P., Rosenfeld, A.: Face recognition: a literature survey. ACM Comput. Surv. **35**, 399–458 (2003)
11. Beveridge, J.R., Givens, G.H., Phillips, P.J., Draper, B.A.: Factors that influence algorithm performance in the face recognition grand challenge. Comput. Vis. Image Underst. **113**(6), 750–762 (2009). https://doi.org/10.1016/j.cviu.2008.12.007
12. Lui, Y.M., Bolme, D., Draper, B.A., Beveridge, J.R., Givens, G., Phillips, P.J.: A meta-analysis of face recognition covariates. In: 2009 IEEE 3rd International Conference on Biometrics: Theory, Applications, and Systems, pp. 1–8. IEEE (2009)
13. Erdogmus, N., Dugelay, J.L.: 3D assisted face recognition: dealing with expression variations. IEEE Trans. Inf. Forensics Secur. **9**(5), 826–838 (2014). https://doi.org/10.1109/tifs.2014.230 9851
14. Grother, P., Quinn, G., Ngan, M.: Face In Video Evaluation (FIVE) Face Recognition of Non-Cooperative Subjects, NIST IR 8173 (2017). https://doi.org/10.6028/nist.ir.8173

15. Gross, R., Baker, S., Matthews, I., Kanade, T.: Face recognition across pose and illumination. In: Li, S., Jain, A. (eds.) Handbook of Face Recognition. Springer, London (2011). https://doi.org/10.1007/978-0-85729-932-1_8

16. Karamizadeh, S., Abdullah, S.M., Zamani, M., Shayan, J., Nooralishahi, P.: Face recognition via taxonomy of illumination normalization. In: Hassanien, A., Mostafa Fouad, M., Manaf, A., Zamani, M., Ahmad, R., Kacprzyk, J. (eds.) Multimedia Forensics and Security. Intelligent Systems Reference Library, vol. 115. Springer, Cham (2017). https://doi.org/10.1007/978-3-319-44270-9_7

17. Basri, R., Jacobs, D.: Illumination modeling for face recognition. In: Li, S., Jain, A. (eds.) Handbook of Face Recognition. Springer, London (2011). https://doi.org/10.1007/978-0-85729-932-1_7

18. Li, S.Z., Yi, D.: Face recognition using near infrared images. In: Li, S., Jain, A. (eds.) Handbook of Face Recognition. Springer, London (2011). https://doi.org/10.1007/978-0-85729-932-1_15

19. Koschan, A., Yao, Y., Chang, H., Abidi, M.: Multispectral face imaging and analysis. In: Li, S., Jain, A. (eds.) Handbook of Face Recognition. Springer, London (2011). https://doi.org/10.1007/978-0-85729-932-1_16

20. Kakadiaris, I.A., et al.: Face recognition using 3D images. In: Li, S., Jain, A. (eds.) Handbook of Face Recognition. Springer, London (2011). https://doi.org/10.1007/978-0-85729-932-1_17

21. Lee, Y.C., Chen, J., Tseng, C.W., Lai, S.H.: Accurate and robust face recognition from RGB-D images with a deep learning approach. BMVC 1(2), 3 (2016)

22. Brauckmann, M., Busch, C.: Large scale database search. In: Li, S., Jain, A. (eds.) Handbook of Face Recognition. Springer, London (2011). https://doi.org/10.1007/978-0-85729-932-1_25

23. Mhatre, A.J., Palla, S., Chikkerur, S., Govindaraju, V.: Efficient search and retrieval in biometric databases. In: Biometric Technology for Human Identification II, vol. 5779, pp. 265–273. International Society for Optics and Photonics (2005). https://doi.org/10.1117/12.604173

24. Smowton, C., Lorch, J.R., Molnar, D., Saroiu, S., Wolman, A.: Zero-effort payments: design, deployment, and lessons. In: Proceedings of the 2014 ACM International Joint Conference on Pervasive and Ubiquitous Computing, pp. 763–774 (2014). https://doi.org/10.1145/2632048.2632067

25. Amazon Go. https://www.amazon.com/go

26. Take & Go. https://tg.shop/

27. Wójtowicz, A., Cellary, W.: New challenges for user privacy in cyberspace. In: Human-Computer Interaction and Cybersecurity Handbook, pp. 77–96. Taylor & Francis Group, Boca Raton (2019)

Privacy and Trust

To Allow, or Deny? That is the Question

Panagiotis Andriotis[1]([⊠]) [iD] and Atsuhiro Takasu[2] [iD]

[1] Computer Science Research Centre, University of the West of England, Bristol, UK
panagiotis.andriotis@uwe.ac.uk
[2] Digital Content and Media Sciences Research Division,
National Institute of Informatics, Chiyoda City, Tokyo, Japan

Abstract. The Android ecosystem is dynamic and diverse. Controls have been set in place to allow mobile device users to regulate exchanged data and restrict apps from accessing sensitive personal information and system resources. Modern versions of the operating system implement the run-time permission model which prompts users to allow access to protected resources the moment an app attempts to utilize them. It is assumed that, in general, the run-time permission model, compared to its predecessor, enhances users' security awareness. In this paper we show that installed apps on Android devices are able to employ the systems' public assets and extract users' permission settings. Then we utilize permission data from 71 Android devices to create privacy profiles based on users' interaction with permission dialogues initiated by the system during run-time. Therefore, we demonstrate that any installed app that runs on the foreground can perform an endemic live digital forensic analysis on the device and derive similar privacy profiles of the user. Moreover, focusing on the human factors of security, we show that although in theory users can control the resources they make accessible to apps, they eventually fail to successfully recall these settings, even for the apps that they regularly use. Finally, we briefly discuss our findings derived from a pen-and-paper exercise showcasing that users are more likely to allow apps to access their location data on contemporary mobile devices (running version Android 10).

Keywords: Human factors · Live analysis · Mobile computing · User profiling · Location · Android 10

1 Introduction

We live in an ever-changing digital world and we constantly benefit from technological advancements. Mobile computing is an unambiguous example of the merits we enjoy. Mobile devices are integral parts of our routines and, as a consequence, they hold and transmit voluminous amounts of our personal data. Unsurprisingly, since the earliest years of the mobile computing era we encountered malicious entities attempting to circumvent security and privacy controls that were set to protect users' information. The lessons learned from recent

© Springer Nature Switzerland AG 2020
A. Moallem (Ed.): HCII 2020, LNCS 12210, pp. 287–304, 2020.
https://doi.org/10.1007/978-3-030-50309-3_20

years, regarding users' inability to effectively protect themselves from intrusive and malevolent actors, led system developers to the implementation of privacy controls that would allow users to easily monitor and regulate the apps' accessibility to sensitive data, sensors and system resources.

Four years after the introduction of the current access control system on Android, which uses request dialogues during run-time (ask-on-first-use, a.k.a AOFU [22]), and a few months after the advent of the anticipated finer-grained model for managing location accessibility while the app is in the foreground (version 10), there still existed approximately 25.2% users that access the Android Play Store on devices running legacy versions of the OS (5.1 and below), as reported on [4]. However, three quarters of Android users (who visit the Play Store) are now familiar with the AOFU model.

This paper reports the results of a study we conducted recruiting 71 participants to voluntarily provide access to the permission settings on their Android devices. For this cause we developed an app that is able to instantly gather appropriate information while it is active, i.e. while it runs on the foreground. Given that any benign app in the Android ecosystem is capable of performing similar data collection, we consider our prototype as a potential tool, able to perform an endemic live digital forensic analysis and extract the current state of the permission settings on the device. This information might be useful for the analyst as it will provide the capability to perform user profiling and acquire some fundamental information about the user's security awareness. Furthermore, we conducted a survey (using the app we developed) asking our volunteers to answer two basic questions, aiming to investigate the following research questions.

- **RQ1:** Which sensitive resources on their devices users aim to protect more frequently?
- **RQ2:** Do they change their privacy-related perceptions when they are dealing with their favorite apps?
- **RQ3:** Are users aware of the permission settings on their devices?
- **RQ4:** Can we categorize users according to their privacy/permission settings?

Therefore, the main contributions of this paper are as follows:

a) We gather system related information from the actual devices used daily by our participants, resulting in the acquisition of high quality permission data which are further used to create representative privacy profiles.
b) We demonstrate that Android users are sceptical about providing access to sensitive resources such as their SMS, microphones and contact lists. However, they become more permissive with their favorite apps; this action is related to the anticipation to gain benefits from the advanced functionality and is based on the foundations of trust.
c) We show that users who are now familiar with the AOFU model are still not fully aware of the resources their favorite apps are accessing on their devices.

d) Finally, we demonstrate that the finer grain location settings introduced in Android 10 will probably positively affect users' intention to allow apps to access their location data.

The rest of this paper is structured as follows. Section 2 discusses recent related work on users' acceptance of the AOFU model. In Sect. 3 we present the methodology we used to collect permission settings from live devices and we also discuss elements of our survey design and implementation. Section 4 reviews the collected information and Sect. 5 analyzes the results. Finally, we discuss our findings in Sect. 6 and draw our conclusions in Sect. 7.

2 Related Work

Prior work that investigates mobile phone permission controls and dialogues has shown that not only users do not pay attention to them, but they also cannot comprehend them [9]. The ask-on-install (AOI) permission model (used on legacy Android OS versions) might also cause frustration to users who feel they do not have control on the personal data they share [8]. Additionally, the AOI system presents the inherit disadvantage that users are not given any contextual information about how and when apps access their sensitive resources [20].

These drawbacks undermine users' secure interaction with the system and therefore novel approaches have been adopted to address them. The AOFU model was long-anticipated and it was initially well-received by Android users [1,3]. However, users' engagement in decision making when they are dealing with the access control management of their mobile devices might lead to the problem of habituation [23]. In addition, although the AOFU model provides some context in the foreground and allows users to make informed decisions, especially at the beginning of the apps' lifespan, it can also be error prone [11,22]. However, users appreciate the fact that they have dynamically been made part of the security chain in the AOFU model and they take into account the "when" and "why" an app requests permissions [11,21].

We have seen numerous papers investigating users' adoption and acceptance of this model [2,6,7,10,16,18,19,21,23]. Andriotis et al. [1,3] recently introduced a method to acquire snapshots of permission settings from Android devices and showed that, in general, users make consistent choices when it comes to allowing access to specific sensitive resources. Although malicious actors can employ side-channel attacks to gain unauthorized access to sensitive resources bypassing the Android system's controls [17], users have a more positive attitude towards the run-time permission model [18]. In order to simplify and enhance its effectiveness, various researchers suggest the accumulation of users' privacy profiles [13,14].

To this end, we use an updated approach of the aforementioned methodology [1–3] to acquire permission snapshots via an app that has to be installed on the users' device. Our scenario/threat model accounts for the fact that any installed app can periodically acquire similar snapshots (while in use) to effectively create representative users' privacy profiles. Therefore, the app can conduct a live forensic analysis to perform a comprehensive user profiling.

3 Methodology

We follow the data collection approach discussed in [3] to collect users' permission settings. First, we develop an Android app that will be used as a survey instrument and at the same time it will collect the current permission settings of the running device. We distribute our application on Google Play and request participants to download the app on their devices. We target users with devices that run Android 6.0 and above, i.e. they implement the run-time permission model. The participants were recruited after viewing our call on various online platforms such as popular social media and university email lists. We did not compensate the respondents for their engagement but we gave them the chance to be included in a prize draw, if they were willing to provide their email address to communicate with them in case they won a prize. We finally got responses from 71 individual Android users from around the world. The project was carried out after ethical approval was acquired by the our RBI (FET Faculty Research Ethics Committee of the University of the West of England (FET.17.03.027)).

3.1 Permission Settings Collection

Our redesigned app utilizes the `PackageManager` and employs the `GET_META_DATA` flag to query the participant's device and acquire a list of application information. Then we use the method `getPackageInfo` with the `GET_PERMISSIONS` and `FLAG_SYSTEM` flags to retrieve non-system applications, i.e. apps that were installed by the users from online app stores. This distinction on the acquired data provides a more accurate representation of users' permission settings because we target only apps that were installed by them. Therefore there is a better probability for creating more representative profiles because we are primarily based on apps that have been used at least once (details in Sect. 5). This is a fundamental improvement compared to the previous work [1–3].

To ensure that this hypothesis stands true, we employ the `UsageStatsManager` to collect app usage information provided by the Android system itself. Furthermore, we store locally on the phone for each app the `requestedPermissions` and `requestedPermissionFlags`, along with additional information such as the: `versionCode`, `firstInstallTime`, `LastUpdateTime`, and `targetSdkVersion`.

The `PackageManager` returns the integer 3 if the permission has been granted and the integer 1 if not. Following this methodology we are able to acquire a snapshot of the user's permission settings. Note that –using this methodology– if the integer that was returned is 1, we do not know if a dangerous permission has been requested by the app in the past. We can only infer that the specific app does not have permission to access the given resource currently. Therefore, following this approach we are able to reconstruct current permission settings on the device for each installed app. In other words we are able to reconstruct information given by the system when the user engages the *Settings* app and requests to see the "App permissions" from the "App info" utility, as seen in Fig. 1e.

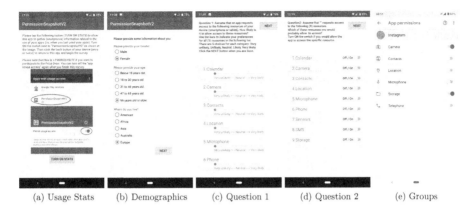

| (a) Usage Stats | (b) Demographics | (c) Question 1 | (d) Question 2 | (e) Groups |

Fig. 1. Screenshots showcasing "Permissions Snapshots V2" application and system's functionality.

3.2 Questionnaire Design

The data collection process and the users' engagement lifecycle is described in detail below. First, participants download the app on their devices. After launching the app, consent is given to the app by the user to collect permission settings information. Then the participant is asked to allow the app to collect usage statistics from the device (Fig. 1a). This functionality must be explicitly given by the user on our targeted devices. However we provide the users the capability to skip this step, if they do not feel comfortable providing this amount of data to a third party (i.e. to our app).

Afterwards the participants are asked to provide basic demographics (Sex, Age, and Residency as seen in Fig. 1b) and answer 2 questions (Fig. 1c, 1d). The first question asked the following: "Assume that an app requests access to the following resources of your device (smartphone or tablet). How likely is it to allow access to these resources? Use the bars to indicate your preferences for all (9) resources in the following list. There are 5 choices for each category: Very unlikely, Unlikely, Neutral, Likely, Very likely". A five-point Likert scale [12] was implemented as a slider to store participants' preferences for each dangerous permission ranging from "Very unlikely" to "Very likely".

Next our survey app asked the participants to provide the name of an app they regularly use: "The second (and last) question is related to your favourite app. Please tap on the following text field and provide the name of an app that you regularly use on this device. Then hit the NEXT button to see the second question". After providing the name of their preferred app, they read the second question: "Assume that "your_favourite_app" requests access to the following (9) resources. Which of these resources you would probably allow to access? Turn ON the switch if you would allow the app to access the specific resource".

The activity contained a sequence of switches representing the state of access privileges the specific user would be willing to provide to the specific app, as seen in Fig. 1d.

Finally, respondents were instructed how to participate in the prize draw and turn off this app's Usage Access privilege after submitting their answers. The rationale behind the design of our short questionnaire is to identify if there exist deviations between the users' ideal privacy preferences (Question 1) and the amendments they are willing to do when they need to enjoy certain functionalities of their favorite apps (Question 2).

4 Data Analysis

The majority of the respondents of our call provided complete survey answers. Additionally the majority provided their app usage data to our app allowing access to the UsageStatsManager. However, there was a small proportion of users that did not allow this action. Additionally, we identified responses from 3 participants that seemed ambiguous. For example, these respondents sent more than one responses while our app was available on Google Play. Therefore, their data were completely removed from the dataset. More details are given in Sect. 5 below.

Data analysis has been performed in two stages. First we accumulated valid survey responses from participants as explained in Sect. 5. We refer to this group of participants as G_s in this paper. Then, we compiled another set of data depending only on the permission settings that were sent from the devices to us. These data do not depend on the survey responses as they are actual representations of the permission settings on the participants' devices the given time (Permissions Snapshots); we call G_d this group in this paper.

In order to translate permission data from each device and reconstruct the permission group settings for each app as shown to any user from the Android system (e.g. Fig. 1e), we are using the same methodology presented in [3]. We focus on dangerous permissions groups and simulate the way Android handles run-time permission requests to allow or deny access to sensitive resources. Hence, permission settings for each app are represented as a sequence of nine "Allow" or "Deny" decisions. The number nine represents the number of dangerous groups, according to the official classification. This classification depends on the Android API level. While collecting our data, the highest available API level was 27 (i.e. devices running up to version O, codenamed as Oreo). The given time, there existed nine dangerous groups. From API level 28 (Android Pie) another group was added (namely CALL_LOG) which practically included some of the older permissions from the PHONE group. Since our app was running on devices with OS versions up to Android Pie, we present results based on the nine group classification.

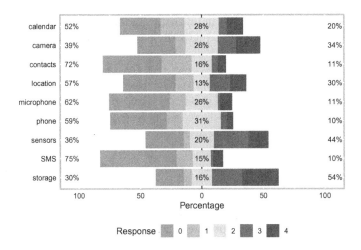

Fig. 2. Responses to Question 1: (0: Very unlikely - 4: Very likely).

5   Results

We received responses from 71 individuals. Among them, 60 allowed access to the `UsageStatsManager`, 8 did not turn on the Usage access switch when requested by our app, and 3 provided ambiguous responses, therefore their data were removed from our study. Additionally, data from one participant were rejected because she claimed she was below 18 years old. Based on the ethical approval terms, respondents had to be 18 years old and above to participate.

5.1   RQ1: Which Sensitive Resources on Their Devices Users Aim to Protect More Frequently?

For the first part of this study (regarding the questionnaire responses) we analyzed survey data provided by 61 participants (group G_s). We rejected the answers from individuals who either they did not provide the name of an app for question 2 or they provided a name that could not be found in the corresponding packages provided by their devices' `PackageManager`. Additionally, some of these participants provided responses baring the default answers only, which made us consider they did not sincerely answer the questions; hence their responses were also removed.

As shown in Fig. 2 respondents in general are reluctant to allow access to their devices' resources. However, they are more positive to allow access to apps requesting to use their devices' "Storage" and "Sensors". This finding aligns with recently presented work [2]. The figure also demonstrates that Android users are hesitant to allow apps accessing their: a) SMS messages (75% negative answers), b) their contact lists (72% negative answers), and, c) their devices' microphones

(62% negative answers). Another noteworthy finding is that responses related to the camera access were almost equally divided (39% negative, 34% positive). On the other hand, participants are disinclined to allow access to their location data (57% negative answers).

Another point related to location data access is that the answers for the certain permission group presented strong polarity between negative and positive views (13% neutral answers). The decreased percentage of neutral views for this group showcases that mobile device users are aware of the importance of their location data, therefore they have clear views when it comes to sharing them with third parties. Compared to similar previous studies [2,3] we identify analogous behavior considering users' acceptance of possible requests from the system. In these studies most of the users do not intend to allow access to their SMS, microphones, contact lists, phone logs and location. Our results showcase that these trends haven't changed a lot since the arrival of the run-time permission model three years ago. Additionally, compared to the previous studies we can see that users nowadays have a stronger perception about which protected resources are willing to allow external apps to access.

5.2 RQ2: Are Users Changing Their Privacy-Related Perceptions When They Are Dealing with Their Favorite Apps?

Next we investigate if users change their behavior when their *favorite apps* request to access protected resources. For this case we focus on the G_s group and gather the answers of the second survey question to compare them with the answers from the first question. We consider as positive the "Likely" and "Very likely" answers and as negative the "Unlikely" and "Very unlikely" answers from the first survey question. Then we count the positive answers representing the resources (i.e. the dangerous groups) they are more positive to allow an app to access. This information is derived from their answers to the first question. Similarly, we count the resources they would allow their favorite app to access, according to their answers to the second question.

Figure 3 shows how participants answered. The blue line shows the number of resources they feel more comfortable to allow an app to access in general, and the orange line shows their responses for their favorite app. We can see that in most cases users would allow more resources to be accessed by their favorite apps compared to their generic response provided to the first question. 18% of the participants provided the same number of positive answers and number of accessible sensitive resources.

In general, from Fig. 3 we can infer that users are inclined to allow access to a larger number of sensitive resources when prompted by their favorite apps.

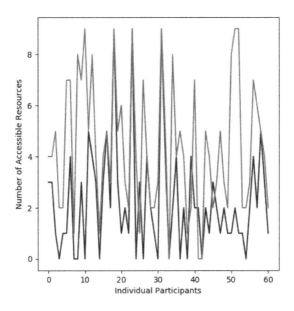

Fig. 3. Deviations among users' survey answers (comparing Q1 vs Q2)

5.3   RQ3: Are Users Aware of the Permission Settings on Their Devices?

The next part of our survey data analysis reflects on the differences between the users' answers on the second question and the actual settings we found on their devices. Therefore, we now evaluate users' answers by comparing them with the users' actual interaction with their favorite apps. This comparison is temporal and adheres to the time we acquired the permission snapshot. Therefore, this is a snapshot that depicts the users' interaction with the system dialogues until that moment.

We are still studying the responses from group G_s in this section. However, due to inconsistencies in some of the users' responses we had to consider only those which did not cause any confusions. For example, one user suggested her favorite app was "messaging" and, at the same time, we found permission settings for more than one messaging applications on her device. Hence, it was not feasible to know the application she was referring to. These ambiguous answers were removed for this part of the study and therefore we report data derived from 47 responses from group G_s.

We use the Jaccard distance (ranges from 0.0 to 1.0) to measure the similarity of two binary vectors for each participant's answer. In general, the Jaccard distance of two vectors equals to 0.0 if the vectors are identical.

The first vector resembles the answers given for question 2 and the second resembles the actual privacy preferences/controls found in the participant's device for the specific app. For example, if the respondent answered that Twitter is her most used/favorite app, we represent as $v_1 = (0, 1, 0, 1, 0, 0, 1, 0, 1)$ her

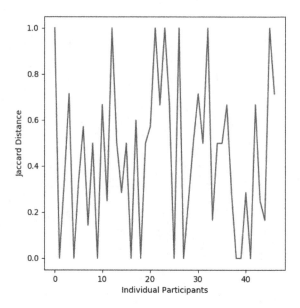

Fig. 4. Jaccard similarity of users' answers to Q2 and their actual permission settings.

answers to the second question, where 0 is "I would not allow access" and 1 is "I would allow access" to the following permission groups: (Calendar, Camera, Contacts, Location, Microphone, Phone, Sensors, SMS, Storage).

The second vector $v_2 = (N, 1, 0, 1, 0, 0, N, 0, 1)$ resembles the actual access settings found on her device for the specific app. Note that some apps do not declare permissions for specific groups; here for example, the Calendar is not used by the app, therefore this group is flagged as N in v_2.

In order to calculate the Jaccard distance we neglect users' choices made for the permission groups flagged as N. Hence, the vectors to be compared are now the following: $v_1 = (1, 0, 1, 0, 0, 0, 1)$ and $v_2 = (1, 0, 1, 0, 0, 0, 1)$. We do that because we do not want to compare users' answers (v_1) with actual settings (v_2) when the particular dangerous permission group is not declared by the app. Hence, we do not impute any missing values. Therefore, the Jaccard distance of v_1 and v_2 is 0.0 in this instance, which means that the user's answer and her actual settings on her device are exactly the same. This can be seen as an indication that the respondent was totally aware of the permission settings on her device related to the specific app.

Figure 4 shows the Jaccard distance between v_1 and v_2 for each participant's entry. In 10 cases the Jaccard distance between v_1 and v_2 was 0.0. This means that only 21.3% of the respondents appeared to have a clear view of the resources they allowed their favorite apps to access. This number is indeed lower if we consider that half of these participants appeared to be 100% permissive when their favorite app requests access to their devices' resources. The average Jaccard distance derived from the 47 participants is approximately 0.71. The last metric shows that there exist misconceptions about the actual state of the permission settings in our participants' devices despite the fact that there were asked to provide their privacy preferences/settings for their favorite (hence most used) apps.

5.4   RQ4: Can We Categorize Users According to Their Privacy/Permission Settings?

As of October 2019, there existed $N = 55$ distinct sub-categories on the Google Play App store (e.g. Art & Design, Auto & Vehicles, Beauty, etc.). Our aim here is to create users' privacy profiles based on their acquired snapshots depicting the permission settings for each category.

Modeling User's Settings. We accumulate permission settings on each device as follows:

App permission settings for each device are reconstructed from the permission snapshots and resembled by vectors $a = (p_1, p_2, \ldots, p_9)$, for $i \in [1,9]$ (9 permission groups), where:

a) $p_i = 1$, i.e. the permission was allowed to this app,
b) $p_i = -1$, i.e. the permission was not allowed (or never requested by the app)
c) $p_i = 0$, i.e. the app did not declare this permission.

When there are cases where more than one apps from one category exist on a device, we perform the following basic calculations. For each permission group we count the "Allow" (i.e. "1") and the "Deny (i.e. "0") decisions and find the more prominent value between them. We transform this value to a float number (percentage) representing the probability of this user to allow or deny access to the resource protected by the permission from this specific dangerous permission group. When the prominent number refers to "Allow" decisions the float number is positive, and it is negative in the opposite case. If there exist apps that do not declare a specific permission from a group (e.g. Sensors), we fill this place with a zero. If there are equal "Allow" and "Deny" decisions for a permission group in a category, we assume that the user is positively inclined to allow access (according to our finding from RQ2).

Therefore, for each device we create a sequence (or a feature set in other words) of $N = 55$ vectors representing the tendency of the user to allow or deny an app from a given category.

In this sub-section we report results gathered from a larger group from our pool of participants (i.e. G_d). G_d consists of data derived from 67 devices. As explained earlier in this Section, we removed data derived from 4 devices. Additionally, we also noted that 7 participants did not provide app usage data. However, we included their permission snapshots in this part of the study because these data are not ambiguous, meaning that they could not be falsified or somehow manipulated, given that they are provided by the Android system itself.

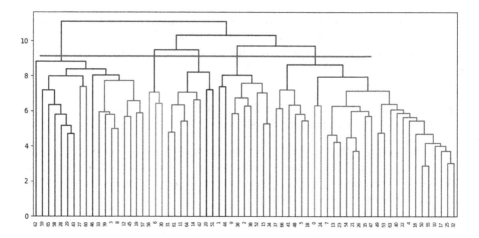

Fig. 5. Dendrogram derived from hierarchical clustering.

However, there is always a small probability that some permission settings in these devices (we refer here to the 7 participants) will describe apps that have never been used before. This is a reasonable concern which might lead to misinterpretations of a user's intention to allow or deny access to an app from a certain category. Indeed this was also a basic limitation of similar previous work [2].

In order to overcome this limitation we examined the data we derived from devices that provided app usage data. We measured the percentage of installed apps in each of these devices and identified from the app usage data if these apps were invoked at least once. We found that on average 94.22% of the installed apps were run at least once. Therefore, it is safe to generalize and assume that the majority of the data provided from the aforementioned 7 devices contain permission settings from apps that were used at least once.

Clustering Profiles. We perform Agglomerative hierarchical clustering using *scikit-learn* [15] to identify clusters in our data (linkage method: *ward*). The same methodology was used by Liu et al. [14] recently to create similar privacy profiles. However, Liu et al. [14] did not consider users' permission settings for all known categories in the Play Store in their work.

We draw a dendrogram to visualize how clusters are formed from our data. After performing a visual inspection, we empirically decide to deviate the users in five big clusters (see the red line in Fig. 5). Liu et al. [14] identified 7 clusters in their analysis. However, they admit that the majority of the users in their study is gathered in one big cluster.

Figure 6 showcases representative samples of the privacy profiles we created. On the vertical axes we place the different app categories and on the horizontal axes we show the nine groups of dangerous permissions. The color of each cell

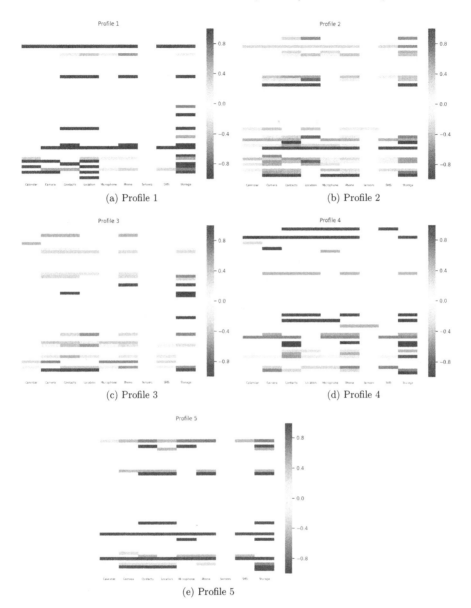

Fig. 6. Users' privacy preferences profiles derived from their permission settings. (Color figure online)

resembles the user's tendency to allow (green) or deny (red) an app from that category to access a resource from this permission group. White spaces denote the lack of knowledge of the user's reaction to access requests from apps from the given categories.

6   Discussion

As expected from the results presented so far, most of the users tend to protect a number of sensitive resources on their devices. Therefore, the majority of the profiles appear to be more restrictive. Profile 2 and Profile 5 are generally permissive. Profile 2 includes users who tend to allow apps access their Location and Storage. Profile 5 appears to be stricter with particular app categories compared to Profile 2. Profile 1 is restrictive in general, but allows access to Location and Sensors. Profile 3 would not usually allow access to the Calendar, Storage and the Microphone. Finally, Profile 4 appears to be generally restrictive.

Looking at the distribution of the population, we can report the following numbers. Profile 1 includes 18 users (26.9% of our sample), Profile 2 includes 8 users (11,9%), Profile 3 is the most populated with 29 users (43.3%), Profile 4 has 9 users (13.4%) and, finally, Profile 5 is the smallest comprising only 3 users (4.5%).

Compared to the work of Lin et al. [13] and Liu et al. [14] we identify similarities between our generally permissive users (Profile 2) and the "Profile 3 users" of [14] and the "unconcerned" users of [13]. Additionally, Profile 4 in our study is similar to the restrictive "Profile 4" that Liu et al. [14] identified as their protective users, and Lin et al. [13] as their "conservative" users. Finally, the derived clusters from our methodology seem to be more equally distributed compared to those presented in [14].

6.1   Android 10 Location Settings

The permission data collection methodology utilized in this study can be applied on the revamped finer-grained permission model for protection of location data in the most contemporary Android version (i.e. Android 10). The current version was released during Autumn 2019 and it features a new approach to location permission management, featuring two levels of protection. The user according to this updated model has the ability to choose between two location accessibility levels: a) Allow an app to access location data all the time (i.e. even when it is on the background), or b) allow access only when the app is in use (i.e. when it is in the foreground).

Compared to the previous models, the only difference in this occasion is the addition of an extra permission; the ACCESS_BACKGROUND_LOCATION. Thus, in order to update users' profiles in the near future to incorporate those users who updated to the most recent OS version (Android 10), we probably need to introduce a 4th choice in the location permission group: "Always Allow", "Allow when in Use", "Deny", "Not requested". Additionally, we need to account for the fact that more consumers will start using devices running versions 9 and above (i.e. API level 28+). This means that we need to implement different profiles for these users which consist of 10 dangerous permission groups. For the moment these remarks form our plans for future work.

6.2 Pilot Study on Android 10 Location Settings

We attempted to measure users' acceptance of the modernized, tristate location permission system on Android 10, conducting a pen-and-paper exercise as follows. We gathered a random group of 25 undergraduate and postgraduate students (studying Cyber Security and Digital Forensics at the University of the West of England) and asked them to participate in a short experiment. We distributed a short questionnaire and asked them to anonymously answer three questions in 5 min.

The questionnaire comprised a screenshot of an app requesting location permission, adhering to the new tristate location permission system introduced in Android 10 [5], followed by 3 short questions. The depicted dialogue message stated: "Allow App 1 to access this device's location?". The message featured the following options: "Allow all the time", "Allow only while the app is in use", "Deny". The participants asked to answer the following questions:

- To comment on the functionality/outcome of each option.
- If the message was clear.
- Which option they would choose.

22 students answered anonymously the questionnaire. We briefly discuss the outcome in this section. 16 participants (i.e. 72.7%) said that the message shown by the system is clear. 3 students (i.e. 13.6%) claimed the opposite, and 3 other students said that "it is misleading", "not very clear", or "a little clear". Therefore, 72.7% thought the message is clear and 27.3% had a different opinion. The most interesting finding however derives from the answers to the last question. 16 students said they would choose the "Allow only while the app is in use" if they were using the app, and only 1 said they would "Allow all the time". Finally, 2 students said they would choose "Deny" and 3 students replied that "it depends on the app". Among these 3 participants, 2 of them said "it depends", but they would probably choose to "Allow only while the app is in use" or "Deny".

Hence, this preliminary study shows that if the users have the choice to allow an app to access the device's location only while the app is in the foreground, they are eventually positively inclined to provide the permission. Also, we saw that almost three quarters of the participants thought the message provided by the system about the tristate location permission was clear enough.

7 Conclusion

We utilized publicly available system information derived from the use of the `PackageManager`, accessible by any installed app on the device[1]. We showed that any app installed on an Android device is able to extract similar information and perform user profiling tasks related to the user's privacy awareness. In this study we gathered permission settings from 71 devices and identified 5 distinct user profiles, related to their inclination to allow or deny access to specific sensitive

---

[1] The dataset can be found at the UWE Research Repository: Output ID: 5296390.

resources on their devices. We found that 13.4% of users in our sample belong to the most restrictive profile, 16.4% belong to generally permissive profiles and the rest of them are protective, allowing access to certain permission groups (Location, Sensors and Storage).

Moreover, our survey responses, and their comparison with participants' actual privacy controls, demonstrated that users do not feel comfortable with allowing apps to read their SMS, contact lists, and using their microphones. However, the results of this study demonstrated that, as users, we are keener to allow our favorite apps to access restricted resources.

Finally, following a cross-examination of the users' responses with their actual permission settings, we concluded that although users are supposed to have a better overview of the protected resources they allowed their favorite apps to access on their devices, they eventually fail to accurately report which groups are accessible and which are not. Also we identified the inclination of users to allow location access to an app only while the app is in the foreground (feature available on devices running Android 10).

As future work we intend to use our profile categorization methodology to investigate the feasibility of embedding these profiles in recommendation systems to efficiently suggest apps that match users' privacy settings. We believe that online app stores (such as the Google Play app store) have the capability to create more accurate privacy profiles using numerous permission snapshots via longitudinal measurements, because they have constant access to app usage statistics.

Acknowledgment. This work has been supported by the UWE Bristol Vice-Chancellor's Early Career Researcher Awards 2017–2018 and the Great Britain Sasakawa Foundation (No. 5303/2017).

References

1. Andriotis, P., Sasse, M.A., Stringhini, G.: Permissions snapshots: assessing users' adaptation to the android runtime permission model. In: 2016 IEEE International Workshop on Information Forensics and Security (WIFS), pp. 1–6, December 2016. https://doi.org/10.1109/WIFS.2016.7823922
2. Andriotis, P., Li, S., Spyridopoulos, T., Stringhini, G.: A comparative study of android users' privacy preferences under the runtime permission model. In: Tryfonas, T. (ed.) HAS 2017. LNCS, vol. 10292, pp. 604–622. Springer, Cham (2017). https://doi.org/10.1007/978-3-319-58460-7_42
3. Andriotis, P., Stringhini, G., Sasse, M.A.: Studying users' adaptation to android's run-time fine-grained access control system. J. Inf. Secur. Appl. **40**, 31–43 (2018). https://doi.org/10.1016/j.jisa.2018.02.004
4. Android Developers: Distribution dashboard (2019). https://developer.android.com/about/dashboards. Accessed 13 Oct 2019
5. AOSP: Tristate Location Permissions (2020). https://source.android.com/devices/tech/config/tristate-perms. Accessed 31 Jan 2020
6. Bonné, B., Peddinti, S.T., Bilogrevic, I., Taft, N.: Exploring decision making with android's runtime permission dialogs using in-context surveys. In: Thirteenth Symposium on Usable Privacy and Security ({SOUPS} 2017), pp. 195–210 (2017)

7. Diamantaris, M., Papadopoulos, E.P., Markatos, E.P., Ioannidis, S., Polakis, J.: REAPER: real-time app analysis for augmenting the android permission system. In: Proceedings of the Ninth ACM Conference on Data and Application Security and Privacy, pp. 37–48. ACM (2019). https://doi.org/10.1145/3292006.3300027
8. Felt, A.P., Egelman, S., Wagner, D.: I've got 99 problems, but vibration ain't one: a survey of smartphone users' concerns. In: Proceedings of the second ACM workshop on Security and privacy in smartphones and mobile devices, pp. 33–44. ACM (2012). https://doi.org/10.1145/2381934.2381943
9. Felt, A.P., Ha, E., Egelman, S., Haney, A., Chin, E., Wagner, D.: Android permissions: user attention, comprehension, and behavior. In: Proceedings of the Eighth Symposium on Usable Privacy and Security, SOUPS 2012, pp. 3:1–3:14. ACM, New York (2012). https://doi.org/10.1145/2335356.2335360
10. Hossen, M.Z., Mannan, M.: On understanding permission usage contextuality in android apps. In: Kerschbaum, F., Paraboschi, S. (eds.) DBSec 2018. LNCS, vol. 10980, pp. 232–242. Springer, Heidelberg (2018). https://doi.org/10.1007/978-3-319-95729-6_15
11. Iqbal, M.S., Zulkernine, M.: Droid mood swing (DMS): automatic security modes based on contexts. In: Nguyen, P., Zhou, J. (eds.) ISC 2017. LNCS, vol. 10599, pp. 329–347. Springer, Heidelberg (2017). https://doi.org/10.1007/978-3-319-69659-1_18
12. Likert, R.: A technique for the measurement of attitudes. Arch. Psychol. (1932)
13. Lin, J., Liu, B., Sadeh, N., Hong, J.I.: Modeling users mobile app privacy preferences: restoring usability in a sea of permission settings. In: 10th Symposium On Usable Privacy and Security ({SOUPS} 2014), pp. 199–212 (2014)
14. Liu, B., et al.: Follow my recommendations: a personalized privacy assistant for mobile app permissions. In: Symposium on Usable Privacy and Security (2016)
15. Pedregosa, F., et al.: Scikit-learn: machine learning in Python. J. Mach. Learn. Res. 12, 2825–2830 (2011)
16. Raval, N., Razeen, A., Machanavajjhala, A., Cox, L.P., Warfield, A.: Permissions plugins as android apps. In: Proceedings of the 17th Annual International Conference on Mobile Systems, Applications, and Services, pp. 180–192. ACM (2019). https://doi.org/10.1145/3307334.3326095
17. Reardon, J., Feal, Á., Wijesekara, P., Elazari Bar On, A., Vallina-Rodriguez, N., Egelman, S.: 50 ways to leak your data: an exploration of apps' circumvention of the android permissions systems. In: 28th USENIX Security Symposium (2019)
18. Reinfelder, L., Schankin, A., Russ, S., Benenson, Z.: An inquiry into perception and usage of smartphone permission models. In: Furnell, S., Mouratidis, H., Pernul, G. (eds.) TrustBus 2018. LNCS, vol. 11033, pp. 9–22. Springer, Cham (2018). https://doi.org/10.1007/978-3-319-98385-1_2
19. Scoccia, G.L., Ruberto, S., Malavolta, I., Autili, M., Inverardi, P.: An investigation into android run-time permissions from the end users' perspective. In: Proceedings of the 5th International Conference on Mobile Software Engineering and Systems, pp. 45–55. ACM (2018). https://doi.org/10.1145/3197231.3197236
20. Thompson, C., Johnson, M., Egelman, S., Wagner, D., King, J.: When it's better to ask forgiveness than get permission: attribution mechanisms for smartphone resources. In: Proceedings of the Ninth Symposium on Usable Privacy and Security, p. 1. ACM (2013). https://doi.org/10.1145/2501604.2501605
21. Votipka, D., Rabin, S.M., Micinski, K., Gilray, T., Mazurek, M.L., Foster, J.S.: User comfort with android background resource accesses in different contexts. In: Fourteenth Symposium on Usable Privacy and Security ({SOUPS} 2018), pp. 235–250 (2018)

22. Wijesekera, P., et al.: The feasibility of dynamically granted permissions: aligning mobile privacy with user preferences. In: 2017 IEEE Symposium on Security and Privacy (SP), pp. 1077–1093, May 2017. https://doi.org/10.1109/SP.2017.51
23. Wijesekera, P., et al.: Contextualizing privacy decisions for better prediction (and protection). In: Proceedings of the 2018 CHI Conference on Human Factors in Computing Systems, p. 268. ACM (2018). https://doi.org/10.1145/3173574.3173842

"Alexa, Are You Spying on Me?": Exploring the Effect of User Experience on the Security and Privacy of Smart Speaker Users

George Chalhoub$^{(\boxtimes)}$ ⬤ and Ivan Flechais$^{(\boxtimes)}$

Department of Computer Science, University of Oxford, Oxford OX1 3QD, UK
{george.chalhoub,ivan.flechais}@cs.ox.ac.uk

Abstract. Smart speakers are useful and convenient, but they are associated with numerous security and privacy threats. We conducted thirteen interviews with users of smart speakers to explore the effect of user experience (UX) factors on security and privacy. We analyzed the data using Grounded Theory and validated our results with a qualitative meta-synthesis. We found that smart speaker users lack privacy concerns towards smart speakers, which prompts them to trade their privacy for convenience. However, various trigger points such as negative experiences evoke security and privacy needs. When such needs emerge, existing security and privacy features were not found to be user-friendly which resulted in compensatory behavior. We used our results to propose a conceptual model demonstrating UX's effect on risk, perceptions and balancing behavior. Finally, we concluded our study by recommending user-friendly security and privacy features for smart speakers.

Keywords: User experience · Smart speaker · Security · Privacy · Behaviors

1 Introduction

The first practical keyboard was invented by Christopher Latham Sholes in 1873 [21]. The keyboard and other peripheral devices were invented because traditional computing devices were not able to decode human voices. However, the rapid development of speech recognition technology is changing the way people interact with technology. Mobile phones are equipped with speech-activated functions supported with advanced and accurate speech-to-text technology. One of the most significant and successful voice technology innovations are smart speakers. Smart speakers like Amazon Echo, Google Home, and Apple HomePod are increasingly becoming a trend in homes and rapidly becoming integrated with other smart devices. Amazon's devices team announced in January 2019 that the company had sold more than 100 million Alexa powered devices worldwide [12]. In 2018, Google revealed that they sold more than one Google Home product every second [19].

© Springer Nature Switzerland AG 2020
A. Moallem (Ed.): HCII 2020, LNCS 12210, pp. 305–325, 2020.
https://doi.org/10.1007/978-3-030-50309-3_21

Smart speakers offer hands-free and eye-free operations allowing users to send voice commands while working on other tasks. Smart assistants like Alexa also emulate social presence due to being equipped with speech synthesis technologies allowing Alexa to artificially produce human-like speeches [13]. To be able to operate in a hands-free environment, smart speakers need to continuously listen to what is being said around the device to catch the wake word (e.g., "Ok Google"). Cybersecurity critics have argued that always-on devices like smart speakers bring a significant threat to privacy and security. Smart speakers were previously vulnerable to security attacks which allowed attackers to turn them into a wiretapping device [13]. Integrating proper privacy and security controls into smart speakers while preserving UX seems to be a continuous challenge.

Users don't just look for privacy and security from those devices; they look for satisfaction, convenience, and well-being. They want to use technology with-out worry while having a good User Experience (UX). The UX of smart speakers involves much more than usability; it includes people's feelings, emotional reactions and psychological needs. The purpose of this research is to allow us to understand better how UX influences users' security and privacy. Therefore, we asked the research question: How do UX factors influence the security and privacy of users of smart speakers?

To tackle our research question, we conducted semi-structured interviews with thirteen users of smart speakers and analyzed the data with Grounded Theory. We summarize our key findings below:

- Users express a lack of privacy concerns towards smart speakers be-cause of individual perceptions (e.g., their perceived notability).
- Users trade their security and privacy for the benefits arising from smart speakers (e.g., convenience and utility).
- Users have various security and privacy needs that result from specific trigger points (e.g., detrimental experiences, adversarial needs).
- Common security and privacy features (e.g., muting) of smart speakers were not found to be user-friendly and were hindering the UX.
- Users reported compensatory behavior (e.g., disconnecting the devices, deleting audio history) resulting from negative experiences with smart security and privacy tools.

We used our results to present recommendations for the security and privacy design of smart speakers. In addition, we proposed a conceptual framework showing how UX interacts with risk and balancing behavior.

This research paper is organized as follows. Section 2 provides background information related to UX and smart speakers. The section also discusses related works. Section 3 describes our study methodology and design. Section 4 presents a detailed description of our results, organized according to the discovered categories. Section 5 introduces design recommendations for security and privacy in smart speakers. In addition, it introduces our proposed conceptual framework. Finally, Sect. 6 presents our conclusion.

2   Theoretical Background

2.1   User Experience

Definition. There is no universally accepted definition of UX. However, we will follow the definition by the international standard of human-system interaction ISO 9241-210, which defines UX as *"a person's perceptions and responses that result from the use or anticipated use of a product, system or service"* [23]. The definition includes a person's emotions, psychological responses, beliefs, perceptions, behaviors, preferences, and accomplishments.

Research Approach. While the Human-Computer Interaction (HCI) community cannot agree on a uniformly accepted UX model that drives research, there is an agreement that UX is subjective, dynamic, and context-dependent [38]. UX research is mainly divided into two research methods: one method which advocates a qualitative design approach and one method that promotes a quantitative model approach. There are two prominent UX frameworks for each approach: McCarthy and Wright's approach [39] which is considered as qualitative design-based and Hassenzahl's approach [30] which is considered as quantitative model-based.

McCarthy and Wright's Framework. McCarthy and Wright's framework [39] draws attention to the significance of a holistic experience view without reductionism [49]. The experience is described as holistic, dynamic, and subjective. The framework suggests threads that help describe experience based on context, time, feelings, emotions and processes which describe how a user subjectively makes sense of an experience.

Hassenzahl's Framework. Hassenzahl's framework [30] focuses on the technological artifacts that affect the experience. The framework specifies distinct properties of experience (e.g. subjective, dynamic, holistic, situated). Based on the self-regulation theory by Carver and Scheier [16], the framework is composed of a tiered hierarchical UX model that describes experiences as being related to motives, actions, and specific conditions.

Factors of UX. UX is influenced by three factors: user, system, and context [45]. These factors act as primary dimensions of UX, where sub-factors emerge from the literature. For the user factor, the related sub-factors that appear are emotions and psychological needs. As for the system factor, the sub-factors are hedonic and pragmatic product quality. For the context dimension, time and situatedness are the sub-factors.

Use in This Paper. For this paper, which is concerned with the security and privacy of smart home speakers, we will apply Hassenzahl's UX framework because it is concerned with the design of technological products and the UX.

2.2 Smart Speakers

Description of Smart Speakers. A smart speaker is a wireless voice command device with a virtual assistant offering multiple hands-free services with the help of activation words known as wake-up words or hot words. Smart speakers consist of one or more microphones which await the wake-up word followed by a command from the user. Smart Speakers provide extra capabilities by allowing third-party developers to create applications that offer services. They can run If This Then That (IFTTT) automation applications that connects cloud services and users' devices. Smart speakers are associated with numerous security and privacy concerns [28,33,50], we summarize them below.

Security of Smart Speakers

Voice Authentication. VAs allow users to communicate remotely by saying the wake-up word followed by the voice command. VAs had struggled in the past to recognize human voices, which prompted any audio within microphone range to send requests to the smart speaker. Smart speaker devices have numerous cases of interaction with television programs and advertisements. In 2017, a cartoon which included repeated Amazon Echo and Google Home commands had wrecked some of the viewer's devices [2]. Moreover, a notable attack on VAs is known as DolphinAttack [52] which sends voice commands in the form of an ultrasonic sound, a high-frequency sound that the human ear cannot detect.

Wiretapping. Smart speakers are at risk of getting turned into wiretapping devices. Security researchers from Tencent demonstrated a security vulnerability at DefCon that would allow attackers to take complete control of the device, which would enable them to eavesdrop on private conversations [32]. Other related security vulnerabilities were discovered by Checkmarx [1] and MWR [10].

Voice Commands. Smart speakers voice commands are transferred and stored in cloud servers [50]. While the data sent to the cloud is encrypted, it does not prevent a network sniffer from knowing there is an interaction happening with smart speakers [8]. Major smart speaker brands like Google Home, Amazon Echo, and Apple HomePod store the audio recordings in the cloud [41]. Google [36] and Amazon [25] allow users to manage and listen to their audio activity online, which adds a security risk in case an account is compromised [50].

Privacy of Smart Speakers

Company Monitoring. Major smart speaker companies (e.g., Google, Apple and Amazon) employ staff to manually listen to consumers' voice commands to improve speech recognition technology [17]. A Bloomberg investigation revealed that Amazon had contracted thousands of humans to work in a secret program with each employee processing up to 1,000 audio clips in 9 h shifts [22]. Amazon responded by saying that their contractors do not have access to customers' personally identifiable information [17]. However, critics argued that contractors may have access to GPS coordinates which can be used to point to users' locations [46]. In addition, companies collect personal information such as names, IP addresses, locations, addresses and payment cards [3]. German magazine Heise reported the story of an Amazon customer who decided to exercise his GDPR rights by requesting his stored personal information from Amazon. The company mistakenly sent 1,700 audio files and a transcribed document containing the interactions of users with Amazon Echo [11].

Misinterpretation. Misinterpretation of wake words and commands raise privacy concerns. An investigation by Symantec revealed that wake-up words could trigger smart speakers even if they are not accurate. The research reports that Google Home woke up for 'Ok Bobo' instead of 'Ok Google' [50]. A case reported by KIRO7 confirms the finding where a family in Portland had their private conversation recorded by Alexa and sent to a random contact due to misinterpretation [31].

Law Enforcement. Smart speakers collect and store a massive amount of personal information, prompting law enforcement to often demand access to data. A double murder investigation in New Hampshire prompted a judge to order Amazon to submit any audio recordings by Echo during the day of the murder [27]. Prosecutors have also sought evidence from Amazon Echo in a case involving the killing of an Arkansas police officer [14]. To protect consumer privacy, Amazon filed a motion against the police warrant issued by the prosecutors [15] but later released the data once the owner of the Echo consented [40]. Although Amazon was able to fight off the judge's orders, some privacy experts warn that laws can be passed to allow law enforcement to remotely activate smart speakers and eavesdrop on suspects [20].

2.3   UX of Smart Speakers

Unlike laptops and mobile phones, smart speakers do not generally have a screen. Even with screen-enabled smart speakers, the interactions remain invisible and the designers often aim at a positive 'voice experience'. The lack of visuals used in interactions makes designing and measuring UX more challenging [5]. Pyae and Joelsson conducted a web-based survey with 114 users and found that Google Home devices result in positive UX but had some usability issues [44]. There are current issues with understanding UX design for Voice Assistants (VA) of Smart Speakers [34]. Traditionally, measuring user satisfaction consisted of analyzing clicks and scroll signals. However, those signals do not exist in smart speakers which makes it challenging to measure user satisfaction. Other researchers have proposed ways to measure new signals. For instance, Hashemi et al. [29] proposed user intent as an original signal for measuring user satisfaction. Moreover, the personification of Alexa is linked to a higher level of user satisfaction due to increased social interactions [43]. The personification of VAs might require UX designers to work with Machine Learning as a design material [34].

2.4   Related Work

Lau et al. [37] ran a diary study and semi-structured interviews with 17 users and 17 non-users of smart speakers to understand users' reasoning for the adoption of those devices, privacy concerns and insights, and experiences. Smart speaker users were found to have a sophisticated trust relationship with companies behind smart speakers, a lack of complete understanding of privacy risks and a dependence on the socio-technical context where smart speakers are. The researchers also found that users rarely use the privacy features of smart speakers. Moreover, non-users expressed distrust for smart speakers' companies and did not find smart speakers useful. Pascal Kowalczuk [35] analyzed more than 2,000 customer reviews and 850 tweets and found that enjoyment has the largest effect on the intention to use smart speakers. Other factors that strongly adopted the use of smart speakers were found to be: usability, equality and diversity of the product, consumer's technology optimism, and the security and privacy risk. Yang et al. [42] ran a questionnaire for 315 individuals in South Korea to study user intentions for adopting smart speakers. They found that the risk of smart speaker use did not have a significant effect on the perceived value of speakers. The authors tried to justify the findings with two possible explanations. The first explanation is that privacy is the major viewed risk in speaker adoption which could have a negligible effect on the perceived value [51]. The second explanation is that smart speaker users may not be knowledgeable of all the risks associated with smart speakers. To the best of our knowledge, there has been no previous work that investigates the role of UX in security and privacy in smart speakers.

3   Research Methodology

Our study aims to explore how UX factors affect security and privacy in smart speakers; therefore, we used a qualitative research approach (Fig. 1). Our approach consisted of collecting data using semi-structured interviews. This exploratory approach allowed us to reveal new information from participants and uncover UX factors (e.g., emotions and motivations).

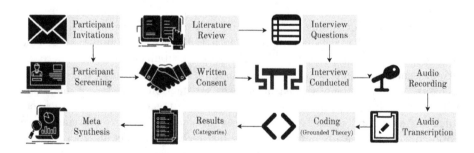

Fig. 1. Summary of our research methodology

3.1   Recruitment

To recruit participants, we printed recruitment flyers and posted them in different department buildings. We also published announcements in local city forum posts (e.g., our city's local subreddit [18]). Furthermore, we sent recruitment emails for participants using university-provided mailing lists. The recruitment message contained eligibility criteria and contact details. Initial communication with potential participants happened via university email.

3.2   Sampling

We used purposive and theoretical sampling to recruit a sample of thirteen smart speaker users to participate in our research study. Purposive sampling allowed us to select specific eligible participants from preselected criteria. The eligibility criteria consisted of users who: (i) were at least 18 years, (ii) used smart speakers in the past three months, (iii) were able to communicate in English and (iv) were able to give consent. Theoretical sampling allowed us to inform the sample size (n = 13) which was determined based on theoretical saturation. We performed data analysis after each interview and we stopped recruitment when interviews did not provide any additional categories. The demography of the participants is summarized below (Table 1).

Table 1. Participant demographics

ID	Age group	Education	Gender	Device
P1	25–30	High School	Female	Google Home
P2	30–35	High School	Male	Amazon Echo Dot
P3	35–40	Bachelors	Male	Amazon Echo Dot
P4	20–25	Bachelors	Male	Google Home Mini
P5	20–25	Doctorate	Male	Google Home
P6	20–25	Masters	Male	Google Home, Apple HomePod
P7	35–40	Bachelors	Male	Amazon Echo Dot
P8	20–25	Masters	Male	Google Home Mini
P9	25–30	Masters	Male	Amazon Echo Dot
P10	40–45	Masters	Female	Amazon Echo, Amazon Echo Dot
P11	20–25	Bachelors	Female	Amazon Echo Dot
P12	25–30	Masters	Male	Amazon Echo
P13	25–30	Bachelors	Male	Amazon Echo

3.3   Data Collection

Interviewees were invited to attend the interview in person. The interviews were conducted within interview rooms in university buildings. Four participants could not be present and were interviewed via Skype. The interview questions were based on the literature review conducted and tackled topics related to UX factors. All the interviews were audio-recorded using a recording device. Written notes were taken during the interview. The length of the interviews varied between 28 min and 62 min. All the participants were thanked with a £10 ($12) Amazon gift card voucher regardless of whether they completed the interview or not.

Interview Process. The experimenter first started with collecting necessary information from interviewees such as their age, gender, education, employment. Interviewees were then asked about the number and type of smart speakers that they use. The experimenter had deeper probing about the environment of the smart speaker. Interviewees were asked to justify all of the decisions they have made such as reasons for using a smart speaker, picking a particular brand and placement of the speaker in a particular location. Interviewees were then asked to explain how they understand the technology behind smart speakers and discuss any unpleasant interactions. This was followed by an open-ended discussion of situations where the interviewees felt uncomfortable or uneasy around the smart speaker. Based on the previous experiences and knowledge of interviewees, circumstances related to privacy and security were further explored.

3.4   Data Analysis

All the recorded interviews were transcribed and repeatedly read for familiarization with the present data. We used Grounded Theory to analyze our data. Interviews were coded with data analysis software Nvivo 12.0. At the end of the analysis, we identified 127 codes. To validate our findings, we consolidated the existing literature and used meta-synthesis [48] to compare our results with the reviewed literature.

3.5   Limitations

We have interviewed smart speaker participants who clearly chose to use and adopt smart speakers. Users of smart speakers are not a representative of all users. Non-users are likely to have different views and perceptions.

3.6   Ethics

Oxford University's Central University Research Ethics Committee reviewed and approved our research study (CUREC/CS_C1A_19_024). At the beginning of each interview session, we gave each participant an information sheet and a consent form which they had to sign before taking part in our study.

4   Results

We extracted six categories (Table 2) from our analysis (Fig. 2).

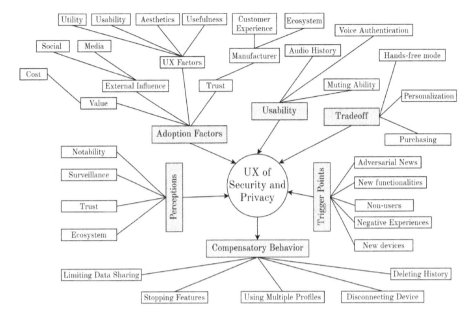

Fig. 2. Summary of our categories and codes

Table 2. Summary of extracted categories

Perceptions and beliefs towards privacy resignation
Perceptions leading to privacy resignation: perceived notability, government surveillance, trust, and product ecosystem
Usability and pragmatic quality of security and privacy controls
Usability of smart speaker's security and privacy controls: muting ability, voice authentication, and audio recording history
Influencers in the trade-off between privacy and convenience
Features affecting the trade-off choice between privacy and convenience: personalization, hands-free mode, and purchasing
Factors and motivators affecting smart speaker adoption
Factors determining smart speaker adoption: usefulness, trust, hedonic quality, cost, and social influence
Trigger points for security and privacy considerations
Occasions prompting security and privacy considerations: adversarial news, non-users and negative experiences
Security and privacy compensatory behavior
Reported compensatory behavior: limited use, disconnecting the device, stopping audio history and using multiple profiles

4.1   Perceptions and Beliefs Towards Privacy Resignation

Users express different perceptions and beliefs towards giving up their personal data to their smart speakers. We identified four perceptions and beliefs:

Perceived Notability. Users of smart speakers are influenced by how notable they think they are. When discussing giving personal data to the speaker, five users said they're not concerned about data collected by smart users because they have nothing to hide. Other users said they do not feel targeted by any external entities. When asked about concerns regarding their data being stolen, two participants responded by saying they are not an interesting target and don't feel targeted as a result. P5 said: *"I think it's easy to kind of get wrapped up in worrying about being followed or being tracked online. But in reality, probably not going to happen to us. We're not a person of particular importance."*

Surveillance. Some participants dismissed privacy concerns since they believe that government and corporate surveillance can obtain their personal data. Quoting P7: *"At the end of the day, if government agencies want to see what I'm doing, they can. I'll never know. So, what's the point of worrying about it?"* Also, some participants dismissed smart speaker microphone concerns because they claimed they are no different than their smartphones. Quoting P6: *"Why does one smart speaker microphone make a difference? Some people wouldn't talk around Alexa because it seems like an over-listening device. But also, ultimately, it is not that different from smartphones."*

Trust. All thirteen participants said that they trust their smart speaker manufacturer (e.g., Google, Apple, Amazon) to secure their personal data. As a result, they feel safe using the devices despite some saying that the companies might use it for *"targeted advertising"* (P6) and *"commercial gains"* (P1).

Ecosystem. Some participants dismiss privacy concerns because their data is shared with the smart speaker's manufacturer through their ecosystem. P6 who massively uses Google's services (e.g., Gmail, Drive, Photos) thought that adding Google Home won't make a difference. P6 said: *"I did think of the privacy of it. But once I saw how it was being used on, I thought about this whole Google ecosystem which I'm already tied into, I thought well"*. Similarly, P6 had used Amazon services for more than two decades and was comfortable using the Echo Dot in their home. Quoting P6: *"Amazon must have an incredible profile on me because I've used it for the last 20 years, they have a total profile of what my hobbies are, what I like and what I don't like. So, I don't care. Really."*

4.2   Usability and Pragmatic Quality of Security and Privacy Controls

We explored the usability of common security and privacy controls.

Muting Ability. Some users wanted to mute the smart speakers for privacy reasons but were frustrated because the devices can only be physically muted. Quoting P10: *"This is unhelpful. Echo devices are on high shelves. I can't just reach up and click it. I have to actually go and get it and pull it down and then press it. Being able to voice control would be more useful"*. Other participants went further by suggesting that they would be annoyed if the smart speaker is remotely muted because they will need *"to get up to unmute it, because it is not listening anymore"* (P11). P1 said they would prefer to have a temporary remote mute feature that would mute the device for a short period: *"I wish there was a feature where you tell Google not to listen to you for like 10 min and it starts listening to you again after 10 min."*

Audio Recording History. Most Amazon Echo users know that they can view their audio recordings using the Amazon app. Two participants said that they regularly delete their audio recording history as part of digital hygiene or housekeeping. Three participants described their stored history as *"pointless"*. Two participants who use the Google Home said that they wanted to check their queries online; however, they found the process to be complicated and confusing. Quoting P4 *"You needed to do like 7–8 steps to be able to see your voice commands. After a few minutes, I gave up."*

Voice Authentication. Echo users expressed feelings of trust and security towards ordering from Amazon due to the Echo's Purchase by Voice feature. The feature prompts Alexa to individually recognize voices using 'Alexa Voice Profiles' and reportedly is easy to set up and effortless. Quoting P3: *"It was easy to set up, Alexa made me say a couple of things and then it easily worked. If someone tries to use the Alexa in my house to order things, they won't be able to, because the voice thing will be able to block it.'* Google Home's voice authentication feature was not supported for UK households during the time of the interview.

4.3   Trigger Points for Security and Privacy Considerations

We identified trigger points prompting users to re-consider their security and privacy.

Adversarial News. Adversarial news originating from news stories or social contacts tend to prompt smart speaker users to consider what they share with the device. User P9 recalled a news article about Amazon: *"You could read in the past that Amazon had some issues with the data, for example, gave data from one person A to person B. They didn't even know each other"*. In addition, P9 felt worried after finding a news article alleging that Alexa would recognize if they were ill.

New Functionalities. New smart speaker functionalities might prompt users to question whether they would use smart speakers. While one participant had the Echo Show 5, which contains a camera, most participants were not comfortable with using a smart speaker with a camera. P11 considers microphones to be less concerning: "*It's just cameras. It's like having CCTV in your home. You don't want people watching you eat peanut butter at 3 am in the morning. It's a bit more concerning, I guess. Audio is less concerning than video for sure*". In addition, when asking participants whether they would bank with their device, many have completely dismissed the idea.

Non-user. Non-users of smart speakers prompt some users to consider their privacy around the device. P1 warns his guests about the device: "*I would tell my guests that the Google Home is listening to them. You know, if they have anything very private to say, or if they would want me to mute it, then I would mute it.*" P2, who possessed multiple Echo Dots at home and work, started having considerations about leaving it active when co-workers are around. P2 said that they have never muted the device at home but when they began using it at work, they thought that it is appropriate to mute it. Similarly, P13 expressed similar behavior when they had their client visiting them at home.

Negative Experiences. Some users reported negative experiences during their use of smart speakers, which prompts them to consider their behavior. Participant P8 who had difficulties checking his Google Home audio log was able to review his logs eventually and discovered that multiple non-intended conversations were recorded. Quoting P8: "*I really thought the Google Home was innocent and all. Until I realized that a lot of unintended conversations were recorded, yikes*". Another negative experience reported by P10 relates to the use of the purchasing feature by Amazon Echo. P10 discovered later that their son had made multiple orders from Amazon by tweaking the device settings. P10's negative experience prompted them to consider whether the purchasing feature on their device is secure enough and whether it should remain activated.

Acquiring New Devices. Acquiring a new smart speaker for the first time might be a trigger point for privacy considerations. Participant P4 explained how receiving a Google Home as a gift triggered a privacy consideration: "*I didn't want to get a smart speaker. And when I got it as a gift, I just kept it in the drawer. Then I thought: Hey, it's not recording me randomly. Why would it be? And then, one time, I just put it on and slowly got over the fear of using them*".

4.4   Factors and Motivators for Smart Speaker Adoption

We discovered six major factors and motivators for smart speaker adoption:

Usefulness. Usefulness is the most common factor for smart speaker adoption. Before acquiring smart speakers, ten participants anticipated that the device will be useful, convenient, and will *"make life easier"* (P13). P1 purchased Google Home to be able to ask the assistant for quick questions: *"I thought the Google Home would be well equipped to answer my queries quickly."* Other widespread purposes that users anticipated to be very useful were: playing music, managing their calendar, checking the weather, messaging and getting the news.

Trust. Participants' trust for smart speaker manufacturers affects whether they would adopt a smart speaker or not. P2 would not have purchased a smart speaker if Google was the only company that manufactured those devices because they don't trust the company. P2 said, *"I really trust Amazon as a company, I've used many of their services before"*. In contrast, P5 trusts Google said *"I like Amazon a lot actually, in terms of products and services. But I don't trust them as much as I trust Google"*.

Aesthetic and Hedonic Quality. The perceived aesthetic and hedonic quality of smart speakers influences their adoption. Before purchasing the product, P13 watched online videos and felt that the *'humanized voice of Alexa'* is satisfying. Not only were the aesthetics considered, but the size, looks and feels. Another user said that they were positively surprised by how small the Echo Dot and they thought the small device can easily hide out of sight if needed. Other reported qualities that were considered are the audio quality of the device, as well as the color and mobility.

Cost. The cost of smart speakers seems to play a significant factor in acquiring and adopting smart speakers. Eight participants had either got smart speakers for free or paid a small amount during a sale period. Participant P10 *"won one"* while P4 *"got it as a gift"*. Other participants acquired the device during sales such as *"black friday sales"* (P11), *"prime day"* (P13) or during a *"promotion"* (P8). Participant P3 was torn between getting Amazon's Echo Dot or Apple's HomePod, but after finding a promotion online for the Echo Dot, they made their decision: *"The Apple stuff is too expensive. We got a deal for the Echo Dots for 30 quid"*. Two participants said they would not have purchased their smart speaker device at the usual price sold.

Social Influence. Social contacts who own smart speakers seem to influence non-users into acquiring them. P6 bought their own Google Home after a Google Home Mini was set up at their family's house. Similarly, P11 purchased their own device after they used the smart speaker of their partner a couple of times.

P12 saw an Echo Dot at his cousin's residence before getting one: "*When I was at his place once, it looked like a very compact tool to have, I got jealous, and I thought that's a device that would like to have*".

Media. Mass media also seems to influence or motivate users to purchase and use smart speakers. Two participants heard about smart speakers on the news before acquiring them. Quoting P7: "*I read an article in the newspaper and it said the next third generation of the Echo Dot is out. I saw something in the paper that was like, very interesting. I just thought this is going to be pretty cool. Actually, I was just kind of intrigued*". Similarly, participant P1 had watched videos and read about the Google Home before making the purchase.

4.5   Security and Privacy Compensatory Behavior

Users reported different cases of compensatory behavior.

Deleting Audio History. When P8 went through his Google Home audio commands history and reviewed their audio history, the discovery of accidental recordings triggered a compensatory behavior. Unintended conversations could be recorded by the accidental triggering of the smart home assistant (e.g., mishearing the wake words). After this experience, P8 mentioned that they regularly review and monitor audio commands and delete queries that are considered to be non-intended or malicious.

Stopping Device Features. P10's negative experience of having unauthorized purchases on their smart speaker from their child prompted a compensatory behavior. P10 had contacted Amazon customer service and was able to turn off the purchasing feature from their smart speaker: "*I was able to chat with customer support and completely stop this feature from working on my Alexa.*" In that case, P10 had a negative experience that caused them to lose money, and this has led them to take a course of action and stop this feature from their Alexa device.

Disconnecting the Device. Another reported example of compensatory behavior involved participant P13 and his client. They were having a regular discussion at P13's residence, which ought to be private and confidential. P13 had noticed that their client seemed very uncomfortable after spotting that the Google Home's LED Light showing "*running lights in white color*" which meant that Google Home is listening. P13 described the situation as very "*awkward.*" After facing this experience, P13 disconnects his smart speakers whenever they have a client visiting: "*We never discussed the matter. But whenever they are in my home, I make sure to plug off all the smart assistants*".

Using Multiple Profiles. Two participants set separate profiles for security or privacy reasons. P3 had enabled different profiles on their account to be the only person able to make purchases on the Alexa app. Quoting P3: *"So they're there, attached to me and set so that only I could make purchases through them."* Another participant set up profiles on the Google Home to be able to receive personalized results on that without feeling uncomfortable. Personalized results include data from Google apps such as Photos, Calendar, Contacts, and Purchases [26].

Limiting Data Sharing. P4 described themselves as *"cautious"* when using their Google Home. In particular, when sending a command to the device, they make sure no compromising information is sent. Quoting P4: *"I make sure I don't say anything risky when it is recording. You know, I'm not going to, like, say my SSN out loud when it's talking."* Some participants do not completely adopt smart speakers. They express reservations when looking at different features. For instance, P11 said they would never use the purchasing feature in the device, whereas P13 said they refuse to give the Alexa app access to their iPhone's list of contacts.

4.6   Deliberations in Privacy/Security and UX Trade-Off

Personalization. Smart assistants like Alexa, Siri, and Google Assistant are personalized; they tend to use customer's data and audio log to provide a personalized experience with the device. We asked users if they prefer a neutral smart assistant that does not store any of their personal data, which might reduce the UX with the smart speaker. Only one user said they wish to have a non-personalized assistant. Most participants said they prefer smart assistants that are personified, personalized and integrated into their daily lives. Some participants express numerous positive emotional reactions that heavily influence their trade-off choice. Quoting P12: *"I feel cognizant of the fact that sometimes I refer to the device as "the device". But sometimes I'll refer to the device as "she" or "her". Kind of like humanizing the device in a sense."* Many users utilize their smart speakers daily for different tasks at different times of the day and the devices seem to be integrated into their lifestyle. P10 discussing personalization: *"Alexa almost feels like a member of the family and we just love her. We want her to stay smart and remembering our details"*.

Hands-Free Mode. We asked participants if they prefer a version of smart speakers without the always-listening mode. 12 out of 13 participants dismissed the idea. When examining the trade-off between privacy and UX, they chose to sacrifice privacy for their comfort. Participants described a not-always-listening mode smart speaker as *"bothersome"* (P5), *"annoying"* (P1), *"a hassle"* (P12), *"difficult"* (P9) and *"defeating the purpose"* (P7) (P11). For disabled users, having a not always-listening mode could significantly impact their comfort. P10 weighted in *"I like the fact that I can wake up and ask what to do Alexa with my* *voice because I'm disabled, I can ask Alexa dozens of things to do for me without having to find my phone or another human being."*

Purchasing. Both Google and Amazon allow users to purchase items through smart speakers. Some non-users of this feature said that they don't trust the whole process of buying via the device. One participant was okay with using for their smart speaker for small purchases but some felt *"uncomfortable sometimes for not knowing what is happening behind the scenes. Where is my credit card stored? What if they overcharged me?"* (P2). Participants who order via smart speakers expressed positive feelings, good UX, and trust towards purchasing and using the devices. Some users expressed feelings of trust and security from ordering off Amazon due to the Echo's "Purchase by Voice" feature. The feature prompts Alexa to recognize voices using "Alexa Voice Profiles" and as a result, only allows the smart speaker owner to order from Amazon.

5   Discussion

5.1   Privacy Design Recommendations

Improvements to Muting. Amazon Echo and Google Home users cannot mute their smart speakers remotely (e.g., Alexa stop listening), which creates an inconvenience. For instance, disabled users suffer from significant disadvantages for not being able to mute their devices remotely. Manufacturers should add a device feature allowing users to remotely mute their speakers. Remote muting would require a physical trigger to unmute the device. Therefore, the feature should be accompanied by two complementary functions: *Temporary Remote Mute* and *Mobile App Unmute*. *Temporary Remote Mute* would allow participants to mute the speaker for a period of time (e.g., 'Ok Google, stop listening for the remainder of the day.'). *Mobile App Unmute* would allow users to unmute their devices via their mobile applications. Manufacturers of such applications should ensure that unmuting from apps is straightforward and easy to use (e.g., using GUI on/off toggle components).

Support for Multiple Devices. It is not unlikely for household users to own multiple smart speakers. Having to remotely mute every device by voice may decrease the usefulness and usability. Manufacturers should support muting all (e.g., Hey Google mute all devices) or part of household devices from one device (e.g., Ok Alexa mute the living room speakers).

Changing Privacy Default Settings. Google and Amazon store the audio history of their customers' commands by default. Google activates the 'Voice & Audio Activity' feature by default storing all of the customer's recordings. Similarly, Amazon turns on two features by default which permits their contractors to manually review a portion of the audio recordings. A significant number of our interviewees were not aware that their audio recordings are cataloged and stored. It seems highly unlikely that smart speaker users will go through the settings and disable features that pose a risk to their privacy or security (e.g., consenting to human review of their audio activity). Companies should ensure that privacy-preserving settings are switched on by default.

Improvements to the Audio Logs Feature. While Google allows its customers to switch off the audio log activity feature, Amazon does not [24]. Users who do not want to have their audio activity stored would still need to delete their log from the device regularly – which would result in decreased UX.

Private Mode. Some users mentioned that they would like to keep their audio recordings for practical reasons, which would increase the UX. Smart speaker manufacturers should introduce a private mode that is equivalent to the private mode of a web browser. Users who wish to have their activity logged could temporarily pause activity logging using the suggested private mode feature. The private mode could be complemented with two additional associated features: *Voice Activation* and *Associated Colors*. *Voice Activation* allows users to toggle the private mode by voice (e.g., Hey Alexa, turn on private mode). *Associated Colors* would change the color of the speaker to a specific color (e.g., red) when private mode is on.

5.2   Security Design Recommendations

Adding Security Layers to Voice Recognition. Voice Recognition technologies have a history of security vulnerabilities (e.g., voice impersonation attacks [4]). Many of our interviewees had difficulties trusting the voice recognition features available on smart speakers – Google uses 'Voice Match' whereas Amazon uses 'Voice Recognition'. Smart speaker companies can add additional security layers to voice recognition (e.g., asking for memorable passphrases) – which is likely to increase the security and nurture trust.

Offline Capabilities. While some participants use their devices for multiple and varied tasks, some report minimal use of the devices. Two participants have suggested they would like to use offline smart speakers. One of the participants' uses of their smart speaker is limited to controlling their smart home. The three major commercial smart speakers send every user query to the cloud for processing even if the command was straightforward (e.g., 'Alexa, shut off the lights').

Creating an offline smart speaker for performing basic tasks is possible. The company Sensory has developed an offline smart speaker that does not require any internet access. The device can perform voice recognition offline and perform many tasks such as setting the timer, control smart homes and playing music via Bluetooth [6]. Offline smart speakers nearly eliminate the security and privacy risks associated with cloud smart speakers.

5.3   UX Conceptual Model

Our results show that UX qualities (e.g., findable, desirable, credible) influence
security and privacy in three areas: the perception of risk, the experience of harm
and the mitigation practice. To present a model showing how UX affects behavior, we explored John Adam's theory of risk compensation, which states that
there is a *"risk thermostat"* influencing human behavior. The theory explains
that users experiencing a safe lifestyle eventually seek out risky behavior; but
overcompensate before returning to safety [7,47]. Using the risk thermostat and
our study findings, we proposed a conceptual model demonstrating how UX qualities interact with the concepts on risk and balancing behavior. In our model,
the experience [39] of impact, vulnerability, and threat strongly influence users'
perceptions of risk which would affect balancing behavior (Fig. 3).

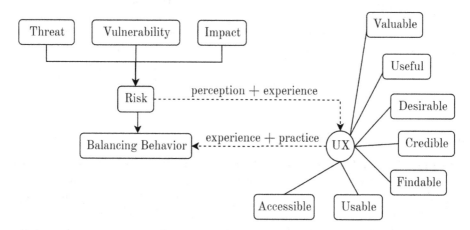

Fig. 3. Conceptual model demonstrating UX effect on risk and balancing behavior

6   Conclusion

With over a quarter of American adults owning a smart speaker [9], there is
no doubt that smart speakers are witnessing considerable growth today. Smart
speakers bring convenience and benefits to their users, but security and privacy concerns may be damaging their market growth. To find out how UX
factors affect the security and privacy of smart speaker users, we conducted
semi-structured interviews with thirteen users of smart speakers. We found that
users reported compensatory behavior due to security and privacy features that
were not user friendly. We used our results to recommend enhanced security and
privacy features for smart speakers. Finally, we proposed a conceptual model
that illustrates how UX qualities are linked with the concepts of risk and balancing behavior.

Acknowledgments. The interview gift cards were funded by Oxford University's Centre for Doctoral Training in Cyber Security. The author of this research paper is funded by a grant from Foundation Sesam, a Geneva-based foundation.

References

1. Amazon Echo: Alexa leveraged as a silent eavesdropper. Technical report, Checkmarx. https://info.checkmarx.com/wp-alexa
2. 'South Park' Episode Triggers Viewers' Amazon Alexa and Google Home, vol. 2019. https://www.hollywoodreporter.com/live-feed/south-park-premiere-messes-viewers-amazon-alexa-google-home-1039035
3. What data does Amazon collect and use? vol. 2019
4. Security Vulnerabilities of Voice Recognition Technologies, vol. 2019 (2015). https://resources.infosecinstitute.com/security-vulnerabilities-of-voice-recognition-technologies/
5. "Alexa, How Will Voice Impact User Experience?" (2018). https://userbrain.net/blog/alexa-voice-user-experience
6. Sensory is Enabling Offline Smart Speakers with No Cloud Connectivity to Maximize Security, vol. 2019 (2019). https://voicebot.ai/2019/01/18/sensory-is-enabling-offline-smart-speakers-with-no-cloud-connectivity-to-maximize-security/
7. Adams, J.: Risk and morality: three framing devices. In: Risk and Morality, pp. 87–106 (2003)
8. Apthorpe, N., Reisman, D., Feamster, N.: A smart home is no castle: privacy vulnerabilities of encrypted IoT traffic. arXiv preprint arXiv:1705.06805 (2017)
9. Auxier, B.: 5 things to know about Americans and their smart speakers. https://www.pewresearch.org/fact-tank/2019/11/21/5-things-to-know-about-americans-and-their-smart-speakers/
10. Barnes, M.: Alexa, are you listening?, vol. 2019, August 2017. https://labs.mwrinfosecurity.com/blog/alexa-are-you-listening
11. Bleich, H.: Alexa, Who Has Access to My Data?
12. Bohn, D.: Amazon says 100 million Alexa devices have been sold. The Verge (2019)
13. Burke, S.: Google admits its new smart speaker was eavesdropping on users, p. 7 (2017). https://money.cnn.com/2017/10/11/technology/google-home-mini-security-flaw/index.html
14. Carman, A.: Police want an Echo's data to prove a murder case, but how much does it really know?, vol. 2019 (2016). https://www.theverge.com/2016/12/27/14089836/amazon-echo-privacy-criminal-investigation-data
15. Carman, A.: Amazon says Alexa's speech is protected by the First Amendment, vol. 2019 (2017). https://www.theverge.com/2017/2/23/14714656/amazon-alexa-data-protection-court-free-speech
16. Carver, C.S., Scheier, M.F.: On the Self-regulation of Behavior. Cambridge University Press, New York (2001)
17. Cellan-Jones, R.: Smart speaker recordings reviewed by humans (2019). https://www.bbc.com/news/technology-47893082
18. Chalhoub, G.: r/oxford - Do you own a smart speaker (Alexa, Google Home)? Get paid £10 for a 30 minutes interview. https://www.reddit.com/r/oxford/comments/cgrxgm
19. Chandra, R., Huffman, S.: How Google Home and the Google Assistant helped you get more done in 2017. blog (2018)

20. Cranz, A.: Amazon's Alexa Is Not Even Remotely Secure and I Really Don't Care, vol. 2019. https://gizmodo.com/alexa-is-not-even-remotely-secure-and-really-i-dont-car-1764761117

21. David, P.A.: Clio and the economics of QWERTY. Am. Econ. Rev. **75**(2), 332–337 (1985)

22. Day, M., Turner, G., Drozdiak, N.: Amazon Workers Are Listening to What You Tell Alexa. Accessed 27 June 2019 (2019)

23. ISO DIS: 9241–210: 2010. Ergonomics of human system interaction-Part 210: Human-centred design for interactive systems (formerly known as 13407). International Standardization Organization (ISO). Switzerland (2010)

24. Fussell, S.: Consumer Surveillance Enters Its Bargaining Phase, vol. 2019 (2019). https://www.theatlantic.com/technology/archive/2019/06/alexa-google-incognito-mode-not-real-privacy/590734/

25. Garun, N.: How to hear (and delete) every conversation your Amazon Alexa has recorded, vol. 2019 (2018). https://www.theverge.com/2018/5/28/17402154/amazon-echo-alexa-conversation-recording-history-listen-how-to

26. Google: Allow personal results on your shared devices. https://support.google.com/assistant/answer/7684543

27. Hamilton, I.A.: A judge has ordered Amazon to hand over recordings from an Echo to help solve a double murder case, vol. 2019. https://www.businessinsider.com/amazon-ordered-to-disclose-echo-alexa-recordings-murder-case-2018-11

28. Hart, L.: Smart speakers raise privacy and security concerns. J. Account. **225**(6), 70 (2018)

29. Hashemi, S.H., Williams, K., Kholy, A.E., Zitouni, I., Crook, P.A.: Measuring user satisfaction on smart speaker intelligent assistants. Anne Dirkson, Suzan Verberne, Gerard van Oortmerssen & Wessel Kraaij p. 22 (2018)

30. Hassenzahl, M.: Experience design: technology for all the right reasons. Synth. Lect. Hum. Center. Inform. **3**(1), 1–95 (2010)

31. Horcher, G.: Woman says her Amazon device recorded private conversation, sent it out to random contact, vol. 2019 (2018). https://www.kiro7.com/news/local/woman-says-her-amazon-device-recorded-private-conversation-sent-it-out-to-random-contact/755507974

32. HuiYu, W., Wenxiang, Q.: Breaking Smart Speakers: We are Listening to You, vol. 2019. https://www.defcon.org/html/defcon-26/dc-26-speakers.html#HuiYu

33. Jackson, C., Orebaugh, A.: A study of security and privacy issues associated with the Amazon echo. Int. J. Internet Things Cyber Assur. **1**(1), 91–100 (2018)

34. Kaye, J., et al.: Panel: voice assistants, UX design and research. In: Extended Abstracts of the 2018 CHI Conference on Human Factors in Computing Systems, p. panel01. ACM (2018)

35. Kowalczuk, P.: Consumer acceptance of smart speakers: a mixed methods approach. J. Res. Interact. Market. **12**(4), 418–431 (2018)

36. Krasnoff, B.: How to stop Google from keeping your voice recordings, vol. 2019 (2019). https://www.theverge.com/2019/5/13/18618156/how-to-stop-google-voice-recordings-storage-assistant

37. Lau, J., Zimmerman, B., Schaub, F.: Alexa, are you listening?: privacy perceptions, concerns and privacy-seeking behaviors with smart speakers. In: Proceedings of the ACM on Human-Computer Interaction, vol. 2(CSCW), p. 102 (2018)

38. Law, E.L.C., Roto, V., Hassenzahl, M., Vermeeren, A.P., Kort, J.: Understanding, scoping and defining user experience: a survey approach. In: Proceedings of the SIGCHI conference on human factors in computing systems, pp. 719–728. ACM (2009)

39. McCarthy, J., Wright, P.: Technology as Experience. MIT Press, Cambridge (2007)
40. McCormick, R.: Amazon gives up fight for Alexa's First Amendment rights after defendant hands over data, vol. 2019 (2017). https://www.theverge.com/2017/3/7/14839684/amazon-alexa-first-amendment-case
41. Moynihan, T.: Alexa and Google Home Record What You Say. But What Happens to That Data? (2016). https://www.wired.com/2016/12/alexa-and-google-record-your-voice/
42. Park, K., Kwak, C., Lee, J., Ahn, J.H.: The effect of platform characteristics on the adoption of smart speakers: empirical evidence in South Korea. Telematics Inform. **35**(8), 2118–2132 (2018)
43. Purington, A., Taft, J.G., Sannon, S., Bazarova, N.N., Taylor, S.H.: Alexa is my new BFF: social roles, user satisfaction, and personification of the Amazon echo. In: Proceedings of the 2017 CHI Conference Extended Abstracts on Human Factors in Computing Systems, pp. 2853–2859. ACM (2017)
44. Pyae, A., Joelsson, T.N.: Investigating the usability and user experiences of voice user interface: a case of Google home smart speaker. In: Proceedings of the 20th International Conference on Human-Computer Interaction with Mobile Devices and Services Adjunct, pp. 127–131. ACM (2018)
45. Roto, V., Law, E., Vermeeren, A., Hoonhout, J.: User experience white paper: Bringing clarity to the concept of user experience. In: Dagstuhl Seminar on Demarcating User Experience, p. 12 (2011)
46. Seals, T.: Amazon Employees Given 'Broad Access' to Personal Alexa Info, vol. 2019. https://threatpost.com/amazon-employees-personal-alexa/144119/
47. Thompson, M.: Taking account of societal concerns about risk
48. Walsh, D., Downe, S.: Meta-synthesis method for qualitative research: a literature review. J. Adv. Nurs. **50**(2), 204–211 (2005)
49. Wright, P., McCarthy, J., Meekison, L.: Making sense of experience. In: Blythe, M., Monk, A. (eds.) Funology 2. HIS, pp. 315–330. Springer, Cham (2018). https://doi.org/10.1007/978-3-319-68213-6_20
50. Wueest, C.: A guide to the security of voice-activated smart speakers (2017)
51. Yang, H., Yu, J., Zo, H., Choi, M.: User acceptance of wearable devices: an extended perspective of perceived value. Telematics Inform. **33**(2), 256–269 (2016)
52. Zhang, G., Yan, C., Ji, X., Zhang, T., Zhang, T., Xu, W.: DolphinAttack: inaudible voice commands. In: Proceedings of the 2017 ACM SIGSAC Conference on Computer and Communications Security, pp. 103–117. ACM (2017)

Clearing the Hurdles: How to Design Privacy Nudges for Mobile Application Users

Susen Döbelt[1,2(✉)], Josephine Halama[1], Sebastian Fritsch[3], Minh-Hoang Nguyen[4], and Franziska Bocklisch[1]

[1] Professorship of Cognitive Psychology and Human Factors, Chemnitz University of Technology, Chemnitz, Germany
susen.doebelt@psychologie.tu-chemnitz.de
[2] Research Group of Cognitive and Engineering Psychology, Chemnitz University of Technology, Chemnitz, Germany
[3] secuvera GmbH, Gäufelden, Germany
[4] Distributed Artificial Intelligence Laboratory, Technische Universität Berlin, Berlin, Germany

Abstract. Many smartphone apps pose a privacy risk to their users and use sensitive data, which is not visible during daily app usage. App permissions are accessible but not comprehensible for average users, thus leading to information asymmetry between app providers and users. We want to minimize information asymmetries by making app information flows visible and understandable. To determine the information needed and how it should be presented, a survey ($N = 227$) and a laboratory study ($N = 31$) were conducted. In sum, users desired a credible tool that shows, explains and valuates information flows of apps. Furthermore, it should provide options to act in a privacy protective way. This led to a framework of user requirements, which can guide the development of analytic tools and nudge mobile application users towards privacy, make informed privacy decisions, and possibly change apps from the provider side.

Keywords: Mobile application · Permission · Nudging

1 Introduction

Starting in 2017, the majority of mobile phone users worldwide (51%) owned a smartphone [32]. An average smartphone user has 33 applications (apps) installed, 12 of which they use every day [3]. Furthermore, two and a half million apps exist in the Google Play Store [1] available on Android, which is the most common operating system for smartphones [2]. Despite the importance and popularity of mobile apps, data protection and privacy issues create potential downsides for the user. Previous analyses revealed that mobile apps might request more permissions than needed to accomplish tasks [5]. Moreover, two-thirds of the tested Android apps suspiciously used sensitive data with implicit or explicit user consent [17]. Therefore, the Android's permission system has attracted a lot of research interest during the last years [27].

© Springer Nature Switzerland AG 2020
A. Moallem (Ed.): HCII 2020, LNCS 12210, pp. 326–353, 2020.
https://doi.org/10.1007/978-3-030-50309-3_22

In Android versions prior to 6.0, the user has to accept permissions during the installation process [28]. Research showed that these permission screens are hardly considered or comprehended [6, 7, 14], and thus users fail to remember granted permissions [15]. Furthermore, users often feel uncertain about the appropriateness of permission requests [14] and are more comfortable with additional explanations [16, 18]. In case of uncertainty, users rather rely on the expectation that apps only incorporate the personal information required by their functionality [15].

Since Android version 6.0. install time are complemented by runtime permission requests [27], asking for user approval once a permission group is needed [19, 27]. However, critically important is that permissions are explained exclusively in the smartphone settings and only permission groups ranked as "dangerous" (e.g., for location or microphone access) are requested during runtime. Permissions classified as "normal" or "signature" are granted by default during installation [19]. One example for an install time permission is the internet access [27], requested from 91% of tested Android apps and often not secured even though used to send personal data [4].

In sum, regardless of the Android version, there are large hurdles for most of the users in making informed privacy decisions during the usage of mobile apps. Particularly, there is an information asymmetry between app users and providers. To address these issues, user-centered designed tools [9] are needed to provide users with clear information about the behavior of their apps. As insufficient usability prevents users from effective use of privacy functionality offered [36], the aim of our studies is to formulate guidelines to design a user-friendly analytic tool to clear hurdles and enable informed privacy decisions for mobile application users.

2 Related Work

Different analytic approaches have been developed to identify possible privacy risks of mobile apps [5]. For example, the static analytic approach analyzes the app code and identifies possible sources and sinks of data leakage. Dynamic monitoring investigates app behavior during runtime. Moreover, permission applications read the manifests of installed applications and notify users about the requested permissions [5]. However, there is little research on how these approaches could be combined to achieve the greatest possible transparency for users [16], and eventually nudge users to preserve privacy.

The aim of nudging is to improve individual well-being without limiting the freedom of choices [13]. In general, nudges are interventions that can, for instance, encourage users towards more beneficial privacy choices by accounting for hurdles in human decision-making [12]. One hurdle is incomplete or asymmetric information [13]. It is conceivable that these decision-making hurdles also apply to mobile app interaction.

In particular, previous authors suggested that "*dedicated mobile apps can assist users with nudges in making beneficial privacy decisions*" [13], p. 30, or for example "*a nudge may take the form of an alert that informs the user of the risk*" [8]. This raises the question of how nudges should be designed. Acquisti et al. [13] already described six design dimensions: 1. Information: reduces information asymmetries and provides a realistic perspective of risks, 2. Presentation: contextual cues in the user interface to reduce cognitive load and convey appropriate risk level, 3. Defaults: configuring the system according to user's expectations, 4. Incentives: motivate users to behave according to stated preferences, 5. Reversibility: limits the impact of mistakes, 6. Timing: defines the right moment to nudge. These nudging dimensions can be assigned to mobile privacy interventions described in the literature. For example, Dogruel, Jöckel and Vitak [24] examined different default settings during the decision procedure. The authors found that privacy default features are highly valued by users.

Bal and colleagues' studied [25] nudges aiming on the presentation and timing dimensions. First, the authors derived design guidelines from the literature and applied them on a permission app. Second, they conducted a user study, which showed that privacy concerns of the permission app group were significantly lower than in the control group. The authors concluded that a permission app designed in a usable manner could be a promising tool to address privacy concerns. However, it remains unclear how the authors designed the alternative approach of the control group in detail and what characteristics account for a usable permission app.

Another study conducted by Almuhimedi et al. [26] focused on information, presentation, and timing. The authors examined behavioral consequences of a weak (daily message) and a strong nudge (daily overlays). Results showed that the weak nudge lead to privacy protective behavior, however strong privacy nudges can reinforce this effect. The authors derived three design recommendations: First, an effective nudge should be personalized (e.g., adapted to previous user decisions). Second, users should be able to configure the nudges (e.g., the timing and form of delivery). Third, a nudge should be salient without being annoying (especially repetitive notifications). The authors' recommendations on the individuality and salience of a nudge are valuable but provide little help to understand the app user and its privacy requirements comprehensively.

Kelley et al. [14] also addressed the information, presentation and the timing dimensions. They compared a Google Play Store permission screen with a modified privacy facts sheet displayed before the app download. Results showed a significant increase in selecting privacy-friendlier apps. However, all participants wanted a better understanding of why apps request certain permissions. Therefore, the authors demanded for information on frequencies and purposes of permission utilization [14].

In summary, previous related work covered the development of different analytic approaches enabling the identification of possible privacy risks raised by and during the usage of mobile apps [5, 18]. Combining these approaches within one tool should achieve the greatest gain for the user [13, 16], and thus offer strong potential to nudge users towards privacy. Previous study results [14, 25, 26] serve as a starting point, however, questions remain how analytic tools should be designed in a user-centered way to clear hurdles regarding information and presentation of complex results of risk analysis.

3   Research Question

The aim of our research was to formulate user-centered design guidelines for a mobile application analytic tool to overcome hurdles of privacy decisions with regard to information asymmetries and the presentation of (complex) information [13, 16]. We derived the following research questions:

1. Which user requirements regarding the information provision and presentation of mobile application analytic tools need to be considered?
2. Which guidelines can be derived from the user requirements for mobile application analytic tools?

We used a two-step approach to investigate our research questions and conducted an online survey to identify users' informational needs. Subsequently, we ran a laboratory study to formulate user requirements, especially in terms of the presentation dimension.

4 Study 1 – Online Study

4.1 Materials and Methods

Sample. Our online survey was conducted in Germany. We received $N = 227$ completed surveys from 81 (36%) female and 146 male respondents. The respondents were on average 35 years old ($SD = 12.22$). Our sample differed from the German population [10] in terms of gender and age, but corresponded to the age distribution of German smartphone users [21, 23]. The majority (78%) held a university degree, which exceeds the average German education level (31%, [10]). Furthermore, our respondents indicated an average smartphone use of 2 hours a day ($M = 109$ min), in accordance with available German studies (140 min of daily usage; [22]). A quarter of our participants indicated using 11 to 20 apps, which is also the most frequently ranked category among German smartphone users [31]. The distribution of mobile operating systems among our survey respondents (69% Android, 25% iOS and 4% Windows) was representative as well [2]. Most respondents indicated using a messenger app (86%) and a navigation/map app (85%). About half of the respondents used a weather app and 27% stated using a shopping app. The ordering followed official download statistics [29, 30]. In sum, our sample was highly representative for German smartphone users.

Procedure. The respondents of our online survey were invited via newsletter, personal and panel based invitations. For compensation, participants could take part in a raffle for 20 Euros. The survey questions included open and closed-ended questions. It took about 30 min to complete the survey, which commenced with a short explanation of it's purpose, a guarantee of data anonymization, and a consent on voluntary participation.

The first part included items examining the respondents' perception of privacy threat for different data types - more or less necessary for the operation of different app groups. To ensure personal relevance, we started with the query whether participants use navigation/map-apps, weather apps, messenger apps, and/or shopping apps. If they confirmed, we asked to indicate the level of agreement (ranging from 1 = "*strongly disagree*" to 6 = "*strongly agree*") with the statement "*I feel my privacy is threatened if my [map/navigation app, messenger app, weather app, or shopping app] uses...*". We always presented 15 different types of data with a short explanation (see Appendix A.1). Although this list is not exhaustive, it provides a reasonable set of necessary and unnecessary data to fulfill an app service. Hence, the level of necessity of each data type varies according to the respective app group.

In the second part, the participants answered an open-ended question: "*How could privacy protection be improved in the mobile sector? Do you have any requests or ideas for implementation?*". The survey concluded with questions about demographics and smartphone/app usage (number of installed apps; operating system; estimation of app usage time) and optional on previous negative experiences with privacy violation.

Data Analysis. Quantitative items were analyzed descriptively using median (*Mdn*), mean (*M*) and standard deviation (*SD*). Depending on the distribution, non- or parametric inferential statistics were applied to identify differences between depending variables. Relationships were analyzed via bivariate parametric or nonparametric correlation coefficients.

We used an inductive category formation [35] to analyze the qualitative answers. Categories were built bottom-up from the participants' answers, which were split up into single suggestion (multiple answers possible). Two levels of categories were formed within this process. To comply with the requirements of exclusiveness comparable degrees of abstraction, the second level categories is reported. A second coder was included to ensure reliability of codings. Intercoder-reliability (unweighted Kappa) account for $\kappa = .79$ indicating an "*excellent*" (>0.75) [37] agreement. Discrepancies of codings have been eliminated and relative response frequency of this consensus solution was analyzed descriptively to identify the most common suggestions.

4.2 Results

Quantitative Results. To obtain an overview of participants' evaluation of privacy threat, we analyzed their ratings on the 15 different data types and the 4 different app groups. The mean evaluation was $M = 5.16$ ("*strongly agree*"; $SD = .97$), indicating respondents feeling their privacy was threatened in general. Further, we calculated participants' mean agreement on the potential threat for each of the 15 data types across all four app groups as well as for each separate app group (for all 15 data types see Appendix A.2). The distribution of descriptive data suggests that the evaluation of data types differed depending on the need for requesting data from the four app groups. To verify this assumption, we defined three different levels of necessity (1 = "*data is necessary*", 2 = "*data is partially necessary*", 3 = "*data is not necessary*" to provide the app service). An expert group ($N = 9$ persons working as researchers in the field of mobile security) allocated each data type and app group combination to these three necessity levels. Figure 1 presents participants' mean agreement with the privacy threatening potential of data requests separated by the data necessity.

Evaluations appeared in the following plausible order: necessary data ($M = 4.53$; $SD = 1.13$; $n = 218$), partially necessary data ($M = 5.14$; $SD = 0.99$; $n = 218$), unnecessary data ($M = 5.29$; $SD = 1.05$; $n = 219$). To identify statistical differences between these three necessity levels, we conducted a Friedman's ANOVA, as the Kolmogorov-Smirnov test showed that the data for all three levels of necessity violated the assumption of distribution normality ($D_{necessary}(217) = .12$; $p < .001$; $D_{partly\_necessary}(217) = .19$; $p < .001$; $D_{unnecessary}(217) = .21$; $p < .001$). Results revealed a significant difference ($\chi^2(2) = 136.75, p < .001$) between the perceived privacy threat across the defined

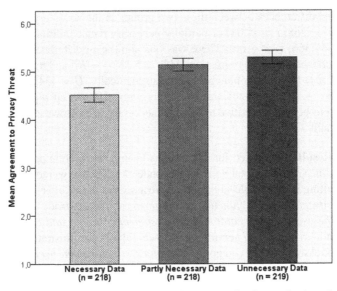

Fig. 1. Mean level of agreement (1 = "*strongly disagree to the threat of privacy*", 6 = "*highly agree to the threat of privacy*") to the degree of privacy threat across three different levels of data necessity; error bars represent 95% confidence intervals.

necessity levels. According to the post-hoc Wilcoxon-signed-rank-tests, the respondents viewed using highly necessary data (*Mdn* = 4.75) as significantly less threatening ($z = 9.74; p < .001; r = .66$) than partially necessary data (*Mdn* = 5.40). They rated unnecessary data (*Mdn* = 5.70) as significantly more threatening ($z = 3.05; p = .002; r = .21$) than partially necessary data, however the effect size was rather small [33]. Accordingly, there was also a significant difference between highly necessary data and unnecessary data ($z = 9.44; p < .001; r = .63$). All comparisons were made using a Bonferroni correction ($\alpha = .0167$).

We examined how individual difference variables in our sample (age, gender, prior experiences with privacy violations) related to users' perceived threat evaluations. We used Spearman's Rho (r_s) for all correlations as the assumption of distribution normality across the different levels of necessity (results are presented above) and for the average perception collapsed across all types of data were violated ($D_{\text{overall}}(219) = .19; p < .001$). The overall perception of privacy threat level indicated slightly increasing levels with advancing age ($r_s = .20; p = .003$). Separated by level of necessity, only the perceptions for highly necessary ($r_s = .20, p = .005$) and unnecessary data ($r_s = .19; p = .005$) showed small significant correlations with users' age. There were no significant differences between males' and females' perception of privacy threat level either across separate data necessity levels or for overall necessity.

The same procedure was applied for analyzing previous experience with privacy violations. No differences existed between those who indicated to have these experiences and those who did not regarding the overall perception of privacy threat level across all data types and app groups ($U = 4471.50; z = -1.78; p = .075; r = -.12$). Furthermore, we did not find differences between these two groups in the necessary ($U = 4700.00$; $z = -1.11$; $p = .268$; $r = -.08$) or partially necessary data condition ($U = 4788.50$; $z = -.90$; $p = .366$; $r = -.06$). There was one significant difference between those who had experienced a privacy violation ($Mdn = 5.83$; $n = 76$) and those who had not ($Mdn = 5.60$, $n = 138$) across unnecessary data specifically ($U = 4345.00$; $z = -2.07$; $p = .038$; $r = -.14$). This indicates that users who experienced a previous privacy violation tend to be more sensitive to using unnecessary data. However, the effect size was rather small.

Qualitative Results. We asked for suggestions to improve mobile privacy protection within our online survey. In total $n = 154$ respondents (68%) answered this open-ended question, resulting in 240 single suggestions. We assigned these suggestions to six categories: *"security techniques"*, *"functions, strengthen the user control"*, *"increased transparency for the user"*, *"legal control and punishment"*, *"social and economic change of values"*, and *"avoidance of service usage"*(see Table 1 for illustration). Most statements could be assigned to the categories *"functions, strengthen the user control"* (36%), *"security techniques"* (26%), and *"increased transparency for the user"* (16%).

4.3 Discussion

The purpose of our online study was to identify users' informational needs regarding privacy invading app behavior and contribute to a set of user requirements. The findings indicate that the users' perception of privacy are linked to the necessity of data requests. The survey respondents perceived using unnecessary data as more threatening towards their privacy than (partially) necessary data. In line with Lin et al. [18], these results emphasize the importance of a reasonable relation between the necessity of data usage and user's decisions on mobile apps. We conclude that transparency in terms of unnecessarily used data should be particularly emphasized by application analytic tools. For this purpose, crowd sourced perceptions or (in our case) app group specific threat perceptions across different data types could supplement automated app analyses and serve as a user based indicator of privacy risk or as a default (in line with [13]).

With regard to individual differences in the survey, we discovered only marginally significant correlations between participants' age and their perceived level of privacy threat. Furthermore, we found a significant difference, although small effect size, for unnecessary data between respondents who did and did not experience a past privacy violation. Even though these effects improve understanding of privacy behavior, they do not warrant adjusting privacy nudges and tools based on individual user characteristics in general. Therefore, we refrain from recommending customized privacy nudges according to these variables per se. An individual adjustment would require access to this personal data, which directly counteracts the privacy protection.

Respondents' qualitative statements underlined requests on *"functions, strengthen the user control"* and *"security techniques"* actively applied to protect privacy. Furthermore, they desired *"increased transparency"* on data access. Additionally, the overall perception of privacy threat caused by data access was high. This underlines the high level of concern app users in Germany generally have.

Table 1. User suggestions for improving mobile privacy protection.*

Freq.	Category	Explanation	Example statement
36%	Functions, strengthen the user control	Accessible functionalities, which allow for control of data release on a granular level such as: flexible definition of permissions, increase of permission granularity, runtime and event based permissions	*"The user should/has to have the option to determine by him/herself what data is released to whom (explicit consent; personal data belongs to the user)."*
26%	Security techniques	Possibilities to avoid the access to, or even the evolution of personal data such as: encryption of transferred data, local data processing, minimized data acquisition of apps, generation of dummy data	*"[…] to feed the app with pseudo data."*
16%	Increased transparency for the user	Comprehensible information about smartphone/app behavior with regard to data handling such as: permission alerts, knowledge transfer to the user, improvement of app store information, app comparisons	*"display comprehensible information about the data on which the app has access to […]"*
10%	Legal control and punishment	Increased enforcement of data protection laws and consequences after data misuse such as: ban of further data processing, facilitate deletion of data, reinforcement of control institutions	*"[…] to bring companies to justice if they misuse personal data, stricter laws, more inspections […]"*
6%	Social and economic change of values	Ethical change from economic use of personal data to a value of personal privacy such as: implement ethical standards into economics, financial payment for services as a standard	*"We need a change in information society. At the moment, large corporations and government institutions are in a collection fever."*
5%	Avoidance of service usage	Abandonment on the usage of services such as: avoidance of certain apps/smartphones, avoidance of data entry	*"Avoid the usage of an app."*

Concluding, these basic results confirm app users perception of incomplete and asymmetric information in Germany. To overcome incomplete and asymmetric information, transparency in app behavior is a prerequisite for privacy-related decision making [20] and privacy preserving behavior. Static and dynamic analyses for example can deliver detailed information on app information flow. The major challenge is to adjust the presentation of this information to fit user requirements. For this purpose, the laboratory study results below could provide valuable assistance.

5 Study 2 – Laboratory Study

The laboratory study's aim was to identify presentation requirements that must be addressed when developing a mobile application analytic tool. We employed the user experience (UX) concept to assess the presentation dimension as suggested by Aquisti [13]. The CUE-Model (components of UX-Model) [34] enabled a subjective evaluation of the applications and thus served as a theoretical background. In the main study, we compared the UX of three privacy apps. In preparation, we conducted a pre-study to adjust UX-facets, enabling the main evaluation of the applications and the selection of the privacy apps.

5.1 Pre-study

Materials and Method. The pre-study's first aim was to identify useful UX-facets for the assessment of privacy apps. The term *"privacy app"* will be used to describe permission apps and mobile application analytic tools. Whereas permission apps only depicted the manifest of a scanned app to provide information about these permissions, mobile application analytic tools use (e.g., static or dynamic) analyses to gain information.

Identifying useful UX-facets for privacy apps assessment was an exploratory process that also incorporated the results of the online survey. First, free available permission applications were downloaded from the Google Play Store. Second, a UX expert explored the apps to obtain a first impression of permission apps. Next, a suitable UX questionnaire (the AttrakDiff2 [11]) was selected that was adaptable for the assessment of privacy apps. Upon choosing a UX-questionnaire, the permission apps were explored again and the facets (see Table 4 in the Appendix) were adapted and extended.

The pre-study's second aim was selecting permission apps serving as comparable tools for a mobile application analytic tool. The mobile application analytic tool (Fig. 2) was used, because it was similar to the tool we wanted to develop (static and dynamic analyses included). For the selection of permissions apps, two UX experts evaluated 17 permission apps using the adjusted facets. They rated the extent to which the permission applications fulfilled the criteria for the facet definitions. Furthermore, the facets were weighted from two other UX-researchers to calculate an aggregated value. After that, two different privacy apps (less and more user-friendly) were selected.

Results. In the pre-study, nine UX-facets (see Table 4) relevant to evaluating permission apps could be identified. The two (more and less) user-friendly apps were compared to the mobile application analytic tool. Figure 2 presents sample screenshots of the three apps.

5.2 Main Study

Material and Method

Sample. Our sample consisted of $N = 31$ participants (65%) females; $M_{age} = 23$ years, $SD_{age} = 2.73$). All participants were students and received credit points for participating.

They stated using their smartphone an average of 116 min per day ($SD = 65$ min), which is representative of the German smartphone users [22]. Most often (29%) the participants indicated using from 11 to 20 apps, typically for German users [31] and the mobile operating systems used (71% Android, 26% iOS, and 3% Windows) was also comparable [2]. Most participants (77%) had never used a permission app before.

Procedure. Two Android smartphones were available to allow for parallel testing of participants. The mobile application analytic tool and the two permission apps were preinstalled. Additionally, four other apps (Skype, eBay Kleinanzeigen, wetter.com, WhatsApp) were installed to examine them via the privacy apps. Participants first received an introduction to the test's purpose and signed a consent form about the data recording. A monitor presented the three tasks (within-subjects design, randomized order) and assessed the privacy apps (closed-ended and open-ended questions). The main study concluded with questions on demographics and individual usage behavior of smartphones.

Study Design and Data Analysis. The main study's independent variable was the tested privacy app (mobile application analytic tool vs. permission app 1 vs. permission app 2; see Fig. 2).

The participants completed three questions for each privacy app: 1. *"Can the application (Skype/WhatsApp/eBay Kleinanzeigen) collect location data?"*, 3. *"Does the permission application provide any information about the risk of eBay Kleinanzeigen/Skype/WhatsApp?"*). The facets identified during the pre-study served as dependent variables to evaluate the apps. The participants indicated the extent to which the three apps fulfilled the criteria of the facets' definitions (from $-3 =$ *"not fulfilled"* to $+3 =$ *"fulfilled"*). In addition, participants assessed the importance of each UX-facet (from $1 =$ *"not at all important"* to $10 =$ *"extremely important"*). The ratings on the UX-facets including *"credibility"* and *"information about the analytic tool and provider"* were omitted because of the time-saving pre-installation of the privacy apps. In addition, the participants could have made qualitative statements on perceived problems and the amount of required support supplied by the app. After completing all tasks, participants recorded their perceived advantages *"What do you like about this permission application?"* and disadvantages *"Do you see room for improvement?"*.

We used inferential statistics to analyze the quantitative data and a deductive category assignment [35] to categorize the qualitative responses. In the subsequent sections, we first present the quantitative assessment results, followed by a summary of the open-ended question responses.

Fig. 2. Selection of privacy apps compared in the main study.

Results

UX-Facets – Assessment of the Privacy Apps. Participants indicated the extent to which the definitions of the UX-facets (Table 4) were fulfilled. Friedman's ANOVA was used to test whether privacy apps differed across facet assessment (Table 3 presents the results). Permission app 2 received the best evaluations across all UX-facets (all differences between permission app 1 and the mobile application analytic tool were significant, except the difference between permission app 2 and 1 in the "*navigation*" facet). Permission app 1 received significantly higher ratings than the mobile application analytic tool in the following UX-facets: "*overall attractiveness*", "*navigation*" and "*comprehensibility*". Neither applications differed across the following facets: "*description and valuation of permissions*", "*options for action*", "*stimulation*" and "*identity*".

UX-Facets – Level of Importance. The participants rated overall importance of the nine UX-facets. The aim of the analysis was to determine which facets were most important for assessing user experience of privacy apps. The Wilcoxon-signed-ranktest was used due to the violation of the distribution normality assumption based on the Kolmogorov-Smirnov test. We tested whether the distribution representing the single facets differed from the median (Mdn=8.00) of all facets. The results (Table 3) show that participants rated the facets "*description and valuation of permissions*", "*credibility*", "*comprehensibility*" and "*navigation*" on average as significantly more important than all facets.

Additionally Required Functions. After assessing the privacy apps, the participants could indicate whether they felt any functions were missing. The most common answers included: (de)activation of single permissions (8 participants), information on the necessity of permissions for the function of a scanned app (4), suggestions for alternative applications with less risk (4), and individualization of the risk score (2).

Frequencies of Qualitative Responses. Participants' responses to open-ended questions (problems/support demand, positive/negative aspects) yielded a total of 536 answers. Common answers (one participant same app) were included only once. The most frequent responses could be assigned to the facets "*description and valuation of permissions*" (40%), "*navigation*" (37%) and "*stimulation*" (15%). Only 6% of the replies could be allocated to the other facets (3% "*overall attractiveness*", 2% "*comprehensibility*", 1% "*options for action*"), whereas 2% could not be assigned to any facet. No answers could be attributed to the facets "*identity*", "*information about the analytic tool and the provider*" and "*credibility*" (Table 2).

Content of Qualitative Responses. Most answers could be assigned to the UX-facet "*description and valuation of permissions*". The evaluation of the mobile application analytic tool reveals that 65% of the participants criticized the English terms and that the permissions were difficult to understand (61%). Furthermore, they criticized the listing of permissions, their poor explanations, and the absence of providing possible consequences for the user's privacy. Participants (42%) were bothered by the use of technical terms and the absence of a risk score (29%). Participants mainly (81%) criticized permission app 1 because of the lack of any risk valuation of a scanned app. On the other hand, almost one third (29%) liked the categorization of single permissions into groups. The participants appreciated that permission app 2 explained all single permissions and the possible consequences/risks (45%). Also valued was an overall numerical risk score for all installed apps (39%) and for a scanned app with additional information (36%).

Table 2. Users' importance ratings of UX-facets for privacy apps.

UX-facet	Distribution of normality test[a]	Median level of facet importance	Significant derivation from overall median[b]
Overall attractiveness	$D = .197, p = .003$	8.00	$z = -0.18, p = .860$
Navigation	$D = .232, p = .000$	9.00	$z = 3.38, p = .001$
Description and valuation of permissions	$D = .254, p = .000$	9.00	$z = 3.95, p < .001$
Comprehensibility	$D = .232, p = .000$	9.00	$z = 3.56, p < .001$
Options for action	$D = .185, p = .008$	8.00	$z = 0.38, p = .707$
Stimulation	$D = .127, p = .200$	6.00	$z = -3.59, p < .001$
Identity	$D = .159, p = .045$	5.00	$z = -4.74, p < .001$
Information about the analytic tool and provider	$D = .149, p = .076$	7.00	$z = -2.52, p = .012$
Credibility	$D = .292, p = .000$	10.00	$z = 3.81, p < .001$

[a]Based on the Kolmogorov-Smirnov test for distribution normality, $\alpha = .05$.
[b]The Wilcoxon signed-rank test for one sample examined if the distributions of the single facets were significantly different from the median ($Mdn = 8.00$) of all facets.

In contrast, some participants remarked that they were not pleased with the lack of a risk valuation for each single app (19%) and the non-transparent calculation of the overall risk score (10%).

Many of the responses could be assigned to the "*navigation*" facet (37%). Most participants (71%) criticized the mobile application analytic tool because of a confusing presentation of information when scanned apps sorted permissions. In contrast, some (26%) stated that the sorting by permission groups supported navigation. Participants broadly assessed the "*navigation*" facet of permission app 1 very positively due to it being "*clear*" (68%) and that the sorting of information by scanned apps and permission group was implemented very well (55%). A few participants (16%) stated that the "*hierarchical structure of the privacy app was good*". Similarly, participants widely assessed the navigation of permission app 2 as "*clear*" (84%) and "*simple, intuitive and fast*" (74%). Here, several participants (39%) felt that the function to sort permissions by permission groups across all scanned apps was missing.

The mobile application analytic tool scored well regarding the "*stimulation*" facet. Participants appreciated the presentation of potential risk (32%), especially with the use of traffic light colors. Nearly one third (29%) criticized the design of the permission list due to the extensive use of red. More specifically, these participants felt that permission app 1 "*seemed to be incomplete and without any highlighting of the potential risk*" of a scanned app. Comparable to the previously described UX-facets, participants responded positively to the permission app 2 regarding the stimulation facet. Respondents stated that the application's design was "*attractive and clear*". They also perceived the presentation of potential risk via traffic light colors as intuitive (32%).

Table 3. Differences between the three evaluated privacy apps across all UX-facets.

UX-facet	Mean[a] (standard deviation)	Significance test Friedman's ANOVA	Post hoc test[b] Wilcoxon rank-sum test
Overall attractiveness	AT: 0.06 (1.86)	$\chi^2(2, 31) = 21.41$, $p < .001$	AT < PA1: $z = -2.45$, $p = .014$, $r = 0.44$
	PA1: 1.03 (1.54)		AT < PA2: $z = -3.98$, $p < .001$, $r = 0.71$
	PA2: 2.16 (0.86)		PA1 < PA2: $z = -3.20$, $p = .001$, $r = 0.58$
Navigation	AT: 0.61 (1.93)	$\chi^2(2, 31) = 14.37$, $p = .001$	AT < PA1: $z = -2,58$, $p = .010$, $r = 0.46$
	PA1: 1.39 (1.61)		AT < PA2: $z = -3.22$, $p = .001$, $r = 0.58$
	PA2: 1.97 (1.08)		PA1 = PA2: $z = -1.92$, $p = .055$, $r = 0.34$
Description and valuation of permissions	AT: −0.06 (1.70)	$\chi^2(2, 31) = 25.49$, $p < .001$	AT = PA1: $z = -1.58$, $p = .114$, $r = 0.28$
	PA1: 0.42 (1.61)		AT < PA2: $z = -4.29$, $p < .001$, $r = 0.77$
	PA2: 2.23 (0.76)		PA1 < PA2: $z = -3.98$, $p < .001$, $r = 0.71$
Comprehensibility	AT: 0.03 (1.84)	$\chi^2(2, 31) = 21.21$, $p < .001$	AT < PA1: $z = -2,71$, $p = .007$, $r = 0.49$
	PA1: 0.97 (1.47)		AT < PA2: $z = -4.04$, $p < .001$, $r = 0.73$
	PA2: 2.00 (0.97)		PA1 < PA2: $z = -3,39$, $p = .001$, $r = 0.61$
Options for action	AT: −0.10 (2.04)	$\chi^2(2, 31) = 15.14$, $p = .001$	AT = PA1: $z = -0.83$, $p = .409$, $r = 0.14$
	PA1: 0.13 (1.82)		AT < PA2: $z = -3.43$, $p = .001$, $r = 0.62$
	PA2: 1.26 (1.57)		PA1 < PA2: $z = -2.49$, $p = .013$, $r = 0.45$
Stimulation	AT: 0.03 (1.92)	$\chi^2(2, 31) = 15.87$, $p < .001$	AT = PA1: $z = -0.53$, $p = .593$, $r = 0.10$
	PA1: −0.26 (1.44)		AT < PA2: $z = -3.22$, $p = .001$, $r = 0.58$

(continued)

Table 3. (*continued*)

UX-facet	Mean[a] (standard deviation)	Significance test Friedman's ANOVA	Post hoc test[b] Wilcoxon rank-sum test
	PA2: 1.61 (1.28)		PA1 < PA2: $z = -3.72, p < .001, r = 0.67$
Identity	AT: −0.61 (1.82)	$\chi^2(2, 31) = 13.41, p = .001$	AT = PA1: $z = -0.72, p = .471, r = 0.13$
	PA1: −0.32 (1.60)		AT < PA2: $z = -3.50, p < .001, r = 0.63$
	PA2: 1.10 (0.98)		PA1 < PA2: $z = -3.16, p = .002, r = 0.57$

[a]T = mobile application analytic tool, PA1 = permission application 1, PA2 = permission application 2.

[b]All comparisons were made using a Bonferroni correction. Therefore, all effects are reported at $\alpha = .0167$ level of significance.

Only a few answers could be assigned to the "*overall attractiveness*" UX-facet. For instance, one participant stated that permission app 1 entailed the essential function and 13% of the participants evaluated permission app 2 as useful. Some statements could be considered as part of the "*comprehensibility*" facet. For example, one participant acknowledged the simple language of permission app 1. Only a few comments about the "*options for actions*" facet existed. Two participants (7%) liked the option to delete scanned apps, whereas another wanted a function that provides suggestions for alternative applications.

Discussion

User Experience Facets

Overall Attractiveness. Participants rated the *overall attractiveness* as fairly important. Qualitative responses could be rarely assigned to this facet. This could possibly be explained by the facet's global nature. Participants were asked if they needed support or if they encountered problems while using the privacy apps. Answers to these questions were mainly specific and could therefore be assigned to other facets.

All three apps tested differed in their attractiveness. Permission app 2 was considered more attractive than permission app 1. However, both were rated more attractive than the analytic tool. This is reflected in the assessment of the other UX-facets. Therefore, we hypothesize that the "*overall attractiveness*" could serve as a global measurement for the overall UX-evaluation of a mobile application analytic tool.

Navigation. The importance level of the navigation facet and the number of assigned qualitative responses were rather high. The participants appreciated a simple, fast, hierarchical and intuitive navigation. In addition, participants acknowledged the opportunity to switch between the sorting of information by a scanned app and by permission groups.

The quantitative assessment partly revealed these navigation aspects. The mobile application analytic tool, lacking a hierarchical navigation structure, received the lowest score. The permission apps did not differ, although permission app 2 provides no information sorting by permission groups. A possible explanation of this balanced assessment of the permission apps is that participants perceived the navigation of permission app 2 as more clear and simple compared to permission app 1. Therefore, the sorting by permission groups seems to be not crucial.

Description and Valuation of Permissions. Participants rated this facet as the most important and provoked the most commentaries. To comprehend the permissions, it was essential that single permissions were explained. Grouping permissions enhanced understanding. In contrast, using another language or technical terms diminished comprehension. In addition to the explanation of permissions, participants felt that a valuation of the arising risks was important. They questioned whether there was a compelling necessity for using certain permissions and what possible consequences could arise. Although participants appreciated an overall risk score, some wanted a numerical score for each scanned app. Based on the open-ended answers regarding additional functions, it appears that individualizing such a risk score would also be useful. Overall, the results indicate that the contents assigned to this facet are the most important for developing a mobile application analytic tool.

Comprehensibility. Participants rated the *"comprehensibility"* facet as important, however the number of qualitative responses was rather small. A small number of responses possibly existed because the tested privacy apps were easy to understand. Another possible explanation is that the privacy apps with their specific functions only had limited components. Thus, there was little potential for it to be considered not comprehensible, which could be assigned to the *"comprehensibility"* facet rather than the *"description and valuation of permissions"* facet.

Options for Action. Participants rated the *"options for action"* as moderately important. There were only a few qualitative responses. Some participants wanted a function to (de)activate single permissions and suggestions for alternative apps. The few qualitative responses received was unsurprising since the tested apps did not differ in their options. Therefore, it was remarkable to find significant differences between the three systems (permission app 2 being rated higher). This result could probably be explained by the halo-effect (permission app 2 received the most positive evaluations). However, because of the main study's procedure, its importance was probably underestimated. Further research should examine the *"options for action"* in greater detail.

Stimulation. This facet received the third most open-ended responses. Participants perceived a simple design and the presentation of the privacy risk of a scanned application through traffic light colors as intuitive. However, they rated importance of the facet rather low, which seems to contradict the number of qualitative responses. However, upon closer inspection, most responses referred to the design of core functions of the apps. In conclusion, the general findings assigned to the *"stimulation"* facet were crucial to support essential contents and functions of a mobile application analytic tool despite the overall rated level of importance.

Identity. Assigned contents of the *"identity"* facet of the mobile application analytic tool did not appear that important given the user rating of its importance and the few qualitative responses. As with other UX-facets, permission app 2 differed significantly from permission app 1 as well as the mobile application analytic tool. A possible explanation could be the high correlation ($r = .55$) between the *"identity"* and *"stimulation"* facets previously reported in the original AttrakDiff 2 literature [11].

Information About the Analytic Tool and the Provider. Based on the rated importance level and the few qualitative responses, this facet does not seem paramount for developing mobile application analytic tools. This result is likely because our participants did not download the privacy apps and therefore were limited in the available information during the study. For this reason, the *"information about the analytic tool and the provider"* facet requires further investigation.

Credibility. A permission app is credible if it refrains from requesting permissions for its own purposes. The participants could not assess whether this facet was fulfilled because the applications were preinstalled. Participants rated importance level for the *"credibility"* facet as very high, receiving the highest median among all evaluated UX-facets. Therefore, *"credibility"* should be further investigated by including the tested tool's download procedure.

Future Work and Limitations
During the assessment, we focused on the usage of mobile application analytic tools. Therefore, investigation of the *"information about the analytic tool and the provider"* and *"credibility"* UX-facets was limited due to the exclusion of the app download process. Thus, future studies should assess these facets via a holistic interaction process including download, scanning, and usage of mobile application analytic tools.

Our test setup most likely influenced the quantitative and qualitative UX-facet results. Basing user evaluations on performing three selected tasks may have led to overestimating the importance of task-related UX-facets and provoking a higher amount of qualitative responses to these facets (e.g., *"description and valuation of permissions"* or *"options for action"*).

Another limitation is that the UX-facets cannot be considered perfectly distinct from each other. However, the general findings (regardless of their facet assignment) were used to derive requirements and guidelines for designing mobile application analytic tools (see Sect. 6. Overall Conclusion).

6   Overall Conclusion

Both studies lead to a collection of user requirements, thus answering the first research question. In this section, these user requirements are used to derive guidelines for developing a mobile application analytic tool (research question 2). In summary, increased transparency is the central purpose. Moreover, a credible tool should explain and valuate information flows of mobile apps. Furthermore, it should provide options to act in a privacy protective way. Figure 3 presents the guidelines and accompanying sub-guidelines, which are not mutually exclusive and thus considered as a framework.

I TRANSPARENCY	II EXPLANATION	III VALUATION	IV ACTION	V CREDIBILITY
Increase transparency of mobile application information flows to overcome incomplete and asymmetric information access.	Explain permissions as simply as possible.	Evaluate and show the mobile application's potential risk.	Provide comprehensive options for action to enable privacy preserving behavior.	Provide a transparent tool to meet moral requirements regarding privacy protection.
		SUB-GUIDELINES		
Combine different analytic approaches to capture the most information possible for the user.	Employ the user's language and avoid acronyms, technical terms or terms in other languages.	Show users possible consequences that could arise from used permissions.	Provide and highlight the option to delete single permissions or the scanned application within the permission application.	Develop an analytic tool that works without requesting permissions for its own purposes.
	Use hierarchical navigation structure to guide users from permission groups to assigned single permissions and explanations.	Provide information about the necessity of data requests to support valuation of permissions.	Show alternatives to a scanned application rated as less risky.	Develop a tool that does not capture user's personal data.
		Use traffic light colors to show and highlight the potential risk of a scanned application.		
		Use a numerical risk score, explain the composition and enable individualization.		

Fig. 3. Guidelines for mobile application analytic tools.

Increase Transparency to Overcome Information Asymmetries. In accordance with previous research [13], our results underline the demand for *increased transparency* about app behavior. Hence, our first guideline is: *"Increase transparency of mobile application information flows to overcome incomplete and asymmetric information access."*. Through a combination of different (static and dynamic) analytic approaches it is possible to gain maximum informational benefit for the user [16]. This guideline clearly refers to the *information* dimension, as the hurdles are asymmetric and incomplete information, availability, and overconfidence biases [13] in human decision making. Furthermore, we - as other authors [20] - concluded that transparency serves as an prerequisite. In other terms, the absence of transparency is the first hurdle to clear for making informed privacy decisions within the mobile app context.

Explain and Valuate Mobile Application Behavior. Previous research has indicated that most app users did not comprehend permissions [6, 7]. This corroborates our lab study findings given the central importance of the *"explanation and valuation of permissions"* UX-facet. The results showed that a mobile application analytic tool should aid comprehension on two different levels: 1). Technical terms, acronyms, or foreign languages should be avoided, since these confused participants in our main study and finally led to the *"Explain permissions as simply as possible."* guideline, assigned to the information dimension [13]. Based on the lab study results, a usable and hierarchical navigation could serve as a support. We attribute his sub-guideline to the presentation dimension [13]. 2). Lab study participants mentioned difficulties understanding potential personal risks. Therefore, we formulated the information guideline: *"Evaluate the potential risk of a mobile application and show possible consequences to the user."* This is closely related to our survey result underlining the high importance for users to understand the data request necessity. This guideline could also be assigned to the default dimension in a broader sense, as crowd sourced privacy risks evaluations [18] can serve as defaults in a tool. In addition, some lab study participants also asked for information on the necessity of data requests. Therefore, we recommend that a tool should provide information about this necessity. The usage of traffic light colors seems to be appropriate to highlight potential risk. Furthermore, a comprehensible numerical score can aid the user's risk assessment.

Provide Options for Action to Enable Privacy Preserving Behavior. To nudge privacy preserving behavior, it is necessary to go beyond show, explain and evaluate. The online survey's results showed a demand for functions that strengthen user control. This corresponds to the lab study participants' statements desiring more options for action. According to these results, mobile application analytic tools should *"Provide comprehensive options for action to enable privacy preserving behavior."*. This could show users possible options for action, for instance altering existing privacy (pre-)settings or switching to another more privacy preserving app. Therefore, we assigned this guideline to the *information* and *reversibility* dimensions [13].

Ensure Credibility of the Mobile Application Analytic Tool. As described above, transparency serves as a prerequisite for other guidelines. Therefore, a mobile application analytic tool itself should be transparent regarding privacy protection. The median rating for the importance of the *"credibility"* facet in the lab study received the maximum possible rating. This suggests that a tool must avoid using permissions for its own purposes. Moreover, the survey revealed an absence of significant correlations between privacy threat evaluations and demographic data. Thus, we conclude that a mobile application analytic tool should refrain from accessing personal demographic data. Therefore, the fifth guideline is to *"Provide a transparent tool to meet moral requirements regarding privacy protection."*. It is associated with the *information* dimension [13] as it reduces incomplete and asymmetric information access or eliminates this hurdle with respect to the mobile application analytic tool itself.

7 Future Work

Our study results led to a user-driven framework of guidelines. They refer to designing privacy nudges and addressing hurdles of informed decision making when using mobile apps. It is conceivable that this framework can guide the design of privacy nudges and respective tools addressing present information asymmetries in another context. Therefore, future work could investigate the transferability of our results (e.g., to intelligent transportation systems or vehicles).

Our guidelines do not address the *timing* and *incentive* dimensions due to the methodology we chose. Enhancing motivation and temporal effects of mobile application analytic tools should be investigated in settings that are more naturalistic and in the long-term. Our future research will address this limitation and we will test our tool during a field trial. If user's privacy preservation decisions are encouraged, this will probably entail changes in app implementation from the provider side.

Acknowledgments. The studies are part of the research project *"AndProtect: Personal data privacy by means of static and dynamic analysis for Android app validation"*, funded by the German Federal Ministry of Education and Research. Furthermore, we want to thank Franziska Hartwich and Christiane Attig for their valuable comments on the first draft of the paper.

Appendix A.1

I feel my privacy threatened if my [map/navigation app, messenger app, weather app, or shopping app] uses…		Strongly disagree	Largely disagree	Somewhat disagree	Somewhat agree	Largely agree	Strongly agree
		1	2	3	4	5	6
…location data	Information about where I am						

(continued)

(*continued*)

I feel my privacy threatened if my [map/navigation app, messenger app, weather app, or shopping app] uses...		Strongly disagree	Largely disagree	Somewhat disagree	Somewhat agree	Largely agree	Strongly agree
...communication data	Dialogues with other persons in terms of text, picture, video and audio messages						
...contacts data	The stored contact information in my contact list (e.g., first name, last name, telephone number, and e-mail address of the contact)						
...motion sensor data	What kind of movements I execute (e.g., climbing stairs, running, walking)						
...app usage data	When and how often I use my [app-group] app						
...data about usage of other apps	What other apps I have installed						
...calendar data	Which appointments (content and timing) I have entered						
...call history data	With whom and when I had a call						

(*continued*)

(*continued*)

I feel my privacy threatened if my [map/navigation app, messenger app, weather app, or shopping app] uses…		Strongly disagree	Largely disagree	Somewhat disagree	Somewhat agree	Largely agree	Strongly agree
…local files	Files which I have stored on my smartphone (e.g., pictures, audio records, download files)						
…camera data	Pictures which are in the focus of my camera						
…WiFi state data	Information with which WiFi I' m connected to, if I used this WiFi before, which wireless networks I have registered on my device and/or which WiFi my device is searching for						
…fitness data	Information about my physical activity (e.g., pedometer, heart rate, sleeping phase)						

(*continued*)

(continued)

I feel my privacy threatened if my [map/navigation app, messenger app, weather app, or shopping app] uses…		Strongly disagree	Largely disagree	Somewhat disagree	Somewhat agree	Largely agree	Strongly agree
…data about social network	Information on who I know, e.g. the names of my contacts, access of my contacts on personal data (pin board, pictures, status of persons), and unrestricted access to my data in a social network						
…shopping data	Information on which products I monitor, which products I bought and which means of payments and shipping address I used						
…audio data	Audio information which my smartphone microphone records						

Appendix A.2

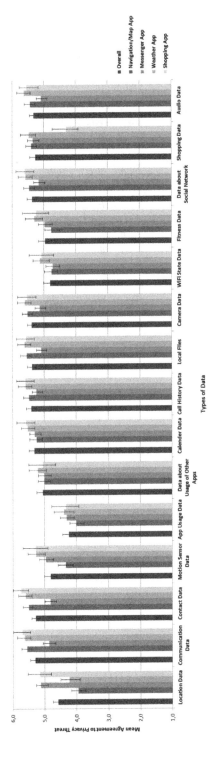

Fig. 4. A.2. Mean privacy threat for different types of data and app-groups evaluated by online survey respondents.

Appendix A.3

Table 4. Overview of adjusted UX-facets.

UX-facet[a]	Definition
Overall attractiveness	"...fulfilled if the application is generally considered humane, simple, practical, direct, predictable, clear, and manageable."
Navigation[b]	"...fulfilled if a permission application is simple, direct, intuitive to use, and if the user can receive help during the navigation."
Description and valuation of permissions[b]	"...fulfilled if the permission application could describe and explain permissions, if it presents a valuation of permissions and if this valuation is customizable."
Comprehensibility[b]	"...fulfilled if the user could comprehend the presented information and if the user can receive support to aid comprehension. The facet does not measure the comprehension of permissions."
Options for action[b]	"...is fulfilled if the user can function within the permission app in a way they consider necessary based on presented information about the permissions and the resulting privacy risk."
Stimulation[c]	"...fulfilled if the application supports the user in his or her personal development. This can be achieved via introducing interesting and stimulating functions, contents, presentation and interaction styles as well as an appealing graphical design."
Identity[c]	"...fulfilled if the user can identify himself with the application. A high level of identification is achieved if the application is describable as professional, stylish, valuable, inclusive, presentable, and brings them closer to people."
Information about the analysis tool and the provider[c]	"...fulfilled if the user receives comprehensive information about the analytic tool and the tool's provider while downloading and using the tool."
Credibility [c]	"...fulfilled if a permission application avoids the use of permissions for its own function."

[a]UX-facets are based the AttrakDiff2 questionnaire [11].
[b]UX-facets that were assigned to instrumental qualities in the UX-concept.
[c]UX-facets that were assigned to non-instrumental qualities in the UX-concept.

References

1. AppBrain: Number of Android applications (2017). https://www.appbrain.com/stats/number-of-android-apps
2. Kantar: Marktanteile der mobilen Betriebssysteme am Absatz von Smartphones in Deutschland von Januar 2012 bis Oktober 2016 [Market shares of mobile operating systems in sales of smartphones in Germany from January 2012 to October 2016] (n.d.). https://de.statista.com/statistik/daten/studie/225381/umfrage/marktanteile-der-betriebssysteme-am-smartphone-absatz-in-deutschland-zeitreihe/
3. Caufield, K.P., Byers: Durchschnittliche Anzahl der installierten und täglich genutzten Apps pro Endgerät in den USA und weltweit im Mai 2016 [Average number of installed and daily used apps per device in the US and worldwide in May 2016] (n.d.). https://de.statista.com/statistik/daten/studie/555513/umfrage/anzahl-der-installierten-und-genutzten-apps-in-den-usa-und-weltweit/
4. Fraunhofer AISEC: 10.000 Apps und eine Menge Sorgen [10,000 apps and a lot of worries] (2014). http://www.aisec.fraunhofer.de/de/presse-und-veranstaltungen/presse/pressemitteilungen/2014/20140403_10000_apps.html
5. Geneiatakis, D., Fovino, I.N., Kounelis, I., Stirparo, P.: A Permission verification approach for android mobile applications. Comput. Secur. **49**, 192–205 (2015). https://doi.org/10.1016/j.cose.2014.10.005
6. Kelley, P.G., Consolvo, S., Cranor, L.F., Jung, J., Sadeh, N., Wetherall, D.: A conundrum of permissions: installing applications on an android smartphone. In: Blyth, J., Dietrich, S., Camp, L.Jean (eds.) FC 2012. LNCS, vol. 7398, pp. 68–79. Springer, Heidelberg (2012). https://doi.org/10.1007/978-3-642-34638-5_6
7. Felt, A.P., Ha, E., Egelman, S., Haney, A., Chin, E., Wagner, D.: Android permissions: user attention, comprehension, and behavior. In: Cranor, L.F. (ed.) Proceedings of the Eighth Symposium on Usable Privacy and Security, p. 3 (2012). http://dx.doi.org/10.1145/2335356.2335360
8. Balebako, R., et al.: Nudging users towards privacy on mobile devices. In: Proceedings of the CHI 2011 Workshop on Persuasion, Nudge, Influence and Coercion (2011)
9. DIN EN ISO 9241-210: Prozess zur Gestaltung gebrauchstauglicher interaktiver Systeme [Process for the design of usable interactive systems]. Beuth, Berlin (2011)
10. Statistisches Bundesamt Deutschland: Statistisches Jahrbuch Deutschland und Internationales [Statistical Yearbook Germany and International]. Statistisches Bundesamt, Wiesbaden (2015)
11. Hassenzahl, M., Burmester, M., Koller, F.: AttrakDiff: Ein Fragebogen zur Messung wahrgenommener hedonischer und pragmatischer Qualität [A questionnaire to measure perceived hedonic and pragmatic quality]. In: Ziegler, J., Szwillus, G. (eds.) Mensch & Computer 2003: Interaktion in Bewegung, pp. 187–196. B.G. Teubner, Stuttgart, Leipzig (2003). http://dx.doi.org/10.1007/978-3-322-80058-9_19
12. Thaler, R.H., Sunstein, C.R.: Nudge: improving decisions about health, wealth, and happiness. Const. Polit. Econ. **19**(4), 356–360 (2008)
13. Acquisti, A., et al.: Nudges for Privacy and Security: Understanding and Assisting Users' Choices (2016) SSRN https://ssrn.com/abstract = 2859227
14. Kelley, P.G., Cranor, L.F., Sadeh, N.: Privacy as part of the app decision-making process. In: Proceedings of the SIGCHI Conference on Human Factors in Computing Systems, pp. 3393–3402. ACM (2013). http://dx.doi.org/10.1145/2470654.2466466
15. King, J.: How Come I'm Allowing Strangers to Go Through My Phone? Smartphones and Privacy Expectations (2012). http://dx.doi.org/10.2139/ssrn.2493412

16. Tan, J., et al.: The effect of developer-specified explanations for permission requests on smartphone user behavior. In: Proceedings of the SIGCHI Conference on Human Factors in Computing Systems, pp. 91–100. ACM (2014). http://dx.doi.org/10.1145/2556288.2557400

17. Enck, W., et al.: TaintDroid: an information-flow tracking system for realtime privacy monitoring on smartphones. ACM Trans. Comput. Syst. (TOCS), **32**(2) (2014), http://dx.doi.org/10.1145/2619091

18. Lin, J., Amini, S., Hong, J.I., Sadeh, N., Lindqvist, J., Zhang, J.: Expectation and purpose: understanding users' mental models of mobile app privacy through crowdsourcing. In: Proceedings of the 2012 ACM Conference on Ubiquitous Computing, pp. 501–510. ACM (2012) http://dx.doi.org/10.1145/2370216.2370290

19. Gerber, P., Volkamer, M., Renaud, K.: The simpler, the better? Presenting the COPING Android permission-granting interface for better privacy-related decisions. J. Inf. Secur. Appl. (2016). http://dx.doi.org/10.1016/j.jisa.2016.10.003

20. Hartwig, M., Reinhold, O., Alt, R.: Privacy awareness in mobile business: how mobile os and apps support transparency in the use of personal data. In: BLED 2016 Proceedings, vol. 46 (2016)

21. Bitkom: Anteil der Smartphone-Nutzer in Deutschland nach Altersgruppe im Jahr 2016 [Share of smartphone users in Germany by age group in 2016]. In Statista - Das Statistik-Portal (n.d.). https://de.statista.com/statistik/daten/studie/459963/umfrage/anteil-der-smartphone-nutzer-in-deutschland-nach-altersgruppe/

22. MyMarktforschung.de: Studie: Smartphones liebster Zeitvertreib der Deutschen [Study: Smartphones favorite pastime of the Germans] (2015). https://www.mymarktforschung.de/de/ueber-uns/pressemitteilungen/item/studie-der-alltag-der-deutschen.html

23. comScore: Geschlechterverteilung der Smartphone-Nutzer in Deutschland in den Jahren 2012 und 2016 [Gender distribution of smartphone users in Germany in 2012 and 2016] (n.d.). https://de.statista.com/statistik/daten/studie/255609/umfrage/geschlechterverteilung-der-smartphone-nutzer-in-deutschland/

24. Dogruel, L., Jöckel, S., Vitak, J.: The valuation of privacy premium features for smartphone apps: the influence of defaults and expert recommendations. Comput. Hum. Behav. **77**, 230–239 (2017)

25. Bal, G., Rannenberg, K., Hong, J.: Styx: design and evaluation of a new privacy risk communication method for smartphones. In: Cuppens-Boulahia, N., Cuppens, F., Jajodia, S., Abou El Kalam, A., Sans, T. (eds.) SEC 2014. IAICT, vol. 428, pp. 113–126. Springer, Heidelberg (2014). https://doi.org/10.1007/978-3-642-55415 5_10

26. Almuhimedi, H., et al.: Your location has been shared 5,398 times!: a field study on mobile app privacy nudging. In: Proceedings of the 33rd Annual ACM Conference on Human Factors in Computing Systems, pp. 787–796. ACM, New York (2015). http://dx.doi.org/10.1145/2702123.2702210

27. Zhauniarovich, Y., Gadyatskaya, O.: Small changes, big changes: an updated view on the android permission system. In: Monrose, F., Dacier, M., Blanc, G., Garcia-Alfaro, J. (eds.) RAID 2016. LNCS, vol. 9854, pp. 346–367. Springer, Cham (2016). https://doi.org/10.1007/978-3-319-45719-2_16

28. Gerber, P., Volkamer, M.: Usability und Privacy im Android Ökosystem [Usability and privacy within the Android ecosystem]. Datenschutz und Datensicherheit **39**(2), 108–113 (2015). https://doi.org/10.1007/s11623-015-0375-y

29. PocketGamer.biz: Ranking der Top-20-Kategorien im App Store im Januar 2017 [Ranking of the top 20 app store categories in January 2017] (n.d.). https://de.statista.com/statistik/daten/studie/166976/umfrage/beliebteste-kategorien-im-app-store/

30. Distimo: Anteil der im Google Play Store weltweit am häufigsten heruntergeladenen Apps nach Kategorien im Februar 2014 [Share of the most downloaded apps in the Google Play Store worldwide by category in February 2014]. In Statista - Das Statistik-Portal (n.d.). https://de.statista.com/statistik/daten/studie/321703/umfrage/beliebteste-app-kategorien-im-google-play-store-weltweit/
31. ForwardAdGroup: Wie viele Apps haben Sie auf Ihrem Smartphone installiert? [How many apps have you installed on your smartphone?] (n.d.). https://de.statista.com/statistik/daten/studie/162374/umfrage/durchschnittliche-anzahl-von-apps-auf-dem-handy-in-deutschland/
32. Website (internetdo.com): Prognose zum Anteil der Smartphone-Nutzer an den Mobiltelefonnutzern weltweit von 2014 bis 2020 [Forecast for the share of smartphone users in mobile phone users worldwide from 2014 to 2020]. In Statista - Das Statistik-Portal (n.d.). https://de.statista.com/statistik/daten/studie/556616/umfrage/prognose-zum-ant eil-der-smartphone-nutzer-an-den-mobiltelefonnutzern-weltweit/
33. Cohen, J.: Statistical Power Analysis for the Behavioral Sciences, pp. 20–26. Lawrence Earlbaum Associates., Hillsdale (1988)
34. Mahlke, S., Thüring, M.: Studing antecendents of emotional experiences in interactive contexts. In: CHI 2007 Proceedings of the SIGCHI Conference on Human Factors in Computing Systems, pp. 915–918. ACM, New York (2007). http://dx.doi.org/10.1145/1240624.1240762
35. Mayring, P.: Qualitative Content Analysis: Theoretical Foundation, Basic Procedures and Software Solution (2014). http://nbn-resolving.de/urn:nbn:de:0168-ssoar-395173
36. Hansen, M., Berlich, P., Camenisch, J., Clauß, S., Pfitzmann, A., Waidner, M.: Privacy-enhancing identity management. Inf. Secur. Tech. Rep. **9**, 35–44 (2004). https://doi.org/10.1016/S1363-4127(04)00014-7
37. Fleiss, J.L., Levin, B., Paik, M.C.: Statistical Methods for Rates and Proportions. Wiley, New York (2013)

Modelling and Presentation of Privacy-Relevant Information for Internet Users

Denis Feth[(✉)]

Fraunhofer IESE, Fraunhofer-Platz 1, 67663 Kaiserslautern, Germany
denis.feth@iese.fraunhofer.de
http://www.iese.fraunhofer.de

Abstract. Privacy policies are the state of the practice technique for data transparency. Oftentimes, however, they are presented in a non-prominent way, are lengthy, and are not written in the users' language. As a result, their acceptance is rather low, even though users are generally interested in privacy. Thus, we need enhanced transparency approaches. In this paper, we present a taxonomy and models that allow to describe privacy-relevant information. These models are based on practical privacy policies and legal regulations, and enable automated processing of privacy-relevant information. Automated processing based on well-defined semantics is the baseline for new ways to represent privacy-relevant information, for example by filtering, step-wise refinement or contextualization.

Keywords: Privacy policies · Taxonomy · Usable security · Transparency

1 Introduction

1.1 Motivation

Modern IT systems and services are getting more and more customized and aligned to the user. This comes along with massive collection, processing, and sharing of personal-related data. Because of that, many users have privacy concerns when using online services [8] and intent to inform themselves about data usage [13]. In addition to the users' demand for privacy, data protection laws (e.g., EU GDPR) are getting stricter. However, most privacy measures can only be effective, if users are able to understand how their data is processed and how their privacy is protected. For example, if users want to meaningfully use their right for objection, they must know and understand their rights, be able to map the abstract right to the current situation or service, know how to use their right, and understand the consequences. In other words: For informed and sound self-determination, data processing and data protection must be transparent for the user.

In the Internet, privacy policies are the standard measure to achieve transparency. Providers textually describe the way they gather, use, manage or disclose user data. However, current privacy policies are neither designed in a way so that they are suited for users to achieve transparency nor do they meet transparency requirements demanded by

© Springer Nature Switzerland AG 2020
A. Moallem (Ed.): HCII 2020, LNCS 12210, pp. 354–366, 2020.
https://doi.org/10.1007/978-3-030-50309-3_23

legal regulations (such as the EU GDPR). In a survey by Obar and Oeldorf-Hirsch [11], it is stated that 74% of users skipped the privacy policy completely. For the remaining 26%, the average reading time was only 73 s—even though the average length of a privacy policy is about 2,700 words [16]. Besides other reasons (e.g., privacy paradox), this lack of acceptance is caused by a number of inherent shortcomings of their presentation. In particular, their length, a complicated language, a high abstraction level and a rather hidden positioning lead to low acceptance [5]. Additionally, privacy policies are not verifiable by users. Thus, we need to find new approaches for modelling and presenting privacy-relevant information to the users.

1.2 Ideas and Contributions

To improve the presentation of today's privacy policies and eventually transparency, we target two main goals: First, privacy policies need to be better navigable and searchable (e.g., based on filtering or improved structure or presentation). Second, privacy-relevant information needs to be better aligned to the current context of use (i.e., users should only be required to read information that is relevant for them now). For this, automatic processing and tailoring of privacy relevant information based on standardized models and well-defined semantics is needed to master the complexity of managing privacy information. Both goals cannot be achieved using plain text policies.

In the paper, we present the results of a privacy policy analysis we executed and show the taxonomy we created based on our findings. This taxonomy consists of various models, which are related to each other. Furthermore, we discuss options regarding how users can access privacy-relevant information in an easy and understandable form based on our concepts. To that respect, we distinguish two major cases: In the first case, users want to know how their data is processed and protected during a concrete task they currently executes (e.g. payment). This can be referred to as "Contextual Privacy Policies" [5] and answers concrete privacy questions that come up during usage of the website or web service. In the second case, users want to learn about their data is being processed and protected by the service in general. Both use cases have their right to exist and can (perhaps even should) be provided in parallel.

2 Approach

In order to build our models and taxonomy, we analyzed the content of existing online privacy policies. We picked two representatives from each of the top 25 websites for Germany from each of the 17 Alexa.com (a web traffic analysis service) categories. We decided to split the category "Society" into "Adult" and "Society (without adult content)", because 24 out of 25 Society pages contained adult content, and we felt that there might be relevant differences in terms of transparency and privacy demands. We also excluded websites that were not in German or English from our analysis. This was due to the simple fact that we do not adequately understand other languages and we did not want to use automated translation tools in order not to falsify the results. Thus, we ended up with 18 categories and analyzed the following 36 privacy policies (as of February 2018), like shown in Table 1.

Table 1. Analyzed privacy policies

Arts & Entertainment	Business & Industry	Computers & Technology	Education	Finance & Economics
netflix.com ubi.com	immoscout24.de dhl.de	whatsapp.com videolan.com	wikimedia.org tu-kl.de	bitpay.com commerzbank.de

Government	Health	Home	Internet	News & Media
europa.eu bremen.de	Weightwatchers.com Baua.de	chefkoch.de cookitsimply.com	pinterest.com twitter.com	spotify.com spiegel.de

Recreation	Reference	Science	Shopping	Society (without Adult)
bet365.com koa.com	gutefrage.net britishmuseum.org	mathoverflow.net zeiss.com	check24.de amazon.de	creativecommons.org vice.com

Society (only Adult)	Sports	Travel & Transport
pornhub.com xtube.com	fifa.com fcbarcelona.com	booking.com volvocars.de

From each of the privacy policies, we extracted the following information that are related to how a provider processes personal-related data:

- Which **entities** are involved in the processing of person-related data?
- How is data **processed**?
- Which **data** is processed?
- Which **users** are affected?
- Which **use cases** require the processing of data?
- For which **purpose** is data processed?
- Which **technologies** are used?
- Under which **conditions** is data processed?

We harmonized and clustered all information. We removed duplicates, merged similar elements (e.g., caused by different language or different terms for same concepts), built clusters and related the remaining elements.

3 Modelling of Privacy-Relevant Information

Eventually, we came up with one model for each of the upper-mentioned topics. Those topics and models relate to each other as shown in Fig. 1. Their relationship can be summarized in the following sentence structure:

```
In <Service>, <Entity> [does|must|can|should|might] (not)
perform <Processing> with <Data> about <Person> during <Use-
Case> for <Purpose> using <Technology> if <Condition>.
```

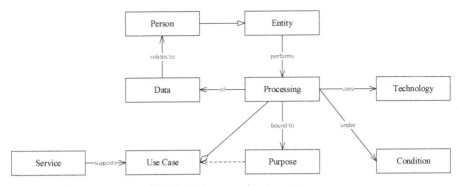

Fig. 1. Data processing taxonomy

For example, an instantiation of the model/sentence structure could be: "In example.com, Example.inc does perform analytics with usage data about registered users during the ordering process for the purpose of personalized marketing with Google AdSense if the user consented".

In our idea, such statements can be used to describe how a service processes personal-related data—a major requirement for data transparency. Also, the structure and the models behind the individual *elements* are the key for an automatic processing of privacy-relevant information: They allow privacy policies to be easily filtered, searched, aligned to the context. Example queries could be: "To whom is my order data transferred?", "Which data is collected when consuming video content?", or "For which use cases and which purposes does the service need my geo location?"

In the following, we describe each model in an own section. The sum of all models builds a taxonomy for privacy relevant information.

3.1 Entities

We start with entities that process personal-related data (cf. Fig. 2). In our analysis, we found three main *entity* groups: The *user* himself, *service providers*, and *external entities*. External entities, or third parties, include *other users* of the service, *subcontractors* of the *providers*, and processors. For the latter, we mainly found examples for *payment*, *logistics* and *advertisement*.

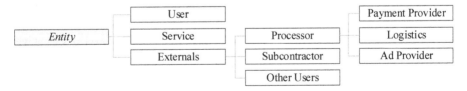

Fig. 2. Entity model

3.2 Data Processing

Next, we took a look at how data is processed. In the analyzed privacy policies, we found seven types of processing (see Fig. 3, left), namely *collect, analyze, store, transfer, share, delete*, and the *generic* description *process*. Those seven types are also described in Art. 4 lit. 2 GDPR. In addition, GDPR describes nine other types of processing which, however, were not explicitly mentioned in the privacy policies we analyzed (see Fig. 3, right). Those are: record, organize, structure, adapt or alternate, retrieve, consult, align or combine, restrict, and destruct.

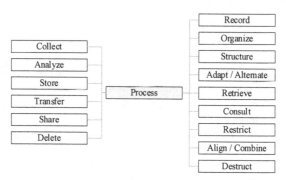

Fig. 3. Data processing model

3.3 Data

The kind of data that is processed, differs depending on the kind of service. Thus, we built quite generic categories of data. In general, only person-related data is relevant from a privacy perspective. Note that the presented categories are not disjunct, and the categories do not make a statement about the sensitivity of the data. For example, the "special categories of personal data" stated in Art. 9 GDPR can be contained in each of our categories.

Master Data is all data about the data subject (e.g., user profile). *Usage Data* is data that describes how a certain user is using the service. *Location Data* relates to data that can be used to identify the position of a certain user (GPS, IP address). *Public Data* is data that is openly available (e.g., via the Internet). Many services offer physical or digital goods that can be purchased. In this case *Order Data* is produced. Also, many services offer the possibility to *communicate* via the service—either between users, or between the user and the service provider. Finally, the content of the service is what we describe as *Application Data* (cf. Fig. 4).

Fig. 4. Data model

3.4 Person

As already stated, we only focus on person-related data. Thus, we analyzed which persons data relates to, according to the privacy policies (cf. Fig. 5). In general, there are four large groups of persons. *Visitors* use the service for free and do not have an account. *Registered Users* are visitors that do have an account at the service. *Customers* pay for the service or goods the service offers. Customers do not necessarily have to be registered users. The last person group is somewhat different. While Visitors, Registered Users and Customers can be considered as direct users of the service, there is data processed about *Uninvolved Persons,* i.e., persons that are not using the service at all. Prominent examples are social plugins that track you, even if you are not using this social network. Also, on social media platforms, users can give access to their address book to the platform. However, these address books typically also contain data about persons that are not on this platform.

Fig. 5. Person model

3.5 Use Cases

Depending on the type of service, there are a lot of different use cases where person-related data is processed. We clustered them in eight categories (cf. Fig. 6).

Oftentimes, services require users to *create an account* for using the full service. Therefore, users need to register, typically with their email address. Besides this classical approach, more and more services allow users to *connect their accounts,* respectively authenticate with a different authentication provider (e.g., login with Google). The actual *service usage* can happen via a *web page,* or an *API.* As many of the services are financed via ads, *ad usage* is also part of our model. Service usage may include the *provision and consumption of content* (e.g., multimedia, posts). Also, it can include the *purchase* of physical or digital goods, in particular *ordering* and *payment. Communication* is another important use case. We differentiate the *correspondence* of a user with *the service provider* (e.g., support, newsletter) and with one or more *other users* of the service. Finally, there are some more special use cases, that also appeared several times, namely the participation in beta tests, surveys and lotteries.

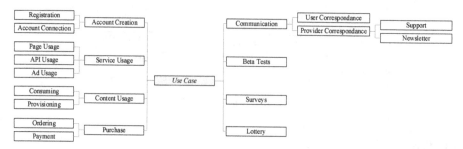

Fig. 6. Use case model

3.6 Purposes

According to regulations like GDPR, the processing of person-related data must always be bound to specified, explicit and legit purposes. So, we categorized the purposes mentioned in the privacy policies (cf. Fig. 7).

In most cases, the purpose is simply the execution of primary business processes as part of the provisioning of the service. Besides that, data is processed for a number of secondary purposes, namely:

- *communication* between the service provider and the user,
- *customizing* the service to the user,
- *financing* the service, either via ads or direct payment,
- *improving* the service,
- *enforcing the security* of the service, and
- *enforcing the terms and conditions* of the service.

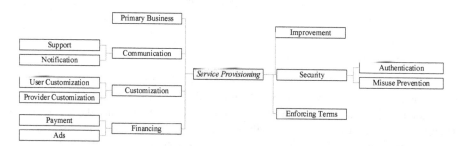

Fig. 7. Purpose model

3.7 Technologies

Regarding the technologies used, four major categories were mentioned in the privacy policies (cf. Fig. 8): the usage of *cookies*, of *social plugins*, *trackers* and *captchas*. The use of cookies in particular was dealt with in great detail. Several services differentiate different kinds of cookies, based on their purpose and allow the user to give explicit consent for cookies that are not mandatory. In particular, these are cookies that are used to improve performance, customize the service and manage advertisements. For the latter, but also for social plugins, third party cookies might be used.

Fig. 8. Technology model

3.8 Conditions

Finally, we looked at whether the privacy policies link data processing to specific conditions. However, most privacy policies stayed vague at this point. Only four conditions were mentioned:

- Explicit consent has been given by the user
- The processing is lawful
- The user has been informed about the processing
- A certain timespan elapsed (e.g., IP address is deleted after 30 days)

Also, more and more services offer privacy settings for their users. These settings influence how data is processed and are thus a part of the condition. These settings give users the option to express their privacy demands and influence how data is processed. In this sense, we differentiate four degrees of freedom, as shown in Fig. 9. Primarily, the processing of data is defined by the application logic of the service and its business processes. At this level, the concept of privacy by design should apply. Typically, the provider then makes default settings when he configures the service (e.g., "posts are publicly visible"). "Privacy by default" has to be implemented on this level. When users are offered privacy settings, they are given the option to override these default settings (e.g., "posts are only visible for my friends"). Ultimately, however, these settings can also be overwritten on a case by case basis (e.g., "this special post is only visible for my family").

4 Presentation of Privacy-Relevant Information

The presented taxonomy, including the individual models, is not an end in itself, but rather a starting point for optimized processing and presentation of privacy-relevant information. In this section we discuss how they can be used to improve transparency for Internet users.

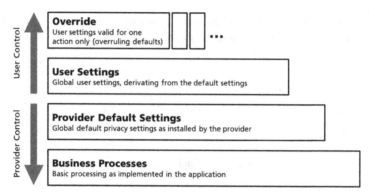

Fig. 9. Degrees of freedom

4.1 Improving Traditional Privacy Policies

In Sect. 3, we presented a sentence structure that covers all relevant information represented by our model. Of course, it is impractical to build a privacy policy solely based on such sentences. Although consistent and precise, the result would be hard to read and not very usable.

In its pure form, the sentence structure is an assistance for policy authors in order to cover all relevant aspects. Also, these sentences can be used to summarize complex or lengthy parts of the privacy policy. This concept of short summaries is a huge help for users and can already be seen on some pages. A very positive example is Wikimedia (cf. Fig. 10), where every paragraph is summarized in parallel and can be expanded for more information. However, this approach has not yet established itself on a broad scale.

The main advantage of the presented taxonomy is that it allows for a consistent semantics across different domains and services. Consistent wording, iconography, glossaries and explanation texts are to be developed as part of our future work.

Fig. 10. Example privacy policy with icon, short summary and layered details (Source: Wikimedia)

4.2 Providing Equivalent Technical Descriptions

We provide a data model in order to allow service providers to offer machine-readable policies by instantiating our model. The major benefit is that it allows for automatic processing, especially searching and filtering. If users search for particular privacy-relevant information, this is oftentimes difficult with plain-text policies. For example, different languages, different or inconsistent wording or filler words complicate search. Additionally, information might be spread over the whole privacy policy, which demands a high mental effort from the user. In contrast, a concrete search query (e.g., "show which of my data is released") can result in a filtered model that in turn can be used to generate a human-readable answer based on the proposed sentence structure. In contrast to complete privacy policies, the representation in this form is reasonable in this case, as only a small subset of the information is shown. As part of our work, we built a data model for our taxonomy and implemented a Chrome extension that injects filtered privacy information into a website based on a technical privacy policy. The screenshot in Fig. 11 shows an example of this.

4.3 Putting Information into Context

All services analyzed by us provide exactly one monolithic privacy policy for their service. In some cases, one privacy policy even applies to several services offered. This requires a large mental load from the user, due to the policy's length, language and abstraction level. As a result, their acceptance is quite low [11, 14, 15].

The idea of contextual privacy policies [5] is to show privacy-relevant information in context of the current use case. This means that concrete information about collection, use and sharing of information is shown at the time a user performs a certain activity.

For example, when a user creates a post on a social media platform, he or she will be interested in the visibility rules and data processing of that post. In this situation, he or she is probably not interested in how the platform uses cookies to authenticate the user. In classic privacy statements, however, both pieces of information are treated in the same document, which is located in a completely different place that has nothing to do with the user's actual activity.

By binding privacy statements to the current activity, privacy statements can be more specific and explicitly relate to the current activity. We assume that this increases understandability. The individual privacy polices presented to the user become shorter, as only currently relevant information is shown. Also, it does not require the user to interrupt his or her activity. This increases the likelihood that users take time to read the privacy statements.

Figures 11 and 12 show fictive examples of contextual privacy policies. The processing of data is explained directly at the point where they are elicited. This can be, for example, when registering a user account (Fig. 11), or when creating a post (Fig. 12). In both cases, information texts and graphics inform about what happens with the data to be entered - without the user having to interrupt his activity. Of course, the presentation must be adapted to the look and feel of the service and the information must be presented in a correspondingly comprehensible way. We are currently working on guidelines for designing such information texts and boxes.

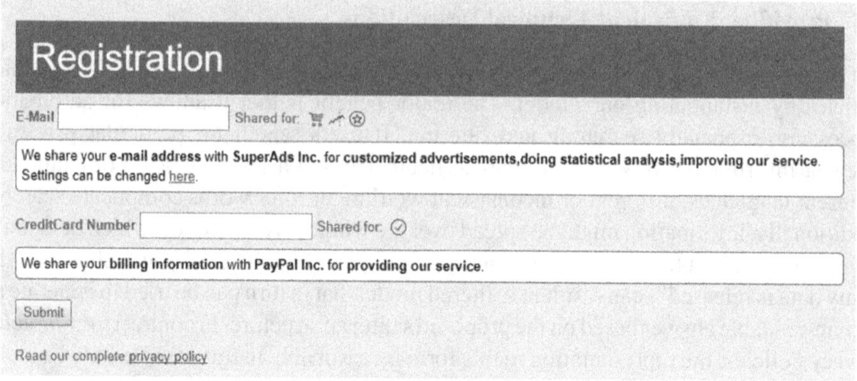

Fig. 11. Idea: Contextual Privacy Policy on a demo registration page

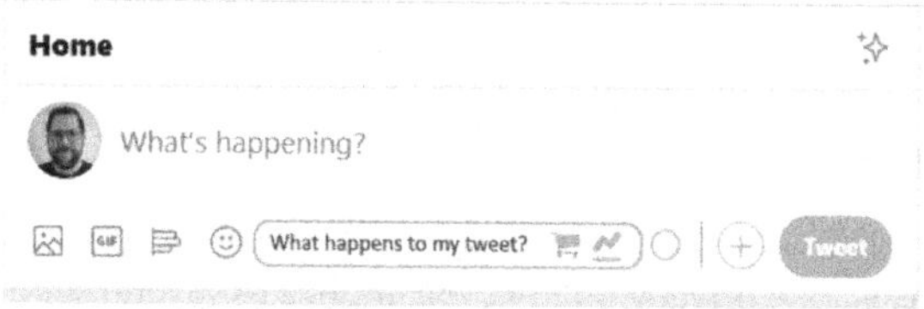

Fig. 12. Idea: Contextual Privacy Policy on Twitter

However, maintaining such distributed privacy statements manually is hard and time-consuming. For example, by filtering the currently relevant data (e.g., e-mail address), the model instance can extract all processing of this data from the model. This reduces the administration effort, because changes in data usage can still be managed at a central location, but a change is automatically made transparent at all relevant points.

5 Related Work

Since the mid-1990s, huge efforts have been made to develop approaches for aligning usability and security. In [6] Garfinkel and Lipfort summarize the history and challenges of the "usable security" domain.

Existing literature on usable security shows that the user is an important and active part of modern security chains. The research field of usable security and privacy has been approached both in a theoretical fashion and in the form of case studies. Famous case studies analyze the usability of email encryption with PGP [17, 18], of file sharing with Kazaa [7], and of authentication mechanisms and password policies [2, 4, 9]. However, case studies are specific to one system, system class, or application domain and can hardly be generalized. On the other hand, theoretical work [1, 3] is typically more abstract and hard to apply in practice.

The acceptance of privacy policies by end users, as well as the consequences of missing acceptance have been analyzed in different surveys [11, 14, 15]. These studies showed that privacy policies are mostly unsuited for users in practice. To improve the situation, there is work targeting readability [1, 10], understandability [12] and design [16] of privacy policies. These are important aspects, but all of these works consider a privacy policy to be a large monolithic document, which is in contrast to our considerations. Tools like the Platform for Privacy Preferences P3P Project[1] targeted transparency of web service privacy, but were not well accepted for usability reasons.

6 Summary and Conclusion

Our main goal is to optimize transparency for Internet users. To this end, we analyzed 36 online privacy policies for information about how the corresponding service processes personal-related data. Based on this information, we created a taxonomy for privacy policies. Eventually, we want to use this taxonomy to create a uniform, cross-system semantics, language and iconography for privacy-relevant information. In the medium term, we expect significant added value in terms of comprehensibility and thus also in terms of acceptance and transparency of privacy policies. In addition, privacy-relevant information can be better adapted to the current situation of the user through the contextual presentation presented. We also expect this to improve acceptance and transparency, as the users' mental load is reduced.

With regard to the effort involved in the administration of privacy policies, manual maintenance of (classical central or contextually distributed) texts and the maintenance of a more formal model are opposed. This evaluation will be part of our future work.

Acknowledgements. The presented research is supported by the German Ministry of Education and Research (BMBF) projects Software Campus (01IS12053) and TrUSD (16KIS0898). The responsibility for the content of this document lies with the author.

References

1. Adams, A., Sasse, M.A.: Users are not the enemy. Commun. ACM **42**(12), 40–46 (1999)
2. Choong, Y.-Y., Theofanos, M.: What 4,500+ people can tell you – employees' attitudes toward organizational password policy do matter. In: Tryfonas, T., Askoxylakis, I. (eds.) HAS 2015. LNCS, vol. 9190, pp. 299–310. Springer, Cham (2015). https://doi.org/10.1007/978-3-319-20376-8_27
3. Cranor, L., Garfinkel, S.: Security and Usability. O'Reilly Media, Inc., Newton (2005)
4. Eljetlawi, A.M., Ithnin, N.: Graphical password: comprehensive study of the usability features of the recognition base graphical password methods. In: Proceedings - 3rd International Conference on Convergence and Hybrid Information Technology, ICCIT 2008, vol. 2, pp. 1137–1143 (2008)
5. Feth, D.: Transparency through contextual privacy statements. In: Burghardt, M., Wimmer, R., Wolff, C., Womser-Hacker, C. (eds.) Mensch und Computer 2017 - Workshopband. Gesellschaft für Informatik e.V, Regensburg (2017)
6. Garfinkel, S., Lipford, H.R.: Usable security: history, themes, and challenges. Synthesis Lect. Inf. Secur. Priv. Trust **5**, 1–124 (2014)

---

[1] https://www.w3.org/P3P/.

7. Good, N.S., Krekelberg, A.: Usability and privacy. In: Proceedings of the Conference on Human factors in Computing Systems - CHI 2003, vol. 5, p. 137 (2003)
8. IControl Networks: 2015 State of the Smart Home Report. Technical report (2015)
9. Inglesant, P., Sasse, M.: The true cost of unusable password policies: password use in the wild, pp. 383–392 (2010)
10. Milne, G.R., Culnan, M.J., Greene, H.: A longitudinal assessment of online privacy notice readability. J. Public Policy Mark. **25**(2), 238–249 (2006)
11. Obar, J.A., Oeldorf-Hirsch, A.: The biggest lie on the internet: ignoring the privacy policies and terms of service policies of social networking services. In: The 44th Research Conference on Communication, Information and Internet Policy (2016)
12. Reidenberg, J.R., et al.: Disagreeable privacy policies: mismatches between meaning and users' understanding. Berkeley Technol. Law J. **30**, 39 (2014)
13. Rudolph, M., Feth, D., Polst, S.: Why users ignore privacy policies – a survey and intention model for explaining user privacy behavior. In: Kurosu, M. (ed.) HCI 2018. LNCS, vol. 10901, pp. 587–598. Springer, Cham (2018). https://doi.org/10.1007/978-3-319-91238-7_45
14. Symantec: State of Privacy Report 2015 (2015)
15. Tsai, J., Egelman, S., Cranor, L., Acquisti, A.: The effect of online privacy information on purchasing behavior: an experimental study (2007)
16. Waldman, A.E.: Privacy, notice, and design (2016)
17. Whitten, A.: Making Security Usable. Comput. Secur. **26**(May), 434–443 (2004)
18. Whitten, A., Tygar, J.: Why Johnny can't encrypt: a usability evaluation of PGP 5.0. In: Proceedings of the 8th Conference on USENIX Security Symposium, vol. 8, p. 14. USENIX Association (1999)

Enabling Medical Research Through Privacy-Preserving Data Markets

Shadan Ghaffaripour$^{(\boxtimes)}$ and Ali Miri

Ryerson University, Toronto, Canada
shadan.ghaffaripour@ryerson.ca

Abstract. A great deal of recent advances in medical research are leveraging machine learning and artificial intelligence techniques. A major impediment to these advances is the reluctance of patients to share personal health data due to privacy concerns and lack of trust. In this paper, we propose a new privacy-preserving data-market platform to tackle this problem. Our novel crowd sourcing platform uses zero-knowledge proofs and blockchains to verify the validity of patients' contributions, while providing strong privacy guarantees for these contributions.

Keywords: Blockchain · Smart contract · Zero-knowledge proof · Data market · Collaborative medical research · Machine learning model · Crowdsourcing

1 Introduction

A great deal of recent advances in medical research are leveraging machine learning and artificial intelligence techniques. Many of these techniques are data driven, and require access to significant amount of patients' data. However, due to privacy and regulatory restrictions, the process of gaining access to such amount of data can be cumbersome, bureaucratic, and sometimes not possible. Statistics show that even though in practice patients are typically supportive of medical research, only a small percentage of them are willing to share their medical data. This is often due to their concerns about unauthorized secondary utilization of their data [8]. These concerns are often reinforced when the promise of anonymity for shared medical data has failed, resulting in release of private medical information [13]. This perceived risk of data misuse and lack of transparency discourages cooperation, and can negatively impact research that relies on these data. In this paper, we propose a new framework to address this important impediment - reluctance to share personal health data due to privacy concerns and lack of trust - in medical research. Our framework provides a mutually beneficial platform for researchers and patients. This platform enables an easy-to-use data collection method to researchers, while ensuring a degree of privacy to patients, who are also provided monetary incentives. It is worth to highlight that although patients can offer their data as part of their contributions to research studies, they are still assured of a high degree of privacy, as no single health record is ever shared with researchers directly.

© Springer Nature Switzerland AG 2020
A. Moallem (Ed.): HCII 2020, LNCS 12210, pp. 367–380, 2020.
https://doi.org/10.1007/978-3-030-50309-3_24

This paper is organized as follows: An overview of the most recent and relevant literature is given in Sect. 2, followed by the background information on blockchain technologies and zero-knowledge proofs in Sect. 3. In Sect. 4, the proposed framework and the description of how patients can collaborate in medical research are presented. This section also shows how patients' contributions can be validated using a zero-knowledge approach. Sections 5 and 6 are dedicated to demonstrate the feasibility of implementation using existing protocols. Section 7 outlines the mathematical underpinnings of the applied zero-knowledge proof for arithmetic circuit satisfiability, based on Quadratic Span Programs (QSP). Conclusions and some possible future work can be found in Sect. 8.

2   Relevant Work

The past decade has seen a growth in the crowdsourcing approach to problem-solving. However, the effectiveness of this approach has yet to be utilized for collection of personal health data for analysis and research purposes, with one of the main challenges being the importance of confidentiality assurance to public for their participation. Many of the work in privacy-preserving data mining and machine learning, rely on the use of secure Multi-Party Computation (MPC) [5] and Differential Privacy [7]. In MPC, participants can jointly compute a function over a set of inputs, while keeping them private in the process. However, the functions over which MPC can be performed are limited. Also, MPC suffers from scalability issues. Differential privacy techniques also try balance the privacy needs with that of results' accuracy by adding an appropriate level of noise. However, the inherent noise in the result can have unintended or unacceptable consequences [3]. Furthermore, they are not designed for data validation, as required by our health data collection application.

Our approach to protecting the privacy of participants is not to share any data in the first place. Instead, allow participants to collaborate in the analytic tasks with their private data and only provide proof attesting to their honest behavior. To enable this aim, we have applied the principle of zero-knowledge proof and have incorporated it in our blockchain transaction validation scheme.

Despite the importance of confidentiality in sharing private information, the incorporation of zero-knowledge proofs in blockchain validation processes has not received much attention. Previous work has been limited to preserving the privacy of users in the context of digital payment. For example, Zcash [6] allows transactions to be verified without revealing the sender, receiver, or transaction amount. Likewise, on Ethereum, the AZTEC protocol [15] enables confidential digital asset transactions. Few studies have examined zero-knowledge proofs in voting systems to ensure anonymity of voters [9,10]. The details of these work are outside scope of this paper. However, we believe that our approach can provide a promising direction in these areas as well.

3 Background

3.1 Blockchain and Smart Contract

Blockchain is a chain of blocks linked by hash pointers, which contains the information about the transition of states in a system. The most important property of blockchain is being immutable; once data is stored in a blockchain, it becomes unchangeable. The implications of immutability are tamper-resistance, auditability, and trust. Blockchain can be used as a secure decentralized data store that is not controlled by a central authority, but instead, maintained by a network of peers.

A smart contract is a self-enforcing agreement, written as a computer program that is managed by a decentralized network [14]. The program encodes a set of rules under which the involved parties agree to interact with one another. Once those rules are met, the terms of the agreement are automatically enforced.

We use smart contracts in our framework, as the framework requires that researchers reimburse patients for their contributions to their research, according to a set of mutually agreed-upon rules. On the other hand, the same rules hold patients accountable for valid contributions. Smart contracts guarantee that neither of the parties deviates from the terms of that agreement.

3.2 Zero-Knowledge Proofs

Proof systems mathematically validate the authenticity of a computation. Zero-knowledge protocols are a subset of proof systems, with an additional requirement of "zero knowledge", which allows a party to prove to another party that a given statement is true without revealing the actual information.

Formally, zero knowledge proofs allow a prover to convince a verifier of a statement of the form "*given a function F and input x, there is a secret w such that $F(x, w) = true$*" [16].

Zero-Knowledge Succinct Non-Interactive Argument of Knowledge (zkSNARKs) [1] is a form of zero knowledge proof that provides an additional useful properties of *succinctness*. The first property allows for extremely small proofs for large statements and efficient verification, regardless of how long it takes to evaluate F. The second property preserves privacy, meaning that the proof reveals no information about the secret w [16].

4 Proposed Framework

4.1 High-Level Description

Our proposed framework uses programmable blockchains as its underlying platform. The decentralized security model of blockchains guarantees that only "valid" updates, verified by the majority of network peers are accepted.

In simple terms, the researcher interested in building a model creates and deploys a smart contract on the system, specifying the desired model structure.

The objective of this contract is to calculate the model parameters according to a learning method.

Patients who are willing to participate in the research, calculate their share, and update the model parameters. As they are preloaded with balance, the contracts automatically reimburse the patients for their contribution.

Ultimately, one of the primary goals of the system is to preserve the privacy of patients. Therefore, unlike other blockchain-based systems, the correctness of calculations cannot be verified by re-execution of the contract by peer nodes. Yet, validation of proposed updates is one of the main processes in blockchain-based systems and it is crucial to check whether patients have correctly evaluated the formula, as given in the contract, with their secret data, and have indeed used their data values in this process. We use a zero-knowledgeproof technique - zkSNARKs (Zero-Knowledge Succinct Non-interactive ARgument of Knowledge) [1,11,16] - to validate patients' participation and that of the values they have used. The core of this technique allows our validation problem to reduce to a very efficient Quadratic Span Program (QSP), which we will discuss in more details later in the paper. With QSPs, the verification task is simplified to checking whether one polynomial divides another polynomial at a single random point. The reduction function translates the transaction to a Boolean formula, such that the formula is satisfiable if and only if the transaction is valid.

4.2 Model Descriptions in Accordance with Zero-Knowledge

Since the computational nature of the application is not customary in the sphere of common blockchain applications that are often geared to financial transactions, we start by providing a mapping between the terminology used in those contexts and that of our proposed framework in Table 1.

Table 1. The different use of blockchain terminology in our application domain

Blockchain core concepts	Equivalent
State	Model parameters
Transaction	Proposed updates to model parameters
Transaction validation	Zero-knowledge proof verification

In our construction, *states* are model parameters that are meant to be updated by transactions. *Transactions* contain proposed updates, issued by patients, on the basis of their data.

For ease of explanation, we examine one of the simplest learning methods, stochastic gradient descent [2] in a linear regression model.

The model parameters, w_j, are updated according to the following equation, where the (x_i, y_i) pair is the private data of the patients and α is the learning rate.

$$w_j = w_j - \alpha(x_i w - y_i)x_{ij} \tag{1}$$

From an instance of QSP, Φ, the system generates proving and verifying keys, pk and vk respectively. The patients compute the update corresponding to their data and generate the zkSNARK proof using pk, a public input X_{public}, and a private input W_{secret} for Φ. The proof attests to the satisfiability of Φ with the (X_{public}, W_{secret}) pair, but reveals no information about W_{secret} [16].

Note that in our example, the private pieces that are not shared are x_i and y_i and model parameters, w_j, are publically accessible at each time instance.

By having the vk, X_{public}, as well as the proof, the verifiers of the blockchain run the verification test, and if the provided proof passes the test, the proposed update will be committed to the model in the blockchain.

Mathematically speaking (see Sect. 7 for more information), the verifying nodes check whether a polynomial divides another polynomial at a random point. In essence, the verifying nodes check whether the patient owns a data piece x_i and y_i such that if substituted in Eq. 1, will result in her proposed update. This statement checks: 1) whether the patient has the data she claims and 2) whether she properly performed the computation as it was expected.

5   Components of the Framework

In this section, the components of our collaborative research platform is described, in accordance with the Decentralized Anonymous Payment (DAP) scheme in [12]. The reason behind this conformity is allowing the platform to be tested using the existing implementations, such as Zcash [6].

5.1   Data Structure

The following data structures are used in the system:

- **Distributed Ledger** L
- **Health Record** a data object c, to which a commitment $cm(c)$, a value $v(c)$, a serial number $sn(c)$ and an address $addr_{pk}(c)$ is associated.
- **Transactions**
    - Health Record Generation: a transaction $tx_{recordGen}$ contains the tuple $(cm, v, *)$ and indicates a health record c with value v and the commitment cm has been generated in the system.
    - Calculation: a   transaction $tx_{calculation}$ contains   the   tuple $(rt, sn_1^{old}, sn_2^{old}, cm_1^{new}, cm_2^{new}, v_{pub}, info, *)$ and   indicates   the   use   of two health records c_1, c_2 with respective serial numbers sn_1^{old}, sn_2^{old} in the calculation of new model updates with respective commitments of cm_1^{new}, cm_2^{new}.
- **List of Commitments**: a list of record commitments at time t: $CMList_t$
- **List of Serial Numbers**: a list of serial numbers of records at time t: $SNList_t$
- **Merkle Tree**: a Merkle tree at time t: $Tree_t$ with root rt over the list of commitments

5.2 Algorithms

Setup. The purpose of this algorithm is to generate the public parameters, available to every party in the system. It is run only once by a trusted third-party (see Algorithm 1).

Algorithm 1: Setup

Input: security parameter λ
Output: public parameters pp
begin

> Construct $C_{\text{calculation}}$ /* Arithmetic circuit for the NP statement, i.e. verification of model-building calculations */

zkSNARK

> $(\text{pk}_{\text{calculation}}, \text{vk}_{\text{calculation}}) := \text{KeyGen}\left(1^\lambda, C_{\text{calculation}}\right)$ /* generates proving key and verifying key */
> $\text{pp}_{\text{enc}} := \mathcal{G}_{\text{enc}}\left(1^\lambda\right)$
> $\text{pp}_{\text{sig}} := \mathcal{G}_{\text{sig}}\left(1^\lambda\right)$
> $\text{pp} := (\text{pk}_{\text{calculation}}, \text{vk}_{\text{calculation}}, \text{pp}_{\text{enc}}, \text{pp}_{\text{sig}})$

Create Addresses. This algorithm generates address key pairs. The public portion is published by researchers who request participation in the research study. The secret portion is then used to receive the model updates performed by the participating patients (See Algorithm 2).

Algorithm 2: Create Addresses

Input: public parameters pp
Output: Address Key pair $(addr_{pk}, addr_{sk})$
begin

> $(pk_{enc}, sk_{enc}) := \mathcal{K}_{enc}(\text{pp}_{enc})$
> randomly sample $a_{sk} \in \{0, 1\}^{256}$
> $a_{pk} := \text{PRF}_{a_{sk}}^{addr}(0)$ /* PRF is a pseudorandom function */
> $addr_{pk} := (a_{pk}, pk_{enc})$
> $addr_{sk} := (a_{sk}, sk_{enc})$

Generate Health Record. This algorithm generates a health record and a $\text{tx}_{\text{recGen}}$ transaction (See Algorithm 3).

Model-Building Calculations. This algorithm takes health records as input and generates new records, the values of which are determined according to a pre-specified logic, for example, the one specified in Eq. 1.

Algorithm 3: Health Record Generation

Input: public parameters pp,
health record value $v \in \{v_{min}, ..., v_{max}\}$,
patient's public key $addr_{pk}$
Output: health record c,
health record generation transaction $tx_{recordGen}$
begin

    randomly sample $\rho \in \{0,1\}^{256}$
    randomly sample COMM trapdoors s, r `/* COMM is a`
    `statistically-hiding non-interactive commitment scheme */`
    $(a_{pk}, pk_{enc}) \leftarrow parse(addr_{pk})$
    $k := COMM_r(a_{pk} \| \rho)$
    $cm := COMM_s(v \| k)$
    $c := (addr_{pk}, v, \rho, r, s, cm)$ `/* health record tuple */`
    $tx_{recordGen} := (cm, v, *), \text{where } * := (k, s)$

To confirm the existence of such records, the algorithm tests the commitment paths to be valid authentication paths with respect to the root in the Merkle tree (See Algorithm 4 for more information). The algorithm also creates a $tx_{calculation}$ transaction, as described in the previous section.

The patients who want to participate in research must have ownership of the qualified health records, existing on the system. In other words, they must know the secret keys pertaining to such health records. By having ownership of the qualified health records, patients use them in calculations and create a new record and commit to its value. The record, whose value is the sought-for model update, is directed to the researcher by encryption via his/her receiving public-key. Patients also calculate proofs using the proving key, the zkSNARK input x, and zkSNARK secret a (see Algorithm 4 for more information) attesting to the validity of their calculations, verifiable by anyone in the system.

Verify Transaction. All the transactions are validated before being permanently recorded in the distributed ledger.

For the case of $tx_{recordGen}$, a valid transaction is simply the one with proper calculation of record commitment. For $tx_{calculation}$ transactions, it is much more complicated. The algorithm first tests whether the serial numbers pertaining to the used health records appear on the ledger or not. If not, meaning that they have not been "double spent", it also checks whether the zkSNARk verification passes with respect to the provided proof and the zkSNARK input extracted from the transaction (See Algorithm 5).

Algorithm 4: Model-building Calculations

Input: public parameters pp

Merkle root rt

patient's health records $\mathbf{c}_1^{old}, \mathbf{c}_2^{old}$

patient addresses secret keys $addr_{sk,1}^{old}, addr_{sk,2}^{old}$

path $path_1$ from $cm(c_1^{old})$ to rt /* path from commitment to Merkle tree root */

path $path_2$ from $cm(c_2^{old})$ to rt

new values (calculations) v_1^{new}, v_2^{new}

new addresses (researchers) public keys $addr_{pk,1}^{new}, addr_{pk,2}^{new}$

transaction string Info

Output: new records $\mathbf{c}_1^{new}, \mathbf{c}_2^{new}$

calculation transaction $tx_{calculation}$

begin

    foreach $i \in \{1,2\}$ **do**

        $(addr_{pk,i}, v_i^{old}, \rho_i^{old}, r_i^{old}, s_i^{old}, cm_i^{old}) \leftarrow parse(c_i^{old})$

        $(a_{sk,i}^{old}, sk_{enc,i}^{old}) \leftarrow parse(addr_{sk,i}^{old})$

        $sn_i^{old} := \mathrm{PRF}_{a_{sk,i}^{old}}^{sn}(\rho_i^{old})$

        $(a_{pk,i}^{new}, pk_{enc,i}^{new}) \leftarrow parse(addr_{pk,i}^{new})$

        randomly sample $\rho_i^{new} \in \{0,1\}^{256}$

        randomly sample COMM trapdoors s_i^{new}, r_i^{new}

        $k_i^{new} := \mathrm{COMM}_{r_i^{new}}(a_{pk,i}^{new} \| \rho_i^{new})$

        $cm_i^{new} := \mathrm{COMM}_{s_i^{new}}(v_i^{new} \| k_i^{new})$

        $\mathbf{c}_i^{new} := (addr_{pk,i}^{new}, v_i^{new}, \rho_i^{new}, r_i^{new}, s_i^{new}, cm_i^{new})$

        $\mathbf{C}_i := \mathcal{E}_{enc}(pk_{enc,i}^{new}, (v_i^{new}, \rho_i^{new}, r_i^{new}, s_i^{new}))$

    $(pk_{sig}, sk_{sig}) := \mathcal{K}_{sig}(pp_{sig})$

    $h_{Sig} := \mathrm{CRH}(pk_{sig})$

    $h_1 := PRF_{a_{sk,1}^{old}}^{pk}(1 \| h_{Sig})$

    $h_2 := PRF_{a_{sk,2}^{old}}^{pk}(2 \| h_{Sig})$

1    $x := (rt, sn_1^{old}, sn_2^{old}, cm_1^{new}, cm_2^{new}, v_{pub}, h_{sig}, h_1, h_2)$ /* zk3NARK input */

2    $a := (path_1, path_2, \mathbf{c}_1^{old}, \mathbf{c}_2^{old}, addr_{sk,1}^{old}, addr_{sk,2}^{old}, \mathbf{c}_1^{new}, \mathbf{c}_2^{new})$ /* zkSNARK secret */

3    $\pi_{calculation} := \mathrm{Prove}(pk_{calculation}, x, a)$ /* zkSNARK proof */

    $m := (x, \pi_{calculation}, info, \mathbf{C}_1, \mathbf{C}_2)$

    $\sigma := \mathcal{S}_{sig}(sk_{sig}, m)$

    $tx_{calculation} := (rt, sn_1^{old}, sn_2^{old}, cm_1^{new}, cm_2^{new}, v_{pub}, info, *)$, where $* :=$

    $(pk_{sig}, h_1, h_2, \pi_{calculation}, \mathbf{C}_1, \mathbf{C}_2, \sigma)$

Receive Updates. Researchers with address key pair $(addr_{pk}, addr_{sk})$ use this algorithm to scan the ledger and receive the records containing update values aimed at their address $addr_{pk}$ (see Algorithm 6).

Algorithm 5: Verify Transaction

Input: public parameters pp,
transaction tx,
current ledger L
Output: bit $b \in \{0, 1\}$
begin

   if $tx = tx_{\text{recordGen}}$ **then**

      $(cm, v, *) \leftarrow parse(tx_{\text{recordGen}})$ **AND** $(k, s) \leftarrow parse(*)$
      $cm' := \text{COMM}_s(v \| k)$
      if $cm' == cm$ **then**

         $b = 1$ `/* valid */`

      else

         $b = 0$ `/* invalid */`

   else

                                   `/* transaction is` $tx_{\text{calculation}}$ `*/`
      $(rt, sn_1^{\text{old}}, sn_2^{\text{old}}, cm_1^{\text{new}}, cm_2^{\text{new}}, v_{\text{pub}}, \text{info}, *) \leftarrow parse(tx_{calculation})$
      $(pk_{\text{sig}}, h_1, h_2, \pi_{\text{calculation}}, \mathbf{C}_1, \mathbf{C}_2, \sigma) \leftarrow parse(*)$ **if**
      $sn_1^{\text{old}}, sn_2^{\text{old}}$ apprear in L **or** $sn_1^{\text{old}} == sn_2^{\text{old}}$ **then**

         $b = 0$

      if Merkle root rt does not appear on L, **then**

         $b = 0$

      $h_{sig} := \text{CRH}(pk_{sig})$ `/* CHR is a collision-resistant hash`
      `function */`
      $x := (rt, sn_1^{\text{old}}, sn_2^{\text{old}}, cm_1^{\text{new}}, cm_2^{\text{new}}, v_{\text{pub}}, h_{\text{Sig}}, h_1, h_2)$
      $m := (x, \pi_{\text{calculation}}, \text{info}, \mathbf{C}_1, \mathbf{C}_2)$
      $b = \mathcal{V}_{sig}(pk_{sig}, m, \sigma) \wedge \text{Verify}(vk_{calculation}, x, \pi_{calculation})$

Algorithm 6: Receive Model Updates

Input: public parameters pp
researcher's address key pair $(addr_{pk}, addr_{sk})$
current ledger L
Output: set of received records, containing model updates
begin

   $(a_{pk}, pk_{enc}) \leftarrow parse(addr_{pk})$
   $(a_{sk}, sk_{enc}) \leftarrow parse(addr_{sk})$
   foreach $tx_{calculation}$ *on the ledger* **do**

      $(rt, sn_1^{\text{old}}, sn_2^{\text{old}}, cm_1^{\text{new}}, cm_2^{\text{new}}, v_{\text{pub}}, info, *) \leftarrow parse(tx_{calculation})$
      $(pk_{\text{sig}}, h_1, h_2, \pi_{\text{calculation}}, \mathbf{C}_1, \mathbf{C}_2, \sigma) \leftarrow parse(*)$
      foreach $i \in \{1, 2\}$ **do**

         $(v_i, \rho_i, r_i, s_i) := \mathcal{D}_{enc}(sk_{enc}, \mathbf{C}_i)$
         if $cm_i^{new} == \text{COMM}_{s_i}(v_i \| \text{COMM}_{r_i}(a_{pk} \| \rho_i))$ **AND**
         $sn_i := \text{PRF}_{a_{sk}}^{\text{sn}}(\rho_i)$ **not in ledger** L **then**

            $\mathbf{c}_i := (addr_{\text{pk}}, v_i, \rho_i, r_i, s_i, cm_i^{\text{new}})$ `/* received record,`
            `containing the model update` v_i `*/`

6 Implementation Using Shielded Payments in Zcash

Zcash protocol [6] is an implementation of the DAP scheme of [12]. In this section, we demonstrate how this protocol can be used to implement our proposed medical application (See Table 2).

In shielded payments terminology, there are three fundamental notions of "notes", "commitments", and "nullifiers". An unspent valid note[1], at a given point on the blockchain, is one for which the note commitment has been publically revealed on the blockchain prior to that point, but the nullifier has not [6].

A note is a tuple (a_{pk}, v, ρ, rcm), where a_{pk} is the paying key of the recipient's shielded payment address; v is an integer representing the value of the note in zatoshi; ρ is used as input to $\mathrm{PRF}^{nf}_{a_{sk}}$ to derive the nullifer of the note; A commitment on note is derived from a_{pk}, v, and ρ, using SHA-256. While note commitments are maintained in a Merkle tree data structure, nullifiers are kept in a list.

Adhering to the same terminology, we describe the main operations in our framework.

Health Record Generation and Commitment Publishment. Every time an Electronic Health Record (EHR) is generated, a new commitment is published to the blockchain network. These commitments consist of the hash of the public key of a patient (a_{pk}), the value of the EHR record(v), and an identifier unique to that newly-generated EHR record (ρ).

Health Record Contribution and Nullifier Publishment. When patients participate in a research study in order to contribute one of their EHR records, they use their private key (a_{sk}) to publish a nullifier. This nullifier is the hash of an EHR unique identifier (ρ) from an existing commitment, which has not been used before and provides a zero-knowledge proof of their authorization to participate. This hash should not already be in the set of nullifiers keeping track of already-used EHR records to avoid double participation.

Verification of Contributions in Zero-knowledge. zk-SNARK is utilized to prove the validity of transactions without revealing the identities of patients or their electronic health records. At a very high level, the senders of such transactions generate a proof that attests to the following statements:

- The patient is authorized to contribute her EHR records. i.e. has the ownership of EHR records (has a_{sk}), existing in the system.
- For each EHR record that the patient wants to use, a revealed commitment exists on the EHR data management system.

---

[1] protected coin.

- The input values- i.e EHR record values- are mapped to the output value-i.e. model parameter updates, with the pre-specified logic[2]. The logic can be the one shown in Eq. 1.
- The secret key of the EHR record(a_{sk}) is linked to a signature over the whole transaction.

More inline with the terminology of the zcash protocol, a valid zk-SNARK proof assures that given a publicly known input(e.g. the note commitment for the output note, the sequence of nullifiers for the input notes, the merkle root tree), the prover knows a secret input (e.g. a sequence of input notes and their secret keys, the output note, a valid merkle tree path and position for the input notes) such that the following conditions [6] hold:

- *Merkle path validity*, i.e. the path and the position of input notes are valid Merkle paths.
- *Balance is preserved*, i.e. the total value of the output must not exceed the total value of inputs.
- *Nullifier integrity*, i.e. the sequence of nullifiers for the input notes are computed correctly.
- *Spend authority*, i.e. shielded payment address and spending key match.
- *Non-malleability*.
- *Uniqueness of ρ* for the output commitment.
- *Note commitment integrity*, i.e. the output commitment is computed correctly.

Table 2. The mapping between notions of shielded payments and our work, demonstrating their relevance

Shielded payment	Our work
Digital coin (Note)	EHR record
Note commitment	EHR existance in the EHR management system
Digital coin amount	EHR record value
Spending	Participating in research studies
Double spend	Double participation
Authorization to spend	Having the ownership of an EHR record on the system that has not been used

7 Mathematical Descriptions of zk-SNARK for QSP

Quadratic Span Program (QSP) is an NP-complete class of problems for which an efficient construction exists to prove a satisfying assignment in zero knowledge [4]. The same construction can be used for any problem in NP, given the reducibility of NP problems to an NP-complete problem in polynomial time.

---

[2] In payment transactions, the sum of inputs has to be larger than the sum of outputs.

In the QSP, we are given two sets of polynomials $\{v_0, ... v_m\}$, $\{w_0, ... w_m\}$, and a target polynomial t (of degree at most d) and a binary input string u of length n.

The prover finds values $\{a_0, ..., a_m\}$, $\{b_0, ..., b_m\}$ and a polynomial h such that:

$$(v_0 + a_1 v_1 + ... + a_m v_m).(w_0 + b_1 w_1 + ... + b_m w_m) = t.h \qquad (2)$$

In what follows, the setup, proof generation and proof validation processes are described. For in-depth details, please refer to [11].

7.1 Setup

In the setup phase, the Common Reference String (CRS) is generated. The CRS consists of:

- Encrypted secret field element s: $E(s^0), E(s^1), ..., E(s^d)$, and the shifted forms $E(\alpha s^0), E(\alpha s^1), ..., E(\alpha s^d)$
- Evaluated polynomial at s in an encrypted form: $E(t(s))$, and $E(\alpha t(s))$
- Evaluated polynomials at s in an encrypted form: $E(v_0(s)), ..., E(v_m(s))$, and $E(\alpha v_0(s)), ..., E(\alpha v_m(s))$
- Evaluated polynomials at s in an encrypted form: $E(w_0(s)), ..., E(w_m(s))$, and $E(\alpha w_0(s)), ..., E(\alpha w_m(s))$
- $E(\gamma), E(\beta_v \gamma), E(\beta_w \gamma)$
- $E(\beta_v v_1(s)), ..., E(\beta_v v_m(s))$
- $E(\beta_w w_1(s)), ..., E(\beta_w w_m(s))$
- $E(\beta_v t(s)), E(\beta_w t(s))$

The encryption function is defined as $E(x) = g^x$ with certain homomorphic properties, wherein g is the generator of a group of order n. Furthermore, d is the maximum degree of all polynomials and s, α, β_v, β_w and γ are random and secret field elements. The purpose of using β_v, β_w and γ is to verify that the designated polynomials were evaluated and to avoid the use of any other arbitrary polynomials.

This setup is similar to the line that has been denoted as zkSNARK in Algorithm 1.

7.2 Proof Generation

The prover computes polynomial factors as well as the polynomial h with a witness-preserving reduction scheme. The SNARK proof consists of:

- $V_{free} = E(v_{free}(s)) = E(\sum_{k \in I_{free}} a_k v_k(s))$, $W = E(w(s))$, $H = E(h(s))$
- $V'_{free} = E(\alpha v_{free}(s))$, $W' = E(\alpha w(s))$, $H' = E(\alpha h(s))$
- $Y = E(\beta_v v_{free}(s) + \beta_w w(s))$

Note that for each input to be verified, an underlying injective function restricts some of the polynomial factors in linear combination. Those that are not restricted are induced with I_{free} and are used in the calculations above. The restricted factors, induced by I_{in}, can be computed directly from the input. For the zero-knowledge property:

- $v_{free}(s)$ is replaced by $(v_{free}(s) + \delta_{free}t(s))$,
- $w(s)$ is replaced by $(w(s) + \delta_w t(s))$,
- $h(s)$ is replaced by $(h(s) + \delta_{free}(w_0(s) + w(s)) + \delta_w(v_0(s) + v_{in}(s) + v_{free}(s)) + (\delta_{free}\delta_w)t(s))$,

where δ_{free} and δ_w are secret random values chosen by the prover.
The underlying idea that leads to zero-knowledge property is shifting some values by a random secret amount and balancing the shift on the other side of the equation.
Proof generation has been shown in line 1 to 3 of the Algorithm 4.

7.3   Proof Verification

The verifier computes the missing part of the full sum of v by computing $V_{in} = E(v_{in}(s)) = E(\sum_{k \in I_{in}} a_k v_k(s))$.

Following that, The verifier checks that the following equalities hold:

1. $e(V'_{free}, g) = e(V_{free}, g^\alpha)$,
2. $e(W', E(1)) = e(W, E(\alpha))$,
3. $e(H', E(1)) = e(H, E(\alpha))$
4. $e(E(\gamma), Y) = e(\beta_v \gamma, V_{free})e(\beta_w \gamma, W)$
5. $e(E(v_0(s))E(v_{in}(s))V_{free}, E(w_0(s))W) = e(H, E(t(s)))$

In the above equalities, e is a pairing function with the property of $e(g^x, g^y) = e(g, g)^{xy}$, for all x and y. The first three checks verify whether the prover evaluated some polynomial using the CRS. The fourth check verifies that the prover used exactly the designated polynomials. Finally, the last item checks the Eq. 2 holds at s.
Proof verification has been shown in the last line of Algorithm 5.

8   Conclusions and Future Work

In this paper, we proposed a privacy-preserving and auditable crowdsourcing platform for medical research. Our platform incentives participants to contribute their medical data to research projects, while maintaining their privacy. In essence, participants also provide proof attesting to the correctness of the calculations over the data to which only they have access. In this manner, the platform enables researchers to verify the validity of contributions in zero-knowledge. In this work, blockchain technology has not only automated the process, but has also provided a means to enforce the rules of this collaboration.

The significance of zero-knowledge proofs in decentralized systems goes far beyond the application described. Whatever the nature of a transaction might be, the validation by a distributed network of peers is essential. The point here is that the validators do not necessarily know or should know every transaction detail for a variety of reasons, including but not limited to privacy. Yet, they need to verify the validity of the transaction based on some application-specific logic. Future work can explore further application possibilities and unlock the full potential of blockchain technology.

References

1. Ben-Sasson, E., Chiesa, A., Tromer, E., Virza, M.: Succinct non-interactive zero knowledge for a von Neumann architecture. In: Proceedings of the 23rd USENIX Security Symposium, pp. 781–796 (2014)
2. Bottou, L.: Stochastic learning. In: Bousquet, O., von Luxburg, U., Rätsch, G. (eds.) ML -2003. LNCS (LNAI), vol. 3176, pp. 146–168. Springer, Heidelberg (2004). https://doi.org/10.1007/978-3-540-28650-9_7
3. Dankar, F., Emam, K.: Practicing differential privacy in health care: a review. Trans. Data Priv. **6**, 35–67 (2013)
4. Gennaro, R., Gentry, C., Parno, B., Raykova, M.: Quadratic span programs and succinct NIZKs without PCPs. In: Johansson, T., Nguyen, P.Q. (eds.) EURO-CRYPT 2013. LNCS, vol. 7881, pp. 626–645. Springer, Heidelberg (2013). https://doi.org/10.1007/978-3-642-38348-9_37
5. Goldreich, O.: Secure multi-party computation. Manuscript. Preliminary version 78 (1998)
6. Hopwood, D., Bowe, S., Hornby, T., Wilcox, N.: Zcash protocol specification. San Francisco, CA, USA, GitHub (2016)
7. Jayaraman, B., Evans, D.: Evaluating differentially private machine learning in practice. In: Proceedings of the 28th USENIX Security Symposium, pp. 1895–1912 (2019)
8. Kaplan, B.: Selling health data: de-identification, privacy, and speech. Camb. Q. Healthc. Ethics **24**(3), 256–271 (2015)
9. Matile, R., Rodrigues, B., Scheid, E., Stiller, B.: CaIV: cast-as-intended verifiability in blockchain-based voting. In: IEEE International Conference on Blockchain and Cryptocurrency (ICBC), pp. 24–28. IEEE (2019)
10. Murtaza, M.H., Alizai, Z.A., Iqbal, Z.: Blockchain based anonymous voting system using zkSNARKs. In: International Conference on Applied and Engineering Mathematics (ICAEM), pp. 209–214. IEEE (2019)
11. Reitwiessner, C.: zkSNARKs in a nutshell. Ethereum Blog 6 (2016)
12. Sasson, E.B., et al.: Zerocash: decentralized anonymous payments from bitcoin. In: Proceedings of the 2014 IEEE Symposium on Security and Privacy, pp. 459–474, IEEE (2014)
13. Sweeney, L.: Simple demographics often identify people uniquely. Health (San Francisco) **671**, 1–34 (2000)
14. Voshmgir, S.: Token Economy: How Blockchains and Smart Contracts Revolutionize the Economy. Shermin Voshmgir (2019). https://books.google.ca/books?id=-Wp3xwEACAAJ
15. Williamson, D.Z.J.: The AZTEC protocol. https://github.com/AztecProtocol/AZTEC. Accessed 15 Jan 2020
16. Wu, H., Zheng, W., Chiesa, A., Popa, R.A., Stoica, I.: DIZK: a distributed zero knowledge proof system. In: Proceedings of the 27th USENIX Security Symposium, pp. 675–692 (2018)

Understanding Users' Relationship with Voice Assistants and How It Affects Privacy Concerns and Information Disclosure Behavior

Charulata Ghosh[✉] and Matthew S. Eastin

University of Texas at Austin, Austin, TX 78705, USA
charulata@utexas.edu

Abstract. It is important to understand users' relationship with technology, particularly considering the large data breaches and privacy concerns that have been plaguing users in the recent years. The CASA paradigm examines individuals' social responses to technology which are triggered by cues in the interface. Emerging technology like voice assistants or conversational assistants are becoming more human-like, thus warranting a closer examination of the psychological mechanisms underlying users' interaction with technology. Current research examining privacy concerns does not separate the agent (i.e. voice assistant like Siri or Alexa) and the device through which users interact with the agent (i.e. smartphone or smart speaker). This is important to consider as the cues triggering social responses could be different for the agent and the device, thereby having different effects on information disclosure behavior and privacy concerns. This paper aims to distinguish between the different psychological mechanisms underlying users' interaction with the agent and the device, and examine how this distinction affects privacy concerns and information disclosure behavior.

Keywords: Privacy concerns · Voice assistants · Information disclosure

1 Introduction

Doordash recently reported that there had been a data breach in their systems which had left 4.9 million users' data exposed, including the driver's licenses of 100,000 delivery personnel (Baca 2019). Although the report assured consumers that crucial payment information had not been compromised, the fact remains that information disclosure remains a risk in today's digital environment. According to the Advertising Research Foundation (2019), individuals were slightly less likely to share data online in 2019 as compared to 2018. That said, even though people express concerns about their information privacy, their behaviors do not adequately reflect these concerns. This phenomenon is called the privacy paradox (Norberg et al. 2007). Simply, the privacy paradox (Norberg et al. 2007) describes the discrepancy between individuals' privacy concerns and their information disclosure behavior. Research has found that a lack of awareness or technical knowledge could not explain the discrepancy between privacy concerns and information disclosure behavior

© Springer Nature Switzerland AG 2020
A. Moallem (Ed.): HCII 2020, LNCS 12210, pp. 381–392, 2020.
https://doi.org/10.1007/978-3-030-50309-3_25

(Bonne et al. 2017; Hallam and Zanella 2016). While individuals may be aware of the potential threats, the use of SNSs, mobile apps, etc. have become so widely entrenched in day-to-day lives, that people do not subject their behavior to possible consequences every time they perform that behavior. Here, it is important to consider the relationship between consumers and technology, especially in light of the integration of new media in everyday life.

The media equation theory states that individuals' interactions with media are fundamentally social and natural (Reeves and Nass 1996), while the Computers are Social Actors (CASA) paradigm (Nass et al. 1994a) examines users' social responses to computers and technology. Within media equation, Nass and Moon (2000) argue that social responses toward media are mindless and triggered by contextual cues. In the current media landscape, technology is advancing with the goal of providing greater efficiency and usefulness to consumers, while increasing the human-likeness of the technology through an increased number of social contextual cues. With the growth of in-home voice assistants or conversational assistants like Amazon's Alexa and Google's Google Home Assistant, consumers are interacting with increasingly human-like technology on a daily basis. Consumers evaluate privacy risks and concerns on the basis of their relationship with the people whom they interact with through technology – mobile advertisers, e-commerce site employees, bank employees, online vendors, etc. Trust has been a consistent factor that impacts privacy concerns in these contexts (Bergström 2015; Eastin et al. 2016). However, research has not delved into consumers' relationship with the technology itself, i.e. the website, the social media platform, the device through which these sites are being accessed, and how this could affect privacy concerns. The device is the only tangible point of contact between the user and the algorithm, the programmer, the online vendor, the mobile commerce site, and the social media platform. Therefore, the device is an integral part of understanding consumers' relationship with data, technology, and privacy concerns regarding both. This study aims to explicate users' relationship with voice assistants using the CASA paradigm, and understand how this relationship affects information disclosure and privacy concerns.

2 Theoretical Premise

2.1 Consumer's Relationship with Technology - Media Equation & CASA Paradigm

The media equation theory explains how individuals treat media as real people and places (Reeves and Nass 1996). This implies that social rules and norms applied to interpersonal communication are extended to interactions with media. Specifically, in media equation studies, the social dynamics surrounding human–human interactions have been shown to exist in human–computer interactions. Initial research on the media equation found that individuals applied gender stereotypes to computers (Nass et al. 1997), as well as applying social rules like flattery (Fogg and Nass 1997) and politeness (Nass et al. 1999) while interacting with computers. The CASA paradigm (Nass et al. 1994) follows the same tenets of the media equation, attempting to further understand users' relationship with technology in the rapidly evolving technological landscape.

Individuals responded socially to computers despite the absence of any feature suggesting human form, which Nass and Moon (2000) suggested was a result of mindlessness. Mindless behavior is a result of conscious attention to contextual cues which trigger certain scripts and expectations, causing individuals to focus their attention on certain information and divert their attention from other (Langer 1992). In the case of computers, the contextual cues trigger scripts in individuals usually reserved for interactions with other individuals while diverting their focus from cues which clearly suggest that computers do not warrant social responses (Nass and Moon 2000). This suggests a balanced number of contextual cues; enough to trigger a mindless social response, but low enough to consciously believe that social responses are not appropriate. Nass (2004) listed a number of cues that trigger social responses to computers including language use, voice, face, emotion manifestation, interactivity, engagement with user, autonomy, and filling of traditional human roles (e.g. teacher). Kim and Sundar (2012) added to existing CASA research by suggesting that social response to technology could also be the result of mindless anthropomorphism – the tendency to attribute human characteristics to non-human objects. The basic premise of CASA paradigm is grounded in the tendency to anthropomorphize technology that does not possess any physical attributes suggesting humanness, but rather, has other cues that elicit social responses. In other words, this area of research focused on how individuals responded to computers as if they were human, despite the existence of a conscious belief that computers were not human. Emerging technology is being created in order to increase perceived human-likeness because it generates positive evaluation of content from consumers through greater credibility and persuasion (Sundar 2008). This means that the number of contextual or anthropomorphic cues are also increasing. With the increased human-likeness of technology, CASA research developed the concept of an agent – a virtual being which is controlled by technology as opposed to controlled by a person (Fox et al. 2015). The agent, be it a voice assistant like Siri and Alexa or a chatbot communicating with consumers on a website, is distinct from the device through which consumers interact with the agent i.e. the smartphone or smart speaker. The human-likeness which is a result of an increased number of anthropomorphic cues, is manifested in the agent because the actual device is still a piece of hardware or machinery that can only achieve a limited amount of human-likeness. This is where it is important to distinguish between the agent and the device, and examine users' relationship with both separately. Voice assistants or conversational assistants like Amazon's Alexa, Apple's Siri, and Google's Google Home Assistant provide the ideal situation for examining this distinction between the agent and the device, because the smart speaker (in the case of Amazon and Google) or smartphone (in the case of Apple) exists simultaneously with the voice assistant (Alexa, Siri, or Google Home Assistant), enabling users to develop a relationship with both the device and the agent in the same space.

Smartphone. While initial CASA research focused on personal computers, the truly ubiquitous media in a user's life today is the smartphone. Smartphones are a vital part of individuals' daily lives with the number of smartphone users in the United States increasing from 62.6 million in 2010 to 257.3 million in 2018 (Statista 2019). Smartphones are portable and serve many functions – traditional calls, video calls, internet services, apps, etc., and therefore have a much greater presence in users' daily lives than computers. On testing the media equation for smartphones, results confirmed "the idea of phones being able to elicit polite behavior and emphasize the importance of ownership and the emotional aspects associated with one's own device" (Carolus et al. 2018, p.10). Furthermore, users appear to draw some form of digital companionship from smartphones characterized by trust, closeness, and coping with the stress of the companionship similar to social relationships (Carolus et al. 2019). This digital companionship from smartphones mimicking various aspects of social human relationships is significant because it can be connected to the set of cues proposed by Nass (2004) – specifically, the filling-of-human-roles cue. Originally, Nass suggested that computers can fulfil the human role of a teacher in an individual's life, while Carolus and colleagues' (2019) study indicates that smartphones fulfil a companionship role in an individual's life. It is important to note how the human role being fulfilled has changed from a primarily functional one (a teacher) to a primarily emotional one (a companion). This illustrates how important smartphones are in a user's life, inasmuch as it is no longer just a device for performing a set of functions efficiently. Belk (1988, 2013) proposed the concept of a person's possessions becoming part of their extended self, which included digital possessions like emails, smartphones, laptops, and social media.

Smart Speaker. The first popular instance of voice assistant usage was in 2011 when Apple introduced Siri (Apple 2011), and it was a few years later that the concept of an intelligent voice-controlled assistant found its way into people's homes with Amazon's Alexa and Google's Google Home Assistant. While Google did not provide a specific name for its voice assistant, Amazon and Apple went ahead with female names for their respective voice assistants with default female voices. In 2019, over 100 million devices installed with Amazon's Alexa had been sold (Matney 2019), while Google enabled its voice assistant on all Android devices in the same year (Tillman and O'Boyle 2019). While previous voice-controlled devices, smartphones, computers, and tablets provided the user with a certain kind of interaction, natural language processing has advanced the interaction capabilities of voice assistants like Alexa, Google Home, and Siri. The fact that users interact with voice assistants through the modality of a human voice sets it apart from other advanced technology. Nass (2004) suggested the presence of voice interface was one of the anthropomorphic cues that triggered social responses from users. Thus, voice assistants fall under emerging technology with an increasing number of anthropomorphic cues that elicit a social response from consumers.

Mclean and Osei-Frimpong (2019) used the tenets of CASA paradigm to study individuals' use of voice assistants and found that social presence of voice assistants was an important factor influencing their adoption and usage. Lombard and Ditton (1997) conceptualized presence as an "illusion of nonmediation" which can either occur when the medium appears to be invisible or transparent, or when the medium appears to become a social entity. Sundar (2008) lists social presence as a heuristic which increases source and content credibility. The social presence heuristic is triggered by cues present in the interface, causing users to feel that presence of another being. Additionally, Apple, Google, and Amazon offer users the ability to customize their voice assistants either by changing the voice, accent, gender, or name of the assistant. Not only does this allow users to change their voice assistant to suit their personal preferences, it affords them with a higher level of agency. Research suggests that user agency increases an individual's feeling of connectedness to digital possessions (Belk 2013). This feeling of connectedness to digital possessions is related to the concept of the extended self (Belk 1988); in other words, user agency causes individuals to view digital possessions as part of their extended self. This contrasts with the notion of social presence which suggests with feeling of having another being present. Therefore, while interacting with technology it comes down to feeling like another being is present versus feeling like the technology is part of oneself. The existence of the contrasting notions of social presence of technology and technology as extended self, can be explained by following the distinction between the device and the agent as suggested earlier. Users experience social presence due to the agent, while the device itself is part of their extended self. In other words, voice assistants trigger the social presence heuristic while the smartphone or smart speaker feels connected to the user as part of their extended self. Customization has been found to increase user agency (Sundar and Marathe 2010), thus, it is logical that customization will increase the feeling that technology is part of an individual's extended self. Consequently, customization will also lower the feeling that another being is present while interacting with technology (i.e., social presence). Following this logic, the following is hypothesized:

H1: Users who have customized their voice assistant will report lower social presence of voice assistants than those who have not customized their voice assistant.

2.2 Information Disclosure

Information disclosure is both a necessity and a risk in today's digital world. Accessing the various advantages and features of the IoT requires individuals to disclose personal data and information such as banking details, location, social media activities, and internet browsing behavior. Mass data breaches since the explosion of social media and smart technology has created an awareness around the risk posed to individuals' data and personal information. When we imagine digital media, it often comes across as a vast, nebulous concept floating somewhere in the worldwide web. However, the truth is that while data exists in the digital space, information disclosure occurs through a tangible source – the point of contact between consumers and world of data. Here, it is important to consider the device through which consumers disclose personal information and data. Voice assistants are mainly used through smartphones (Siri through iPhone) or smart speakers (Alexa through Echo and Google Assistant through Google Home) (Fingas 2019). Comparing smartphones and smart speakers - while both can be used to interact with voice assistants, each one provides affordances in different ways. For instance, smartphones are used for a variety of functions, the frequency and depth of usage has almost made it into an extension of the user (Brasel 2016). In such a situation, users do not consciously think about why they use their smartphones - is it because of the usefulness of smartphones features, how well it aligns with their own needs, or how intuitive it is. Existing without a smartphone in today's technologically interconnected world is almost unimaginable. However, smart speakers are relatively new to consumers' lives and their primarily fixed location does not afford the same conveniences as a smartphone. Research suggests that users are more likely to disclose information using their smartphone keypad than through voice assistants (Easwara Moorthy and Vu 2015). Users were also more likely to disclose information using voice assistants in private versus public settings, as well as more likely to disclose non-private versus private information using voice assistants. Although we see the difference in information disclosure, it is still not evident whether motivations regarding information disclosure using voice assistants would be influenced by the same factors in the case of smartphones and smart speakers.

In the current media landscape, technology adoption and usage is inextricably linked with some form of information disclosure. Therefore, motivations regarding adoption and usage of technology should also be linked to motivations regarding information disclosure through those technologies. Uses and Gratification theory (U&GT) is grounded on the premise that media users are primarily goal-oriented and select media to fit their needs (Katz et al. 1973). U&G has also been used to understand motivations regarding usage of newer media and technology like social networks (Osei-Frimpong and McLean 2018), and virtual and augmented reality (Rauschnabel et al. 2017; 2018). Lee and colleagues (2008), conceptualized motivations regarding information disclosure in a similar manner - which included factors like information sharing and entertainment, amongst others. This study utilizes both these perspectives to conceptualize motivations regarding information disclosure through voice assistants. According to the Technology Acceptance Model, perceived ease of use and perceived usefulness play a major role in the adoption of new technology (Davis 1989). Venkatesh and colleagues (2012) found that enjoyment influenced technology usage and adoption, thus suggesting both hedonic and utilitarian factors influence adoption and usage of technology. Here we conceptualize the hedonic factor as attitude towards voice assistants as it includes elements of enjoyment and entertainment. Considering that voice assistants are relatively newer technology, perceived ease of use, and perceived usefulness of voice assistants will have an impact on their information disclosure using voice assistants.

H2: Ease of use will significantly predict information disclosure through voice assistant.

H3: Usefulness will significantly predict information disclosure through voice assistant.

H4: Attitude towards voice assistants will significantly predict information disclosure through voice assistant.

3 Privacy Concerns in a Digital World

Due to recent large data breaches and increased privacy concerns regarding personal data, about six-in-ten U.S. adults believe it is not possible to go through daily life without having data collected about them by companies or the government (Auxier et al. 2019). Bergström (2015) found that privacy concerns increased with age, while ideological standing and previous internet experience were also predictors of privacy concerns. Experience using mobile applications was also found to moderate the effect of individual preferences and contextual factors on privacy related judgments, suggesting that frequent users of mobile applications have more trust in them (Martin and Shilton 2015). Searches conducted on the Internet, using e-mail, using social media, and using a debit card on the Internet were four major areas of privacy concern for consumers, and trust was found to be the most important factor for each area, such that people who were more inclined to not trust people had greater privacy concerns (Bergström 2015). Trust in mobile advertisers was found to have a positive impact on consumers' mobile commerce activity, even though consumers' concerns about perceived control and unauthorized access to their personal information had a negative influence on mobile commerce activity (Eastin et al. 2016). It is evident that trust has an important relationship with consumers' privacy concerns. Previous research has examined trust towards e-marketers, online vendors, mobile advertisers, i.e. the context of measuring trust involves the actual people communicating with consumers through e-market sites, websites, blogs, etc. However, trust towards the technology itself was not measured specifically. Users tend to disclose more information through their smartphone keypad than through voice assistants; and even when they disclose information voice assistants, they are more likely to disclose non-private rather than private information (Easwara Moorthy and Vu 2015). This could be due to greater privacy concerns regarding information disclosure through voice assistants. Applying the distinction between device and agent, it appears that consumers disclose more information through the device than through the agent. By considering the device as part of the consumer's extended self (Belk 2013), it is logical to conclude that consumers will have more trust in the device than in the agent whose social presence indicates the presence of another being. Therefore, greater trust should indicate lower privacy concerns. Here, it is important to consider the privacy paradox. Norberg et al. (2007), coined the term 'privacy paradox' to explain the phenomenon where consumers express concerns regarding privacy of their information, yet continue to disclose their information to companies. The privacy paradox has primarily been studied as a decision-making process guided by a rational cost-benefit calculation (Barth and Jong 2017). In other words, individuals calculate the risks and benefits associated with activity on mobile devices, apps, and SNSs, and choose to disclose their information after evaluating that the benefits - functionality, app design, costs, outweigh the risks (Barth et al. 2019). Social rewards on SNSs, often seen as more concrete and psychologically near, were significantly related to the self-disclosure behavior as opposed to potential privacy breaches (considered more psychologically distant), which were not significantly related to self-disclosure behavior (Hallam and Zanella 2016). In this case as well, the benefits (social rewards) appear to outweigh the risks (potential privacy breach) associated with information disclosure. While examining voice assistants, it is important to note that in the case of voice assistants functioning through smartphones (Apple's Siri), information disclosure is possible through the agent and the device, but in the case of voice assistants functioning through smart speakers (Amazon's Alexa), information disclosure is only possible through the agent. Therefore, in order to apply the device-agent distinction proposed in this study to understand the discrepancy between information disclosure behavior and privacy concerns, it is more suitable to consider voice assistants functioning through smartphones. As explained earlier, greater trust in the device should lead to lower privacy concerns and greater information disclosure. However, the existence of the privacy paradox indicates that greater privacy concerns will be associated with greater information disclosure. Additionally, lower trust in the agent should lead to greater privacy concerns and lower information disclosure.

H5a: Privacy concerns will have a significant positive relationship with information disclosure through smartphones.

H5b: Privacy concerns will have a significant negative relationship with information disclosure through voice assistants in the case of participants using smartphones to interact with voice assistants.

H6: Privacy concerns will significantly predict information disclosure through smartphones.

Easwara Moorthy and Vu (2015) also found that users were more likely to disclose information through voice assistant in a private versus public setting, and voice assistants functioning through smart speakers are mainly situated in consumers' homes. In that case, lower information disclosure using voice assistants could also be related to the device through which users interact with the voice assistant. As mentioned, smart speakers only function through voice interaction while smartphones also possess touch functions. Brasel (2016) found that touch versus voice interfaces produced different consumer reactions to online content. Touchscreens encouraged the consumer to incorporate technology into their extended self, increasing the feeling that the technology is part of themselves. On the other hand, voice controls established the device as more of a social entity or assistant. This further strengthens this study's argument separating the device and the agent. By incorporating technology into the extended self, the device becomes increasingly transparent in the interaction (Brasel 2016). With the gradual erasure of the technological object or device in the interaction, privacy concerns related to the device would also decrease.

H7: Privacy concerns will be higher for participants who interact with voice assistants through smart speakers than those who interact with voice assistants through smartphones.

4 Methodology

4.1 Procedure

Participants were recruited using an online student participation pool at a public university in South U.S.A, and were asked to fill out a Qualtrics survey regarding their usage of voice assistants, attitude towards information disclosure, and privacy concerns, amongst other things. The study was approximately 15 min in length and 29 incomplete responses were removed from the dataset.

4.2 Sample

A total of 289 participants voluntarily took the survey. After removing incomplete responses, the final sample consisted of 260 participants of whom 80% were female, while the average age was below 20 years (M = 19.91, SD = 1.53). In terms of ethnicity, 72% identified themselves as White, 13% as Asian, 3% as African American, while the remaining 12% identified as 'Other'.

4.3 Measures

Motivations regarding information disclosure using voice assistants was measured using a 16-item 7 point Likert type scale (M = 2.83, SD = 1.18, α = 0.95) adapted from Lee and colleagues (2008). Items included "I disclose information while interacting with voice assistants because it is convenient" and "I disclose information while interacting with voice assistants because it is an efficient use of my time".

Privacy concerns was measured using a 14-item 7 point Likert type scale (M = 5.46, SD = 1.07, α = 0.94) adapted from existing scales (Malhotra, Kim and Agarwal 2004; Shin (2010); Tan and Qin (2012)). Items included "It usually bothers me when online companies ask me for personal information."

Ease of use of voice assistants was measured using a 5-item 7 point Likert type scale (M = 4.59, SD = 1.27, α = 0.9) adapted from Venkatesh and Davis (2000). Items included "My interactions with voice assistants are clear and understandable."

Usefulness of voice assistants was measured using an 8-item 7 point Likert type scale (M = 3.36, SD = 1.24, α = 0.91) adapted from Mclean and Osei-Frimpong (2019). Items included "Completing tasks using a voice assistant fits my schedule."

Attitude towards voice assistants was measured using a 4-item 7 point Likert type scale (M = 4.14, SD = 1.36, α = 0.91) adapted from Mclean and Osei-Frimpong (2019). Items included "I find using my voice assistant to be enjoyable."

Social presence of voice assistants was measured using a 4-item 7 point Likert type scale (M = 2.83, SD = 1.36, α = 0.85) adapted from Mclean and Osei-Frimpong (2019). Items included "When I interact with the voice assistant it feels like someone is present in the room".

Participants were asked "On what device do you interact with your voice assistant the most?" in order to group them according to device usage. 67% said they interacted with their voice assistant through a smartphone, while 25% said they used a smart speaker.

4.4 Analysis

Independent samples t-test was run for H1 and H7. Regression analyses were run for H2, H3, H4, and H6. Correlation tests were run for H5a and H5b.

4.5 Results

People who customized their voice assistants (M = 2.93, SD = 1.42) did not report higher social presence than those who did not customize (M = 2.92, SD = 1.49) their voice assistant (t125 = 0.25, p > 0.05). Therefore, H1 was not proven. However, when turning to H2-H4, ease of use (β = −0.15), usefulness (β = 0.5), and attitude towards voice assistant (β = 0.22) were all significant predictors of information disclosure through voice assistants, explaining 35% of the variance in information disclosure through voice assistants (R = 0.59, F = 34.78, p < 0.05). Thus, H2-H4 were supported by the data.

Turning to privacy concerns, data indicate privacy concerns (β = 0.25) significantly explained 6% of the variance in information disclosure through smartphones (R = 0.25, F = 17.32, p < 0.05). Therefore, H6 was supported by the data. Regarding H5a and H5b, data indicated a significant positive relationship between privacy concerns and information disclosure using smartphones (r = 0.25, p < 0.01), but indicated a non-significant negative relationship between privacy concerns and information disclosure through voice assistants in the case of participants who interacted with voice assistants through their smartphone (r = −0.04, p = 0.58). Thus, H5a was supported but H5b was not.

People who primarily interacted with their voice assistant through smart speakers (M = 5.69, SD = 0.94) reported higher privacy concerns than those who interacted with their voice assistant through a smartphone (M = 5.37, SD = 1.08) (t244 = 2.10, p < 0.05). Therefore, H7 was supported by the data.

5 Discussion

As technology advances at an unprecedented rate, it is becoming increasingly difficult to limit the amount of data and information that is available for companies and apps to access and use. Smart speakers like Amazon Echo and Google Home provide a variety of functions to consumers, but it comes at the cost of their personal data. This study proposed that the increased human-likeness of emerging technology is bringing about a distinction between the device and the agent, such that the consumer's relationship with either is established through different psychological mechanisms. In the case of the device, consumers feel connected to it as it becomes a part of the consumer's extended self, while the social presence of the agent influences the relationship between the agent and the consumer. Customization was expected to increase user agency and lower social presence, however, users who customized their voice assistant did not report lower social presence of voice assistants compared to those who had not customized their voice assistant. Ease of use, usefulness, and hedonic factors were all significant predictors of motivations regarding information disclosure through voice assistant. This was in accordance with both the Technological Acceptance Model and Uses and Gratification Theory. Privacy concerns had a significant positive relationship with information disclosure through smartphones, but had a non-significant negative relationship with information disclosure through voice assistants in the case of participants who used their smartphone to interact with the voice assistant. Privacy concerns also significantly predicted information disclosure through smartphones. Finally, participants who interacted with voice assistants through smart speakers reported higher privacy concerns than those who interacted through smartphones.

This study uses a student sample, and further research should test these observations on a general sample.

References

Auxier, B., Rainie, L., Anderson, M., Perrin, A., Kumar, M., Turner, E.: Americans and privacy: concerned, confused and feeling lack of control over their personal information (2019). https://www.pewresearch.org/internet/2019/11/15/americans-and-privacy-concerned-confused-and-feeling-lack-of-control-over-their-personal-information/

Advertising Research Foundation: 2nd Annual ARF Privacy Study. Advertising Research Foundation, August 2019. https://thearf.org/category/articles/findings-from-the-2nd-annual-arf-pri vacy-study/

Apple: Apple Launches iPhone 4S, iOS 5 & iCloud. Apple.com (2011). https://www.apple.com/pr/library/2011/10/04Apple-Launches-iPhone-4S-iOS-5-iCloud.html

Baca, M.: DoorDash data breach affects 4.9 million users. The Washington Post, 26th September 2019. https://www.washingtonpost.com/technology/2019/09/26/doordash-data-breach-aff ects-million-users/. Accessed 26 Sept

Bonné, B., Rovelo, G., Quax, P., Lamotte, W.: Insecure network, unknown connection: understanding wi-fi privacy assumptions of mobile device users. Information **8**(3), 76 (2017)

Brasel, S.A.: Touching versus talking: alternative interfaces and the extended self. ACR North American Advances (2016)

Barth, S., De Jong, M.D.: The privacy paradox–investigating discrepancies between expressed privacy concerns and actual online behavior–a systematic literature review. Telematics Inform. **34**(7), 1038–1058 (2017)

Barth, S., de Jong, M.D., Junger, M., Hartel, P.H., Roppelt, J.C.: Putting the privacy paradox to the test: online privacy and security behaviors among users with technical knowledge, privacy awareness, and financial resources. Telematics Inform. **41**, 55–69 (2019)

Carolus, A., Schmidt, C., Schneider, F., Mayr, J., Muench, R.: Are People Polite to Smartphones? In: Kurosu, M. (ed.) HCI 2018. LNCS, vol. 10902, pp. 500–511. Springer, Cham (2018). https://doi.org/10.1007/978-3-319-91244-8_39

Carolus, A., Binder, J.F., Muench, R., Schmidt, C., Schneider, F., Buglass, S.L.: Smartphones as digital companions: characterizing the relationship between users and their phones. New Media Soc. **21**(4), 914–938 (2019)

Davis, F.D.: Perceived usefulness, perceived ease of use, and user acceptance of information technology. MIS Q. **13**, 319–340 (1989)

Eastin, M.S., Brinson, N.H., Doorey, A., Wilcox, G.: Living in a big data world: predicting mobile commerce activity through privacy concerns. Comput. Hum. Behav. **58**, 214–220 (2016)

Easwara Moorthy, A., Vu, K.P.L.: Privacy concerns for use of voice activated personal assistant in the public space. Int. J. Hum. Comput. Interact. **31**(4), 307–335 (2015)

Fingas, R.: Apple's Siri ties with Google Assistant for most-used voice assistant. Apple Insider, 29 April 2019. https://appleinsider.com/articles/19/04/29/apples-siri-ties-with-google-assistant-for-most-used-voice-assistant. Accessed 29 Dec

Fogg, B.J., Nass, C.: Silicon sycophants: the effects of computers that flatter. Int. J. Hum. Comput. Stud. **46**, 551–561 (1997)

Fox, J., Ahn, S.J., Janssen, J.H., Yeykelis, L., Segovia, K.Y., Bailenson, J.N.: Avatars versus agents: a meta-analysis quantifying the effect of agency on social influence. Hum. Comput. Interact. **30**(5), 401–432 (2015)

Hallam, C., Zanella, G.: Online self-disclosure: the privacy paradox explained as a temporally discounted balance between concerns and rewards. Comput. Hum. Behav. **68**, 217–227 (2017)

Holmes, A. (2019). https://www.businessinsider.com/biggest-hacks-and-data-breaches-of-2019-capital-one-whatsapp-iphone-2019-9

Katz, E., Blumler, J.G., Gurevitch, M.: Uses and gratifications research. Public Opin. Q. **37**(4), 509–523 (1973)

Kim, Y., Sundar, S.S.: Anthropomorphism of computers: is it mindful or mindless? Comput. Hum. Behav. **28**(1), 241–250 (2012)

Langer, E.J.: Matters of mind: Mindfulness/mindlessness in perspective. Conscious. Cogn. **1**(3), 289–305 (1992)

Lombard, M., Ditton, T.: At the heart of it all: the concept of presence. J. Comput. Mediated Commun. **3**(2), JCMC321 (1997)

Lee, D.H., Im, S., Taylor, C.R.: Voluntary self-disclosure of information on the Internet: a multimethod study of the motivations and consequences of disclosing information on blogs. Psychol. Mark. **25**(7), 692–710 (2008)

Malhotra, N.K., Kim, S.S., Agarwal, J.: Internet users' information privacy concerns (IUIPC): the construct, the scale, and a causal model. Inf. Syst. Res. **15**(4), 336–355 (2004)

Matney, L.: More than 100 million Alexa devices have been sold. Tech Crunch, 4 January 2019. https://techcrunch.com/2019/01/04/more-than-100-million-alexa-devices-have-been-sold/. Accessed 29 Dec

McLean, G., Osei-Frimpong, K.: Hey Alexa… examine the variables influencing the use of artificial intelligent in-home voice assistants. Comput. Hum. Behav. **99**, 28–37 (2019)

Nass, C.: Etiquette equality: exhibitions and expectations of computer politeness. Commun. ACM **47**(4), 35–37 (2004)

Nass, C., Moon, Y.: Machines and mindlessness: social responses to computers. J. Soc. Issues **56**(1), 81–103 (2000)

Nass, C., Steuer, J., Tauber, E.R.: Computers are social actors. In: Proceedings of the SIGCHI conference on Human factors in computing systems, pp. 72–78. ACM (1994a)

Nass, C., Moon, Y., Green, N.: Are computers gender neutral? Gender stereotypic responses to computers. J. Appl. Soc. Psychol. **27**, 864–876 (1997)

Nass, C., Moon, Y., Carney, P.: Are people polite to computers? Responses to computer-based interviewing systems. J. Appl. Soc. Psychol. **29**(5), 1093–1110 (1999)

Norberg, P.A., Horne, D.R., Horne, D.A.: The privacy paradox: personal information disclosure intentions versus behaviors. J. Consum. Aff. **41**(1), 100–126 (2007)

Osei-Frimpong, K., McLean, G.: Examining online social brand engagement: a social presence theory perspective. Technol. Forecast. Soc. Chang. **128**, 10–21 (2018)

Rauschnabel, P.A., He, J., Ro, Y.K.: Antecedents to the adoption of augmented reality smart glasses: a closer look at privacy risks. J. Bus. Res. **92**, 374–384 (2018)

Rauschnabel, P.A., Rossmann, A., Dieck, M.C.T.: An adoption framework for mobile augmented reality games: the case of Pokemon Go. Comput. Hum. Behav. **76**, 276–286 (2017)

Reeves, B., Nass, C.I.: The media equation: How people treat computers, television, and new media like real people and places. Cambridge University Press, Cambridge (1996)

Shin, D.H.: The effects of trust, security and privacy in social networking: a security-based approach to understand the pattern of adoption. Interact. Comput. **22**(5), 428–438 (2010)

Statista: Number of smartphone users in the United States from 2010 to 2023 (in millions)*. In: Statista - The Statistics Portal, May 9 2019. https://www.statista.com/statistics/201182/for ecast-of-smartphone-users-in-the-us/

Sundar, S.S., Marathe, S.S.: Personalization versus customization: the importance of agency, privacy, and power usage. Hum. Commun. Res. **36**(3), 298–322 (2010)

Sundar, S.S.: The MAIN Model: A Heuristic Approach to Understanding Technology Effects on Credibility, pp. 73–100. MacArthur Foundation Digital Media and Learning Initiative, Chicago (2008)

Tan, X., Qin, L.: Impact of privacy concern in social networking web sites. Internet Res. **22**(2), 211–233 (2012)

Tillman, M., O'Boyle, B.: What is Google Assistant and what can it do? Pocket-lint, 8 October 2019. https://www.pocket-lint.com/apps/news/google/137722-what-is-google-assist ant-how-does-it-work-and-which-devices-offer-it. Accessed on 29 Dec

Venkatesh, V., Thong, J.Y., Xu, X.: Consumer acceptance and use of information technology: extending the unified theory of acceptance and use of technology. MIS Q. **36**, 157–178 (2012)

Smart Home Security and Privacy Mitigations: Consumer Perceptions, Practices, and Challenges

Julie M. Haney[1]([✉]), Susanne M. Furman[1], and Yasemin Acar[2]

[1] National Institute of Standards and Technology, 20899 Gaithersburg, MD, USA
{julie.haney,susanne.furman}@nist.gov
[2] Leibniz University Hannover, Hannover, Germany
acar@sec.uni-hannover.de

Abstract. As smart home technology is becoming pervasive, smart home devices are increasingly being used by non-technical users who may have little understanding of the technology or how to properly mitigate privacy and security risks. To better inform security and privacy mitigation guidance for smart home devices, we interviewed 40 smart home users to discover their security and privacy concerns and mitigation strategies. Results indicated a number of concerns, but a general willingness to accept risk in lieu of perceived benefit. Concern was sometimes, but not always, accompanied by users taking mitigating actions, although most of these were simplistic and not technical in nature due to limited options or lack of user technical knowledge. Our results inform how manufacturers might empower users to take protective actions, including providing security tips and more options for controlling data being collected by devices. We also identify areas that might benefit from third-party involvement, for example by providing guidance to manufacturers on minimum privacy and security standards or developing a security and privacy rating system to aid users in selecting devices.

Keywords: Smart home · Internet of Things · Security · Privacy · Usability

1 Introduction

As Internet of Things (IoT) smart home technology is becoming pervasive, smart home devices are increasingly being used by non-technical users [10] who may have little understanding of the technology or awareness of the implications of use, including considerations for privacy and security. Since their inception, smart home devices have become the target of security attacks, placing consumers' data, privacy, and safety at risk [13, 16]. In addition, concerns about the privacy and protection of potentially sensitive consumer data are surfacing [6, 12]. In fact, the U.S. Federal Bureau of Investigation (FBI) recently issued security and privacy warnings about smart televisions and other IoT devices [18, 19]. Therefore, it is critical

© Springer Nature Switzerland AG 2020
A. Moallem (Ed.): HCII 2020, LNCS 12210, pp. 393–411, 2020.
https://doi.org/10.1007/978-3-030-50309-3_26

that users are provided with the means to safeguard their information and households while still enjoying the convenience of these devices.

Unfortunately, smart home device manufacturers may not provide privacy and security protections and configuration options [4], or, if they do, these options may not be transparent to the user. In addition, smart home users may not be knowledgeable enough to discern which mitigations would be most effective, or may only implement simplistic mitigations that might be inadequate [1,11,15,26]. This inadequacy was demonstrated by recent stories of weak user-configured passwords being responsible for parents and children being surveilled and terrorized after their smart home devices were exploited [13].

Understanding consumers' interactions with smart home devices and their current privacy and security mitigation strategies is a first step towards developing guidance for manufacturers and third-party organizations to aid consumers. We sought to gain this understanding via an in-depth interview study of 40 smart home consumers to discover their overall experiences with, perceptions of, and challenges regarding their smart home devices. This paper addresses a subset of research questions (RQs) from the broader study that were focused on security and privacy:

RQ1: What are smart home users' privacy and security concerns, if any?
RQ2: What mitigation actions, if any, do users take to address their concerns?
RQ3: What are the factors affecting users' implementation (or lack of implementation) of privacy and security mitigations?
RQ4: What do users want (actions to take on their own or from others) in order to feel like their privacy and security are adequately protected?

We found that many users have privacy and security concerns but are mostly implementing simplistic mitigations to counter those concerns. However, some smart home users displayed a lack of concern or failed to take mitigation actions even if they do have concerns. The interviews revealed several challenges to the implementation of effective security mitigations, including users having incomplete threat models, privacy resignation, lack of transparency, poor usability of privacy and security-related device features, and lack of user technical knowledge to discern or implement appropriate mitigations. Our study makes several contributions:

- We confirm and expand upon prior studies that investigated smart home users' privacy and security concerns and mitigations [3,20,26] with a larger, more diverse participant sample.
- We identify several mitigations not previously described in the literature, including a more in-depth examination of smart home device updates.
- We distill participants' privacy and security "wishlist," which provides insight into potential areas for improvement in smart home device design and data handling.
- Our results inform how manufacturers and third-party evaluators might provide a more usable security and privacy experience.

2   Related Work

Prior work has examined perceptions of smart home privacy and security. Security and privacy concerns can be barriers to adoption of smart home devices. Lau et al. find that some non-users are privacy conscious and distrustful of privacy and security of smart home devices and their manufacturers, and that smart home devices generally cross these non-users' perceived privacy thresholds [11]. This finding is corroborated by Parks Associates [14], Worthy et al. [25], Emami-Naeini et al. [3], and Fruchter and Liccardy [7], who find that a lack of trust in vendors to properly safeguard personal data is a major obstacle to adoption of smart home technology. From a broader IoT perspective, Williams et al. [24] found that IoT is viewed as less privacy-respecting than non-IoT devices such as desktops, laptops, and tablets.

Adopters were found to share the same concerns, and often expressed a lack of agency in the control of their data [11]. However, they generally have higher tolerances for privacy violations, and willingly or reluctantly accept the trade-off in exchange for the convenience and utility offered by smart home devices [11]. They are generally more trusting towards well-known manufacturers and often express that they have "nothing to hide" [11,20]. They also have complex, but incomplete threat models, which includes a general sense of being surveilled by manufacturers or the government, and the possibility of being attacked by hackers, but a lack of awareness of botnets and the sale of inferred data [1,3,27]. A main security concern was the possibility of a breach in the cloud that would expose user data [20].

Multiple studies discovered both technical and non-technical mitigations to address security and privacy concerns, for example passwords, secure configurations for the home network, and altering behavior around the devices [1,11, 15,20,26]. However, they also identified lack of action. Reasons may be lack of awareness and availability of these options, privacy resignation, trust in the manufacturers, and assignment of responsibility to entities other than the users themselves [11,20,26].

Our study confirms many of the findings identified in prior literature while identifying additional mitigations such as device selection, access control, and updates. In addition, unlike other studies, we collected a wish list of mitigations that can help inform manufacturers and other entities in making privacy and security protections for smart home devices more usable for consumers.

3   Methods

We conducted semi-structured interviews of 40 smart home consumers to understand their perceptions of and experiences with smart home devices from purchase decision, to implementation, to everyday usage. The in-depth interviews afforded more detailed data than could be collected via anonymous surveys and the ability to ask follow-up questions to explore responses [2]. To protect participants' confidentiality, data were recorded with generic identifiers (such as P10) and not linked back to individuals. The study was approved by the National Institute of Standards and Technology (NIST) research protections office.

We hired a consumer research company to recruit 33 general public participants, and identified seven participants via professional contacts. To determine study eligibility, adult participants interested in the study completed an online screening survey about their smart home devices, role with the devices (i.e., decision maker, purchaser, installer, administrator, troubleshooter, or user), professional background, basic demographic information, and number of household members. To ensure information-rich cases, we then purposefully selected participants who had two or more smart home devices for which they were active users.

The interview protocol addressed the following areas: understanding smart home terminology, purchase and general use, likes and dislikes, installation and troubleshooting, privacy, security, and physical safety. Interviews lasted an average of 41 min. Prior to the interviews, we informed the participants about the study and how we would protect their data by not recording any personal identifiers that could be linked back to the participant. All interviews were audio recorded and transcribed. General public participants were compensated with a $75 gift card.

Using widely-accepted qualitative data analysis methods [9], all three authors individually coded a subset of four interviews, then met to develop and operationalize a codebook to identify concepts within the data. Based on the codebook, we then performed iterative coding on the remainder of the interviews, with two coders per transcript. Each pair of coders met to discuss and resolve areas of difference in code application. As a group, we then progressed to the recognition of relationships among the codes and examined patterns and categories to identify themes. In this paper, we focus on themes related to privacy and security mitigations and concerns.

4   Participant Demographics

We interviewed 40 participants, 32 of whom were the installers and administrators of the devices (indicated with an A after the participant ID) and eight who were non-administrative users of the devices (indicated with a U). 55% were male, and 45% were female. Multiple age ranges were represented, with the majority (70%) between the ages of 30 and 49. Overall, participants were highly educated with all but one having at least a bachelor's degree and almost half (45%) having at a graduate degree. Table 1 shows participant demographics.

All but one participant had three or more individual smart home devices, with 34 (85%) having three or more different types of devices. Figure 1 shows the general categories of smart home devices in participants' homes. Represented categories, along with examples of devices in that category, were:

Table 1. Participant Demographics. ID: A - smart home administrators/installers, U - smart home users; Education: M - Master's degree, B - Bachelor's degree, C - some college, H - High school.

ID	Gender	Age	Education	Occupation
P1_A	F	50–59	M	Liaison
P2_A	M	30–39	M	Lead engineer
P3_A	F	40–49	M	Professor
P4_A	M	60+	M	Retired
P6_U	F	30–39	B	Events manager
P7_A	M	30–39	B	Software engineer
P8_A	M	30–39	B	Federal employee
P9_A	F	30–39	M	Educationist
P10_A	M	30–39	B	Computer scientist
P11_A	M	50–59	M	Electrical engineer
P12_U	F	30–39	M	Administrative assistant
P13_A	M	50–59	M	Manager, Cognitive scientist
P14_U	F	40–49	H	Information specialist
P15_A	M	30–39	B	Computer scientist
P16_A	M	40–49	M	Research chief
P17_A	F	30–39	M	Systems engineer
P18_A	M	30–39	B	Business consultant
P19_A	M	50–59	B	Retail services specialist
P20_A	F	30–39	B	Administrator
P21_U	F	18–29	B	Human resources manager
P22_A	M	30–39	B	Executive admin assistant
P23_A	F	40–49	M	Community arts specialist
P24_A	M	40–49	B	Operational safety analyst
P25_A	M	30–39	B	Program management analyst
P26_A	M	30–39	B	Analyst
P27_A	F	40–49	M	Program coordinator
P28_A	F	50–59	B	Consultant
P29_A	M	18–29	M	Events coordinator
P30_U	F	18–29	B	Event planner
P31_A	F	30–39	M	Lobbyist
P32_A	M	30–39	B	Health educator
P33_A	M	18–29	B	Senior technology analyst
P34_A	M	40–49	B	Financial analyst
P35_A	M	40–49	M	Accountant
P36_A	F	30–39	B	Project manager
P37_A	F	40–49	M	Assistant principal
P38_U	F	60+	M	Special educator
P39_U	M	60+	M	Retired
P40_U	F	30–39	C	Customer service rep
P41_A	M	40–49	B	Security

Smart security: security cameras, motion detectors, door locks.

Smart entertainment: smart televisions, speakers, streaming devices, other connected media systems.

Home environment: smart plugs, energy monitors, lighting, smoke and air quality sensors, thermostats.

Smart appliances: refrigerators, coffee pots, robot vacuums, washers.

Virtual assistants: voice-controlled devices such as Amazon Echo (colloquially called Amazon Alexa) and Google Home.

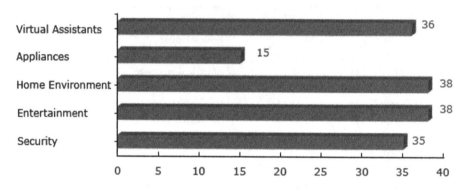

Fig. 1. Types of Smart Home devices owned by participants.

5   Results

In this section, we report results from a subset of the interview data specific to privacy and security concerns, mitigations, and mitigation wish lists. Counts of the number of participants mentioning various concepts are provided in some cases to illustrate weight or unique cases and are not an attempt to reduce our qualitative data to quantitative measures.

5.1   Concerns

We present an overview of concerns identified in our study to provide context for what our participants believe might need to be addressed by mitigations. Participants' privacy and security concerns are summarized in Table 2. For each concern in the table, we include whether the concern was discussed in a privacy or security context (or both), the number of participants mentioning each concern, and an example participant quote to illustrate the concern.

The most frequently mentioned concerns that were discussed within both the privacy and security contexts included: audio and video access via smart home devices such as virtual assistants and cameras; data breaches of the manufacturer; foreign and domestic government access to data; and exposure of financial information via smart home device credentials and apps. Participants

Table 2. Smart Home Privacy and Security Concerns. # - number of participants mentioning the concern

	Concern	#	Example participant quote
Security and Privacy	Audio/video access	34	*"I was reading some article where [a virtual assistant] listens in on some of the conversations we have in our house without it being awake... That kind of freaks me out in the sense that we could be talking about something, and they have that information." (P21_U)*
	Data breaches	17	*"Manufactures can say they can protect things, but in reality, if someone wants something bad enough, I don't know if they really can." (P33_A)*
	Government access	12	*"I would hate to sound like a conspiracy theorist, but I'm pretty sure the government and places like that can actually see what you do." (P14_U)*
	Exposure of financial information	8	*"I wouldn't want anybody committing fraud and taking my credit card information to do things they shouldn't be doing." (P37_A)*
Privacy	Household profiling	19	*"If someone was in control of this [device], they might be able to know what my schedule is, when I'm usually home, when the house is empty." (P34_A)*
	Selling data	17	*"That's what I'm really afraid of, is them packaging my information to get trends and marketing it." (P13_A)*
	Unknowns of data collection	16	*"I'm concerned because I think we're unaware of the types of information that these smart devices store of us or have of us." (P21_U)*
Security	Device hacking	22	*"There's some just people who are really smart and they're sitting somewhere, all they're thinking about is how to get into stuff... And if people could hack into the Department of Defense, they can hack into yours." (P28_A)*
	Safety	17	*"It could be life threatening... If you rely on the smart device to keep your home locked,... if it does misfunction, there could be extreme circumstances." (P19_U)*
	Gaining Wi-Fi access	6	*"Many of these devices, you're giving it your network password, so it has full access to everything on your network." (P11_A)*
	Linked accounts	4	*"If you use a password commonly across different accounts, the same password, if that gets hacked... If I log into my Google account they might be able to get in because I might use the same exact password and user name." (P2_A)*
	Poor default security settings	2	*"I would be disturbed if I saw a device that, for example, had a password you couldn't change or restricted you to something like a 4-digit key code that's more easily hacked." (P15_A)*
	Update issues	2	*"I guess one area where I would be worried about would be adding features that may threaten my privacy and security." (P15_A)*

talked about the following privacy-specific concerns: household habit profiling; the selling of data and targeted ads; and unknowns about what data is being collected and how it is being used. Security-specific concerns included: general exploitation/hacking of devices; physical security/safety; gaining access to the Wi-Fi network and other devices on that network via smart home devices; gaining access to linked accounts (e.g., email or social media accounts) by exploiting device apps; poor default security settings (e.g., default passwords); and updates potentially having harmful consequences.

We also found examples of various levels of lack of concern, with seven participants having neither privacy nor security concerns. In 24 cases, participants did not think that the information collected by smart home devices was valuable or interesting to others. For example, one participant commented, *"I live a life that you could probably watch. I could probably have cameras in my house, and I wouldn't feel guilty about that... That's a concern I know some people have. But I didn't have an issue with that"* (P2_A). We also identified evidence of participants exhibiting privacy and security resignation [11,17] (8 participants). They are of the opinion that, since so much of their data is already publicly available via other means (e.g., social media, data breaches), smart home devices pose no additional risk. One smart home user said, *"I do dislike having all of my information out there, but I think that, regardless of these smart devices, it's already out there"* (P17_A). Finally, five participants viewed exploitation of devices (hacking) as a low-probability event. This feeling was often tied to them not valuing information collected by smart home devices: *"Somebody would have to pluck us at random to really be at risk"* (P25_A).

Ultimately, even if they had concerns, participants were more than willing to accept privacy and security risks because of the perceived benefits. One participant commented, *"It's an acceptable risk if you don't think you're doing anything that's illegal or bad. It's not like I do anything weird in front of the TV besides exercise, and nobody wants to see that"* (P14_U). Another said, *"It makes my life easier, so I will continue to do it unless I have a major security concern that comes up"* (P17_A).

5.2   Mitigations

Our study discovered a variety of mitigations that participants or others in their household implement to address privacy and security concerns. All mitigations were mentioned in both the privacy and security contexts. Figure 2 shows the number of participants mentioning each mitigation. We describe the mitigations in more detail below.

Authentication. Participants mentioned using various forms of authentication (e.g., passwords, face recognition, two-factor) when asked what actions they take to address their concerns. However, this action was typically not a user choice, but rather prompted during installation. Authentication was most often referenced with regards to the device companion apps, which are often controlled via a cellphone.

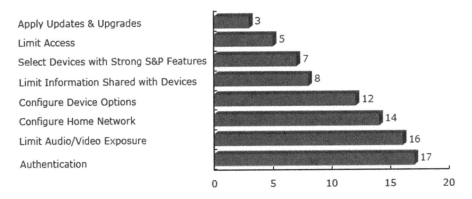

Fig. 2. Security and Privacy mitigations mentioned by participants.

Passwords were the most common authentication mechanism afforded by device companion apps, and often the only mitigation mentioned. One participant said that he addressed his concerns by *"password protecting the devices so nobody can connect to them... It's not very convenient, but... that's what I need to do" (P20_A)*. Several participants specifically discussed their attempts at having strong passwords: *"I have my own unique passwords that aren't dictionary words, so that's how I mitigate" (P10_A)*. Another participant used a password manager for her smart home device apps. Two others said that they made sure that they change any default passwords during installation.

Only one participant mentioned two-factor authentication in the context of mitigations: *"If I know that I can do two factor authentication for something, I'll do that" (P2_A)*. When asked about how they authenticate to their devices in a later, separate question, only one additional participant mentioned two-factor authentication, which was an option offered by his smart thermostat.

Limiting Audio and Video Exposure. To address concerns about audio and video being exposed to manufacturers or unauthorized users, study participants mostly mentioned non-technical mitigations. They were careful about where they placed cameras and virtual assistants, avoiding more private rooms in the house. For example, one participant talked about the location of his virtual assistant: *"Bedrooms are just a little more personal. I make sure not to keep it there because... if it does record, I don't want maybe those conversations and things that happened in the bedroom to be on there" (P32_A)*. Several participants were also cognizant of not having sensitive conversations in the vicinity of listening devices: *"I try to keep [my virtual assistant] in a central location and kind of avoid being close to it when having certain conversations" (P22_A)*. Others covered cameras not being used. For instance, a participant remarked that her husband took action: *"The [virtual assistant] device has a video camera that you can use, but he's taped it over" (P1_A)*. Finally, several users turned off devices in certain circumstances. One user talked about how her husband unplugs their virtual assistants when he is teleworking to guard against potentially sensitive conversations being recorded. Another said, *"With the security camera, sometimes I switch it off. . . It's when I'm really like out of town, that's when I like to switch it on back again"* (P34_A).

Network Configuration. The security and privacy of smart home devices can be contingent on the security of the home network. There were a few advanced users that mentioned more sophisticated network security mitigations, for example, segmenting their home network, installing virtual private networks (VPNs), or monitoring network traffic. For example, a do-it-yourselfer who customizes his smart home devices was diligent in securing his home network: *"I have a protective network where all these devices live in, and you can't get to it from the outside. I can get to it from within my house, and if I have to I can get to it via a VPN from the outside"* (P16_A). Another also made use of VPNs *"to mask the IP address. It's not that I'm doing anything illegal. . . It's just I don't feel like being tracked"* (P20_A).

However, most participants' extent of network security configuration was to password-protect their Wi-Fi. One participant commented, *"When it comes to my internet that I use to connect a lot of them, you know, it is password protected. So you know, it's not like anyone can just log on and use my network"* (P32_A). Another said, *"I'm always switching passwords with my Wi-Fi"* (P34_A).

Option Configuration. Twelve participants configured options that were at least loosely related to privacy and security. This mostly entailed disabling default functionality. For example, one participant disabled online ordering on her virtual assistant: *"We have cut off some functionality just to prevent the $400 order of mystery items"* (P1_A). A tech-savvy participant mitigated his concerns by *"turning off certain features that I think might share more information or provide more access to the device than is necessary"* (P15_A), giving the example of how he had disabled the microphone in his smart TV. Another participant was one of the few who knew about options in virtual assistants to limit audio recording usage: *"For the [virtual assistant], it records everything. But I did see one of the options was to regularly delete it every day or something, so that kind of took the concern off the table"* (P27_A).

Limiting Shared Information. Eight participants mentioned limiting the information they share with device manufacturers, mostly when setting up companion apps. A participant said, *"I have my email address that I use for signing up for accounts that I'm never going to check and email address that I use for signing up for things that I actually care about. The latter is a very small number"* (P17_A). Another remarked, *"When it comes to, especially I think my [virtual assistant], I don't keep certain information stored on it. Like, I know some people will keep their actual address or even sometimes even credit card information to be able to buy things right away"* (P32_A). One participant discussed using false information when setting up her smart home device app accounts: *"I always put in fake birthdays... You need to know I'm eighteen, but you don't need to know everything" (P37_A)*.

Device Selection. Some participants were proactive in their mitigation efforts by considering security and privacy in their purchase decisions. One participant remarked that, prior to selecting devices, he *"paid a lot of close attention to the security of those devices and what's happening with the data, what sorts of data they might record, how others might be able to access the system" (P15_A)*. Another commented on the importance of buying secure devices: *"Even if you have to spend more money to get more into that security, we would definitely do that as we are so much dependent on this. We have to protect ourselves" (P9_A)*. Others made decisions based on whether or not they trusted particular manufacturers to provide secure products. For example, a participant commented, *"I'm looking for devices that, if they're going to communicate with a cloud service, they use a well-known cloud service" (P11_A)*. One made the conscious choice to buy products from well-known, larger companies: *"These are pretty big companies... We're paying money for the brand itself... Maybe that's why I'm feeling a little more secure than not... If something happens, hopefully, they have the money to figure it out" (P6_U)*.

Limiting Access. Five participants made a variety of attempts to limit access to smart home devices and their apps. Three discussed limiting access of devices by visitors and service providers entering the house. One discussed making decisions on which device to use for potentially sensitive tasks, for example, *"I don't place orders via [my virtual assistant]... I do everything mostly on my computer, which has a VPN on it" (P14_U)*. Another mentioned securing access to her cellphone (which contained device companion apps) as a mitigation:

> *"I'm very secure with my phone. I make sure that it's not easily accessible... I keep my phone right on me, I don't set it down, I don't let people look at stuff, I don't access the [public Wi-Fi] internet in other areas when I'm using those apps" (P37_A)*.

Updates. Although updates can be a powerful mitigation against device vulnerabilities, only three participants mentioned updates or upgrades in the context of mitigations. A user said, *"I found that I'm updating everything a lot more... just kind of keeping up with the technology because it is so important" (P31_A)*. A do-it-yourselfer purchased a smart camera with dubious ties to a foreign government, so he *"modified the firmware so it's no longer using the [untrusted] web service or cloud service" (P11_A)*.

Prior to the security and privacy portions of the interviews, we asked participants about their experiences with device updates. Participants rarely associated updates with security or privacy and mentioned that they often do not know whether updates are available or have been installed due to inconsistent notifications and user interfaces. While updates are often viewed as potentially being security-related with traditional IT products (e.g., Microsoft's "Patch Tuesday"), we did not find that same association in our study. In addition, users often do not apply updates if they feel their devices are still working without issue. These findings indicate both a usability problem and a perception that updates are only functionality-based and not related to security.

Lack of Mitigations. We also discovered reasons for participants not implementing mitigations. Several participants cited a lack of privacy/security options or them not being aware of available options: *"Usually the description of the controls aren't specific enough... They're like, 'Check this for our privacy settings,' and sometimes the description of the settings aren't very specific" (P13_U)*. Similar to reasons behind lack of concern, users often exhibited resignation and feelings of lack of control: *"I wish we could [limit data collection], but I don't think there'll ever be a way to control it" (P12_U)*. Others cited a lack of knowledge or skill, especially with respect to cybersecurity: *"I'm not going to educate myself on network security... This stuff is not my forte. I'm very accepting to the fact that it is what it is" (P8_A)*. Of course, some participants were simply not concerned enough to take any kind of action: *"I go on faith that they don't find me interesting enough. I guess that's it" (P23_A)*.

5.3   Mitigation Wish List

Even though users have ultimately accepted privacy and security risks by introducing the devices into their homes, we found that they still desire greater control, especially with respect to privacy. We asked participants what they would like to do to protect their smart home privacy and security but are not doing, cannot do, or do not know how to do. Examination of the participant "wish list" provides insight into what would make users feel more empowered to take mitigating action and what options or instructional information they think manufacturers should provide.

Data Collection Transparency. Users desire manufacturers to be more forthcoming about what data is being collected, where it is going, and how it is being used (mentioned by 12 participants). Manufacturers claim that user level agreements provide this information. However, participants said that they rarely read the long agreements and generally do not find those useful because they are in *"lawyer speak. You don't really know what they're collecting because they can use language to mislead you" (P31_U)*. The lack of transparency leaves users wanting more: *"At least give us notice in terms of who has access to it... We would appreciate that and make us feel more comfortable around the security behind it" (P21_U)*. One user desired a more concise, clear statement of data usage: *"if these companies provided a manifesto of what information they're interested in or how they use information and how they're collecting information and provide* *that - a one pager - that would be great"* (P2_A). Realizing that it might not be in manufacturers' best interest to clearly disclose data usage, P31_A saw the government as having a role since *"we've got to do something to protect people's information, or at least make them more aware of what exactly is being utilized and sold."*

Privacy and Security Controls. Ten participants would like more control over the devices and data. This includes the ability to opt in/out of various data collections, limit how data is shared, and configure security and other privacy options. For example, a participant remarked, *"there would be some of these products that I have been avoiding purchasing that I might purchase if they provided more granular control over... all aspects of the security and privacy"* (P15_A). Another participant said he would like to be able to use two-factor authentication for his devices' companion apps: *"There would be features that would be nice to have, I guess one being a two-factor authentication. If my phone is close to my thermostat, that's my second factor"* (P10_A). Options should also be easy-to-configure, as mentioned by one participant: *"I think the ability to control that data should be simpler than a multi-step process"* (P29_A).

Technically advanced users were more specific about what they would like to do and wanted granular controls. A computer scientist said, *"I would really be happy actually if a lot of them had APIs [application programming interfaces] that I could use to directly program their behavior and get more control over them programmatically"* (P15_A). An electrical engineer commented:

> *"I'd like to have the ability to potentially allow or disallow the functionality of all these devices, maybe at given times. I'd like to be able to define what are allowable communications or protocols"* (P11_A).

Five participants wished that they had the ability to keep smart home data on their local network when possible instead of the common business model of data being sent to manufacturers or their cloud services. A participant said, *"If I could not have accounts and just have it on my own home network, I would prefer that"* (P17_A). P15_A commented that he wished *"some of these devices used the voice control features locally only rather than sending clips of your voice over the Internet to be analyzed."*

Security Feature Transparency. Four participants would like to know the level of security provided by the devices. One stated, *"it would be nice to know what security features are already there because they're not advertised or transparent at all. And maybe to have an option to get some kind of enhanced security if you wanted to"* (P24_A). Wishing to know if he needed to bolster the security of his home network to counter potentially weak smart home security, another participant said, *"I wish I knew more about what kind of encryption they use"* (P3_A).

Assistance for Users. Within the security context, four participants expressed their desire to be provided with suggestions and instructions on how to better secure their devices. A participant unfamiliar with security best practices commented, *"I think I need to be advised on good practices that I could take. . . And then I probably would implement them"* (P35_A). Another suggested, *"maybe the apps that I have could throw out reminders in a more frequent manner that says are you doing something like this to protect yourself?"* (P19_A). A heavy user of smart home devices said that he would like to know how best to protect his devices against vulnerabilities: *"I would like the vulnerability identified well enough so I know what it is and then some directions on how to solve it"* (P13_A).

6 Implications

The users we interviewed were diverse in their mitigation approaches to smart home devices. Some were proactive from a privacy and security perspective and knowledgeable about the technology. Others had very little understanding of the technology and implications of use. Our results suggest that users do the best they can with the skills and the options available to them.

Most of the mitigations identified in our study were simplistic (e.g., setting passwords) or not technical in nature (e.g., placement of devices). From a privacy perspective, participants expressed the desire to be able to control what happens to their data but do not know what options are available, or, in many cases, no options exist. Security concepts and implications were more difficult for participants to grasp, with many lacking the knowledge to implement effective mitigations, for example, by properly securing their home networks. Overall, we observed that many of the participants were left with a feeling of discomfort because they had privacy and security concerns but felt powerless to address those.

Based on study results, we describe possible ways in which manufacturers could empower users to make appropriate security choices through usable interfaces and where further research may be helpful. We also identify areas that could benefit from third-party evaluation and guidance.

6.1 Considerations for Usable Security and Privacy Options

Participants' current mitigation strategies (or lack thereof) and their wish lists for privacy and security can inform what additional options manufacturers could provide and other areas where they might alleviate user burden by defaulting to strong privacy and security.

Note that since our interview study was broader than privacy and security, we had the opportunity to delve into users' installation and administration experiences with their smart home devices. Participants revealed that they rarely change settings after initial setup. Therefore, additional research may be warranted to investigate if installation is the best time to prompt users on security and privacy options.

Secure and Private by Default: As revealed in prior usable security research, people are often reluctant to change default security settings [28, 29]. Therefore, to alleviate undue burden on users, there may be settings which manufacturers could configure to be the most secure/private by default. However, more research should be conducted to understand how setting defaults to the most secure/private options may contribute to or detract from usability.

Opt In/Out: Currently, opting out of data collection and various uses may not be possible or may be burdensome. For example, P17_A said that one manufacturer required a letter be mailed requesting to limit data sharing. Based on participants desiring more control on data usage, more research is needed regarding how manufacturers could offer easy-to-configure opt in/out options.

Data Usage Transparency: Device privacy policies and user agreements are rarely read and difficult to understand, leaving users uninformed about data collection practices. Manufacturers could provide greater transparency about what data is collected, where the data goes, how long it is stored, and who it is shared with.

Data Localization: Our participants were often concerned about manufacturer profiling of their households, selling of their data, and possible data breaches of manufacturer data storage. To counter these concerns, manufacturers could provide options to localize whatever data processing can be localized instead of sending everything to the manufacturer's cloud.

Securability: In situations where security settings might be dependent on user context, there could be a focus on "securability," which is the "ability and knowledge to enable and configure the appropriate security features" [23]. To achieve product securability, manufacturers could facilitate secure use by providing users with real-time assistance, such as configuration wizards, to help them set the level of security appropriate for their situation. For example, users might be given the option of configuring low, medium, and high levels of security based on clear criteria (e.g., network environment, context of use, risk tolerance) gleaned through a security configuration wizard. The securability concept can also be applied to privacy settings.

Granular Options for Advanced Users: We interviewed several advanced users who were well-versed in technology and security. These users wanted more control over security settings. Therefore, in addition to supporting less technical users with guided wizards and instructions, manufacturers could offer more granular security controls for those who want them. We acknowledge that striking the right balance between an abundance of granular options and a minimal set for less-technical users may be difficult. Therefore, we recommend additional research into interface solutions that may attempt to balance these considerations.

Update Transparency: Updates are especially important as they might be the only mitigations for certain kinds of smart home device vulnerabilities (e.g., those in the code). In line with the NIST Interagency Report 8267 (Draft) Security

Review of Consumer Home Internet of Things (IoT) Products [5] recommendation that users receive update notifications in a timely manner, manufacturers might either provide an option for automatic updates or push notifications to users with clear installation instructions and descriptions of the importance of applying the update.

Network Security Tips: Home networks need to be secured to protect smart home devices. However, people often lack the knowledge and motivation to take action. For example, the FBI recommends that users segment their network [13] even though few participants in our study had the technical knowledge to be able to do so. Several of our study participants said they would like manufacturers to provide step-by-step tips on home network security (e.g., setting up secure Wi-Fi, password-protecting all devices on the network) that complement the security options provided by the devices themselves.

6.2   Third-Party Opportunities

Our results suggest that users may be open to third-party organizations (e.g., government agencies, industry groups, standards organizations) playing a bigger role in suggesting guidance for manufacturers concerning the usability of smart home security and privacy features and options. For example, the guidance produced by NIST [4,5] provides recommendations but emphasizes that these should be tailored to specific contexts of use while not placing undue burden on the user.

The wide variety of mitigations mentioned by participants may also indicate a need for more standardization of privacy and security best practices for smart home users by trusted third parties (e.g., government agencies or an IoT industry consortium). To help users understand privacy and security implications of smart home devices, we also recommend exploring the usability considerations of having an independent, third-party ratings system similar to that which has been proposed by the Canadian Internet Society [21] and the U.S. Government Departments of Commerce and Homeland Security [22]. This ratings system would help consumers to make informed decisions about which devices to bring into their homes.

7   Limitations

In addition to typical limitations of interview studies (e.g., recall, self-report, and social desirability biases), our study may be limited in generalizability. The small sample of participants, the majority of whom were well-educated individuals living in a high-income metropolitan area, may not be fully representative of the U.S. smart home user population. However, our study population appears to mirror early adopters of smart home devices, which have been characterized in prior industry surveys [8]. We also recognize that smart home users in the U.S. may have different privacy and security attitudes from users in other countries because of political or cultural factors, for example those related to privacy expectations. Finally, our study does not capture perceptions of those choosing not to adopt smart home technologies or limited adopters (those with only one device). Non-adopters' and limited adopters' perceptions of privacy and security could shed light on additional areas needing improvement. However, even given the limitations, our exploratory study is a solid step in investigating smart home users' perceptions and practices and can inform subsequent surveys of broader populations, for example via quantitative surveys distributed in multiple countries.

8 Conclusion

We interviewed 40 smart home users to discover their security and privacy concerns and mitigation strategies. Results indicated a number of concerns, but a willingness to accept risk in exchange for perceived benefit. Concern was sometimes, but not always, accompanied by users taking mitigating actions, although most of these actions were simplistic due to limited options or lack of user technical knowledge.

Improving the security and privacy of smart home devices will be critical as adoption of these technologies increase. Efforts should be joint between consumers, manufacturers, and third-party organizations with special consideration made for designing usable interfaces that empower users to take protective actions while not overburdening them.

Disclaimer

Certain commercial companies or products are identified in this paper to foster understanding. Such identification does not imply recommendation or endorsement by the National Institute of Standards and Technology, nor does it imply that the companies or products identified are necessarily the best available for the purpose.

References

1. Abdi, N., Ramokapane, K.M., Such, J.M.: More than smart speakers: security and privacy perceptions of smart home personal assistants. In: Proceedings of the Fifteenth Symposium on Usable Privacy and Security (2019)
2. Corbin, J., Strauss, A.: Basics of Qualitative Research: Techniques and Procedures for Developing Grounded Theory, 4th edn. Sage Publications, Thousand Oaks (2015)
3. Emami-Naeini, P., Dixon, H., Agarwal, Y., Cranor, L.F.: Exploring how privacy and security factor into IoT device purchase behavior. In: Proceedings of the 2019 CHI Conference on Human Factors in Computing Systems. ACM (2019)
4. Fagan, M., Megas, K.N., Scarfone, K., Smith, M.: NISTIR 8259 Foundational Cybersecurity Activities for IoT Device Manufacturers (2020). https://csrc.nist.gov/publications/detail/nistir/8259/final
5. Fagan, M., Yang, M., Tan, A., Randolph, L., Scarfone, K.: Draft NISTIR 8267 security review of consumer home Internet of Things (IoT) products (2019). https://nvlpubs.nist.gov/nistpubs/ir/2019/NIST.IR.8267-draft.pdf

6. Federal Trade Commission: VIZIO to pay \$2.2 Million to FTC, State of New Jersey to settle charges it collected viewing histories on 11 million smart televisions without users' consent (2017). https://www.ftc.gov/news-events/press-releases/2017/02/vizio-pay-22-million-ftc-state-new-jersey-settle-charges-it

7. Fruchter, N., Liccardi, I.: Consumer attitudes towards privacy and security in home assistants. In: Extended Abstracts of the 2018 CHI Conference on Human Factors in Computing Systems. ACM (2018)

8. GfK: future of smart home study global report (2016). https://www.gfk.com

9. Glaser, B.G., Strauss, A.L.: Discovery of Grounded Theory: Strategies for Qualitative Research. Routledge, London (2017)

10. GutCheck: Smart home device adoption (2018). https://resource.gutcheckit.com/smart-home-device-adoption-au-ty

11. Lau, J., Zimmerman, B., Schaub, F.: Alexa, are you listening?: privacy perceptions, concerns and privacy-seeking behaviors with smart speakers. In: Proceedings of the ACM on Human-Computer Interaction. ACM (2018)

12. Lee, T.B.: Amazon admits that employees review small "sample" of Alexa audio, April 2019. https://arstechnica.com/tech-policy/2019/04/amazon-admits-that-employees-review-small-sample-of-alexa-audio/

13. Murdock, J.: Ring security cameras pose a threat to families and the public, privacy campaigners claim amid surge in hack attacks, December 2019. https://www.newsweek.com/amazon-ring-camera-hacking-privacy-groups-fight-future-threat-families-public-1477709

14. Parks associates: state of the market: smart home and connected entertainment (2019). http://www.parksassociates.com/bento/shop/whitepapers/files/ParksAssoc-OpenHouseOverview2018.pdf

15. PwC: smart home, seamless life, January 2017. https://www.pwc.fr/fr/assets/files/pdf/2017/01/pwc-consumer-intelligence-series-iot-connected-home.pdf

16. Security Research Labs: Smart spies: Alexa and Google Home expose users to vishing and eavesdropping (2019). https://srlabs.de/bites/smart-spies/

17. Stanton, B., Theofanos, M.F., Prettyman, S.S., Furman, S.: Security fatigue. IT Prof. **18**(5), 26–32 (2016)

18. Steele, B.A.: Oregon FBI Tech Tuesday: securing smart TVs, November 2019. https://www.fbi.gov/contact-us/field-offices/portland/news/press-releases/tech-tuesdaysmart-tvs

19. Steele, B.A.: Tech Tuesday: Internet of things (IoT), December 2019. https://www.fbi.gov/contact-us/field-offices/portland/news/press-releases/tech-tuesday-internet-of-things-iot

20. Tabassum, M., Kosinski, T., Lipford, H.R.: "I don't own the data": end user perceptions of smart home device data practices and risks. In: Fifteenth Symposium on Usable Privacy and Security (2019)

21. The Internet Society: Securing the Internet of Things: a Canadian multistakeholder process draft report (2019). https://iotsecurity2018.ca/wp-content/uploads/2019/02/Enhancing-IoT-Security-Draft-Outcomes-Report.pdf

22. U.S. Departments of Commerce and Homeland Security: A report to the president on enhancing the resilience of the internet and communications ecosystem against botnets and other automated, distributed threats, May 2018. https://www.commerce.gov/page/report-president-enhancing-resilience-against-botnets

23. Vasserman, E., Fitzgerald, B.: Cyber-"securability", presentation at FDA Science Forum, September 2019

24. Williams, M., Nurse, J.R., Creese, S.: Privacy is the boring bit: user perceptions and behaviour in the Internet-of-Things. In: 15th Annual Conference on Privacy, Security and Trust, pp. 181–18109. IEEE (2017)
25. Worthy, P., Matthews, B., Viller, S.: Trust me: doubts and concerns living with the internet of things. In: ACM Conference on Designing Interactive Systems, pp. 427–434. ACM (2016)
26. Zeng, E., Mare, S., Roesner, F.: End user security and privacy concerns with smart homes. In: Thirteenth Symposium on Usable Privacy and Security (2017)
27. Zheng, S., Apthorpe, N., Chetty, M., Feamster, N.: User perceptions of smart home IoT privacy. In: Proceedings of the ACM on Human-Computer Interaction, vol. 2, no. CSCW (2018)
28. Zurko, M.E.: User-centered security: stepping up to the grand challenge. In: Proceedings of the 21st Annual Computer Security Applications Conference, p. 14 (2005)
29. Zurko, M.E., Kaufman, C., Spanbauer, K., Bassett, C.: Did you ever have to make up your mind? what notes users do when faced with a security decision. In: Proceedings of the 18th Annual Computer Security Applications Conference, pp. 371–381 (2002)

Multi-method Approach Measuring Trust, Distrust, and Suspicion in Information Technology

Sarah A. Jessup[1], Gene M. Alarcon[1]([✉]), August Capiola[1], and Tyler J. Ryan[2]

[1] Air Force Research Laboratory, Wright-Patterson AFB, Dayton, OH, USA
gene.alarcon.1@us.af.mil
[2] General Dynamics Information Technology, Dayton, OH 45431, USA

Abstract. In two studies, we examined the measurement of complex state variables with length of response, construct word counts, Likert-type responding, self-reports of past behaviors, and implicit associations. In the first study, participants were primed to write in a control condition and a suspicion condition, which were also used as referents for self-reports, past behaviors, and priming for implicit associations. In the second study, participants were primed for trust and distrust. Results indicated length of response, construct word counts, Likert-type responding, and self-reports of behavior were all affected by the manipulations, indicating they measure the state constructs adequately. However, length of response was also influenced by which condition participants received first, indicating a possible exhaustion effect. Implicit associations indicated no change due to the manipulations.

Keywords: Trust · Suspicion · Distrust · Information technology

1 Introduction

The measurement of psychological constructs has been at the forefront of psychology since the inception of the discipline. Researchers today have a litany of methods for assessing psychological constructs, but it remains to be seen which measure is best for complex constructs (ones that comprise both affective and cognitive attributes) such as suspicion, trust, and distrust. While the latter two constructs are more established in the psychological literature [e.g., 1, 2], state suspicion is relatively new and has only recently been defined to incorporate aspects from a multitude of literatures [3, 4]. Suspicion is an evaluation of a referent possibly having malicious motives [3]. Trust has been defined as the willingness of a person to be vulnerable to a referent, with the expectation of a positive outcome [2], whereas distrust has been described as a negative unilateral judgement [5] or confidence in a negative outcome from another's actions [6]; suspicion suggests an unknown but possibly negative outcome. In summary, suspicion, trust, and distrust are complex states in which a person assesses a referent's intentions. What is currently unanswered is how to best measure state suspicion, trust, and distrust,

© Springer Nature Switzerland AG 2020
A. Moallem (Ed.): HCII 2020, LNCS 12210, pp. 412–426, 2020.
https://doi.org/10.1007/978-3-030-50309-3_27

which may account for variance in human decision-making. To better understand the measurement of these constructs, the present research aimed to measure each through a multi-method approach across two studies.

1.1 Measuring Complex State Variables

There are a variety of methods to measuring complex state variables, with self-report being one of the most common [7]. Although self-report may be a great tool for assessing some state variables such as affect [8] and pain [e.g., 9], it remains to be seen if self-report is the non-invasive measure of choice for assessing more complex constructs that are both affective and cognitive. Constructs such as social desirability, faking, and social norms may influence measures with ratings on self-report scales [10], indicating alternative measurement methods may be necessary. Other methods exist that can assess psychological constructs without the issues mentioned above, such as measures of cognitive associations [e.g., 11, 12]. While no method of assessing psychological constructs is perfect, each method has unique contributions and may account for unique variance [13]. We attempt to apply a multi-measurement approach towards investigating suspicion, trust, and distrust using non-invasive assessments of state variables with self-reports and implicit associations.

Self-reports. Self-reports have been implemented in information technology contexts to measure trust and suspicion [14]. Self-reports rely on explicit ratings from the individual being assessed, which may be in the form of qualitatively coded writing assessments (e.g., construct word counts), surveys, and reports of past behavior.

Self-reports can be valuable and economical for measuring complex state variables. In terms of value, the respondent may be the best individual to make any claims about perceptions of their own internal state [15]. Self-reports are quick and cost-effective to administer in real-world contexts [16, 17]. However, an issue with self-report measures is that participants may not always be explicitly aware of everything they are experiencing at the time of report, which may skew their responses [e.g., 18, 19].

Cognitive Associations. Researchers often wish to take a more indirect approach to quantify a psychological construct by identifying implicit associations that may not be accurately measured if the individual is asked directly [11]. These methods can include implicit measurement [e.g., implicit associations; 11] and structural assessments [e.g., pathfinder networks; 20]. Cognitive association methods help researchers to assess implicit associations that may be difficult to measure explicitly [19] but can take much longer to gather compared to self-report measures.

Convergence Between Measurement Strategies and the Present Research
Previous researchers have investigated the association between self-reports and cognitive associations on certain constructs [21]. Some attitudes associated with an object are better assessed through implicit measures due to the participant not being aware of their true sentiments [22] or being reluctant to report their true sentiments towards an attitude object [23]. Researchers have called for such assessments when the subject

matter concerns issues that may be difficult for participants to report due to cultural and social constraints [24].

Explicitly and implicitly reported measures of complex state variables are multi-faceted and complex in nature. Each type of measure may account for unique variance in dependent measures, suggesting the limitations of any one metric can be overcome by assessing these constructs with multiple measures. In this way, convergent validity between multiple measures of complex state variables may be obtained. The present research explores suspicion, trust, and distrust with a multi-method approach, and explores convergent validity between self-reported and cognitive-associative measures of state suspicion, trust, and distrust. In study 1, we investigated state suspicion using a multi-method approach to account for variance between disparate measures. Study 2 explored state trust and distrust using the same methodology.

2   Study 1 – State Suspicion

State suspicion has been defined as "a person's simultaneous state of cognitive activity, uncertainty, and perceived malintent about underlying information" [4, p.336]. State suspicion is the evaluation of a stimulus [e.g., person or situation] as having questionable motives, and there is uncertainty as to the maliciousness of the motives [3, 4]. Behavioral trust and distrust may be laden with suspicion if the person is uncertain about the outcome of their actions.

The construct of state suspicion grew out the trust-distrust literature; while trust and distrust entail perceived certainty of an outcome of a decision, suspicion entails uncertainty by "questioning motives" [25] and entertaining "plausibly rival hypotheses" [26]. Recently, Bobko and colleagues [3] created a theoretical model of suspicion, in which suspicion comprises uncertainty, cognitive activity, and perceived mal-intent. Uncertainty refers to the perceived ambiguity of the outcome, and arises when one cannot determine if the outcome from their behavior or action will be positive or negative. Cognitive activity refers to a high cognitive load attributed to one's evaluation of a referent [3, 25]. That is, when suspicion is aroused, it leads to further examination for a better assessment of the stimulus in question. There must also be perceived mal-intent, or an inference that the action (such as purchasing from a website) or trusting the referent may result in harm due to maliciousness [3]. The mal-intent aspect comprises questioning the motives and potential hidden interests of the referent. All three aspects must be present for state suspicion: uncertainty, cognitive activity, and perceived mal-intent.

Study 1 examines the state suspicion construct, a complex state variable which comprises uncertainty, cognitive activity, and perceived mal-intent. We hypothesize self-reports and implicit associations will both accurately assess state suspicion. Lastly, we explore the convergent validity of self-report and implicit association, as they measure the same constructs, albeit through different routes. It is hypothesized that the type of measures (self-reports and implicit associations) will correlate within measurement type. Exploratory analyses examine correlations between measurement types.

2.1   Method

Participants. Participants consisted of 120 undergraduate students enrolled in introductory psychology courses at a medium-sized university in the Midwestern United States. Demographic data were not collected, but participants were likely to be similar to the average incoming freshman class, which comprised predominantly Caucasian (71.3%), male (51%) students with an average age of 20.12 years ($SD = 3.43$). All participants earned course credit in their introductory psychology course, and were entered into a random drawing to receive one of four online retailer gift cards if their responses were admissible. Several participants performed the tasks incorrectly; these cases as well as missing data were excluded from the analysis, leaving a total of 57 cases.

Materials

Episode Elicitation Questionnaire. Two versions of the episode elicitation questionnaire were constructed (i.e., suspicion-event and control-event). Both versions were presented to each participant in a random order. The purpose of each version was two-fold: 1) prime the participant's memory for the given event and 2) collect open ended-response data from which to later qualitatively code for suspicion. The suspicion-event version instructed participants to "Think of a time you were making an online purchase and became extremely suspicious" while the control-event version instructed participants to simply "Think of a time you were making an online purchase." For both versions, participants were instructed to keep the given event in mind while completing the questionnaire, which asked specifics of the event through prompts such as "Describe the event in detail." The length of response and number of suspicious words/phrases from the "Describe the event in detail" prompt were coded by four subject matter experts by counting the total number of words written and the number of suspicious words and phrases used to describe the situation. Participants were also asked whether they followed through with using the website to make a purchase online, a behavioral assessment.

Likert-Type Responses. We adapted 20 items from Bobko et al. [4] to assess state suspicion in online contexts. Each suspicion item was measured on a five-point scale (1 = *strongly disagree* to 5 = *strongly agree*), with higher scores indicating more state suspicion. For both the suspicion and control conditions, the items composed a reliable scale (suspicion $\alpha = .91$; control $\alpha = .97$).

Implicit Measurement. Implicit associations were measured using a Java applet version of jImplicit software [27], an adapted version of the task described in [28]. In the first phase, participants are presented with a randomized ordering of single stimulus terms (target words) on a computer monitor and instructed to press a key to categorize them as "suspicion" or "trust" so that baseline latency scores can be calculated. The second phase is a priming task, where participants are primed with attitude object words before each categorization trial and instructed to commit the primes to memory, over a total of 32 randomly presented test trials. The difference was calculated between the latency at which the participants classified the target words as either suspicion or trust in the second phase and the target baseline scores to compute final latency scores used in subsequent analyses. Greater values indicated greater polarity in one's implicit associations between suspicion and trust words [see [28] for full discussion].

Procedure. Participants sat at a station consisting of a standard desktop-computer, mouse, keyboard, and monitor. After the informed consent process, the experimenter instructed participants to follow all on-screen instructions. On each computer, a Qualtrics [29] survey first presented either the suspicion or control version of the episode elicitation questionnaire, followed by a self-report of state suspicion questionnaire. Then, participants were presented with the implicit association task. Upon completion of this first half of the experiment, the survey then presented the alternate version of the episode elicitation questionnaire, with self-report measures and the implicit associations task. Upon completion of all measures, participants were debriefed and thanked before leaving the experiment room.

2.2   Results

We analyzed the data using a 2 × 2 repeated measures multivariate analysis of variance (MANOVA), with a null hypothesis of no significant differences between suspicion and control conditions on four dependent variables. Although we did not expect the order of the manipulation condition to have a significant effect [i.e., suspicious condition first (manipulation first) or suspicious condition second (manipulation second)] we ran MANOVAs with one within factor containing two levels (suspicious condition vs control condition) and one between factor containing two levels (manipulation first vs manipulation second) to ensure any between factor variance was accounted for. Using the Wilks' criterion we were able to determine the combined DVs were significantly affected by condition, $F(4, 52) = 43.48, p < .001$ $\eta_p^2 = .77$, but the order of the manipulation was not significant, $F(4, 52) = 2.03, p = .10, \eta_p^2 = .14$. The interaction of condition and manipulation order was significant, $F(4, 52) = 12.24, p < .001, \eta_p^2 = .49$. Below, we present the univariate results for each dependent measure assessed. All means and standard errors for repeated measures MANOVA analyses are presented in Table 1.

Table 1. Means (*SDs*) for univariate analyses on condition (suspicion/control) by order of manipulation (SC/CS).

Outcome	Suspicion		Control	
	SC	CS	SC	CS
1. Total Response Length	72.85 (39.88)	46.42 (28,87)	35.54 (25.52)	62.87 (31.14)
2. Suspicion Word Count	3.31 (1.87)	2.39 (1.71)	0.27 (.72)	0.42 (0.96)
3. Likert-type Suspicion	3.45 (0.63)	3.62 (0.48)	2.10 (0.82)	2.29 (0.73)
4. Suspicion Prime Latency	0.68 (0.68)	0.58 (0.72)	0.73 (0.78)	0.51 (0.67)

Note. Time for latency scores are reported in seconds.

Writing Assessment. Univariate tests suggested significant differences between conditions for response length, $F(1, 55) = 7.22, p = .01, \eta_p^2 = .12$, suspicion word count,

$F(1, 55) = 90.27, p < .001, \eta_p^2 = .62$, and suspicion self-reports, $F(1, 55) = 138.60$, $p < .001, \eta_p^2 = .72$. Participants wrote significantly longer responses, more suspicion words, and reported higher state suspicion in the suspicion condition compared to the control condition. The interaction of condition and order of manipulation was significant on total word count $F(1, 55) = 63.67, p < .001, \eta_p^2 = .40$, and suspicious word count, $F(1, 55) = 5.10, p = .03, \eta_p^2 = .05$.

Implicit Associations Task. Univariate tests showed that there were not significant differences in implicit associations between conditions, $F(1, 55) = 0.02, p = .89, \eta_p^2 = .00$.

Behavior. The outcomes for each online experience were qualitatively coded to reflect whether or not they followed through with making a purchase using the website they described. In the control condition, 54 participants reported they followed through with purchasing from the website (indicating trust), and 3 reported they abstained from purchasing from the website (indicating suspicion). In contrast, 32 participants reported trust behavioral outcomes in the suspicious condition with 19 choosing to abstain from purchase (6 did not specify if they completed the purchase or not in the suspicion condition). Differences in reported past behaviors between conditions were tested using McNemar's chi-square test of independence. The proportion of purchase behaviors to abstinent behaviors significantly differed between the suspicion and control conditions, $\chi^2 (1) = 15.06, p < .001$. More participants abstained from purchasing from the website in the suspicious condition compared to participants in the control condition.

Convergent Validity. Correlations within conditions are presented in Table 2.

Table 2. Study 1 correlations between measures within each condition.

	1	2	3	4	5	6
1. Response Length	–	.58**	−.23	.05	−.19	−.04
2. Suspicion Word Count	.28*	–	.21	−.24	−.01	.03
3. Likert-type Suspicion	.14	−.27*	–	−.44**	.05	.10
4. Behavior	.27*	.33*	−.24	–	−.09	−.17
5. Suspicion Prime Latency	.01	.17	.02	.40	–	.55**
6. Control Prime Latency	−.09	.29*	.00	.18	.68**	–

Note. Control condition correlations below the diagonal, Suspicion condition correlations are above the diagonal. Time for latency scores are reported in seconds. $^*p < .05, ^{**}p < .01$.

2.3 Discussion

When primed to write about a suspicious interaction with a website online, self-reports were affected the most, as demonstrated by the large effect size ($\eta_p^2 = .72$). Suspicious words and phrases were higher than in the control condition. Participants indicated cognitive activation and uncertainty with phrases such as "Upon further inspection…" and mal-intent with words such as "skeptical," "sketchy," and "fake," respectively. These results resemble those of [5] who found significant differences in attributions when explaining trust behaviors after being primed for suspicion. In the suspicion condition, participants wrote longer responses when describing the event. Uncertainty about the outcome of using the website leads to increased cognitive activity [3, 14], as was evidenced by the increased length of response by participants. However, the order in which participants received conditions had an influence on the total response lengths. As such, length of response may not be an optimal assessment of suspicion; factors such as response fatigue and personality may influence the data. In addition, state suspicion, measured by Likert-type response scales, was higher in the suspicion condition than in the control condition, supporting the scale's capacity to measure suspicion.

Participants were less likely to report making an online purchase in the suspicion condition, possibly due to perceived malintent. Individuals that perceive something or someone is going to harm them are less likely to perform a behavior [30]. Although suspicion was associated with a decrease in the use of the website, it is premature to say suspicion leads to avoidance of the behavior; the majority of participants still performed the behavior despite being suspicious of the website. Although suspicion may lead to suspended judgement [3], people might still perform trusting behaviors while monitoring the referent. For example, tracking a package after having purchased the item from a website may indicate suspicion, not trust. In contrast to our hypotheses, writing about a suspicious condition did not influence implicit associations.

We obtained some measure of convergent validity between self-report measures. In the control condition, self-reported suspicion was related to total response lengths and suspicion word counts. This supports the hypothesis that suspicion is associated with higher cognitive activity [3, 4] indicated by increased word counts. However, no convergent validity was demonstrated within implicit associations. Only suspicion word count demonstrated convergent validity across measurement types, which may have been spurious as it was not replicated across conditions.

3   Study 2 – Trust and Distrust

Study 2 attempts to extend the investigation of measurement strategies on two other complex state constructs – state trust and state distrust. Trust is the willingness of a person to be vulnerable to a referent, with the expectation of a positive outcome [2]. Although trust has been traditionally thought of as being between two persons, recent research indicates trust is also an important aspect of a relationship between a person and a non-person such as in automation [31, 32] and online [33] contexts.

Distrust has rarely been explored in the psychological literature [3]. Researchers have considered distrust to be the lack of trust either implicitly or explicitly, indicating they are the same construct [2, 5]. Distrust has been described as a negative unilateral judgement [5] or confidence in a negative outcome from another's actions [6]. An important distinction between trust and distrust is the expected positive outcome if one is vulnerable to the referent (e.g., person, machine, website) for trust and an expected negative outcome for distrust [6]. Despite the moniker - distrust indicating a lack of trust – some postulate that trust and distrust are orthogonal [6].

Previous research offers conflicting views on the relationship between trust and distrust. Some research on trust and distrust in information technology contexts indicate trust and distrust are orthogonal [14]. Similarly, a card sort analysis found a weak relationship between trust and distrust from in-depth interviews in organizations [34]. In contrast, research [35] and theory [2] has suggested trust and distrust are part of the same continuum. Indeed, trust and distrust involve a degree of perceived certainty the stimulus will lead to positive or negative outcomes, respectively. However, if the constructs are orthogonal it is difficult to envision a scenario when a person believes that trusting a referent will result in *both* positive and negative outcomes [36], as trusting and distrusting behaviors are almost always mutually exclusive.

Study 2 explores ways to measure trust and distrust. We hypothesize self-reports will accurately assess state trust and distrust. In addition, self-report methodologies should correlate moderately. We also hypothesize cognitive associations will accurately assess state trust. Furthermore, cognitive associations will moderately correlate with each other as they are based on the associations of words. As in Study 1, we investigated the convergent validity between and within self-report and cognitive association measures.

3.1 Method

Participants. Study 2 had the same number of factors as Study 1. We obtained 120 undergraduate students enrolled in introductory psychology courses at a medium-sized university in the Midwestern United States to participate in Study 2. Demographic data were not collected, but participants were likely to be similar to the average incoming freshman class, which are the same demographics as Study 1. Participants were compensated and incentivized the same as Study 1. Computer crashes and missing data left a total of 90 cases on which we conducted our analyses.

Materials

Episode Elicitation Questionnaire. Two versions of the episode elicitation questionnaire were constructed (i.e., trust-event and distrust-event); both versions were presented to each participant in a random order as described in the procedure section. The method and coding were the same as in Study 1.

Likert-Type Responses. We adapted 10 items from Lyons, Koltai, Ho, Johnson, Smith, and Shively [37] to assess self-reported trust in the trust and distrust conditions. Items assessed general trust in a website. Participants respond to items such as "I would rely on the website without hesitation" on a 7-point response scale (1 = *not at all* to 7 = *extremely*), with higher scores indicating more self-reported trust. The items comprised a reliable scale in both the trust ($\alpha = .86$) and distrust ($\alpha = .86$) conditions, respectively.

Implicit Measurement. The data collection instrument for the implicit measurement was a Java applet version of jImplicit software [see Study 1, 27].

3.2 Study 2 Results

We analyzed the data using a 2×2 repeated measures multivariate analysis of variance (MANOVA) tests, with a null hypothesis that no significant differences exist between trust and distrust conditions on six dependent variables. We conducted a MANOVA with one within factor containing two levels (trust manipulation vs distrust manipulation) and one between factor containing two levels (trust manipulation first vs distrust manipulation second) to ensure any between factor variance was accounted for. Using the Wilks' criterion we were able to determine the combined DVs were significantly affected by condition, $F(6, 83) = 43.25, p < .001$ $\eta_p^2 = .76$, and by order of the manipulation, $F(6, 83) = 2.74, p = .02, \eta_p^2 = .17$. Also, the interaction of condition and manipulation order was significant, $F(6, 83) = 2.32, p = .04, \eta_p^2 = .14$. All means and standard deviations for repeated measures MANOVA analyses are presented in Table 3.

Table 3. Means (*SD*s) for univariate analyses on condition (trust/distrust) by order of manipulation (DT/TD).

Outcome	Trust		Distrust	
	DT	TD	DT	TD
1. Total Word Count	53.86 (37.1)	67.61 (34.2)	84.35 (46.8)	73.37 (80.54)
2. Trust Word Count	3.20 (2.75)	3.63 (2.31)	1.29 (1.78)	0.83 (1.00)
3. Distrust Word Count	0.12 (0.53)	0.20 (0.81)	1.10 (1.21)	0.95 (1.26)
4. Likert-type Trust	3.57 (0.52)	3.01 (0.57)	1.97 (0.70)	1.83 (0.60)
5. Trust Prime Latency	0.16 (0.12)	0.19 (0.17)	0.16 (0.09)	0.17 (0.12)
6. Distrust Prime Latency	0.19 (0.18)	0.25 (0.16)	0.21 (0.13)	0.20 (0.11)

Note. Time for latency scores are reported in seconds.

Univariate Results. The main effect of condition was significant on response length, $F(1, 88) = 8.92, p = .00, \eta_p^2 = .09$, trust word count, $F(1, 88) = 71.83, p < .001, \eta_p^2 = .45$, distrust word count, $F(1, 88) = 34.30, p < .001, \eta_p^2 = 0.28$, and self-reported levels of trust, $F(1, 88) = 223.13, p < .001, \eta_p^2 = .72$. Trust word counts and self-reported trust levels were higher in the trust condition, while total word counts and distrust word counts were higher in the distrust condition. Condition had no main effect on trust prime latencies or distrust prime latencies.

Order of manipulation had a main effect on self-reported trust, $F(1, 88) = 15.97, p < .001, \eta_p^2 = .15$, such that trust was higher when participants received the distrust manipulation first. There were no significant main effects of manipulation order on response length, trust word counts, distrust word counts, trust prime latencies, or distrust prime latencies.

The interaction between condition and manipulation order significantly affected self-reported trust, $F(1, 88) = 4.97, p = .03, \eta_p^2 = .05$. There were no significant interaction effects of condition and manipulation order on response length, trust word counts, distrust word counts, trust prime latencies, or distrust prime latencies.

Behavior. Differences in reported past behaviors between conditions were tested using McNemar's chi-square test of independence. The proportion of purchase behaviors to abstinent behaviors significantly differed between the trust and distrust conditions, χ^2 (1) = 21.19, p < .001, such that more persons reported purchase behaviors in the trust condition (88) than in the distrust condition (64), and more persons reported abstinent behaviors in the distrust condition (26) than in the trust condition (2).

Convergent Validity. Correlations within and between conditions are presented in Table 4.

Table 4. Study 2 correlations between measures within each condition.

	1	2	3	4	5	6	7
1. Response Length	–	.33**	.42**	−.17	.15	−.18	−.01
2. Trust Word Count	.59**	–	.12	.00	.37**	−.07	.10
3. Distrust Word Count	.19	−.02	–	−.22*	.00	−.11	.28**
4. Likert-type Trust	−.05	.15	−.17	–	.31**	−.10	−.33**
5. Behavior	.14	.11	.04	.17	–	−.04	.03
6. Trust Prime Latency	.23*	.10	.23*	−.23*	.02	–	.29**
7. Distrust Prime Latency	.14	.05	−.01	−.01	−.04	.10	–

Note. Trust condition correlations below the diagonal, Distrust condition correlations are above the diagonal. Time for latency scores are reported in seconds. *p < .05, **p < .01.

3.3 Study 2 Discussion

Study 2 explored the measurement of state trust and distrust with the same methodologies as Study 1. In the trust condition, responses were shorter and trust phrase and word counts were higher. In the distrust condition, total responses were longer, distrust word counts and phrases were higher, and trust word counts were lower. Distrust may evoke salient thoughts about the referent, such as reasons why the website was distrustful in this instance. Participants used phrases such as "the website looked old and not well updated" when describing their interaction.

The Likert-type self-report measure of state trust was reliable in both conditions and higher mean scores in the trust condition, supporting the scale's capacity to measure trust as a state-based construct. The significant interaction supports this conclusion. Moreover, there were more reports of purchase behaviors in the trust condition than in the distrust condition. This may be because individuals believed something or someone was going to harm them, making them less likely to make a purchase [30]. Trust and distrust did not influence implicit associations. Implicit associations may assess more stable associations [18, 22] such as trait suspicion or neuroticism, which may be associated with state suspicion [3].

We found several instances of convergent validity between self-report measures in the distrust condition, but not in the trust condition. It may be that distrust caused an increased memory recall from the bad experience, supporting past researching that has found that when people are in a negative mood or have a negative experience, the quality and precision of their memories is improved [38]. In addition, some convergent validity was found across measurement types, however no discernable pattern was detectable and thus the results may have occurred by chance.

4 General Discussion

The current studies sought to explore the best methods for assessing the complex state constructs of suspicion, trust, and distrust. Based on the multivariate analyses, self-report measures were effective in measuring complex state variables. In contrast, the implicit association measure was not effective in measuring suspicion, trust, and distrust across conditions. The assessments of convergent validity on the self-report measures across the studies demonstrate these measures are capturing variance in state suspicion, trust, and distrust, whereas implicit associations are not. In this study, we found that self-report measures are more effective at assessing complex state variables. States of suspicion, trust, and distrust can change depending on which context they are assessed. As such, self-reports may be the non-invasive measure of choice compared to the others assessed in the present research.

All measures of self-report were affected by conditions in the direction hypothesized. The length of response was longer when prompted for suspicion or distrust. The advantage of using length of response as a measure is that this measure is an indirect assessment of the constructs. In both studies there was an interaction effect of condition and order effect. If the suspicion or distrust condition was first, the effects of the condition were stronger than if the condition was last. Length of response has significant issues, such as exhaustion, for assessing the constructs in question. Length of response may be best suited for scenarios when only one condition is presented to a participant. Construct word counts were also significantly affected by the conditions. The construct word counts were not affected by the order effects, as opposed to the length of response discussed above. The construct word counts are directly related to the constructs in question; when primed to discuss the interaction in the appropriate condition, primes elicit the construct-related information.

Likert-type scales were adequate predictors of complex state variables. The ability to create statements that participants agree or disagree with has high face validity [39] and have been successful in the past at assessing state variables in the psychological literature, such as state anxiety [40] and state stressor appraisals [41]. For state constructs such as suspicion, trust, and distrust, the individual may be the best person to report how they perceive the referent.

Interestingly, reports of past behaviors were adequately influenced by the suspicion and control manipulations in Study 1 and the trust and distrust manipulations in Study 2. An important finding of the current study was that reliance behavior, or trust actions, were not always representative of trust. In Study 1, 59% of the participants reported purchasing from the website, despite being suspicious. This contrasts with Bobko and colleagues' [3] assertion that suspicion is a suspension of judgement and thus a suspension of action. Instead, suspicion may involve action (i.e., purchasing from a website), but the judgement is still suspended as participants reported tracking the package, emailing the vendor, and other information seeking behaviors. Purchasing behaviors were also reported in the distrust condition of Study 2. Research has demonstrated people have a tendency to perform trusting behaviors even when faced with information that indicates the referent may not perform the desired behavior [30]. As such, although 98% of the participants performed a trusting action in the trust condition, it may not always be that trust motivates a trusting action. If the trustor is still seeking information and making assessments, suspicion may be occurring despite the trust action. It is important to note, we are not advocating the abonnement of examining behaviors in the psychological literature. Instead, we acknowledge that behaviors such as "trust actions" have their short-comings in that subsequent behavior is often multiply determined [42]. Self-reports such as construct word counts or Likert-type scales help to elucidate the underlying antecedents, which lead to behaviors.

4.1 Cognitive Associations

Implicit associations were not influenced by the writing conditions. It is possible that implicit associations are stronger held beliefs that are not easily manipulated by writing about a situation and would thus explain why this had no effect on latency scores in the priming task. The implicit associations of suspicion, trust, and distrust may be closely associated with personality variables, which are relatively stable across time [43]. It may be that the implicit associations individuals hold are heuristics they employ in new situations to process information, such as trust [44]. The task in the current study was to reflect on a past experience of suspicion, trust, or distrust. The participants may have chosen scenarios that fit their cognitive model of these constructs. Situations that fit these cognitive models should come to the forefront of cognitive accessibility [11]. In contrast, in a new situation such as a job interview, people may have to rely on their heuristics, which may be formed by the cognitive associations that are exemplified in implicit associations.

4.2 Limitations and Future Research

The current study is not without limitations. First, the current study did not conduct construct validity of the measures of suspicion. Although some of the measures do associate with each other, it remains to be seen if the constructs are reliably different from other more established constructs. Future research should attempt to study the divergent validity of measures. Second, participants received all conditions and spillover effects of suspicion, trust, and distrust in both within-subjects designs. However, the within-subjects design controlled for possible individual differences in writing length that may have unduly influenced results. The current study used repeated measures design because of possible individual differences in word counts. Future research should implement a between-subjects design to investigate the influence of suspicion, trust, or distrust. Third, future research should investigate the association of specific words that have a high consensus across the population at evoking state suspicion, trust, and distrust. This can be done by assessing a large sample's ratings of many words as being associated with suspicion, trust, or distrust, ad hoc. Future research should investigate words that are classified as "suspicion," "trust," or distrust" based on the consensus in a large sample.

4.3 Implications

There are several implications of the present research. First, the study adds to the burgeoning literature on state suspicion [3, 4] and its relation to state trust and distrust constructs [2, 5, 6]. Second, we quantified the convergent validity of multiple self-report and cognitive association measures of state suspicion, trust, and distrust to determine the variance accounted for by multiple measures of complex state variables. In comparison to cognitive association measures, future research investigating complex state variables may benefit by using self-report measures in terms of not only their economy but also their efficacy and convergent validity. Third, we found behaviors, typically labeled "trust actions" do not necessarily indicate trust. Trust actions were found in the suspicion and distrust condition, with the majority performing the behavior despite the condition they were primed to write about.

Acknowledgements. This research has been approved for public release: 88ABW Cleared 4/27/17; 88ABW-2017-1800. This research was supported in part by an appointment to the Postgraduate Research Participant Program at the U.S. Air Force Research Laboratory, 711th Human Performance Wing, Airman Systems Directorate, Warfighter Interface Division, Collaborative Interfaces and Teaming Branch administered by the Oak Ridge Institute for Science and Education through an interagency agreement between the U.S. Department of Energy and USAFRL.

References

1. Jones, S.L., Shah, P.P.: Diagnosing the locus of trust: a temporal perspective for trustor, trustee, and dyadic influences on perceived trustworthiness. J. Appl. Psychol. **101**, 392–414 (2015)
2. Mayer, R.C., Davis, J.H., Schoorman, F.D.: An integrative model of organizational trust. Acad. Managc. Rev. **20**, 709–734 (1995)
3. Bobko, P., Barelka, A.J., Hirshfield, L.M.: The construct of state-level suspicion: a model and research agenda for automated and information technology (IT) contexts. Hum. Factors **56**, 489–508 (2014)
4. Bobko, P., Barelka, A.J., Hirshfield, L.M., Lyons, J.B.: The construct of suspicion and how it can benefit theories and models in organizational science. J. Bus. Psychol. **29**, 335–342 (2014)
5. Sinaceur, M.: Suspending judgment to create value: suspicion and trust in negotiation. J. Exp. Soc. Psychol. **46**, 543–550 (2010)
6. Lewicki, R.J., McAllister, D.J., Bies, R.J.: Trust and distrust: new relationships and realities. Acad. Manage. Rev. **23**, 438–458 (1998)
7. Clark, L.A., Watson, D.: Constructing validity: basic issues in objective scale development. Psychol. Assess. **7**, 309–319 (1995)
8. Watson, D., Clark, L.A., Tellegen, A.: Development and validation of brief measures of positive and negative affect: the PANAS scales. J. Pers. Soc. Psychol. **54**, 1063–1070 (1988)

9. Jensen, M.P., Karoly, P.: Self-report scales and procedures for assessing pain in adults. In: Turk, D.C., Melzack, R. (eds.) Handbook of pain assessment, 3rd edn, pp. 19–44. Guilford Press, New York (2011)
10. Podsakoff, P.M., MacKenzie, S.B., Lee, J., Podsakoff, N.P.: Common method biases in behavioral research: a critical review of the literature and recommended remedies. J. Appl. Psychol. **88**, 879–903 (2003)
11. Fazio, R.H., Sanbonmatsu, D.M., Powell, M.C., Kardes, F.R.: On the automatic activation of attitudes. J. Pers. Soc. Psychol. **50**, 229–238 (1986)
12. Nosek, B.A., Greenwald, A.G., Banaji, M.R.: The implicit association test at age 7: a methodological and conceptual review. In: Bargh, J.A. (ed.) Automatic processes in social thinking and behavior, pp. 265–292. Psychology Press, New York (2007)
13. Goldring, J., Strelan, P.: The forgiveness implicit association test. Pers. Individ. Differ. **108**, 69–78 (2017)
14. Lyons, J.B., Stokes, C.K., Eschleman, K.J., Alarcon, G.M., Barelka, A.: Trustworthiness and IT suspicion: an examination of the nomological network. Hum. Factors **53**, 219–229 (2011)
15. French, J.R., Kahn, R.L.: A programmatic approach to studying the industrial environment and mental health. J. Soc. Issues **18**, 1–47 (1962)
16. Gupta, N., Beehr, T.A.: A test of the correspondence between self-reports and alternative data sources about work organizations. J. Vocat. Behav. **20**, 1–13 (1982)
17. Spector, P.E., Jex, S.M.: Development of four self-report measures of job stressors and strain: interpersonal conflict at work scale, organizational constraints scale, quantitative workload inventory, and physical symptoms inventory. J. Occup. Health Psychol. **3**, 356–367 (1998)
18. Banaji, M.R., Greenwald, A.G.: Implicit stereotyping and prejudice. In: Zanna, M.P., Olson, J.M. (eds.) The Psychology Of Prejudice: The Ontario Symposium, vol. 7, pp. 55–76. Erlbaum, New Jersey (1994)
19. Greenwald, A.G., McGhee, D.E., Schwartz, J.L.: Measuring individual differences in implicit cognition: the implicit association test. J. Personality and Soc. Psychol. **74**, 1464–1480 (1998)
20. Schvaneveldt, R.W.: Pathfinder Associative Networks: Studies in Knowledge Organization. Ablex, New Jersey (1990)
21. Hofmann, W., Gawronski, B., Gschwendner, T., Le, H., Schmitt, M.: A meta-analysis on the correlation between the implicit association test and explicit self-report measures. Pers. Soc. Psychol. Bull. **31**, 1369–1385 (2005)
22. Greenwald, A.G., Banaji, M.R.: Implicit social cognition: attitudes, self-esteem, and stereotypes. Psychol. Rev. **102**, 4–27 (1995)
23. Gaertner, S.L., Dovidio, J.F.: The aversive form of racism. In: Gaertner, S.L., Dovidio, J.F. (eds.) Prejudice, Discrimination, and Racism, pp. 61–89. Academic Press, New York (1986)
24. Dovidio, J.F., Fazio, R.H.: New technologies for the direct and indirect assessment of attitudes. In: Tanur, J. (ed.) Questions about Questions: Inquiries into the Cognitive Bases of Surveys, pp. 204–237. Russell Sage Foundation, New York (1992)
25. Hilton, J.L., Fein, S., Miller, D.T.: Suspicion and dispositional inference. Pers. Soc. Psychol. Bull. **19**, 501–512 (1993)
26. Fein, S.: Effects of suspicion on attributional thinking and the correspondence bias. J. Pers. Soc. Psychol. **70**, 1164–1184 (1996)
27. Schuelke, M.J.: jImplicit (Version 1.0) [Software] (2014). http://spark.myftp.org:1200/jImplicit/. Accessed 27 Dec 2019
28. Fazio, R.H., Jackson, J.R., Dunton, B.C., Williams, C.J.: Variability in automatic activation as an unobtrusive measure of racial attitudes: a bona fide pipeline? J. Pers. Soc. Psychol. **69**, 1013–1027 (1995)
29. Qualtrics [Software]. http://www.qualtrics.com. Accessed 27 Dec 2019

30. Dunning, D., Anderson, J.E., Schlösser, T., Ehlebracht, D., Fetchenhauer, D.: Trust at zero acquaintance: more a matter of respect than expectation of reward. J. Pers. Soc. Psychol. **107**, 122–141 (2014)
31. Lee, J.D., See, K.A.: Trust in automation: designing for appropriate reliance. Hum. Factors **46**, 50–80 (2004)
32. Merritt, S.M., Ilgen, D.R.: Not all trust is created equal: dispositional and history-based trust in human-automation interactions. Hum. Factors **50**, 194–210 (2008)
33. Flavián, C., Guinalíu, M.: Consumer trust, perceived security and privacy policy: three basic elements of loyalty to a web site. Ind. Manage. Data Syst. **106**, 601–620 (2006)
34. Saunders, M.N., Dietz, G.: Thornhill, A: Trust and distrust: polar opposites, or independent but co-existing? Hum. Relat. **67**, 639–665 (2014)
35. Schoorman, F.D., Mayer, R.C., Davis, J.H.: An integrative model of organizational trust: past, present, and future. Acad. Manage. Rev. **32**, 344–354 (2007)
36. Bigley, G.A., Pearce, J.L.: Straining for shared meaning in organization science: problems of trust and distrust. Acad. Manage. Rev. **23**, 405–421 (1998)
37. Lyons, J.B., Koltai, K.S., Ho, N.T., Johnson, W.B., Smith, D.E., Shively, R.J.: Engineering trust in complex automated systems. Ergon. Des. **24**, 13–17 (2016)
38. Spachtholz, P., Kuhbandner, C., Pekrun, R.: Negative affect improves the quality of memories: trading capacity for precision in sensory and working memory. J. Exp. Psychol. Gen. **143**, 1450–1456 (2014)
39. Spector, P.E.: Summated Rating Scale construction: An Introduction, vol. 82. Sage Publications, California (1992)
40. Spielberger, C.D., Gorsuch, R.L., Lushene, R., Vagg, P.R., Jacobs, G.: Manual for the State-Trait Anxiety Inventory (form Y): Self-Evaluation Questionnaire. Consulting Psychologists Press, California (1983)
41. Schneider, T.R.: Evaluations of stressful transactions: what's in an appraisal? Stress Health **24**, 151–158 (2008)
42. Ajzen, I.: The theory of planned behavior. Organ. Behav. Hum. Decis. Process. **50**, 179–211 (1991)
43. Terracciano, A., McCrae, R.R., Brant, L.J., Costa Jr., P.T.: Hierarchical linear modeling analyses of the NEO-PI-R scales in the baltimore longitudinal study of aging. Psychol. Aging **20**, 493–506 (2005)
44. Tortosa-Edo, V., López-Navarro, M.A., Llorens-Monzonís, J., Rodríguez-Artola, R.M.: The antecedent role of personal environmental values in the relationships among trust in companies, information processing and risk perception. J. Risk Res. **17**, 1019–1035 (2014)

Did I Agree to This? Silent Tracking Through Beacons

Edden Kashi[(✉)] and Angeliki Zavou[(✉)]

Department of Computer Science, Hofstra University, Hempstead, NY, USA
EKashi2@pride.hofstra.edu, Angeliki.Zavou@hofstra.edu

Abstract. Users' personally identifiable information (PII) collection is a primary revenue model for the app-economy, and consequently user tracking has become increasingly invasive and ubiquitous. Smart and IoT devices provide even more access to users' personal information by utilizing their exact location and default device settings. Although users in most cases must grant permission before their personal information is collected and shared with third-parties, this is not the case when user tracking happens through email or just by owning and using Bluetooth dependent devices. In any case, the average user is willing to accept the terms of the often unread "Privacy Policy" in order to receive the advertised "better user experience", without really being aware of the consequences of this decision. In this work, we investigate the latest popular technologies for user tracking through mobile and web applications and demonstrate how much information about users can be gathered without user awareness or acknowledgment as well as in which cases and how we were able to limit this tracking. Finally, in our work, we attempt to create unified user profiles by combining our findings from the different tracking techniques against targeted users. We hope that our extensive analysis of beacon tracking will lead to greater awareness of the privacy risks involved with web beacons and Bluetooth tracking and motivate the deployment of stricter regulations and a more effective notification mechanism when such tracking is in place.

Keywords: Security and privacy technologies · User awareness of privacy threats · Ethical, economic and societal issues in cybersecurity · Tracking · Web beacons · Bluetooth beacons

1 Introduction

In the digital age, billions of users are using Web and mobile applications on a daily basis and while doing so, are creating a *digital footprint* and a roadmap that can reveal a significant amount of personally identifiable information (PII) as well as their activity patterns. Such digital traces are leveraged by advertising companies, online retailers as well as data brokers to craft targeted advertisements and marketing messages in the hopes of driving sales and creating a deeper level of customer engagement.

© Springer Nature Switzerland AG 2020
A. Moallem (Ed.): HCII 2020, LNCS 12210, pp. 427–444, 2020.
https://doi.org/10.1007/978-3-030-50309-3_28

Numerous studies in the last two decades have discussed a wide range of techniques of user tracking across the Web ranging from standard stateful cookie-based tracking [12,21], to advanced cross-browser device fingerprinting [20] and more recently email tracking through web beacons [11,22]. With the popularity of smartphones and IoT devices on the rise, it is no surprise that new methods of user tracking through Bluetooth and GPS have flourished [13,15,16]

In an effort to limit potential legal liability for the abundant collection of user data, most service providers display lengthy, easily accessible privacy policies to regulate their engagement with customers and inform them about the data that is collected by the service as well as the ways this data will be treated. Still, despite their importance to users, multiple user studies [9,14,26] have shown that it is common practice for users to quickly *accept* services' privacy policies without ever reading them with the foresight of a *better user experience* (tailored ads, better streaming content, location-based suggestions, etc.). But even in the cases where users are aware of this situation, they are still willing to give up their data if they feel it's going to help them in their day-to-day lives. For example, surprisingly many consumers (more than 100.000 downloads in Google Play) were willing to share their "first name, user name, profile picture, email address, gender, birthday/age, country, language and password" [23,25] in order to receive personalized advice and recommendations on how to improve their brushing and oral hygiene habits.

In this work, we conducted empirical research for online user tracking using popular email-tracking services and Customer Relationship Management (CRM) systems as well as location-tracking through mobile and IoT devices. Our goals were to simulate and better understand how much personal user information can be gathered without users' knowledge, combine information from different tracking methods in order to build unified profiles for targeted users and explore if/how these means of tracking can be limited.

The rest of the paper is organized as follows. Section 2 provides background information on web beacons and Bluetooth technology and discusses the related work. Section 3 details the tracking methodologies used for our data-collection experiments. Section 4 presents our experimental results and compares the effectiveness of the different tracking mechanisms we used while Sect. 5 discusses countermeasures against these types of tracking. Finally, the paper concludes in Sect. 6 where we also discuss our future work.

2   Background and Related Work

2.1   Personally Identifiable Information (PII)

Personally Identifiable Information (PII) is any representation of information that permits the identity of an individual to whom the information applies, to be inferred by direct or indirect means. According to the Bridge Corp [8], PII can be divided into two categories, linked and linkable information. Linked information is any piece of personal information that can be used to identify an individual on its own. Linkable information, on the other hand, is information that on its own cannot identify a person per se, but when combined with other information gathered, has the ability to identify, trace, or locate a person. Table 1 highlights the difference between the two types. The PII that we have investigated in this paper are (1) device owner's name, (2) device name, (3) MAC address, (4) IP address, (5) device type and (6) distance.

Table 1. Linked PII vs. Linkable PII

Linked PII	Linkable PII
Name: full name, maiden name, last name, alias	Date of birth
Personal identification numbers: social security (SSN), passport, credit card	Place of birth
Personal address information: street address, email address	Business telephone number
Telephone numbers	Business mailing or email address
Personal characteristics: images, fingerprints, handwriting	Race
Biometrics: retina scan, voice signature	Religion
Asset information: IP address, MAC address, Mobile Device Unique Identifier	Employment information (location)

2.2 Stateful vs. Stateless Web Tracking

Stateful web tracking, the most common practice of online user tracking, uses persistent cookies to identify unique users across multiple websites. These cookies stay in a user's browser until they are either deleted by the user or they exceed their expiration date. And it is not a surprise that these tracking cookies are usually set to expire in several years. Regardless, most users are at least aware of this tracking since they often need to accept these cookies to continue browsing the website.

To the contrary, *stateless* web tracking, or fingerprinting, the method that relies on device-specific information and configurations (e.g., screen size, WiFi on/off, browser type & version, operating system, etc.) to identify unique users, is not as known to the regular users as it doesn't require user approval to proceed. Note that the device- and/or browser-identifying data cannot be hidden, as they are part of the requests to websites and without this data these requests will be blocked.

The distinction between the two tracking techniques lies in how users can block and avoid tracking. With stateful tracking, it is possible to block tracking by preventing the code on a webpage from executing and storing information on the machine, i.e., disabling cookies and 3rd party tracking in a browser could accomplish this. *In this project, we utilize stateless tracking methods in relation to web beacons which is harder to detect and prevent due to the opaque nature of fingerprinting.*

2.3   Web and Email Tracking with the Use of Web Beacons

The main purpose of email tracking is for senders to know which emails have been read by which recipients and when. Although user tracking through email views and URL-shorteners is not a new thing in the marketing world, it seems to be evolving very fast lately due to the freely available CRM systems and all the new browser extensions that can be setup with minimal effort. To prove that claim, Engelhardt et al. [11] looked at emails from newsletter and mailing-list services from the 14,000 most popular websites on the web, and found that 85% contained trackers and 30% were leaking email addresses not only to the owner of the mailing list but to outside corporations, without the subscribers consent. Surprisingly, all current email tracking services are utilizing one of the very basic mechanisms of stateless web-tracking, the web-beacons [19]. These are just very small invisible images (1×1 `gif`) that are included in emails (or in websites) and are supposed to "retrieve" detailed user data (i.e., IP address, geolocation, device type, timestamp, and email client – results vary depending on user's settings) from targeted victims every time an email is opened. These invisible images are automatically downloaded on most systems with standard, default browser settings and are creating a log-entry at the tracking server at every email view or visit to a tracking website. So email tracking is possible because modern graphical email clients allow rendering a subset of HTML and although JavaScript is invariably stripped, embedded images and stylesheets are allowed. As the authors of [11] mentioned there hasn't been much research done lately on the privacy implications of CRMs and email trackers.

2.4   Bluetooth - and Bluetooth Low Energy (BLE) Devices

Bluetooth and BLE have emerged as the *de facto communication* protocols for many of the new Internet of Things (IoT) devices, e.g. smart TVs, smart speakers, cameras, fitness trackers, wireless headphones, cars, medical devices, and even shoes. And although these two different categories of Bluetooth enabled devices are incompatible with each other, some devices, like smartphones and laptops, tend to support both protocols and therefore can communicate with both types of devices.

In both cases, there are three main states that these devices can operate on: *advertising*, *scanning*, and *connected* (aka. *paired*). To get two Bluetooth- (or BLE-) devices connected, one device should be in "*advertising*" mode, broadcasting packets, whereas the other has to scan for such packets. The scanning device may then decide to initiate a connection if the advertisement packets indicate that the advertising device allows it. In our experiments (see Sect. 3.2 we simulated both of these modes. We used small BLE-transmitters, i.e., *Bluetooth beacons*, to simply broadcast data (e.g, a URL) that could be discovered by any Bluetooth-enabled device, e.g., a smartphone equipped with an application (e.g. a retailers' application) that is silently scanning for such packets. Once the smartphone application gets close (within 70 m) to the beacons and discovers their packets, it will send data back to the retailers' server and the application on the smartphone will probably be prompted to display a targeted advertisement based on this user's browsing history. Retail chains in the U.S., including Target, Walmart, Urban Outfitters, Sephora, have embraced such Bluetooth-based technology to connect and interact with customers [15].

But scanning Bluetooth-devices are not necessarily used with mobile applications. Instead they can also be used to *"fingerprint"* individual users by listening to advertising packets broadcasted by nearby Bluetooth-discoverable devices and record information contained in them, including but not limited to (1) device name, (2) MAC address, (3) services' ids (UUIDs) and signal strength (RSSI), which also implies the distance from the scanner. More details on this are included in Sect. 3.2. Fawaz et al. [13] conducted an extensive study across 214 BLE-enable devices to conclude that Bluetooth (and BLE) advertising messages, leak an alarming volume of artifacts that permits the tracking and fingerprinting of users. Similarly, the study in [10] focuses on BLE-enabled fitness trackers and finds that the majority of them use static hardware address while advertising, which allows user tracking.

Based on these conclusions of these studies, a couple of empirical research works were conducted to leverage the broadcasted data from BLE-devices to locate and profile individual users. Apart from our work, Kolias et al. [16] also utilized the broadcasted information by nearby-BLE devices for profiling users but in our case we were able to combine and verify the data gathered by the email and web-tracking experiments for our targeted group of users. Korolova et al. [17] also tried to identify real users using BLE-packets but their threat model is involving malicious mobile applications that allow for cross-app tracking, i.e., linking pseudonymous users of different apps to each other.

3   User Tracking Methodologies

With the term **user profiling** we refer to the collection of PII (i.e., email, MAC address, IP address, etc.) for targeted unsuspected users through beacons located on webpages or in a close proximity to these users' Bluetooth-enabled mobile devices. According to the results from our experiments, many users are susceptible to this kind of tracking through emails, websites, hyperlinked content, and Bluetooth mostly because their *default* user settings do not block the aforementioned tracking techniques.

Testing Environment: In order to simulate the setup of actual email marketing campaigns our testing email campaign was implemented using the Mailchimp CRM tool. Our case study consisted of 85 participants, who signed up for our email campaigns accepting the Mailchimp user agreement rules, as they would for every other marketing campaign. Geolocation by Mailchimp [18] is done through collecting the user's IP-address during every email viewing. The accuracy of the geolocation varies significantly between different device types and settings.

As for tracking over Bluetooth, we mimicked a typical retail environment that utilizes multiple Bluetooth Beacons, specifically we used two Estimote LTE Beacons, three iBKS105 Beacons by Accent Systems, and a RadBeacon USB,

Fig. 1. Web-Stat analytics collected information

all acting as Eddystone Beacons broadcasting URLs. We then used the *Physical Web* iOS app [4] on an iPhone to capture the Bluetooth signals sent out from our Beacons (as retailers apps would do). To monitor users' reoccurring appearances for longer periods of time, we utilized a Raspberry Pi 3 B+. The Raspberry Pi was used for general scanning in multiple intervals of 5 consecutive days. This way we were able to identify Bluetooth-discoverable devices in a 70 m range and log reoccurring appearances unbeknownst to the target user. This information was then cross referenced with the information collected through email campaigns to create **user unified profiles**.

Threat Model: We assume that our adversary has access to all the web-, online-, and Bluetooth-tracking mechanisms described in Subsects. 3.1 and 3.2 and not only wants to monitor users' online activity, but more importantly, gather information about the locations they frequent and the times they do so. The adversary can have various motives depending on their end goals: a) marketing and campaigning; b) profit through a sale; c) personal-interest (stalking). Finally, we assume that the attacker can be in a certain proximity to their victims in order to complete the second stage of user profiling using Bluetooth-enabled devices.

3.1 Web Beacons

Based on our own user study [14], and previous user surveys [24], Chrome, Safari, and Firefox are the three most used browsers. With this in mind, we chose to conduct our case study using these browsers to best simulate a user's environment when they are subject to tracking. Apart from the three popular browsers we also tested widely known privacy focused browsers (i.e., Brave and Tor). In addition to this, we tested different email providers i.e., Gmail, Outlook, AOL, Yahoo, Apple Mail. Each email provider was tested on all 5 browsers in terms of which one would provide the most detailed and accurate information when a web beacon was injected in the email. CRM applications and several tracking browser extensions (e.g., Streak and ContactMonkey) were used for injecting the web beacon. To further the scope of our investigation and collect more information for our targeted users, web analytics services i.e., Google Analytics, Stat-Counter, Web-Stat were added to our targeted test website. Our monitored users were lured to our website through campaign-emails, which happen to include the shortened-URL by Grabify of our tracking website.

Figures 1 and 2 depict the information collected by the methods mentioned above.

Recipients	Subject	Sent Date ∨	Opens	Clicks	Cities	Devices	Last Open
eck1242@outlook.com	VM - Firefox - Outlook	Nov 17, '19 20:27	1	2	1	1	Nov 17, '19 20:29

👤 eck1242@outlook.com						
Nov 17, 2019 08:29:17 PM		74.101.244.64		Valley Stream, NY, US		Firefox WebMail

Links Clicked

https://t.shhtrk.com/e/aAVg...	Nov 17, 2019 08:27:41 PM	74.101.244.64	Valley Stream, NY, US	Firefox WebMail
https://t.shhtrk.com/e/aAVg...	Nov 17, 2019 08:29:20 PM	74.101.244.64	Valley Stream, NY, US	Firefox WebMail

Fig. 2. ContactMonkey collected information

Email Tracking: To simulate email tracking through marketing campaigns, we used the most popular free CRM tool i.e., Mailchimp. Table 2 demonstrates a side by side comparison of the findings from Mailchimp tracking versus findings from free email tracking browser extensions i.e., Streak and ContactMonkey. To follow the email marketing trend, in the first stage of our tracking procedure, 27 email campaigns using the Mailchimp service, were sent to our targeted group of users, in the span of four months. For each user engaging with an email from these campaigns, MailChimp was recording the view- and URL-click-rate.

Note that users of Mailchimp are not *explicitly* informed about the collection of their IP, geolocation, and other private information through these emails neither at the time of subscription to the service and mailing list nor at any later point in time. Through these email campaigns, we were able to collect also device fingerprinting data and retrieve the participants' most frequent locations. The automatically generated user profiles and a sample of the collected data for one of our test users are shown in Fig. 3.

Table 2. Email tracking services comparison

Service	IP address	Date and time	Number of opens	Location provided	Location accuracy
MailChimp - CRM		✓	✓	✓	Location used most frequently when opening email campaigns
Streak - Browser Extension		✓	✓	✓	Specific Town with WiFi enabled, General City without WiFi
ContactMonkey - Browser Extension	✓	✓	✓	✓	Specific Town with WiFi enabled, General City without WiFi

URL Shorteners and Web Analytics. To improve the accuracy of the unified user profiles, we employed free URL-shorteners (e.g., Grabify, Bitly) to mask the URLs (*i.e*, https://grabify.link/HXYE4S *vs.* google.com). Once the URL was clicked, no matter the settings enabled on the user's device (i.e., load remote

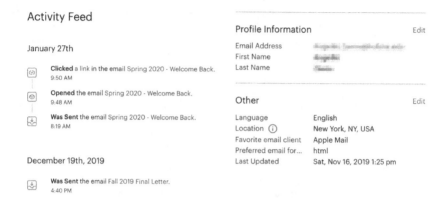

Fig. 3. Mailchimp's generated user profile & tracking statistics

images, incognito mode, etc.), a log would be collected, as seen the one seen in Fig. 4, for this figure WiFi was enabled. Moreover, when users clicked the shortened URL, they were redirected to our test website that was being monitored by web analytics (i.e., Google Analytics, StatCounter, Web-Stat). Figure 1 shows a log from Web-Stat, the tracking of this service was not affected by the presence of ad-blockers on the user's side.

3.2   Tracking Through Bluetooth

Taking advantage of users' willingness to enable Bluetooth at all times, we were able to collect user information through Bluetooth-discoverable devices. To simulate the Bluetooth tracking done by retailers we used Bluetooth Beacons (see *Testing Environment*) and the *Physical Web* iOS application to capture the signals broadcasted by the beacons. We were also able to direct users to our website through our test beacons without the need for a user to have downloaded our own app. To initially explore tracking through Bluetooth, we used free applications such as BlueCap [1] and NRFConnect [3] to identify nearby beacons and Bluetooth-enabled devices (including those of our targeted users). Through our scans, we were able to collect data which included linkable PII such as device name, UUID, and device type of our target users. However, the disadvantage of these scanning apps is that they don't keep any log of reoccurring users.

To bypass this limitation we used a Raspberry PI to simulate what these scanning apps were doing for a longer period of time, created a permanent log of reoccuring users. In general, any computer with BLE capabilities running any Linux distribution with the Bluez stack [2] suffices for our tracking tasks. In addition to the data we could recover from the scanning apps, with the Raspberry Pi we were able to recover the MAC address of the Bluetooth enabled devices within close proximity to the scanner. However, it is important to note that with Bluetooth scanning applications iPhones and iPads do not include the full device name that includes the owner's name, however with the Raspberry Pi scanning,

Date/Time	2020-01-18 18:45:04
IP Address	74.101.244.64
Country ❷	United States, Woodmere
Orientation	landscape-primary
Timezone	America/New_York EST
User Time	Sat Jan 18 2020 18:43:50 GMT-0500 (Eastern Standard Time)
Language	en-US
Incognito/Private Window	No
Ad Blocker	No
Screen Size	1440 x 900
Local IP	3915b0f5-78e4-4e3d-804c-f6eef5751fb1.local
GPU	Intel(R) Iris(TM) Plus Graphics 640
Browser	Chrome (79.0.3945.117)
Operating System	Mac 10.14.6
Device	Apple
Touch Screen	No
User Agent	Mozilla/5.0 (Macintosh; Intel Mac OS X 10_14_6) AppleWebKit/537.36 (KHTML, like Gecko) Chrome/79.0.3945.117 Safari/537.36
Platform	MacIntel
Referring URL	*no referrer*
Host Name	pool-74-101-244-64.nycmny.fios.verizon.net
ISP	MCI Communications Services, Inc. d/b/a Verizon Business

Fig. 4. Grabify link shortener collected information

the full device name (which often includes owner's name) is given. In order to track a specific user using only scanning applications we would have to manually collect the data of appearance. Using the Raspberry Pi we continuously scanned for BLE, Bluetooth, and IoT devices (i.e., fitness watches, wireless headphones, etc.) based on their MAC address and automatically created a permanent log of every appearance for a targeted user.

4   Results and Conclusions

4.1   User Study

We conducted an online anonymous survey of 325 participants recruited through popular forums and groups online and over email in order to better understand user browsing habits and whether users' are aware of the online tracking we described in Sect. 3.1. The main section of the survey included also questions regarding subscription to retailer's email campaigns and familiarity of the participants with privacy-related online common practices (e.g., Ad-blockers, private browsing). A separate section was added for participants who themselves used email tracking tools (e.g. Browser extensions, CRMs) to better understand their motives as well as their understanding of these technologies.

Of our 325 participants, 86.5% of participants were between 18 and 44 years old, 6.2% were between 45 and 54, 4.7% were over 55 and 2.2% were younger than 18. 42.2% of the participants described their "knowledge of computers and new technology" as proficient, 39.7% as competent, 6.5% as experts and 11.7% as advanced beginners or novice users. Regardless of their self-identified computer knowledge though, there was great consent in the answers to the question *"Have your ever chosen "I agree" to legal terms and conditions agreement after hardly giving it a glance?"*, with 98.8% of the participants answering "yes" to this question as shown in Fig. 5.

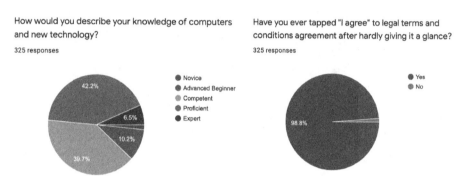

Fig. 5. Results: users knowledge and agreeing to privacy policies

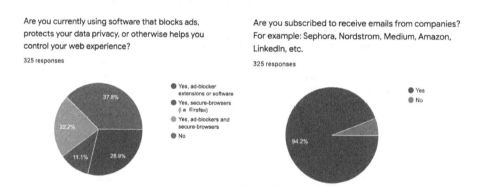

Fig. 6. Results: software & extensions for blocking and email campaign users

Our survey also showed that although the majority of our participants are aware that their online activity is tracked and therefore 62.2% of them use at least one of the popular practices to limit this tracking (e.g. ad-blocking software or privacy-focused browsers), still 94.2% are subscribed to email campaigns from retailers and other popular services (e.g. LinkedIn), shown in Fig. 6. This leads us to believe that users are mostly unaware of the tracking they are subject to through email-campaigns and web-analytics tools.

4.2   Comparison of Email Tracking Extensions

When testing with various email providers and methods of opening emails, we found a varied outcome of user information collected depending on device settings, email provider, and how the emails were opened (i.e, Apple Mail, App, Desktop). With default email settings on, the most insecure method of opening emails was found to be Apple Mail application which shares location, IP, device fingerprint, etc. no matter the email provider, as seen in Table 3. However, the Wi-Fi setup (on or off) skewed the accuracy of the location retrieved. Our results indicated that having Wi-Fi on gave the IP address which was then geolocated to the user's current address. Without Wi-Fi enabled, a less precise location was collected, showing the surrounding city rather than the specific town when (results from Wi-Fi on). The most secure emails were opened via the Gmail mobile or desktop application, which did not reveal any info other than when the email was opened. With the Gmail app (on either mobile device or Desktop) no information was revealed apart from the date and time of the email views.

Table 3. Tracking browser extensions through various email clients

Services	Information collected
AOL opened on Apple Mail	- Streak: City, Date & Time, Device, # opened
	- Saleshandy: City, Date & Time, Device, # opened
	- Docsify: City, Date & Time, Device type, # opened
	- ContactMonkey: IP, City, Date & Time, Device, # opened
Outlook opened on Apple Mail	- Streak: City, Date & Time, Device type, # opened
	- Saleshandy: City, Date & Time, Device, # opened
	- Docsify: City, Date & Time, Device type, # opened
	- ContactMonkey: IP, City, Date & Time, Device, # opened
Gmail opened on Chrome Incognito Mode	- Streak: "gmail - unknown location", date & time, # opened
	- Saleshandy: "read using gmail", date & time, # opened
	- Docsify: "gmail proxy", date & time, # opened
	- ContactMonkey: "using gmail", date & time, # opened

4.3   Comparison of Web Analytics Tools in Terms of Tracking

After understanding how a user profile can be engineered as well as the extent of information the average user is vulnerable to sharing, we then began to search for ways to stop or limit this profiling. Various methods of blocking tracking were tested (in Table 4) to determine whether or not these methods deemed to live up to their pre-conceived functions. Ad-blockers which claim to block invisible trackers, including Ghostery, PrivacyBadger, uBlockOrigin, etc. all deemed unsuccessful in blocking tracking through emails and did not block web-analytics tool Web-Stat, still able to retrieve PII which includes the IP address. However, common web-analytics services including StatCounter and Google Analytics were successfully blocked. On a different note, popular "Private" browsing options, including DuckDuckGo, Brave, and Firefox were still susceptible to email tracking, however, two forms of web-analytics were blocked (StatCounter, Google Analytics), but Web-Stat remained unblocked and logged user visit information.

Table 4. Web analytics services

Service	Information collected	Private browsers (Brave, DuckDuckGo, Firefox)
StatCounter	IP address Location Data • wifi on: specific town • wifi off: surrounding city Number of visits User engagement (i.e clicks, scrolling)	Successfully blocked by private browsers
Google Analytics	Location Data • wifi on/off: surrounding city Number of visits User engagement (i.e clicks, scrolling)	Successfully blocked by private browsers
Web-Stat	IP address Location Data • wifi on: specific town • wifi off: surrounding city Number of visits User engagement (i.e clicks, scrolling)	Not blocked by private browsers
Grabify	IP address Location Data • wifi on: specific town • wifi off: surrounding city Number of visits Browser fingerprint Device fingerprint	Not blocked by private browsers

A misconception we have also come to find is that the "Incognito" and "Do Not Track" modes are frequently thought to block tracking while browsing. Through the use of survey studies [14], we found that most users do not use and others have misconceptions about incognito mode browsing. While 27.1% do not use these modes, 16% of users believed their IP address was hidden from web tracking when using incognito modes. In reality, incognito mode is an internet browser setting that prevents browsing history from being stored. In contrast, with normal browsing, when you visit any web page, any text, pictures, and cookies required by the page are stored locally on your computer, and any searches or forms filled out are stored in the autocomplete field. Although nothing is stored on your computer in private mode, users are definitely not anonymous. Each page that a user visits reveals their IP address therefore geolocation can still occur, and user profiling techniques can still be applied.

Table 5. Bluetooth scanning services/techniques comparison

Application	Device name	UUID	MAC address	RSSI	Device model number	Device manufacturer name	Services UUID and properties (e.j., write, notify)
BlueCap	✓	✓		✓	✓	✓	
NRFConnect	✓	✓		✓	✓	✓	✓
Raspberry Pi	✓	✓	✓	✓		✓	

When using incognito mode/do not track mode/private mode, do you believe your IP address is hidden from web tracking tactics?

325 responses

- Yes
- No
- I do not use any of those modes with my browser

27.1%
56.9%
16%

Fig. 7. Results: incognito mode

4.4 Bluetooth Tracking Tools

Our experiments proved that using a combination of the BlueCap BLE and NRFConnect scanning application to first identify a user, then a Raspberry Pi for reoccurring scanning and logging of the user's device successful in learning a users habits at a specific location. The Raspberry Pi detects IoT devices (i.e., fitness watches, wireless headphones, etc.), laptops, and phones. By collecting a specific user's device name, which we assume includes a variation of their first name, we are able to collect information about this device including the MAC address and RSSI. The detection of phones in our scanning though is dependent on the manufacturer and user settings, for example, Huawei smartphones were always detected but iPhones and Samsungs phones had to be paired to an IoT device in order to be detected. To define user habits of a specific location, we logged the timestamp and distance (RSSI) of a specific user with each reappearance. Table 5 includes the details of the data collected by each one of the technologies mentioned above.

4.5   Unified User Profiles

To simulate unified user profiles, a combination of all tracking methods were applied to each of the our target users. As Fig. 8 shows, there are two ways we do user tracking, through web and Bluetooth tracking. First, we track a targeted user online given the users email address. We track a user everytime they open an email sent from our marketing campaign on their desktop, mobile, or laptops. Each marketing campaign that is sent has web beacons and includes hyperlinked content using URL shortener loggers. Then either the user will visit our tracking website, or they are requested to fill out a form with their information, either way we will collect the same end information.

On the other hand, we integrate tracking of targeted users through their Bluetooth-enabled devices. We can either have the same result as web tracking through our beacons that are broadcasting a tracking website; so in this case, our targeted users do not have to be subscribed to our email campaigns. Or, we can take advantage of their Bluetooth devices and create a log of each reoccurring appearances and timestamp when the user, or their IoT devices, are within a certain range. The comprehensive unified user profile is then created combining both methods of user tracking, as shown in Table 6.

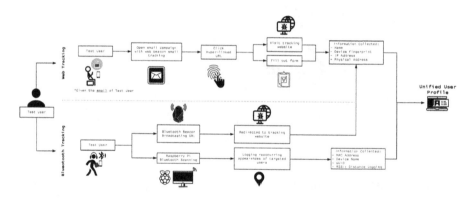

Fig. 8. Different tracking methods for a single test-subject.

5   Countermeasures

In the final stage of our work, we looked into **countermeasures** against those prevalent tracking methods. We examined widely known techniques that are thought to be solutions to limit user tracking.

5.1   Web Beacon Tracking

Blocked Images: The only permanent solution we have found to end tracking via emails that doesn't involve the email providers is disabling the "*load remote*

Table 6. Comprehensive unified user profile

Information	Technology used	Final user profile of test user
IP address	Grabify URL Shortener, Email Tracking, Web Analytics	147.4.36.79
Physical address	Geolocated	1000 Hempstead Turnpike, Hempstead, NY 11549
Device name	Raspberry Pi, Bluetooth Scanners	Edden's MacBook Pro
Device fingerprint	Grabify URL Shortener, Email Tracking, Web Tracking	Date/Time: 2020-01-18 18:45:04 Country: United States City: Hempstead, New York IP Address: 74.101.244.64 Incognito/Private Window: No Screen Size: 1440 × 90 GPU: Intel(r) Iris(TM) Plus Graphics 640 Browser: Chrome (79.02945.117) Operating System: Mac 10.14.6 Device: Apple User Agent: Mozilla/5.0 (Macintosh; Intel Mac OS X 10_14_6) AppleWebKit/537.36 (KHTML, like Gecko) Chrome/79.0.3945.117... Platform: MacIntel
MAC address	Raspberry Pi	38:F9:D3:88:58:B0
UUID of device	Raspberry Pi, Bluetooth Scanners	B9407F30-F5F8-466E-AFF9-25556B57FE6D
User name or email	Mailchimp, User Survey	Edden
Distance logged	Raspberry Pi, Bluetooth Scanners	Sat Feb 22 19:03:41 2020, RSSI: -72; Sat Feb 22 19:03:47 2020, RSSI: -66; Sat Feb 22 19:04:03 2020, RSSI: -57; Sat Feb 22 19:06:29 2020, RSSI: -65; Sat Feb 22 19:07:08 2020, RSSI: -52; Sat Feb 22 19:07:45 2020, RSSI: -62; Sat Feb 22 19:08:43 2020, RSSI: -70; Sat Feb 22 19:10:29 2020, RSSI: -52; Sat Feb 22 19:10:53 2020, RSSI: -42...

images" setting, essentially blocking all images from the email and giving the user the option to decide on their own and for every email separately whether they want to view the images. Although this is a viable solution against user tracking through email web-beacons, it severely diminishes the quality of campaign emails that users have signed up for so this will not be a decision that the regular user will make lightly. Another solution against email tracking are some web browser extensions (i.e., Trocker [6], UglyMail [7], PixelBlock [5]) that detect, notify, and block tracking pixel within emails. All three pixel-blocking extensions mentioned are available for Chrome and Firefox browsers, and used with Gmail and Trocker is used on Outlook as well. Although based on their reviews they do not seem to be always successful, they are still a good compromise. That being said, not all email providers and browser types would have this option to specifically block tracking pixels in emails.

VPNs: Another blocking technique we tested to limit web tracking was using a VPN. Although this creates another problem since VPN are just glorified proxies, in the sense that the VPN provider gets access to all user traffic.

Despite this, when using a VPN with web-analytics, email- and link- tracking were successfully bypassed, providing the VPN location, instead of the user location. However, device types, client settings, timestamps and number of views were still accurate.

Cookies: As for web-based tracking, even though again user experience will be affected, we found when disabling all (third-party) cookies on Google Chrome and Firefox the tracking methods were severely affected, however, enabling this setting restricts the usage of many websites. For example, websites such as Gmail, LinkedIn, Facebook, etc. will not allow a user to log in without having cookies enabled. Even when adding these websites to the whitelisted links will not allow users to log in, unless cookies are enabled. Note that on Google Chrome and Firefox blocking third party cookies was successful in stopping web analytics based tracking, however this same setting on Safari did not block web analytics tags. However, blocking cookies is not effective against link tracking as our tests on Google Chrome, Safari, and Firefox showed.

Ad-Blockers: Ad-blockers proved effective against widely known web analytics (i.e., Google Analytics, StatCounter), however, they did not block email trackers, or WebStat analytics tracking, or URL shorteners. Ad-blockers are a good solution to block from well known services, but are still not a bulletproof solution.

5.2 Bluetooth Tracking

Turn Off Bluetooth: The most secure way to prevent all Bluetooth based tracking would be to turn off Bluetooth on our mobile and laptop devices, and not utilizing and Bluetooth dependent technologies such as fitness watches, wireless headphones, automobile handsfree speakers, etc. However, it is highly improbable that users will be willing to stop using these devices. Especially as technology is becoming more Bluetooth dependent (i.e., wireless devices).

Rename Devices: To limit the tracking that can be done through Bluetooth, we suggest renaming devices to protect against **personal interest tracking**. This will not mask all information about a device, but only the owner's name.

6 Discussion and Future Work

While there are advantages in targeted advertising and BLE services for the convenience of end-users, they can be overcome by the inherent privacy risks of such systems, especially since in most cases no user approval is required for this tracking. We have demonstrated how even low-skilled adversaries with inexpensive equipment can successfully achieve tracking of targeted users, violating end-users privacy. And although there are countermeasures to limit user tracking if users decide to protect themselves from this constant tracking (e.g., install Ad-blockers, change default settings on email-providers, use VPNs, deactivate Bluetooth), we should not take for granted that the average end-user understands the consequences of such tracking, or knows how to activate these countermeasures on their devices. Especially for the very young and the very old users, that usually lack the knowledge and/or the willingness to protect themselves. In such cases, privacy-focused browsers, e.g. Brave, that by design block user tracking and data collection, through built-in Ad-blockers, might be a good compromise.

Our future work will focus on the development of user-friendly notification mechanisms, for email-campaign tracking, so that the regular user can easily be aware of the extent and the frequency of this tracking in their day-to-day communications. We also plan to build a mobile application for logging the use of the Bluetooth-controller on mobile-devices so that the privacy-aware owners of smartphones will be able to easily identify the installed applications that are sending out data over Bluetooth so that they can make informed decisions regarding the applications on their device.

References

1. BlueCap. https://apps.apple.com/us/app/bluecap/id931219725. Accessed 24 Feb 2020
2. Bluez Project. Official Linux Bluetooth protocol stack. http://www.bluez.org/. Accessed 24 Feb 2020
3. nRF Connect for Mobile. https://www.nordicsemi.com/Software-and-tools/Development-Tools/nRF-Connect-for-mobile. Accessed 24 Feb 2020
4. Physical Web App. https://google.github.io/physical-web/. Accessed 24 Feb 2020
5. PixelBlock. https://chrome.google.com/webstore/detail/pixelblock/jmpmfcjnflbco idlgapblgpgbilinlem. Accessed 24 Feb 2020
6. Trocker: a tracker blocker. https://trockerapp.github.io/. Accessed 24 Feb 2020
7. Ugly Email. https://uglyemail.com/. Accessed 24 Feb 2020
8. Bridge: PII vs. non-PII data: what the heck is the difference? https://www.thebridgecorp.com/pii-vs-non-pii-data/. Accessed 24 Feb 2020
9. Cakebread, C.: You're not alone, no one reads terms of service agreements, November 2017. https://www.businessinsider.com/deloitte-study-91-percent-agree-terms-of-service-without-reading-2017-11. Accessed 24 Feb 2020
10. Das, A.K., Pathak, P.H., Chuah, C., Mohapatra, P.: Uncovering privacy leakage in BLE network traffic of wearable fitness trackers. In: Proceedings of the 17th International ACM Workshop on Mobile Computing Systems and Applications, (HotMobile), pp. 99–104 (2016)
11. Englehardt, S., Han, J., Narayanan, A.: I never signed up for this! privacy implications of email tracking. In: Proceedings of Privacy Enhancing Technologies (PETS), pp. 109–126 (2018)
12. Englehardt, S., et al.: Cookies that give you away: the surveillance implications of web tracking. In: Proceedings of the 24th ACM International Conference on World Wide Web (WWW), pp. 289–299 (2015)
13. Fawaz, K., Kim, K.H., Shin, K.G.: Protecting privacy of BLE device users. In: Proceedings of 25th USENIX Security Symposium, pp. 1205–1221 (2016)
14. Kashi, E.: User privacy and security research survey (2019). https://docs.google.com/forms/d/13xPDjB2OOACHn94ZVHz-8KH_6HCRbrXb16lAEiYQJNc/viewanalytics
15. Kirkpatrick, K.: Tracking shoppers. ACM Commun. **63**, 19–21 (2020). https://doi.org/10.1145/3374876

16. Kolias, C., Copi, L., Zhang, F., Stavrou, A.: Breaking BLE beacons for fun but mostly profit. In: Proceedings of the 10th European Workshop on Systems Security (EuroSec), pp. 1–6 (2017)
17. Korolova, A., Sharma, V.: Cross-app tracking via nearby bluetooth low energy devices. In: Proceedings of the 8th ACM Conference on Data and Application Security and Privacy, CODASPY, pp. 43–52 (2018)
18. Mailchimp: about geolocation. https://mailchimp.com/help/about-geolocation/
19. Naik, B.I.I.: Tracking user activities using web bugs (2013). https://resources.infosecinstitute.com/tracking-user-activities-using-web-bugs/
20. Nikiforakis, N., et al.: Cookieless monster: exploring the ecosystem of web-based device fingerprinting. In: 2013 IEEE Symposium on Security and Privacy, S&P 2013, Berkeley, CA, USA, 19–22 May 2013, pp. 541–555. IEEE Computer Society (2013). https://doi.org/10.1109/SP.2013.43
21. Roesner, F., Kohno, T., Wetherall, D.: Detecting and defending against third-party tracking on the web. In: Proceedings of the 9th USENIX Symposium on Networked Systems Design and Implementation (NSDI), pp. 155–168 (2012)
22. Ruohonen, J., Leppánen, V.: Invisible pixels are dead, long live invisible pixels! In: Proceedings of the 2018 Workshop on Privacy in the Electronic Society (WPES@CCS), pp. 28–32 (2018)
23. Schlesigner, J., Day, A.: Most people just click and accept privacy policies without reading them–you might be surprised at what they allow companies to do, March 2019. https://www.cnbc.com/2019/02/07/privacy-policies-give-companies-lots-of-room-to-collect-share-data.html
24. Shanhong, L.: Global market share held by the leading web browser versions as of November 2019, December 2019. https://www.statista.com/statistics/268299/most-popular-internet-browsers/
25. Sonicare, P.: Philips sonicare privacy notice, July 2019. https://www.usa.philips.com/a-w/mobile-privacy-notice/sonicare-connected-app-gdpr.html
26. Zaeem, R., German, R., Barber, S.: Privacycheck: automatic summarization of privacy policies using data mining. ACM Trans. Internet Technol. **18**, 1–18 (2018)

Perspectives on Information Technology Artefacts in Trust-Related Interactions

Holger Koelmann(⊠)(iD)

Department of Information Systems, University of Muenster,
48149 Muenster, Germany
holger.koelmann@ercis.uni-muenster.de

Abstract. Current research often tries to measure trust in technology or argues about the possibility or plausibility of trust in technology, while neglecting other influences Information Technology artefacts (IT) might have on situations involving trust. To broaden the outlook on this area, this article focuses on perspectives that can be taken in terms of the roles IT might play in interactions that involve trust. The results of this theoretical approach provide a role framework for IT in trust-related interactions distinguishing the role of IT between a) a simple interaction enabler between two other entities, b) a mechanism for mitigating risk in an interaction between two other entities, c) a tool used in an interaction, and d) a trustee in an interaction. In addition, assumptions on the differences these roles might have on the perception of the users, i.e. reliability, control, and trust, are given for each role. Giving future research and practitioners the possibility to use the roles of the framework as lenses for further work in the area.

Keywords: Trust · Human Computer Interaction · Information Technology Artefacts · Theory · Framework

1 The Trust and IT Controversy

A recent article about seven *Grand Challenges* in Human Computer Interaction (HCI)[25], identifies trust issues as an important factor in three of the uncovered challenges, i.e. *"human-technology symbiosis"*, *"ethics, privacy, and security"*, as well as *"well-being, health, and eudaimonia"*. A deeper look into the interplay of trust and technology seems therefore necessary to further develop the field of HCI.

The role of Information Technology artefacts (IT) in trust-related interactions between entities is a disputed topic in academia, where most literature focuses on examining IT as the trustee, the object or party into which is trusted [11], of an interaction. These studies have tried to measure trust in technology with specifically developed measures in recent years [13,26]. Besides this application of measures, a long ongoing debate exists, if it is reasonable or even possible to consider the perception of trust in human-made, non-living objects, such as IT. On the one hand, Friedman et al. have once stated *"people trust people, not*

© Springer Nature Switzerland AG 2020
A. Moallem (Ed.): HCII 2020, LNCS 12210, pp. 445–457, 2020.
https://doi.org/10.1007/978-3-030-50309-3_29

technology" [6], which is backed by Solomon and Flores [24], thereby arguing that what we perceive when interacting with IT is only technical reliability and not trust. On the other hand though, Computers are Social Actors (CASA) [15] and Social Response Theory (SRT) [14] show people applying social norms to technology in experiments. The interplay between IT and trust thus remains disputed, which often resulted in an undifferentiated view as rather a question of faith to the general possibility of trusting IT, fading out other potential influences IT might have on trust-related interactions, and raising the question, if IT's only purpose in these interactions is the role of a potential trustee.

This article therefore aims to discuss the different roles that IT can take in interactions involving trust in a more differentiated way. Instead of a general understanding about trusting IT as either always possible or not, a set of different roles these artefacts can take in interactions with humans, depending on the specific context of the situation, is proposed. This includes additional relations between IT and trust, besides specifying IT as the object of trust. It should also provide scholars and practitioners with a better understanding on how trust and IT can be linked and influence each other. Consequently, the research questions of this work are:

RQ1: *What are the roles that IT artefacts can take in trust-related interactions?*

RQ2: *What might be the effects of these roles on the perception of the user?*

Due to the abstract nature of the above stated research questions, a theoretical *approach* is used in this article to propose a novel framework, which analyzes and describes, according to the classification of theory in the information systems discipline by Gergor [8], the roles of IT in trust-related interactions and their effects on the user's perception. In this case, relying on social sciences and psychology for an understanding of trust, which is then applied to a generalized interaction model involving IT, providing a more comprehensive perspective on the problem at hand.

Resulting from this approach, the rest of the article is *structured* as follows. In Sect. 2, the relevant fundamentals of trust are discussed. Then, a general interaction model for interactions that are related to trust and IT is deduced in Sect. 3. Based upon this, a framework showing perspectives, roles, and resulting effects on user's perception for IT in trust-related interactions is presented in Sect. 4, followed by a discussion of the work's limitations and implications for research and practice in Sect. 5. In the end, a conclusion of this work is provided in Sect. 6.

2 Trust

Trust has been researched for many decades with different definitions and conceptualizations for its application fields, such as psychology, sociology, economics, and computer science [1]. In this section, a definition and conceptualization of interpersonal trust is given in 2.1, with risk, as an important contextual factor, discussed in 2.2, and trust in technology, as a specific form of trust involving IT, introduced in 2.3.

2.1 Trust as an Interpersonal Concept

For the purpose of this article, trust is defined according to Mayer, Davis, and Schoorman as

> *"the willingness of a party to be vulnerable to the actions of another party based on the expectation that the other will perform a particular action important to the trustor, irrespective of the ability to monitor or control that other party"* [11].

Important elements from this definition are the willingness to make oneself vulnerable, the expected action of another party, the importance of that action to the first party, and the incapability to monitor or control the situation [11]. This definition is widely used and integrates elements of many other often used definitions, such as the one from Rousseau, Sitkin, Burt, and Camerer, who set out to create an interdisciplinary definition, which states that *"[t]rust is a psychological state comprising the intention to accept vulnerability based upon positive expectations of the intentions or behaviour of another"* [18]. One benefit of using the interpersonal trust definition by Mayer et al. is that they also conceptualized a model for measuring and further breaking down trust and its surrounding factors (see Fig. 1)[11].

The model describes the relationships between the relevant constructs for trust, which are [11]:

- an entity who is trusting, the trustor, with its general propensity to trust others,
- an entity in whom is trusted, the trustee, with its trustworthiness, based upon different antecedents,
- perceived risk in a situational context, and
- a resulting behaviour leading to an outcome, which then effects the trustworthiness of the trustee.

It should be noted, that there is no clear finite set of properties that influence a trustee's perceived trustworthiness. Mayer et al. have identified ability, benevolence, and integrity to be crucial antecedents for interpersonal trust [11]. Other studies though have identified additional potentially important antecedents, influencing the perceived trustworthiness, often depending on the properties of the selected trustee [10].

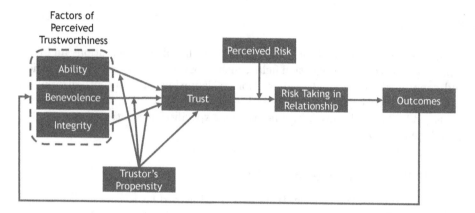

Fig. 1. Interpersonal trust model according to Mayer, Davis, and Schoorman [11]

2.2   Risk as a Contextual Factor

Besides the properties of trustor and trustee, the situational context is also highly relevant for trust to result in behaviour, a so-called trusting action [4,11]. One key contextual factor of trust is perceived risk, which is directly linked to vulnerability. Mayer et al. describe this relation as:

> "Making oneself vulnerable is taking risk. Trust is not taking risk per se, but rather it is a willingness to take risk." [11].

Trust is therefore important to overcome risk in a situation, because an action under risk involves willingly making oneself vulnerable, which is a key component of the definition of trust.

2.3   Trust in Technology

Under the assumption that IT can be trusted, a few changes to the interpersonal trust model above become necessary. With the conceptualization of IT as a trustee, the properties of the trustee that work as antecedents of trustworthiness, had to be changed away from properties of people to properties of technology. One commonly used translation of these properties was done by McKnight et al. [13]. In order for this to work, they remapped the trustworthiness factors identified by Mayer et al. [11] in the following way [13]:

- instead of ability, the degree of supporting the required *functionality* of an IT artefact is used,
- instead of benevolence, the degree of *helpfulness* through helper functions of IT is used, and
- instead of integrity, the *reliability* of IT is used.

With this remapping of antecedents of trustworthiness, it is possible to measure the trustworthiness of IT and consider it as a trustee in a trust relationship or interaction.

When evaluating IT or assessing its broader societal effects, models and theories, such as the Technology Acceptance Model (TAM)[5] and the Unified Theory of Acceptance and Use of Technology (UTAUT)[27] can be used to measure the acceptance, intention to use, and adoption of IT. The question of users trusting technology can be important in this context, with multiple studies identifying trust in IT or its trustworthiness as an important additional factor in a user's acceptance, intention to use, or adoption of an artefact [7,13,20,23]. Besides these outcomes, Thielsch et al. have also discovered the influence of trust in information systems on well-being, performance, and stress [26], which could relate to IT itself as well.

3 Trust-Related Interactions

Resulting from the given definition and conceptualization of trust (see 2.1), an interaction between trustor and trustee can be used to abstract and analyze a situation involving trust and IT. To find additional roles IT can play in these situations, a model of trust-related interactions with their potential ways of IT involvement is derived. As a starting point, a person (or user) is defined to be the trustor in the interaction. In terms of relevant trustees, with whom a person can interact, interpersonal trust and trust in technology have already been covered in 2.1 and 2.3. They are also included in the interaction model. Besides these, various other trustees have also been researched in the literature. For the purpose of this article, it can be argued that especially trust in organizations is of additional interest, because organizations provide the user with IT and are therefore potentially perceived to be associated with it [17,21], e.g. governments [28] and companies [9]. Therefore, organizations will be considered in the abstraction of the interaction as well. The trust-related interaction itself takes place between trustor and trustee in a situational context that involves risk. The resulting interaction model is illustrated in Fig. 2.

In the model, IT is already included as a trustee. But besides being a potential direct interaction partner, IT may serve other purposes in the context of the interaction as well. Following Söllner et al. [22] in differentiating between IT as a mediator or as a trustee, the positioning of the IT artefact in the interaction is set accordingly. Hence, an IT artefact is either a mediator within an interaction between two other entities, effectively providing a form of infrastructure, or the target of an interaction. It is noteworthy to say, while one IT artefact may serve as the trustee of the interaction, another may act as a mediator at the same time.

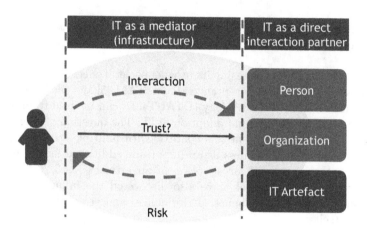

Fig. 2. Trust as an interaction between different entities.

4 Perspectives on IT Artefacts in Trust-Related Interactions

This trust-related interaction model can now be analyzed to find potential roles that IT artefacts can take within the interaction. In this section, the following identified roles for IT are discussed:

1. an interaction enabler between two other entities (see 4.1),
2. a mechanism for mitigating risk in an interaction between two other entities (see 4.2),
3. a tool used in an interaction (see 4.3), and
4. a trustee in an interaction (see 4.4).

In addition, different terms for the influence on the interaction as perceived by its users are assigned to the roles and discussed further in the article. These include the perceived reliability of an artefact, the change of perceived control during the interaction, and a distinction for IT as interaction partners for which either reliability or trust is perceived. These roles and perception concepts are also visualized in Fig. 3.

It is important to note that IT can potentially fulfill each of these roles depending on the interaction or the scientific perspective taken on the interaction. To further clarify the roles and their interplay, an encrypted messaging service is used as a running example throughout this section.

4.1 IT as an Interaction Enabler

The first identified role is IT as an interaction enabler. It can clearly be identified when seeing IT as a mediator or infrastructure between a trustor and a trustee. IT can be used as a platform or channel for trustee and trustor to act, enabling

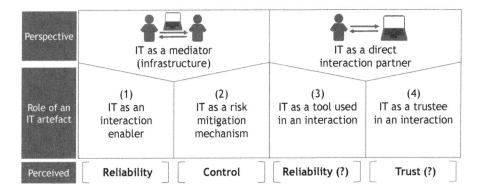

Fig. 3. Roles of IT in trust-related interactions.

the interaction. The parties represent themselves digitally or use digital channels within their trusting relationship. In this case, the interaction is based upon the use of technology to facilitate the interaction in any form possible. The interaction involving that role is visualized in Fig. 4.

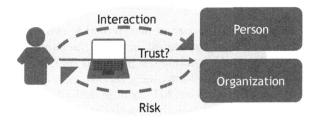

Fig. 4. IT as an interaction enabler

By using IT as an enabler for the interaction, IT can introduce new risk, such as potential system failures, affecting the interaction [6] and possibly alter or distort the perceived trust between parties involved, due to differences in media compared to non-digital alternatives [3]. In terms of the trusting relationship, the involved parties rely on it to work, to be able to interact with one another. Therefore, IT needs to be reliable in this trust interaction. The important factor for the user's perception is therefore *reliability*.

Every IT artefact that is capable of providing the basis of an interaction can potentially take this role. In the example of an encrypted messaging service, the service provides the means to interact digitally on which users rely upon to work as a basis for their interaction.

4.2   IT as a Risk Mitigation Mechanism

The second identified role is IT as a risk mitigation mechanism. From the perspective of IT as an infrastructure, IT can be used to mitigate the involved perceived risk in the context of an interaction. Hereby not affecting trust between the two parties per se, but rather the outcome of a trust evaluation against the perceived risks involved, resulting in a potentially different trust-based action [4]. This role is depicted in Fig. 5.

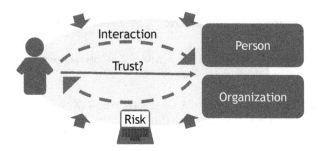

Fig. 5. IT as a risk mitigation mechanism

By actively mitigating the amount of perceived risk involved in a situation, IT acts as a control system for the context in which the interaction takes place [19]. IT taking this role is thus affecting the perceived *control* over a situation.

In the example of an encrypted messaging service, especially the encryption of the transferred massages stands out to be of importance for mitigating the risk in an interaction, e.g. involving to talk about activities that involve high amounts of risks, such as submitting information out of crisis regions [12]. Other examples of IT use mitigating risk can be found in additional forms of transparency or obfuscation technology. Recent developments in blockchain technologies are even often called trust-free technologies or ecosystems [2,16], because trust becomes irrelevant through control in their contexts.

4.3   IT as a Tool Used in an Interaction

The third identified role is IT as a tool used in an interaction. In this case, IT is viewed from the perspective of IT as the interaction partner, which is visualized in Fig. 6.

According to Solomon and Flores, trust, as *"a function of human interaction"* [24], only applies to beings with agency, responding to our actions according to their own attitudes towards the situation and their own intentions [24]. Following this logic, IT artefacts cannot be considered to be trustworthy in a reciprocal relationship on which trust usually is based [24]. Shneiderman put the perception and related behavior of a human user towards IT the following way:

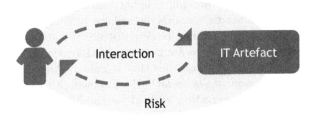

Fig. 6. IT as an interaction partner

"If users rely on a computer and it fails, they may get frustrated or vent their anger by smashing a keyboard, but there is no relationship of trust with a computer." [21]

For any trust-related interaction involving IT, this would mean that we won't be able to view IT as the trustee in the interaction, but would have to refer to IT's perceived *reliability* when using the perspective of IT as the interaction partner.

When considering the example of an encrypted messaging service, this would mean, using the perspective of IT being the direct interaction partner, the importance of the perceived reliability of the service is the important perception for its user.

4.4   IT as a Trustee in an Interaction

The fourth and last identified role is IT as a trustee in an interaction. This role is depicted in Fig. 7, which strongly resembles Fig. 6, differing only in an added trust relationship. When directly interacting with IT, the IT artefact might also be seen as the trustee in a user-to-IT trust relationship.

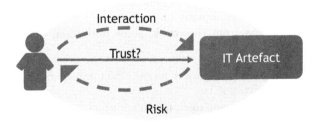

Fig. 7. IT as a trustee in an interaction

CASA [15] and SRT [14] provide insights into how people apply human behaviour, such as social norms, towards technology. It is important to note, the people in the experiments, examined to demonstrate the attribution of human traits to IT through users, were aware that their behaviour might seem unreasonable [15]. Nass et al. derived from this that human *"individuals' interactions with computers are fundamentally social"* [15]. Following this line of argument, a user's perception in an interaction with IT as the direct interaction partner may include the perception of *trust* in IT.

Looking back into the example of an encrypted messaging service, the user might perceive trust in the service and therefore be willing to use it even in situations involving a high amount of perceived risk.

5 Discussion

The proposed framework of roles that IT can take in trust-related interactions, has some limitations and implications for academics as well as practitioners.

Limitations of the Framework. Since this is a theoretical article, the conceptual framework still needs to be tested to fully prove its actual usefulness for academia in future research and practice. Specifically, the distinction in terms of IT as an interaction partner into reliability and trust needs to be clarified and checked for proof, if this holds true. Therefore, the question of the plausibility of trust in IT still remains open.

Implications for Research. This work shows that IT can have multiple implications on situations that involve trust, providing the possibility to use roles of the framework as scientific lenses for research to fixate a certain perspective on the analyzed artefact, while further examining it. Using these roles as lenses on IT, scientists can differentiate properly, what effects they can expect for their studies and measurements when using IT in a trust-related situation. It shows that IT can fulfill different purposes in relation to trust, providing a more differentiated look into what is actually happening.

In addition, resulting from this work, some additional open questions for future research arise:

- How does IT as a risk mitigation factor affect interpersonal or person-to-organizational interactions?
- Is trust in IT actually reasonable and under which circumstances?
- What are processes surrounding IT or attributes of IT that lead to the perception of trust in IT artefacts by its users?
- How can IT be developed and used to work best according to the role or roles it is fulfilling in relation to trust?
- What are roles in case of a more sociotechnical information systems perspective?

Research hence still needs to guide practice towards a better understanding of the social interplay their developments encounter as well as what influences their IT may have on their users.

Implications for Practice. Practitioners can use the proposed roles to think about the influence their IT artefacts may have on the trust-related interactions of their users and can evaluate as well as develop them according to the social role they fulfill. Further work from researchers and practitioners should find guidelines and best practices to better understand their influence points in designing IT according to each potential role.

6   Conclusion

This articles answered what roles IT artefacts can take in trust-related interactions and what the effects of these roles on the perception of the user might be from a theoretical perspective. The resulting framework (Fig. 3) for IT and trust shows clear roles IT can take in trust-related interactions. With the proposed distinction between these roles, research and practice can gain better insights into the effects of IT on the real social world.

Acknowledgements. This work was supported by the *"Trust and Communication in a Digitized World"* research project (promotion reference 1712/1), funded by the German Research Foundation (DFG).

References

1. Alzahrani, L., Al-Karaghouli, W., Weerakkody, V.: Analysing the critical factors influencing trust in e-government adoption from citizens' perspective: a systematic review and a conceptual framework. Int. Bus. Rev. **26**(1), 164–175 (2017). https://doi.org/10.1016/j.ibusrev.2016.06.004
2. Beck, R., Stenum Czepluch, J., Lollike, N., Malone, S.: Blockchain-the gateway to trust-free cryptographic transactions. In: Proceedings to the European Conference on Information Systems, ECIS, Research Papers (2016). https://aisel.aisnet.org/ecis2016_rp/153
3. Daft, R.L., Lengel, R.H.: Organizational information requirements, media richness and structural design. Manage. Sci. **32**(5), 554–571 (1986). https://doi.org/10.1287/mnsc.32.5.554
4. Das, T., Teng, B.S.: The risk-based view of trust: a conceptual framework. J. Bus. Psychol. **19**(1), 85–116 (2004). https://doi.org/10.1023/B:JOBU.0000040274.23551.1b
5. Davis, F.D., Bagozzi, R.P., Warshaw, P.R.: User acceptance of computer technology: a comparison of two theoretical models. Manage. Sci. **35**(8), 982–1003 (1989). https://www.jstor.org/stable/2632151
6. Friedman, B., Khan Jr., P.H., Howe, D.C.: Trust online. Commun. ACM **43**(12), 34–40 (2000). https://doi.org/10.1145/355112.355120

7. Gefen, D., Karahanna, E., Straub, D.W.: Trust and tam in online shopping: an integrated model. MIS Q. **27**(1), 51–90 (2003). https://doi.org/10.2307/30036519
8. Gregor, S.: The nature of theory in information systems. MIS Q. **30**(3), 611–642 (2006). https://doi.org/10.2307/25148742
9. Lankton, N.K., McKnight, D.H.: What does it mean to trust facebook? Examining technology and interpersonal trust beliefs. ACM SIGMIS Database DATABASE Adv. Inf. Syst. **42**(2), 32–54 (2011). https://doi.org/10.1145/1989098.1989101
10. Lee, J.D., See, K.A.: Trust in automation: designing for appropriate reliance. Hum. Factors **46**(1), 50–80 (2004). https://doi.org/10.1518/hfes.46.1.50_30392
11. Mayer, R.C., Davis, J.H., Schoorman, D.F.: An integrative model of organizational trust. Acad. Manag. Rev. **20**(3), 709–734 (1995). https://doi.org/10.5465/AMR.1995.9508080335
12. McGregor, S.E., Charters, P., Holliday, T., Roesner, F.: Investigating the computer security practices and needs of journalists. In: 24th {USENIX} Security Symposium ({USENIX} Security 15), pp. 399–414. {USENIX} Association, Washington, D.C. (2015). https://www.usenix.org/conference/usenixsecurity15/technical-sessions/presentation/mcgregor
13. McKnight, D.H., Carter, M., Thatcher, J.B., Clay, P.F.: Trust in a specific technology: an investigation of its components and measures. ACM Trans. Manage. Inf. Syst. **2**(2), 1–25 (2011). https://doi.org/10.1145/1985347.1985353
14. Nass, C., Moon, Y.: Machines and mindlessness: social responses to computers. J. Soc. Issues **56**(1), 81–103 (2000). https://doi.org/10.1111/0022-4537.00153
15. Nass, C., Steuer, J., Tauber, E.R.: Computers are social actors. In: Proceedings of the SIGCHI conference on Human Factors in Computing Systems, pp. 72–78 (1994). https://doi.org/10.1145/191666.191703
16. Notheisen, B., Cholewa, J.B., Shanmugam, A.P.: Trading real-world assets on blockchain. Bus. Inf. Syst. Eng. **59**(6), 425–440 (2017). https://doi.org/10.1007/s12599-017-0499-8
17. Rosenbloom, A.: Trusting technology: introduction. Commun. ACM **43**(12), 31–32 (2000). https://doi.org/10.1145/355112.355119
18. Rousseau, D.M., Sitkin, S.B., Burt, R.S., Camerer, C.: Not so different after all: a cross-discipline view of trust. Acad. Manage. Rev. **23**(3), 393–404 (1998). https://doi.org/10.5465/amr.1998.926617
19. Schoorman, F.D., Wood, M.M., Breuer, C.: Would trust by any other name smell as sweet? reflections on the meanings and uses of trust across disciplines and context. In: Bornstein, B.H., Tomkins, A.J. (eds.) Motivating Cooperation and Compliance with Authority. NSM, vol. 62, pp. 13–35. Springer, Cham (2015). https://doi.org/10.1007/978-3-319-16151-8_2
20. Shareef, M.A., Archer, N., Dwivedi, Y.K.: An empirical investigation of electronic government service quality: from the demand-side stakeholder perspective. Total Qual. Manage. Bus. Excel. **26**(3–4), 339–354 (2015). https://doi.org/10.1080/14783363.2013.832477
21. Shneiderman, B.: Designing trust into online experiences. Commun. ACM **43**(12), 57–59 (2000). https://doi.org/10.1145/355112.355124
22. Söllner, M., Hoffmann, A., Hoffmann, H., Wacker, A., Leimeister, J.M.: Understanding the formation of trust in IT artifacts. In: Proceedings of the International Conference on Information Systems, ICIS (2012)
23. Söllner, M., Hoffmann, A., Leimeister, J.M.: Why different trust relationships matter for information systems users. Eur. J. Inf. Syst. **25**(3), 274–287 (2016). https://doi.org/10.1057/ejis.2015.17

24. Solomon, R.C., Flores, F.: Building Trust: In Business, Politics, Relationships, and Life. Oxford University Press, Oxford (2003)
25. Stephanidis, C., et al.: Seven HCI grand challenges. Int. J. Hum. Comput. Inter. **35**(14), 1229–1269 (2019). https://doi.org/10.1080/10447318.2019.1619259
26. Thielsch, M.T., Meeßen, S.M., Hertel, G.: Trust and distrust in information systems at the workplace. PeerJ **6**, e5483 (2018). https://doi.org/10.7717/peerj.5483
27. Venkatesh, V., Morris, M.G., Davis, G.B., Davis, F.D.: User acceptance of information technology: toward a unified view. MIS Q. **27**(3), 425–478 (2003). https://doi.org/10.2307/30036540
28. Welch, E.W., Hinnant, C.C., Moon, M.J.: Linking citizen satisfaction with e-government and trust in government. J. Public Adm. Res. Theor. **15**(3), 371–391 (2005). https://doi.org/10.1093/jopart/mui021

Mental Model Mapping Method
for Cybersecurity

Kaur Kullman[1]($\boxtimes$), Laurin Buchanan[2]($\boxtimes$), Anita Komlodi[3]($\boxtimes$), and Don Engel[3]($\boxtimes$)

[1] Tallinn University of Technology, Tallinn, Estonia
m4c@coda.ee
[2] Secure Decisions, Northport, NY, USA
laurin.buchanan@securedecisions.com
[3] University of Maryland, Baltimore County, Baltimore, MD, USA
{komlodi,donengel}@umbc.edu

Abstract. Visualizations can enhance the efficiency of Cyber Defense Analysts, Cyber Defense Incident Responders and Network Operations Specialists (Subject Matter Experts, SME) by providing contextual information for various cybersecurity-related datasets and data sources. We propose that customized, stereoscopic 3D visualizations, aligned with SMEs internalized representations of their data, may enhance their capability to understand the state of their systems in ways that flat displays with either text, 2D or 3D visualizations cannot afford. For these visualizations to be useful and efficient, we need to align these to SMEs internalized understanding of their data. In this paper we propose a method for interviewing SMEs to extract their implicit and explicit understanding of the data that they work with, to create useful, interactive, stereoscopically perceivable visualizations that would assist them with their tasks.

Keywords: Visualization design and evaluation methods · Cybersecurity · Data visualization

1 Introduction

Cybersecurity visualizations provide Cyber Defense Analysts[1], Cyber Defense Incident Responders[2] and Network Operations Specialists[3] (all three roles will collectively be referred to as Subject Matter Expert (SME) in this paper from here forward) with visual representation of alphanumeric data that would otherwise be difficult to comprehend due to its large volume. Such visualizations aim to efficiently support tasks including detecting, monitoring and mitigating cyberattacks in a timely and efficient manner. For more information about these and other cybersecurity related roles, see [1]. As noted in [2], cybersecurity-specific visualizations can be broadly classified into a) network analysis, b) malware analysis, c) threat analysis and situational awareness. Timely and

---

[1] As designated PR-CDA-001 and bearing responsibilities for tasks identified in [18].

[2] As designated PR-CIR-001 and bearing responsibilities for tasks identified in [18].

[3] As designated OM-NET-001 and bearing responsibilities for tasks identified in [18].

© Springer Nature Switzerland AG 2020
A. Moallem (Ed.): HCII 2020, LNCS 12210, pp. 458–470, 2020.
https://doi.org/10.1007/978-3-030-50309-3_30

efficient execution of tasks in each of these categories may require different types of visualizations addressed by a growing number of cybersecurity-specific visualization tools (for examples and descriptions of such see [3, 5] and [6]) as well as universal software with visualization capabilities. These tools could be used to visualize data in myriad ways (for examples and descriptions of such see [7]) so that SMEs could explore their data visually and interactively (for interaction techniques see [8]). These are crucial qualities for SMEs, with emphasis on the importance of the low latency between SME's request for a change in visualization (change in applied filter, time window or other query parameters) and rendering of the visualized response from the system [9].

The challenge in creating meaningful visual tools for cybersecurity practitioners is in combining the expertise from specialists from the fields of data visualization and cybersecurity so that the resulting visualizations are effective and indeed useful for their intended users [10]. Further, creating visualizations useful for SMEs is not possible without an in-depth understanding of the tasks which the visualizations will support [11]. Hence, we describe here a multi-part, semi-structured interviewing method for extracting from an individual SME their internalized understanding of the dataset[4] that represents their protected environment, in order to create visualizations that align with their own understanding of that dataset and that will enhance the SMEs and their colleagues' ability to understand and work with that dataset.

The proposed interview method is rooted in the tradition of participatory design [12], a democratic form of design originating in Scandinavia. In participatory design all stakeholders are involved in the design by directly designing the user experience. Stakeholders are asked to not simply inform the design process but to contribute by actually designing interfaces and interactions.

2 Background

Although there are other design approaches for developing data visualizations [13], we identified the need for a cybersecurity specific method that would allow SMEs to create spatial three-dimensional layouts of visualized elements, referred to as data-shapes, that are specific to these SMEs datasets or data sources, in order to benefit from the novel capabilities of Virtual and Mixed Reality headsets that can provide users with stereoscopic perception of the data visualization environment.

We acknowledge that the efficiency of 3D data visualization has been subject to controversy (as thoroughly explained in [14]) and that the usability of visualizations overall are hindered by biological factors of the user (e.g. impaired color vision, impaired vison): these and other concerns were covered in earlier papers of our project [15] and [4]. Despite that, for the users who can use and who do find 3D visualizations useful, we should provide methods they can use to create, and suitable technical tools to use useful visualization of their data. Other research [16] has previously shown that stereoscopically perceived, spatialized data visualizations may provide advantages for understanding

---

[4] In the context of this paper, "dataset" refers to the collection of individual data sources, e.g., network flow data, log files, PCAP, databases and other stores (Elasticsearch, Mongo, RDB-s) used by an SME at a particular organization.

and exploring the types of multidimensional (often partially deterministic) datasets and sources that SMEs work with.

The Virtual Data Explorer (VDE) software that may be employed for visualizing cybersecurity specific datasets was covered in previous research [15] and [4]. For a data-shape or their constellations to be useful, the SME must be able to readily map data into a data-shape and choose visual encoding for its attributes so that the resulting visualization will enhance their understanding of that data. Only once an SME is intimate with the composition of the visualization and its relation to the underlying dataset or source can the SME use that visualization to extract information from it.

In this paper we describe a mental model mapping method that may be used to extract the necessary information for creating such data-shapes from SMEs while they're working with their actual data. To validate the usefulness of the new visualizations created with this method, it would be beneficial to involve at least three SMEs from the same group or company who are working with the same data so that the visualizations created with each participant could be evaluated at the end of the process with other members of the same group.

Visualization examples in this paper are showing NATO CCDCOE Locked Shields CDX networks traffic dataset [4], Figures feature screen captures from VDE Virtual Reality sessions.

2.1 Assumptions

The following assumptions underlie our work:

Assumption 1: Visualizations of different dimensions of network topology (functional, logical, geographic) using stereoscopically perceivable 3D can enhance an SME's understanding of their unique protected network environment if the visualizations are designed to match the individual SMEs mental model(s) of their environment's raw cyber data.

Assumption 2: It is possible to create data-shapes by interviewing SMEs in order to identify hierarchies of entities and entity[5] groups in their data that, when grouped by their functions, could be arranged into a 3D topology.

2.2 Hypotheses

We hypothesize that enriching the 3D data-shapes with additional contextual information that is derived from the queries that SMEs typically execute to find all relevant information to their data-focused tasks could be of benefit, specifically:

1. 3D data-shapes enriched with contextual information will provide significant insights more effectively in comparison with their alphanumerical representations and/or 2D visualizations on flat screens.
2. 3D data-shapes enriched with contextual information will improve the efficiency of operators' workflow, e.g., seeking answers to their analytical questions.

---

[5] "Entity" refers to any atomic unit that the user could encounter in the data that's being investigated. In the context of this paper for example: a networked computer, IoT device, server, switch, but also a human actor (known user, malicious actor, administrator).

3 Process

The overarching goal of the SME interview process is to identify the properties that an SME seeks within the raw cyber data of their environment, i.e., their dataset, in order to obtain answers to the analytic questions for their work role. To do this, we must identify the relevant attributes of the data which enable the SME to form, verify, or disprove hypotheses about possible incidents or noteworthy events relevant to their work role. Based on the SME's role and specific inquiry goal, we determine the desired dimensions of data (entities, the relations of groups, subgroups, and sub-subgroups, etc.) to be visualized. We then consider which properties should be represented by which elements; an example of these dimensions and properties can be seen in Fig. 1, where names of groups (e.g. "..Siemens Spectrum 5 power management..", "Substation equipment network") are visible above the "blades" of a data-shape, while names of subgroups (inside each group) (e.g. "Windows 10 workstations", "PLC-s", "Servers") are visible inside the "blades", above the entities of that subgroup. To better grasp the three-dimensionality of these shapes, see videos at https://coda.ee/M4C.

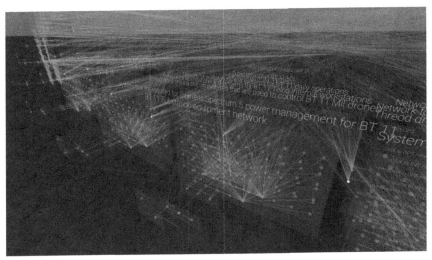

Fig. 1. Examining relationships and behavior of the entities of a group of groups.

This information is initially elicited through the first individual interviews with the SME group (Session 1 Interviews) by asking a series of specific questions designed to identify these groups and entities. In our example case, where we are visualizing the functional topologies of computer networks, the entities are networked devices (server, laptop, fridge, gas turbine's controller, etc.) that can be classified into multiple different groups (e.g., logical subnetwork, physical topology, geolocation, etc.). The relevant grouping (i.e., business functions, found vulnerabilities, etc.) depends on the goal of an SME's inquiry. If the visualization goal was different, for example, to visualize application logs, the initial interview questions should be adjusted accordingly.

Once all the first interviews have been completed, we evaluate the layouts created during the interviews (see Sect. 3.3). All or some of the layouts will be implemented using VDE (as described in [4]), either by creating new configuration files or implementing necessary components in C# (or with another visualization tool). Once done, the resulting data visualizations shall be tested with the data that the interviewed SMEs would be using it with (or an anonymized version of it), prior to a second round of SME interviews.

During Session 2 interviews, subjects are expected to use the custom visualizations with a VDE instance, that is rendering the data-shapes from actual data from the SME's environment to enable the SME to adequately evaluate the usefulness of the visualization.

3.1 Prescreening Questionnaire

Participants should be pre-screened to verify their level of expertise and work roles to the participant pool. In our example case, SMEs working subject matter (e.g., computer network activity data) for at least a year with the specific dataset of their protected network environment (e.g., flow data, captured packets, Intrusion Detection System logs, logs of endpoints and servers, vulnerability scan reports, etc.,) may be invited to participate in the study.

3.2 Session 1 Interviews

In the beginning of each session, the interviewer explains the purpose behind the knowledge elicitation and asks the SME for written permission to record audio and video during the session. The interviewer then conducts a semi-structured interview using guiding questions to learn the SME's understanding of the norms, behaviors, structure, context etc. of the available dataset (e.g., their computer network's topology, logfiles, etc.). In cases where the tasks or roles of the group being studied are different than described in this paper, the questions should be adjusted accordingly.

To gather actionable information from an interview, it is imperative that the interviewer quickly builds rapport with the SME to a level, that allows the SME to validate the level of subject matter competence of the interviewer [17]. If the interviewee, a seasoned SME, determines that the interviewer does not have a strong understanding of the related tasks, data, or concerns, they may choose to skip through the interview with minimal effort, rendering the efficiency and usefulness of the resulting visualization negligible.

Throughout the interview, equipment to support and capture the SME's participation in the design process must be available. Equipment could include a whiteboard, large sheets of paper with colored pens, LEGO sets, a computer with access to the datasets the SME could refer to, or other tools, that would help and encourage the SME to express their perception of the structure of the data in three-dimensional space. With LEGO sets, for example, they could lay out the structure of groups on the table and build them vertically, to a limit. With whiteboard SME could sketch the possible visualizations, while the interviewer may need to help with capturing its dimensionality.

The questions below are examples for how to enable the SME to think through their knowledge of the targeted data and lay out the groups. Not only should these questions be adjusted for the specifics of the role of the person and data source or data set, but also to the personality of the SME. The interviewer may need to adjust or rearrange the sequence of the questions based on the responsiveness of the SME.

Question 1: What are the primary everyday tasks that require you to use large data sources (datasets, data collections)?

The intent of this question is to build rapport with the SME, while finding out the specific role of the interviewee and identifying the data that the interview should focus on. To help the SME articulate their tasks, a list of tasks from the Reference Spreadsheet for the NICE Framework [18] (respectively for PR-CDA-001, PR-CIR-001 and OM-NET-001 or others) could be shown to the interviewee. Depending on the tasks identified, interviewer could then choose which one(s) of the data source(s) relevant to the tasks to focus on.

Question 2: What groups of networked entities participate in your computer networks?

The intent of this question is to identify the nested groups of additional groups and entities (in the data source that was identified in Q1) that could be laid out spatially. If the interviewee can't name any such groups spontaneously, the interviewer may suggest the following examples:

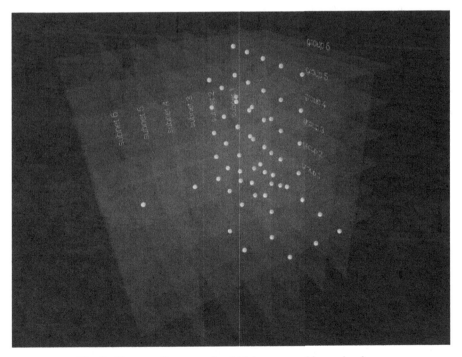

Fig. 2. Closeup of an example of triples arranged in a cube shape.

1. Physical entities, e.g., users, administrators, guests, known external actors (including intruders).
2. Endpoints, e.g., user workstations and laptops.
3. Network infrastructure devices, e.g., switches, routers.
4. Virtual or physical networked services, e.g., Active Directory Domain Controller, a file server, databases, network security services (DLP, SIEM, traffic collectors, etc.), as well as physical computers running the virtualized containers, containing the offered services.
5. Special purpose equipment, e.g., physical access control, Industrial Control Systems.
6. External partners' services inside or outside the perimeter.
7. Unknown entities.

Question 3: What subgroups [and further subgroups] could there be within those groups?

The intent of this question is to help the interviewee to consider different ways of thinking about the dimensions of data and choose the better candidates to be represented by the three axes in a 3D visualization, and the relative positioning of these groups.

See Fig. 2, where entities' positions on XYZ axes are determined by:

Z) the group this entity belongs to (a subnet).
Y) subgroup (a functional group in that subnet: servers, networks devices, workstations).
X) entity's sequential (arbitrary) position in that subgroup (for example the last octet of its IP address).

Question 4: How would you decide to which group an entity belongs, based on its behavior?

The intent of this question is to understand how to build the decision process for the VDE (or other visualization interface) that determines where and how to show each entity in the visualization.

Question 5: While working on task X (identified in Q1), what data source do you investigate first (second, third, etc.), and what would you be looking for in that data?

1. What questions are you asking while building a query to find relevant data in that data source?
2. What clauses would you use to build a query on that data source to acquire relevant information for this question?
3. How do you determine if the result returned by the query contains benign information or if it requires further investigation from the same or other data sources?
4. What other data sources would you consult to validate if a finding is benign or deserves further investigation?
5. If you've identified a recurring identifier, how do you implement its automatic detection for the future?
6. Repeat {1–5} for other data sources relevant for the interviewee.

Question 6: Please group the most relevant query conditions (or categories of indicators) that you use in your tasks to group the found entities into groups of three

This question elicits triples that will then be aligned on 3 axes to create 3D data-shapes. Examples of potential triple groupings are shown in Table 1, while Figs. 1 and 2 show a 3D data-shape for an individual triple. Multiple related triples can be presented in constellations of data-shapes, as shown in Figs. 3 and 4.

Table 1. Examples for mapping identified groups to 3D axes (triples).

Axis	Example 1 (see Fig. 2)	Example 2 (combination of addressing components)	Example 3 (functional topology of groups of entities in an organization)	Example 4 (private ad-dress space)
Z	Entity group	Subnet (e.g., 10.0.x.0/8)	Organizational group (marketing, admin, HR, etc.) the entity is part of	10.x.0.0/8
Y	Entity subgroup	last octet of entity's IP address	Team within larger Org. group (accounts payable/receivable) the entity is part of	10.0.x.0/8
X	Inter-subgroup sequence	Active ingress/egress port nr	Sequential position in the team (team manager or staff; HQ or satellite office)	10.0.0.x/8

The intent of this question is to gather necessary knowledge to create or identify the queries that should be run to gather data for rendering the visualization of groups identified in Question 3.

Question 7: Please arrange triples (see examples in Table 1) into a relational structure on the whiteboard

The intent of this question is to encourage the SME to reimagine (and redraw if needed) the groups and their arrangement into subgroups so that instead of just 3 × 3 relations, triples would be positioned spatially into a stereoscopically perceivable constellation data-shape (see Fig. 3), adding additional dimensions for potential additional data encoding.

At this stage the interview should be ripe for in-depth discussion about the findings and possible enhancements of the sketches of visualizations that were created by the SME and the interviewer to make sure there is enough details for its implementation.

Based on the sketches created during the interview by the interviewer and SME, they will select one or more layouts as potential designs to be implemented in VDE (or other) software for further evaluation. Once the SME's understanding of their dataset has been

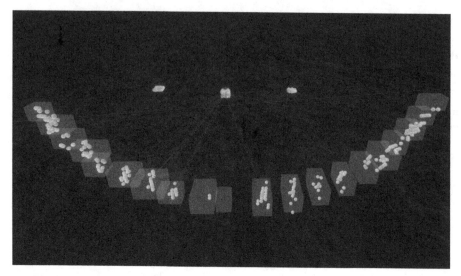

Fig. 3. Overview of a set of groups of groups of entities arranged into a constellation.

documented, the interviewer will explain further steps (e.g., timeline of implementation, further testing with her/his data, if necessary).

3.3 Implementation of Data Visualization

After conducting Session 1 interviews, the data-shapes identified during those interviews will be evaluated by the conductor of the study with the following criteria:

1. The proposed visualization differs from existing 2D or 3D data-shapes that either the SMEs referred to, or which are previously known to authors (for example, Figs. 1, 2, 3 and 4). If the visualization described by an SME could be achieved using an existing module of VDE (by reconfiguring it) or with another software, that shall be employed instead of creating the visualization anew.
3. The data-shape can be rendered functional using the data that the SME referred to during their Interview Session 1.

Layouts that meet the evaluation criteria are implemented with chosen software. In case the VDE is used, the visualization layouts are either created via new configuration files, or by implementing the necessary new components with C# and Unity 3D.

Once all the data-shapes identified during the Session 1 interviews have been implemented in the visualization software, and each SME's visualization has been reviewed with the data sources specified by the SME and found to support the analytical goals provided by the interviewee that it was designed with, Session 2 interviews will be scheduled.

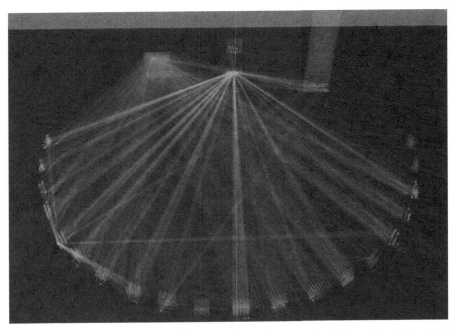

Fig. 4. Overview of a constellation of groups, where subgroups of entities can be distinguished afar, and examined in detail when user zooms in (moves closer with the VR headset).

3.4 Interview Session 2

The goal of these interviews is for each SME to evaluate the usefulness of the visualization(s) developed based on their interview and other visualizations that were created for their colleagues for the same data and/or role. At the start of the interview, the SME will be reminded about the findings from the Session 1 interview and asked for permission to record the audio and video during the current session. When each visualization is introduced, the interviewer will thoroughly explain the logic of the visualization process to the SME, to make sure they fully understand what is being visualized and why, and ensure the SME knows how to use the visualization with their data and interpret its results.

The SME will then be asked to answer some task-related questions while using each of the visualizations: for example, can the visualization enable the SME to identify whether (a) *a suspicious host* has initiated a connection targeting an entity that is currently (b) *vulnerable* and/or the physical or functional provenance of the targeted entity is (c) *part of the protected network* at the (d) *time* when this behavior was observed. Afterwards, the SME will be asked to provide feedback on the visualizations. This feedback will be subjective measures of mental workload and usability, measured using standard survey instruments, respectively the Modified Cooper-Harper (MCH) [19] Scale and the System Usability Scale (SUS) [20]. MCH uses a decision tree to elicit mental workload; the SME simply follows the decision tree, answering questions regarding the task and system in order to elicit an appropriate workload rating. In the SUS, participants are asked to respond to 10 standard statements about usability with a Likert scale that ranges from "Strongly Agree" to "Strongly Disagree". The SUS can be used on small sample sizes with reliable results, effectively differentiating between usable and unusable visualizations. Once done, the SME is asked, using open ended questions to provide overall feedback on the visualizations used, as well on the process of the interviews.

4   Conclusion

The mental model mapping method described in this paper could be used to create data visualizations with SMEs that would be beneficial for them and their immediate peers' purposes. Visualizations that originate from the same SME group could be evaluated by peers from that same group, preferably with the same dataset or using the same original data sources.

The participatory design method described in this paper focuses on creating 3D visualizations for Virtual Data Explorer. With appropriate changes, it may be also applicable for developing 2D visualizations for cybersecurity.

Our follow-up study will describe the results of applying this interviewing method, including an overview of the results of Session 1 interviews, descriptive visualizations of the data-shapes created during the study, lessons learnt from applying the interviewing method and overview of SME feedback on the visualizations used during Interview Session 2.

Later studies could investigate whether data-shapes created based on interviews with experienced SMEs are more accurate and detailed than the data-shapes for the same data that were created during interviews with less experienced SMEs. Another area ripe for research is evaluating what impact these 3D data-shapes developed based on experienced users' interview might have in teaching the (functional, physical, logical) topology of a protected network environment. It is possible that this would speed up the onboarding of new team members by assisting them in learning the functional topology and the behavior of entities that are present in their datasets, for example, the logs from various devices in the protected computer networks.

Further evaluation of the qualitative differences between the 3D visualizations created with SMEs could be done with a follow up study, where the control group's members are not granted access to these 3D visualizations, while experimental group will be taught to use the 3D visualizations created during the study.

Acknowledgements. For all the hints, ideas and mentoring, authors thank Jennifer A. Cowley, Alexander Kott, Lee C. Trossbach, Jaan Priisalu, Olaf Manuel Maennel. This research was partly supported by the Army Research Laboratory under Cooperative Agreement Number W911NF-17-2-0083 and in conjunction with the CCDC Command, Control, Computers, Communications, Cyber, Intelligence, Surveillance, and Reconnaissance (C5ISR) Center. The views and conclusions contained in this document are those of the authors and should not be interpreted as representing the official policies, either expressed or implied, of the Army Research Laboratory or the U.S. Government. The U.S. Government is authorized to reproduce and distribute reprints for Government purposes notwithstanding any copyright notation herein.

References

1. NIST: National Initiative for Cybersecurity Education (NICE) Cybersecurity Workforce Framework (NIST Special Publication 800-181). NIST, Gaithersburg (2017)
2. Sethi, A., Wills, G.: Expert-interviews led analysis of EEVi — a model for effective visualization in cyber-security. In: IEEE Symposium on Visualization for Cyber Security, Phoenix, AZ, USA (2017)
3. Marty, R.: Applied security visualization (2008)
4. Kullman, K., Asher, N.B., Sample, C.: Operator impressions of 3D visualizations for cybersecurity analysts. In: ECCWS 2019 18th European Conference on Cyber Warfare and Security, Coimbra (2019)
5. Kullman, K., Ryan, M., Trossbach, L.: VR/MR supporting the future of defensive cyber operations. In: The 14th IFAC/IFIP/IFORS/IEA Symposium on Analysis, Design, and Evaluation of Human-Machine Systems, Tallinn (2019)
6. Shearer, G., Edwards, J.: Vids Cyber Defense Visualization Project. US Army Research Laboratory, Adelphi (2020)
7. Munzner, T.: Visualization Analysis & Design, p. 428. A K Peters/CRC Press, Boca Raton (2014)
8. Ward, M.O., Grinstein, G., Keim, D.: Interaction techniques. In: Interactive Data Visualization: Foundations, Techniques, and Applications, 2nd edn., pp. 387–406. A K Peters/CRC Press (2015)
9. Wu, Y., Xu, L., Chang, R., Hellerstein, J.M., Wu, E.: Making sense of asynchrony in interactive data. J. Latex Cl. Files **14**(8), 11 (2018)
10. Mckenna, S., Staheli, D., Meyer, M.: Unlocking user-centered design methods for building cyber security visualizations. In: 2015 IEEE Symposium on Visualization for Cyber Security (VizSec), Chicago, IL (2015)
11. Buchanan, L., D'Amico, A., Kirkpatrick, D.: Mixed method approach to identify analytic questions to be visualized for military cyber incident handlers. In: IEEE Symposium on Visualization for Cyber Security (VizSec), Baltimore, MD (2016)
12. Simonsen, J., Robertson, T.: Routledge International Handbook of Participatory Design. Routledge, Abingdon (2012)
13. Marriott, K., et al.: Just 5 questions: toward a design framework for immersive analytics. In: Marriott, K., et al. (eds.) Immersive Analytics. LNCS, vol. 11190, pp. 259–288. Springer, Cham (2018). https://doi.org/10.1007/978-3-030-01388-2_9
14. Marriott, K., et al.: Immersive analytics: time to reconsider the value of 3D for information visualisation. In: Marriott, K., et al. (eds.) Immersive Analytics. LNCS, vol. 11190, pp. 25–55. Springer, Cham (2018). https://doi.org/10.1007/978-3-030-01388-2_2
15. Kullman, K., Cowley, J., Ben-Asher, N.: Enhancing cyber defense situational awareness using 3D visualizations. In: 13th International Conference on Cyber Warfare and Security, Washington, DC (2018)
16. Stuerzlinger, W., Dwyer, T., Drucker, S., Görg, C., North, C., Scheuermann, G.: Immersive human-centered computational analytics. In: Marriott, K., et al. (eds.) Immersive Analytics. LNCS, vol. 11190, pp. 139–163. Springer, Cham (2018). https://doi.org/10.1007/978-3-030-01388-2_5
17. Klein, G., MacGregor, D.G.: Knowledge Elicitation of Recognition-Primed Decision Making. US Army Systems Research Laboratory, Alexandria, Virginia (1988)
18. NIST: Applied Cybersecurity Division, National Initiative for Cybersecurity Education (NICE). Reference Spreadsheet for the NICE Framework, NIST SP 800-181, 18 January 2018. https://www.nist.gov/itl/applied-cybersecurity/nice/nice-cybersecurity-workforce-framework-resource-center/current. Accessed January 2020

19. Jordan, P.W., Thomas, B., McClelland, I.L., Weerdmeester, B.: Modified Cooper-Harper (MCH) Scale. In: Usability Evaluation In Industry, pp. 189–194. CRC Press (1996)
20. Donmez, B., Brzezinski, A.S., Graham, H., Cummings, M.L.: Modified cooper harper scales for assessing unmanned vehicle displays. Massachusetts Institute of Technology (2008)

Parents Unwittingly Leak Their Children's Data: A GDPR Time Bomb?

Suzanne Prior[✉] and Natalie Coull

Abertay University, Dundee, UK
s.prior@abertay.ac.uk

Abstract. There are many apps available for parents that are designed to help them monitor their pregnancy or child's development. These apps require parents to share information about themselves or their children in order to utilise many of the apps' features. However, parents remain concerned about their children's privacy, indicating a privacy paradox between concerns and actions. The research presented here conducted an analysis of parenting apps alongside a survey of parents to determine if their concerns regarding sharing information about their children was at odds with their use of parenting apps.

A survey of 75 parents found that they had strong concerns around the availability of information about their children but were using apps within which they shared this information. Parents were not giving consideration to the information requested when using apps. This should be of concern to developers given the growing awareness of users' rights in relation to managing their data.

We propose new guidelines for app developers to better protect children's privacy and to improve trust relationships between developers and users.

Keywords: Privacy · Security · Mobile apps · Parenting

1 Introduction

Jack's mum shares information about her son's ADHD using a child development tracker and social network app. Eight years later she wants to enroll her child in an exclusive private school. Unbeknown to her, they search online to find evidence of behavioural issues before they decide whether or not to admit him. They find the original posting, and the ensuing discussion where others give her behavioural advice. The school decides not to admit her child.

Pregnancy and the experience of becoming a parent is a life changing event and in this digital age it is not surprising that parents look to online resources and mobile applications to provide them with information and support during this period (Prior 2016). Mobile application developers have responded to this and there are apps for a large variety of parenting issues from conception to pregnancy development, contraction monitors and baby development trackers. Parents are becoming used to sharing information about their children before they are even born (Lupton and Pedersen 2016).

However, by sharing information about their children through these apps, parents are unwittingly creating a digital footprint for their child and potentially compromising their

© Springer Nature Switzerland AG 2020
A. Moallem (Ed.): HCII 2020, LNCS 12210, pp. 471–486, 2020.
https://doi.org/10.1007/978-3-030-50309-3_31

child's privacy. Recent breaches in privacy in apps such as Sitter (an app used for hiring babysitters), in which information including address, credit card details and information on users' children were leaked in a data breach highlights the potential risks in having this information stored online, even in trustworthy apps (Abel 2018).

At the same time parents report being concerned about what information is available about their child online (Madden et al. 2012). This research seeks to build on previous work in the area of sharing children's information on social media, and in the security and privacy of mobile health applications to examine how parents' views of privacy match with the mobile apps they install and use on their phones and the permissions they grant to these apps.

By better understanding how parents' concerns may impact on their use of these apps there is the potential for designers and developers of parenting apps to reach out to parents by including usable security and privacy measures which are clear and straight forward for users. These could be applied in similar manner to other HCI guidelines such as accessibility.

2 Related Work

2.1 Parenting and Privacy

In recent years there has been an increasing interest in parenting and data privacy within the HCI community (Ammari *et al.* 2015; Moser et al. 2017).

Previous work in the field has looked at the information teenagers and children share about themselves on social media, and the implications this has on their privacy (Marwick and Boyd 2014; Silva *et al.* 2017). There has been a growing awareness in recent years, particularly as the digital native generation has aged and become parents of young children themselves that parents are increasingly sharing private information about their children with online audiences.

Much of this work has been conducted from a sociological perspective and examined sharenting – a term used to describe parents who over share information about their children online. There have been concerns over how children of so called "mummy bloggers" (professional bloggers who post regularly about parenting and updates on their children) may feel in the future when reading posts about themselves (Blum-Ross and Livingstone 2017; Orton-Johnson 2017). One large study looking at Facebook sharenting was conducted by Marasli et al. (2016) who examined the Facebook profiles of 94 parents and looked at the information shared through these profiles about their children. The study considered the social implications of this information being shared but also briefly touched on the potential for the children to become victims of identity theft. However, hiding this information from so called "big data" companies can be a considerable challenge, Vertesei (2014) looked at the steps necessary to prevent corporations from discovering a pregnancy and likened the necessary steps to being similar to those used by people wishing to commit criminal acts.

There has also been research into the data theft implications of this information being shared. Brosch (2016) examined the Facebook profiles of participants and noted the significant number of parents uploading photos of birth certificates or sharing their child's date of birth. The risks in sharing this sort of information was discussed by Minkus et al. (2015) who crawled a large number of adult profiles on Facebook for evidence of children in their public profiles and then combined this with public records to identify information on the children. Minkus highlights the value of this information to a data broker. It is possible that parents are not aware of the dangers in sharing information about children online, Steinberg (2017) offers suggestions for protecting children's privacy and suggests that this model could be viewed in a similar manner to the "back to sleep" and second hand smoking campaigns of the 1990s and early 2000s. Most of the work done into sharenting to date has focussed on social media, however the growing availability of parenting and pregnancy apps means that these are increasingly becoming another avenue for parents to share information about their children with others.

2.2 Mobile Apps and Privacy

The number of apps available to provide information and guidance on a range of topics beginning at ovulation tracking through to pregnancy, childbirth and parenting continues to grow at a rapid rate (Lupton et al. 2016). According to market research from 2013, pregnancy apps are more popular than fitness apps (Dolan 2013), and while there has been less research done into this recently it is thought that their popularity continues to grow (Haelle 2018). It is possible that parents feel that by searching for information, sharing images and monitoring the development of their children they are performing good parenthood (Lupton et al. 2016) and there is an increasing awareness that users are sharing a large volume of information through these mobile apps.

There has been interest in the amount of information being shared in mHealth apps (mobile phone apps related to health) in general for several years. One concern since health apps began to appear was the trustworthiness of the information, however this has now grown into concerns regarding the security of users' health information (Adhikari and Richards 2014). It has been suggested that data breaches in mHealth apps are more common than might have been thought (Adhikari and Richards 2014), and this may be due to a limited understanding of security and privacy in mHealth apps and the risks associated with this information being leaked (Dehling *et al.* 2015). Plachkinova et al. (2015) created a taxonomy of mHealth apps in order to investigate their security and privacy concerns and suggest that information on privacy should be available in an app's description so that users can read it before downloading.

It is argued that the rush to produce mHealth apps has led to some aspects of privacy and security not being considered (Martínez-Pérez et al. 2014). At the same time there appears to be a paradox in that users have high concerns about their privacy online but are also willing to trade their personal information freely when they feel there is a benefit to them (Wilson and Valacich 2012). It is still not clear whether this paradox is due to users' desire for instant gratification and is a behavioural mechanism which cannot be altered (Acquisti and Gross 2006), or a case of learned helplessness. Learned helplessness describes a situation in which users feel that it is inevitable that at some point their data will be compromised and as a result feel there is no point in taking privacy protecting actions (Shklovski *et al.* 2014).

Research into privacy concerns surrounding parenting apps has been more limited than general mHealth apps, however it is now a growing concern. An Australian study found that many women using pregnancy apps were not concerned by the privacy of the information shared or the accuracy of the information they receive (Lupton and Pedersen 2016). Lupton (2016) argues that monitoring apps related to conception and pregnancy may have been created for the purpose of acquiring data for data breaches. There is a risk that by sharing information in order to use apps, parents and their children could effectively become recruited as unpaid contributors to the "digital labour workforce" (Lupton and Williamson 2017).

This study examines the links between the security concerns of parents when considering sharing information about their children, and the information they are willing to provide in order to use parenting apps. It differs from previous studies such as Lupton and Pedersen's work (2016) in that it is targeted specifically at users of parenting and pregnancy apps and looks at a wider range of privacy issues.

In this study we will investigate the extent to which parents are aware of the interaction between data sharing on apps and their privacy and propose the following hypothesis:

H1. Parents are conscious of security and privacy dangers in sharing information about their children.
H2. Parents with privacy and security concerns install, use and grant permissions to apps on their mobile phone without considering the security implications.
H3. Parents do not consider data sharing implications while selecting and installing apps.

Using these hypothesis, we look to answer the research question, what consideration do parents give to security and privacy concerns when installing parenting apps?

3   Methodology

In this present study, we explore the extent to which parents consider the security and privacy implications of providing data about themselves and their children in mobile apps and whether this influences the decisions they make about installing apps related to pregnancy and parenting.

A two stage approach was taken within this study. Firstly a poll was conducted with members of online parenting groups to discover popular parenting and pregnancy apps. This was combined with an analysis of trending Apps for Parents from the App Store.

The initial poll involved asking members of Parenting Facebook Groups which apps they used, and collating those responses. This was then followed by a survey of users of these apps to determine the extent to which they consider the security implications when installing apps.

3.1   App Analysis

Eleven of the most popular parenting apps were selected for this study. These apps were then further analysed to ascertain which data types the apps requested during registration, and to review the terms and conditions of these apps. All of the apps were available through Google Play or the Apple Store.

Table 1. Apps selected for study

App	App description (Android downloads)
Peanut	Peanut is a social networking app, designed to help mothers connect with, and learn from, other mothers in their local area (50,000)
Ovia Parenting	Ovia Parenting is designed to help parents keep track of their child's milestones and provides advice on child development and parenting. Parents can use the app to share information about their children, including photographs and videos (100,000)
Mush	Mush is a social networking app, designed to help mothers to meet similar, like minded-mothers in their local area (100,000)
Baby center	Babycenter produce a pregnancy tracker and baby development calendar app for parents. The app contains parenting advice and tips (10, 000,000)
Sprout	Sprout is a pregnancy tracker with some premium content available for a fee, for example health information and 3d videos of in-utero foetus development (1,000,000)
Bounty Parenting	Bounty Parenting is a pregnancy and baby tracking app, with vouchers and free samples available for pregnancy and baby related products, and links to UK relevant health guides and hospital information packs (100,000)
Ovia Pregnancy	Ovia lets users track the development of a foetus and provides further advice and information on pregnancy and health tracking (1,000,000)
Parentune	Parentune is a social networking app for parents, and provides access to parenting experts and online advice (500,000)
Glow Baby	Glow Baby is designed to help parents track their baby's activities, including breast/bottle feeds, diaper changes, nap times and duration, medication, and record milestones (100,000)
Glow Nurture	Glow Nurture is a pregnancy tracker, designed for expectant parents to track the growth of the foetus and provide advice on pregnancy related health matters (500,000)
What to Expect	What to Expect is a pregnancy and baby tracking app to help parents keep track of foetal development and record their baby's milestones (1,000,000)

The identified apps are shown in Table 1, along with a description of the purpose of the app.

We installed these apps onto our own personal mobile devices (one Android and one iOS), and logged the data that each app requested during the registration process. Table 2 shows the data that each app requested from the user.

Data Collected by Apps. It is evident from Table 2, that there is a very broad range of data collected by the various apps. Some of the data requested relates exclusively to the user, for example name, email address and photo, while other data types relate to the user's child(ren), for example child's date of birth, child's medical history, and

Table 2. App analysis

App	Peanut	Ovia Parenting	Mush	Baby Center	Sprout	Bounty Parenting	Ovia Pregnancy	Parentune	Glow Baby	Glow Nurture	What to Expect
Your name	X	X	X	X		X	X	X	X	X	
Your child's name	X	X	X	X	X	X	X	X	X		X
Current location (P)	X	X	X								
Address	X	X	X			X					
Email Address	X	X	X	X		X	X	X	X	X	X
Phone number (P)								X			
Your Photo	X	X	X	X		X	X	X	X	X	
Your child's photo	X	X	X	X		X			X		
Your date of birth		X	X			X		X			
Child's date of birth	X	X	X	X		X	X	X	X	X	X
Your child's due date (P)			X	X		X	X	X	X	X	X
Your contacts (P)								X			
Your social media profiles	X	X	X			X	X				
Your medical history (P)								X		X	X
Your child's medical history (P)		X						X	X	X	
Your child's place of birth (P)						X	X				

child's place of birth. To appreciate the sensitivity of the different data types, we further categorised the data depending on the longevity of the data. For each data type stored by the app, we categorised the data type depending on whether the data was static (i.e. would not change during the course of the owner's lifetime), flexible (may change over time) or dynamic (likely to change frequently). If there was a data breach, static and flexible data will be of more value in constructing a further attack on a victim, as the data is more likely to be accurate and useful in generating an attack hook that could appear authentic to the victim. In Table 2, the static data types have been coloured red, flexible as orange and dynamic as green. Some of the data could be considered publicly available, (e.g. if the data is already available in the public domain, e.g. from websites such as 192.com), while others would be considered private. For each of the data types, those considered private (i.e. not generally shared online or via social media) are denoted by (P). Some of this information is considered private by certain organisations, and used to confirm identity (e.g. date of birth, place of birth).

Privacy Threats from Apps. Privacy threats relating to the use of parenting apps include: a breach of user confidentiality, failure to protect the data, and client or server end bugs that could lead to a security breach. Given the sensitivity of some of the data collected, it is important that users are fully aware of what data is being collected, how and where it is being stored, and how the data is going to be used. We reviewed the Privacy Policies of each of the apps, to ascertain where data was stored and how it was used. Typically, the paid apps had the best level of privacy protection, where the user's data was generally stored only on the user's phone. This would ensure that a breach of the organisation's infrastructure would not lead to compromisation of the user's data, and the data was not being passed to third parties for marketing purposes.

Any threats to the user's privacy from these types of apps is limited to app security on the device itself, and the ease with which malicious apps installed on the device may be able to access the data on the device. The free apps stated various levels of data sharing within their privacy policies, with all of them requesting permission to store user data on the organisation's servers, with that data being passed to third parties for marketing purposes. Typically, the social media apps required the user to agree to share their data with other users.

Based on the information that is stored by these apps, a list of potential attacks that could be conducted using this information was compiled. A description of these potential attacks and how information could be used to help orchestrate such an attack is described below:

Spear phishing is an email spoofing attack that targets a specific user or organisation, using information that has been harvested to make the email look more authentic. Spear phishing emails are generally designed to gain unauthorised access to sensitive information, either by persuading the user to click on a link in the email or open a malicious attachment. If someone's email address was leaked from a parenting app, along with other personal information, this information could be used to construct an authentic looking spear phishing attack.

Identity fraud can occur if personal information has been stolen, for example following a breach of user confidentiality. Information such as name, address, date of birth can be used to gain access to existing accounts, or used to obtain goods or services by impersonating the user to open new accounts.

If a user's details are breached, this information could be used to construct a password guessing attack, or reset a user's password if 'security questions' can be guessed. If a user's password hash has been stolen, user's details could be used to generate a password dictionary, unique to that particular user that could be used to then orchestrate a hybrid password attack.

It would be relatively easy for someone who was seeking access to children, or vulnerable mothers, to use the apps to gain access to this demographic for grooming purposes.

App Reviews. The reviews of the apps in Table 1 which were posted in both the Google Play and Apple App stores were examined for any mention of privacy or security. Over 500 reviews were examined, eleven reviews were related to security or privacy, these were spread across seven apps.

Three reviews mentioned issues in deleting data, either users could not work out how to delete their data, or having thought they deleted it they discovered that it was still stored by the app provider. Four reviews expressed concern over the amount of data which was being collected, these reviews related to two apps. While many reviews revealed users' frustration at being forced to create a Facebook account to log into some apps only one review related this back to a concern around their personal privacy. Of the remaining three reviews, one raised concern around the other users of the app and how they were vetted, one commented that it was not easy to change the privacy settings of photos stored on the app and the remaining review stated that they liked not having to give special privacy permissions to install the app.

3.2 Survey

Following analysis of the parenting apps selected for the study, we conducted a survey of parents who used parenting apps to determine what consideration they gave to security concerns when using the apps.

Participants and Design. An online survey was used to gather parents' views on security, privacy and app use. The use of an online survey enabled us to reach a wider geographical area than would have been possible through other methods. The survey questions were trialled with seven participants prior to validate the survey and ensure there were no barriers to survey completion. The survey was designed to be completed in under ten minutes.

Recruitment. Participants were recruited to the survey over the period of one month between April and May 2018. Recruitment took place through a variety of online mediums including Twitter, Facebook groups targeted at parents and parenting websites (such as NetMums and BabyCentre). We were aware that some parents who used parenting apps may not use social media and so leaflets about the study were put in playgroups, parenting cafes and children's recreation centres in the local area.

Following the informed consent process there were four sections to this survey.

Demographics. Participants were asked for their age, gender, level of education, if they had children, if they used parenting apps and their country of residence. If participants selected no to either having children or using parenting apps they were excluded from the study. As the survey was examining the amount of personal information which participants are willing to share we deliberately avoided asking for information by means of which participants could be identified. This meant that the demographic information elicited was limited but still ensured that any themes in participant groups could be identified.

Use of Apps. Before participants were asked about their privacy concerns they were asked to identify which of the apps in Table 2 they used. There were eleven apps available for them to select and the option of none of the above.

Privacy Concerns. The questions on privacy concerns were separated into two sections. The first section asked questions relating to general attitudes to security and privacy on a five point Likert scale ranging from Strongly Disagree to Strongly Agree.

The second section looked specifically at the information participants were willing to share in order to use an app. The following information asked for by the apps were listed and participants rated on a five point Likert scale their level of comfortableness with sharing this information, ranging from Very Uncomfortable to Very Comfortable.

Reaction to Apps. The final stage of the survey revealed a grid which presented the types of information stored by each of the apps. Once participants had examined this grid they were asked whether they were comfortable or uncomfortable with this information being collected. Depending on their answer they were then directed either to a question asking why they felt comfortable sharing this information or to a question asking them given they were uncomfortable with this what they were likely to do with these apps in the future.

Ethical consent was sought and obtained by the authors' institution prior to the commencement of the survey. The survey asked for no identifiable information and provided details at the end on websites which could provide participants with further information on keeping their data private if they wished.

4 Results

4.1 Descriptive Statistics

During the month that the survey was available 101 participants began the study, 26 were excluded because they were either not parents or did not use parenting apps. In total 75 participants completed the survey. Of those participants 97% ($n = 73$) were female. Participants were composed predominantly of the millennial generation, the majority of participants were aged between 26 and 35 see Table 3.

Table 3. Participant demographics

Variable name	% (n)
Age	
18–25	9.33 (7)
26–35	60 (45)
36–45	29.33 (22)
46–55	1.33 (1)
Country	
United Kingdom	89.33 (67)
USA	6.67 (5)
Australia	1.33 (1)
Singapore	1.33 (1)
Ukraine	1.33 (1)
Education	
Did not complete HS	2.66 (2)
Completed HS	12 (9)
Some higher education	30.67 (23)
Undergraduate Degree	50.67 (38)
Postgraduate Degree	32 (24)
PhD	1.67 (5)

The participants were mainly from the United Kingdom with the remainder coming from USA, Australia, Singapore and Ukraine. Participants had a variety of educational experiences ranging from not completing high school to having a PhD. The majority of participants had at least an undergraduate degree. All participants in the study had used at least one app with the average being 2.6 (sd = 1.6). The most popular app used was Baby Center (52%, $n = 39$).

4.2 Levels of Concern

When asked how concerned they were about the data being collected and shared about themselves and their children, the participants were above neutral in their level of concern for every category - see Table 4. Participants were more concerned about the data being gathered about their children than they were about themselves. The highest average level of concern related to information being collected about children for advertising purposes ($n = 4.04$), followed closely by concerns around who could see information about their children ($n = 4$). When considering information being shared about their children, only three participants (4%) were completely unconcerned with the volume of information stored about their children online, and with whom could see it. One participant (1.33%) was completely unconcerned about the information stored about their child for marketing purposes (Fig. 1).

Table 4. Hypothesis

Hypothesis	Supported/not supported
H1. Parents are conscious of security and privacy dangers in sharing information about their children	Supported
H2. Parents with privacy and security concerns install, use and grant permissions to apps on their mobile phone without considering the security implications	Supported
H3. Parents are not conscious of the information they are sharing on apps	Supported

4.3 Levels of Comfort

The examination of the information participants would be comfortable sharing revealed that there were only two categories of information in which participants on average rated feeling comfortable or very comfortable in sharing, these were their own name ($n = 3.45$) and their email address ($n = 3.45$). By contrast the average level of comfort for their child's name was 2.56. Participants were least comfortable in sharing their child's medical history (n = 1.56), followed closely by their own medical history (n = 1.6). The median for both these forms of data was 1 (Fig. 2).

4.4 Continued Use of Apps

Having been presented with the information regarding what information is stored by the apps, the participants were asked if they were happy to continue using the app, 81.3% of participants ($n = 61$) were not happy.

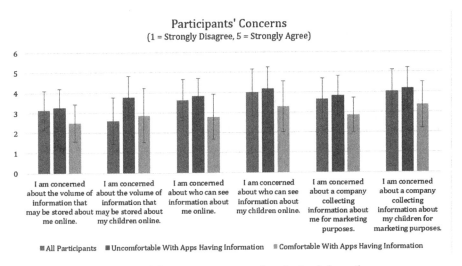

Fig. 1. Participants concerns regarding sharing information

Participants who were unhappy were asked about their future plans for use of these apps and the majority (65%, $n = 39$) said that they would consider altering the settings on the apps. Only two participants (3.3%) planned to continue using the app as before and 31.7% ($n = 19$) would consider deleting the app.

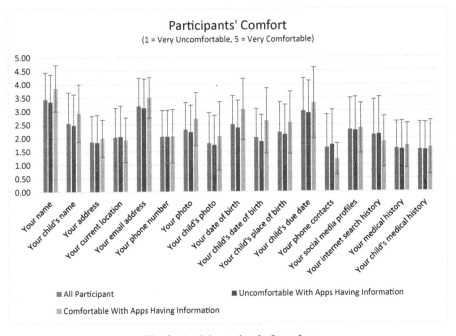

Fig. 2. Participants level of comfort

The participants who were happy with the information being stored on the app were asked for the reason behind this. For the majority (78.6%, $n = 11$) this was because they trusted the app providers to use the data appropriately, while the remaining three participants (21.4%) were not concerned about how this data was used.

By splitting the participants into two groups it is possible to examine any differences between them in their levels of concerns around issues about their data being shared and in their degrees of comfort in sharing specific forms of information.

In both cases the data was normally distributed and application of the MannWhitney U test shows that participants who were unhappy with the data being stored on the apps had reported higher levels of concerns around data sharing issues than the participants who were happy with the data stored on the apps ($z = 3.01$, $p = 0.003$). However there was no significant difference between their levels of comfort in sharing specific items of information ($p = 0.14$).

5   Discussion

5.1   H1. Parent's Consciousness of Security and Privacy Dangers

Parents in the study on average were concerned about the information stored about them and their children. Areas of particular concern were who could have access to this information and how this information could be used for marketing purposes. This suggests they are conscious of the dangers in sharing information about their children.

5.2   H2. Installation and Use of Apps

There were no significant differences in the amount of information parents with high security concerns were potentially sharing through apps compared to those with lower security concerns. This indicates that despite having privacy and security concerns, parents are installing apps which request large amounts of information. It should be noted that this study did not specifically ask what information was being shared, but from our analysis of the apps we can conclude that this information would be required in order to use the app effectively.

5.3   H3. Sharing of Information

When participants were shown the amount of information that could be stored by the different apps they were using, 81.3% ($n = 61$) they stated that they were uncomfortable with this and of these the majority ($n = 39$, 65%) would be looking to change the settings on these apps. This indicates that parents are installing apps which request information about their children and are not taking on board that they are sharing information in doing this.

The results suggest that although the majority of parents are concerned by online security and privacy issues surrounding their children, they give little to no consideration to this when installing mobile parenting apps.

5.4 Parents Views and Actions

Parents in the study reported being highly concerned about the information being shared about themselves and their children and uncomfortable with many types of information being shared. However, this appeared to be in contrast with their behaviour of using many apps which stored personal information on them. This privacy paradox has been noted in previous studies (Norberg et al. 2007), in which it has been noted that despite their disclosed intentions users frequently share personal data. Much of this previous work has looked at social media however, as this study has shown, this behaviour can also be found in the use of apps. This study's results are in contrast to those found in Lupton and Pedersen's work (2016) which found participants were not overly concerned with the data being stored or used by parenting apps.

One potential reason why this contrast can be seen so clearly in this study could have been due to stories in the media during the time period the survey was available. The Cambridge Analytica/Facebook scandal was first covered in the press in the UK in March 2018, shortly before we deployed this survey and during the study was being discussed at on many popular parenting websites (Babycentre 2018; Mumsnet 2018). The heightened awareness is often that users' data is a commodity may have explained this difference.

5.5 Guidelines for Developers

Those participants who responded that they were unhappy with the apps having their information indicated that they were likely to have been unaware of the amount of information being stored before the survey – only 3.3% would continue to use the apps with no changes. As pointed out by some commentators, by raising awareness of how data is processed there is the opportunity to build trust between app providers and their users. If user awareness in this area continues to rise then app providers may find themselves at risk of losing users if this trust is not present. Parental app providers could be at an additional risk, as this study shows parents are more guarded about their child's data than their own.

There are existing guidelines for developers regarding how much data they should request from and store about users. However, what our study suggests is that parents are particularly concerned about the amount of information being stored on their children and that should they become aware of this it may impact upon their use of the app.

We suggest that in addition to complying with current data legislation and only storing the minimum required amount of information, developers of parenting apps should work with parents to determine the levels of information they are comfortable in sharing with specific applications. Developers should also give consideration as to how they present the terms and conditions of their apps. If parents feel confident that they understand the digital footprint they are creating for their child then there is the possibility that they may be more inclined to continue to use the app.

In addition there may be benefits in allowing parents to use the apps without providing specific information about their child. For example will it affect the advice given by the app if they don't provide their child's gender or exact date of birth. Consider if there are less identifying ways to gather this data such as the child's age, could an icon be used instead of a photo of their child? Developers should give consideration to these issues when designing parenting apps.

5.6 Limitations

There are several limitations within this survey. Firstly by asking adults to self report on their concerns around data privacy there is the risk of a social desirability bias, we were not able to validate how accurate this reporting was. Secondly we did not investigate if parents who are concerned about the data being stored are actually sharing their child's data or using dummy data.

When asking participants about their comfort in sharing specific pieces of information this was on a very general form, there would be benefit in future studies examining in which situations they would be comfortable sharing these different pieces of information.

Finally we have not been able to follow up on the study to determine if the participants took any action after discovering the amount of data they were sharing.

6   Conclusion and Future Work

There has been a large growth in recent years in pregnancy and parenting apps, and data on parents is of interest to many corporations. At the same time parents are becoming increasingly concerned with what data is available online about their children and who can access this. This study has shown that despite these concerns many parents are using apps which store this information and have not given consideration as to who may have access to this information.

This survey showed that despite being unhappy with the information stored by app providers, the majority of participants were still planning to continue using the apps. However of those who were planning to continue using the apps, many would look to alter the settings on the apps, it should be noted that this is behavioural intention and it is not clear if it became actual behaviour.

Future studies should investigate if after being informed about the data stored by apps, participants make any changes to the settings on apps or the information, and if this has been influenced by the recent press stories regarding the commoditization of data. It would also be beneficial to work with parents who are non-users to discover any privacy concerns that have stopped them from using these apps.

References

Abel, R.: Babysitting app Sitter exposed the data of 93,000 customers, SC Media (2018). https://www.scmagazine.com/home/network-security/babysitting-app-sitter-exposed-the-data-of-93000-customers/. Accessed: 19 Nov 2018

Acquisti, A., Gross, R.: Imagined communities: awareness, information sharing, and privacy on the facebook. In: Danezis, G., Golle, P. (eds.) PET 2006. LNCS, vol. 4258, pp. 36–58. Springer, Heidelberg (2006). https://doi.org/10.1007/11957454_3

Adhikari, R., Richards, D.: Security and privacy issues related to the use of mobile health apps. In: 25th Australasian Conference on Information Systems (ACIS 2014), Auckland, New Zealand, pp. 1–11 (2014)

Ammari, T., et al.: Managing children's online identities: how parents decide what to disclose about their children online. In: Proceedings of the 33rd Annual ACM Conference on Human Factors in Computing Systems (CHI 2015), pp. 1895–1904. ACM, New York (2015). https://doi.org/10.1145/2702123.2702325

Babycentre: Cambridge Analytica and your social media use (2018). https://community.babycentre.co.uk/post/a31540953/cambridge-analytica-and-your-social-media-use. Accessed 4 June 2018

Blum-Ross, A., Livingstone, S.: "Sharenting", parent blogging, and the boundaries of the digital self. Popul. Commun. 15(2), 110–125 (2017). https://doi.org/10.1080/15405702.2016.1223300

Brosch, A.: When the child is born into the internet: sharenting as a growing trend among parents on facebook. New Educ. Rev. 43(1), 225–235 (2016). https://doi.org/10.15804/tner.2016.43.1.19

Dehling, T., et al.: Exploring the far side of mobile health: information security and privacy of mobile health apps on iOS and Android. JMIR mHealth uHealth (2015). https://doi.org/10.2196/mhealth.3672. Edited by G. Eysenbach. Toronto, Canada

Dolan, B.: Report finds pregnancy apps more popular than fitness apps, mobihealthnews (2013) http://www.mobihealthnews.com/20333/report-finds-pregnancy-apps-more-popular-than-fitness-apps. Accessed 4 June 2018

Haelle, T.: Pregnancy Apps: Your Patients Use Them—Are You Up to Speed? Medscape (2018). https://www.medscape.com/viewarticle/892945. Accessed 4 June 2018

Lupton, D.: "Mastering your fertility": the digitised reproductive citizen. In: McCosker, A., Vivienne, S., Johns, A. (eds.) Negotiating Digital Citizenship: United States, pp. 81–93. Rowman & Littlefield Publishers (2016)

Lupton, D., Pedersen, S.: An Australian survey of women's use of pregnancy and parenting apps. Women and Birth 29(4), 368–375 (2016). https://doi.org/10.1016/j.wombi.2016.01.008

Lupton, D., Pedersen, S., Thomas, G.M.: Parenting and digital media: from the early web to contemporary digital society. Sociol. Compass 10(8), 730–743 (2016). https://doi.org/10.1111/soc4.12398

Lupton, D., Williamson, B.: The datafied child: the dataveillance of children and implications for their rights. New Media Soc. 19(5), 780–794 (2017). https://doi.org/10.1177/1461444816686328

Madden, M., et al.: Parents, Teens, and Online Privacy, Washington, USA (2012). https://files.eric.ed.gov/fulltext/ED537515.pdf

Marasli, M., et al.: Parents' shares on social networking sites about their children: sharenting. Anthropologist 24(2), 399–406 (2016). https://doi.org/10.1080/09720073.2016.11892031

Martínez-Pérez, B., de la Torre-Díez, I., López-Coronado, M.: Privacy and security in mobile health apps: a review and recommendations. J. Med. Syst. 39(1), 181 (2014). https://doi.org/10.1007/s10916-014-0181-3

Marwick, A.E., Boyd, D.: Networked privacy: how teenagers negotiate context in social media. New Media Soc. 16(7), 1051–1067 (2014). https://doi.org/10.1177/1461444814543995

Minkus, T., Liu, K., Ross, K.W.: Children seen but not heard: when parents compromise children's online privacy. In: Proceedings of the 24th International Conference on World Wide Web, Florence, Italy, pp. 776–786. International World Wide Web Conferences Steering Committee (WWW 2015) (2015). https://doi.org/10.1145/2736277.2741124

Moser, C., Chen, T., Schoenebeck, S.Y.: Parents' And children's preferences about parents sharing about children on social media. In: Proceedings of the 2017 CHI Conference on Human Factors in Computing Systems (CHI 2017), pp. 5221–5225. ACM, New York (2017). https://doi.org/10.1145/3025453.3025587

Mumsnet: MN, FB, marketing companies and our data (2018). https://www.mumsnet.com/Talk/site_stuff/a3199266-MN-FB-marketing-companies-and-our-data. Accessed 4 June 2018

Norberg, P., Horne, D., Horne, D.: The privacy paradox: personal information disclosure intentions versus behaviors. J. Consum. Aff. **41**(1), 100–126 (2007). https://doi.org/10.1111/j.1745-6606.2006.00070.x

Orton-Johnson, K.: Mummy blogs and representations of motherhood: "bad mummies" and their readers. Soc. Media Soc. **3**(2), 2056305117707186 (2017). https://doi.org/10.1177/2056305117707186

Plachkinova, M., Andrés, S., Chatterjee, S.: A taxonomy of mHealth apps – security and privacy concerns. In: 2015 48th Hawaii International Conference on System Sciences, pp. 3187–3196 (2015). https://doi.org/10.1109/hicss.2015.385

Prior, S.: The millennial mum – technology use by new mothers. In: Proceedings of British HCI 2016 - Fusion, Bournemouth, UK, pp. 20.1–20.3 (2016)

Shklovski, I., et al.: Leakiness and creepiness in app space: perceptions of privacy and mobile app use. In: Proceedings of the 32nd Annual ACM Conference on Human Factors in Computing Systems (CHI 2014), pp. 2347–2356. ACM, New York (2014). https://doi.org/10.1145/2556288.2557421

Silva, C.S., et al.: Privacy for children and teenagers on social networks from a usability perspective: a case study on facebook. In: Proceedings of the 2017 ACM on Web Science Conference (WebSci 2017), pp. 63–71. ACM, New York (2017). https://doi.org/10.1145/3091478.3091479

Steinberg, S.B.: Sharenting: children's privacy in the age of social media. Emory Law J. **66**(4), 839–884 (2017)

Vertesi, J.: My Experiment Opting Out of Big Data Made Me Look Like a Criminal, Time (2014). http://time.com/83200/privacy-internet-big-data-opt-out/. Accessed 11 June 2018

Wilson, D.W., Valacich, J.: Unpacking the privacy paradox: irrational decision-making within the privacy calculus. In: International Conference on Information Systems, ICIS 2012, vol. 5, pp. 4152–4162 (2012)

An Emerging Strategy for Privacy Preserving Databases: Differential Privacy

Fatema Rashid and Ali Miri[✉]

Department of Computer Science, Ryerson University, Toronto, Canada
{fatema.rashid,Ali.Miri}@ryerson.ca

Abstract. *Data De-identification* and *Differential Privacy* are two possible approaches for providing data security and user privacy. Data de-identification is the process where the personal identifiable information of individuals is extracted to create anonymized databases. Data de-identification has been used for quite some time in industry to sanitize data before it is outsourced for data-mining purposes. Differential privacy attempts to protect sensitive data by adding an appropriate level of noise to the output of a query or to the primary database so that the presence or the absence of a single piece of information will not significantly alter the query output. Recent work in the literature has highlighted the risk of re-identification of information in a de-identified data set. In this paper, we provide a comprehensive comparison of these two privacy-preserving strategies. Our results show that the differentially private trained models produce highly accurate data, while preserving data privacy, making them a reliable alternative to the data de-identification models.

Keywords: Differential privacy · Data De-identification · Separate architecture · Privacy preserving databases

1 Introduction

In today's ultra-connected world, huge volume of data are being produced and consumed. Therefore, there has been a tremendous increase in the collection of private information in areas such advertising, health care, and financial services. Repositories for these types of data are also commonly shared with third parties, either for commercial or research purposes. In this setting, there are growing number of users who need adequate levels of data privacy and security protection against all types of adversaries. Accessible users' data made available by storage or service providers are often hidden and de-identified based on policy and regulatory requirements. However, given the level of access and variety of data analytic tools available, such efforts provide minimal or no privacy protection to users.

The growing need of the organizations to mine, research and analyze data has created a need for sharing data within and among the organizations like

© Springer Nature Switzerland AG 2020
A. Moallem (Ed.): HCII 2020, LNCS 12210, pp. 487–498, 2020.
https://doi.org/10.1007/978-3-030-50309-3_32

never before. For example, a central department may need to access the data of the other departments to evaluate the effectiveness of services delivered and consequently revise funding provided. In all such cases, there must be a rule of law for sharing the information within and among the departments since the personal information of users is at stake along with their privacy. The Freedom of Information and Protection of Privacy Act *(FIPPA)* and Municipal Freedom of Information and Protection of Privacy Act *(MFIPPA)* have been enacted in Canada as a standard guide for information sharing within and among organizations. The motivation for FIPPA and MFIPPA was that the need to access data has to be balanced with the rights of individuals to have control over their own informations. These acts mandates that all organizations take necessary measures and controls to protect private data. However, over recent years there have been a large number of breaches of anonymized data sets [3] that highlights the needs for better solutions and strategies to address these problems.

The term differential privacy was first introduced in a seminal work by Dwork, McSherry, Nissim and Smith in 2006 [1], who in addition to providing a formal definition, also demonstrated various properties of this concept. Differential privacy relies on building a scheme that provides privacy for a given piece of information by ensuring that what is learnt as the result of an adversary's efforts will not significantly change whether that piece of information was included in, or removed, from the database. This aim is achieved by adding an appropriate level of noise to the output of the query or the primary database so that the difference in the results of the output due to the presence or the absence of a single piece of information will be insignificant.

In the remainder of this paper, we provide a detailed comparison between de-identification and differential privacy. In our comparison, we also leverage recent results in [14] that illustrate that even highly anonymized data sets are not likely to satisfy the standards for anonymization set out by EU General Data Protection Regulation (GDPR), and that the risk of re-identification in these types of data sets is very high. In this paper, we provide a concrete solution for data anonymization through differential privacy. We will provide a complete analysis of differential privacy along with its three different architectures namely: *Data Publication architecture, Separated architecture* and *Hybridized architecture*, with a number of case studies based on the privacy and efficiency requirements. We propose and validate through a statistical model, that the likelihood of re-identification will be reduced. We demonstrate the accuracy of results when using differential privacy, and we will compare the probability of re-identification between the two approaches. We use different types of benchmarks as used in [14], to perform comparison between de-identification and differential privacy and establish that differential privacy is definitely a better alternative to de-identification in the modern world of data science.

2   Differential Privacy vs De-identification

2.1   Differential Privacy

One of the early seminal work on Differential Privacy (DP) was done by Dwork, Nissim, McSherry and Smith [1], with much follow up since. Generally, DP works by embedding a layer between queries made by an examiner and the database itself. Differential privacy is provided using the following equation [1]:

$$Pr\left[K\left(D1\right) \in S\right] \leq exp\left(\epsilon\right) x Pr\left[K\left(D2\right) \in S\right] \tag{1}$$

A randomized function K provides differential privacy, if the above equation holds for all data sets $D1$ and $D2$ differing on at most one element. The function K satisfying this definition can address concerns that any participant might have about the disclosure of her personal information x. That is, even if the participant removed her data from the data set, the output would not significantly change. DP [2] will provide privacy by process; specifically, it will present randomness in the form of noise. Noise additions can be done before or after queries have been made to a database. Differential privacy can also be considered as privacy-preserving statistical analysis of data. Different types of noise can also be used. Some of the most prominent differential privacy mechanisms are PINQ [9], AIRAVAT [15], GUPT [10] and that used in Apple iOS [8].

In all the differentially private analysis, there is a trade-off between minimizing privacy loss and maximizing utility [3]. Privacy is measured via the parameter ϵ. The choice of ϵ depends upon how much privacy is required, as the information is presented to multiple analysis, as well as in multiple databases. The choice of ϵ also depends on the behaviour of the underlying algorithms used. Different genre of problems belonging to different sectors like education, health, financial, military etc, require specialize differential privacy algorithms for better insight. Laplace mechanism, the Gaussian mechanism (i.e., addition of Gaussian noise), the exponential mechanism and the propose-test-release paradigm are the most popular choices [7]. The Laplace mechanism is a popular solution for real-valued or vector-valued functions and is used to generate noise. The Laplace distribution is also known as the double exponential distribution because its distribution function looks like the exponential distribution function with a copy reflected about the y-axis [16]. The two exponential curves join at the origin to create a tent shape. The absolute value of a Laplace random variable is an exponential random variable. Objective perturbation methods have yielded better results (lower error, smaller sample complexity) for certain techniques in machine learning such as logistic Regression. In order to achieve near to perfect results, special-purpose solutions may be of higher quality than general solutions. In order to find methods for any particular analytical problem or sequence of computational steps that yield good utility on data sets of moderate size, challenging computations are required [16]. There are different implications as well associated with differential privacy. Some of the common implications of using DP are that it protects individuals' privacy regardless of prior knowledge. DP makes it impossible to guess whether one participated in a database with large probability or not. The main goal of differential privacy is to allow the user to know the properties of the population of the underlying sample population and at the same time protect the private information of the individuals. In short, differential privacy aims at developing strategies which allow to reveal the information about the database but preserve the privacy of the individuals [3].

Properties of Differential Privacy. The following are some of the key properties of DP [3]: *Arbitrary risks* - DP algorithm ensures that even if the user's data is removed from the database, no outputs would become significantly more or less likely. *Worst-case guarantees* - Differential privacy is a worst-case, when compared to alternative paradigms that are mostly average case guarantee. That means, it protects privacy even in the case of nontraditional databased or those databases that do not conform to the normal distributions and templates. *Group privacy* - DP automatically yields group privacy. DP can hide the absence or presence of any group of a particular size with a specific quality of hiding depending upon the size of the group. Having said that, the inference will not include the characteristics of the group and also will not reveal any particular information about the group irrespective of it's size. Automatic and oblivious composition of more than one databases, is also a useful characteristic of differentially private databases. DP ensures and minimizes the cumulative risk undergone by participating in both the databases to a number related to the individual databases' differential privacy factor. Learning the distributions is a very important characteristic of DP since it will allow the results to be more accurate and close to correctness while ensuring the privacy of the individual rows. Learning distributions and correlations between publicly observable and hidden attributes is the key to accurate data analysis and data mining research results. As we discuss later, DP has also can have a performance advantage when compared to de-identification. Furthermore, it can avoid the re-identification attacks that can pose a serious concern to protecting the privacy of the database.

Technical Issues. Depending upon the architecture used, a number of the security consideration should be undertaken by the data owner. The first issue is that of the side channel attacks originating from releasing the noisy results. The data owner must consider strong strategies to minimize the leakage of information to the adversary from such attacks. The second issue is to limit the number of times queries can be made to the database, as the higher this number is, the more the information will be available to an attacker.. Therefore, the owner of the data should allocate number of sessions and number of query limits to in his privacy-preserving architecture.

2.2   Data De-identification

Data de-identification is commonly considered as a vital strategy for ensuring personal data privacy and protection. It is used in many different areas such data communications, big data analytics, cloud computing and data storage.

Data de-identification is the process where all or most of the personally identifiable information of individuals are extracted and removed to from an anonymized database. This anonymized database can then be used without disclosing private information. One guideline on how to use de-identification with databases that contain the personal information of the individuals is that of the privacy protection provision section of the Freedom of Information and Protection of Privacy Act *(FIPPA)* and the Municipal Freedom of Information and Protection of Privacy Act *(MFIPPA)* [5]. The term data de-identification is also commonly interchanged with the term *data anonymization*. One of the main goals of data de-identification techniques is to provide the opportunity to analyze the characteristics of the raw data without violating the privacy of the individuals associated with the database [5].

We will next explain different terminologies and practices involved in the different steps of the process of data de-identification [5]. The first step is to determine the target of the model: *publicly released, semi-publicly released* or *non-publicly released*. Each of these release models is associated with a specific level of availability and protection of information. Depending on the sensitivity nature of the database, the usability of each model varies. The amount of de-identification chiefly depends on these release models. For example, the public data releases requires the most availability and the least protection and therefore significant amount of de-identification has to be applied. On the other hand, non-public data only requires smaller amount of de-identification due to its limited public availability requirement. The second step is to identify the variables. These variables, referred to as *direct identifiers* are those which can directly identify individuals. For example, name, address, driver license number, telephone number, photograph or biometrics are direct identifiers. Other variables may release information about the individuals, when used in combination with other variables and they are called *indirect* or *quasi identifiers*. For example, date of birth, gender, profession, ethnic origin, marital status etc are often considered indirect identifiers. Depending upon the requirements of the data de-identification, specific identifiers should be removed. Third step involves determining an acceptable re-identification risk threshold. Re-identification is the process that re-creates the relation between identifiable information and a real individual. The amount of required de-identification is directly proportional to the level of re-identification risk in case of the release of the database. The higher the re-identification risk of a data release, the greater the amount of de-identification is required. The level of re-identification can be evaluated by estimating the risk which the release of the database would incur on the individual's privacy. The risk could be categorized as high, medium and low. The fourth step is to measure the data risk. After the re-identification risk threshold has been determined, the organization should measure the re-identification risk in the data itself. This risk will give an estimate of the privacy loss in case of the release of re-identified data. This measurement is a two step process which includes first to calculate the probability of re-identification of each tuple in the database and the second is to apply the risk measurement method based on the release model used. Fifth step is to measure the context risk in terms of re-identification context risks produced. This measure will provide the probability of one or more re-identification attacks against the database. The impact of the attacks differ and depend upon the type of the release model used. According to the safe harbour de-identification standards, there are mainly three types of release attacks to be considered. For public data, the organization has to take measures in keeping the worst case scenario in assumption which clearly needs to cater the highest risk of re-identification. For a nonpublic data set, three types of attacks are considered: a deliberate re-identification by the data recipient; an inadvertent re-identification by the data recipient; and a data breach, where data are accidentally exposed to an open audience. The final step in the calculation of the risk is to measure the overall risk associated with the re-identification. Over-all risk is actually the product of data risk and context risk. This overall risk gives the probability of one or more data tuples being exposed in case of an attack. The last two steps includes to actually de-identify the database by adopting a suitable strategy, assess the trade off between the privacy of de-identification and the accuracy for the research purposes according to the domain of the research.

Pros and Cons of Data De-identification. Data de-identification can offer advantages over other data concealing strategies. Data de-identification is com-putationally lighter to perform as compared to data encryption and also gives better efficiency as compared to differential privacy. It also provides customiza-tion since it allows different identifiers for individuals without identifying the actual identity as per the requirements of the research domain. If shared within the organization, data can be de-identified with lesser quantifiers as compared to the situation where data is outsourced to a third party. Within the orga-nization as well, employees at different levels of the hierarchy, need to share different layers of data which can be produced by changing the identifiers for data de-identification. Other uses of de-identified data may require the ability to retain unique identifiers for individuals in the data set, without identifying the actual identity of the individuals [14]. For example, a researcher may need to know that certain actions were all taken by the same individual, in order to form conclusions about how individuals use the data or service. A web site designer may want to determine how long individuals stay on the site, or how individuals traverse the site in order to find the information sought. Systems development, test, and training environments may require the use of data that simulates real production data, while not actually consisting of real data ele-ments such as Social Security numbers. In such cases, de-identification processes are complicated by the need to replace unique identifiers such as Social Security numbers or IP numbers with alternate unique identifiers that cannot be used to identify the actual individual While de-identification techniques protect against the disclosure of individuals' identities, they do not protect against the disclo-sure of attributes relating to groups of individuals that may be denouncing to those individuals. In a number of recent work, it has also been shown that given the variety of data analytic tools and having access to a wide range of (possibly anonymized) data can result in serious privacy breaches against databases using de-identification approach as their protection tool.

Examples of De-identification. Data de-identification is being used extensively in practice in order to protect the privacy of the patients, consumers, individuals or students in different fields. We mention only a few examples here to emphasis upon the utility and application of data de-identification in the industry. A research team from Harvard University and MIT has released a de-identified version of learning data from their blackboard portal named as edX [11]. The data is focused on the online learning of each institution's first year courses. Specifically, the data set contains the original learning data from the 16 HarvardX and MIT xcourses offered in 2012–13. The data set was de-identified using anonymization via random identifiers, and blurring techniques to completely remove any personal identification information of the students. This de-identified database has been vastly used for research purposes.

Data de-identification is also being used in the health care sector for protecting the privacy of patients across the world. The Canadian Primary Care Sentinel Surveillance Network (CPCSSN) needed to outsource and mine their data for the health practitioners and researchers in order to help improve treatment and care [17]. They developed a multi-disease electronic record surveillance system that would allow for research and analytic, by using data de-identification of the health information in order to protect patient privacy. Through securely de-identifying patient data from practices and care centers across Canada, researchers and healthcare practitioners are now able to conduct research on chronic disease and at the same time protect the patients' private information. Another application of data de-identification is the program named "Enabling Better Health Care Outcomes for Mothers and Infants: BORN Ontario" [13]. The researchers and the practitioners received a de-identified version of the database for the mothers and infants primary health at the time of the birth. Subsequently, researchers can share EMR and population-based de-identified birth data in order improve maternal health care. Through this data, they can use to support performance measurement, quality improvement, answer policy questions, enable research and inform funding inquiries. One of the most prominent examples of differential privacy is The Health Information Trust Alliance's (HITRUST), which is designed to "enhance innovation and streamline the appropriate use of healthcare data". The framework was also very useful in promoting the utilization of de-identification and improve the understanding of the healthcare organizations regarding the de-identified data, its classifiers and it's utility in developing fine research [12]. HITRUST privacy framework uses "multiple levels of anonymization" and recommend specific use cases for each variant in order to provide customized de-identification services to specific healthcare units according to their needs.

3   Experimental Analysis

In [14], the authors demonstrated that an individual can be re-identified correctly
in a de-identified database with a high probability, including the cases where the
data set is incomplete and de-identified at a high level.

Their work mostly focused on using health care data, socio demographic and
survey data sets. Their [14] results exhibits that the with a mean absolute error
(MAE) of 0.018 on average, their model was able to estimate the population
uniqueness. For a population sample of 1%, their model was able to uniquely re-
identify the individual with a MAE of 0.041. On a trained model, an individual is
identified at a false discovery rate if <6.7% for a 95% threshold with an error rate
of 39% lower than the best population level estimator. They also gave evidence
that as the number of attributes increase, the probability of an individual being
re-identified correctly within a heavily sampled data set increases. Their results
pointed to the fact that re-identification can occur with high probabilities in de-
identified datasets. They also argued that therefore the present de-identification
policies in the market does not satisfy the GDPR and CCPA standards set by
the European Governments.

Our comparisons includes two of the datasets used in this work [14]. Our
experiments were aimed at proving that differential privacy is a better strategy
than de-identification of the data. We started with original data sets, trained
them with differentially private AI algorithms. We used differential private
library developed by IBM [4], and applied classification models namely Gaussian Naive Bayes (NB) and Logistic Regression respectively. The NB model is
based on the key idea of deriving the sensitivity for each attribute appropriately

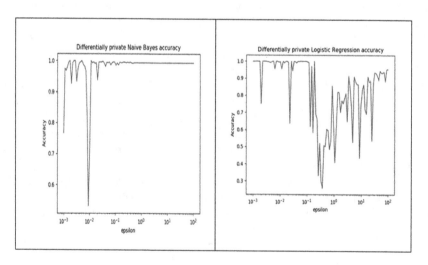

Fig. 1. Naive Bayes and Logistic Regression results for ADULT database

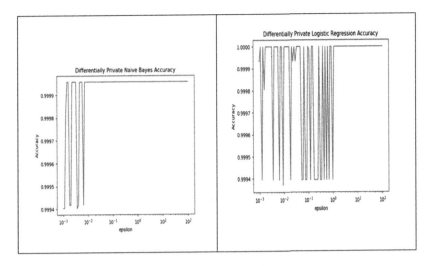

Fig. 2. Naive Bayes and Logistic Regression results for MIDUS database

based on whether it is categorical or numeric [4]. Further, an appropriate Laplacian noise was added to the counts for categorical attributes, the means and the standard deviations for numeric attributes. These parameters are then used to classify a new instance in the NB environment. Secondly we used the Logistic regression algorithm to make the data set differentially private and train our model. We used Python version 3.7 and JetBeans as our IDE, for our implementation. The processor used was an Intel core $i5$.

This class implements regularized logistic regression using an optimize minimum approach. ϵ-Differential privacy is achieved relative to the maximum norm of the data, as determined by datanorm parameter of the algorithm, through the vector method which adds a Laplace-distributed random vector to the objective [CMS11]. The maximum norm of the data is basically $l2$ norm of any row of the data which is actually the spread of data that will be protected by differential privacy. If not specified, the max norm is taken from the data itself when the model is trained for the first time. Differential privacy is completely implemented by selecting datanorm parameter independent or irrespective of the data characteristics or data domain. We then compare the performance of each algorithm in terms of the accuracy of the model to accurately estimate the values of a differentially private data set. For ADULTS data set, obtained from UCI [18] and also used by [14], our accuracy came upto 100% with the ϵ value of 1 as seen in Figure 1. For ϵ values less than 1 and more than 0.001, the accuracy was fluctuating between 0.90 and 1. After that, the accuracy was 1 for larger values of ϵ. The same phenomenon was seen with Logistic Regression. The accuracy was fluctuating between 0.3 and 1 for ϵ values between 0.0001 and 1. After ϵ values of 1, the accuracy tends to increase but unlike the NB, it takes higher values of ϵ to reach to the point of 1 moreover, increased fluctuation is seen in the Logistic Regression than in the Naive Bayes. The same database tends to perform differently under both the algorithms before reaching to the accuracy level of 1. Our results for MIDUS [18] data sets, as used by [14], can be seen in the Fig. 2. The behaviour of the database is same in this case for both the algorithms. The MIDUS database does not show any change in fluctuation for both the algorithms but it does take higher value of $\epsilon(1)$ to reach to the maximum accuracy with Logistic Regression algorithm. On the other hand, it reaches to the accuracy of 1 at the lower value of $\epsilon(0.01)$ in case of Naive Bayes.

The inference drawn is actually the proof that differential privacy has higher accuracy and more security than the ones provided by de-identification. Our results illustrates that through differential privacy injected into the database, the noisy data can still provide results with high accuracy, while reducing the risk of leakage of original information. Our observations also shows that the performance of the algorithm depends upon certain characteristics of the data and that is why we have slightly different accuracy levels for the same values of the ϵ for the two different algorithms. The higher accuracy levels allow the data owners to outsource the differentially private databases to the third party, without the concern of privacy breach. We also noticed from the graphs, that the fluctuating noise before reaching to a stable state, should further be investigated and needs to be regularized.

4   Proposed Architectural Models

The three basic DP architectures used in our experiments were first introduced in [6] These three architectures are: *data publication architecture, separated architecture* and *hybridized architecture*. The following is a brief description of each. In the Data Publication Architecture, the database service uses a particular data schema to publish a synthetic data set which has been injected with noise. Because of the fact that the noisy database is not prone to privacy attacks, the data mining services can be implemented and run on the published database with no security concerns. The Separated Architecture separated the database services from the data mining services through the differential privacy interface in between the two. The data mining services should support the classical queries like count and mean queries. The database service is independent of the data mining algorithms used and the logic of both the database and data mining are independent of each other and can be run by different users. The Hybridized architecture adds the differential privacy interface into Data mining services. In this architecture, the database is specifically tailored to facilitate particular queries for specific data mining services.

In our implementation, we set up and used the Separate Architecture model. The benefit of separate architecture is that the classical databases do not need any modifications or editions to support specific data mining services. The data mining services are curated in such a way that they use the query results only for pattern predictions. The architecture yields higher accuracy results as compared to the data publication architecture since it is simply using the results of the query. The data mining services are limited in this architecture because their implementation is limited to the type of queries supported by the database. In this way, the data owning organization can train the original database with the appropriate AI model and add noise to the database. Secondly, they are able to release the noisy database to the third party for further mining. The third party can perform different analytics tasks and identify the trends in the data. Our results also show a high level of accuracy, while providing protection of individual identifiable information when releasing the noisy database. This architecture does not allow complicated queries, however it also can represent huge cost saving for the data owning organization as no database scheme modifications are required.

5   Conclusions

In this paper, we illustrated that differentially private databases can be used for accurate machine learning outputs, while not having re-identification risks associated with the de-identification techniques. Differential privacy can also allow for designing platforms in which where data owners can train their models and release the noisy data for further analysis by third parties. The accuracy of model can be further improved by considering characteristics of data. Future work can include further exploration of the relationships between the characteristics of data and that of machine learning algorithms used.

References

1. Dwork, C., McSherry, F., Nissim, K., Smith, A.: Calibrating noise to sensitivity in private data analysis. In: Halevi, S., Rabin, T. (eds.) TCC 2006. LNCS, vol. 3876, pp. 265–284. Springer, Heidelberg (2006). https://doi.org/10.1007/11681878_14
2. Dwork, C., Pottenger, R.: Toward practicing privacy. J. Am. Med. Inform. Assoc. **20**(1), 102–108 (2013)
3. Dwork, C., Roth, A., et al.: The algorithmic foundations of differential privacy. Found. Trends® Theor. Comput. Sci. **9**(3–4), 211–407 (2014)
4. Holohan, N.: Welcome to the IBM differential privacy library. https://diffprivlib.readthedocs.io/en/latest/. Accessed 21 Dec 2019
5. Information, of Ontario, P.C.: De-identification guidelines for structured data. White Paper, pp. 1–28 (2016)
6. Jain, P., Gyanchandani, M., Khare, N.: Differential privacy: its technological prescriptive using big data. J. Big Data **5**(1), 1–24 (2018). https://doi.org/10.1186/s40537-018-0124-9
7. Kim, J., Winkler, W.: Multiplicative noise for masking continuous data. Statistics **1**, 9 (2003)
8. McSherry, F., Talwar, K.: Mechanism design via differential privacy. In: Proceedings of the 48th Annual IEEE Symposium on Foundations of Computer Science (FOCS 2007), pp. 94–103. IEEE (2007)
9. McSherry, F.D.: Privacy integrated queries: an extensible platform for privacy-preserving data analysis. In: Proceedings of the 2009 ACM SIGMOD International Conference on Management of Data, pp. 19–30. ACM (2009)

10. Mohan, P., Thakurta, A., Shi, E., Song, D., Culler, D.: GUPT: privacy preserving data analysis made easy. In: Proceedings of the 2012 ACM SIGMOD International Conference on Management of Data, pp. 349–360. ACM (2012)
11. Office, N.: MIT and Harvard release de-identified learning data from open online courses. http://news.mit.edu/2014/mit-and-harvard-release-de-identified-learning-data-open-online-courses. Accessed 15 May 2019
12. Organization, H.: Hitrust de-identification framework. https://hitrustalliance.net/de-identification/. Accessed 30 Jan 2020
13. Registry, B.O., Spafford, O.: Requesting data. https://www.bornontario.ca/en/data/requesting-data.aspx. Accessed 12 Aug 2019
14. Rocher, L., Hendrickx, J.M., De Montjoye, Y.A.: Estimating the success of re-identifications in incomplete datasets using generative models. Nat. Commun. **10**(1), 1–9 (2019)
15. Roy, I., Setty, S.T., Kilzer, A., Shmatikov, V., Witchel, E.: Airavat: Security and privacy for mapreduce. In: Proceedings of the 7th USENIX Symposium on Networked Systems Design and Implementation, NSDI 2010, vol. 10, pp. 297–312 (2010)
16. Sarathy, R., Muralidhar, K.: Evaluating laplace noise addition to satisfy differential privacy for numeric data. Trans. Data Priv. **4**(1), 1–17 (2011)
17. Spafford, K.: Will my personal information be safe? http://cpcssn.ca/faq-posts/will-my-personal-information-be-safe/. Accessed 10 Aug 2019
18. UCI: Center for machine learning and intelligent systems. https://cml.ics.uci.edu/. Accessed Aug 2020

Personal Data Discoverability to Human Searchers: Observations on Personal Data Availability

Kirsten E. Richards[✉]

United States Naval Academy, Annapolis, USA
`krichard@usna.edu`

Abstract. Personal data is widely and readily available online. Some of that personal data might be considered private or sensitive, such as portions of social security numbers [1]. Prior research demonstrates the knowledge of personal acquaintances of data used in secondary authentication protocols [1]. We explored discoverability and location of personal data online and gathered observation actors making the data available.

To empirically understand online data discoverability, we sought to identify select personal data of 32 volunteers. United States Naval Academy (USNA) Midshipmen and recent graduates of the USNA cyber operations major used publicly available online information to assemble personal data of participants. On average, the investigations took 10–20 min and accurately recovered substantial personal data.

Of the sample, 68.75% of *mother's maiden names*, 34.38% of *nicknames* and 28.13% of *mobile phone numbers* were accurately identified. Searchers noted that data was most readily obtained by performing a "social pivot" from the original participant and tracing social relationships on commercial sites (e.g. *WhitePages*) and social media (e.g. *Facebook*). Personal data was most frequently revealed as a result of social connections rather than direct, first person information provided by participants though their own web presence.

Measuring the discoverability of personal data online provides insights into data vulnerabilities and actors in data availability. Data discoverability has ramifications on discussions of privacy beliefs and behaviors and current and future authentication protocols.

Keywords: Authentication and identification · Privacy implications of authentication technologies · Authentication and identification: security and usability of combinations of authentication factors · Human factors: behavior-based cybersecurity · Human factors: human identification of websites

1 Introduction

Posting personal data on the web is increasingly ubiquitous in developed countries. Pew's 2019 social media update places Youtube usage at 73% of the United States adult

© Springer Nature Switzerland AG 2020
A. Moallem (Ed.): HCII 2020, LNCS 12210, pp. 499–512, 2020.
https://doi.org/10.1007/978-3-030-50309-3_33

population and Facebook usage at 69% [2]. Other social media are significant, but trail the leaders with Instagram at 37%, Pinterest at 28%, LinkedIn at 27%, Snapchat at 24%, Twitter at 22%, WhatsApp at 20% and Reddit at 11% [2]. These social media, and other online venues of personal data make locating personal data for a very large demographic of individuals exceptionally easy. Sharing data is both socially and fiscally significant, with multiple actors with various motivations involved in personal data availability [3]. The presence of personal data online represents a complex interplay of individuals, society and risk-benefit decision. The nuanced nature of those choices is not well reflected in currently available technology [4, 5]. While many studies limit the examination of privacy attitudes and behaviors to individuals information sharing behaviors are contextual and societal. Social media users to do not only share personal data about themselves, but also personal data about others.

This study examines the origins of personal data online by performing searches for personal data online for 32 individuals. The search team observed the relative difficulty of obtaining information, whether information obtained was accurate, and where information was likely to be located. Through the process of collecting personal data of consenting individuals, the research team was also able to observe social relationships that reveal data as well as the most likely locations of personal data availability.

Motivations for the study were two-fold. Of primary interest was observing data availability directly and understanding factors affecting availability. Also of interest was observing which data were most susceptible to easy discovery. The relative ease of discovery is a significant aspect of personal privacy and control and is significant in the discussion of authentication protocols, both those currently in use and proposed future protocols.

One important consideration in the discussion of data privacy is the consistent use of personal data in authentication mechanisms. Literature establishes the availability of a wide amount of personal data online and supports the general tendency towards use of personal data as authenticators. The security concern lies at the intersection of personal data availability and the utility of that data for perpetrating security breaches. This personal data may be used in numerous ways, from targeted spear phishing attacks to more generalize password or secret question guessing based attacks. Of specific interest here was the intersection of personal data posted online and data frequently used in authentication. Specific personal data was selected for its ubiquity in personal knowledge authenticators and also for the previous known difficulty in detecting the particular personal data [6].

The study's objective is to observe and report on observations of relative availability of personal data online and explore the location of that data online as an indirect observation of behaviors that make personal data available. Personal data discoverability allows insight into the outcomes of various behaviors – how user sharing influences the availability of personal data online. The availability of personal data online has ramifications on discussions of privacy and cyber security.

2 Background

Previous studies lay a clear foundation for this work. Prior work demonstrates that personal data is available online and provides some insight into motivations and rational for personal data disclosure online. Choices to disclose personal information online represent a complex interplay between privacy and trust [7]. Multiple studies and literature reviews provide insights into user's choices to disclose data [8, 9]. The locations, and implications of locations, of personal data availability have also been explored in recent literature [10]. Research clearly establishes the prevalence of online data availability, various explanations for privacy behaviors and the significance of personal data in the context of authentication.

2.1 Personal Data Availability

Personal data online is a complex and multifaceted issue. Personal data is made available by a wide variety of actors who may act intentionally or unintentionally and with various degrees of good intentions and with nefarious goals. This personal data is exposed online to companies, individual, and government through a variety of venues.

Personal data is exposed on online social media, where seemingly insignificant data could compromise security [11]. With increasing frequency, data made public about individuals online has led to significant personal consequences for actions that might otherwise go unnoticed, such as hiring and firing decisions made on the basis of social media [12].

A movement towards real identities online requirement altered the nature of online identity and made individuals identifiable by name across platforms [13, 14]. One study demonstrated links in social networks reveal private information that users do not wish to reveal, such as political affiliation [15]. Very sensitive personal information, such as portions of social security numbers are also predictable from public data [1]. Data used in authentication and security protocols, such as a mother's maiden name, can be retrieved from public records [16]. Pet's names were slightly harder to guess than human names, but are also vulnerable to statistical analysis [17, 18]. Current work demonstrates that significant personal data is available online and that the personal data may cause individuals harm.

2.2 Personal Data and Privacy Behaviors

Modern technology provides unprecedented abilities to self-propagate personal data [3]. The data is in fact, so easily accessible, that breaches can and have been perpetrated without technical knowledge, but only on the basis of social media acquired personal knowledge, as in the breach of Vice-Presidential candidate Sarah Palin's email account [19] "Neither criminal skill, nor advanced technical knowledge, nor even rudimentary understanding of password cracking tools, is required to access this personal information which is believed to be attainable readily." [6].

Previous studies have indicated that personal data exposure may vary widely and while many studies have explored privacy attitudes and sharing behavior [20, 21]. Privacy behaviors include complex motivations that may fall on a spectrum between helpful and detrimental [22]. Behaviors are directly related to trust [7] and the perceived reward of interaction balanced against privacy concern [23].

Observed privacy behaviors and the resulting data availability may also not reflect actual user intentions. Studies of social media privacy settings reveal that many users have different beliefs about the behaviors of their privacy settings than those settings actually afford [5]. Differences between user expectations and belief, user knowledge, and design driven errors obfuscate user intentions. User's privacy control is minimal at best and the cost and difficulty of maintaining privacy through actions like reading privacy policy is quite high - often requiring multiple years of collegiate level education [24].

Furthermore, information sharing behaviors can be manipulated, either positively or negatively. Commercial actors vested interest in encouraging users to share data. Users provide data for a variety of purposes and for a variety of rewards. Those rewards might include personal rewards such as enjoyment or reputations and inter-personal rewards such as such increasing social capital [25]. Individuals are also willing to part with their data for quite minor rewards and appear to value sharing over protecting personal data [26].

2.3 Secondary and Ternary Actors in Personal Data Privacy

In addition to sharing their own personal data, users are also parting with the personal data of others [27]. Personal data beliefs and sharing behaviors are highly individual and factors such as personality play a role in sharing decisions [28]. Personal information is increasingly collected in a wide variety of circumstances [29].

However, personal control of data is highly ephemeral [30]. Personal data shared in a specific, high trust context, can quickly and easily be moved and re-shared in a different environment by secondary and ternary actors with different beliefs, motivations and potential rewards.

Data may also be recombined in different forms and with the application of machine learning and datamining techniques, yield derived data that was never intended or shared by the original source personal data [13]. At times, this data has been reverse engineered to reveal personal information [31, 32], demonstrating the secondary nature of data control. The real consequences, both positive and negative, of personal data sharing online raise concerns about personal data availability – especially if the data are made available by a secondary source.

2.4 Personal Data Use in Authentication

One potential consequence of personal data misuse is account compromise as a result of personal data availability. The contribution of personal data to account compromise are recognized and well addressed in the literature [3, 33–35]. Despite the known availability of personal data online, personal data continues to form a key aspect of authentication systems in use as well as proposed potential systems. Understanding the overlap of personal data online with personal data that may cause compromise to authentication systems is key.

There is a fundamental gap between "good" passwords and human cognition [36–39]. The design of a "good" password is a superb example of failure to attend to the "human" in technical systems. At one time, when personal data was not highly available online, the threat model for personal data use in passwords was quite different and might potentially be limited to acquaintances or insider threats. The knowledge of acquaintances of personal data relate to authentication is also established in literature [40].

Users frequently compensate for the difficulty of remembering passwords by the use of personal data [37]. Even in the context of better passwords created by users who do not use personal data, secondary authenticators, such as authentication by personal knowledge question may provide an opportunity for compromise [11].

Additionally, personal data are used in other proposed authentication schemes. Personal knowledge in the form of 5th factor authentication might also be compromised by social knowledge obtainable by social media [6, 41]. While this study only addresses common data for primary and secondary knowledge-based authentication, awareness of personal data control and availability is a significant discussion for proposed authentication models.

2.5 Background Summary

Research supports privacy as a complex, multi-faceted concept with a wide variety of beliefs and motivations driving user behavior. The secondary nature of significant portions of personal data sharing is also observed. Personal data is also clearly important to security, particularly in the area of authentication.

Prior work examined the connection between particular personal data and authentication discoverability [10]. Prior research used untrained undergraduate students as participants to locate personal data online. The current study describes online information availability to trained searchers and provides secondary observations of privacy behaviors that are used to obscure personal data on social networks. The study seeks confirm prior observations of data availability, using trained searchers, and observe location of data availability to provide insight into primary and secondary actors in data availability and observe variances in data availability.

3 Methods

The study reflects previous models based around acquaintances, friends, or family members guessing personal data of other individuals [40]. Replacing the acquaintances in the model, strangers to the participants volunteered to search public, online spaces and make their best guess about the personal data. The study explores the data availability of personal data used in authentication and particular data points which were more difficult for searchers to identify in previous studies [6]. Searchers made their best guess or guesses regarding personal data, made observations about the data locations, the apparent actors providing availability, and factors affecting availability, recorded URLs, and time spent searching.

3.1 Participants

Thirty-two individuals were recruited and provided permission to search for their data, provided correct answers to personal data questions, answered a brief demographic questionnaire about age and gender, and provided some initial data to allow for accurate search, which included photographs, name, and a city state location. The participants are all undergraduate students and represent an age demographic between 18 and 22, with an average age of 20.09. The participants provided an HRPP approved consent. Efforts were made to recruit similar numbers of male and female participants. Ultimately, seventeen female and fifteen male students agreed to participate. Two male students originally recruited withdrew from the study.

3.2 Trained Searchers

Three searchers participated in locating personal data. These searchers, all trained in ethical research and approved by the USNA HRPP (Human Research Protection Program), were either graduating seniors in their final semester at the United States Naval Academy or recently graduated officers, who majored in cyber operations. The searchers had access initially only to the name, city and state location and photograph of the participants.

3.3 Procedure

Participants were first recruited and provided with the HRPP approved consent. After consent, they provided their name, city and state location and a photograph. Personal data was also collected, and subsequently separated from identifying information. A master copy of the data with both identifications and personal data was retained by the researcher.

The searchers were provided with the name and city and state of the source participants and asked to identify the source participant as a stranger, that is, someone with which they have not previously communicated directly either in person or online. None of the biographical description includes any part of the personal data sought.

Personal data selected for search included Nicknames, Mother's Maiden Names, and Mobile Phone Numbers. These datum points were selected because of their significance to authentication and the relative difficulty of identifying those particular data points in previous work [6, 10].

For each point of personal data, the searcher provides the requested personal data and may supply multiple guesses, if desired. This design is reflected in other studies as well [40]. Additionally, the approximate time as reported by the seeker spent locating the data, the location of the data, and the perceived difficulty of locating the data were obtained. The searchers recorded additional observations about data location, particularly whether the data was self-propagated or appeared to come from a secondary source. Original URLs of data were also recorded for further analysis after the search process was complete. In addition, searchers rated the difficulty of identifying information and recorded notes on their search process.

4 Analysis

Following the data collection process, the researcher compared searcher supplied guesses with participant supplied correct answers. The comparison between participants supplied answers and searcher supplied answers was also validated *post facto* by one searcher as well. No inconsistencies between the comparisons were noted.

After comparing results for accuracy, analysis of locations was conducted. Location was evaluated *post facto* with analysis of similarities and differences between source participants to providing insight into areas of vulnerability in personal data on the web [10]. URLs were categorized by the researchers as a reflection of location – such a particular social media site and type – social media, commercial or government.

Observations were made comparing gender availability, the most common and readily available locations of data, the most easily discovered data, and the actors most likely supplying data. Through the search process, searchers also noted cases when participants seemed to take additional steps to safeguard their data. These cases were examined comparatively and similarities and differences in approaches to privacy were noted. These cases were also compared for success – whether the personal data was more difficult to discover.

5 Results

The methodology allowed for extensive exploration of multiple factors of data availability and personal privacy behavior. The final results provide an ability to compare discoverability with previous studies that used untrained searchers and acquaintances [6, 10, 40]. Gender differences were also explored, as were the relative difficulty of each data point.

The searchers were able to successfully identify many of the personal data points. There were clearly distinct differences in the availability of personal data availability by data type. In searching for personal data, searchers also noted that additional data, such as physical home addresses, would have been very easy to obtain as well.

Search time was often quite brief with the majority of searches taking approximately 15 min. The fastest search time was 2 min and correctly identified all three datapoints. The mean search time was 16.57 min of recorded searches. Only two searches were rated as very "difficult" by searchers and took 60 min. One of these searches succeeded in all categories and one failed in all categories.

5.1 Mother's Maiden Name

Twenty-two *mother's maiden names* were successfully located. In twenty-one instances only one guess was required. Searchers were confident that they had correctly identified a single correct answer. In the remaining instance, the name was guessed within two guesses. Correct name guesses represent 68.75% of cases. Three of the nine names that were not found were guessed incorrectly by searches. In the remaining six instances, the searchers were aware that they had not located a correct answer. No significant differences in the gender of participants discovered was noted. The total number of discovered cases was 11 (64.71%) for women and 11 (73.33%) for men.

Searchers cited White Pages as the primary source of correct data for *mother's maiden name*. Data for *mother's maiden name* was provided by secondary sources. The majority of discoveries occurred through observation of social relationships on WhitePages. Eighteen successful identification occurred using Whitepages. In addition, three names were successfully located using Facebook. In one case Youtube provided personal information leading to a *mother's maiden name*. The Youtube video that provided the data was not posted directly by the participant but is believed to represent a posting by a significant personal relationship. In no case did searchers find the data directly in self-propagated formats, such as the participant's own social media site.

Searchers described, "social pivoting" as a successful tactic. In this case, using the participant as an informational beginning to their search. Focusing on identifying social relationships and searching the personal data provided by the social circle about the original participant frequent provided *Mother's maiden names*.

5.2 Nicknames

Eleven *nicknames* were correctly obtained. Of the thirty-two participants, two reported not using *nicknames*. *Nicknames* were more likely than *mother's maiden name* to be found directly on from the participant's own web postings. Social media, especially Facebook, was the most consistent discovery location accounting for ten of eleven correct identifications. In one case, LinkedIn provided the *nickname*.

Nicknames were likely to be rated as difficult by the searchers. In four instances, the searchers commented on the ambiguity of nicknames. Also noteworthy, searchers guessed *nicknames* incorrectly twice of nineteen unidentified nicknames.

In one case, searchers noted that one participant used two different names consistently – one name on LinkedIn and a different variant of the name on Facebook. This case, labeled as the most difficult by searches, took a full hour, but did ultimately yield correct answers in all three categories.

5.3 Mobile Phone Numbers

Mobile phone numbers were the most difficult to identify correctly. Nine mobile numbers were correctly identified. A gender difference was noted here, although the number of participants precludes any type of generalization. Seven *mobile numbers* belonging to women were located and two belonging to men representing 41.18% and 13.33% respectively. All participants reported having a cell phone.

Mobile phone numbers were located using White pages, LinkedIn, Youtube and Facebook. In two of the nine correct identifications, *Mobile phone number* was provided by a secondary source such as an apparent relative or friend's social media post. In one instance, the phone number was clearly self-propagated, appearing on a resume posted publicly on LinkeIn from the participant's profile. Searches noted that this case was particularly easy – they successfully located all three data points in two minutes. In all other cases, *mobile phone number* was noted as the most difficult data point to correctly identify.

There were twenty-three misidentifications of *Mobile phone numbers*. The incorrect numbers were discovered on either LinkedIn or WhitePages. Searchers notably struggled to quickly and easily identify mobile phone numbers belonging to participants compared to other numbers.

5.4   Results Summary

Thirty-two searches were conducted over the course of 4 weeks. These searches, using only public web data and free resources correctly identified the majority of data for *Mother's maiden names*, a significant percentage of *nicknames* and over 40% of female participants *mobile phone numbers* but only a little over 13% of male participant's *mobile phone numbers*.

These particular data points were selected because previous studies indicated that they might represent more difficult information to locate compared to personal data studied elsewhere [6]. The studies are not directly comparable due primarily to differences in methodology necessitated by HRPP requirements. The previous study demonstrated a much lower accuracy, with a correct Mother's Maiden Name identified correctly seven times, nicknames, thirty-two times and mobile phone number was correctly identified nine times. Each of four subjects' data were searched for by approximately fifty information seekers [6]. In the current study, much higher accuracy of mother's maiden name and mobile phone numbers were achieved, however, nicknames proved more elusive comparatively (Table 1).

Table 1. Successful information identification

Successful information identification			
	Mother's maiden names	Nicknames	Mobile phone numbers
Female participants *(N 17)*	11 (64.71%)	6 (35.29%)	7 (41.18%)
Male participants *(N 15)*	10 (66.67%)	5 (33.33%)	2 (13.33%)
Total *(N 32)*	22 (68.75%)	11 (34.38%)	9 (28.13%)

6   Discussion

Current and future authentication and secondary authentication models should be evaluated for data discoverability. If personal data is available through statically informed guessing or easily accessible from a web search that data represents a significant and measurable security risk.

There are clear differences in the availability of personal data to correct identification. Some data appears to be treated as "more private" behaviorally compared to other data. Furthermore, the data pertaining to the participants is less likely to be found directly self-propagated. These findings have implications on discussions of privacy belief and behaviors and the development of current and future authenticators.

6.1   Privacy and Personal Data as a Group and Societal Construct

The study demonstrates that a great quantity of the information sough is readily available due to the social construct of users. Previous work suggests that the volume of online data creates a level of obscurity, that while not a substitute for privacy, provides some level of protection, arguing that, "information is obscure online if it exists in a context of missing one or more key factors that are essential to discovery or comprehension" [42]. *The search team observed that the most successful strategy employed was that of observing the web content of "digital neighbors" and social communities as revealed through commercial venues – not the information directly propagated by individuals.* The actual availability of personal data to discovery is not a construct of individual privacy beliefs alone, but of the beliefs and behaviors of groups and societies.

Data privacy of individuals is clearly impacted by groups and societies. Groups might include social relationships, such as friendship or parents. Broader societal decisions also impact data availability – such as the availability of data on commercial and government sites. Based on the location of data we discovered, *it is unlikely the individuals acting alone have significant influence over the availability of the data studied.*

The prior observation impacts our study of the "privacy paradox" Much research supports various explanations for the "privacy paradox" on individual and interactive levels of behavior [8]. Lutz and Strathoff [43] provide support for privacy decisions as a societal and group construct. The study of the *outcome* of privacy behaviors and beliefs of individuals, groups and societies, as evidenced in this study, supports a social construct for data discoverability. *Therefore, the study of privacy beliefs and attitudes about other members of society may be worthy of consideration.* Many studies, to date, focus on the privacy beliefs of individuals about their own data. *Extending discussions of privacy to a group's sense of obligation to protect the data of other's in their group may be a meaningful contribution to unraveling the privacy paradox, particularly with meaning to the actual results in online data discoverability.*

6.2   Human Search and Machine Learning

Prior discussions have quantified the risk of guessing and the likelihood of users forgetting personal information [40]. We expand prior knowledge by providing quantification of the discoverability of personal data to human searchers. Human searchers are often able to perform very well in contexts that computers are not yet able to navigate. However, advances in AI and machine learning are rapidly impacting data availability and prior work highlights the ability of machine learning to identify potentially sensitive personal information. In particular, Acquisti and Gross [1] demonstrated the ability to predict partial social security numbers from public data.

Human search, combined with machine learning, would potentially render very complete data sets on individual with relatively little effort. The effort required to obtain the personal data was often quite low with good accuracy – a level of accuracy that would once have only been achievable by a friend, acquaintance or significant family member.

The relatively difficulty of finding copious amounts of personal data is likely to continue decreasing as machine learning continues to advance. Many new ways to identify ourselves have been recommended [40] however, passwords remain both the most prevalent and user preferred mechanism for authentication [44]. Knowing that the next adopted authentication scheme will be very difficult to replace, potential authentication processes should be evaluated for empirical data availability.

7 Limitations

All participants for study were volunteers. The impact of privacy attitudes on data availability was outside of the scope of the study and the impact of either individual or collective attitudes about privacy were not collected. Volunteers privacy attitudes may not reflect more broadly. A limited number of volunteers were available, and the sample were entirely recruited from university students, which, in effect, limited the age of the sample to eighteen to twenty-two year old adults.

Ethics considerations limited searchers to trained volunteer researchers. Trained volunteers were limited in number, so relatively few actual searches by unique searcher were conducted. This limits the broader application of search results. A larger pool of searchers might have very different results and factors influencing search success were not possible given the limited availability of searchers. Future work, exploring the relative skill of searchers may be of interest.

A limited set of personal data were selected based on prior work, primarily due to limited searcher time and to protect participants by limiting points of data collection. Extremely personal or sensitive data, such as social security numbers or partial credit card numbers were excluded for ethical reasons. Additional study is needed to establish empirical information on data discoverability for other examples of personal data or authentication protocols.

8 Future Work

Data discoverability is clearly a social construct. Individuals have limited ability to control their own personal data exposure. Additional work is needed to address group and social dynamics in privacy. Of interest is the possibility of clusters of privacy attitudes in social groups. Understanding the value individuals place on the personal data of others is also significant given the likelihood of data availability through secondary actors.

The ownership of data and the authorization to provide personal data pertaining to self or others is both a social and legal construct. As technology for sharing and obtaining data has evolved rapidly, laws and social rules are evolving much more slowly. Future work in social construct and law and policy must recognize the current gap between evolutionary speeds and attempt to anticipate the needs of individuals and society considering evolving technologies that impact data discoverability.

Current studies are underway to further explore the impact of personality and privacy beliefs on sharing behaviors as they pertain to participant's own data and to the data of others. A survey instrument for measuring the privacy beliefs of individuals with regards to sharing both their own and other's data is also in development as a result of this study.

Acknowledgements. The assistance of USNA Midshipmen and USN Ensigns in collecting data is gratefully acknowledged. The advice and assistance of the HRRP staff is also acknowledged. HRPP Approval #2018.0061-IR-EP7-A.

References

1. Acquisti, A., Gross, R.: Predicting social security numbers from public data. Proc. Natl. Acad. Sci. **106**(27), 10975–10980 (2009)
2. Anderson, M., Perrin, A.: Share of U.S. adults using social media, including Facebook is mostly unchanged since 2018 (2019). https://www.pewresearch.org/fact-tank/2019/04/10/share-of-u-s-adults-using-social-media-including-facebook-is-mostly-unchanged-since-2018/. Accessed 16 January 2020
3. Schneier, B.: Schneier on security: privacy and control. J. Priv. Confid. **2**(1), 3–4 (2010)
4. Ackerman, M., Darrell, T., Weitzner, D.J.: Privacy in context. Hum. Comput. Interact. **16**(2–4), 167–176 (2001)
5. Madejski, M., Johnson, M., Bellovin, S.M.: A study of privacy settings errors in an online social network. In: 2012 IEEE International Conference on Pervasive Computing & Communications Workshops, p. 340 (2012)
6. Richards, K.E.: Risk analysis of the discoverability of personal data used for primary and secondary authentication. University of Maryland Baltimore County, MD, US (2017)
7. Joinson, A., et al.: Privacy, trust, and self-disclosure online. Hum. Comput. Interact. **25**(1), 1–24 (2010)
8. Kokolakis, S.: Privacy attitudes and privacy behaviour: a review of current research on the privacy paradox phenomenon. Comput. Secur. **64**, 122–134 (2017)
9. Buchanan, T., et al.: Development of measures of online privacy concern and protection for use on the Internet. J. Am. Soc. Inf. Sci. Technol. **58**(2), 157–165 (2007)
10. Richards, K.E., Norcio, A.F.: Exploring the discoverability of personal data used for authentication. In: Nicholson, D. (ed.) AHFE 2017. AISC, vol. 593, pp. 97–105. Springer, Cham (2018). https://doi.org/10.1007/978-3-319-60585-2_11
11. Reeder, R., Schechter, S.: When the password doesn't work: Secondary authentication for websites. IEEE Secur. Priv. Mag. **9**(2), 43 (2011)
12. Drouin, M., et al.: Facebook fired: Legal perspectives and young adults' opinions on the use of social media in hiring and firing decisions. Comput. Hum. Behav. **46**, 123–128 (2015)
13. Schau, H.J., Gilly, M.C.: We are what we post? Self-presentation in personal web space. J. Consum. Res. **30**(3), 385–404 (2003)
14. van Dijck, J.: 'You have one identity': performing the self on Facebook and LinkedIn. Media Cult. Soc. **35**(2), 199–215 (2013)
15. Lindamood, J., et al.: Inferring private information using social network data. In: Proceedings of the 18th International Conference on World Wide Web, Madrid, Spain, pp. 1145–1146. ACM (2009)
16. Griffith, V., Jakobsson, M.: Messin' with texas deriving mother's maiden names using public records. In: Ioannidis, J., Keromytis, A., Yung, M. (eds.) ACNS 2005. LNCS, vol. 3531, pp. 91–103. Springer, Heidelberg (2005). https://doi.org/10.1007/11496137_7
17. Bonneau, J., Just, M., Matthews, G.: What's in a name? Evaluating statistical attacks on personal knowledge questions. In: Lewis, D.E. (ed.) Financial Cryptography and Data Security, pp. 98–113. Springer, Berlin (2010)
18. Rabkin, A.: Personal knowledge questions for fallback authentication. In: ACM International Conference Proceeding Series, p. 13 (2008)
19. Khanna, S., Chaudhry, H.: Anatomy of compromising email accounts. In: 2012 IEEE International Conference on Information and Automation. IEEE (2012)
20. Acquisti, A., Gross, R.: Imagined communities: awareness, information sharing, and privacy on the facebook. In: Danezis, G., Golle, P. (eds.) PET 2006. LNCS, vol. 4258, pp. 36–58. Springer, Heidelberg (2006). https://doi.org/10.1007/11957454_3

21. Beldad, A., de Jong, M., Steehouder, M.: A comprehensive theoretical framework for personal information-related behaviors on the internet. Inf. Soc. **27**(4), 220–232 (2011)
22. Chen, H.-T., Kim, Y.: Problematic use of social network sites: the interactive relationship between gratifications sought and privacy concerns. CyberPsychol. Behav. Soc. Netw. **16**(11), 806–812 (2013)
23. Hallam, C., Zanella, G.: Online self-disclosure: the privacy paradox explained as a temporally discounted balance between concerns and rewards. Comput. Hum. Behav. **68**, 217–227 (2017)
24. McDonald, A.M., Cranor, L.F.: The cost of reading privacy policies. J. Law Policy Inf. Soc. **4**, 543 (2008)
25. Liu, L., Cheung, C.M., Lee, M.K.: An empirical investigation of information sharing behavior on social commerce sites. Int. J. Inf. Manag. **36**(5), 686–699 (2016)
26. Grossklags, J., Acquisti, A.: When 25 cents is too much: An experiment on willingness-to-sell and willingness-to-protect personal information. In: WEIS (2007)
27. Benson, V., Saridakis, G., Tennakoon, H.: Information disclosure of social media users: does control over personal information, user awareness and security notices matter? Inf. Technol. People **28**(3), 426–441 (2015)
28. Gratian, M., et al.: Correlating human traits and cyber security behavior intentions. Comput. Secur. **73**, 345–358 (2018)
29. Il-Horn, H., et al.: Overcoming online information privacy concerns: an information-processing theory approach. J. Manag. Inf. Syst. **24**(2), 13–42 (2007)
30. Acquisti, A., Adjerid, I., Brandimarte, L.: Gone in 15 seconds: the limits of privacy transparency and control. IEEE Secur. Priv. **11**(4), 72–74 (2013)
31. Lee, N.: Consumer privacy in the age of big data. facebook nation, pp. 139–147. Springer, New York (2014). https://doi.org/10.1007/978-1-4939-1740-2_7
32. Lo, B.: Sharing clinical trial data: maximizing benefits, minimizing risk. JAMA **313**(8), 793–794 (2015)
33. Oravec, J.A.: Deconstructing "personal privacy" in an age of social media: information control and reputation mangement dimensions. Int. J. Acad. Bus. World **6**(1), 95–104 (2012)
34. Dlamini, M.T., Eloff, J.P., Eloff, M.M.: Information security: the moving target. Comput. Secur. **28**(3/4), 189–198 (2009)
35. Pavlou, P.A.: State of the information privacy literature: where are we now and where should we go? MIS Q. **35**(4), 977–988 (2011)
36. Bonneau, J., et al.: The quest to replace passwords: a framework for comparative evaluation of web authentication schemes. In: IEEE Symposium on Security and Privacy, pp. 553–567 (2012)
37. Brown, A.S., et al.: Generating and remembering passwords. Appl. Cogn. Psychol. **18**(6), 641–651 (2004)
38. Vu, K.-P.L., et al.: Improving password security and memorability to protect personal and organizational information. Int. J. Hum Comput Stud. **65**(8), 744–757 (2007)
39. Sasse, M., Brostoff, S., Weirich, D.: Transforming the 'weakest link' a human-computer interaction approach to usable and effective security. BT Technol. J. **19**(3), 122–131 (2001)
40. Schechter, S., Brush, A.J.B., Egelman, S.: It's no secret. Measuring the security and reliability of authentication via "secret" questions. In: 2009 30th IEEE Symposium on Security and Privacy (2009)
41. Polakis, I., et al.: All your face are belong to us: breaking Facebook's social authentication. In: Proceedings of the 28th Annual Computer Security Applications Conference, Orlando, Florida, USA, pp. 399–408. ACM (2012)

42. Hartzog, W., Stutzman, F.: Obscurity by design. Wash. Law Rev. **88**(2), 386–418 (2013)
43. Lutz, C., Strathoff, P.: Privacy concerns and online behavior–Not so paradoxical after all? Viewing the privacy paradox through different theoretical lenses. Viewing the Privacy Paradox Through Different Theoretical Lenses, 15 April 2014
44. Zimmermann, V., Gerber, N.: The password is dead, long live the password – a laboratory study on user perceptions of authentication schemes. Int. J. Hum Comput Stud. **133**, 26–44 (2020)

Understanding Privacy and Trust in Smart Home Environments

Eva-Maria Schomakers$^{(\boxtimes)}$, Hannah Biermann , and Martina Ziefle

Human-Computer Interaction Center, RWTH Aachen University,
Campus-Boulevard 57, 52074 Aachen, Germany
{schomakers,biermann,ziefle}@comm.rwth-aachen.de
http://www.comm.rwth-aachen.de

Abstract. Smart homes – a residence with innovative, interconnected, and automated technologies – can enhance the resident's quality of life and well-being. Despite these potentials, users' may have concerns about the increased automation which negatively influence their technology acceptance. Missing trust in automated technologies and privacy concerns have been identified as crucial barriers for smart home adoption. Still, privacy and trust perceptions in smart homes have not yet been deeply understood. Also, the effect of different automation levels has not been studied so far. In a qualitative empirical approach, we examine perceptions of privacy and trust in smart home technologies depending on the level of automation (using two juxtaposed scenarios: partially automated vs. highly automated). 10 adults (20 to 87 years) were interviewed. Trust in smart home technologies comprises multiple dimensions of not only trust in the functionality of the technology but also in the human stakeholders involved and in connected technologies. Privacy in smart home does not only regard informational privacy (data protection) but also physical, social, and psychological dimensions of privacy which are often neglected. The results show that privacy and trust in smart home are interdependent. The degree of automation strongly influences privacy and trust perceptions – with a higher automation leading to more concerns. Our results contribute to a deeper understanding of privacy and trust in smart homes. The negative impact of the level of automation on privacy and trust perceptions is a guide for the development of smart home technologies that meet users' acceptance.

Keywords: Smart home · Technology acceptance · Privacy · Trust in automation

1 Introduction

Increasing digitization entails global progress and change that affect many areas of life [12], also domestic environments that become "sensitive, adaptive, and responsive to human needs" [30]. Smart homes offer great potentials for the control of energy usage, improvement of security, comfort, entertainment, and communication, but also in terms of health management with regard to aging and

© Springer Nature Switzerland AG 2020
A. Moallem (Ed.): HCII 2020, LNCS 12210, pp. 513–532, 2020.
https://doi.org/10.1007/978-3-030-50309-3_34

vulnerable residents [22]. Though research and development concerning home automation is growing rapidly, the use of holistic environments is still rare in practice compared to single technologies that have already become popular (e.g., surveillance camera, smart speaker) [22]. With regard to the users' perspective, a possible reason is that automation may lead to uncertainties, particularly related to privacy and trust concerns. To this, previous research showed that, although users appreciated smart home advantages (especially energy management), they also feared perceived disadvantages in terms of being dependent on technology along with the feeling of loosing control [3,44]. Future scenarios of smart homes with more advanced automation may provide even more benefits but may also increase concerns and feelings of loss of control. Therefore, the technology acceptance by the users is a decisive factor for the successful roll-out of smart home environments. User requirements, especially regarding privacy and trust concerns, need to be understood and considered in the development of smart home technologies.

To better understand perceptions of privacy and trust in this context, further research is needed to identify future users' needs and demands, but also concerns regarding life in smart home under consideration of different automation levels – especially as previous studies are limited to either specific technologies and systems or generic smart home descriptions as basis for use evaluation – to derive acceptance-relevant factors as implications for the technical development.

1.1 Smart Home Environments

Smart homes are provided with integrated sensor and actuator networks for data collection and task performance based on wireless communication to support residents in their personal living environment for improved quality of life [9,11]. Smart home technologies and applications are manifold, including monitoring systems (video tracking, biometrics control, etc.), integrated pressure pads (e.g., in the floor or furniture), light and temperature sensors, smart meters, emergency buttons, and home robots, appropriately designed for security, entertainment and communication, convenience and comfort, energy efficiency, ambient assisted living (AAL) and health care [3]. To give one example, lighting and temperature in a room can be regulated using (floor) sensors, such as for motion or pressure, that detect the presence or absence of a person, allowing the lights and heating systems to be switched on or off accordingly [32].

So far, users are provided with an intuitive handling of the smart home technology using speech, gestures, and familiar interfaces, such as smartphone or tablet, to easily control and operate their living environment [18]. For example, if residents receive visitors, they can recognize and communicate with them through a monitoring system (camera, microphone, speaker) and remotely open the door (e.g., at the push of a button or via voice control) [32]. With regard to advanced home automation, the idea is to have fully networked appliances that operate without human involvement [39]. To stay with the example of home visitors, the security system automatically performs access control by identifying (un)welcome visitors (e.g., via face recognition and pre-set information) to open respectively lock the door [31]. Consequently, when the active performance of tasks is provided by highly automated systems, users take a more passive role. The repercussions on users' acceptance of smart home, especially regarding privacy concerns and trust in the technology have not yet been investigated.

1.2 Technology Acceptance

Research on technology acceptance engages in the comprehension of factors that influence the intention to adopt and use technologies. A very influential model on technology acceptance is the TAM (*Technology Acceptance Model* [10]) and its extensions [21]. Here, central influencing factors on acceptance are the perceived usefulness and the perceived ease of use. As measurement for acceptance the behavioral intention to use a technology is used based on the *Theory of Reasoned Action* [1]. The TAM and most of its extensions are originally developed for the use of Information and Communication Technologies (ICT) on the workplace. For consumer technologies, the UTAUT2 (*Unified Theory of Adoption and Use of Technology 2* [42]) has been developed which includes additional factors which are important to consumers like hedonic motivation and price value.

Still, research shows that regarding digital technologies like the Internet of Things (IoT) and special contexts like smart homes, these models do not consider the whole diversity of factors that influence acceptance [2,29,38]. In order to increase users' confidence and acceptance, Wilson et al. [44] found that smart home technology needed to be reliable and guarantee privacy, corresponding to the findings of Balta-Ozkan et al. [3] who revealed information disclosure (data security) and hacker attacks (the system's physical security) as major barriers to use. In addition, it was apparent that users tended to distrust governments and industries out of the concern for profit-making when it comes to the use of automated smart home technology [3].

This shows that when technologies are integrated into the intimate space of the own home, collect manifold data, and take over control of actions – as it is the case in smart homes – factors like privacy concerns and trust become decisive [36].

1.3 Privacy

Privacy is a key element of personal freedom, autonomy, and well-being [33]. Privacy can be defined as the **control** over access to the self [7]. Control being the core element, privacy is not about absolute withdrawal but about having the ability to achieve the optimal level of withdrawal and disclosure in each situation [26].

In regard to digital technologies, the aspect of *informational privacy* is often focused, meaning the control over access to personal information [7]. But especially regarding smart home technologies the other three dimensions of privacy must not be neglected: *Physical privacy* describes the control over access to the physical self like freedom from surveillance and unwanted intruders; *Social privacy* constitutes of control over the who, what, when, and where of personal encounters with others; and *psychological privacy* is the protection from intrusions upon one's thoughts, feelings, and values [7]. All four privacy dimensions may be infringed by smart home technologies and thus need to be considered to understand privacy requirements regarding the acceptance of smart homes.

In various studies, concerns about privacy have been identified as important barrier to the use of ICT in general [4] and smart home technologies in particular [43,46]. Potential users see risks and concerns regarding access and misuse of personal information, invasion of personal space, feelings of surveillance, obtrusiveness and more [5,14,17]. Influencing factors on privacy concerns are, e.g., the perceived sensitivity of data that is collected by the technology [41], characteristics of the technology like the type or location of sensors [15], who has access to the data [37], and the ability to control the technology [13].

1.4   Trust

Trust is the key to situations characterized by uncertainties [19] that may arise when different stakeholders are involved (*Can I rely on the other?*). This applies to interactions between humans with varying roles, needs, and demands as well as to those involving humans and machines [20].

Considering trust in automated technology, previous studies have already identified a wide range of influencing factors, including the environment (e.g., organizational and cultural setting), situation (e.g., tasks and related risks), previous experiences, as well as user characteristics (demographics, personality, attitudes, etc.), cognition (e.g., ability and expertise), emotion and affection (e.g., technology liking) [16,24,25,34]. Besides, trust in automation was found to be application-sensitive. Brell et al. [6] revealed that trust in home automation was significantly higher in contextual comparison with autonomous driving, provided that the participants also showed a higher willingness to use smart homes. Against the background of increasing home automation, it is of great interest to what extent these findings differ regarding diverse automation levels.

As home automation concerns a particularly private and intimate application field, it is therefore not perceived without risks [22]. Two strong research directions focus on aging in place (given the demographic change) and energy management (as a major motive for use). Steinke et al. [40] identified reliability and ease of use as trust predictors in AAL, provided that trust also depended on the type of technology and varied with regard to user diversity. Wilson et al. [44] found that, in general, dependencies on infrastructure (technologies and networks) and third parties (experts) were perceived as risky. With special focus given to energy management, Paetz et al. [28] and Balta-Ozkan et al. [3] revealed concerns about being betrayed and manipulated by politics and companies for economic reasons. To this, Yang et al. [45] identified trust in the service provider as a central acceptance factor for smart home technologies.

Understanding the role of trust in the decision-making whether or not to use home automation requires further research to explore user requirements in balancing perceived (dis)advantages with regard to multiple applications of use, but also in-depth knowledge of conditions and aspects that can create (dis)trust.

1.5   Research Questions

For the development of smart home technologies that fit the users needs and wishes it needs to be understood what influences the perception of technologies and the technology acceptance by potential users. Much research on technology acceptance in smart homes focuses on the confirmation and extension of existing models, using quantitative approaches [22]. This research shows that privacy concerns and trust in automation are important factors that indeed need to be included into the modeling of technology acceptance in smart homes (e.g., [6,38]). But this quantitative and confirmatory research still falls short in two important aspects.

Firstly, technology acceptance, trust, and privacy are context-dependent [6,26,35]. Still, not much is yet known about privacy and trust perceptions in the special context of smart homes. Therefore, further exploratory examinations are needed to study how these differences affect the perceptions of privacy and trust, respectively, in smart homes. Only then can technological developments be perfectly fitted to users wishes.

Secondly, privacy and trust are mostly examined as two independent variables. Trade-offs between conflicting factors, like privacy concerns and benefits, like energy savings and quality of life, are a core element of the genesis of acceptance [27]. First results show that there are interactions between trust and privacy [6,35]. In a way, trust can mitigate privacy concerns [35]; but privacy concerns also lower trust into automation [6]. To better understand how these two important factors interact with and influence each other regarding smart home acceptance further qualitative research is needed.

Also, an important factor for privacy and trust in automation, respectively, is the perceived control over the technology [37] and correspondingly the level of automation [16]. The level of automation has not yet been considered regarding the acceptance of smart home nor for users' perceptions of trust and privacy in this context. It may help to understand key aspects of smart home acceptance.

This study aims to close these research gaps using an exploratory, qualitative research approach to answer the following research questions:

- What are perceptions of and influences to privacy and trust in smart homes?
- How does the level of automation influence perceptions of privacy and trust?
- How do privacy and trust perceptions interact and depend on one another?

2   Method

The study aim was to explore privacy and trust perceptions of smart homes as regards two automation levels (semi-automated vs. fully-automated). To this, a qualitative research approach was designed with $N = 10$ participants using guided group interviews (two or three participants each) for a reciprocal sharing of opinions between the respondents to maximize the diversity of perspectives. The participants were acquired in the personal environment of the research team on voluntary basis without gratification. As interview location, a familiar environment was chosen, usually at one of the participants' own places.

The sample consisted of $n = 5$ women and $n = 5$ men. The participants' age ranged from 20 to 87 years ($M = 43$; $SD = 24.05$). The interviews were recorded (audio) and transcribed verbatim. Data analysis based on qualitative content analysis [23]. The categories were developed guided by theory and inductively supplemented based on the research material.

Prior to the interviews, the participants were given an introduction to the topic, procedure, and privacy policy. The interview guideline consisted of three parts with open questions and interactive elements. PART I provided a deeper understanding of the content by discussing the use of technology and experiences with home automation. Each participant received a ground plan in which they were asked to draw technologies they regularly used at home (see Fig. 1).

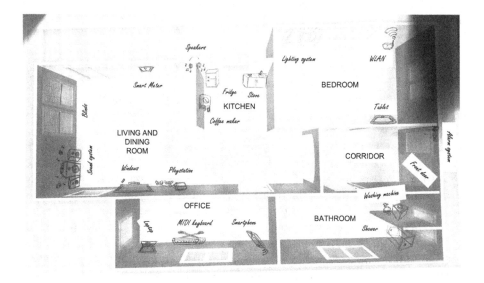

Fig. 1. Ground plan drawing: technology use at home (translated from German).

PART II explored perceptions of and influences to privacy and trust in smart homes with special regard given to the degree of automation. Two scenarios were designed, based on the state of art (see for example [8, 22, 30]), contrasting "semi-automated" (Scenario A) and "fully-automated" (Scenario B) home environments, which were randomized for evaluation within each interview group. First, the participants were provided with clearly illustrated text descriptions of an everyday situation for detailed but easy-to-understand scenario presentations. The integration of smart home technology into daily routines was outlined by demonstrating the active role of users in semi-automated respective the passive role of users in fully-automated smart homes. The understanding of the scenarios for all participants was ensured prior to the study in pretests with participants of different age groups and technology generations.

Next, pictures of smart home technologies were handed out, selected under consideration of diverse application fields (e.g., comfort, entertainment, security, health care, and energy efficiency), including explanations on how they work for each automation scenario (listed in Table 1). A ranking system was used for evaluation to ensure comparability. The assessment of perceived privacy based on a traffic light system with the colors green (= "I have no privacy concerns"), yellow (= neutral), and red (= "I have privacy concerns"). To assess the participants' trust, three emoticons were used with a positive (= "I trust the technology"), neutral, and negative (= "I distrust the technology") facial expression. Subsequently, the participants were asked to discuss further issues of privacy and trust related to the presented technologies, such as *What aspects and conditions are particularly important to you in terms of privacy and trust? What are exclusion criteria for use? Do you think to have control over your data? Do you think the technologies presented are reliable?* etc.

PART III concluded the interview, in which the participants were asked to decide and reason on which smart home scenario (semi-automated vs. fully-automated) they would like to use in practice.

Table 1. Technologies in semi-automated (Scenario A) vs. fully-automated (Scenario B) smart home environments.

Technology	Scenario A (semi-automated)	Scenario B (fully-automated)
Blinds	Opening and closing at the push of a button	Opening and closing based on sensor information (e.g., light)
Fridge	Food stock monitoring	Food stock monitoring and reordering if necessary
TV	Networked with smartphone (screen display)	Networked with smartphone (screen display), lighting (dimming), and external speakers (sound)
Front door	Remote access control via app	Automated access control via face recognition
Bed	Sleep monitoring	Sleep monitoring with automated SOS call in case of emergency
Alarm system	Emergency notification	Automated SOS call
Lighting	Networked lighting controlled via app	Networked lighting adaptive to individual user needs
Smart speaker	Activated via voice control ("Play music!")	Activated via motion detection (music is played automatically)
Smart Meter	Visualization of energy consumption	Automated energy management
Shower	Access to user profile (temperature preference) at the push of a button	Automated user recognition and preference setting

3   Results

In the following, trust perceptions, influences on these, and their dependence on the automation level are described. Thereafter, privacy is focused. The results are illustrated with statements from the participants that are presented at the end of each section. These are indicated in italics, referenced by number and the speaker is identified regarding their gender (f/m) and age (in years).

3.1   Composition of Trust in Smart Home

Trust in a smart home is based on multiple trust perceptions (see Fig. 2). One factor is the **trust into the functionality** with trust in the *reliability* of the technology as a decisive part (see Q1). But also the trust in *data protection* by the technology is important (see Q1, Q2).

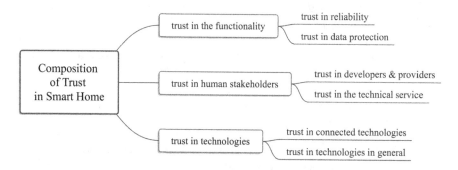

Fig. 2. Composition of trust in smart home.

Also foreground is the **trust in human stakeholders**. This is, on the one hand, the *trust in the developers and providers* (Q3). Very important to many participants was, on the other hand, *trust in a good technical service* (Q3), as they did not trust the technology to be totally reliable.

As smart home technologies rely on technical infrastructure like networks and the internet, **trust in connected technologies** and IT is also important for trust in smart home (Q4). Related to trust in smart home is also **trust in technologies in general** (Q5).

> Q1: "I think trust refers to two things: how reliable the technology is and how much I trust the company to handle my data." (f, 27)
> Q2: "[What conditions are needed for you to trust these technologies?] Data security. That it is ensured that my data cannot be accessed by unauthorized persons." (f, 53)
> Q3: "Any technology is only as good as the people who are behind it and who make the technology work or who are responsive in case of failure." (f, 53)
> Q4: "I would not necessarily trust that the Wi-Fi will always work. So I think it's more about trusting other things that are not the technology itself." (f, 28)
> Q5: "If the standard technology, i.e. a mobile phone wouldn't break after two years, [...] then I would be happy to look into smart home." (m, 57)

3.2   Influences on Trust in Smart Home

Influences on trust in smart home can be structured into three aspects: the technology, the user, and the context (Fig. 3).

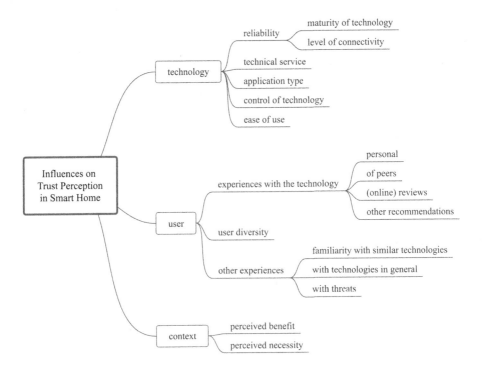

Fig. 3. Influences on trust perception in smart home.

Technology. Multiple characteristics of the technology influence trust. Again, the *reliability* plays the decisive role. This perceived reliability is influenced by the *maturity of the technology* (Q6) and *level of connectivity* with other technologies (Q7). However, as most participants do not trust the technology to be, absolutely reliable, they perform a risk evaluation based on the *application type*: the less risky the task taken over by the smart home technology is, the more they trust that technology (Q8). Therefore, it is also important how they perceive privacy risks: the more severe potential privacy infringements, the lower the trust into the technology. Additionally, the participants search for a safety net in case the technology fails. Here, particularly a good *technical service* and manual *control over the technology* or task at hand are important (Q9). Moreover, the *ease of using* the technology influences trust.

User. Also, individual users vary in their trust perceptions in smart home. An important user factor is the *experience* with the technology. On the one hand, *personal experiences* with the smart home build trust (Q10). On the other hand, *experiences of peers* (Q10) and shared experiences in *(online) reviews* (Q11) are considered. Besides experiences with the technology in question other experiences influence trust perceptions. Here, especially the *familiarity with similar technologies* (Q12) and *technologies in general* (Q13) are important. Also, having *experienced a threat* like a break-in may impact users trust perceptions (Q14).

Additionally, the participants state that *user diversity* factors like age may have an impact on trust in smart home (Q15).

Context. Besides technology characteristics and user factors, also the *context* influences trust in smart home. For once, user do not regard trust independently from the *benefits* of the technology (Q16). Similarly, the *necessity* to use a technology overrides distrust (Q17).

> Q6: "I also think it's important to say that all the systems you just introduced are in absolute, not even beta, but alpha phase, which is not and will not work in any way feasible." (m, 20)
>
> Q7: "Before it didn't work. And now think about upgrading from three to seven or eight technologies. That means there's a better chance that something won't work." (m, 57)
>
> Q8: "I trust such systems more the less tasks they take over. So I don't trust a system that takes over driving my car while I'm on the highway at 160 miles per hour. But if the system is only there to play music in my car, I trust it 100%, because if the music doesn't work, it's not that bad." (m, 20)
>
> Q9: "But as I said, always with the option of manual operation in case I don't like it or want to have it otherwise. The individual adjustment must still be possible." (f, 53)
>
> Q10: "What would create trust would be if a friend bought it, recommended it to me, and then I would try it at his home. So with people who are close to me, who I trust 100%, if they tell me it's safe." (m, 20)
>
> Q11: "[Is there something that would create trust?] Customer reviews" (m, 21)
>
> Q12: "Yeah I think that's more familiar to what we have right now. That makes it easier for me to move to smart technologies." (f, 28)
>
> Q13: "That's the worst, because when I think about what technologies are not working for me right now ..." (f, 53)
>
> Q14: "I would also say that everyone's trust limits are different. If you have had an incident, for example a burglary, you will have more confidence in such a system." (m, 20)
>
> Q15: "Because for us younger people that would not be too much change. But older people may be more concerned regarding technologies or changes." (f, 28)
>
> Q16: "I trust the big picture. This smart meter is super useful." (f, 27)
>
> Q17: "[What would create trust for you?] Once it becomes vital." (m, 20)

3.3   The Impact of the Automation Level on Trust

All participants agreed that trust is higher in the semi-automated smart home regarding all ten technologies on average than in the fully-automated one. Risks are perceived as more severe (Q19) and giving up control increases distrust in the fully-automated smart home (Q18). Still, for some applications, trust is still perceived as positive in the fully-automated smart home, and some applications are perceived negatively in the semi-automated one (see Fig. 4).

Fig. 4. Ratings for (dis)trust in the smart home technologies juxtaposed by scenario.

Q18: "I think I would trust things here [in the semi-automated smart home] more. I think it's the fact that you have more control here." (f, 28)
Q19: "[Which of the two smart homes would you prefer?] That is quite clear. The second [semi-automated] one. It has the least technical risk." (m, 87)

3.4 Composition of Privacy in Smart Home

In smart homes, all four dimensions of privacy [7] are important. **Informational privacy** is the most often mentioned aspect describing the control of access to personal data. Informational privacy in smart home means *no unwanted access* (without consent) to the data collected by smart home technologies (Q20), *no misuse* and *no user profiling* of that data (see Fig. 5). **Physical privacy** is centrally about being alone. In smart home, this particularly means *no visual surveillance* and *no unwanted intrusion to the home* (Q21), e.g., no break-ins.

Also the **social privacy**, i.e. the *control over conversation partners & listeners*, can be confined in a smart home, e.g. by *recordings of conversations* (Q22). **Psychological privacy** is not mentioned directly by the participants. However, their statements show that they do not want technologies to be *insufficiently adjusted to personal needs* as that does not correspond to individual wishes and preferences (Q23).

Q20: "Because this smart home knows almost everything about me and what I'm doing, my privacy is no longer protected when someone can access this data." (f, 27)
Q21: "[Is there something that is very important for your privacy?] That there are not suddenly strange people in my home." (m, 87)
Q22: "[What does privacy mean for you in a smart home?] That conversations are not overheard." (m, 21)
Q23: "This is like a prison for me, because the technology always does what others think is right for you." (m, 20)

3.5 Influences on Privacy in Smart Home

Influences on the perception of privacy in smart home again stem from three sources, the technology, the user, and the context (Fig. 6).

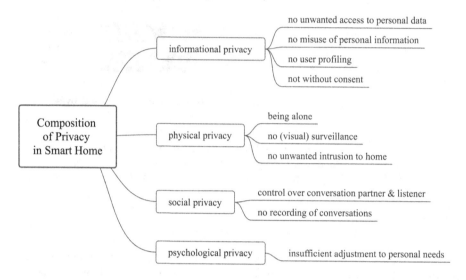

Fig. 5. Composition of privacy in smart home.

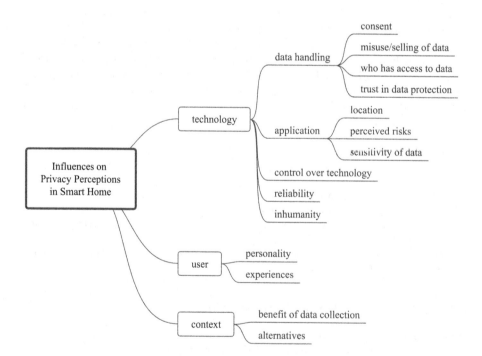

Fig. 6. Influences on the perception of privacy in smart home.

Technology. Technology-wise the *data handling* and data protection are important. Users again perform a risk evaluation and want to prevent *misuse & selling of data* (Q24). Important criteria for this risk evaluation are *who has access to data* (Q24, Q25) and *trust in data protection* in general. In more detail, it is also important where the data is stored and whether the devices are connected to the internet or other technologies. Data provision with consent is no privacy infringement.

The type of technology and *application* is decisive for the privacy perception. In the participants' statements, we again observe the risk evaluation they perform (Q26, Q27). The riskier for the personal privacy, the less a technology is accepted. Decisive criteria besides the application are the *location* of the technology in the home and the *sensitivity of the collected data*.

A feeling of *control over the technology* can mitigate privacy concerns. Also, **reliability** is mentioned as influence on privacy perceptions. Moreover, one participant explains that there is a difference between humans knowing data and an *inhuman* machine doing so (Q28).

User. Also for privacy perceptions, user diversity is influential. On the one hand, users differ in their *personality* and thereby disposition to value privacy (Q29). On the other hand, *experiences* with privacy infringements and technologies play again an important role.

Context. Context-related influences on privacy perceptions stem from the *benefit of data collection* (Q30) and how privacy infringing *alternatives* are (Q31), e.g., moving into a nursing home.

Q24: "Fear of abuse of this data would be a big problem. If the information is for me it is okay. If it is used in the medical field, in the physiotherapy field also good. But if it is used for advertising purposes, marketing strategies development, then I am not willing to provide this data." (f, 53)

Q25: "I think it depends on whom you refer to for privacy. To my neighbors and friends I am still as private or not private as before. But the question is where the data is stored and who can access this data." (f, 27)

Q26: "So with the fridge I think to myself who cares what I eat. Blinds too, I don't know if they interfere with my privacy. I think the front door is super critical. If my front door just lets people in, I it's not cool.' (f, 27)

Q27: "Well, I think it is important to know what the data is used for, because it brings with it dangers." (m, 30)

Q28: "When a milkman analyses my daily routine and then stands outside my door at the exact time of day to bring me milk when I've just been awake for ten minutes, I'm happy to see that milkman. But if you wake up and suddenly he is standing in front of your door because the computer has told him to, I find that strange. I would not feel comfortable with that." (m, 20)

Q29: "I think it depends on you personality regarding privacy." (f, 27)

Q30: "If the information is for me it is okay. If it is used in the medical field also good. But if it is used for advertising purposes, I don't want that." (m, 57)

Q31: "With the blinds, every neighbor can also see when I do this." (m, 20)

3.6   The Impact of the Automation Level on Privacy

All participants agreed that the perceived privacy is higher in the semi-automated smart home when they regard all technologies together. The main argument is even more surveillance in the fully-automated smart home which infringes on privacy as well as less control (Q32). Still, the ratings vary between applications: every rating (positive, neutral, negative) is prevalent for each automation level (see Fig. 7).

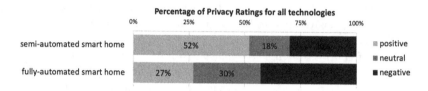

Fig. 7. Ratings for perceived privacy with the smart home technologies juxtaposed by scenario.

– *Q32: "[Do you feel like you'd get your privacy in this [fully-automated] apartment?] No, even less. There is even more data being collected, and even more is controlled by the technology." (m, 57)*

4   Discussion

In an exploratory group interview approach, users' notions and perceptions of privacy and trust in smart homes were investigated with special regard to increasing automation – which has been identified as an important factor in other application fields [16] but not yet investigated in this context. Using two juxtaposed scenarios of a semi-automated vs. fully-automated smart home, the impact of automation level on trust and privacy was studied. To this, interactive empirical research methods were used to sharpen the participants' understanding of the research subject (through groundplan drawings) and discuss results at a detailed level (by means of comparative rating systems). As privacy and trust perceptions are highly context-dependent [6,26,35], in-depth knowledge of both concepts in the sensitive context of home automation is needed. Only then, a user-tailored development of smart home technology can be provided.

4.1   Understanding Trust and Privacy in Smart Home

Trust: The results confirm reliability as a core element of trust from a technological perspective, similar to the acceptance of smart home technology [22]. Also, trust in data protection is an important element. However, because users actually do not fully trust the reliability and data protection, two aspects are important: On the one hand, risks of failure should not be too high. Here the participants perform a risk evaluation based on the application of the technology. On the other hand, users search for a safety net in case of failure wishing for a good technical service and manual control over the technology or task at hand. For developers and provides, the reliability as well as a good safety net should be foreground. This is even more stressed by the results regarding user diversity, where the personal experience with smart home and other technologies is most influential. Correspondingly, time is needed to convince users about the reliability via good experiences.

Our results highlight the high importance of trust in human stakeholders like developers, providers, and particularly the technical support thereby confirming previous results [45]. This human centered perspective needs to be integrated into trust models. For providers, trust-building measures into their performance and the technical support are key factors for users' trust and thereby their acceptance.

As third aspect, trust in the connected technological infrastructure can be confirmed as important factor [44]. Here again, experiences with internet failures, complex installation processes, and more diminish trust in such a dependent and interconnected technology as smart homes. Consequently, the extension of the infrastructure needs to be driven forward for a successful roll-out of advanced technologies like smart homes. As well, compatibility between technologies and simple installation processes are important requirements for smart home technology development.

Privacy: In smart homes, informational privacy and data protection are core elements for privacy perceptions which is closely linked to the trust in data protection. However, physical, social, and psychological dimensions of privacy are also important in smart home. Feelings of being alone and free from unwanted intruders, of unobserved conversations, and control over the environment to adjust to personal preferences are key aspects. Smart home technologies should correspondingly be most unobtrusive into the personal space of the home. As for trust, a risk evaluation is a core element for perceived privacy. This highlights the importance of data the principle of data minimization: only collect and store data when it is needed.

Both, privacy and trust were not regarded independently from the benefits. Here, trade-offs between barriers like privacy and trust concerns and benefits become prevalent that are key to the genesis of technology acceptance [27]. These trade-offs are not yet fully understood and should be focused in future research.

4.2 The Relation of Privacy and Trust

Interdependence of Privacy and Trust: Our study shows first indications that privacy and trust are more interconnected than is often assumed. Comparing the composition of and influences on privacy and trust in smart home, several similarities and interdependence emerge.

a) Privacy and trust perceptions are both based on a risk evaluation. The more severe potential consequences are, the less trust and the less privacy is prevalent for the users.
b) The perception of privacy and the trust in the technology influence each other. Trust in data protection is important for the perceived privacy in smart home, and the perceived privacy influences the technological risks and thereby trust perceptions.
c) Multiple factors influence both, privacy and trust. For example, the reliability, connection with the internet, application type, control of technology, and perceived benefits. For user diversity, experiences play an important role in both cases.

We could observe in the interviews that the participants had a hard time separating privacy and trust. Participants who first answered questions regarding privacy often started referring to trust in data protection when answering questions about trust. Similarly, participants often directly mentioned reliability for privacy when trust was discussed beforehand.

Follow-up studies should investigate this relationship to advance the comprehension of privacy and trust for technology acceptance.

4.3   The Impact of the Automation Level

Faced with the decision to choose one out of the two smart home scenarios presented for living, the participants commonly agreed on the semi-automated environment often motivated by trust and privacy related issues.

Especially for trust perceptions, the level of automation has previously been identified as important influencing factor [16]. Our results confirm that privacy and trust perceptions in smart home are fundamentally based on and influenced by feelings of control and are strongly influenced by the degree of automation. All participants preferred less automated smart home technologies to fully automated ones regarding privacy and trust. These results can be explained by the influencing factors on privacy and trust: higher automation is accompanied by less (felt) control over the technology resulting in higher risk perceptions, more data collection and interconnection between several data sources, as well as more dependence on the reliability of the smart home and the connected technologies and infrastructure. As one participants plainly puts it: "because one trust oneself more than one trusts the technology".

This strong, negative impact of the level of automation has to be confirmed and quantified in future studies. It gives a clear direction to the development of smart home technologies: there are adjusting screws to improve privacy and trust in fully-automated smart homes, e.g. data minimization and data protection, reliability of the technology and connected infrastructure, as well as always providing users with fail-safe technical support and manual control options. However, the use of fully-automated technologies is critical for users and should be guided by a high benefit to convince potential users.

4.4   Limitations

Our results contribute to a deeper understanding of privacy and trust in smart homes and their dependence on each other and the level of automation. Still, methodological limitations have to be considered when interpreting the results. The qualitative approach was suited to identify perceptions and influencing factors for trust and privacy in smart home and to indicate important research directions. These have to be further confirmed and quantified in quantitative empirical approaches. The sample size of 10 interviewees was sufficient for this exploratory study. Still, the impact of user diversity in privacy and trust perceptions needs to be further studied. Hence, more diverse samples are needed regarding age, technical affinity and expertise, and experiences with smart homes. Moreover, the study was conducted in Germany with a German sample. Perceptions of privacy, trust, and technology acceptance vary between cultures and countries. Therefore, the perspective should be widened to analyze cultural differences as well as to better understand further influencing factors.

To engage participants into the discussion and promote in-depth reasoning about privacy and trust in smart home, a interactive approach with drawings of ground plans as introduction to the topics as well as ratings of privacy and trust for each technology was chosen. For the results, this assured that each participants considered and evaluated every technology. At the same time, for the participants this made the interview more engaging and fun resulting in good cooperation.

Another important aspect is the approach to interview *potential* smart home users about *hypothetical* technologies. The participants were neither experienced with smart homes nor could they try out the technologies. Therefore, the results are based on perceptions and images of smart homes that are mostly based on hearsay and experiences with other, partly similar technologies. Still, that does not belittle the meaningfulness of our results as in the current beginning phase of the roll-out of smart home technologies this is what guides most potential users and buyers.

References

1. Ajzen, I., Fishbein, M.: Understanding attitudes and predicting social behaviour (1980)
2. Al-Momani, A.M., Mahmoud, M.A., Ahmad, M.S.: A review of factors influencing customer acceptance of Internet of Things services. Int. J. Inf. Syst. Serv. Sector **11**(1), 54–67 (2019). https://doi.org/10.4018/IJISSS.2019010104
3. Balta-Ozkan, N., Davidson, R., Bicket, M., Whitmarsh, L.: Social barriers to the adoption of smart homes. Energy Policy **63**(2013), 363–374 (2013). https://doi.org/10.1016/j.enpol.2013.08.043
4. Bélanger, F., Crossler, R.: Privacy in the digital age: a review of information privacy research in information systems. MIS Q. **35**(4), 1–36 (2011). https://doi.org/10.1159/000360196

5. Boise, L., Wild, K., Mattek, N., Ruhl, M., Dodge, H.H., Kaye, J.: Willingness of older adults to share data and privacy concerns after exposure to unobtrusive home monitoring. Gerontechnology **11**(3), 428–435 (2013). https://doi.org/10.4017/gt. 2013.11.3.001.00

6. Brell, T., Biermann, H., Philipsen, R., Ziefle, M.: Trust in autonomous technologies. In: Moallem, A. (ed.) HCII 2019. LNCS, vol. 11594, pp. 371–384. Springer, Cham (2019). https://doi.org/10.1007/978-3-030-22351-9_25

7. Burgoon, J.K.: Privacy and communication. Ann. Int. Commun. Assoc. **6**(1), 206–249 (1982)

8. Cook, D.J.: How smart is your home? Comput. Sci. **335**, 1579–1582 (2012)

9. Cook, D.J., Das, S.K.: How smart are our environments? An updated look at the state of the art. Pervasive Mob. Comput. **3**, 53–73 (2007)

10. Davis, F.D.: Perceived usefulness, perceived ease of use, and user acceptance of information technology. MIS Q. **13**(3), 319–340 (1989)

11. Dengler, S., Awad, A., Dressler, F.: Sensor/actuator networks in smart homes for supporting elderly and handicapped people. In: 21st Conference on Advanced Information Networking and Applications Workshops (AINAW 2007), vol. 2, pp. 863–868. IEEE Computer Society (2007)

12. European Commission: Digitalisation research and innovation - transforming European industry and services. Technical report (2017). https://doi.org/10.2777/858080

13. van Heek, J., Himmel, S., Ziefle, M.: Helpful but spooky? Acceptance of AAL-systems contrasting user groups with focus on disabilities and care needs. In: Proceedings of the 3rd International Conference on Information and Communication Technologies for Ageing Well and e-Health (ICT4AWE 2017), pp. 78–90 (2017). https://doi.org/10.5220/0006325400780090

14. van Heek, J., Himmel, S., Ziefle, M.: Privacy, data security, and the acceptance of AAL-systems – a user-specific perspective. In: Zhou, J., Salvendy, G. (eds.) ITAP 2017. LNCS, vol. 10297, pp. 38–56. Springer, Cham (2017). https://doi.org/10. 1007/978-3-319-58530-7_4

15. Himmel, S., Ziefle, M.: Smart home medical technologies: users' requirements for conditional acceptance. I-Com **15**(1), 39–50 (2016). https://doi.org/ 10.1515/icom-2016-0007. http://www.degruyter.com/view/j/icom.2016.15.issue-1/icom-2016-0007/icom-2016-0007.xml

16. Hoff, K.A., Bashir, M.: Trust in automation: integrating empirical evidence on factors that influence trust. Hum. Factors **57**(3), 407–434 (2015). https://doi.org/ 10.1177/0018720814547570

17. Kirchbuchner, F., Grosse-Puppendahl, T., Hastall, M.R., Distler, M., Kuijper, A.: Ambient intelligence from senior citizens' perspectives: understanding privacy concerns, technology acceptance, and expectations. In: De Ruyter, B., Kameas, A., Chatzimisios, P., Mavrommati, I. (eds.) AmI 2015. LNCS, vol. 9425, pp. 48–59. Springer, Cham (2015). https://doi.org/10.1007/978-3-319-26005-1_4

18. Kleinberger, T., Becker, M., Ras, E., Holzinger, A., Müller, P.: Ambient intelligence in assisted living: enable elderly people to handle future interfaces. In: Stephanidis, C. (ed.) UAHCI 2007. LNCS, vol. 4555, pp. 103–112. Springer, Heidelberg (2007). https://doi.org/10.1007/978-3-540-73281-5_11

19. Lee, J., See, K.: Trust in automation. Designing for appropriate reliance. Hum. Factors **46**(1), 50–80 (2004). https://doi.org/10.1518/hfes.46.1.50_30392

20. Madhavan, P., Wiegmann, D.: Similarities and differences between human-human and human-automation trust: an integrative review. Theor. Issues Ergon. Sci. **8**(4), 277–301 (2007)

21. Marangunić, N., Granić, A.: Technology acceptance model: a literature review from 1986 to 2013. Univ. Access Inf. Soc. **14**(1), 81–95 (2015). https://doi.org/10.1007/s10209-014-0348-1
22. Marikyan, D., Papagiannidis, S., Alamanos, E.: A systematic review of the smart home literature: a user perspective. Technol. Forecast. Soc. Change **138**, 139–154 (2019). https://doi.org/10.1016/j.techfore.2018.08.015
23. Mayring, P.: Qualitative Inhaltsanalyse. Grundlagen und Techniken (Qualitative Content Analysis. Basics and Techniques), 12th edn. Beltz, Weinheim (2015)
24. Merritt, S.M.: Affective processes in human-automation interactions. Hum. Factors **53**(4), 356–370 (2011). https://doi.org/10.1177/0018720811411912
25. Moran, S., Oonk, H., Alfred, P., Gwynne, J., Eilders, M.: Developing a context framework to support appropriate trust and implementation of automation. In: Karwowski, W., Ahram, T. (eds.) IHSI 2019. AISC, vol. 903, pp. 738–743. Springer, Cham (2019). https://doi.org/10.1007/978-3-030-11051-2_112
26. Nissenbaum, H.: Privacy in Context: Technology Policy and the Integrity of Social Life, p. 304 (2010)
27. Offermann-van Heek, J., Ziefle, M.: Nothing else matters! Trade-offs between perceived benefits and barriers of AAL technology usage. Front. Public Health **7**(June), 134 (2019). https://doi.org/10.3389/fpubh.2019.00134
28. Paetz, A.G., Dütschke, E., Fichtner, W.: Smart homes as a means to sustainable energy consumption: a study of consumer perceptions. J. Consum. Policy **35**(1), 23–41 (2012). https://doi.org/10.1007/s10603-011-9177-2
29. Peek, S.T.M., Wouters, E.J.M., van Hoof, J., Luijkx, K.G., Boeije, H.R., Vrijhoef, H.J.M.: Factors influencing acceptance of technology for aging in place: a systematic review. Int. J. Med. Inform. **83**(4), 235–248 (2014). https://doi.org/10.1016/j.ijmedinf.2014.01.004
30. Rashidi, P., Mihailidis, A.: A survey on ambient-assisted living tools for older adults. IEEE J. Biomed. Health Inform. **17**(3), 579–590 (2013). https://doi.org/10.1109/JBHI.2012.2234129
31. Robles, R.J., Kim, T.: A review on security in smart home development. Security **15**, 13–22 (2010). https://doi.org/10.1145/1764810.1764818
32. Robles, R.J., Kim, T.: Applications, systems and methods in smart home technology: a review. Int. J. Adv. Sci. Technol. **15**, 37–48 (2010)
33. Rössler, B.: Der Wert des Privaten. Suhrkamp Verlag, Frankfurt, erste aufl edn (2001)
34. Schaefer, K.E., Chen, J.Y., Szalma, J.L., Hancock, P.A.: A meta-analysis of factors influencing the development of trust in automation: implications for understanding autonomy in future systems. Hum. Factors **58**(3), 377–400 (2016). https://doi.org/10.1177/0018720816634228
35. Schomakers, E.M., Lidynia, C., Ziefle, M.: Listen to my heart? How privacy concerns shape users' acceptance of e-health technologies. In: 2019 International Conference on Wireless and Mobile Computing, Networking and Communications (WiMob), pp. 306–311. IEEE (2019)
36. Schomakers, E.-M., Offermann-van Heek, J., Ziefle, M.: Attitudes towards aging and the acceptance of ICT for aging in place. In: Zhou, J., Salvendy, G. (eds.) ITAP 2018. LNCS, vol. 10926, pp. 149–169. Springer, Cham (2018). https://doi.org/10.1007/978-3-319-92034-4_12
37. Schomakers, E.M., Ziefle, M.: Privacy perceptions in ambient assisted living. In: Proceedings of the 5th International Conference on Information and Communication Technologies for Ageing Well and e-Health (ICT4AWE 2019) (2019)

38. Shuhaiber, A., Mashal, I.: Understanding users' acceptance of smart homes. Technol. Soc. **58**(January), 101110 (2019). https://doi.org/10.1016/j.techsoc.2019.01.003

39. Singh, H., Pallagani, V., Khandelwal, V., Venkanna, U.: IoT based smart home automation system using sensor node. In: 4th International Conference on Recent Advances in Information Technology (RAIT), pp. 1–15. IEEE (2018)

40. Steinke, F., Fritsch, T., Brem, D., Simonsen, S.: Requirement of AAL systems: older persons' trust in sensors and characteristics of AAL technologies. In: Proceedings of the 5th International Conference on PErvasive Technologies Related to Assistive Environments (PETRA 2012), Article No. 15, pp. 1–6. ACM (2012). https://doi.org/10.1145/2413097.2413116

41. Valdez, A.C., Ziefle, M.: The users' perspective on the privacy-utility trade-offs in health recommender systems. Int. J. Hum.-Comput. Stud. (2018). https://doi.org/10.1016/j.ijhcs.2018.04.003

42. Venkatesh, V., Walton, S.M., Thong, J.Y.L., Xu, X.: Consumer acceptance and use of information technology: extending the unified theory of acceptance and use of technology. MIS Q. **36**(1), 157–178 (2012). https://doi.org/10.1111/j.1540-4560.1981.tb02627.x. (Forthcoming)

43. Wilson, C., Hargreaves, T., Hauxwell-Baldwin, R.: Smart homes and their users: a systematic analysis and key challenges. Pers. Ubiquitous Comput. **19**(2), 463–476 (2014). https://doi.org/10.1007/s00779-014-0813-0

44. Wilson, C., Hargreaves, T., Hauxwell-Baldwin, R.: Benefits and risks of smart home technologies. Energy Policy **103**, 72–83 (2017). https://doi.org/10.1016/j.enpol.2016.12.047

45. Yang, H., Lee, H., Zo, H.: User acceptance of smart home services: an extension of the theory of planned behavior. Ind. Manag. Data Syst. **117**(1), 68–89 (2017)

46. Yusif, S., Soar, J., Hafeez-Baig, A.: Older people, assistive technologies, and the barriers to adoption: a systematic review. Int. J. Med. Inform. **94**, 112–116 (2016). https://doi.org/10.1016/j.ijmedinf.2016.07.004

Privacy Apps for Smartphones: An Assessment of Users' Preferences and Limitations

Tanusree Sharma[1] and Masooda Bashir[2]([✉])

[1] Illinois Informatics Institute, University of Illinois at Urbana-Champaign, Champaign, IL 61820, USA
tsharma6@illinois.edu
[2] School of Information Sciences, University of Illinois at Urbana-Champaign, Champaign, IL 61820, USA
mnb@illinois.edu

Abstract. Smartphones are becoming our most trusted computing devices for storing and dealing with highly sensitive information which makes smartphones an essential platform to take under control utilizing privacy-preserving applications (apps). There exists a variety of privacy preserving apps on the mobile platform which claims to offer a potential way for people to protect data on their mobile phone. However, there has been no systematic study of these apps and what features and functionalities they offer or what may contribute to their under-utilization by mobile users. In this study, we analyzed the general functionalities of iOS privacy preserving apps by examining features designed to support user engagement and their privacy preserving functionalities. In addition, we examined user experiences, through a thematic analysis of publicly available user reviews of sampled apps. Our findings provide insight from users' reviews and their usability challenges in use of these privacy apps as well as the fundamental privacy features they are seeking. We believe these findings will guide privacy application developers in building appropriate functionalities that is more realistic and relevant to mobile users' daily life. In addition, this study provides the preliminary steps towards a comprehensive and actionable privacy tools/architecture for mobile phones that is human centered.

Keywords: iOS privacy apps · Usable privacy · Content analysis

1 Introduction

In the age of hashtag, you-tubing, trending faceapps, tweets, snaps, we are not only able to share all aspects of our lives, but we are also able to experience interactions like no other time in human history. Smartphones play a vital role in making these interactions and functionalities possible. We rely on smartphones to assist us in all aspects of our daily lives such as messaging, performing

© Springer Nature Switzerland AG 2020
A. Moallem (Ed.): HCII 2020, LNCS 12210, pp. 533–546, 2020.
https://doi.org/10.1007/978-3-030-50309-3_35

financial transactions, accessing medical records, etc. According to a recent Pew research study, large majorities of people around the world own or share mobile devices where smartphones are generally the most common type of mobile device [1]. Smartphones combining with the internet have been prevailing the way to the economy, education, politics, and other fields. In this course of information sharing practices on smartphones, we are often voluntarily sharing our personal information that may be accessible to cybercriminals, different adversaries and unauthorized third parties. Besides, there are potential privacy vulnerabilities due to smartphones' advanced processing capabilities of storing and processing data like location, list of contacts, personal photographs, and health information which are all personal and sensitive information. For example, in 2019 smartphone users downloaded 178.1 bn mobile apps which shows the great success of mobile applications [2]. Furthermore, under the big umbrella of the internet, we are doing different activities through our smartphones: web browsing, text messaging, emailing, storing our photos and videos, using different types of apps. Therefore, persevering privacy becomes a crucial concern for many smartphone users. Among the variety of privacy-enhancing technologies (PETs) for preserving privacy, one strategy available to mobile users is the availability of many privacy preserving applications (privacy apps).

While there are numerous studies on different types of mobile apps, to the best of our knowledge there has been no published studies that have investigated this privacy preserving apps for iOS, evaluating their functionality or usability. Therefore, in our investigation we aimed to analyze both apps specific features and users' perception through their reviews to identify the relationship between these two aspects and to determine if there are parallels and insight to be learned. According to Wasserman, an important challenge with mobile application development is that of finding effective solutions for achieving nonfunctional qualities in mobile applications and defining suitable techniques and tools to support their testing [3]. However, application testing and analysis represents a challenging activity, with several open issues, specific problems, and questions. Much of previous research has solely focused on improving the technological aspect of designing better system and architecture [4–8] or have focused on automated testing to validate by utilizing different tools and most of those studies investigated android apps [9–12] while there is a lack of research studies with iOS apps. We also observed a lack of experimentation with iOS apps. Other researchers have concentrated on utilizing more advanced techniques, for example machine learning and deep learning approaches in system level for authorization, verification to preserve certain level of privacy [13–15]. Meanwhile we know that mobile apps' utilization among users primarily depends on the user-friendly functionalities and appearance. While privacy apps are developed and meant to provide additional privacy preserving measures, in most cases, these apps include some complex configuration and settings components in their architecture. In those cases, it is difficult for users to easily follow new orientation and commands and utilize the user interface and application environment [26]. In the worst-case scenario, people might not be able to use it and therefore, the usage of those apps is significantly decreased.

In this study, we focused our research on iOS privacy apps that were free and investigated the apps' specific functionalities and characteristics and users' experiences and expectations through analyzing their reviews and comments. We believe that the results of this study will help app developers in considering alternative or additional functionalities which could lead to increased privacy preservation for mobile users as well as usage of the apps.

2   Background and Literature Review

Smartphone Privacy vulnerabilities and data leakage has become an important and concerning issue worldwide [17,36]. At the same time sensitive data breaches continue to increase, for example, the entire Verizon-USSS dataset from 2004 to 2009 has shown over 900 breaches [18]. Thus, existing smartphone users' privacy protections needs to be assessed. As mentioned above, a number of privacy apps having been developed to combat these vulnerabilities. In order to improve on these apps' functionality and effective use, there is an urgent need for research in respect to nonfunctional requirements and human factors. Much of previous studies have focused on the development and evaluation of apps' technological functionalities [19,20] and UI testing but even those UI studies have mainly focused on reliability which is mainly also a technological focus [16,21–23].

Our literature review reveals that there are several papers that have assessed apps' content in a form of review and feedback in respect to users' perspective. However, these studies reports on the relationship among different factors and how apps are geared towards users perspective [24–26] or it evaluates the effectiveness of expert involvement [27–30]. These findings have suggested a common view that current apps testing and iterative improvement lack evidence-based requirement analysis on features and functionalities [37]. According to these studies there is evidence of inconsistency in those reports on the correlation between different factors (ratings, download counts) which suggests that there is a need for further research and systematic investigation in this area. Moreover, most of these research studies are conducted in the domain of eHealth, eBanking, fitness and another kind of apps [31–35]. To date, there haven't any published research studies on privacy-preserving apps and users' perceptions toward those apps. Our research study aims to utilize app reviews from app stores which contains a large amount of data regarding users' experiences, type of use, usability difficulties, and favorite features. Previous literature in Human Computer Interactions (HCI) has demonstrated the benefits of using public reviews to investigate users' attitudes toward and experiences of existing apps [37,39].

Accordingly, in our study, we have done content analysis to determine the shortcomings in particular areas such as non-functional requirements by analyzing usability comments, reliability, and compatibility in apps from our collected users' reviews. We have conducted descriptive and distributional statistics to interpret our results.

3 Methodology

This section describes the process of searching, screening, and selecting the apps to be included in our systematic study, as well as the analysis procedures to demonstrate the users' perception towards privacy apps and its' functional and non-functional requirements.

3.1 Sampling

Our sample apps for this study were collected from the iOS Apps store from Dec 2019–Jan 2020. Apps were searched directly from the App Store using an iPad device. The search terms "Privacy", "Data Protection", "Hide", "Block", "Concealment", "Confidentiality", "Privateness", "Seclusion", "Solitude" resulted in 532 privacy apps.

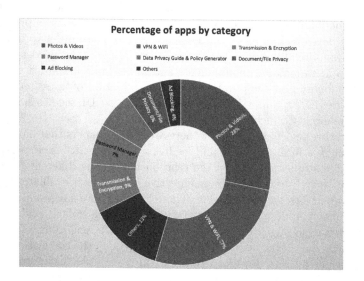

Fig. 1. Collected information of apps

As it can be seen in Fig. 2, initial selection of the apps for analysis were made if they met the following inclusion criteria: (1) English-language app, (2) focused on preserving privacy on users' portable device and mobile phone, (3) free during installation. Hence several apps were excluded before analysis. Upon this initial collection of apps, we noticed that the apps offered different types of privacy protections, for example, photo and video privacy apps, VPN/ Wifi privacy, password manager, transmission and encryption, ad blocking, document/ file privacy, and others including guidelines and privacy specific conference apps. Figure 1 presents our overall 532 collected apps and its privacy categories. To make our follow-up evaluation manageable and systematic, we used the total number of reviews for a given as our main selection criteria. The mean for the number of reviews at the time of our app collection was 10769 (where the maximum and minimum review counts are 426729 and 0). Privacy apps that had slightly below and above 10769 review mean were chosen. Since our assessment is on usability, technology, and interactivity measurement, we randomly selected apps rather than selecting apps with higher number of reviews only. This yielded 12 selected apps, 6 of them are above the mean and 6 of them are under the mean of number of reviews. The selected group of 12 apps were representative of the 6 different privacy categories identified in Fig. 1 (VPN, photo and videos, password, texting, browser, ad-block). The final sample of apps that were downloaded, installed and coded for our subsequent analysis was 12.

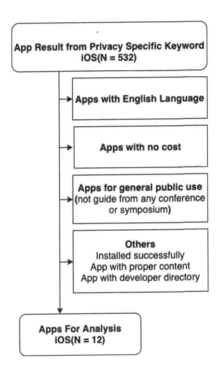

Fig. 2. Apps inclusion chart

3.2 Coding Process

We first downloaded each app to an iPad and got familiarized with the apps' main features. Next, we assessed each app and classified its general characteristics based on the listed description in the App Store. Since our motivation for this research is to understand and interpret' users expectations, experiences, and reviews of privacy apps, we recorded the recent reviews (from Dec, 2019 to Jan,

2020) and its content available from the App store. To analyze this content, we explored similar content analysis coding process/scheme used by previous researchers to guide our coding methodology [38], because there was no specific coding scheme available for privacy apps. Table 1 provides our finalized coding scheme that is literature driven.

Table 1. Collected information from apps web page

Category	Definition
General characteristic	
1. Option to Change Preferred Language	User can change language
2. Actionable Application Lock	Lock to open
3. Auto suggest and option	Automatic suggestion
4. Storage Backup	To store the data from users' input
5. Screen lock	Lock to prevent unauthorized access
6. One-tap connect	Easier to configure
7. Simpler Interface	Friendly user interface to use
8. Well-described policy	Brief privacy policy
9. Two-Factor Authentication	Secure authentication mechanisms
10. Privacy and Security Certification	Validation on products
11. Apps category	Particular types of security
User review	**Comments left by users on application specific page**
1. Rating	Perception and feedback in a numerics
2. Review	Feedback on text format
3. Date	Date when users left any comment
4. Version	Particular version of apps

3.3   Coding Scheme

General Characteristics were coded based on the information that was captured from the App Store, such as price, option for preferred language for app users, availability of application lock for user screen, storage backup, screen lock, one tap connect, simpler interface, well-organized privacy policy, enhanced authentication, for example, two-factor authentication, privacy/security certification, rating, review counts, apps category/particular types of privacy and security.

Purpose of the App. For perceived purpose of the app functionality, we coded each app under one or more of the following six categories: (1) Wifi and VPN privacy, (2) Photos and Videos Privacy, (3) Password Privacy, (4) Ad blocking, (5) Texting Privacy and (6) Document/file privacy.

Users' Perception (Apps Store Review Content). In our overall coding process, coding the review content was considered the most critical and challenging part of our coding scheme. Since Privacy apps include multiple features, general information, privacy-specific functionalities, all of which can be subject to content analysis. Previous studies analyzed their content by directly downloading the app or exploring the features list and description mentioned on app web pages [39]. In our study, we analyzed the actual reviews collected from the App store so that we can gain better insight from users' direct experiences for the selected privacy apps. Again, to make this coding manageable we used their most recent reviews (Dec 2019–Jan 2020) on the most recent version for each app. This is measured and coded as a composite of (1) Text reviews, (2) Rating given, (3) Tag line (Categories of frequent issues of operating those apps). For our analysis, we have conducted content analysis which is a research methodology that involves coding and interpreting qualitative, usually text-based material [40].

Design Principles. Our aim for this evaluation criteria was to systematically study the features and content of the selected 12 privacy apps. Using Table 1's coding for the two main categories: General characteristics and users review we developed Table 2. As it can be seen Table 2 extends the analyses of users reviews content into an additional 6 categories that is been established in ISO 25010 [41] guidelines recently. ISO 25010 is a guideline for product quality evaluation process that determines which requirements and quality should be taken into account [41]. We believe our study is the first one that has unfolded the classification of users' reviews based on ISO guidelines and classifications. Further insights from these classifications will be reported in future papers.

3.4 Assessment

In this study our assessment strategy for evaluating usability, interactivity, and technology was to utilize users' feedback that was available via their reviews. More specifically, we aimed to address the following two main research questions:

1. What does users' reviews reveal about their experiences in their use of these apps interface and general functionality
2. What design and functionality improvements does the reviews reveal for app developers

To address the above questions, we designed the following assessment and validation steps to carry out our systematic research study.

1. The first step included registering and installing all the 12 selected iOS privacy apps that was described in previous sections. Some of them required a valid apple account to create an app-specific account during installation. Next, we manually assessed the usability and functionality of each app and recorded them in Table 1.

Table 2. Categories of users' review on Apps Store

Type	Description	Example from user review
Usability	Degree to which a product can be used by specified users to achieve specified goals with effectiveness	*"Really love the app but I cant take pics or videos in the app now"*
Reliability	Degree to which a product performs specified functions under specified conditions for a specified period of time	*"Every time I try to share an image through the Signal app on iPad, the app crashes"*
Performance	The extent to which a function must be executed under stated conditions	*"Huge battery drain after updating to latest version. Jan 11, 2020"*
Security	Degree to which a product protects information so that persons or other products have the degree of data access appropriate to their types and levels of authorization	*"The develops need to pull their heads out of their collective behinds and instead of introducing more #34;social#34; garbage onto the platform...FIX EXISTING SECURITY FLAWS!!!"*
Compatibility	Degree to which a product can exchange information with other products while sharing the same hardware or software environment	*"You will lose all your conversation history when switching phones since Signal messages are not included in iOS/iTunes backup. Developers have been ignoring feature request for years"*
Portability	Degree of effectiveness and efficiency with which a product can be transferred from one hardware, software or other usage environment to another	*"Not OK, tons of safety security messages for my partner and me with her new iPhone Xr. Verifying us both makes no difference ...We are not able to delete them, it than becomes even more!!!!"*

2. We conducted content analysis for the users reviews and recorded the concerns raised in the reviews in terms of usability, interactivity and functionality. Our preliminary analysis revealed our categorization for the most frequent concerns that is listed in Table 2.

3. Descriptive and distributional statistics was used to interpret the overall evaluation of those apps on their usability, functionality, and interactivity. Statistical software R version 3.6.1 was used to calculate descriptive statistics which yielded to identify associations between app characteristics and user ratings and review tags.
4. Findings were summarized for each app and recommendations and suggestions for app developers were identified.

4   Results

4.1   Road Map

Our aim in this study is to better understand the features and content of privacy elated iOS apps available to the public, with a focus on their purpose, general and privacy-related features and users' reviews. Guided by the newly developed ISO standards for Mobile apps guideline [41], we developed our entire analysis scheme. Our Result include quantitative measures through a descriptive and distributional statistic.

4.2   Sample Description and General Characteristics

Our initial overall privacy apps collection was $N = 532$. All of these apps were free. We calculated the mean score for the number of reviews counts to be 10769 (median $= 6$, SD $= 43215.83$) where the maximum and minimum review counts are 426729 and 0. And the median of users' ratings in apps store is 4.200 (mean $= 3.042$, SD $= 2.035412$). The final sample of apps that met our selection criteria and was used in the final analysis ($N = 12$). These selected apps were randomly selected in respect of mean number of reviews which was 10769. 50% ($N = 6$) of selected apps' are above the reviews mean and 50% ($N = 6$) are below the mean.

4.3   Purpose of the Apps and General Features

The analysis for this part included classifying the goals for each of the apps into one of the six main categories. These categories were established based on literature on recent trend of privacy-enhancing technologies, namely, (1) Wifi and VPN privacy, (2) Photos and Videos Privacy, (3) Password Privacy, (4) Ad blocking, (5) Texting Privacy and (6) Document/file privacy. Majority of the apps were categorized under Photos and Videos which is accounts for more than one fourth of total counts of collected apps. From the total apps collection, 28% are privacy preserving of Photos and Videos, 16.5% is for VPN and WiFi, 8.60% are for protection of data during transmission and encryption, 7% are for Password Manager, 6.60% are specific and a privacy guide for conferences and symposiums (not for general use), 6.37% are saving for documents and files, 3.75% for adblocking, and 13.13% are others including privacy guidelines and conference specific apps (Fig. 1).

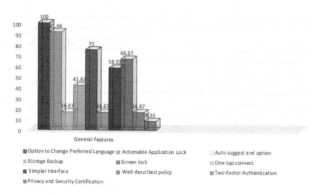

Fig. 3. Percentage of apps' general characteristics

4.4   Evaluating Users' Reviews (Apps Store Review Content)

We assessed actual users' reviews from the Apps store for the 12 selected apps and classified them into seven categories established by ISO 25010. We collected 1248 user reviews from the App store on the most recent version of the app available in the timeline between Dec 2019–Jan 2020. Then we manually identified reviews with concerns related to the non functional categories mentioned in Table 2. From those reviews, we randomly parse sentences and manually classified them into those categories (mentioned in Table 2), which led to 348 total user review sentences. We used this randomly chosen 348 review sentences for subsequent analysis.

All sampled user review sentences were manually classified by following a non-functional standard described in (ISO 25010 [41]). Table 3 shows the numbers and percentages of manually labeled user review sentences in the dataset that were classified as certain types (Usability, Reliability, Performance, Security, Compatibility, Portability, and others) for each of the selected apps for our analysis. From that table, it is quite clear that all the apps have frequent reliability related comments which may indicate that those apps are not performing as users expected them to do so. The other frequently stated comments in the reviews is related to performance, compatibility, and usability (Fig. 4).

Table 4 shows the overall apps non-functional requirements results from randomly selected sentences from users' review regarding the interactions reported while using the selected privacy app. The most highlighted and larger proportion of users' comment were on reliability issues of those apps. For example, one review said "I updated the app and now it just crashes whenever I try to open" "One day I opened it and FOUR YEARS OF INFORMATION HAS DISAPPEARED!!!"

"I updated the app and now it just crashes whenever I try to open"
"One day I opened it and FOUR YEARS OF INFORMATION HAS DISAPPEARED!!!"

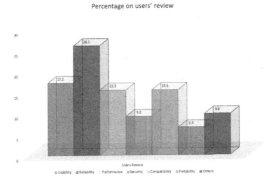

Fig. 4. App characteristics and user review percentage

Table 3. Apps' review classification and percentage

App no	Usability	Reliability	Performance	Security	Compatibility	Portability	Others
App 1	29%	20%	22.7%	10.7%	5.33%	6.67%	5.33%
App 2	36.07%	14.75%	18.03%	6.56%	6.56%	8.2%	9.83%
App 3	11.54%	7.7%	0	23.08%	11.54%	0	46.15%
App 4	4.26%	44.68%	6.38%	12.77%	10.64%	2.13%	19.15%
App 5	37.5%	25%	0	12.5%	0	12.5%	12.5%
App 6	2.18%	30.9%	23.64%	0	21.82%	18.2%	3.64%
App 7	17.85%	25%	14.28%	3.57%	10.71%	0	0
App 8	0	37.5%	37.5%	12.5%	0	0	12.5%
App 9	0	29.41%	0	11.76%	52.94%	5.88%	0
App 10	0	58.06%	0	0	38.71%	0	3.23%
App 11	0	50%	0	50%	0	0	0
App 12	0	36.36%	27.27%	0	18.18%	0	18.18%

Table 4. Proportion and number of manually labeled users' review sentences

Type	No. of sentences	Proportion
Usability	60	0.172
Reliability	91	0.261
Performance	54	0.155
Security	32	0.092
Compatibility	54	0.155
Portability	23	0.066
Others	34	0.098

5   Discussion

In this study, we examined the availability of privacy-preserving apps, their specific privacy preserving functionality, general characteristics, design features, app-specific information (price, rating, review counts, category, description), direct user reviews and comments. At the time of our data collection, 532 privacy preserving apps were identified in the iOS App Store. This high number of privacy preserving apps demonstrates the increasing need from smartphone users for such apps as well as the interest/market from the app developers point of view. The majority of our sampled apps were developed to provide privacy for photos and videos, WiFi, Documents, Passwords, text and calls.

When analyzing users' review content we found the majority of the comments were related to reliability followed by comments related to usability and then related to compatibility. In addition, our evaluation shows that the majority of the apps does not employ "Auto" suggestions such tap connection or two-factor authentication that may ease usability. However, further research is needed to determine if such features would actually provide ease of usability. Consistent with previous studies mentioned above we also noticed that between the free privacy apps that we had selected and those that had a premium price on it had more usability features then the ones that were examined in our study.

6   Conclusion

In this study we investigated the current landscape of the smartphone apps related to preserving privacy. Our research presents a systematic assessment of free privacy apps in the iOS App store. Our analyses not only reveal the type of privacy these apps provide but it also provides, smartphone user concerns and evaluations. We believe this study provides the initial steps towards the importance of not only functionality but also human factors, and interface design considerations. In addition, this study provides support for the potential of using reviewer comments and ratings to learn about user experiences and expectations for privacy apps. Future studies should explore users' expectations from apps' composite usability instances in the context of privacy and data protection. Furthermore, this study provides important insights into the implementation and design strategies for the app developers.

References

1. Silver, L., et al.: Mobile connectivity in emerging economies. Pew Research Center, 7 March 2019. https://www.pewinternet.org/2019/03/07/use-of-smartphones-and-social-media-iscommon-across-most-emerging-economies/
2. Mobile App Usage - Statistics & Facts, Statista. https://www.statista.com/topics/1002/mobile-app-usage/
3. Amalfitano, D., Fasolino, A.R., Tramontana, P., De Carmine, S., Memon, A.M.: Using GUI ripping for automated testing of Android applications. In: Proceedings of the 27th IEEE/ACM International Conference on Automated Software Engineering, pp. 258–261. ACM, September 2012
4. Samarati, P., Sweeney, L.: Generalizing data to provide anonymity when disclosing information. In: PODS, vol. 98, no. 10.1145, pp. 275487–275508, June 1998
5. Lioudakis, G.V., et al.: A middleware architecture for privacy protection. Comput. Netw. **51**(16), 4679–4696 (2007)

6. Luo, W., Xie, Q., Hengartner, U.: FaceCloak: an architecture for user privacy on social networking sites. In: 2009 International Conference on Computational Science and Engineering, vol. 3, pp. 26–33. IEEE, August 2009

7. Allison, D.S., Capretz, M.A., ELYamany, H.F., Wang, S.: Privacy protection framework with defined policies for service-oriented architecture. J. Softw. Eng. Appl. **5**(3), 200 (2012)

8. Sharma, T., Bambenek, J.C., Bashir, M.: Preserving Privacy in Cyber-Physical-Social Systems: An Anonymity and Access Control Approach (2020)

9. Xiao, X., Tillmann, N., Fahndrich, M., de Halleux, J., Moskal, M., Xie, T.: User-aware privacy control via extended static-information-flow analysis. Autom. Softw. Eng. **22**(3), 333–366 (2014). https://doi.org/10.1007/s10515-014-0166-y

10. Villanes, I.K., Costa, E.A.B., Dias-Neto, A.C.: Automated mobile testing as a service (AM-TaaS). In: 2015 IEEE World Congress on Services, pp. 79–86. IEEE, June 2015

11. Penn, J.: Test iOS Apps with UI Automation: Bug Hunting Made Easy. Pragmatic Bookshelf (2013)

12. Zimmeck, S., et al.: Automated analysis of privacy requirements for mobile apps. In: 2016 AAAI Fall Symposium Series, September 2016

13. Ma, X., Ma, J., Li, H., Jiang, Q., Gao, S.: PDLM: privacy-preserving deep learning model on cloud with multiple keys. IEEE Trans. Serv. Comput. (2018)

14. Rahman, S., Sharma, T., Reza, S.M., Rahman, M.M., Kaiser, M.S.: PSO-NF based vertical handoff decision for ubiquitous heterogeneous wireless network (UHWN). In: 2016 International Workshop on Computational Intelligence (IWCI), pp. 153–158. IEEE, December 2016

15. Shovon, A.R., Roy, S., Sharma, T., Whaiduzzaman, M.: A RESTful E-governance application framework for people identity verification in cloud. In: Luo, M., Zhang, L.-J. (eds.) CLOUD 2018. LNCS, vol. 10967, pp. 281–294. Springer, Cham (2018). https://doi.org/10.1007/978-3-319-94295-7_19

16. Murmann, P., Fischer-Hübner, S.: Usable transparency enhancing tools. A literature review (2017)

17. Laurila, J.K., et al.: From big smartphone data to worldwide research: the mobile data challenge. Pervasive Mobile Comput. **9**(6), 752–771 (2013)

18. Baker, W., et al.: 2011 data breach investigations report. Verizon RISK Team (2011). http://www.verizonbusiness.com

19. Jutla, D.N., Bodorik, P., Ali, S.: Engineering privacy for big data apps with the unified modeling language. In: 2013 IEEE International Congress on Big Data, pp. 38–45. IEEE, June 2013

20. Kim, B., Lim, J.I., Jo, Y.H.: Privacy situation and countermeasures of financial apps based on the Android operating system. J. Inst. Internet Broadcast. Commun. **14**(6), 267–272 (2014)

21. Kochhar, P.S., Thung, F., Nagappan, N., Zimmermann, T., Lo, D.: Understanding the test automation culture of app developers. In: 2015 IEEE 8th International Conference on Software Testing, Verification and Validation (ICST), pp. 1–10. IEEE, April 2015

22. Gilbert, P., Chun, B.G., Cox, L.P., Jung, J.: Vision: automated security validation of mobile apps at app markets. In: Proceedings of the Second International Workshop on Mobile Cloud Computing and Services, pp. 21–26. ACM, June 2011

23. Li, Y., Yang, Z., Guo, Y., Chen, X.: DroidBot: a lightweight UI-guided test input generator for Android. In: 2017 IEEE/ACM 39th International Conference on Software Engineering Companion (ICSE-C), pp. 23–26. IEEE, May 2017

24. Stawarz, K., Preist, C., Tallon, D., Wiles, N., Coyle, D.: User experience of cognitive behavioral therapy apps for depression: an analysis of app functionality and user reviews. J. Med. Internet Res. **20**(6), e10120 (2018)

25. Genc-Nayebi, N., Abran, A.: A systematic literature review: opinion mining studies from mobile app store user reviews. J. Syst. Softw. **125**, 207–219 (2017)

26. Mollee, J.S., Middelweerd, A., Kurvers, R.L., Klein, M.C.A.: What technological features are used in smartphone apps that promote physical activity? A review and content analysis. Personal Ubiquitous Comput. **21**(4), 633–643 (2017). https://doi.org/10.1007/s00779-017-1023-3

27. Franklin, J.M., et al.: Mobile Device Security Corporate-Owned Personally-Enabled (COPE). UMBC Faculty Collection (2019)

28. Mueller, B., Schleier, S.: OWASP Mobile Security Testing Guide. Early Access (2017)

29. Gilbert, P., Chun, B.G., Cox, L., Jung, J.: Automating privacy testing of smartphone applications. Technical report CS-2011-02 (2011)

30. Gao, J., Bai, X., Tsai, W.T., Uehara, T.: Mobile application testing: a tutorial. Computer **47**(2), 46–55 (2014)

31. Plachkinova, M., Andr, S., Chatterjee, S.: A Taxonomy of mHealth apps-security and privacy concerns. In: 2015 48th Hawaii International Conference on System Sciences, pp. 3187–3196. IEEE, January 2015

32. Zhang, L.L., Liang, C.J.M., Li, Z.L., Liu, Y., Zhao, F., Chen, E.: Characterizing privacy risks of mobile apps with sensitivity analysis. IEEE Trans. Mobile Comput. **17**(2), 279–292 (2017)

33. Sharma, T., Shithil, S.M., Bubly, N.J., Rahat, N.Z.: Feasibility analysis of immunization alert system in the context of developing countries. Int. J. Innov. Trends Eng. **23**, 37 (2017)

34. Caldeira, C., Chen, Y., Chan, L., Pham, V., Chen, Y., Zheng, K.: Mobile apps for mood tracking: an analysis of features and user reviews. In: Proceedings of the AMIA Annual Symposium, Bethesda, MD, USA. American Medical Informatics Association. Presented at American Medical Informatics Association Annual Symposium, 4–8 Nov 2017, Washington (2017)

35. Zyskind, G., Nathan, O.: Decentralizing privacy: using blockchain to protect personal data. In: 2015 IEEE Security and Privacy Workshops, pp. 180–184. IEEE, May 2015

36. Sharma, T., Bashir, M.: Use of apps in the COVID-19 response and the loss of privacy protection. Nat. Med. 1–2 (2020)

37. Crane, D., Garnett, C., Brown, J., West, R., Michie, S.: Behavior change techniques in popular alcohol reduction apps: content analysis. J. Med. Internet Res. **17**(5), e118 (2015)

38. Erlingsson, C., Brysiewicz, P.: A hands-on guide to doing content analysis. Afr. J. Emerg. Med. **7**(3), 93–99 (2017)

39. BinDhim, N.F., Hawkey, A., Trevena, L.: A systematic review of quality assessment methods for smartphone health apps. Telemed. J. E-Health **21**(2), 97–104 (2015). https://doi.org/10.1089/tmj.2014.0088. (Medline: 25469795)

40. Duriau, V.J., Reger, R.K., Pfarrer, M.D.: A content analysis of the content analysis literature in organization studies: research themes, data sources, and methodological refinements. Organ. Res. Methods **10**(1), 5–34 (2016). https://doi.org/10.1177/1094428106289252

41. ISO, ISO, IEC 25010: Systems and software engineering. Systems and software quality requirements and evaluation. System and software quality models. ISO/IEC FDIS 25010(2011), pp. 1–34 (2011)

Cyberspace and Cyberculture: The New Social and Governance Field

Rodolfo Ward[1]([✉]), Cleomar Rocha[2], and Suzete Venturelli[3]

[1] Medialab/UnB, University of Brasília, Brasilia, Brazil
rodolfoward@unb.br
[2] Medialab/UFG, Federal University of Goiás, Goiania, Brazil
cleomarrocha@gmail.com
[3] Medialab/AM, Anhembi Morumbi University, São Paulo, Brazil
suzeteventurelli@gmail.com

Abstract. This paper discusses how governance on cyberspace used cyberculture elements and is increasingly using data to homogenize behaviors and social groups. It is intended to discuss historical and philosophical issues through transdisciplinary study, gathering political sciences, communications, sociology and international relations to demonstrate that people are taking social network platforms, exposing their privacy and facilitating data capture by large companies. We will see social behaviors on social network platforms and how power groups have used data to manipulate social groups.

Keywords: Cyberspace · Cyberculture · Cybersecurity · Privacy

1 Cyberspace and Post-modern Condition

With the quick scientific and technological advance, technological devices became more accessible and were exponentially being incorporated by society to facilitate routine activities, and are used both at work and in personal relations. We can notice that the scientific and technological advance created better life conditions to the population. The social transformations in the last decades involve not only economic and technological changes, but deep social transformations as well, still in turmoil. This paper presents some explanations on how data are produced, consumed and shared on social networks, in addition to how and where these networks are structured today. It is also shown how the construction of social identity changed and is changing due to the break with concepts of truth and modern meta-narratives.

For researcher and artist Rocha (2018, p. 113) "technology is not technique, or device"; "technology is a knowledge that spreads in a community, after the understanding by science evidences". For him, "device is not a technology, but uses this knowledge, as it incorporates this knowledge to execute its function". This thought is aligned with anthropologist François Sigaut who says that we can't directly "observe" techniques. What we can see is people doing things: a plumber fixing a leakage in your bathroom; a

A. Moallem (Ed.): HCII 2020, LNCS 12210, pp. 547–557, 2020.
https://doi.org/10.1007/978-3-030-50309-3_36

mechanical shovel digging a hole in your street (Sigaut 2012 [1994]:424). For anthropologist Coupaye (2017, p. 476) the "speeches produced" by usages, artifacts (works of art of "new Technologies" products) are no longer passive witnesses, reflexes or signifiers, but rather "actors" of social life, and that, sometimes, not metaphorically".

Today, the idea is to have everybody connected to the internet, producing and sharing data. Not very long ago, mobile phone devices were used only to make calls (verbal language), then text messages prevailed (graphic language), and today everybody has cameras (visual language) and connectivity with internet. Internet is part of people's daily life, and the trend is that we will be increasingly more connected to devices linked to internet, making connectivity a common space in social construction and in the identity of the social being, so that there will be no longer distinction of "online", "off line", "real" and "virtual" (Hine 2015; Teixeira et al. 2017). "The internet is no longer a mere instrument and becomes part of the political action of a wide network of social actors" (Teixeira et al. 2017). Some theorists view connectivity as characteristic of our age, placing it above simple connection between persons and things and linking it to the time we live – the connectivity age, where participation becomes self-motivating as contents are exponentially received and shared on the network, many of them images.

Cyberspace is increasingly becoming more important as stage for political debate, attracting companies and public agents to social media platforms. It is therefore necessary to understand the context and the global conjuncture, to understand why, who and where discussions occur, because they form the collective agenda. Next, syntheses are presented of the thought of scholars who study the post-modernity[1] or super modernity and how social movements are being developed in this new field.

1.1 New Technologies, Conceptions of the World and New Truth Regimes

With the emergence of new technologies, the cyberspace assumed a place of central power promoting the exhaustion of hierarchically rigid institutions like church and academy, making way to relationship networks, with fluid, transversal and cooperative structures.

Studies on contemporaneity address global and collective themes that reflect and are expressed in the individual life, having as initial historical Mark the break with the previous period, modernity, by means of the decline of the Soviet Union and the fall of Berlin wall, which promoted intense socio-economic changes at global level, breaking with the modern model of the Cold War (Maffesoli 2015, *online*) and "changing the global geopolitics[2]" (Castells et al. 2000, p. 39).

---

[1] "As of the 1950s, the term started to be used in North-American literary theory to classify the main schools in the 20th century. At first, the term was used in pejorative sense, that is, to name a poorly inspired moment compared to previous productions in modern languages area. But in the mid of the 1960s, the word gained affirmative connotation. In 1969, the American literary critic Leslie Fiedler (*Cross the border*) describes his time as a death fight between modern and post-modern literature. The post-modern watchword would be: "transpose the border" between a supposedly elitist art and a more popular art" (Feitosa 2004).

[2] Geopolitics is a study of States in their relation in the world context (Bofim 2005).

The new conceptions of the world and reality arise due to several contemporary phenomena, among them, the expansion of concepts of identity, gender and race. They create doubts and promote reflection on economic, social and environmental problems that have been widely discussed both in academic ambit and outside it. These analyses on our historical condition are focused on the globalization and fragmentation paradox. On one side, globalization hegemonizes cultural manifestations and imposes the neoliberal economic model based on large scale consumerism that generates large scale production and disposal. On the other hand, the fragmentation of this process by means of impacts on the nation-state political system "due to local regional and institutional differences that emerge not only across geopolitical groups, but also inside them" (Martins 2013). For Martins, these two contradictory forces create conflicts in social spaces that are intensified, in the post-modernity, by the participation of the mass in social networks located in the cyberspace.

For theorists, this socio-economic and cultural transformation, somehow, has recently promoted some divergence among authors and schools on our current historical period and its definitions; however, there is consensus that we are undergoing a dense social, economic, cultural and symbolic transformation, possible and potentiated by the new information and communication technologies. To theoretically ground this research, post-modern, super-modern and hyper-modern concepts will be presented along with their relations with cyberspace and contemporary social movements.

Post-modernity, or super-modernity, or hyper-modernity definitions are linked to the social changes that the contemporary society is undergoing due to breaks with truth regimes and modern meta-narratives already consolidated in the social culture. These three terms were coined by researchers from different schools in order to define the state of the arts of the contemporary period and also o make theoretically possible the development of methodological studies on the theme. Some definitions on this theme will be presented for a better understanding of the time we live.

Maffesoli (2015), while approaching post-modernity, remarks the difficulty to define the term, but creates a provisional definition that would be "the synergy of archaic phenomena and the technological development" and explains that the main objects of study of post-modernity are the Nation-State, institutions and ideological systems with emphasis on local, urban tribes and mythological bricolage[3]. For Bauman et al. (2001) there is a transition from the modern model (solid) to the post-modern model (liquid), where human relations are increasingly becoming more ephemeral. Giddens et al. (1991) understands that we are still in modernity and that the term post-modernity is the "attempt to ground epistemology" on social life and the patterns of social development that escaped from the control of philosophy and contemporary epistemology and proposes to analyze the nature of modernity itself, which has been insufficiently covered by social sciences.

---

[3] "Bricolage" is a term originated from the French term "bricòláge", whose meaning refers to the execution of small household works without need to use the services of a professional. Available on: <https://www.significados.com.br/bricolagem>. Access on: 04/23/2018. In this paper we use the concept in the sense that the "scientific objectivity does not exclude the human mind, the individual subject, culture, society: it mobilizes them. And objectivity is grounded on the uninterrupted mobilization of the human mind, its constructive powers, as socio-cultural and historical ferments" (Morin et al. 2007, p. 58) (our translation).

Augé (1994) rejects the term post-modernity for considering that there is no break with modernity, as suggested by the term 'post', defending the continuation with modernity, however, modernity with acceleration factors defined as "figures of excesses" rather than "non-places" which he characterizes as space super-abundance, individualization of references and transformation in time categories, which would be super-modernity. Lipovetsky (2004), one of the theorists that made the term "post-modern" popular, today disagrees that there is break with modernity and defends the term 'hyper-modern' based on excesses to define the current age. He explains that in the moment when the expression "post-modern" emerged, by the end of the 1970s, researchers analyzed social, political, economic and cultural transmutation of the time and needed a term to explain it. The term coined at the time was "post-modern". Lyotard et al. (1970) was one of the pioneers in the use of the term post-modern in philosophy, crossing philosophy connected to art and politics to emphasize the study on post-industrial society and post-modern culture. The author states that due to the loss of credibility of great discourses that legitimate reality, that is, modern meta-narratives, spaces emerged to be filled by pluralism and affirmation of differences.

People can connect to others through social networks via text, video, voice or images, regardless of the location or time zone. Contemporary life is objectified, originates elements as data, shared among digital media platforms' participants, from sad and indignation moments to joyful moments. We understand that these deep transformations, in a short period of time, have influenced the creation of urban tribes with highly consumerist use of these data generated.

This conception of consumerist society is aligned with Baudrillard et al. (1981) thought, that proposes to explain the contemporary personal behavior by means of the consumption society and objectification of things and of life, creating a reality where the object is more valuable than its functionality, that is, consuming a given object is more important that its utility. Advertising uses it with branding[4], promoting the image of a given object, company, known brand, transforming the product itself into its purpose. This conception, defined by Baudrillard et al. (1981) as "sign-market" is different from all the previous societies had lived so far.

All these aspects are potentiated by the capitalist and globalized system model of today that influences society by means of the cultural industry and guides daily discussions, as clarified by studies on the setting agenda theory.[5] These instruments of power are used in large scale and impoverish personal relations, objectifying these relations and transforming them into goods, disqualifying those who opt for life styles that are not linked to consumerism (Adorno 1992).

"The characteristic feature of this time is that no human being, without exception, is capable of determining his life in a sense to a certain extent transparent, such

---

[4] "*Branding* is the system for brands management oriented by the significance and influence that brands can have in people's life, aiming at generating value for their publics of interest" (Cameira 2012, p. 44) (our translation).

[5] "(..) daily selection in the presentation of news, editors and editorial directors focuses our attention and influences our perceptions of those that are the most important issues of the day. This ability to influence the emphasis of topics in the public agenda was called the agenda setting of news vehicles" (McCombs et al. 2009, pp. 17–18) (our translation).

as occurred in the past in the assessment of market relations. In principle, all are objects, even the most powerful" (Adorno 1992, p. 31) (our translation).

Individuals start to behave as goods and attempt, by means of image, to add value to themselves. This value in the consumption society is associated to ostentation of material and consumption goods, in addition to public demonstration of buying power or political power that elevates them as consumption product before the other individuals who live in this symbolic system where fewer likes, fewer followers, represent invisibility, and, in the connectivity age "invisibility is equal to death" (Bauman 2009, p. 21).

"[...] people do as much as they can and use the best resources available to them to increase the market value of products they are selling. And the products that they are encouraged to place in the market, promote and sell are themselves" (Bauman 2009, p. 13) (our translation).

For Debord et al. (1997) we live in a "society of the spectacle", where goods and appearance became more marketable in the context of social relations, becoming a form of social relations where having and pretending to be momentarily nurture the living, objectifying and making artificial experiences, which are not lived in their essence. The image that the individual attempts to transmit of himself or his way of life exceeds reality and makes of the image, the representation, a new reality. Debord et al. (1997, p. 8) says that "the spectacle, understood in its totality, is at the same time the result and the project of the existing production mode" (our translation). The spectacle is not just a set of images posted or shared on social media platforms, it is inserted in the context contemporary social relations, mediating the relations of people with images, narratives and framing. And this spectacle, this social action, contributes to create the collective reality of our days.

As presented since the beginning of this text, society is quickly undergoing transmutations in all spheres. When Debord et al. (1997) analyzes and explains the "society of the spectacle", he is analyzing the 1960s and, even later, in 1988, when the author re-assesses the society of the spectacle, it is still very different from the reality we live in 2020.

We agree with Debord et al. (1997), though, nowadays, technological devices multiplied, like platforms and social networks have done, in addition to the number of people with access to the new conceptions of reality and metanarratives. These *prosumers*[6] became fixers and maintainers of the way of life grounded on spectacle, consumption,

---

[6] In 1979, Alvin Toffler coined the term *prosumer*, which derives from the union of two words that are antagonistic at first, producer and consumer. These consumers, in addition to interfering with the form of production, could also customize their products. Kirsner Scott (2005) sees the term *prosumer* as the union of "*professional-consumer*" who is not seeking capital, but rather to improve their distribution channels for creative works. In the marketing field, Mcfedries (2002) identifies it as "*proactive-consumer*", which would be the one that take measures to attempt to solve problems in companies. These studies collaborated for companies to create departments specialized in contact with prosumers and the creation of the concept of branding in advertising, which is "the system of management oriented by the significance and influence that brands can have in people's life, aiming at generating value for their publics of interest" (Cameira 2012, p. 44) (our translation).

fiction, and "everything that was directly lived became representation" (Debord et al. 1997, p. 15) (our translation). The way of living life is very personal, but, analyzing through Debord thought, we constantly see advertising build images of the products that will be consumed. In this case, the image becomes more than the products themselves, and people also become products that need a good image. Thus, the image plays a role that carries desire and starts to form the person.

We are bombed on a daily basis by images of people with ruined marriages posting photos of the last travel in family to Europe, in the best restaurants, wearing expensive clothes indicated by personal stylists, faces marked with beauty products and esthetic procedures smiling to the photo that will form an album with family records on Facebook or Instagram intended to put them in this imagetic market under the view of a family success image and, therefore, encouraging other families to do the same. All that contributes to maintain this social system that became hegemonic. This photo – this product, where these people appear enacting a happy life – is used as instrument of construction of a self-image that represents moral and cultural values of the class or social group to which they belong or want to belong.

The current hegemonic power regime, for knowing the functioning of today society, has used the power of images and personal information transformed into algorithms to create regimes of truth and regimes of power to watch and control society. It is not something new. The photograph technique, since its creation in the 19th century was used to create regimes of truth that stigmatized peoples and cultures, contribution to the Eurocentric domination at global level.

Next, we will deepen the understanding on how power groups have used scientific and academic knowledge – like the concepts of connectivity civilization and image civilization – to control and subdue entire societies, initiating a new phase, the psychocapitalism. Cameroonian researcher Achille Mbembe (2017, s/p) alerts that the age of "humanism is coming to the end". For Mbembe, "another long and mortal game started. The main shock of the first half of the 21st century will not be between religions or civilizations, but rather between liberal democracy and neoliberal capitalism, between the government of finances and the government of people, between humanism and nihilism" (2017, s/p) (our translation).

Based on the understanding of concepts of sign-market, society of the spectacle, age of connectivity and civilization of image – which result from social researches produced in the last decades – we can enter the current discussion on the contemporary society,[7] also called society of transparency. The concept of society of transparency comprises all concepts presented, unifies them in one single definition and proposes a systematized analysis of the current society's way of life, simplifying this dense subject for academic studies.

1.2 Internet and Social Movements

Online social networks let people, wherever they are, whatever the form they are, interact, keep contact with friends, and individuals can express and be heard by a local or even global audience and are increasingly becoming target of campaigns of marketing,

---

[7] Here we are referring to large urban conglomerates, mainly.

advertising, in addition to being stage of political and ideological disputes (Benevenuto et al. 2010, p. 3) (our translation). Social movements on the internet seek to create identities that will put them far from old movements while providing a new garb or approach to old problems.

Attracting these different groups creates political capillarity, which strongly favors the expansion of the group's ideas and domain. However, this expansion also fragments the group due to a series of factors explained by the dilemma of cohesion and expansion. Cohesion considers the group unity by means of identity; identification that people have with the cause, the group, the action, the theme, the framing. Expansion, in its turn, refers to the flexibilization of identity commitments to reach a higher number of individuals (Gobbi 2016, p. 42).

Bennet and Segerberg (2012) divide the actions on networks in three main topics: organizationally negotiated networks; organizationally activated networks; and networks activated by the crowd. In the three cases individuals hold certain freedom and autonomy in actions – "personalizable action framings" – which differ from the logics of collective action.

New forms of mobilization and activism have emerged using social network platforms that became important instruments to organize and mobilize the society, drawing the attention of several social actors for their capacity to engage people and disseminate ideas in conflicting processes. "The new technologies provide approximation of the citizen to political representatives and also to the object of political discussion in a space of autonomy, much beyond the control by governments and companies" (Castells 1999, p. 11) (our translation), creating an appropriate place for the development of digital activism, or online activism.

Online activism has led to changes in the political culture and guided the combat to varied forms of gender, sexuality, race, belief or class oppression. "It is an engagement that aims not exclusively at confronting or connecting to formal political mechanisms, but mainly at generating and fomenting behavior changes in the society" (Teixeira et al. 2017, p. 7) (our translation). Gerbaudo (2016), on the other hand, analyzes this activism as "moments of digital enthusiasm" generated by the synergy of the page administrator, who creates narratives and framings and plays the role of a kind of *prosumer* while receiving, reinforcing and sharing. The author also reflects on the liquidity of social media, where events are fugacious and movements start to decline when they are no longer "alive" becoming ephemeral and are replaced by other events, which is characteristic of the consumption society and the society of the spectacle.

We understand that there are highly complex factors for leaders of social movements to keep the group united and engaged while expanding the group's territory and domain coverage. Tarrow (2009) states that the power of promoting collective actions is not the same power to provide continuation to them. Control and strategy of leaders is necessary to balance internal disputes in organizational processes and to keep the group cohesive while taking advantage of the internet in political processes (vön Bullow 2016; Gobbi 2016). The new communication and information technologies were assimilated by the market creating a digital economy that makes capital circulate through selling of data; as examples we have the scandal of data sales by Facebook (2018), and the USA and Brazil elections, which had massive use of artificial intelligence. The groups of power linked to the financial capital use the new possibilities of CITs to influence political elections, democracies, people's ways of life, chiefly for using and applying the complexity of academic knowledge for purposes of domination.

With the emergence of new technologies and the expansion of networks and social media, populists have created their agendas and shared without filters from gatekeepers,[8] journalists, mass media professionals. This relation involving politics, social media and populism is referred to in the study by Bimber (1998, p. 137; Engesser et al. 2017), who clarifies the potential to promote non mediated communication among politicians and citizens, and, thus, "restructure the political power in a populist direction". While analyzing the political growth on social media and the expansion of the populist language for social mobilization, Bartlett (2014, p. 94), remarks that "the bitter and short nature of populist messages works well in this medium".

Han et al. (2014) sees a possible escape for the civilization crisis we experience in art and contemplation. Art is a possible solution for us to find other narratives to live the "I", to better understand the world and its functioning, to achieve self-knowledge. The author states that for us to live better moments of emptiness, deep reflections on our lives are required, moments when we explore ourselves.

For a better understanding of the questions raised so far, we created a table with the main characteristics of the modern world with regard to the globalized world that exemplifies cultural, political and socio-economic transformations experienced by the society in the last three centuries (Table 1).

With this brief bibliographic survey on cyberspace and social relations in the contemporary world, we tried to explain the current context and the contemporary conjuncture of social organization in the cyberspace and how groups of power have acted inside this new social construct. Our objective was not to exhaust the subject, but rather to provoke the reader's attention to facts that are inherent in our society, showing, through authors from different areas, that there is a dense social transformation that is directly influencing the social re-organization by means of the power that images and their representations and perception exert on humanity. We also sought to demonstrate that social movements on the internet seek to create identities that will put them far from old movements while providing a new garb or approach to old problems.

We understand that the academy has also its share of accountability for the distancing of the society. We also raised questions for future research: Which are the academy responsibilities with regard to social issues and democratization of teaching and knowledge? To where and to whom knowledge is being produced in the academic ambit?

---

[8] *Gatekeeper* may also be understood as the "doorman" of the newsroom. It is that person responsible for filtering the news, that is, he will define, according to editorial criteria, what will be communicated. With the effervescence and a certain trend in the practice of collaborative journalism, the gatekeeper function has undergone changes. The audience, increasingly less passive and more participative, leaves this function less centralized, however without losing the importance in the structure of news construction. Available on: <https://pt.wikipedia.org/wiki/Gateke eping>. Access on: 05/19/2018.

Table 1. Characteristics of the modern world and the globalized world

Modern/documental world 19th–20th centuries	Globalized/fictional world 21st century
Industrial society	Society on networks
Responsibility with the real	Fictional narrative
Vertical	Multiple
Static/slow	Movable/fast
Paternal	Collective
Disciplinary	Risk/transparency
Homeland	Global
Physical support	Digital support
Unisexual	Transexual
Digital	Hyperdigital
Consumer	Prosumer
Oneness	Horizontal

We suggest the trans-disciplinary study for future research and discussions in the academic ambit to develop methodological studies on the theme and promote real democratization of knowledge, besides a probable reduction in manipulation of the population on themes already outdated in university chairs.

2   Conclusions

Considerations on the digital construct in the society and its implications are far from being dimensioned, since we are still immerse in this historical moment that remains in dynamic operations, therefore still changing. Meanwhile, acknowledging development vectors and even movements may serve as diapason to inspect the relations among social, cultural and technological dimensions, in order to navigate supported by a compass, with respect to studies on culture, technologies and media.

Far from exhausting such discussions, the intention was to punctuate how networks and this locus of interaction achieves protagonism in the culture, in a performativity that, sometimes, builds meta narratives motivations that impact the objective and subjective ballast of persons, of the social body itself. From historical and philosophic approaches, with the notes brought in the present paper, a social emergence with few rules is deflagrated, which makes the direction oscillate among truths, realities and quasi-fictions, creating a problematic complex that, differently from the virtual one, is not solved in the current one. It rather re-dimensions the social complexity, wrapped up in a thousand persons, thousand vectors, requiring critical densification to overcome the evident, the apparent, and reaches the immanent in the transcendent, the heart in the leftover, and the essence in the abundance.

It is exactly in this perspective that the glimpse emerged to make see social, political and cultural tensions that networks formulate in the social body and in the historical moment, full of futures, requiring the prenatal that will indicate the nature of this fetus. And if this socio-cultural tensioning shows its face on social networks as in the ballast appointed in this paper, it is essential that studies on the naturalization of the cyberspace and cyberculture find, for once, the umbilical cord that deauthorizes, once and for all, the split between them and the natural world and culture, but, before that, acknowledges them as trace of one single body, the social body, even when we can glimpse their personas, complex, contradictory and incomplete, as they always were.

References

Adorno, T.W., Horkheimer, M.: Minima Moralia. Ática, São Paulo (1992)

Augé, M.: Pour une anthropologie des mondes contemporains. Paris, Aubier (1994)

Bartlett, J.: Populism, social media and democratic strain. In: Lodge, G., Gottfried, G. (eds.) Democracy in Britain: Essays in honour of James Cornford, pp. 91–96. Institute for Public Policy Research, London (2014)

Baudrillard, J.: Simulacres et simulations. Galilée, Paris (1981)

Bauman, Z.: Vida para consumo: a transformação das pessoas em mercadoria. Zahar, Rio de Janeiro (2009)

Bauman, Z.: Modernidade líquida. Zahar, Rio de Janeiro (2001)

Bennett, L., Segerberg, A.: The Logic of Connective Action. Infor. Comm. Soc. 15, 1–30 (2012). https://doi.org/10.1080/1369118X.2012.670661

Benevenuto, F.: Redes sociais on-line: técnicas de coleta, abordagens de medição e desafios futuros. In: Tópicos em Sistemas Colaborativos, Interativos, Multimídia, Web e Banco de Dados, pp. 41–70 (2010)

Bimber, B.: The internet and political transformation: Populism, community, and accelerated pluralism. Polity 31(1), 133–160 (1998). https://doi.org/10.2307/3235370

Bonfim, U.C.: Curso de política, estratégia e alta administração do exércitoensino a distância cpeaex/ead. escola de comando eestado-maior do exército. geopolítica, p. 101 (2005)

Cameira, S.R.: História e conceitos da identidade visual nas décadas de 1960 e 1970. In: Braga, M.D.C., Moreira, R.S. (eds.) Histórias do design no Brasil. Annablume, São Paulo (2012)

Castells, M.: La era de la información. La sociedad red, vol. I. Alianza, Madrid (1999)

Castells, M.: A era da informação: economia, sociedade e cultura. A sociedade em rede, vol. 1. Paz e Terra, São Paulo (2000)

Coupaye, L.: Cadeia operatória, transectos e teorias: algumas reflexões e sugestões sobre o percurso de um método clássico. In: Sautchuk, C. (Org.). Técnica e transformação: perspectivas antropológicas, pp. 475–494. ABA Publicações, Rio de Janeiro (2017)

Debord, G.: A sociedade do espetáculo. Contraponto, Rio de Janeiro (1997)

Engesser, S., Ernst, N., Esser, F., Büchel, F.: Populism and social media: How politicians spread a fragmented ideology. Inf. Comm. Soc. 20(8), 1109–1126 (2017). https://doi.org/10.1080/136 9118X.2016.1207697

Feitosa, C.: Pensamento pós-moderno. In: Teixeira, F.C. (Org.) Enciclopédia de guerras e revoluções do século XX, pp. 702–703. Campus, Rio de Janeiro (2004)

Gerbaudo, P.: Populism 2.0. In: Trottier, D., Fuchs, C. (Eds.) Social media, politics and the state: Protests, revolutions, riots, crime and policing in the age of Facebook, Twitter and YouTube, pp. 16–67. Routledge, New York (2014)

Giddens, A.: As consequências da modernidade. Editora da Unesp, São Paulo (1991)

Gobbi, D.: Identidade em ambiente virtual: uma análise da Rede Estudantes Pela Liberdade (2016). http://repositorio.unb.br/handle/10482/22245

Han, B.-C.: A sociedade da transparência. Relógio D'Água Editores, Lisboa (2014)

Hine, C.: Ethnography for the Internet: Embedded, Embodied and Everyday. Bloomsbury, London (2015)

Kirsner, S.: Are you a prosumer? Take this hand quiz quelle (2005). http://archive.boston.com/business/globe/articles/2005/06/13/are_you_a_prosumer_take_this_hand_quiz/

Lipovetsky, G.: Os tempos hipermodernos. Editora Barcarolla, São Paulo (2004). 129 p.

Lyotard, J.-F.: Discours, figure. Klincksieck, Paris (1970)

Maffesoli, M., Strohl, H.: O conformismo dos intelectuais. Tradução de Tânia do Valle Tschiedel. Sulina, Porto Alegre (2015). 182 p.

Martins, R., Tourinho, I., Martins, A.: Entre subjetividades e Aparatos Pedagógicos: O que nos Move a Aprender? Visualidades (UFG) **11**, 59–71 (2013)

McCombs, M.: A teoria da agenda–A mídia e a opinião pública. Vozes, Petrópolis (2009)

McFedries, P., Mary-Lou Galician: Manual de colocação de produtos na mídia de massa: Novas estratégias em teoria, prática, tendências e ética de marketing (2002)

Mbembe, A.: Crítica da razão Negra. Lisboa: Antígona. Comunicação e Sociedade, **34**, 457–462 (2017). https://doi.org/10.17231/comsoc.34(2018).2959

Morin, E.: Ciência com consciência, 10 edn. Bertrand Brasil, Rio de Janeiro (2007)

Rocha, C.: Inquietações: sociedade, inteligência e tecnologia. Dados eletrônicos. Gráfica UFG, Goiânia (2018). 72 p.

Sigaut, F.: Comment homo devint faber comment l'outil fit l'homme. CNRS Éditions, Paris (2012)

Sven, E., Nayla, F., Anders, O.L.: Populist onlinecommunication: introduction to the special issue. Infor. Comm. Soc. **20**(9), 1279–1292 (2017). https://doi.org/10.1080/1369118X.2017.1328525

Tarrow, S.: Ballots and Barricades: On the Reciprocal Relationship Between Elections and Social Movements (2009)

Teixeira, A.C., Zanini, D., Meneses, L.: O fazer político nas mídias sociais: aproximações teóricas sobre ação coletiva em rede. In: 41° Encontro Anual da Anpocs GT2 – Ciberpolítica, ciberativismo e cibercultura (2017)

Bullow, V., Gobbi, D.: Identidade em ambiente virtual: uma análise da Rede Estudantes Pela Liberdade. (2016). http://repositorio.unb.br/handle/10482/22245

Usable Security Approaches

Evaluation of Secure Pad Resilient to Shoulder Hacking

Kokoro Kobayashi[1]([✉]) [iD], Tsuyoshi Oguni[2], and Masaki Nakagawa[1] [iD]

[1] Tokyo University of Agriculture and Technology, Koganei-shi 184-8588, Japan
dryassy1ac@gmail.com, nakagawa@cc.tuat.ac.jp
[2] NTT DATA, Minato-ku 108-0075, Japan
oguni.tsuyoshi@nifty.com

Abstract. This paper presents evaluation of a series of secure PIN/password input methods named Secure Pad. When a PIN or password is input to a smartphone, tablet, banking terminal, etc., the risk of the PIN or the password being peeped and stolen by other persons arises, which is called shoulder hacking or shoulder surfing. To decrease the risk, we have proposed a method that erases key-top labels, moves them smoothly and simultaneously, and lets the user touch the target key after they stopped. The user only needs to trace a single key, but peepers have to trace the movements of all the keys at the same time. Secure Pad does not have the highest security, but it is easy to use and does not require any changes to the server side. This paper presents detailed evaluation of Secure Pad and demonstrates that it has high resistance to shoulder hacking while providing satisfactory usability without large input errors.

Keywords: PIN code · Password · User authentication · Shoulder hacking · Cognitive difficulty

1 Introduction

A Personal Identification Number (PIN) is a secret sequence of digits and a password is that of characters both to authenticate the user and protect against illegal access to the information or resources possessed by the user. We can consider PINs as a type of passwords here and discuss PINs inclusively. In daily life, passwords are increasingly being used to authenticate user access to ATMs, to pay by credit cards, to open up smartphones/tablets, to enter computer and network services, and so on.

An instance where a password is peeped by others over the victim's shoulder (or from the reflection off glass) is called shoulder hacking or surfing. Once this happens, the information or resource possessed by the user is subject to illegal access or attack.

In this paper, we propose a series of methods for secure password input against shoulder hacking that requires less mental load for the user while incurring cognitive difficulties for peepers. It is not resilient to video recording, but can easily be made so by introducing another secret or calculation. Moreover, it does not require any changes to

© Springer Nature Switzerland AG 2020
A. Moallem (Ed.): HCII 2020, LNCS 12210, pp. 561–574, 2020.
https://doi.org/10.1007/978-3-030-50309-3_37

the hardware and software on the server side. Its effectiveness is demonstrated through an evaluation experiment.

This paper extends two preceding conference publications [1, 2] and formulates them into a series of methods with an added evaluation. Section 2 presents related works and clarifies the position of our approach among others. Section 3 describes our basic method and its extensions, and Sect. 4 reports their evaluation. Section 5 draws conclusion with future work.

2 Related Works

Several technologies have been proposed or invented to protect password input from shoulder hacking. Randomizing key allocations every time a key is pushed may prevent the key from being read by the positions of the user's arm and finger, thus providing resilience against the so-called replay attack [3, 4]. Makita et al. proposed another replay-attack resilient method that displays the input panel partially and has the user scroll it to show and push the desired key [5]. This is more suitable for larger keyboards than the smaller ten numerical keypads. Kakinuma et al. proposed another method within the category of graphical passwords [6] that utilizes a sequence of colors as a password and lets the user touch the color appearing in a presented picture in the sequence of the password. Sakurai et al. proposed a method that is not only resilient to the replay attack but also to peeping [7]. It classifies characters for passwords into several groups, and for every character in a password, the user searches for the character, finds the group that includes it, and selects a random number assigned every time to the group. KyuChoul et al. invented another method [8] that randomizes the key arrangement for a password and then lets the user push the key displaced to the fixed direction with the fixed distance from the target key for each password character. The direction and distance of the displacement is identified from the first character "*" of the password. This method is resilient to replay and peeping attacks, but not to video recording.

Takada et al. proposed a video recording resilient method that introduces "fakePointer" in addition to a password [9, 10]. fakePointer is a mask that may point to several keys. The user manipulates a specific position in the mask to point to a password character and repeats this to input the password. Its specific position is secret and peepers cannot identify which key is selected. However, since the characters are limited in fakePointer, the password is confined within a certain sequence. To avoid this, the method is extended to interleave false characters, which can be detected by the system. It is resilient to peeping and video recording but introduces another secret to remember. Kita et al. proposed another video recording resilient method that displays graphical password keys on a 4 × 4 grid and the user input keys on positions shifted from the target keys by a secret amount [11]. The drawback of this method is that the user needs to make a mental calculation to locate the shifted positions every time. Watanabe et al. proposed another video recording resilient method that introduces "cursor camouflage" [12]. It shows multiple dummy cursors moving in random directions, and while the user can find the real cursor by comparing with the mouse movement, potential peepers cannot identify it. It is resilient to peeping and video recording but it imposes a burden on the user to find the real cursor. Luca et al. proposed a similar method [13].

Information theoretic methods have also been proposed [14–16]. They are resilient even to video recording, but introduce additional secrets and require complex mental operations.

Another stream of authentication is emerging in the form of biometric information such as fingerprint, iris, retinal pattern, finger or palm vein pattern, face, speech, and handwriting [17, 18]. Biometric information is unlikely to be forgotten or stolen compared to passwords or physical objects, and implementing it is both easy and user-friendly. Once such information is stolen, however, it cannot be recovered. Moreover, authentication of the true user may fail due to noises, and false users may pass through a gate as a result of various errors.

Another stream of research has focused on reducing the mental load of the user, though most of the methods are not resilient to video recording. Roth et al. proposed a method [19] that colors half of the ten numerical keys black and the other half white. The user selects the color of the key that he/she wants to input, and then the system scrambles the keyboard to show a different coloring and the user selects the color again. When this is repeated four times, the key is identified uniquely. User testing showed that this method is resilient to peeping, but it takes about ten times as long as entering simple PINs on a number pad. In order to enhance its recording resilience, they proposed reducing color inputs to less than four times and making the PIN number unidentifiable uniquely. The authentication is allowed if the correct one is within the probable candidates. Tan et al. proposed a software keyboard that displays 42 keys and two "Interactor Tiles" at the bottom of the keyboard [20]. Just as each key on a standard keyboard represents two characters, each key is randomly assigned a lowercase letter (on the top row with red background), an uppercase letter (middle with green background), and either a number or a symbol (bottom with blue background). Rather than having a fixed shift state for the entire keyboard, each key has a randomly assigned shift state, indicated by the red line under the active character. In order to select a character, the user first locates the key containing the character to be typed. Next, the user clicks on one of the Interactors to cycle through shift states and move the red underline to the desired character. Finally, the user drags the Interactor to the key on which the desired character resides. Upon the start of the drag interaction, the system blanks all key-top labels. Without knowing where the user is going to drop the Interactor, adversarial observers have to memorize the locations of all characters on the keyboard. The keyboard re-randomizes characters and the user repeats the process to select the next character. The results of a user study conducted on a digital whiteboard showed that, when 8-character passwords were input, the security level was highly improved (a magnitude) while the input time was just doubled in comparison with a common soft keyboard. As their future work, they appended an idea to move multiple keys, but it has not been evaluated yet.

So far, we have proposed a series of methods for secure password input against replay-attack and peeping in shoulder hacking. It requires less mental load for the user while incurring cognitive difficulties for peepers.

We assign colors, shapes, and/or various sizes to keys in a keypad/keyboard, erase key-top labels, move them simultaneously, and let the user touch the target key. Peepers have cognitive difficulty in tracing the movements of all the keys at the same time, but the user only needs to trace a single key and touch it. An extension of this method is to move all the keys instantaneously after erasing key-top labels and let the user touch the target key. Another extension is to introduce a "move backward/forward" function for the user to confirm the traces of movements. It is not resilient to video recording, but it can easily be made so by introducing another secret or calculation in similar ways as [7–9, 19]. A simple example is to let the user touch a key displaced by an agreed distance from the correct key. In our study, however, we limit our focus to presenting a new dimension for defending against shoulder hacking.

3 Basic Method and Extensions

In this section, we present a series of password input methods that require less mental load for the user while incurring cognitive difficulties for peepers, thus providing resilience to replay-attack and peeping. We have named this series of methods Secure Pad.

3.1 Basic Method

When there is no risk of shoulder hacking, the user inputs a password character by touching displayed keys directly. When there is a risk, however, the user triggers the function of Secure Pad by tapping the "shuffle" button. Secure Pad then erases the key-top labels, moves them smoothly and simultaneously, and lets the user touch the target key after they stopped, as shown in Fig. 1. Meanwhile, the shuffle button is renamed as "retry" to let the user retry the process if the target is lost. Peepers are expected to find it cognitively difficult to trace the movements of over four objects at the same time [21, 22], but the user needs only to trace a single target key and touch it without having to remember another secret or to make any calculation. Therefore, we discard key-movement candidates when fewer than four keys overlap while moving. This can be used without any special hardware and without any changes to the server side.

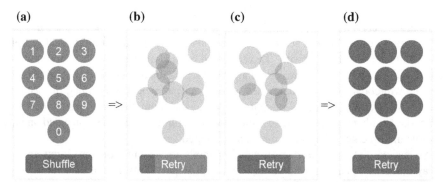

Fig. 1. Secure Pad display: (a) initial state, (b) erasing key-tops, (c) moving them smoothly and simultaneously, and (d) stopped state for accepting key-tap. The retry button initiates another cycle when the target key is lost.

3.2 Extensions

We can extend the basic method by assigning different colors, shapes, and/or sizes to keys for enhancing distinguishability, as shown in Figs. 2 and 3.

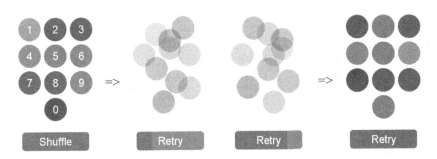

Fig. 2. Secure Pad display with various colors.

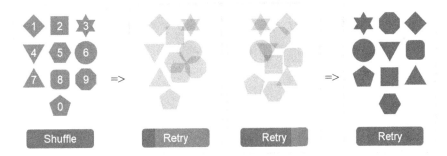

Fig. 3. Secure Pad display with various shapes.

Enhanced distinguishability due to different colors, shapes, and/or sizes allows all the keys to be moved instantaneously after key-top labels are erased and the user to touch the target key.

Table 1 summarizes the dimensions of variations for Secure Pad. Key color may include variations of texture, figure, or even pictures on the tops of keys. However, a set of colors undistinguishable by people with color weakness should be avoided. In such a case, gray level variations could be utilized. We can combine variations of key color, key shape, key size, and key movement to enhance distinguishability, but this may lower the difficulty of peepers to trace key movements.

The combination of variations can be applied for both the ten numerical keypads and the alphanumeric (QWERTY) keypads. Figure 4 shows the color and shape variations applied for the latter.

Table 1. Dimensions of variations for Secure Pad.

Dimension	Variation	Detail
Key color	Single color	Single color for all keys
	Multiple colors	Different color for each key
Key shape	Single shape	Single shape for all keys (e.g., circle, square)
	Multiple shapes	Different shape for each key (e.g., circle, polygon, star)
Key size	Single size	Single size for all keys
	Multiple sizes	Different size for each key
Key movement	Smooth	Move all keys smoothly and simultaneously
	Instantaneous	Move all keys instantaneously and simultaneously

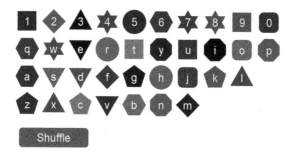

Fig. 4. Secure Pad for the QWERTY keyboard.

4   Evaluation

This section presents evaluation of the variations of Secure Pad through an experiment on the robustness to peeping and usability.

4.1 Variations of Secure Pad

We evaluate the robustness to peeping by others and the user's ease of use of the Secure Pad variations. We prepared 12 variations of Secure Pad for the ten numerical keys (ten keys in short) and the QWERTY keys with regard to key color, key shape, and key movement as well as two benchmark key configurations, as shown in Table 2.

For color variations, we divided the hue into ten (for ten keys) or 36 (for QWERTY) at equal intervals while fixing the brightness and saturation (as all the participants in the experiment had normal color vision). Then, we assigned these different hues randomly to the keys. For shape variations, we utilized circles, upward triangles, downward triangles, squares, rounded squares, diamonds, pentagons, hexagons, octagons, and stars. We felt that more than ten different shapes would be too confusing. When combining color and shape variations for QWERTY, we chose three or four colors, at approximately equal

Table 2. List of keypads for evaluation.

Type	Dimension			
	Key set	Key color	Key shape	Key movement
Benchmark 1	Ten keys	Single (Blue)	Single (Circle)	No movement
Benchmark 2	QWERTY			
Secure Pad 1	Ten keys	Single	Single	Smooth
Secure Pad 2		Multiple		
Secure Pad 3		Single	Multiple	
Secure Pad 4		Multiple		
Secure Pad 5		Multiple	Single	Instantaneous
Secure Pad 6		Single	Multiple	
Secure Pad 7		Multiple		
Secure Pad 8	QWERTY	Single	Single	Smooth
Secure Pad 9		Multiple		
Secure Pad 10		Single	Multiple	
Secure Pad 11		Multiple		
Secure Pad 12		Multiple	Multiple	Instantaneous

hue intervals, and assigned them for each shape. We do not examine key size dimension here because we assumed it would have the same or less effect as the key color and key shape. As for key movement, we considered straight movement and set the duration of the smooth movement to 1 s considering the balance between the difficulty of peepers tracing multiple keys and the user's ease of tracing the target key and time to input a password. For instantaneous movement, keys must be clearly distinguishable, and combination with single color, single shape, and single size is meaningless. When instantaneous movement was used for the QWERTY keys, we only tested the combination with multiple (36) colors and multiple (ten) shapes because color or shape variations alone seems hard to distinguish with 36 keys.

4.2   Details of Experiment

We formed a pair of participants—one as a user and one as a peeper—and changed their roles for each type of Secure Pad. Peepers were allowed to stand at the easiest distance from the display for peeping, which was about 30 cm on average. This is similar to the conditions on a crowded train, so the experiment should illuminate the worst-case scenario for peeping resilience. Table 3 lists the profiles of participants. The PINs used for Secure Pad with ten keys (Secure PIN Pad) were 4-digit numeric strings, and the passwords used for Secure Pad with the QWERTY keys (Secure QWERTY Pad) were 4-character alphanumeric strings. They were randomly generated for each pad and each role in a pair. We denote the sequence of actions where the user inputs a PIN or password and the peeper tries to read it as a trial. We asked each pair and role to perform three trials with the same password (note that PIN is included) on each type of Secure Pad. When the peeper succeeded in reading the password completely at the first or second trial, the subsequent trials are considered "success" and are skipped. In contrast, when the user retried inputting a single character three times, the input and the peeping conditions were marked as "failure" and the user was forced to input the next character. In each trial, we recorded whether the password was successfully peeped and the time required for actions. The experiment was performed using a 7-in 1024×600 tablet oriented horizontally without tilt.

Table 3. Experiment participants.

Pair no.	Age	Gender
1	22	Male
	23	Male
2	22	Male
	23	Male
3	22	Female
	21	Male
4	54	Female
	55	Male
5	59	Female
	59	Male

Each pair took part in the following procedure:

1. Be explained on how to use Secure Pad and the procedure for the experiment.
2. Do a few practice runs on Secure Pad 1 and Secure Pad 12 (QWERTY).
3. Perform the trials on Benchmark 1 and Benchmark 2.
4. Perform the trials on various types of Secure Pad. In order to eliminate bias due to the order of use, the types of Secure Pad used were randomized for each pair.
5. Answer a simple questionnaire after completing the experiment.

4.3 Results

We present the results on the robustness to peeping, ease of input, input time, and verification.

Robustness to Peeping. Table 4 shows the average numbers of successful peeping of individual characters and the average rate of peeping all four characters for each type of keypad. Although the password was typically peeped in the 1st or 2nd trials with the benchmark keypads, which do not feature moving keys, Secure Pad was robust to peeping even in three trials with many types. With Secure PIN Pad for numeric keys, only one PIN was peeped in two trials, some were peeped in the third trial, and the number of characters successfully peeped was less than half in three trials. With Secure QWERTY Pad, no password was peeped in three trials, and only less than a single character was peeped with some types on average (at most two characters).

Table 4. Average number of peeped characters and rate of all four characters peeped.

Type	Measure					
	Number of characters peeped			Rate of all four characters peeped		
	1st trial	2nd trial	3rd trial	1st trial	2nd trial	3rd trial
B1 (Ten, Kc:Sin, Ks:Sin, M:No)	4.00	4.00	4.00	1.00	1.00	1.00
B2 (Qw, Kc:Sin, Ks:Sin, M:No)	3.10	3.80	4.00	0.60	0.90	1.00
SP1 (Ten, Kc:Sin, Ks:Sin, M:S)	0.90	1.50	1.50	0.00	0.00	0.20
SP2 (Ten, Kc:Mul, Ks:Sin, M:S)	0.60	0.90	1.50	0.00	0.00	0.10
SP3 (Ten, Kc:Sin, Ks:Mul, M:S)	1.20	1.30	1.90	0.00	0.10	0.10
SP4 (Ten, Kc:Mul, Ks:Mul, M:S)	0.80	1.40	1.80	0.00	0.00	0.10
SP5 (Ten, Kc:Mul, Ks:Sin, M:I)	0.00	0.30	0.70	0.00	0.00	0.00
SP6 (Ten, Kc:Sin, Ks:Mul, M:I)	0.50	1.00	0.70	0.00	0.00	0.00
SP7 (Ten, Kc:Mul, Ks:Mul, M:I)	0.50	0.60	1.10	0.00	0.00	0.00
SP8 (Qw, Kc:Sin, Ks:Sin, M:S)	0.00	0.10	0.10	0.00	0.00	0.00
SP9 (Qw, Kc:Mul, Ks:Sin, M:S)	0.10	0.10	0.30	0.00	0.00	0.00
SP10 (Qw, Kc:Sin, Ks:Mul, M:S)	0.00	0.00	0.20	0.00	0.00	0.00
SP11 (Qw, Kc:Mul, Ks:Mul, M:S)	0.10	0.20	0.30	0.00	0.00	0.00
SP12 (Qw, Kc:Mul, Ks:Mul, M:I)	0.10	0.10	0.20	0.00	0.00	0.00

Under "Type", B and SP denote Benchmark and Secure Pad, Ten and Qw denote Ten keys and QWERTY, KC:Sin and KC:Mul denote key color being single and multiple, KS:Sin and KS:Mul denote key shape being single and multiple, and M:No, M:S, and M:I denote movement being no movement, smooth, and instantaneous, respectively.

Ease of Input. Table 5 shows the average number of characters successfully input and the number of retries performed on each type of keypad. The former divided by four shows the input success rate. Participants in their 20s had no large difference in this rate between Secure Pad and the benchmarks, and their numbers of retries were small. In contrast, the input success rates were lower and the numbers of retries increased on Secure Pad for participants in their 50s. Moreover, instantaneous movement was liable to cause input failure. As the color and/or the shape variations were added under the same condition, however, the input success rate was improved and the number of retries decreased.

Input Time. Table 6 shows input time, where the "Time" column shows the average time (in sec) taken to input all four characters on each type of keypad and the "Time/char." column shows the average time per character from pushing the shuffle button to key input. Note that B1 and B2 do not have the shuffle button, so there is no value for the latter column. For Secure Pad, the value in the Time column does not equal four times the value in the Time/char. column since the former includes the time from key input to the next shuffle and that for retries. With Secure Pad, it takes lager input time. It is from 2.8 to 11.5 times compared with the benchmarks (27.34 s on SP8 v.s. 9.70 s on B2 to 38.62 s on SP4 v.s. 3.34 s on B1 by participants of 50 s). Moreover, Secure QWERTY Pad took a long time for users in their 50 s (discussed in more detail later).

Verification. We performed paired t-testing on the number of characters successfully peeped, the rate of all four characters being peeped, the input time, and the number of characters successfully input between each type of keypad and the benchmarks (B1 or B2). The number of characters successfully peeped and the rate of all four characters being peeped were significantly smaller with $p < 0.001$, which supports the peeping resilience of Secure Pad in these respects. On the other hand, the input time was significantly larger with $p < 0.05$, while the number of characters successfully input was not significantly different with $p > 0.01$.

We also preformed paired t-testing between the smooth movements (SP2, SP3, SP4 and SP11) and the instantaneous movements (SP5, SP6, SP7 and SP12) under the same conditions. Specifically, we took the n-th ($n = 1$ to 3) trial of a pair of participants for SP2 and the n-th ($n = 1$ to 3) trial of the same pair of participants for SP5. We repeated this for SP3 and SP6, for SP4 and SP7 and for SP11 and SP12. Then, we applied paired t-testing for all of these pairs. The number of characters successfully peeped and the rate of all four characters being peeped by the instantaneous movements were significantly smaller than those by the smooth movements ($p < 0.05$), which shows that the peeping resilience of the instantaneous movements is stronger than that of the smooth movements. On the other hand, the number of characters successfully input by the smooth movements was significantly larger ($p < 0.01$), which shows that the ease of use of the smooth movements is better compared to that of the instantaneous movements. For the input time, no significant difference was observed ($p > 0.05$).

Feedback from the participants. We received the following opinions from the participants after the experiment:

- When a single color and shape is used, neither inputting nor peeping are easy.
- Instantaneous movement is difficult both to trace and to peep from a single observation.
- Ease of peeping depends on the distance of key movement.
- Without shape variation, the user is not confident in deciding the target key.
- When the target key and surrounding keys are similar in shape and color, the user is confused in tracing the target key.
- When movements cross over, both tracing and peeping are difficult.
- It takes time to input all four characters.

Table 5. Average number of successfully input characters and number of retries.

Type	Group of participants & measure					
	All participants		Age: 20s		Age: 50s	
	No. of chars.	No. of retries	No. of chars.	No. of retries	No. of chars.	No. of retries
B1 (Ten, Kc:Sin, Ks:Sin, M:No)	3.97	N/A	4.00	N/A	3.92	N/A
B2 (Qw, Kc:Sin, Ks:Sin, M:No)	3.87	N/A	3.94	N/A	3.75	N/A
SP1 (Ten, Kc:Sin, Ks:Sin, M:S)	3.80	0.13	3.78	0.00	3.83	0.33
SP2 (Ten, Kc:Mul, Ks:Sin, M:S)	4.00	0.07	4.00	0.00	4.00	0.17
SP3 (Ten, Kc:Sin, Ks:Mul, M:S)	3.97	0.03	4.00	0.00	3.92	0.08
SP4 (Ten, Kc:Mul, Ks:Mul, M:S)	4.00	0.00	4.00	0.00	4.00	0.00
SP5 (Ten, Kc:Mul, Ks:Sin, M:I)	3.77	0.30	3.94	0.28	3.50	0.33
SP6 (Ten, Kc:Sin, Ks:Mul, M:I)	3.67	0.33	3.67	0.22	3.67	0.50
SP7 (Ten, Kc:Mul, Ks:Mul, M:I)	3.93	0.10	3.94	0.00	3.92	0.25
SP8 (Qw, Kc:Sin, Ks:Sin, M:S)	3.80	0.27	3.94	0.00	3.58	0.67
SP9 (Qw, Kc:Mul, Ks:Sin, M:S)	3.80	0.33	3.94	0.28	3.58	0.42
SP10 (Qw, Kc:Sin, Ks:Mul, M:S)	3.80	0.27	3.94	0.06	3.58	0.58
SP11 (Qw, Kc:Mul, Ks:Mul, M:S)	3.90	0.10	3.94	0.11	3.83	0.08
SP12 (Qw, Kc:Mul, Ks:Mul, M:I)	3.93	0.10	3.94	0.06	3.92	0.17

4.4   Considerations

The experimental results, as shown in Table 5 and discussed in Robustness to peeping section, demonstrate that Secure Pad is robust to peeping. However, the success rate of inputting a password character dropped when a single color and shape were specified. In addition, instantaneous movement was liable to cause input failure, but failures could be prevented by the color and shape information. Likewise, the number of retries decreased when there were more color and shape variations. These results suggest that the user's mental load is not excessively increased by the color and shape information, compared with the benchmark keypads that do not feature moving keys.

As for the input time, it took several times with Secure Pad than with the benchmarks. This is the price of enhancing the security, the same as with other methods [11, 17]. In Secure Pad, however, users can touch keys without having to move them, which means they can shorten the input time when there is no need to worry about security. It took users in their 50s a longer time with the Secure QWERTY pad, presumably because two of them were not accustomed to using the QWERTY keyboard.

A comparison between the smooth movements and the instantaneous movements shows that the instantaneous movements have higher peeping resilience but the input success rate deteriorates. Each has advantages and disadvantages so that an appropriate method can be chosen according to the required peeping resilience and the ease of use.

Table 6. Average input time (sec).

Type	Group of participants & measure					
	All participants		Age: 20s		Age: 50s	
	Time	Time/char.	Time	Time/char.	Time	Time/char.
B1 (Ten, Kc:Sin, Ks:Sin, M:No)	2.81	–	2.51	–	3.34	–
B2 (Qw, Kc:Sin, Ks:Sin, M:No)	4.60	–	1.53	–	9.70	–
SP1 (Ten, Kc:Sin, Ks:Sin, M:S)	15.75	2.06	10.80	1.77	22.76	2.47
SP2 (Ten, Kc:Mul, Ks:Sin, M:S)	18.60	2.18	9.54	1.76	32.18	2.81
SP3 (Ten, Kc:Sin, Ks:Mul, M:S)	20.88	2.10	9.89	1.75	36.45	2.60
SP4 (Ten, Kc:Mul, Ks:Mul, M:S)	21.35	2.21	9.84	1.75	38.62	2.91
SP5 (Ten, Kc:Mul, Ks:Sin, M:I)	19.89	1.71	10.41	1.39	34.12	2.20
SP6 (Ten, Kc:Sin, Ks:Mul, M:I)	21.80	2.04	13.12	1.69	34.81	2.56
SP7 (Ten, Kc:Mul, Ks:Mul, M:I)	20.17	1.49	9.42	1.06	36.30	2.14
SP8 (Qw, Kc:Sin, Ks:Sin, M:S)	20.55	2.31	15.75	1.97	27.34	2.79
SP9 (Qw, Kc:Mul, Ks:Sin, M:S)	22.85	2.26	15.63	1.87	34.65	2.84
SP10 (Qw, Kc:Sin, Ks:Mul, M:S)	22.28	2.31	14.00	1.89	34.70	2.94
SP11 (Qw, Kc:Mul, Ks:Mul, M:S)	22.59	2.33	12.05	1.83	38.40	3.08
SP12 (Qw, Kc:Mul, Ks:Mul, M:I)	3.93	0.10	3.94	0.06	3.92	0.17

5   Conclusion

We presented a series of replay-attack and peeping resilient PIN/password input methods named Secure Pad and detailed evaluation. The key idea is to associate colors and shapes with keys, erase key-top labels, move them smoothly and simultaneously or instantaneously, and let the user touch the target key. The user only needs to trace a single key, but peepers have to trace the movements of all the keys at the same time.

We conducted an experiment to evaluate the resilience, ease of input, and input time. It has demonstrated that Secure Pad is robust to peeping even over three trials. Although the success rate of inputting a password character dropped in the case of single color and shape, especially for older people, the input success rate improved and the number of retries decreased when color and shape variations were added under the same condition,. As for the input time, it took several times longer with Secure Pad compared with the benchmarks featuring no key movement. This is the price of enhancing security, as with other methods. In Secure Pad, however, users can touch keys without moving them, which shortens the input time when there is no need to worry about security. We compared the smooth and the instantaneous movements with the result that the instantaneous movements have higher peeping resilience but a worse success rate of input. An appropriate method can be chosen based on the required peeping resilience and the ease of use. As a whole, Secure Pad achieves high resilience to shoulder hacking while providing satisfactory usability without large input errors.

There are still a few issues pointed out by the users, including speed and crossover of movements and arrangement of different colors and shapes among keys, which need to be addressed. Moreover, movements along curvilinear or polygonal lines should also be considered.

Acknowledgements. This work is partially supported by JSPS KAKENHI (A) 19H01117 and (S) 18H05221. We would like to thank all of the people who joined the evaluation experiment.

References

1. Kobayashi, K., Oguni, T., Nakagawa, M.: PIN code/password input method resilient to shoulder hacking using difficulty of tracing multiple button movements. In: Proceedings of the Computer Security Symposium 2017, pp. 728–733 (2017). (in Japanese)
2. Kobayashi, K., Oguni, T., Nakagawa, M.: Usability improvement of an anti-shoulder-hacking PIN code/password input method exploiting tracing difficulty of multiple button movements. In: Proceedings of the IPSJ Interaction 2018, pp. 565–568 (2018)
3. Willeby, G.T.: Secure key entry using a graphical user interface. U.S. Patent Application No. US 20020188872 A1 (2002)
4. Tanaka, S., Takahashi, S.: 暗証番号入力装置及び暗唱番号入力方法. Japanese Patent Application No. 2002-134808 (2002). (in Japanese)
5. Makida, K.: パスワード入力装置及びパスワード入力方法. Japanese Patent Application No. 2005-340699 (2005). (in Japanese)
6. Kakinuma, Y., Maruyama, K.: Color distance based authentication smartphone lock screens. In: Proceedings of the 76th National Convention of IPSJ, vol. 1, pp. 121–122 (2014). (in Japanese)
7. Sakurai, S., Takahashi, W.: Authentication methods for mobile phones. IPSJ SIG Technical reports, No. 122 (CSEC-19), pp. 49–54 (2002). (in Japanese)
8. KyuChoul, A., Ha, Y.A.: Password security input system using shift value of password key and password security input method thereof. U.S. Patent Application No. US 20130047237 A1 (2013)
9. Takada, T.: フェイクポインタによる暗証番号入力装置及び暗唱番号入力方法. Japanese Patent Application No. 2007-175073 (2007). (in Japanese)
10. Takada, T.: fakePointer: a user authentication scheme that makes peeping attack with a video camera hard. Trans. IPS. Japan **49**(9), 3051–3061 (2008)
11. Kita, Y., Sugai, F., Park, M., Okazaki, N.: Proposal and its evaluation of a shoulder-surfing attack resistant authentication method: secret tap with double shift. Int. J. Cyber Secur. Digit. Forensics **2**(1), 48–55 (2013)
12. Watanabe, K., Higuchi, F., Inami, M., Igarashi, T.: CursorCamouflage: multipledummy cursors as a defense against shoulder surfing. In: SIGGRAPH ASIA 2012 Emerging Technologies (2012). https://doi.org/10.1145/2407707.2407713
13. Luca, D.A., von Zezschwitz, E., Pichler, L., Husmann, H.: Using fake cursors to secure on-screen password entry. In: Proceedings of the CHI 2013, Paris, France, pp. 2390–2402 (2013). https://doi.org/10.1145/2470654.2481331
14. Matsumoto, T., Imai, H.: Human identification through insecure channel. In: Davies, Donald W. (ed.) EUROCRYPT 1991. LNCS, vol. 547, pp. 409–421. Springer, Heidelberg (1991). https://doi.org/10.1007/3-540-46416-6_35
15. Li, X.-Y., Teng, S.-H.: Practical human-machine identification over insecure channels. J. Comb. Optim. **3**(4), 347–361 (1999). https://doi.org/10.1023/A:1009894418895
16. Hopper, Nicholas J., Blum, M.: Secure human identification protocols. In: Boyd, C. (ed.) ASIACRYPT 2001. LNCS, vol. 2248, pp. 52–66. Springer, Heidelberg (2001). https://doi.org/10.1007/3-540-45682-1_4

17. Jain, A., Hong, L., Pankanti, S.: Biometric identification. Commun. ACM **43**(2), 90–98 (2000). https://doi.org/10.1145/328236.328110

18. Sakano, S.: Astate of the art of biometric authentication technology. Japan. J. Forensic Sci. Technol. **12**(1), 1–12 (2007). https://doi.org/10.3408/jafst.12.1. (in Japanese)

19. Roth, V., Richard, K., Freidinger, R.: A pin-entry method resilient against shoulder surfing. In: Proceedings of the 11th ACM Conference on Computer and Communication Security, Washington DC, USA, pp. 236–245 (2004). https://doi.org/10.1145/1030083.1030116

20. Tan, S.D., Keyani, P., Czerwinski, M.: Spy-resistant keyboard: More secure password entry on public touch screen displays. In: Proceedings of the OZCHI 2005, Canberra, Australia, pp. 1–10 (2005)

21. Intriligator, J., Cavanagh, P.: The spatial resolution of visual attention. Cogn. Psychol. **43**, 171–216 (2001). https://doi.org/10.1006/cogp.2001.0755

22. Pylyshyn, W.Z., Storm, W.R.: Tracking multiple independent targets: evidence for a parallel tracking mechanism. Spat. Vis. **3**, 179–197 (1998). https://doi.org/10.1163/156856888X00122

Smart Assistants in IT Security – An Approach to Addressing the Challenge by Leveraging Assistants' Specific Features

Michael Kubach$^{(\boxtimes)}$ ⓘ and Heiko Roßnagel

Fraunhofer IAO, Nobelstraße 12, 70569 Stuttgart, Germany
{michael.kubach,heiko.rossnagel}@iao.fraunhofer.de

Abstract. Smart assistants, also known as ubiquitous personal assistants, intelligent assistants or digital personal assistants, have already entered the private sphere and are at the brink of real productive application in the business sphere as well. While those developments can make life easier for end users and increase productivity of businesses, they, at the same time, lead to concerns from the perspective of IT security and privacy. This article presents an approach to address these challenges – not through restricting these assistants but through leveraging their specific features.

Keywords: Digital personal assistants · Smart assistants · IT security · Privacy · Enterprise security

1 Introduction

New technologies regularly promise to make life easier for end users and provide companies with large productivity gains, while these growth promises are at the same time usually met with skepticism [1, 2]. From the point of view of the IT security and privacy discipline, however, it is mainly the associated dangers that are regularly pointed out [3, 4]. In the past, such new technologies were for example cloud computing or mobile (smart) phones. Experience shows that, already in the medium term, ignoring or banning new technologies is not a promising strategy. Useful technologies eventually spread and employees simply establish "shadow IT systems" that are not monitored or sanctioned by the IT department [5]. If cloud services for collaboration, such as Google Drive or Dropbox are not available, employees simply use private accounts.

When it comes to new technologies, it is therefore necessary to develop viable solutions that balance IT security and data protection aspects holistically with (socio)-economic and usability aspects. The technologies should therefore be examined with regard to the security challenges and solutions must be developed to leverage the potential of the new technologies for the organizations on the one hand, and to ensure IT security and data protection on the other.

More recently, some technologies inducing major challenges from the perspective of IT security and privacy discipline are the Internet of Things (IoT) and Artificial Intelligence (AI) [6, 7]. In the wave of these developments, so called smart assistants (also

© Springer Nature Switzerland AG 2020
A. Moallem (Ed.): HCII 2020, LNCS 12210, pp. 575–587, 2020.
https://doi.org/10.1007/978-3-030-50309-3_38

known as digital personal, intelligent, or ubiquitous personal assistants) are coming into use. Such assistants are usually based on IoT devices and use big data and AI technologies. Various definitions of smart assistants have been proposed. A definition of an ideal smart assistant could be that it should employ many, if not all of the following properties: some form of personalization, context awareness, enable intelligent interaction, act proactively and have a network connection. This definition by [8] is in line with the definition for fuzzy cognitive agents [9] and personal digital assistants [10]. As such, smart assistants are now getting into the focus of attention for those responsible for IT security and data protection in organizations. The reason for this is that we are moving towards the ubiquity of smart assistants, often equipped with voice interfaces [11]. Well-known implementations of such assistants are Siri, Alexa, and Google Now, but also more and more domain specific assistants are being released, for example "MBUX - Hey Mercedes" in cars [12, 13].

Voice controlled smart assistants or simply speech interfaces, also referred to as "Conversational AI" (potentially in order to benefit from the current hype around AI, the most recent Gartner Hype Cycle for Emerging Technologies features plenty of AI technologies [14]), are proclaimed to become the interface of the future [15]. In a first step, such speech assistants are already spreading in the private sphere. They currently appear as stationary "intelligent" loudspeakers in the smart home, mobile on the wrist via smart watches and in the trousers' pocket in smart phones, in headphones connected to smart phones and watches, in the car and kitchen appliances as well. Diffusion among the population is already considerable [16, 17].

As smart assistants will soon be everywhere, it will become more or less impossible to avoid getting in contact with them. Employees bring smart watches to work, drive in rental cars with smart assistants and sleep in hotel rooms with smart speakers. At the same time, businesses increasingly look at smart assistants to optimize their processes. This means that non-authorized employees as well as visiting employees of other companies will get into contact with these smart assistants that smart might also overhear confidential conversations of the employees. We see that there is no escape from smart assistants and that separating the private and the business sphere seems is another serious challenge when it comes to this technology. Therefore, we need to analyze more closely, what IT security and privacy challenges are posed by smart assistants. This will be the topic of the next section. However, those challenges are not everything that has to be taken into consideration when drafting a strategy about how to deal with smart assistants. We have to account for their potential as well (Sect. 3), in order to evaluate potential strategies (Sect. 4). Section 5 will then outline an approach for a strategy ensuring secure and privacy-friendly use of smart assistants while still being able to profit from their potential.

2   IT Security and Privacy Challenges Through Smart Assistants

In the following, we will focus on voice-based smart assistants such Amazon's Alexa, Google's Assistant and Apple's Siri that can be based on smart speakers such as Amazon's Echo, Apple's Home Pod and on smart phones as well. Their very basic functionality is as follows (of course architectures can vary): Via their built-in microphones these devices continuously listen into the surrounding sound using a local voice interpreter detecting wake words such as "Hey Siri" or "Hello Google". On smart phones this is often the default setting that can be deactivated, while on smart speakers this is the setting that enables the basic functionality of the device. The microphones can usually be deactivated via hardware buttons. Once the specific wake-word(s) is (are) detected, the device switches to recording mode where the recorded sound is sent to the cloud. If no wake word is detected no sound recordings are stored. In the cloud of the smart assistant provider, the recordings are decoded using natural language processing to capture the intention of the user. This intention can trigger an action that is performed or triggered directly in the cloud of the smart assistant and sent back to the device where the assistant is located. An example could be the setting of a timer. Another possibility is that an action of a third party is supposed to be triggered. Then a request is forwarded to the web service of the third party where it is again processed, an answer is sent back to the assistant provider's cloud and back to the user's device. Maybe even another cloud service is triggered to control another Internet of Things device such as a remote controlled light switch.

2.1 Challenges Resulting from the Technical Architecture

Various privacy and security challenges arise from the described technical architecture as such. The cloud-based architecture of smart assistants requires that the sound that is recorded after the wake-word is detected will be sent from the private network of the assistant's user through the internet to the cloud of the smart assistant provider for processing. The wake-word can be triggered intentionally or unintentionally or the interpretation of the smart assistant can be false. Most of the current smart assistants provide no means for authentication of users or controlling the access to functionality of the assistant. This means that everyone in range of the device is able to issue voice commands and to perform sometimes security critical tasks. Moreover, it has been demonstrated that so called "Dolphin" attacks can be used to call functions on voice assistants without the owner or user of the assistant noticing. This is achieved through broadcasting audio signals, e.g. through smart phones, TVs or other devices, which are inaudible to humans [18]. Replay attacks on voice assistants are another technical attack vector. These are performed through somehow acquired recordings of authenticated voices (if such an authentication is even implemented) that are played back to trick voice assistants into assuming the authenticated person would actually interact with the assistant. Recently, Amazon has applied for a patent that is supposed to protect speech assistants against replay attacks on voice-based authentication systems [19].

In any case, the sound recording that is supposed to contain the voice command is processed and stored in the cloud of the smart assistant provider that builds up a rich pool of data sourced by all smart assistant users and their potentially highly sensitive information overheard by the smart assistants. This means that this can pool be a valuable target for attackers. Moreover, the smart assistant provider could perform profiling tasks with the recorded data. A simple profile would be when and where a user is present. That such a profiling can even be achieved through traffic analysis of encrypted traffic by external attackers has been demonstrated by [20]. If actions from third parties, e.g. for smart devices are triggered and web and/or cloud services of these providers are involved in the process, these services and devices can be used for profiling as well, become attack points for attackers and serve as entry points [21], for example, have demonstrated how an attack on a smart device can spread in a private network. There is also the question about which data is exactly shared with the third party provider. A systematic overview of technical security and privacy challenges from smart assistants can be found at [22].

2.2   Challenges Resulting from the Usage Scenarios

Other security and privacy challenges are less related to the technical architecture as described above, but arise from the manner the assistants are used. While the challenges mentioned above seem to be in the focus of current research efforts, less sophisticated attacks do not seem to be as much in the current focus of the scientific discussion. The current usage scenarios can look as follows.

Users communicate to the assistants via the voice interface. The assistants are based on smart devices that are located in environments that are visited by various known and potentially not so well known people (visitors). These locations might be conference rooms in companies, hotel rooms, a (rental) car, the private living room etc. Moreover, the assistants might be carried around by users on smart watches or smart phones that meet other known or unknown people in various locations. The smart devices and thus the smart assistants as well can have some knowledge of their current location, e.g. through GPS. The communication to the smart assistant provider's cloud either is routed through the local network (usually for smart speakers) or through the cellular network (usually smart phones, possible for smart watches as well).

The diffusion of intelligent assistants in the private sphere makes it increasingly difficult to keep private smart assistants out of the professional sphere. This means that it could easily occur that an employee's private smart watch with voice assistant listens in on confidential professional meetings – even without the employee's malicious intent, this implies a security challenge. Moreover, it may appear undesirable that the voice assistant in the office reminds its user out lout of sensitive private topics like your therapy session in the afternoon and colleagues or business partners listen in. This could happen as you have entered this appointment into your office calendar to block the time (or as private and business calendars are synchronized). Alternatively, a manager could be reminded of a confidential business appointment with a competitor when playing semi-private golf with business partners. These examples highlight the privacy and security challenges that such assistants might induce. The particular context and (potential) recipient(s) of the information have to be taken into account. Depending on the sphere: private or business, privacy challenges in one sphere can also be seen as security challenges in the other sphere. These challenges apparently have been only partially addressed so far.

To summarize, from a security and privacy perspective, significant challenges for voice assistants that originate from usage scenarios are:

1. Who is talking/asking? *(Authentication)*
   Voice authentication of current voice controlled smart assistants is basic – if existent at all. Anyone can control the assistant with his voice.

2. What is asked, is the questioner entitled? *(Authorization)*
   Current smart assistants do not support different users, roles and respective rights. However, it might be reasonable to distinguish between users being able to tell the smart assistant in a conference room to close the shades and others being able to end the meeting and change the conference room schedule. One limited possibility to approach this can be verbal password prompts. Those are integrated into Amazon's Alexa as protection against Kids going shopping via the voice assistant. However, those password prompts are obviously very vulnerable to eavesdropping as well as replay attacks and only provide very limited security gain.
3. Who else might be standing there? *(Authentication, Authorization, Context)*
   The smart assistant might be used by an authorized person while other persons are present that are not authorized for information that the assistant is providing. This could be the case in a company conference room with external visitors. In such a situation, classified information should not be shared.
4. Where is the assistant located? *(Context)*
   While Smart Assistants already have some knowledge about their current location, they do not use this for security or privacy features. It would, for example, be advisable that smart phone-based smart assistants disable any sound recording as soon as they enter sensitive areas such as corporate research and development facilities.

Besides the challenges related especially to the voice interface of smart assistants, other vectors might be exploited by attackers or can passively leak sensitive information as well. There are, for example, GPS functionalities tracking the location of their users to share it through APIs with web services. In early 2018, it became known that through a social network for fitness tracker users that aggregates and publishes heat maps of the routes run by its users, the locations of secretive US military bases and patrol routes were unintentionally leaked. Apparently, it was even possible to identify and locate interesting individuals and track them. The US military reacted by tightening its policies and restricting the use of such trackers [23]. From an industrial espionage perspective, it could be promising for an attacker to trace if certain high-ranking individuals from a certain company meet business partners in their facilities to prepare a certain deal or to derive information whether the activities in a certain research or production facility of a competitor is higher or lower. This illustrates that besides the voice interface, other functionalities of smart assistants pose a challenge as well. Therefore, smart assistants as a whole should be addressed.

The challenges described are both relevant for the business (as security challenges) as well as for the private sphere (as privacy challenges). In the business sphere, they seem to hinder the adoption of smart assistants, as IT security professionals are hesitating to permit the introduction of these technologies into productive processes. This could result in missed opportunities to optimize productive processes (see following section for examples). Private users apparently do not seem to care as much about those challenges, as can be observed from the fast adoption that is reflected in the statistics mentioned in the introduction. However, for privacy-aware private persons it could become virtually impossible to avoid contact with such smart assistants if most persons they meet and places they visit are equipped with them. Moreover, from a societal point of view, it could be regarded problematic if these smart assistants collect such a huge amount of personal data that in the end is aggregated and exploited by a few big platform corporations.

3   The Potential of Smart Assistants in the Business Sphere

The challenges mentioned above would not be as relevant, if smart assistants had no potential in the business sphere. Then companies could just avoid using them, there would not be a security challenge and all that remained was the privacy problematic in the private sphere. However, there is a significant potential for smart assistants in the business sphere. By leveraging this potential, companies could improve their business processes, make work for their employees easier and gain competitive advantages. This will be illustrated through the following examples.

Amazon Alexa already features a number of skills that are useful for programmers and users of cloud services like Amazon Web Services (AWS). These skills allow for the easy voice query of the current status of the cloud resources and start or stop certain cloud instances. Others let you create or manage service tickets and to learn about the open or recently closed tickets of a JIRA bug-tracking system [24]. Authentication and authorization are not really covered by these skills, which makes it questionable if using them is worth the danger of everyone entering the office being able to stop a cloud instance or spamming the helpdesk with new service tickets. Microsoft focusses with his Cortana smart assistant now specifically on business applications, e.g. to schedule meetings, book conference rooms and aims at more sophisticated applications [25].

Another example is the Nami Assistant, presented in 2018. This smart assistant with chat interface and natural language processing is supposed to support finance traders in routine and monitoring tasks. As such, it monitors the market and notifies the trade of fluctuations. Moreover, it can be instructed to place orders depending on defined rules. The assistant is supposed to be self-learning to increase his performance over time [24], but his current functionality looks more like a technology demo and not yet ready for the professional application. Nevertheless, it gives an outlook on the potential on such assistants.

Examples can be found on the shop floor as well. Industrial machine manufacturing company Trumpf has presented a laser marking workstation that can be controlled with a voice interface. So far, the product is a technology study that is not on the market yet, less of a smart assistant or powered with artificial intelligence as Trumpf claims but it already demonstrates both some potential as well as challenges of voice-controlled smart assistants. The voice interface is intuitive – even for unexpected users and more accessible for operators with disabilities. Navigation through sub-menus is no longer necessary, so that complicated or unusual tasks can be executed faster. Moreover, as operators do not have to press any buttons at the machine, they can already prepare the next element to be worked on, while using the voice interface to execute instructions. This should increase productivity. The next step in the development would be to combine the voice interface with image recognition and further sensors so that the machine could recognize elements and execute the respective programs automatically [26]. The public statements that are available do not address questions about how users are authenticated and whether anyone passing by the machine could simply issue voice commands in order, for example, to cancel current tasks. Is known neither whether the voice commands are processed on premise or in the cloud and which kind of infrastructure is used.

The examples show that there is a significant potential for smart assistants in the professional sphere, while the security challenges remain. Therefore, the following sections will investigate how to counter these challenges.

4 Strategies to Counter the Security and Privacy Challenges Posed by Smart Assistants

The challenges presented above, posed by the increasing proliferation of smart assistants, raise the question, which measures organizations, society, and individuals can take. At the same time, the potential, as described in the previous section for professional applications, needs to be taken into account as well. So how can or should smart assistants be regulated, considering the security and privacy risk as well as the benefits of smart assistants:

- Not at all?
- Through a complete ban?
- By blocking the network for assistants?
- Through completely different strategies?

The current strategy seems to be a mix between not really reacting and trying to ban the assistants. The first one is followed by the general society, while many responsible for IT security in organizations tend follow to the second strategy. Privacy-aware individuals try to avoid smart devices that are equipped with (voice-controlled) smart assistants and, as such, try to enforce such a ban in their sphere of influence. However, as we have shown above, these strategies do not seem to be very successful.

In view of the challenges outlined above, the strategy to do nothing does not seem appropriate for organizations. We will therefore go straight to the second strategy. A general ban on intelligent assistants – whether private ones, brought into the organization by employees, as well as their professional application, may be a strategy that organizations like the military can enforce for sensitive areas. However, for average companies or organizations, this does not seem like an advisable strategy. On the one hand, the potential of intelligent assistants in a professional context, i.e. for reasons of efficiency, argues against this and could lead to the aforementioned shadow IT that is then without any regulation of corporate IT security professionals. On the other hand, a ban would hardly be effectively enforceable, since intelligent assistants cannot be kept out of organizations at a reasonable cost. To this end, employees would first have to leave their private smart phones, smart watches and potentially other future smart devices, such as fitness trackers, off the firm's premises. It is, however, questionable to what extent modern smart watches and fitness trackers can still be identified as such and in which mobile gadget intelligent voice assistants will be integrated next. In addition, business travelers use hotel rooms equipped with intelligent loudspeakers or drive rental cars with voice controlled smart assistants. In this respect, there appears to be no viable way to avoid smart (voice) assistants – already in the medium term.

Individuals concerned of their privacy in the age of ubiquitous smart assistants face similar challenges. They can certainly chose not to buy any smart devices or disable the respective functions. Nevertheless, they will encounter more and more smart assistants when leaving their house. The person that sits next to them in the subway might carry a smart watch, and friends might own a smart speaker. There is virtually no escape from smart assistants.

Blocking the network for smart assistants could be a solution that organizations can enforce in the network that is under their control. Smart speakers, for example, then would not be operational anymore in the organization's facilities. However, smart assistants that are based on smart phones using the cellular network or smart watches that increasingly also feature cellular connections would still work. Hence, this appears as an only partly promising strategy. It is also related to the "banning strategy" and could lead to the establishment of a shadow IT. Employees might just use cellular connections to operate their "shadow smart assistants".

For individuals the blocking-strategy does not seem to be fruitful at all. While they could block their home network for smart assistants, they can also just chose not to buy such devices or disable respective functionalities. As argued above, this does not help them at all as soon as they leave their personal sphere of influence.

Those simple strategies are apparently insufficient. What is required is a comprehensive strategy for dealing with smart assistants, which includes both technical and organizational measures. Such a strategy will be outlined in the next section.

5 Outline of a Solution Approach Leveraging Smart Assistants for IT Security

We have illustrated the privacy and security challenges that smart assistants produce. Private and business sphere need to be separated and the particular context and (potential) recipient(s) of the information need to be taken into account. These challenges have only been partially addressed so far and the simplistic strategies described in the previous sections are not sufficient.

Our thesis in the paper, summing up what was already described above, is that the privacy challenges in the private sphere are quite comparable to the IT security challenges in the business sphere:

- Unauthorized persons (assistants, organizations) obtaining certain data and processing it,
- smart assistants leaking data to unauthorized persons (organizations),
- unauthorized persons triggering functions in assistants, manipulating data, and so forth.

In the private sphere, "unauthorized persons" are generally unauthorized third parties, the state or private or public organizations that are not supposed to receive the data or that a person does not willingly interact with. Another possibility is that organizations, which are in fact authorized to receive the data, are able to aggregate huge amounts of data about the private user. The consequences of this might be non-transparent and contrary to the users' interest. Thus, this gathering of data could be regarded as not explicitly authorized.

In the business environment, these unauthorized persons or organizations could be (former) employees, competitors or other (state) actors performing industrial espionage. Unauthorized employees could also simply trigger functions there are not trained for and provoke unintended malfunctions.

If the challenges are comparable, the approaches to solve them might also similar. In the following, we present a combined technical and organizational approach to address the IT security and privacy challenges that smart assistants pose – not through trying to ban assistants but through leveraging their specific features. The proposed approach is based on the architecture developed in the ENTOURAGE research project [27].

The ENTOURAGE project has developed the reference architecture (see Fig. 1) and components of an open ecosystem for trustable smart assistants. The following sections will briefly outline how an approach building on its security and privacy architecture [8] could be used to address the aforementioned challenges.

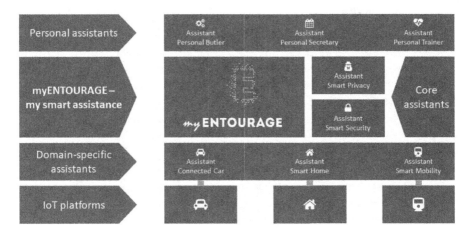

Fig. 1. ENTOURAGE reference architecture

The ENTOURAGE "Core Assistants" (see Fig. 1) Security and Privacy Assistant support in addressing the challenges mentioned above. According to the architecture, those are smart assistants supporting end users and those responsible for IT security and data protection in setting up and controlling their smart devices according to their individual preferences or their organization's policies as well as the specific context. Manual control in the multitude of different settings of various IoT-devices and assistants would be highly complex and overwhelm both end users and administrators. In addition, as already shown above, a general ban of those devices is not viable.

Following the ENTOURAGE Architecture, Core Assistants could implement organizational security policies and help to separate the business and private spheres. This is achieved by personalized, context-sensitive and proactive interventions and reminders of the assistants. Where automated interventions are not possible, the awareness of the user could be increased through push messages, audio reminders or notifications – depending on the respective context. As an example, those could be triggered when a sensitive meeting is pending, and ask the end user to switch off the voice assistant on his smart watch and the like (and notify him when the assistant can be switched back on). Stationary smart devices, such as smart speakers in conference rooms, could be plugged in via smart power sockets that can be switched on and off by the security assistant.

Context information and different data sources combined with policies that could be trained through AI enable the security assistants to increase security. This can be achieved using ENTOURAGE interfaces to calendars, other assistants and data sources. Geofencing for sensitive (world) regions or company divisions/premises (research departments etc.) could be implemented as well. As appropriate interfaces become available – which is the goal and already foreseen in the architecture – this can be achieved automatically. Before that, one has to rely largely on push notifications and user engagement. For this, as illustrated in Fig. 2, the architecture specifies (1) interfaces to other assistants or data sources in the ecosystem, (2) privacy and security interfaces that enable direct control of security, transparency, and intervenability functions, and (3) composition interfaces that enable platform-independence by providing standardized interfaces for typical platform functions and components (out of scope for this paper, see [8]).

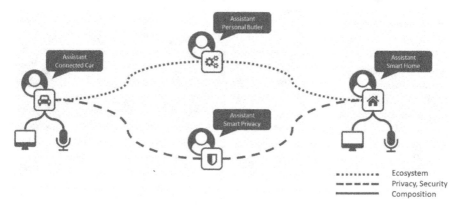

Fig. 2. Interfaces in the ENTOURAGE ecosystem

Such interfaces should be based on open standards that are agreed upon and implemented by the industry. This would enable different vendors to compete in developing security and privacy assistants with separate functionalities and business models. Customers (both private end users as well as business customers) would then be able to opt for the assistant of their preference. Moreover, companies could decide to develop their own security assistants that are specifically designed according to their requirements and completely under their control – both code as well as deployment on corporate IT resources. It would also enable privacy supporting nonprofit organizations to develop and offer privacy assistants. A related example could be the Mozilla Foundation with its web browser that is not, as competing browsers are, developed by platform and advertisement-financed corporations. We see that standardization could make a major contribution here. Industrial self-regulation that would lead to appropriate international standards would certainly be preferable. However, if this cannot be achieved, regulative approaches that set standards and force the industry to adhere to them could be an alternative.

6 Conclusion

The widespread diffusion of smart assistants in our daily lives as well as in the professional sphere leads to significant challenges for privacy and IT security. While many authors focus on the technical IT security and privacy challenges that smart assistant induce, this paper considers their potential as well and presents an approach that leverages their specific features to deal with this challenge.

The presented approach outlines a technical solution that needs to be complemented by non-technical initiatives. First, it is required to involve the employees to create awareness and ensure their cooperation. They are the ones that would have to connect their private assistants with the security and privacy assistants of the organization – in exchange for that they are allowed to use them on premise. In addition, legislative measures would also be necessary to bring manufacturers of smart assistants to implement the necessary interfaces in order to enable access to security- and privacy-relevant functions of assistants. In general, the legislator could persuade or force manufacturers to open up to ecosystems in order to simplify the combination of different assistants from different manufacturers and to connect to privacy and security assistants selected by end users and organizations. While this might seem utopian at first glance, examples like the "European Directive on Payment Services (PSD2)" that forces banks and payment service providers to implement specific security functions and open up interfaces for access through competitors, show that such legislative actions are possible if the political will is there. Antitrust policies could be used for this purpose as well. This has already been applied in the past in the IT-industry, for example, when the linking of browsers and operating systems was broken up. Through that, not only IT security and privacy standards could be enhanced, but the dominant positions of individual platform giants that accumulate more and more data and gain more and more power could be broken up as well.

References

1. Pisa, M., Juden, M.: Blockchain and Economic Development: Hype vs. Reality. CGD Policy Paper 107, Center for Global Development, Washington (2017)
2. Aghion, P., Jones, B., Jones, C.: Artificial Intelligence and Economic Growth. NBER Working Paper No. 23928. National Bureau of Economic Research (2017). https://doi.org/10.3386/w23928
3. Chung, H., Iorga, M., Voas, J., Lee, S.: Alexa, can i trust you? IEEE Comput. **50**(9), 100–104 (2017). https://doi.org/10.1109/MC.2017.3571053
4. Lei, X., Tu, H.-H., Liu, A.X., Li, C., Xie, T.: The insecurity of home digital voice assistants - Amazon Alexa as a case study. Paper presented at the IEEE Conference on Communications and Network Security, Beijing (2018)

5. Myers, N., Starliper, M.W., Summers, S.L., Wood, D.A.: The impact of shadow IT systems on perceived information credibility and managerial decision making. Account. Horiz. **31**(3), 105–123 (2017)
6. Sadeghi, A-R, Wachsmann, C., Waidner, M.: Security and privacy challenges in industrial internet of things. Paper presented at the 52nd ACM/EDAC/IEEE Design Automation Conference (DAC), San Francisco, 8 June 2015
7. Wirkuttis, N., Klein, H.: Artificial intelligence in cybersecurity. Cyber Intell. Secur. J. **1**(1), 103–119 (2017)
8. Zibuschka, J., Horsch, M., Kubach, M.: The ENTOURAGE privacy and security reference architecture for internet of things ecosystems. In: Roßnagel, H., Hühnlein, D., Wagner, S. (eds.) Proceedings of the Open Identity Summit 2019, pp. 119–130. Gesellschaft für Informatik, Bonn (2019)
9. Miao, C., Yang, Q., Fang, H., Goh, A.: A cognitive approach for agent-based personalized recommendation. Knowl.-Based Syst. **20**(4), 397–405 (2007)
10. Milhorat, P., Schlogl, S., Chollet, G., Boudy, J., Esposito, A., Pelosi, G.: Building the next generation of personal digital assistants. Paper presented at the 1st International Conference on Advanced Technologies for Signal and Image Processing, Sousse (2014)
11. Singleton, S.: AI in the Workplace: How Digital Assistants Impact Cybersecurity. Infosecurity Magazine. https://www.infosecurity-magazine.com/opinions/ai-workplace-digital-assistants/. Accessed 6 Jan 2020
12. López, G., Quesada, L., Guerrero, L.A.: Alexa vs. Siri vs. Cortana vs. Google Assistant: a comparison of speech-based natural user interfaces. In: Nunes, I. (ed.) Advances in Human Factors and Systems Interaction, pp. 241–250. Springer, Cham (2017). https://doi.org/10.1007/978-3-319-60366-7_23
13. Mercedes-Benz: A-Class MBUX (2019). https://www.mercedes-benz.com/a-class/com/en/mbux/ Accessed 16 Jun 2019
14. Gartner: 5 Trends Appear on the Gartner Hype Cycle for Emerging Technologies, 2019 (2019). https://www.gartner.com/smarterwithgartner/5-trends-appear-on-the-gartner-hype-cycle-for-emerging-technologies-2019/ Accessed 6 Jan 2020
15. Wired: Conversational AI: making technology more human (2017). https://www.wired.co.uk/article/conversational-ai-making-technology-more-human. Accessed 6 Jan 2020
16. Statista: Smart speaker household penetration rate in the United States from 2014 to 2025, Loup Ventures (2019). https://www.statista.com/statistics/1022847/united-states-smart-speaker-household-penetration/. Accessed 16 Dec 2019
17. Statista: Number of digital voice assistants in use worldwide from 2019 to 2023 (in billions), Voicebot.ai, Juniper Research (2019). https://www.statista.com/statistics/973815/worldwide-digital-voice-assistant-in-use/. Accessed 16 Dec 2019
18. Zhang, G., et al.: DolphinAttack: inaudible voice commands. Paper presented at the ACM Conference on Computer and Communications Security (CCS), Dallas (2017)
19. Bhimanai, B.K., Hitchcock, D.W.: Detecting replay attack in voice-based authentications. In: United States Patent Application Publication, Pub. No.: US 2019/0013033 AI (2019)
20. Apthorpe, N., Reisman, D., Feamster, N.: A Smart Home is No Castle: Privacy Vulnerabilities of Encrypted IoT Traffic. arXiv, arXiv:1705.06805v1 [cs.CR] (2017). https://arxiv.org/abs/1705.06805. Accessed 6 Jan 2020
21. Ronen, E., O'Flynn, C., Shamir, A., Weingarten, A.O.: IoT goes nuclear: creating a ZigBee chain reaction. In: Proceedings - IEEE Symposium on Security and Privacy, San Jose, pp. 195–212 (2017)
22. Edu, J.S., Such, J.M., Suarez-Tangil, G.: Smart Home Personal Assistants: A Security and Privacy Review. arXiv, arXiv:1903.05593v2 [cs.CR] (2019). https://arxiv.org/abs/1903.05593v2. Accessed 7 Jan 2020

23. Wired: The Strava Heat Map and the End of Secrets (2018). https://www.wired.com/story/str ava-heat-map-military-bases-fitness-trackers-privacy/. Accessed 20 Dec 2019
24. Computerworld: 15 Alexa skills for business success (2018). https://www.computerworld. com/article/3249710/15-alexa-skills-for-the-enterprise.html. Accessed 21 Jan 2020
25. Sayer, P.: Why Microsoft is building Cortana for business interactions. Techrepub-lic (2019). https://www.techrepublic.com/article/why-microsoft-is-building-cortana-for-bus iness-interactions/. Accessed 21 Jan 2020
26. Trumpf GmbH + Co.KG.: Künstliche Intelligenz zieht in die Lasermaterialbearbeitung ein (2018). https://www.trumpf.com/de_DE/unternehmen/presse/pressemitteilungen-global/pre ssemitteilung-detailseite-global/release/kuenstliche-intelligenz-zieht-in-die-lasermaterialbe arbeitung-ein/. Accessed 21 Jan 2020
27. Entourage: Projekt Webseite (2019). http://entourage-projekt.de/. Accessed 21 Jan 2020

An Improved Method of Time-Frequency Joint Analysis of Mouse Behavior for Website User Trustworthy Authentication

Wei Li, Shuping Yi$^{(\boxtimes)}$, Qian Yi, Jiajia Li, and Shiquan Xiong

Chongqing University, Chongqing 400044, China
874794328@qq.com, yshuping@cqu.edu

Abstract. With the increasingly prominent problem of information security, the research on user trustworthy authentication technology becomes more and more important. Identification and authentication methods based on user's biological behavior characteristics have attracted widespread attention due to their low cost and difficulty in imitation, which represented by mouse dynamics. This study proposed an improved method for time-frequency joint analysis of mouse behaviors for trustworthy authentication of website users. We collected the behavior data of the user's natural mouse operation under real website environment, and analyzed the timing and spatial characteristics of the user's mouse movements. Based on extracting the time-frequency joint distribution characteristics and spatial distribution characteristics of the temporal signals of the user's mouse movements, we used the random forest algorithm to establish a user's trustworthy authentication model. Mouse behavior data of five users during twenty-eight months had been used as a case study to explore the effectiveness of this method in user trustworthy authentication. The results of case analysis showed that, comparing to the original research, the method proposed in this study significantly improved the accuracy of the website user trustworthy authentication.

Keywords: Trustworthy authentication · Mouse behavior · Time-frequency joint analysis · Random forest

1 Introduction

With the popularization of computer network, the problem of information security is increasingly prominent. User trustworthy authentication refers to the process of verifying whether the identity of the online account login user is the true owner of the account. As an important means to ensure the privacy of computer systems and networks, user trustworthy authentication technology has received widespread attention. The existing website user trustworthy authentication technologies include credential authentication and biometric authentication. Credential authentication technology suffers from the shortcomings that its credentials are vulnerable to be theft and counterfeiting. Biometric authentication technology can be divided into identity authentication based on physiological characteristics and identity authentication based on behavior

© Springer Nature Switzerland AG 2020
A. Moallem (Ed.): HCII 2020, LNCS 12210, pp. 588–598, 2020.
https://doi.org/10.1007/978-3-030-50309-3_39

characteristics [1]. The former has a good authentication effect due to its unique biological characteristics [2], but common biometric methods require the addition of additional hardware equipment, which is costly and not universal. Malathi and Jeberson proved that when fingerprints, iris and other biological characteristics are damaged or aging, it will affect the recognition accuracy [3]. Biological behavioral characteristics have their traits which are difficult to be intercepted and imitated [4, 5]. Due to its advantages of difficult to be imitated and low cost, the trustworthy authentication methods based on behavioral biometrics characteristics represented by mouse dynamics has attracted researchers' attention.

Shrobe, Shrier and Pentland studied the information search and selection characteristics of network users [6]; Yi, Li and Yi established a user behavior flow diagram based on the user's network behavior data, and performed trustworthy interaction detection based on the user behavior flow diagram [7]; Ho, Kang and Dae-Ki studied the user's keystroke characteristics, and constructed a user's keystroke behavior pattern to detect user identity [8]. Shen, Cai & Guan used a pattern-growth-based mining method to extract frequent-behavior segments in obtaining stable mouse characteristics, and used these mouse behavior characteristics for continuous verification tasks [9]. Among many biological behavior characteristics, mouse dynamic characteristics have attracted the attention of researchers because of their widespread existence and easy access.

Pusara used mouse trails to detect abnormal behaviors in experiments [10]. Shen, Cai, Liu, Guan & Maxion used the speed characteristics of mouse movement to characterize the dynamic process of mouse movement [11]. Wang, Xiong, Yi, Yi & Yan used the speed, angle, curvature and other characteristics of mouse movement to identify mouse behavior in the research [12]. Some researchers analyzed the 11-dimensional temporal signals of the user's mouse movement, such as the coordinates and speed, and expressed the dynamic process with the five statistical features of maximum, minimum, mean, standard deviation and range, which were used for user trustworthy authentication [13–16].

These studies have indicated that the characteristics of mouse behavior could be used for trustworthy authentication of website users. The user's mouse movement is a typical temporal signal, which has the dual characteristics of time and frequency domains. The above studies had used statistical description methods to explore the characteristics of user's mouse movement from the perspective of the time domain. These studies had not involved to the frequency domain characteristics of the user's mouse behavior. In the previous research, my group had performed Time-Frequency Joint Analysis (TFJA) on the temporal signals of the mouse movement of web users, and had explored the time-frequency joint distribution characteristics. In the case study, the Wavelet Packet Transform (WPT) was used to extract the time-frequency joint distribution characteristics of temporal signals of mouse movement and used for trustworthy authentication. We found that using the time-frequency joint distribution characteristics could achieve better results in website user trustworthy authentication than using the time-domain characteristics of the mouse movement temporal signal.

In order to effectively improve the authentication effect of the trustworthy authentication model, this paper analyzed the user's mouse behavior characteristics from two dimensions of time and space. On the one hand, the temporal signals of the user's mouse movement had been analyzed by multi-resolution using the WPT to further explore the time-frequency joint distribution characteristics. On the other hand, this paper had analyzed the differences of the user's mouse movements in different directions and different interaction areas, and had explored the spatial distribution characteristics of the user's mouse movement behavior. Finally, based on the time-frequency joint distribution and spatial distribution characteristics of the user's mouse movements, this paper used Random Forest (RF) algorithm to establish a website user trustworthy authentication model, and had verified the model's authentication effect in a case study. The trustworthy authentication process of the method proposed in this paper is shown in the Fig. 1:

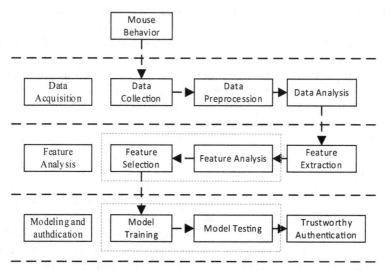

Fig. 1. Schematic diagram of website user trustworthy authentication

2 Data Collection and Preprocessing

2.1 Data Collection

The data set used in the study was derived from the academic research website (http://www.cquieaml.com/), which is the research group's official website system. This website was mainly used for resource sharing and learning exchange among members of the research group. The website has eight sections, including the home page, academic research, scientific research results, corporate communication, forum interaction, research team, resource sharing and management. The backstage of the website had recorded the mouse behavior data of users in the state of natural use of the mouse in a real web environment. This study had collected data recorded on the website from April 7, 2017 to November 5, 2019, with a total of more than 1.94 million pieces of data.

The raw data includes five dimensions: mouse operation type, system time stamp, cursor X-axis coordinate, cursor Y-axis coordinate, and user ID. As shown in Table 1.

There are five types of mouse operations: left mouse button press, left mouse button release, right mouse button press, right mouse button release, and mouse movement. The system timestamp unit is "millisecond". The cursor X-axis coordinate unit and the cursor Y-axis coordinate unit both are "pixel". The data set contains a total of 40 user operations. All data in the original data set are arranged in order of time stamp size.

Table 1. Schematic diagram of raw data

Options	Times	Point X	Point Y	Username
slide	1493900902128	226	132	0
slide	1493900902144	227	132	0
click_left	1493900902297	227	132	0
release_left	1493900902394	227	132	0
slide	1493900902403	227	132	0
slide	1493900902553	225	133	0

2.2 Data Preprocessing

Data preprocessing is the basic condition of data preliminary processing to make it meet the following application. In order to extract features from the mouse behavior data of users, it is necessary to preprocess the original mouse behavior data recorded by the website. The pre-processing flow is shown in Fig. 2.

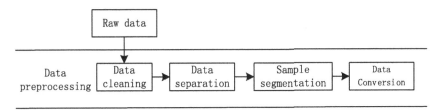

Fig. 2. Schematic diagram of data preprocessing

The first step is data cleaning, the purpose of which is to organize the data set. Its work is to remove redundant data and abnormal data from the original data. The second step is data separation. Its purpose is to divide user data. The work is to split the mouse operation data of different users and store them separately in chronological order. The third step is sample segmentation, the purpose of which is to obtain a sample of the user's mouse behavior. This study uses the time slice sample method. We set three thresholds for dividing the data set of a single user to obtain a sample of the user's mouse behavior, including threshold of mouse behavior interval, threshold of time slice length, and threshold of sample data size. The fourth step is data conversion, the purpose of which is to obtain sufficient temporal signals of mouse behavior required for the study, based on the mathematical transformation of the three-dimensional data of the time stamp, horizontal coordinate, and vertical coordinate in the initial sample.

Temporal signals of mouse movement required in the study include horizontal axis coordinates, vertical axis coordinates, horizontal rate, vertical rate, tangential rate, tangential acceleration, rate of change of acceleration, Angle, rate of change of Angle, curvature, rate of change of curvature.

3 Feature Extraction

According to the properties and extraction methods, the user's mouse behavior characteristics used in this study can be divided into two parts, one is the time-frequency joint distribution characteristics of mouse behavior signals, and the other is the spatial distribution characteristics of mouse behavior signals.

3.1 The Time-Frequency Joint Distribution Characteristics

From the perspective of engineering signals, any temporal signal has its unique time and frequency domain characteristics. To fully highlight the characteristics of a temporal signal, we can combine time-domain analysis and frequency-domain analysis. This means that TFJA should be used to mine the signal distribution. In the previous research of this research group, we had analyzed the characteristics of the temporal signals of the user's mouse behavior, and we had explored the TFJA of the user's mouse behavior. In these studies, the time-frequency joint distribution characteristics of the user's mouse behavior temporal signals were successfully extracted and used for user trustworthy authentication. User's mouse behavior data used in this study is a kind of typical non-stationary discrete digital signal, with obvious local characteristics. We used wavelet packet transform method to perform time-frequency joint analysis on this signal.

WPT satisfies the requirements of TFJA of mouse behavior signals. It constructs a family of wavelet functions based on the mother wavelet, and uses multi-scale wavelet functions to implement multi-resolution analysis (MRA) of the signal. WPT is a classical time-frequency joint analysis method of non-stationary signals, with excellent local analysis ability. The WPT formula of the mouse behavior signal is as Formula (1):

$$WT(a, \tau) = \frac{1}{\sqrt{a}} \int_{-\infty}^{+\infty} f(t) * \psi\left(\frac{t - \tau}{a}\right) d_t \tag{1}$$

Among them, "$\psi((t - \tau)/a)$" is the wavelet function family obtained from the wavelet basis function through the scaling and translation operation. "a" (scale) controls the expansion and contraction of the wavelet function, which corresponds to the frequency (inverse ratio). "τ" (translation) controls the translation of the wavelet function, which corresponds to time. Using wavelet basis functions of different scales to decompose and reconstruct mouse behavior signals, we had realized the MRA of mouse behavior signals, and decomposed the original signals into sub-signals of different frequency bands. Based on WPT, we can decompose the low frequency part and high frequency part of the signal at the same time, and we can obtain sub-signal groups with the same bandwidth, as shown in Fig. 3.

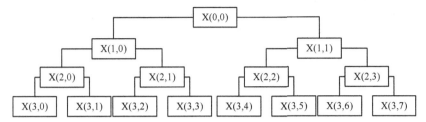

Fig. 3. Schematic diagram of the WPT of mouse behavior signals

For the sub-signals of different frequency bands obtained by wavelet packet transformation, we used nine eigenvalues to describe them. Including Maximum, Mean, Minimum, Range, Variance, Power, Power ratio, Skewness and Kurtosis.

Power (P) is a characterization of the average signal strength. The formula for calculating the P of the sub-signal is shown in Formula (2). "N" is the discrete signal length, and "x(k)" is the signal amplitude. "j" is the serial number (integer) of the sub-signal, and the value range is 0–7.

$$P_i = \frac{1}{N} \sum_{k=0}^{N} |x(k)|^2 \tag{2}$$

Power ratio (Pr) is the ratio of sub-signal power to total power. The formula for calculating Pr of the sub-signal is shown in Formula (3). "j" is the serial number (integer) of the sub-signal, and the value range is 0–7.

$$Pr_i = P_i / \sum_{j=0}^{7} P_j \tag{3}$$

Skewness (Skew) is a numerical feature which characterizes the degree of asymmetry between the probability distribution density curve and the mean of the signal. The formula for calculating the Skew of the sub-signal is shown in Formula (4).

$$Skew[X] = \frac{E(X - EX)^3}{\left[E(X - EX)^2\right]^{3/2}} \tag{4}$$

Kurtosis (Kurt) is a numerical feature that characterizes the peak height of the probability density distribution curve at the mean of the signal. The formula for calculating the Kurt of the sub-signal is shown in Formula (5).

$$Kurt[X] = \frac{E(X - EX)^4}{\left[E(X - EX)^2\right]^2} - 3 \tag{5}$$

3.2 The Spatial Distribution Characteristics

Mouse movement directions were usually divided into 8 categories [17]. This study classified the user's mouse movement behavior into eight categories based on the movement direction, as shown in Fig. 4. For each category of mouse movement behavior data in the sample, we selected the tangential rate and tangential acceleration rate as the objects, and use the maximum, minimum, mean, range, and variance to represent it.

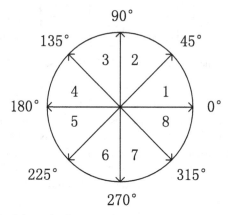

Fig. 4. Schematic diagram of the mouse movement direction

At the same time, we divided the mouse behavior into 9 categories according to the range of user interaction positions in the study, as shown in Fig. 5. For the mouse behavior data in each position range in the sample, the tangential rate and tangential acceleration rate were also selected as the objects, and the maximum, minimum, mean, range, and variance of these were used to represent the data.

1	2	3
4	5	6
7	8	9

Fig. 5. Schematic diagram of user interaction positions

4 Modeling and Trustworthy Authentication

4.1 Trustworthy Authentication Based on Random Forest

This study used RF to model for website user trustworthy authentication. RF is a classification algorithm that combines bootstrap and Decision Tree (DT). The size of the original sample set is N. The algorithm obtains m subsample data sets with a size of n by random sampling m times from the original data set. Then DT will be used to build classification model for each subsample data set. The final model output is determined by absolute mode classification based on m decision trees.

RF is an improvement of DT, Comparing with DT, RF algorithm obtains strong anti-noise ability through the random selection of samples and features, which avoids the model over-fitting problem to a certain extent.

4.2 Evaluation Indicators

Trustworthy authentication of website user is a binary classification problem. When using RF to solve this problem, we must establish binary classification models for each account owner. The original sample set of the model consists of two types: positive and negative samples. Positive samples are credible samples of account owners, and negative samples are obtained by random sampling of untrusted samples of other non-account owners.

The results of trustworthy authentication are divided into four categories:

True Positive (TP): True positive samples are judged as positive samples.
False Positive (FP): True negative samples are judged as positive samples.
True Negative (TN): True negative samples are judged as negative samples.
False Negative (FN): True positive samples are judged as negative samples.

In the research of website user trustworthy authentication, the higher the accuracy of the authentication, the better the model performs in the trustworthy authentication. In this study, we selected three indicators for evaluating the effectiveness of trustworthy authentication models, including True Positive Rate (TPR), False Positive Rate (FPR), and Areas Under Curve (AUC) of the Relative Operating Characteristic Curve (ROC).

TPR: The proportion of TP to positive samples. The value range of TPR is from 0 to 1. The larger the TPR is, the better the model performance.

FPR: The proportion of FP to negative samples. The value range of FPR is from 0 to 1. The smaller the FPR is, the better the model performance.

AUC of ROC: It is a model performance evaluation index that integrates TPR and FPR. The value range is from 0 to 1. The larger the AUC value is, the better the model performance.

4.3 Results

In the case study, we had selected 5 users with the richer mouse behavior samples from the 40 users in the dataset to perform website user trustworthy authentication. In the practice of trustworthy authentication of five users, the training set and test set sample had been divided according to the ratio of 7:3. In order to improve the reliability of the model evaluation index, two cross-validations had been performed on the results of the user's trustworthy authentication in the study. The first item was cross-validation within the group. Ten trustworthy authentication models had been established for each user, and the average evaluation indicators of the ten model is used as the authentication result of the user in the practice of trustworthy authentication. The second item was cross-group verification, which took the average of the trustworthy authentication results of five users as the final result of this method in the practice of trustworthy authentication.

This study had compared the results of trustworthy authentication with the previous research of my group, as it shown in Table 2. In the case where only the time-frequency joint distribution characteristics of the user's mouse behavior had been used, the trustworthy authentication results are shown in Table 2 (a). The trustworthy authentication results of this study are shown in Table 2 (b), which was from a trustworthy authentication combined time-frequency joint distribution characteristics and the spatial distribution characteristics.

Table 2. Schematic diagram of trustworthy authentication results

(a) Previous research				(b) This paper			
Username	TPR	FPR	AUC	Username	TPR	FPR	AUC
A	86.51%	7.78%	96.74%	A	95.06%	0.21%	99.57%
B	93.05%	10.44%	98.13%	B	96.67%	6.54%	99.13%
C	90.02%	10.00%	97.82%	C	92.22%	6.00%	97.59%
D	89.61%	12.02%	95.29%	D	90.27%	9.66%	96.25%
E	91.98%	8.99%	98.07%	E	98.61%	6.48%	99.42%
Mean	90.23%	9.84%	97.21%	Mean	94.56%	5.78%	98.39%

As shown in the figure above, the average TPR in this study was 94.56%, the FPR was 5.78%, and the AUC value of the ROC was 98.39%. The results show that the improvement method in this paper has significantly improved the accuracy of user trustworthy authentication compared with previous studies.

5 Conclusions

Based on the previous research, this study combined user time-frequency joint distribution characteristics and spatial distribution characteristics of mouse movement to identify users, and had built a user trustworthy authentication model based on random forest algorithm. The trustworthy authentication results prove that this method effectively improved the accuracy of user trustworthy authentication based on the original research, and that is an effective method of user trustworthy authentication.

Future research will include:

(1) Increasing the number of users to verify the universality of this method.
(2) Deeper mining of the time-frequency joint distribution and spatial distribution characteristics of the user's mouse movement behavior.
(3) Adding the characteristics of user's mouse click behavior to the research to improve the effect of user identity authentication.

Acknowledgment. This work was supported by the National Natural Science Foundation of China under Grant No. 71671020.

References

1. Xu, J., Li, M., Zhou, F., Xue, R.: Identity authentication method based on user's mouse behavier. Comput. Sci **43**(2), 148–154 (2016)
2. Grother, P., Tabassi, E.: Performance of biometric quality measures. IEEE Trans. Pattern Anal. Mach. Intell. **29**(4), 531–543 (2007)
3. Malathi, R., Jeberson, R.R.R.: An integrated approach of physical biometric authentication system. Procedia Comput. Sci. **85**, 820–826 (2016)
4. Jain, A.K., Pankanti, S., Prabhakar, S., Hong, L., Wayman, J.L.: Biometrics: a grand challenge. In: Proceedings of ICPR, vol. 2, no. 4, pp. 935–942 (2004)
5. Zweig, M.H., Campbell, G.: Receiver-operating characteristic (ROC) plots: a fundamental evaluation tool in clinical medicine. Clin. Chem. **39**(4), 561–577 (1993)
6. Shrobe, H., Shrier, D.L., Pentland, A.: New Solutions for Cybersecurity. The MIT Press, Boston (2018)
7. Yi, S., Li, J., Yi, Q.: Trustworthy interaction detection method in view of user behavior flow diagram. Control Decis. 1–8 (2019)
8. Ho, J., Kang, D.-K.: One-class naive Bayes with duration feature ranking for accurate user authentication using keystroke dynamics. Appl. Intell.: Int. J. Artif. Intell. Neural Netw. Complex Problem-Solving Technol. **48**(6), 1547–1564 (2018)
9. Shen, C., Cai, Z., Guan, X.: Continuous authentication for mouse dynamics: a pattern-growth approach. In: 42nd IEEE/IFIP International Conference on Dependable Systems & Networks, Boston, pp. 1–12. IEEE Computer Society (2012)
10. Pusara, M., Brodley, C.: User re-authentication via mouse movements. In: 11th Workshop on Visualization and Data Mining for Computer Security, Washington, pp. 1–8. ACM (2004)
11. Shen, C., Cai, Z., Liu, X., Guan, X., Maxion, R.A.: MouseIdentity: Modeling mouse-interaction behavior for a user verification system. IEEE Trans. Hum.-Mach. Syst. **46**(5), 734–748 (2016)
12. Wang, B., Xiong, S., Yi, S., Yi, Q., Yan, F.: Measuring network user trust via mouse behavior characteristics under different emotions. In: Moallem, A. (ed.) HCII 2019. LNCS, vol. 11594, pp. 471–481. Springer, Cham (2019). https://doi.org/10.1007/978-3-030-22351-9_32
13. Sayed, B., Traore, I., Woungang, I., Obaidat, M.S.: Biometric authentication using mouse gesture dynamics. IEEE Syst. J. **7**(2), 262–274 (2013)
14. Nakkabi, Y., Traore, I., Ahmed, A.A.E.: Improving mouse dynamics biometric performance using variance reduction via extractors with separate features. IEEE Trans. Syst. Man Cybern. Part A: Syst. Hum. **40**(6), 1345–1353 (2010)

15. Feher, C., Elovici, Y., Moskovitch, R., Rokach, L., Schclar, A.: User identity verification via mouse dynamics. Inf. Sci. **201**, 19–36 (2012)
16. Chen, Y.: Research and Implementation of User Identification Based on Mouse Dynamics (2018)
17. Zheng, N., Paloski, A., Wang, H.: An efficient user verification system using angle-based mouse movement biometrics. ACM Trans. Inf. Syst. Secur. **18**(3), 1–27 (2016)

Cyber Security Threats and Incidents in Industrial Control Systems

Jens Mehrfeld[(⊠)]

Bundesamt für Sicherheit in der Informationstechnik, Godesberger Allee 185-189, 53175 Bonn, Germany
jens.mehrfeld@bsi.bund.de

Abstract. Cyber attacks on companies pose a real threat. The number of incidents is rising and industrial control systems are increasingly affected by the attacks. The reasons for this are organizational and technical. Practical and user-friendly solutions must be found to mitigate cyber security threats.

Keywords: Industrial security · Cyber security threats · Incidents

1 Introduction

With digitization and trends like "Industrie 4.0", the use of IT systems and their connections, as well as the use of cloud applications, have a firm place in production companies. Among other things, this will lead to predictive maintenance, simplified and faster engineering. However, the new technology and interconnection brings up new ways attacker can use and dependencies that have not existed up to now or have not been considered yet.

Overall, the number of attacks on the IT infrastructure in companies has increased massively in the recent years. This ranges from undirected mass attacks on home users to targeted attacks on specific companies. Estimates predict that by 2019 cyber-crime damage will exceed $2 trillion [1]. The average cost of a ransom attack or data breach is between $2.6 million [2] and $3.9 million [3]. Public sources report between 100 and 150 attacks on businesses or user campaigns per month [4]. These figures affect the economy in general. Manufacturing companies are a subset. In the following, a closer look at incidents for these will be taken.

2 Problems in ICS

2.1 Architecture

In order to investigate the attack paths and their consequences of attacks, the architecture must first be examined. Industrial Control Systems (ICS) are classically divided into 5 layers (see Fig. 1).

© Springer Nature Switzerland AG 2020
A. Moallem (Ed.): HCII 2020, LNCS 12210, pp. 599–608, 2020.
https://doi.org/10.1007/978-3-030-50309-3_40

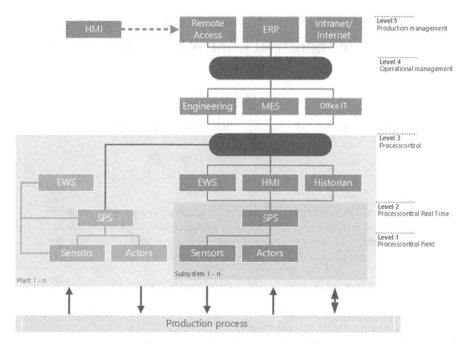

Fig. 1. General architecture of an ICS

Layer 1 contains actuators and sensors that interact directly with the physical environment. These can be, for example, temperature sensors, light barriers, motors or pumps. Programmable logic controllers (PLC) are in the layer above which implement real time control. Cyclic programs control sensors and actuators and transmit the status upwards or receive commands from above. Layer 3 contains human-machine interfaces (HMI), historians, or engineering workstations. This level is responsible for local operation of a plant. Layer 4 is used for operations management with Manufacturing Execution Systems (MES) or control rooms, which are responsible for planning and operation of the ICS. This is where higher-level operational decisions are made and production planning is carried out. The top layer comprises the office IT with Internet and Intranet applications, Enterprise Resource Planning (ERP) and the office workstations. In the Reference Architecture Model Industrie 4.0, a further layer has been introduced, which covers the "External World". This includes all services, functions, and applications that run outside the company [5]. These include remote maintenance and monitoring or other cloud applications.

In addition to the systems that are necessary for the actual function, there are additional safety systems at layers 1–3. These are responsible for the protection of people and the environment against hazards from the system. Typical examples are emergency stop switches. They put the ICS into a safe state. These are usually designed as separate systems. However, there is a trend to integrate them [6].

3 Incidents

3.1 General

As already described in the introduction, most attacks are motivated by cyber-crime. The Federal Office for Information Security in Germany sees a high threat level from malware, botnets, and identity theft [7]. Denial of service attacks by botnets with bandwidths of up to 300 Gbit/s have been observed. In addition, attackers are becoming more professional. This is reflected in more and better publicly available tools and also service providers for illegal services.

Dissemination takes place via phishing and spam messages, drive-by exploits or remote maintenance access, among other things [7]. "Emotet" was the most relevant ransomware variant last year and has caused damage in a large number of companies by data encryption. Only by paying a ransom should the victims be able to access the data again. However, there is no guarantee that the data will be decrypted in the event of a payment.

Various agencies have analysed and published a large number of attacks with Ransomware. The most common errors are [8]:

- Not deploy security updates
- Missing or insufficient network segmentation
- Insufficient and unprotected backups
- Local administration accounts
- Poor protection of the Active Directory

Attacks on companies and the implementation of protective measures present many companies with challenges. In office IT, the problems described have been known for many years and there are many documents and support materials. In addition, the innovation cycles are significantly faster. As a consequence, companies can respond faster to threats.

3.2 Ransomware in ICS

An evaluation of public sources, such as blogs and news sites, after cybersecurity incidents in manufacturing companies shows a clear trend. Ransomware caused the majority of incident in this sector and sometimes affected the production enviroment. The consequences of a successful Ransomware attack vary among companies.

Three variants can be distinguished:

1. The ransomware does not affect the ICS. Only systems in layer 5 become infected. All data and systems relevant for production are still available. There are only impairments in the office IT, which for example concerns invoicing and the processing of new orders. If problems persist for a longer period of time, this can also affect production, as no new orders are received. This applies to companies that operate mass production without customer individualization.

2. The ransomware does not affect the ICS. Systems in layer 5 (partially layer 4) become infected. Systems relevant to production, such as production orders, production planning or warehousing are affected or have to be shut down to protect them from infection. This applies to companies that produce customer specific products. As a result, the production gets impaired. Probably, the production has to be stopped, because the relevant information are not available in the machines. An alternative workaround it is to transfer the production-relevant data manually to the machines. This decreases productivity and is not always possible.
3. The complete ICS or parts are directly affected by the ransomware. All layers become infected. This means that systems like HMI or database servers have been encrypted and they cannot be used anymore. Therefore, it will be necessary to interrupt production at least to remove the ransomware and restore the systems. Depending on the production environment, certifications or other documentation must be updated before ramping up the production. This is the case in e.g. in pharmaceutical industry.

The described variants one and two can be traced in the case of the norwegian group "Norsk Hydro". The company was victim of an attack with the "Locker Goga" malware in March 2019. The company itself has provided detailed information on the current status of various divisions [9–15]. To prevent further spread, all central services were shut down and employees were not allowed to start their office workstations [16]. In particular, automated processes could no longer be used and the company had to switch to manual operation and paper processes again. The "Building Systems" division, which manufactures customer-specific products, was affected most severely and for the longest time [17].

A large number of examples of variant three have become known in the context of the "NotPetya" malware in 2017. A lot of ICS were affected.

3.3 Targeted Attacks on ICS

In addition to the incidents caused by ransomware, targeted attacks on ICS have been reported in recent years repeatedly. Table 1 shows an exemplary list of investigated incidents.

Table 1. Selected list of targeted attacks on ICS.

Year	Title	Sector
2010	Stuxnet	Manipulation of view and control on uranium enrichment centrifugen
2014/2016	Dragonfly	Cyber-espionage in ICS
2016	Crashoverride/Industroyer	Attack on electrical grid in the Ukraine
2017	TRITON	Attack on safety controller

Stuxnet is the most famous attack on ICS. It involved the Iranian uranium enrichment centrifuges. The attacker manipulated the programmable logic controller (PLC), in this way the operators saw wrong information and the centrifuges got manipulated commands.

The Dragonfly-campaign focused on the energy sector [18]. The attacker tried to get information about the targeted energy companies. The malware had the potential to do sabotage, but there is no evidence that this was used.

The "Industroyer" malware was used in the attacks on the Ukrainian power grid in 2016 [19]. It supported various ICS-specific protocols. On this way it could communicate directly with the ICS-components used in the substations (layer 1 to 3 in Fig. 1). The attackers benefited from the missing security mechanism in the protocols.

The case "TRITON" or "TRISIS" is special because the target was a safety controller. It is an incident from 2017 in the Middle East. Safety controllers protect people and the environment from the dangers posed by the ICS. The safety system moves the machine or plant to a safe state. Typical examples are emergency stop switches or light barriers that stop a machine. In complex plants, such as in the chemical industry, there is usually no simple stop. Measures that are more extensive are taken, such as opening a valve and stopping pumps. The nice control program is stored on the safety controller.

The attackers wanted to change this control program. To do this, they reverse-engineered the protocol of the engineering workstation software for the safety controller. The malware developed was then able to load the manipulated control program onto the safety controller. However, this failed and the safety controller stopped the system in the specified way (but without the need for this). This resulted in an impairment of operation, but no physical damage to the plant or harm to people.

These attacks show that attacker groups exist that target ICS also. The technical skills of the attackers differ. In most cases the typical weaknesses and problems in operation play into the hands of the attackers.

3.4 Future Attack Scenarios

The core of "Industrie 4.0" is formed by data in machines and companies, which are exchanged, evaluated and used to optimize or redesign processes and procedures. Machines, plants and IT systems are being networked more closely with one another. This enables better utilization and planning, for example. The same applies to the exchange of data between companies. The aim can be to increase availability through predictive maintenance and monitoring or to accelerate development and design by exchanging CAE data [20].

Some of the new possibilities are already being used. This can be seen in the increasing connection of machines to the Internet. What has not changed is how to deal with the resulting risks, especially with regard to IT security. One reason for this is that this was not necessary in the past. The systems were isolated, had little or no networking and there was therefore no reason for this. In this case, progress not only makes work easier or provides opportunities for optimisation. It also brings with it dangers and risks, such as the outflow of production information or blackmail by criminals by locking up machines.

4 Challenges

The Ransomware incidents show that attackers are able to penetrate into the production facilities. Once there, the attacker can act comparatively unhindered due to the lack of security mechanisms.

4.1 Asset Management

Some reasons for the problems with ransomware and targeted attacks on ICS have already been mentioned in the general remarks. Especially the distribution of security updates is a challenge due to the requirements for the availability of the systems. Especially updates of the operating system require a restart, which in turn requires an interruption of production. In some systems, this is only possible once a year in planned maintenance windows.

But the installation is not the only problem. The manufacturers are required to provide security updates over the entire service life. For ICS components this can be 10–20 years. This is a challenge for developers and vendors. Most vendors and developers just begin to establish a secure development lifecycle. For example, IEC 62443-4-1 describe the tasks and requirements that must be met. Nevertheless, in currently available product, this was not taken into account. Moreover, some integrators forbid the installation of updates, because they cannot assure that the update causes conflicts.

To be able to plan the updates, an asset directory is necessary. This contains information about the components used in the ICS, the installed firmware and software versions. This forms the basis for deciding to react to a message from a manufacturer about an update. However, this information is rarely available. In many cases, it is distributed over different systems or is not up-to-date. This makes it difficult to obtain an overview of the update to be installed and to plan the installation.

In addition to the inadequate asset management, there is also a lack of an overview of the communication relationships. It is often not documented which components or services communicate with each other and which protocol is used. This makes the segmentation of the network more difficult, as this cannot be planned and implemented without obstacles.

Without network segmentation, an attacker can move through the different layers. In most cases, attackers get into the company trough phishing or drive-by-downloads. This way he enters layer 5. Without segmentation, he can move to deeper layers and infect the ICS or he can move from one ICS to another in the company.

4.2 Availability and Usability of Security Functions

In addition to the organizational problems described above, there are technical obstacles. Necessary security functions are partly not implemented, are difficult to use in practice or are not used in ICS.

An example for all three problems is OPC-UA. In the specification 1.02.38, a Global Discovery Service was specified. This should provide an automated solution for the distribution of certificates for authentication, encryption and signature in ICS. The OPC-Foundation published the specifications in 2012 [21]. However, a first product was only available in 2015 [22]. A sample implementation by Microsoft followed in 2017 [23]. In 2019 no further products providing a complete product-ready implementation of a Global Discovery Service was available.

As a consequence, the distribution of the certificates is not standardized. This results in complex and time-consuming solutions. In smaller ICS, a manual change of the certificates is possible. As the number of devices increase, this is no longer practicable as it is very costintensive and error-prone.

In addition, every vendor develops a different solution. This solution fits the problems of one vendor. Another vendor chooses a different solution. In the end, an operator has to deal with several ways to configure the devices. This leads to solution that

1. are not interoperable, because only one or small group of vendors implement a solution or
2. are unsecure because of security vulnerabilities (e.g. infinite lifespan of the certificate).

The consequence of these problems is that encryption and signature functions of the protocol are not or rarely used.

5   Conclusion

There are many threats to ICS in use. The incidents described make it clear that the risk will increase with Industry 4.0. At the same time, there are possible solutions for many threats. On the provider side, it is important that the implementations do not overburden the operator. In this context, existing technologies must be integrated into products in a more user-friendly way.

Essential tasks for protection relate to the development and provision of components. According to the Mechanical Engineering Industry Association in Germany, by 2015 "30% of the manufacturing costs for a mechanical engineering product will be accounted for by IT and automation technology" [24] with a further increasing trend. It is therefore important to protect the development process and programs from misuse and manipulation. This also applies to the avoidance and handling of weak points and the distribution of software or updates.

With the networking of the systems, a changed threat situation arises. Machines and systems are more vulnerable. Therefore more effort must be put into secure development and operation. At this point the employees have a key position. They must be sensitized to the risks and threats and provided with the appropriate knowledge. This has already been addressed in the Industry 4.0 platform in the context of recommendations for training and further education [25]. However, the general shortage of skilled workers also poses a challenge in this area.

In principle, the thoughts of security-by-design and security-by-default should be followed when developing components. The former aims at a secure design and development. Weak points should be avoided from the beginning if possible. The second is to prevent unsecure operation by delivering the component in a secure basic configuration. This is intended to prevent an unnecessarily large area of attack during rapid commissioning. This is the case, for example, with wireless interfaces activated by default.

The new possibilities for better evaluation, optimization and utilization of machines and systems as well as more flexible production are not only associated with advantages. There are also risks to the systems to which they have not been exposed up to now.

The challenge of cyber security in Industry 4.0 could only be touched on individual points. Component manufacturers, integrators and operators are responsible for dealing with cyber security. Because they can only guarantee together the protection of the systems. Safe components are necessary for this. These must be suitably, secure and safely assembled, configured and programmed by the integrator. The operator must guarantee secure operation over the period of use.

Due to increasingly professional attackers, it is not an option to bury one's head in the sand and ignore challenges. Solutions already exist or are being worked on for a variety of problems. It is important that value is placed on usability. It is important to find the right balance between ease of use and an appropriate level of security. After all, the employees must be integrated into the overall concept.

The PDCA cycle has established itself as the solution. This describes the four phases:

1. Plan
2. Do
3. Check
4. Act

This involves the analysis of risks and the planning of protective measures. This is followed by the implementation. The implementation must then be checked and errors or problems must be eliminated in the final step. This cycle is repeated after each run. It is carried out during product development from one version to the next, during the operation of systems in the context of changes or after a deadline has expired.

For the proof of such implementations, certifications according to IT-Grundschutz of the BSI [26] or according to the ISO 27001 ff. series of standards can be used. This confirms the implementation of an information security management system by an independent third party.

Operators must become more aware of the risks and their responsibility for secure operation. Among other things, the IT Security Act and the specifications for operators of critical infrastructures have contributed to this. Operators must also realize that IT security is not available at zero cost on the one hand. On the other hand, optimizations and developments such as Industry 4.0 are only made possible in the first place.

Therefore, practicable technical solutions and a targeted sensitization of developers, integrators and operators are needed.

References

1. Juniper Research: Cybercrime will Cost Businesses Over $2 Trillion by 2019 (2015). https://www.juniperresearch.com/press/press-releases/cybercrime-cost-businesses-over-2trillion. Accessed 29 Feb 2020

2. Accenture: Ninth Annual Cost of Cybercrime Study (2019). https://www.accenture.com/us-en/insights/security/cost-cybercrime-study. Accessed 29 Feb 2020
3. IBM: 2019 Cost of a Data Breach Report (2019). https://www.ibm.com/security/data-breach. Accessed 29 Feb 2020
4. Passeri, P.: Q1 2019 Cyber Attacks Statistics (2019). https://www.hackmageddon.com/2019/05/23/q1-2019-cyber-attacks-timeline/. Accessed 29 Feb 2020
5. Plattform Industrie 4.0: RAMI 4.0 – Ein Orientierungsrahmen für die Digitalisierung (2018). https://www.plattform-i40.de/PI40/Redaktion/DE/Downloads/Publikation/rami40-einfuehrung-2018.pdf?__blob=publicationFile&v=7. Accessed 29 Feb 2020
6. Siemens: Safety Integrated for industrial safety technology (2019). https://new.siemens.com/global/en/products/automation/topic-areas/safety-integrated.html. Accessed 29 Feb 2020
7. Bundesamt für Sicherheit in der Informationstechnik: Lagebericht 2019 (2019). https://www.bsi.bund.de/SharedDocs/Downloads/DE/BSI/Publikationen/Lageberichte/Lagebericht2019.pdf?__blob=publicationFile&v=7. Accessed 29 Feb 2020
8. Hungenberg, T.: Emotet, Trickbot, Ryuk – ein explosive Malware-Cocktail (2019). https://www.heise.de/security/artikel/Emotet-Trickbot-Ryuk-ein-explosiver-Malware-Cocktail-4573848.html. Accessed 29 Feb 2020
9. Hydro: Hydro subject to cyber attack (2019). https://www.hydro.com/de-DE/medien/news/2019/hydro-subject-to-cyber-attack/. Accessed 29 Feb 2020
10. Hydro: Update on cyber attacks March 21 (2019). https://www.hydro.com/fi-FI/media/news/2019/update-on-cyber-attacks-March-21/. Accessed 29 Feb 2020
11. Hydro: Update on cyber attacks March 26 (2019). https://www.hydro.com/fi-FI/media/news/2019/update-on-cyber-attack-March-26/. Accessed 29 Feb 2020
12. Hydro: Update on cyber attacks March 28 (2019). https://www.hydro.com/fi-FI/media/news/2019/update-on-cyber-attack-March-28/. Accessed 29 Feb 2020
13. Hydro: Update on cyber attacks April 5 (2019). https://www.hydro.com/fi-FI/media/news/2019/update-on-cyber-attack-April-5/. Accessed 29 Feb 2020
14. Hydro: Update on cyber attacks March 12 (2019). https://www.hydro.com/fi-FI/media/news/2019/update-on-cyber-attack-March-12/. Accessed 29 Feb 2020
15. Hydro: Update: Hydro subject to cyber attack (2019). https://www.hydro.com/fi-FI/media/news/2019/update-hydro-subject-to-cyber-attack/. Accessed 29 Feb 2020
16. Ilascu, I.: LockerGoga Ransomware Sends Norsk Hydro Into Manual Mode (2019). https://www.bleepingcomputer.com/news/security/lockergoga-ransomware-sends-norsk-hydro-into-manual-mode/. Accessed 29 Feb 2020
17. Hydro: Building systems (2019). https://www.hydro.com/en-DE/products-and-services/building-systems/. Accessed 29 Feb 2020
18. Symantec: Dragonfly: Western energy sector targeted by sophisticated attack group (2017). https://www.symantec.com/blogs/threat-intelligence/dragonfly-energy-sector-cyber-attacks. Accessed 29 Feb 2020
19. Cherepanov, A., ESET: Industroyer: Größte Bedrohung für kritische Infrastruktur seit Stuxnet (2017). https://www.welivesecurity.com/deutsch/2017/06/12/industroyer-bedroht-kritische-infrastrukturen/
20. Plattform Industrie 4.0: Sicherer Bezug von CAE-Daten (2018). https://www.plattform-i40.de/I40/Redaktion/DE/Downloads/Publikation/sicherer-bezug-von-cae-daten.pdf?__blob=publicationFile&v=5. Accessed 29 Feb 2020
21. https://opcfoundation.org/developer-tools/specifications-unified-architecture/part-12-discovery-and-global-services. Accessed 29 Feb 2020
22. https://www.automation.com/products/ge-releases-global-discovery-server-based-on-opc-ua. Accessed 29 Feb 2020
23. https://opcconnect.opcfoundation.org/2017/10/microsoft-announces-global-discovery-server/. Accessed 29 Feb 2020

24. Reimann, G.: Trendstudie: IT und Automation in den Produkten des Maschinenbau bis 2015. Frankfurt/Main: Verband Deutscher Maschinen- und Anlagenbau e.V. (VDMA) (2015). https://itatautomation.vdma.org/article/-/articleview/792227. Accessed 29 Feb 2020
25. Plattform Industrie 4.0: Ergebnispapier: Industrie 4.0-Security in der Aus- und Weiterbildung: Neue Aspekte für Unternehmensorganisation und Kompetenzen (2016). https://www.plattform-i40.de/I40/Redaktion/DE/Downloads/Publikation/i40-securityaus-und-weiterbildung.html. Accessed 29 Feb 2020
26. Bundesamt für Sicherheit in der Informationstechnik: IT-Grundschutz (2019). https://www.bsi.bund.de/grundschutz. Accessed 29 Feb 2020

Usable Security by Design: A Pattern Approach

Bilal Naqvi[1,2]([⊠]) [iD] and Jari Porras[1] [iD]

[1] LUT Software, LENS, LUT University, 53850 Lappeenranta, Finland
syed.naqvi@student.lut.fi

[2] Software Engineering, Mirpur University of Science and Technology, MUST, Mirpur, Pakistan

Abstract. Security and usability are often in conflict. There is a recognition that security cannot be achieved in real sense unless it incorporates the human factor (usability elements). Despite this recognition, the state of the art identifies many challenges and reasons for conflicts between security and usability. This paper discusses some of these challenges while proposing the use of design patterns to handle those challenges. While justifying the use of patterns as one of the effective ways of handling the problem (conflicts), the paper presents a proposal for participatory usable security design patterns workshop. The workshop provides a forum for discussing a variety of issues concerning the usability and security conflicts while documenting the instances of conflicts and suitable tradeoffs as design patterns for use by other designers and developers. A catalog of usable security design patterns can assist the system designers and developers by positively influencing their decision-making abilities when it comes to conflicts.

Keywords: Patterns · Security · Usability · Usable security

1 Introduction

Security and usability are essential quality characteristics in today's software systems. To address the quality demands, security and usability are considered in specialized teams where the focus of each team is specific, the security team focuses on making the system security as robust as possible against internal and external attacks, however, usability is a minor concern for them. Whereas the usability team focuses on improving usability issues arising with the use of the system while providing a positive user experience (UX). With this specific focus, the need for usable security is realized when the instances of conflicts between security and usability are identified. A classic example in this regard is the password for authentication. The security dimension suggests that the passwords should be sufficiently long, frequently changed, have different cases and special characters, etc. However, from the user's (usability) point of view, such passwords are hard to memorize. If the suggested security guidelines are implemented, they have an adverse impact on the usability of the system, and if not implemented the system security is at stake.

Recently, there has been a realization that security cannot be implemented effectively unless we pay attention to the usability aspects [1]. US National Institute of Standards and Technology (NIST) report NIST Special Publication 800-63B states "evaluating the

© Springer Nature Switzerland AG 2020
A. Moallem (Ed.): HCII 2020, LNCS 12210, pp. 609–618, 2020.
https://doi.org/10.1007/978-3-030-50309-3_41

usability of authentication is critical, as poor usability often results in coping mechanisms and unintended workaround that can ultimately degrade the effectiveness of security controls" [4]. Initially, usable security was considered as limited to the usability of security interfaces, however, with time aspects like, (1) correspondence between systems' internal procedures and user's thoughts, (2) incorporating user values into security design [2, 3], were identified as important aspect to be considered in development of simultaneously usable and secure systems. With correspondence between the system's internal procedures and human thoughts, it is meant that there should be compliance between user perceptions and the way security procedures are performed on the system. Such compliance could be achieved in two ways, (1) training the users, and, (2) designing the security systems while considering the human aspects, thereby decreasing the chances of human errors as the system works the same way as the user thinks it does.

Similarly, incorporating user values into security design can also contribute towards implementing security effectively. In the development of security systems, the goals are set by experts who are unaware that users might have different priorities and values concerning security [3]. Certain user value-based objectives associated with security include objectives such as minimize system interruptions, maximize information retrieval, maximize ease of use, enhance system-related communication, etc. [2]. Therefore, the elements of value-sensitive design (VSD) can improve users' engagement with security.

Despite the realization of aligning security and usability in the development of systems and services, the state of the art concerning usable security identifies many challenges. While considering all the challenges identified via literature review and conducting exploratory studies in the industry, this paper advocates the concept of 'usable security by design'. The usable security by design concept is aimed at aligning security and usability right from the start of the system development lifecycle [5]. The concept is centered on the development of a catalog of usable security design patterns to assist the system designers and developers in dealing with the conflicts, thus delivering simultaneously secure and usable solutions. The fundamental question addressed in this paper is 'how do we develop a catalog of usable security patterns?'. The paper presents a proposal for a participatory usable security design patterns workshop [6]. To conduct such a workshop, various templates to be used during the workshop are also presented.

The remainder of the paper is structured as follows. Section 2 presents the background. Section 3 presents the proposal for a participatory usable security design patterns workshop. Section 4 presents the related work and Sect. 5 concludes the paper.

2 Background

2.1 Challenges in the State of Art

The authors [8] state that "usable security assumes that when security functions are more usable, people are more likely to use them, leading to an improvement in overall security. Existing software design and engineering processes provide little guidance for leveraging this in the development of applications". Based on an analysis of existing literature and exploratory studies in the industry, the following are some of the challenges in aligning security and usability during the system development lifecycle.

- *Security and usability handled independently*: Security and usability are considered by different teams, where the focus of each team is specific i.e. the team working on security is focused on making the system secure; whereas the team focusing on usability and UX is focused on improving the human interaction with the system. There does not exist a mechanism where concerns from both teams can be integrated towards achieving the goal of simultaneously usable secure systems, therefore it is a tradeoff between security and usability.
- *Reliant on Skill of Developers*: Handling usable security in an organizational setting is reliant on the skill of developers [8]. Developers are either experts in security or usability. Despite this, there does not exist a mechanism (in practice) to assist developers in handling the issues where security and usability are in conflict.
- *Lack of emphasis during the early phases of development*: Security requirements are usually improperly specified, due to lack of emphasis on security during the early stages of development; the same holds for usable security [9]. The authors [10] argue that system security is usually considered in the production environment by employing protections like firewalls, IDS/IPS, AV servers, etc., which identifies the state of consideration on security during the system development phases, let alone its usability.
- *Existence of suitable technique for assessing adequacy*: Concerning the adequacy of security, techniques like vulnerability scan and penetration testing can be employed to check the robustness of security features, however, there is no such technique for evaluating the adequacy of usable security [16].
- *Constraint to a Constraint*: The requirement engineering community defines security as a constraint to the system's functional requirements [11]. The question is, if security is a constraint to the system's requirements, then usability of security could be a constraint to a constraint, which is one of the reasons that usable security requirements are neither specified nor addressed adequately.

The challenges discussed above often serve as contributing factors to the complexity of usable security problem. Furthermore, the standards concerning software quality in general and usability, security in particular, do not provide any guidance when these characteristics are in conflict. While considering all these aspects, this paper advocates the use of design patterns for handling security and usability conflicts.

2.2 Why Patterns?

A pattern expresses a relationship between three things, *context, problem,* and *solution*. Furthermore, the patterns have three dimensions: descriptive, normative, and communicative [6]. In its *descriptive* dimension, a pattern is an analytic form to describe problems, context and solutions. However, in the *normative* dimension, a pattern is a meta-design tool to identify key issues and propose a method for addressing them. It is a *communicative* tool to allow different communities to discuss and address issues [6].

Moreover, for multidisciplinary fields such as usable security, it is important to consider the concerns from both perspectives. Patterns can incorporate multiple concerns due to their descriptive nature and enable different communities to discuss design issues and solutions due to their communicative ability. Patterns' ability to evolve with time

Table 1. Challenges in the state of art with a description of how pattern addresses it

Challenges	Description	Involved patterns' dimension
Usability and security handled independently	Patterns allow concerns from both usability and security to incorporated before documenting a final solution	*Communicative*
Reliant on skill of developers	Information provided by the pattern including problem addressed, solution, context facilitates the developers in making reasonably accurate decisions in other similar contexts	*Descriptive*
Lack of emphasis during the early phases of development	Patterns can be incorporated right from the beginning of development life cycle and can be used by designers and developers as a meta-design tool for identification of key problems and solution for resolving them	*Descriptive/communicative*
Existence of suitable technique for accessing adequacy	Patterns ability to be improved with time helps in establishing adequacy of the solution presented by the pattern. Even when the patterns are disseminated, they are monitored and reviewed and proposal for amendments can be incorporated at any stage	*Descriptive/normative*
Constraint to a constraint	Security and usability are considered together thereby decreasing the chances of being considered as constraint to constraint or as after thoughts	*Normative*

also makes them suitable for problems like usable security. A pattern has different states, a *proto pattern* is a pattern which is newly documented after the first iteration, and it captures the basic elements of problem, context, and solution. However, after undergoing various refinement stages it is in *alpha-state,* ready to be released for use and testing by designers and developers.

Furthermore, patterns provide benefits like means of common vocabulary, shared documentation, improved communication among the different stakeholders during product development [5]. Patterns provide real solutions by explicitly mentioning the context and problem and summarizing the rationale for their effectiveness. Since the patterns provide a generic "core" solution, its use can vary from one implementation to another [7]. All the challenges in the state of art identified earlier along with how the pattern approach helps in addressing them are presented in Table 1. The Table 1 also presents the dimension of the pattern involved in addressing a particular challenge.

As stated earlier, security and usability have evolved independently as different domains, therefore, expertise in both security and usability is hard to find in one person. Todays' industrial practices reflect that handling the security and usability conflicts is reliant on the skill of the developers [8]. The use of patterns provides a way of assisting developers at work by influencing their decision-making abilities when it comes to the conflicts between security and usability. Moreover, the patterns can be incorporated right from the start of the systems' development lifecycle, which helps in saving significant costs and effort associated with rework in contrast to the cases where security and usability are afterthoughts.

3 Proposal for Participatory Usable Security Design Patterns Workshop

Having discussed the problem and motivation for using design patterns, the question is how we can identify such patterns to be able to build a catalog of patterns for dissemination among common developers. One mechanism for creating such a catalog is a participatory usable security design patterns workshop. The activities during the workshop are to be performed in groups (3–5 participants each). Participants of the workshop are security and usability developers and designers. The key activities during the workshop are presented in Fig. 1, which include:

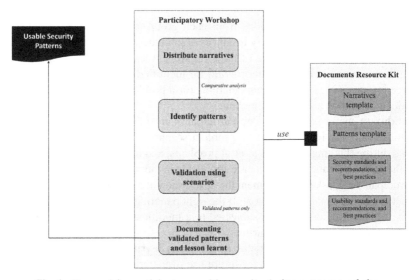

Fig. 1. Proposal for participatory usable security design patterns workshop

1. **Distribute narratives**: The narratives describing a usable security problem are distributed among the participants in groups. The narrative elicits a case story describing a usable security problem. The groups are tasked to design a solution of their own for the problem under consideration. The narrative template used during the first activity of the workshop is presented in Fig. 2.

- **Name of the case story:** A meaningful name for the case story. Name should reflect the essence of the story, so that the reader is able to know what's coming.
- **Summary:** A concise summary of the story for which the narrative has been written for.
- **Problem:** Concise statement representing the problem to be considered. The reader must be able to relate the problem statement with the case story.
- **Context:** Explicit mention of the context in which the problem was presented, this should be considered while devising the solution.

// Fields marked with * are mandatory

- ***Solution:** Based on the context and the problem, you can propose a solution in this field. You may use extra page to describe your solution.
- ***Intended impact:** What will be the intended impact of your proposed solution on the problem in the considered context.
- ***Lessons learned:** Any aspects to be considered while implementing this solution. You may add the concerns raised during the group discussion.
- **Notes, Links and references:**

Fig. 2. The narrative template to be used during the workshop

2. **Identify patterns**: The solutions from each group are subjected to comparative analysis in an attempt to identify instances of good design. The 'Rule of Three' also comes into play here. The rule of three requires at least three instances of similar implementations before a pattern could be identified and documented [6]. Once three instances of similar implementations for a problem are identified, the pattern is documented on a standard template.
3. **Validation using scenarios**: The participants are provided with a list of design patterns (already identified) and a problem scenario. The problem scenario being used during this stage involves a set of problems, and the task involves the selection of the patterns (from the list) that are applicable in the context being considered. The participants are tasked to document the description of a solution derived by applying a pattern in the considered context. If the right pattern is applied in the right context, it is validated; otherwise, it is subjected to a modification to ensure the use of the right patterns in the right scenarios.
4. **Documenting validated patterns and lessons learned**: In the end, the lessons learned and recommendations for future use of patterns are documented. The outcome of the activity is a catalog of validated usable security design patterns, which will be disseminated among the community of designers and developers to positively influence their decision-making abilities when it comes to conflicts.

An example of how a usable security pattern looks like is presented in Fig. 3. It is imperative to state that the pattern is documented on a standard template.

- **Title:** Toggle Password Visibility
- **Classification:** Authentication
- **Prologue:** To ensure secure authentication and users' privacy while preserving the usability element of feedback.
- **Problem statement**: Password for authentication is masked by default to protect against attacks such as shoulder surfing. This is done to preserve breach of privacy and authentication, but at the cost of 'feedback'. If the user makes an error while typing the long password s/he has to retype the entire password without just knowing and correcting the error.
- **Context of Use:** Whenever the password is masked to protect against shoulder surfing and other similar attacks.
- **Affected Sub Characteristics:** The sub characteristics of usability and security being affected/involved when this pattern is applied.
  - o   Usability: satisfaction, effectiveness in use, desirability
  - o   Security: privacy, confidentiality, authentication
- **Solution:** Provide the user with option to toggle password visibility by providing an icon or button. The button/icon should unmask the users' password. The password should remain unmasked until the button/icon is being clicked. The button/icon should be accessible with the mouse pointer.
- **Discussion:** This solution enhances the usability element of feedback while preserving users' privacy and security of the authentication process. The button/icon can be presented at the far end of password field or below it. This would help users in correcting the mistyped character in the password rather than retyping the entire password.
- **Type of service**: Desktop/ Web application requiring authentication with passwords.
- **Epilogue:** Increased user satisfaction, desirability of the service while providing the effectiveness in use.
- **Related Patterns:** To be added from the catalog

Fig. 3. Toggle password visibility pattern

The pattern presented in Fig. 3. addresses the conflict between authentication (security mechanism) and feedback (usability element) in cases where the user is confident that the password is not readable by the adversary. There are instances of this pattern on the authentication screens by major service providers, however, it is documented and intended for other designers and developers for consideration in newer versions of the system they develop. Moreover, other usable security patterns are available elsewhere [5, 7, 13, 15].

4   Related Work

The authors [7] presented a four staged framework for identification of conflicts and elicitation of suitable tradeoffs as patterns. In the first stage, the usable security problems are identified, which are modeled and quantified during the second stage. Standards and best practices on security and usability are accessed while developing suitable tradeoffs (solutions) to be documented as patterns. The documented patterns are applied to the software ecosystem.

Furthermore, the authors [15] presented a methodology for deriving usable security patterns during the requirements engineering stage of system development. The methodology is aimed at handling the conflict from the requirement engineering stage of system development. It does so by enumerating all security-related features. For all the enumerated features the security concerns are listed, and usability concerns arising from security features are identified. Once the concerns from both security and usability perspectives are known, the tradeoffs are explicitly elicited and then documented as patterns.

The authors [12], while listing 20 usable security patterns presented the results after analyzing applications such as Internet Explorer, Mozilla Firefox, and Microsoft Outlook. The authors state "patterns make sense and can be useful guide for software developers". However, the work was limited to listing the patterns and justifying their usage.

The authors [13] presented a list of patterns to align security and usability. They classified the patterns into two categories: data sanitization patterns and secure messaging patterns. Different patterns listed include, 'explicit user audit', 'complete delete', 'create keys when needed', among others.

The authors [14] proposed a set of user interface design patterns for designing information security feedback based on elements of user interface design. In addition, the authors created prototypes incorporating the user interface patterns in the security feedback to conduct a laboratory study. The results of the study showed that incorporating the elements of usability interface design patterns could help in making security feedbacks more meaningful and effective.

What distinguishes this work from others just discussed is that it provides a mechanism to involve a wider group of developers and designers during a workshop and identifying patterns based on their expertise. Though the work [7, 15] provides an avenue for identifying patterns, their scope and intended environment of application is during a project or in a team. However, the current proposal has been designed to hold good for participants from multiple projects and teams. We believe that the workshop proposal discussed in this paper can help attract a wider audience and identify usable security patterns.

5   Conclusion

There is a recognition that security and usability need to be handled together and integrated during the entire system development life cycle, rather than being considered as afterthoughts. With reference to the literature, we identified various challenges in the state of the art concerning usable security and proposed the use of design patterns as a way to handle the usable security challenge. While justifying the use of patterns in handling the usable security problem, we presented the proposal for a workshop for identifying and developing a catalog of usable security patterns. The catalog of patterns can help common security and usability designers and developers by influencing their decision-making abilities when it comes to security and usability conflicts in other but similar contexts.

Developing such catalogs requires a community-level effort and arranging various participatory workshops. We hope to gather the attention of the HCI community during the conference towards establishing a joint effort framework for arranging such workshops and collecting more usable security design patterns.

Moreover, the research advocates the shift in approach from 'user is the weakest link in security chain' to achieving, (1) correspondence between systems' internal procedures and human thoughts, and, (2) incorporating user values into security design. As an instance of the patterns' approach, a usable security pattern was also presented in the paper.

References

1. Garfinkel, S., Lipford, H.R.: Usable Security History, Themes and Challenges. Morgan and Claypool, San Rafael (2014)
2. Dhillon, G., Oliveira, T., Susarapu, S., Caldeira, M.: Deciding between information security and usability: developing value-based objectives. Comput. Hum. Behav. **61**, 656–666 (2016 2016
3. Dodier-Lazaro, S., Sasse, M.A., Abu-Salma, R., Becker, I.: From paternalistic to user-centered security: putting users first with value-sensitive design. In: CHI 2017 Workshop on Values in Computing, p. 7 (2017)
4. Grassi, P.A., Newton, E.M., Perlner, R.A., et al.: Digital identity guidelines: authentication and lifecycle management. Special Publication (NIST SP)-800-63B (2017). https://doi.org/10.6028/NIST.SP.800-63b
5. Naqvi, B., Porras, J., Oyedeji, S., Ullah, M.: Aligning security, usability, user experience: a pattern approach. In: IFIP Joint WG 13.2 & WG 13.5 International Workshop on Handling Security, Usability, User Experience and Reliability in User-Centered Development Processes held during International Conference on Human Computer Interaction (INTERACT) (2019)
6. Mor, Y., Winters, N., Warburton, S.: Participatory Patterns Workshops Resource Kit. Version 2.1 (2010). https://hal.archives-ouvertes.fr/hal-00593108/document
7. Naqvi, B., Seffah, A.: Interdependencies, conflicts and trade-offs between security and usability: why and how should we engineer them? In: 1st International Conference, HCI-CPT 2019 Held as Part of the 21st HCI International Conference, HCII 2019, Orlando, FL, USA, pp. 314–324 (2019)
8. Caputo, D.D., Pfleeger, S.L., Sasse, M.A., Ammann, P., Offutt, J., Deng, L.: Barriers to usable security? Three organizational case studies. IEEE Secur. Priv. **14**(5), 22–32 (2016)
9. Riaz, M., Williams, L.: Security requirements patterns: understanding the science behind the art of pattern writing. In: Requirements Patterns (RePa 2012), pp. 29–34. IEEE (2012)
10. Parveen, N., Beg, R., Khan, M.H.: Integrating security and usability at requirement specification process. Int. J. Comput. Trends Technol. **10**(5), 236–240 (2014)
11. Xuan, X., Wang, Y., Li, S.: Privacy requirements patterns for mobile operating systems. In: IEEE 4th International Workshop on Requirements Patterns, pp. 39–42. IEEE (2014)
12. Ferreira, A., Rusu, C., Roncagliolo, S.: Usability and security patterns. In: Second International Conference on Advances in Computer-Human Interaction, pp. 301–305 (2009)
13. Cranor, L., Garfinkel, S.: Patterns for aligning security and usability. In: Symposium on Usable Privacy and Security (SOUPS), Poster (2005)
14. Munoz-Arega, J., et al.: A methodology for designing information security feedback based on user interact patterns. Adv. Eng. Softw. **40**(2009), 1231–1241 (2009)

15. Naqvi, B., Seffah, A.: A methodology for aligning usability and security in systems and services. In: 2018 Third International Conference on Information Systems Engineering, pp. 61–66 (2018)
16. Wang, Y., Rawal, B., Duan, Q., Zhang, P.: Usability and security go together: a case study on database. In: 2017 Second International Conference on Recent Trends and Challenges in Computational Models (ICRTCCM), pp. 49–54 (2017)

Understanding Insider Threat Attacks Using Natural Language Processing: Automatically Mapping Organic Narrative Reports to Existing Insider Threat Frameworks

Katie Paxton-Fear[1]($\boxtimes$) (iD), Duncan Hodges[1] (iD), and Oliver Buckley[2] (iD)

[1] Centre for Electronic Warfare, Information and Cyber, Cranfield University, Defence Academy of the United Kingdom, Swindon SN6 8LA, UK
{k.paxton-fear,d.hodges}@cranfield.ac.uk
[2] School of Computing Sciences, University of East Anglia, Norwich NR4 7TJ, UK
o.buckley@uea.ac.uk

Abstract. Traditionally cyber security has focused on defending against external threats, over the last decade we have seen an increasing awareness of the threat posed by internal actors. Current approaches to reducing this risk have been based upon technical controls, psychologically understanding the insider's decision-making processes or sociological approaches ensuring constructive workplace behaviour. However, it is clear that these controls are not enough to mitigate this threat with a 2019 report suggesting that 34% of breaches involved internal actors. There are a number of Insider threat frameworks that bridge the gap between these views, creating a holistic view of insider threat. These models can be difficult to contextualise within an organisation and hence developing actionable insight is challenging. An important task in understanding an insider attack is to gather a 360-degree understanding of the incident across multiple business areas: e.g. co-workers, HR, IT, etc. can be key to understanding the attack. We propose a new approach to gathering organic narratives of an insider threat incident that then uses a computational approach to map these narratives to an existing insider threat framework. Leveraging Natural Language Processing (NLP) we exploit a large collection of insider threat reporting to create an understanding of insider threat. This understanding is then applied to a set of reports of a single attack to generate a computational representation of the attack. This representation is then successfully mapped to an existing, manual insider threat framework.

Keywords: Insider threat · Natural Language Processing · Organic narratives

© Springer Nature Switzerland AG 2020
A. Moallem (Ed.): HCII 2020, LNCS 12210, pp. 619–636, 2020.
https://doi.org/10.1007/978-3-030-50309-3_42

1   Introduction

An insider threat can be defined as 'a current or former employee, contractor, or business partner who has or had authorised access to an organisation's network, system, or data and intentionally exceeded or misused that access in a manner that negatively affected the confidentiality, integrity, or availability of the organisation's information or information systems' [6] and represents a major security risk to organisations. A 2019 report compiled by Verizon suggests that 34% of all data breaches involved an internal actor and 15% of actions taken during a breach were misuse of a system by authorised users [32]. Insiders were shown to be particularly common in specific sectors such as the Public Sector (30% of all breaches), Finance (36% of all breaches) and Healthcare (59% of all breaches). It is clear that despite the increased availability of technical solutions and the increased awareness of the insider threat, insiders are still able to plan and commit attacks.

The current state of the art approaches to understand, and ultimately prevent insider threat, usually consider either technical [1,8,11], psychological or sociological [4,12,17] approaches with a small number of models which encapsulating a number of these factors (e.g. [27]). Within this domain, technical solutions usually aim to restrict or detect insider threat activity, distinguishing malicious activity from non-malicious activity; this is often very challenging as, by definition, the insider activity can closely resemble normal, 'everyday' activity. Alternatively, the psychological and sociological approaches aim to understand the factors and decision-making processes involved in initially becoming a threat and then the process of moving from a threat to committing a malicious act.

However, in isolation these approaches are usually not enough to fully understand and contextualise the threat from an insider attack within an organisation. There are also a number of frameworks which attempt to bring together these approaches to create a more holistic understanding of the problem, acknowledging that the threat from insiders is a nuanced socio-technical problem [7,19]. These frameworks can provide an abstract appreciation for the relevant factors but it can be challenging to map this understanding to a tangible set of mitigations which can reduce the risk from insider threat.

Following a security breach from an insider it is important to gather information regarding the incident, gathering data from co-workers including the individual's peers, juniors and seniors, human resources and those in a staff management role, in addition to IT or security personnel. This represents a diverse community of individuals all of whom may have important information pertaining to the incident. With research showing that these individuals are willing to write reports about an incident when one has occurred, giving investigators important information regarding an attack [10]. This research acknowledges that casting this evidence base into an insider threat framework will help to evaluate the incident, however the mechanism by which this model integration could lead to erroneous sense-making.

Requiring this variety of individuals to cast their understanding into framework, may bias individuals' recollections of the events and exhibited behaviours as individuals attempt to cast their story into the model framework. In addition there is a cognitive load associated with performing this activity, particularly with those who are not familiar with the framework being used. These factors can result in a view of the incident which is distorted to fit into existing understandings of insider threat, rather than accurately encapsulating the events associated with the insider attack.

In this paper we describe a computational approach to collecting reports of insider attacks that uses organic narratives describing the insider attack to build a model representation of the incident. It is important to understand that these organic narratives are created by non-experts and represent 'free' text written in 'natural' language. The aim is that this reduces both the security expertise, and the cognitive load required to contribute information to an investigation of an insider threat attack. This computational approach is unsupervised and delivers a model representation of the attack derived from a corpus of organic narratives, this model is free from assumptions about how insider threat attacks have traditionally been committed allowing a rich understanding of new and emerging attacks.

In this paper we first discuss the background to this work, then introduce our approach and describe an experiment validating the ability for our approach to produce models that accurately represent insider threat. We finally discuss the implications of our approach and highlight future research directions exploiting this technology.

2 Background

2.1 Insider Threat

As previously discussed insider threat is defined as 'A current or former employee, contractor, or business partner who has or had authorised access to an organisation's network, system, or data and intentionally exceeded or misused that access in a manner that negatively affected the confidentiality, integrity, or availability of the organisation's information or information systems' [6]. These attacks can be more dangerous than attacks from external actors as insider often have access to privileged information, valid credentials and knowledge of potential security systems. Security compromises form insider actions often follow 4 primary archetypes [6]. The first three archetypes are associated with a malicious insider, these include insider fraud, insider IT sabotage and insider IP theft; the final archetype is the so-called unintentional insider threat which can be defined as an insider who '... through action or inaction without malicious intent unwittingly causes harm or substantially increases the probability of future serious harm' [13].

The current approaches for understanding insider threat can be characterised into three general approaches; the first is a technical approach that aims to understand the technical artefacts an insider leaves on an IT system and from this identify or block activity associate with an insider threat, (e.g. [25]). The challenges in this approach is that by the nature of insider activity, it often closely resembles everyday activity and is often perpetrated by those who have the knowledge to reduce their exposure to technical detection mechanisms.

The psychological and sociological approaches aim to understand any predisposition resulting from personality which increases the risk of becoming an insider threat (for example, [22]), additionally, there are other approaches which attempt to model the decision-making during the transition of an employee to becoming an insider threat (for example, [14]).

The socio-technical characterisation of the insider threat is typically brought together in the third approach to understanding insider threat, using a framework or model in order to understand the complex and nuanced interactions between the different elements. The relationships between these elements associated with insider threat can form complex feedback loops, which attempt to model the individual, the environment or organisation and the security incident itself. These typically acknowledge that technical controls are often insufficient to manage the risk from insider threat [9] and a holistic understanding of the risk and hence controls is essential to begin to manage the risk.

These models of insider threat (for example [5, 20, 23, 27]) typically identify a set of themes as related to insider threat and then identify connections between the themes, typically highlighting causal relationships. These relationships demonstrate opportunities for mitigations or detection, whilst also highlighting possible feedback loops that look to increase the likelihood of, for example a successful attack or an employee becoming a threat in the first place. In an academic sense these models are very useful for understanding the interactions between a variety of environmental and technical elements as well as the effect of individual differences, however when translated into an organisational workplace or as a tool for post-hoc exploration of an incident they typically require a knowledgeable security professional to carefully explore the evidence from a number of sources and then contextualise this evidence within the model.

There are two approaches to post-hoc exploration of an incident using a model, the first involves collecting the evidence surrounding the incident directly in a model with individuals who are providing evidence doing so directly into a model representation. This relies on those reporting the incident to be able to contextualise their observations into a model, insider attacks are often nuanced and complex [7] which can mean this contextualisation is very challenging and requires a significant amount of domain knowledge, it can also result in observations of incident being unconsciously adjusted to fit the model, rather than accurately represent the incident.

The alternative approach to post-hoc exploration of an incident is for an investigator to collect a number of different reports of the incident and then contextualise these within a model. This potentially represents a more accurate approach as by encouraging individuals to report their observations as organic narratives written in 'natural' language allows an individual to represent the incident to the best of their ability. However, this approach requires a significantly skilled individual to gather this information and contextualise it within a model, this will typically be a security domain expert. They will likely have individual bias as to what is expecting to be seen, based on both previous experience and the common threads within the model itself. This confirmation bias will potentially result in a model representation which is a convolution of both the individual reports and what the security professional is expecting to see and has seen in the past.

The approach outlined in this paper attempts to support this second approach to the post-hoc exploration of a security incident by automatically generating a model representation of the reports of an insider attack. In our approach we have focused on taking organic narrative reports, these are a narrative that links all actions and actors which provides more information about the incident and the protagonists as the narrative continues (rather than an episodic narrative which considers a report constructed of a number of small incidents)—in our experiments performed with non-experts it is clear that non-experts tend to construct reports of these attacks as organic narratives. By computationally summarising these documents into a model representation our approach simplifies this task and also removes elements of cognitive bias from the model synthesis, we also anticipate that it should be able to resolve new attack vectors previously unseen as the approach purely considers the corpus of natural, organic narratives from the attack rather than previous examples of attacks.

2.2   Natural Language Processing

Natural Language Processing (NLP) is a collection of methods to computationally process and understand human language [24]. NLP is used for many applications that involve natural language such as machine translation [16], question answering [16], information retrieval [30], speech recognition [31] and speech production [31]. These allow computational activities to infer, enrich or perform other operations on human-generate texts.

These approaches typically exploit a large corpora (collection of documents) to build statistical, computational models of the text. These models can then either be used to generate new insight from an existing corpus, or by applying the models to previously unseen text and generate new insight as evidence is gathered.

One popular approach to information retrieval and understanding the content large documents is the use of Topic Modelling [18]. A topic model groups statistically related words, in essence creating a statistical representation of what a piece of text is 'about'. The most common algorithm used to create topic models is the LDA (Latent Dirichlet Allocation) algorithm [3]. The LDA algorithm assumes that every document contains a number of topics, and every unique word has a probability of being in every topic. Some words are more discriminative than others, meaning the presence is more indicative of a text being related to a particular topic. It should be noted that this is an unsupervised technique, individual topics are not 'curated' they are statistical representations that elements to emerge from the corpus.

It is common practice in Natural Language Processing to perform a set of preprocessing tasks to normalise and prepare the corpus. This ensures that the topic modelling approach is efficient and also increases the performance of the model itself. First stopwords are removed, for example an English stopword list contains the most common English words that do not provide additional information for topic modelling but slow down the training process, these include words such as: 'the', 'a', 'to', 'of'. Stopwords can also be domain specific, as some words in certain contexts can similarly provide no additional information for example when analysing news articles potential stopwords could include 'BBC' or other news organisations [21]. Next the tense of text is normalised using stemming, for example this process normalises 'walk', 'walking' and 'walked' to 'walk', for topic modelling tense does not offer additional context [24]. These processes are important to reduce the cost of training models and to ensure the output topic models represent the most important words in the text and are standard practice when using topic models [18].

The use of topic models to identify the relevant topics in human-generated text provides an ideal approach to ingesting reports of insider threat, this allows individuals to generate their own descriptions of what occurred in their own writing style. This approach to creating narratives reduces the cognitive load of those generating the reports, NLP can then be used to extract the topics which appear across the entire set of narratives. We could hypothesise that these topics would include topics related to, for example, the method used to conduct the attack, the potential impact of the attack, information about the individual and even social elements relating to the perpetrator and their interactions with other staff members. This unsupervised approach will create topics which are derived from the statistical relationships between words in the text rather than a security professional who may be influenced by the existing body of knowledge and what is expected to be seen or confirmation bias [26].

3   Method

The method can be separated into a data gathering phase and three main steps. During the data gathering phase 2 corpora are created:

1. A corpus of insider threat cases taken from news articles
2. A corpus of reports relating to a single insider threat case, these are the organic narratives from observers of the incident

Once these corpora have been collected the main three stages of the modelling approach can be applied, first the creation and labelling of a corpus of individual insider threat reports, second the creation and tuning of a final topic model, and finally the creation of the final mapped report corpus. This full method is shown visually in Fig. 1.

3.1   Data Gathering

As previously discussed two corpora are required for this method, first a corpus of many different types of insider threat cases, which are used to generate a topic

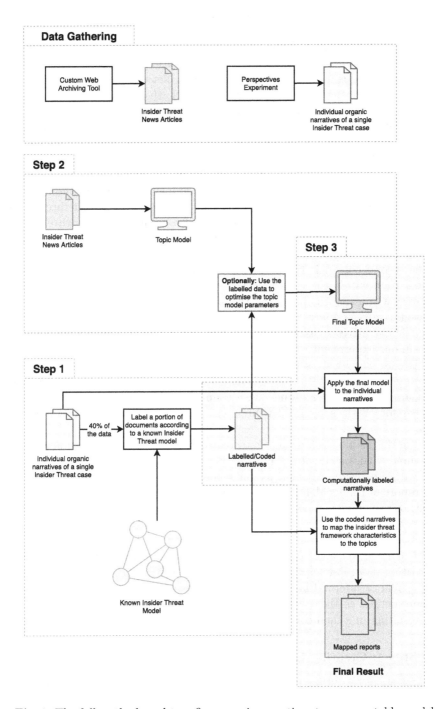

Fig. 1. The full method used to refine organic narratives to a computable model

model. This model encapsulates the various elements of an insider attack from different attacks, that could be written about, for example how the attack was performed, who perpetrated the attack, whether or not the insider has accomplices etc. These are used to build a model to computationally 'understand' insider threat and is labelled as `Insider Threat News Articles` in Fig. 1. The second corpus are the reports of a single incident, these are written as organic narratives and are the corpus we wish to explore.

To create the initial corpus a number of internet sites were identified that report on insider attacks documented on news sites, this includes mainstream news (e.g. BBC News), technology specific sites (e.g. ZDNet) and security specific sites (e.g. Naked Security). A custom web archiving tool was created and these were gathered automatically, this corpus was supplemented by a complex web-scraper that used machine-learning to identify articles about insider threat from news feeds [28]. This creates the final corpus, with a range of insider threat cases all following a similar writing style (that of news articles), with a total document count of 2,700 articles.

The second corpus is the corpus of organic narratives we wish to explore, in application within the workplace these will be gathered from any number of employees witnessing the incidents, the after-effects of the attack or the preceding events, or indeed have simply met the perpetrator. To simulate this corpus of organic narratives a case of insider threat attack was identified from the literature. In our experiment we chose an example case from Nurse et al. [27] (Case 1), this case was ideal as the insider threat model had already been applied, there were clear witnesses to the insider attack and the case matched the insider threat archetype 'Insider Fraud' [6], a common insider threat attack. This corpus, therefore, is the same insider threat case written with many different writing styles.

Using this as a basis a dramatic recreation was produced presenting the case from three witnesses creating multiple perspectives on the same event. These three witnesses were presented as audio recordings, one witness presented as a news report of the incident, one was presented as relating to a colleague of the perpetrator the final perspective represented the perspective of the event from an IT professional. These three recordings were co-created with professionals in the respective domains to ensure the perspectives were relevant. Study participants were then asked to listen to or read these perspectives and retell the story in their own writing style. Participants were encouraged to write however they preferred using formal or informal language, bullet points or full sentences and as few or as many details as they wanted. Participants were recruited from Mechanical Turk resulting in a final corpus of 107 documents.

3.2   Step 1: Creating Labelled/Coded Reports

The first stage as outlined in Fig. 1 is to create a subset of organic narrative reports of the incident. In order to validate the modelling approach this subset is then manually labelled or coded according to a known insider threat model, in our example the model from Nurse et al. [27]—this also has the added advantage that since the case study is taken from this same paper we have the case study already in the framework as intended by the original authors. In essence each sentence was allocated a code based on the element of the insider threat model to which it was discussing, e.g. attack step, vulnerability, organisational outcome. This was cross-coded by five independent security researchers and the code with the highest majority was chosen.

This provided a 'human-coded topic model', and provides a guide to which the final computational topic model could be compared.

3.3 Step 2: Creating and Optimising the Computational Models

The second step of the computational process is to use the large corpus of reports to create a model related in insider threat, this is shown as step 2 in Fig. 1. This used topic modelling, specifically the LDA algorithm to discover the topics in the documents and create a model for the topics we expect to see in reports of insider threat. It is worth reiterating that this is an unsupervised technique which is solely guided by the statistical relationships between words in the corpus. Exploiting a large corpus of different insider threat news articles which refer to different events, we expect to draw out topics related to a range of insider threat activity, without being reliant on a single case or archetype.

To create the topic models we must choose a value of k, the number of topics. For a large amount of documents this is likely high, although there are methods to automatically compute potential values of k, such as [2].

In this case we do a custom optimisation step which allows us to automatically generate a potential value of k by comparing the characteristics of the computational topic model to the characteristics of the topic model generated by the human-labelling. We make the following assumption, that two sentences that appear within the same code or label are related and therefore we assume that they should appear together in the same topic (or one topic is a subset of the other). Using this desirable characteristic as a metric we can then tune the model hyper-parameters such that this characteristic is maximised. Therefore, the final topic model could have been computed using alternative methods such as [2,15] or with this custom optimisation step. This forms the final output of step 2, from our corpus the final model was generated with a k (number of topics) of 370, and with the removal of stopwords related to both english language and news domain-specific. It is worth noting that all the 370 topics will not be populated when applied to a single case—these represent the putative topics that the unsupervised approach identified as being present in the corpus.

3.4 Step 3: Applying and Mapping the Computational Model

The third and final step in the process as shown in Fig. 1 is to apply the model of insider threat to the organic narratives. To do this we exploit a feature of the topic model called a priori probabilities [29]. This takes a segment of text such as a sentence and calculates the probability of that sentence being 'about' each topic, in our case we simply take the highest probability topic and assign the sentence to this topic. This does mean that some sentences can be difficult to place in a single topic, as there can be multiple high scoring topics. Once we have applied the model all sentences from the organic narratives are associated with a topic.

To evaluate the modelling approach we then need to associate each of these computational topics to the manually coded topics. Since the manually coded topics used a subset of these organic narratives we can identify the topics which contain the same topics, i.e. if a particular sentence appears in topic Y of the human generated topic model and topic X of the machine generated topic model then we can apply the insider threat label (e.g. attack step) from topic Y to topic Y of the machine generated model. This process allows us to add domain context to the unsupervised computational model. It can be noted that this process is not necessarily always accurate, as it relies on a small subset of the data that has been coded in order to appropriately label each topic, however even with this naive approach to labelling each topic we can see that it performs very well.

The output of this final step and indeed the final result of the whole approach is a corpus of organic narratives associated with one insider attack, each sentence of this corpus is mapped to a 'topic' and each of these 'topics' is mapped to the insider threat framework created by Nurse et al. [27].

4 Results

In this section we will discuss in depth the results of this process and the performance of model overall. In this we highlight several results from the model, these results are provided as the sentences from the organic narratives which are clustered to one particular topic and the insider threat framework entity to which it is related. A representative subset of these topics is shown in Figs. 2 to 7. It is worth noting in this section that the original topic model was only trained on a corpus of insider threat news reports and not from the corpus of organic narratives, hence these results demonstrates the training of a generic model that 'understands' insider threat and it's application to a specific 'instance' of insider threat.

When the topics are evaluated, there are some topics that can link to several characteristics from the original framework or the approach is unable to map the topic to a particular characteristics. There are many reasons this could happen, a sentence can map to multiple characteristics or there is no strong link to an existing characteristic. For example a sentence may contain information regarding the behaviour of an individual, this could be considered historical behaviour or observed physical behaviour, and often a single element will have aspects of both characteristics, an example is shown in Fig. 3 where the topic contains both a characteristic of an attack and the vulnerability that is exploited. In Fig. 2, there is no strong link between the sentences and a characteristic so it remains unlabelled.

An alternative

In addition, the topic model, since it is unsupervised tends to be more specific than a human, for example Topic 265 in Fig. 4 and Topic 146 in Fig. 5 show

Topic 6

Closely related to:

- No one of the coworkers believed because she never seemed to be suspicious, only a IT manager did saw something. *(Document: 5d039b5fd1d3a)*
- She said it was from an inheritance, and people believed her, others joked that she gambled and won the money. *(Document: 5d03983ac17c8)*
- She was caught and no one could believe it to be true, especially since she was so generous with everyone. *(Document: 5d024811e412e)*

Fig. 2. Topic 6

Topic 205

Closely related to: Attack Characteristics - Attack Step Goal/Organisation Characteristics - Vulnerability/Opportunity

- come up with a new computerized system but she insisted she could not work with it and was allowed to exempt her Dept. *(Document: 5d03baf2e2694)*
- Despite a recently implemented computer system, designed to avoid the possibility of fraud, the manager was allowed to operate outside the system allowing her scheme to continue for so long. *(Document: 5d036a7f85570)*
- She was able to commit the fraud by manipulating paper based records without detection as, at her insistence, higher management allowed an exception to be made: her department were allowed to operate outside the recently implemented computer system which added a layer of auditing and accounting. *(Document: 5c73c9a927a4c)*
- She began to help IT install a new, computer-based system, and upon realising that this would expose her she used her nine associates and managed to get her team to stay on paper, thus allowing her to continue her theft. *(Document: 5c6fc9bcf2c2e)*

Fig. 3. Topic 205

two different topics which contain sentences humans both coded as 'Personality Characteristics'. However the computational approach has separated these into one topic that described her kindness and influence with a focus on how her colleagues perceived her, the other topic supplements this with additional elements that describe her as 'quirky' and 'flaky'.

These examples demonstrate that the approach is able to correctly identify the various elements and themes associated with insider threat frameworks, however we are also interested in the relationships between these themes. These causal and temporal relationships are particularly important in helping identify opportunities for the reduction of the risk from insider threats as well as better-understanding the 'catalysts' and pathways that enabled a particular incident. A naive approach to linking these themes builds on the identification of the reports as organic narratives in which the report is fundamentally structured in a temporally monotonic manner, with a causal relationship that is linked to this temporal evolution.

From this observation we can then assume that if a sentence that occurs in Topic N is followed by a sentence in Topic Q, there is the potential of a relationship between Topics N and Q. The directed graph of these relationships is shown in Fig. 6. Here we can see strong links between the Attack Step and the Asset that was being attacked and the Skill Set of the attacker; between the Precipitating Event and the Attack; between Attack step goal and Attack step and between all Actor Characteristics which are well connected in the graph.

This initial work demonstrates that not only can the approach outlined in this paper be used to in an unsupervised manner map organic narrative reports to an insider threat framework but also begin to identify some of the underlying structure in the framework. This naive approach makes an assumption that

Topic 265

Closely related to: Actor Characteristics - Personality characteristics

- The employee, a middle level manager, was said to be kind and generous. *(Document: 5d07afae00e24)*
- The news came as a surprise to many who say that she was kind and generous. *(Document: 5d07ad29c4338)*
- The manager is described as kind and generous by her colleagues. *(Document: 5d0481de7bb2e)*
- The news came as a shock to the office because the manager had always behaved in a kind and generous way with everyone. *(Document: 5d037c3adef6c)*
- The news came as a shock to the office who had found the manager to be a kind and generous co-worker who frequently supported those in need. *(Document: 5d036a7f85570)*
- Reports say that the manager was a kind and friendly person and no one suspected her of being a thief, despite her oddities. *(Document: 5d02dc8e97cb6)*
- The woman spun a web of lies to hide where the money was coming from and was kind to her friends and staff, enabling her to keep her secret. *(Document: 5c7f9270c1494)*
- But she was kind and generous to her colleagues and was known to frequently support those in need. *(Document: 5c73c9a927a4c)*
- Therefore due to her kindness and generosity, the fraud seemed out of character and came as a shock to her colleagues. *(Document: 5c73c9a927a4c)*
- A new IT system was brought in which would have made it harder to manipulate the records, therefore making it harder to commit fraud, but the manager used her influence to give her department exemption from using the new system. *(Document: 5c6ecc9f2513e)*
- The manager appeared kind, generous and supportive of people in her group. *(Document: 5c6e877f639e8)*
- The actions of the manager, who was described as kind and generous by one of her colleagues, was discovered after a teller at the bank questioned a cheque she had written for over $400,000. *(Document: 5c6e80c32e77a)*
- Colleagues perceived the manager as kind and generous, but there were some jokes and rumours about where they got their money from. *(Document: 5c6d857487398)*
- A middle manager, female, known as kind and generous/nice and understanding committed financial fraud. *(Document: 5c6d530129acc)*

Fig. 4. Topic 265

Topic 146

Closely related to: Actor Characteristics - Personality characteristics

- She probably wanted the money, but she was a nice and generous person with her employees, like buy food and drinks and help those who needed help. *(Document: 5d079eb114fb4)*
- All of her coworkers thought she was a nice person. *(Document: 5d056c1ca9952)*
- Everybody thought she was weird, but was nice. *(Document: 5d03fbe74cb6c)*
- When uncovered, everyone was surprised because the employee was always nice and generous towards everyone and could never imagined her stealing money for so long. *(Document: 5d03d561c08b4)*
- Staff thought she was a little quirky and sometimes joked about where she got her money, but they never did anything about it because she bought the occasional round at the bar and did other nice things for staff. *(Document: 5d03cbf7e42dc)*
- Co-workers were shocked as she seemed really nice. *(Document: 5d035b56d3d10)*
- Her colleagues were somewhat surprised by this as she always came across as a nice person to be around, although some did point at her being a bit flaky. *(Document: 5c6fee6c3665a)*
- Her colleagues had viewed her as being nice, caring and happy. *(Document: 5c6e9bcfbe44c)*
- The manager was seen to be a nice person, always willing to help and be there for her staff - even though some of them thought she was a 'bit flaky'. *(Document: 5c6d591491dac)*

Fig. 5. Topic 146

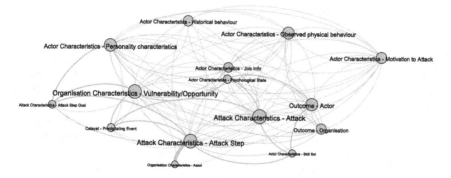

Fig. 6. The topics mapped with the naive approach

there is a temporal and causal link between sentences, whilst this is at times true (particularly in organic narratives) there is also a causal relationship which may not be directly temporally correlated.

5   Discussion

The results presented demonstrate the model's ability to map sentences from organic narrative reports written by non-experts to an existing framework for modelling insider threat. This is shown by exploring various topics, their links to the insider threat model and the sentences within. However there are some areas for potential improvement, firstly some topics do not map well to the existing insider threat model, some topics link to multiple elements of an insider threat model and there are some mistakes made by the model.

In general the sentences match well with the models description of each element, following similar structures, further demonstrating the effectiveness of this technique. For example the element 'Attack Characteristics Attack' is defined in the initial report from which the case study was drawn [27] as 'Manipulating Company Records', although this is more general the majority of sentences within topics that link to this characteristic are related to the overall idea of writing fraudulent cheques as a manager in the tax office seen in topic 340 in Fig. 7. This is also true for the element 'Organisation Characteristics - Vulnerability/Opportunity' which was described in [27] as 'Manual records, easily manipulated' and 'Inadequate security and processing (of records)', in Topic 132 in Fig. 8 we see sentences regarding the auditing of records, a clear example of the inadequate security and sentences regarding the paper based system in use, once again an example of manual records. These two examples clearly demonstrate the unsupervised computational approach identifying similar characteristics that the authors of the initial case study expected to identify.

As discussed above some topics do not map well to the insider threat model, and therefore may not be associated with a characteristic within the insider threat framework. However this may also highlight a missing piece of a framework, emerging factors of an incident which have not yet been considered or as parts of other characteristics which have not been fully understood. An example from this case study is that the computational approach separated the 'outcome' theme from the framework into an outcome associated with the actor (the perpetrator of the attack) and an outcome associated with the organisation. This is an interesting reflection with respect to our understanding of insider threat.

In addition to the issues with assigning topics to characteristics, another issue is the mislabelling of some sentences. For example, consider Topic 84 shown in Fig. 9, the majority of sentences refer to the insider being caught, investigated, sent to court and asked to pay a fine, however, the final sentence 'The computer system was difficult to use and tax office staff found it an extra burden' is clearly an outlier. Although this is an issue, many of the mislabelled sentences are semantically different, this allows these sentences to be filtered out from the overall topic. To reduce the number of these sentences this we take the

Topic 340

Closely related to: Attack Characteristics - Attack

- She was only caught because a bank teller questioned a cheque she wrote. *(Document: 5d07bded75b16)*
- There was a person who was a manager at the bank that some would describe as a nice woman who had been stealing millions from the bank overtime. *(Document: 5d03c707b6dfa)*
- She ended up getting caught when a bank teller marked a check as suspicious. *(Document: 5d039950a0ffa)*
- the bank manager was stealing checks she got away with it by telling everyone it was a family inheritance she was able to hide the transactions becasue the bank used a paper based system she was caught by a bank teller who thought a check looked suspicious the bank manager was caught and fined 60 million dollars *(Document: 5d028986a93c6)*
- A female bank manager was caught stealing money from the bank. *(Document: 5c7939498b4b6)*
- generally well-liked and popular female tax office manager had been stealing from taxes over 18 years by exploiting loopholes in paperwork systems and was very against an electronic system which she probably knew would make her theft harder to carry out and easier to detect, and was caught by a bank teller who noticed/questioned a suspicious cheque for $400,000; there were at least nine other accomplices; required to pay at least $45 million in restitution/taxes and other costs *(Document: 5c6fc0970bcac)*
- A bank teller helped catch her when they spotted a suspicious cheque for $400'000. *(Document: 5c6ecc9f2513e)*

Fig. 7. Topic 340

Topic 132

Closely related to: Organisation Characteristics - Vulnerability/Opportunity

- In the world new system to manage financial transaction, but we have worked old auditing and accounting paper systems, So did not provide & operating new system. *(Document: 5d03c9147ba66)*
- This old system did not have any controls for auditing or inspection. *(Document: 5c77c731bba1c)*
- However it was not straightforward to discover the extent of her fraudulent activities as there was no clear audit trail for her as she had been operating outside the computer system. *(Document: 5c73c9a927a4c)*
- Person was a female middle-manager at a company, operating with the assistance of nine others, managing to abuse the paper auditing (?) system to steal large amounts of money. *(Document: 5c6fc9bcf2c2e)*
- From a work perspective she was deemed experienced, important and knowledgeable enough to be involved in the creation of the new auditing system, but when it was implemented and she protested that it was not workable within her group, and despite the IT Group's insistence, did not have to work to it. *(Document: 5c6d6e434c6a8)*

Fig. 8. Topic 132

approach representing the sentences as a graph using co-reference resolution to join matching actors such as 'co-workers' to 'her office', and 'accomplices' to 'co-fraudsters'. The directed graph from these co-references would create highly connected graph referring to the intended characteristic, and a disjointed sub-graph referring to the computer system and tax office.

It is clear that there are potential improvements that can be made, however the results still demonstrate the ability of topic models to computationally map a set of non-technical organic narratives to an existing technical security framework. Using topic modelling allows for additional advantages such as a model evolving as new reports are added, improving the model over time for a specific organisation.

The initial work in reconstructing a framework demonstrates that it is possible to link these topics together and to create a custom insider threat framework. Although further work needs to be done to explore causal links or temporal links, initial work shows that strongly linked characteristics already exist in the framework.

Topic 84

Closely related to: Outcome - Actor

- Eventually they were caught and found guilt of the fraud. *(Document: 5d07a0d1acdfa)*
- After being found guilty, the manager was required to pay back $60 million of funds, in addition to $3.2 milllion in state taxes. *(Document: 5d079fc2cf7ce)*
- --> Her office was surprised when they found out this news. *(Document: 5d0481de7bb2e)*
- She got caught when a bank teller found a suspicious check for 400,000 GBP. *(Document: 5d04581fba50e)*
- She was caught when a teller reported a suspicious large check, and once found guilty, made to pay restitution to the bank as well as taxes on the ill-gotten gains. *(Document: 5d03998389dc8)*
- Law enforcement officials found that some scammers who were easily manipulating documents without anyone noticing. *(Document: 5d037c3adef6c)*
- a lady has been found to be stealing from her company for over 18 years at a total of 60 million dollars. *(Document: 5d024dc0f1798)*
- As consequence, she was found guilty in a court and fined in the order of millions, purportedly to set an example. *(Document: 5c87a852e0b46)*
- She was found to be manipulating paper based records, and now everyone is mandated to use the new IT system. *(Document: 5c77c731bba1c)*
- The cheque that she was found out from was a 400,000 dollars cheque. Investigations found that 9 other people were involved but their charges were not yet determined. *(Document: 5c6e9bcfbe44c)*
- Despite the co-worker being surprised at the fraud it is indicated that a further 9 co-fraudsters and also been found. *(Document: 5c6e877f639e8)*
- Once found out the manager was brought before the courts, found guilty, ordered to pay back the money with taxes. *(Document: 5c6e877f639e8)*
- The manager was found guilty and suffered sever penalties, including fines of over $60M. *(Document: 5c6e867e1b300)*
- The computer system was difficult to use and tax office staff found it an extra burden. *(Document: 5c6e867e1b300)*

Fig. 9. Topic 84

6 Conclusion

In this paper we have demonstrated an approach using Natural Language Processing (NLP) to computationally map organic narrative reports of insider threat attacks written in 'natural' language to an existing insider threat framework. This significantly reduces the barriers to gathering and generating actionable insight from a wide range of employees within an organisation. Reducing the cognitive load and the requirement for security knowledge we can improve the breadth of viewpoints of the incident and also reduce the effect of any confirmation bias in the model synthesis and hence improve the accuracy of a post-hoc model representation of the incident. In turn, this improved model representation improves the evidence used to generate an organisation's response to an incident with the ultimate aim of making organisations more secure.

By empowering the entire employee base to engage in an exercise, it is also possible to generate a more insightful study of an incident, it is also possible to hypothesis a study where an entire employee base write a short piece of prose of how they would compromise an organisation. These would form an interesting set of narratives that could be used to generate hypothetical models which represent the 'everyday' vulnerabilities that employees note as they go about their daily business.

This work forms a small part of a larger project to use NLP in understanding the threat from insider activity. The aim of which is to create a custom framework for each incident, which can merge, grow and evolve as the organisation experiences different attacks. With the ultimate goal of helping organisations develop appropriate and proportionate security decision to manage the risk from insider attack whilst empowering the entire employee-base to support the security of the organisation.

References

1. Agrafiotis, I., Nurse, J.R., Buckley, O., Legg, P., Creese, S., Goldsmith, M.: Identifying attack patterns for insider threat detection. Comput. Fraud Secur. **2015**(7), 9–17 (2015). https://doi.org/10.1016/S1361-3723(15)30066-X
2. Arun, R., Suresh, V., Veni Madhavan, C.E., Narasimha Murthy, M.N.: On finding the natural number of topics with latent dirichlet allocation: some observations. In: Zaki, M.J., Yu, J.X., Ravindran, B., Pudi, V. (eds.) PAKDD 2010. LNCS (LNAI), vol. 6118, pp. 391–402. Springer, Heidelberg (2010). https://doi.org/10.1007/978-3-642-13657-3_43
3. Blei, D.M., Ng, A.Y., Jordan, M.I.: Latent dirichlet allocation. J. Mach. Learn. Res. **3**(Jan), 993–1022 (2003)
4. Brown, C.R., Watkins, A., Greitzer, F.L.: Predicting insider threat risks through linguistic analysis of electronic communication. In: 2013 46th Hawaii International Conference on System Sciences, pp. 1849–1858 (2013). https://doi.org/10/gdrb3z
5. Butts, J.W., Mills, R.F., Baldwin, R.O.: Developing an insider threat model using functional decomposition. In: Gorodetsky, V., Kotenko, I., Skormin, V. (eds.) MMM-ACNS 2005. LNCS, vol. 3685, pp. 412–417. Springer, Heidelberg (2005). https://doi.org/10.1007/11560326_32
6. Cappelli, D., Moore, A., Trzeciak, R.: The CERT Guide to Insider Threats: How to Prevent, Detect, and Respond to Information Technology Crimes (Theft, Sabotage, Fraud). Addison-Wesley Professional, Boston (2012)
7. Coles-Kemp, L., Theoharidou, M.: Insider threat and information security management. In: Probst, C.W., Hunker, J., Gollmann, D., Bishop, M. (eds.) Insider Threats in Cyber Security, pp. 45–71. Springer, Boston (2010). https://doi.org/10.1007/978-1-4419-7133-3_3
8. Eberle, W., Graves, J., Holder, L.: Insider threat detection using a graph-based approach. J. Appl. Secur. Res. **6**(1), 32–81 (2010). https://doi.org/10.1080/19361610.2011.529413
9. Elmrabit, N., Yang, S.H., Yang, L.: Insider threats in information security categories and approaches. In: 2015 21st International Conference on Automation and Computing (ICAC), pp. 1–6 (2015). https://doi.org/10.1109/IConAC.2015.7313979
10. Forte, L.: Insider Threat Report 2019. Insider Threat Report 2019, Red Goat Cyber Security (2019)
11. Gavai, G., Sricharan, K., Gunning, D., Hanley, J., Singhal, M., Rolleston, R.: Supervised and unsupervised methods to detect insider threat from enterprise social and online activity data. J. Wirel. Mob. Netw. Ubiquit. Comput. Dependable Appl. (JoWUA) **6**(4) (2015). https://doi.org/10.1145/2808783.2808784
12. Greitzer, F.L., Kangas, L.J., Noonan, C.F., Brown, C.R., Ferryman, T.: Psychosocial modeling of insider threat risk based on behavioral and word use analysis. e-Serv. J. **9**(1), 106 (2013). https://doi.org/10/gdrb4d
13. Greitzer, F.L., et al.: Unintentional insider threat: contributing factors, observables, and mitigation strategies. In: 2014 47th Hawaii International Conference on System Sciences, pp. 2025–2034, January 2014. https://doi.org/10.1109/HICSS.2014.256
14. Greitzer, F.L., Hohimer, R.E.: Modeling human behavior to anticipate insider attacks. J. Strateg. Secur. **4**(2), 25–48 (2011). http://www.jstor.org/stable/26463925

15. Griffiths, T.L., Steyvers, M.: Finding scientific topics. Proc. Natl. Acad. Sci. **101**(Suppl. 1), 5228–5235 (2004)
16. Hirschberg, J., Manning, C.D.: Advances in natural language processing. Science **349**(6245), 261–266 (2015). https://doi.org/10/f7kfrk
17. Ho, S.M., Hancock, J.T., Booth, C., Burmester, M., Liu, X., Timmarajus, S.S.: Demystifying insider threat: language-action cues in group dynamics. In: Proceedings of the Annual Hawaii International Conference on System Sciences, vol. 2016-March, pp. 2729–2738 (2016). https://doi.org/10.1109/HICSS.2016.343
18. Jacobi, C., van Atteveldt, W., Welbers, K.: Quantitative analysis of large amounts of journalistic texts using topic modelling. Digit. Journal. **4**(1), 89–106 (2016). https://doi.org/10/f3s2sg
19. Johnston, A.C., Warkentin, M., McBride, M., Carter, L.: Dispositional and situational factors: influences on information security policy violations. Eur. J. Inf. Syst. **25**(3), 231–251 (2016). https://doi.org/10.1057/ejis.2015.15
20. Kandias, M., Mylonas, A., Virvilis, N., Theoharidou, M., Gritzalis, D.: An insider threat prediction model. In: Katsikas, S., Lopez, J., Soriano, M. (eds.) TrustBus 2010. LNCS, vol. 6264, pp. 26–37. Springer, Heidelberg (2010). https://doi.org/10.1007/978-3-642-15152-1_3
21. Lo, R.T.W., He, B., Ounis, I.: Automatically building a stopword list for an information retrieval system. In: Journal on Digital Information Management: Special Issue on the 5th Dutch-Belgian Information Retrieval Workshop (DIR), vol. 5, pp. 17–24 (2005)
22. Maasberg, M., Warren, J., Beebe, N.L.: The dark side of the insider: detecting the insider threat through examination of dark triad personality traits. In: 2015 48th Hawaii International Conference on System Sciences, pp. 3518–3526, January 2015. https://doi.org/10.1109/HICSS.2015.423
23. Magklaras, G., Furnell, S.: Insider threat prediction tool: evaluating the probability of it misuse. Comput. Secur. **21**(1), 62–73 (2001). https://doi.org/10.1016/S0167-4048(02)00109-8. http://www.sciencedirect.com/science/article/pii/S016704802001098
24. Manning, C.D., Manning, C.D., Schütze, H.: Foundations of Statistical Natural Language Processing. MIT Press, Cambridge (1999)
25. Meng, F., Lou, F., Fu, Y., Tian, Z.: Deep learning based attribute classification insider threat detection for data security. In: 2018 IEEE Third International Conference on Data Science in Cyberspace (DSC), pp. 576–581, June 2018. https://doi.org/10.1109/DSC.2018.00092
26. Nickerson, R.S.: Confirmation bias: a ubiquitous phenomenon in many guises. Rev. General Psychol. **2**(2), 175–220 (1998). https://doi.org/10.1037/1089-2680.2.2.175
27. Nurse, J.R.C., et al.: Understanding insider threat: a framework for characterising attacks. In: 2014 IEEE Security and Privacy Workshops, pp. 214–228, May 2014. https://doi.org/10.1109/SPW.2014.38
28. Paxton-Fear, K., Hodges, D., Buckley, O.: Corpus expansion using topic modelling: creating a library of insider threat attacks. Hum.-Centric Comput. Inf. Syst. (in review)
29. Riedl, M., Biemann, C.: Topictiling: a text segmentation algorithm based on LDA. In: Proceedings of ACL 2012 Student Research Workshop, pp. 37–42. Association for Computational Linguistics (2012)

30. Smeaton, A.F.: Using NLP or NLP resources for information retrieval tasks. In: Strzalkowski, T. (ed.) Natural Language Information Retrieval. Springer, Dordrecht (1999). https://doi.org/10.1007/978-94-017-2388-6_4
31. Trilla, A.: Natural language processing techniques in text-to-speech synthesis and automatic speech recognition. Departament de Tecnologies Media, pp. 1–5 (2009)
32. Verizon: 2019 data breach investigations report. https://enterprise.verizon.com/en-gb/resources/reports/dbir/

Predicting Tap Locations on Touch Screens in the Field Using Accelerometer and Gyroscope Sensor Readings

Emanuel Schmitt[1] and Jan-Niklas Voigt-Antons[1,2]([⊠]) [iD]

[1] Quality and Usability Lab, Technische Universität Berlin, Berlin, Germany
jan-niklas.voigt-antons@tu-berlin.de
[2] German Research Center for Artificial Intelligence (DFKI), Berlin, Germany

Abstract. Research has shown that the location of touch screen taps on modern smartphones and tablet computers can be identified based on sensor recordings from the device's accelerometer and gyroscope. This security threat implies that an attacker could launch a background process on the mobile device and send the motion sensor readings to a third party vendor for further analysis. Even though the location inference is a non-trivial task requiring machine learning algorithms in order to predict the tap location, previous research was able to show that PINs and passwords of users could be successfully obtained. However, as the tap location inference was only shown for taps generated in a controlled setting not reflecting the environment users naturally engage with their smartphones, the attempts in this paper bridge this gap. We propose TapSensing, a data acquisition system designed to collect touch screen tap event information with corresponding accelerometer and gyroscope readings. Having performed a data acquisition study with 27 participants and 3 different iPhone models, a total of 25,000 labeled taps could be acquired from a laboratory and field environment enabling a direct comparison of both settings. The overall findings show that tap location inference is generally possible for data acquired in the field, hence, with a performance reduction of approximately 20% when comparing both environments. As the tap inference has therefore been shown for a more realistic data set, this work shows that smartphone motion sensors could potentially be used to comprise the user's privacy in any surrounding user's interact with the devices.

Keywords: Tap locations · Prediction · Test environment · Input modality · Body posture

1 Introduction

The utilization of smartphones has become an integral part of our everyday life. We use them to perform various tasks ranging from highly privacy-sensitive tasks as for bank transactions or personal communication to more casual tasks such

© Springer Nature Switzerland AG 2020
A. Moallem (Ed.): HCII 2020, LNCS 12210, pp. 637–651, 2020.
https://doi.org/10.1007/978-3-030-50309-3_43

as setting an alarm clock or checking the weather. This universal applicability is one important factor that has contributed to the immense success of the smartphone. A second factor is the rich set of embodied sensors, such as an accelerometer, digital compass, gyroscope, GPS, microphone and camera [12] which have enabled developers to introduce highly interactive applications. Location based services, for instance, utilizing the GPS sensor [13] can lead users on the fastest route to their desired destination while health tracking applications [6], enabled by the motion sensors, can recommend health beneficial behavior based on the amount of physical activity sensed. Furthermore, newly introduced augmented reality applications utilize the camera and the motion sensors to enhance our perception of our immediate surroundings resulting in a whole new interactive experience. The motion sensors, gyroscope and accelerometer, which are typically used for detecting the device orientation and for gaming applications [8], can be used to infer the locations of touch-screen taps. As the striking force of a tapping finger creates an identifiable signature on the 3-axis motion sensors, previous research has shown that the granularity of inference is adequate to obtain PINs and passwords [5,15,20]. However, as the motion data used to train the inference systems in previous research was acquired from users in a laboratory setting [5,15,20], the feasibility of tap location inference has not been shown for a more realistic data set that is capable of modeling natural user behavior as well as their changing environments. It is plausible that when a user interacts with the touch screen, for instance, while walking in the park or during a public transportation ride, the sensory data will be effected by this activity potentially mitigating the predictions. In order to address this issue, we propose *TapSensing*. TapSensing is a data acquisition system designed to acquire tap information with corresponding accelerometer and gyroscope readings. After having conducted a laboratory and field study, we have collected over 25,000 taps from 27 participants to investigate if the inferability of tap locations also applies to an uncontrolled setting.

2   Related Work

Tap location inference falls into the category of side-channel attacks as the motion sensor signals are used as a side-channel to obtain the initial position of taps on a touch screen. In literature, various forms of side-channel attacks have been revealed by researchers in the past enabling attacks that eavesdrop on confidential information. One way of spying on electrical devices is by utilizing the acoustic channel [1,4,27]. Many electronic devices deploy tiny mechanics that generate sounds as a byproduct during interactions or during operation. These distinct sounds can differ in their characteristics making them adequate to identify the original information currently being processed by the machine. Researchers have examined the problem of acoustic emanations of dot matrix printers and were able to recover whole sentences the printer was processing [4]. In a related study, researchers investigated acoustic emanations produced by hitting keystrokes on desktop and notebook keyboards. In an experiment 79%

of the characters could be correctly recognized based on audio recordings of the individual keystrokes [1]. Besides acoustic emanations, optical emanations can also pose a valuable source of information for a potential side-channel attack. Most electronic devices, such as notebook, smartphones and tablet computers, provide graphical user interfaces through their own built-in screens. Even though these screens are meant to target the human eye, they can reflect off other surfaces. These reflections can be caught by high resolution camera sensors. In one example, researcher aimed to eavesdrop on cathode-ray-tube (CRT) monitors at distance [10] were the researcher could show that the information displayed on the monitor can be reconstructed from its distorted or even diffusely reflected light. Moreover, a similar approach that comprises reflections has been shown focusing on LCD displays [3]. In this experiment, the researchers caught reflections in various objects that are commonly to be found in close proximity to a computer screen. Such objects included eyeglasses, tea pots, spoons and even plastic bottles. This work was later extended to additionally capture screens based on the reflections on the human eye's cornea [2]. A third way of spying on devices is through the use of electrical emanations. Back in 1943, a research group under the codename TEMPEST, a subdivision of the NSA[1], were able to infer information from the infamous Bell Telephone model 131-B2, a teletype terminal which was used for encrypting wartime communication [19]. Using an oscilloscope, researchers could capture leaking electromagnetic signals from the device and by carefully examining the peaks of the recorded signals, the plain message the device was currently processing could be reconstructed [19]. This technique was later advanced and used in the Vietnam war where the US military could detect approaching Viet Cong trucks giving them an immense competitive advantage over their enemies [16]. Today, TEMPEST is a security standard for electronic devices ensuring that certified devices do not accidentally emanate confidential information [17]. Moreover, research has shown that side-band electromagnetic emanations are present in keyboards [25], computer screens [7,11], printers [22], computer interfaces, such as USB 2 [18] and the parallel port [24] and in so-called Smart Cards [23].

Concerning emanations from motion sensor signals, it has been shown that it is possible to use the iPhone's accelerometer to predict key presses on a regular keyboard when the smartphone lies in close proximity [14]. The initial paper showing the possibility of tap location inference was published by Chai and Chen [5]. In their proof-of-concept study both researchers successfully analyzed the predictability of a 10-digit PIN-pad area [5] based on accelerometer recordings with 70% accuracy. A similar study, ACCessory, predicted accelerometer readings onto a 60-cell grid with 30% accuracy [20]. The most comprehensive study regarding motion sensor emanations is TapPrints [15]. While the previous studies are both evaluated on Android smartphones, TapPrints investigates the tap inference on both iOS and Android platforms including tablets and smartphones alike. TapPrints could show that a 20 cell-grid could be predicted with an accuracy of approx. 80% [15].

---

[1] National Security Agency.

3   Methods

3.1   Hypothesis

Previous research has shown that is it possible to predict locations on a smart-phone touch screen based on accelerometer and gyroscope recordings [5,15,20]. However, since the data used for classification in these approaches was collected in a controlled environment, it has not been shown that the feasibility to predict tap locations also applies to a field environment. We therefore define the following Hypothesis:

H1 The environment of recorded sensor data has an effect on the prediction accuracy.
H1.1: The prediction accuracy for a classifier trained with the data in the laboratory environment will score higher than one trained with data collected in the field.

Moreover, assumptions are made concerning the way the user interacts with the device. A user can either use the thumb to touch or the index finger while holding the device in the other hand. Assuming that the input modality also has an effect on the behavior of the estimator, data sets for both hands will be evaluated.

H2: The input modality has an effect on the prediction accuracy.
H2.1: The prediction accuracy for a classifier trained with index finger tap data will score higher than one trained with thumb tap data.

Finally, assumptions are made based on the body posture a user has while tapping. Overall, a difference in classification results is assumed between standing and sitting.

H3: The body posture has an effect on the prediction accuracy.
H3.1: The prediction accuracy for a classifier trained with taps where a user sat will score higher than one trained with taps where a user stood.

3.2   Data Acquisition System

The TapSensing application consists of two main components: the mobile and the server-side application. The mobile application provides a tap input screen for the user to perform on-screen taps on buttons arranged on a 20-cell grid, which is illustrated in Fig. 1. Each button on a grid references a specific grid class for later classification. While the user enters tap information, the accelerometer and gyroscope readings are recorded at a frequency of 100 Hz. Once taps are entered, the application asks the user to label the data in order to gain information on the body posture and input modality. Finally, all the sensor recordings including the labeled data are sent to the backend application for persistence.

Fig. 1. The figure shows the tap input user interface with buttons aligned in a grid shape structure. The red area on screen indicates where the user has to tap. (Color figure online)

3.3 Experimental Approach

The overall experiment consists of a three step process. In the first step, labeled data is acquired from subjects in the field and in the laboratory. After the data is successfully acquired, the continuous sensor recordings are preprocessed to obtain the portion of recording which represents each individual tap. To extract certain characteristics of the sensor signature, feature are extracted in a further step. These features are then used to train an SVM-RBF and a Neural Network classifier [9,21]. In order to compare individual estimators, as for instance for the comparison between laboratory and field, classifiers are evaluated using a 10-fold cross-validation. The individual accuracy scores of the cross-validation are then compared by means of a Wilcoxon signed-rank test.

3.4 Labeled Data Acquisition

A total of 27 participants were invited to participate in the study, 12 (44%) females and 15 (56%) males. Participants had an average age of 26.4 years (Min = 17, Max = 53, SD = 6.39) and all 27 were right-handed (100%). The devices have been restricted to the Apple iPhone 6, 6s and 7 based on their mutual screen size. The data acquisition is done in two distinct settings:

1) **Laboratory Environment**: Participants were invited to a laboratory room which had a standard office ergonomics setup. Participants have been asked to either sit at the desk or stand in the room while tapping.
2) **Field Environment**: Participants were asked to generate taps using their smartphone at any place they are currently located. For example, this could be at home, at work or during leisure activity.

Besides the environment of the recorded sensor data, the collected data varies in the input modality and body posture. Participants are either allowed to use the index finger (while holding the device in the other hand) or the thumb to generate taps. Sitting and standing are allowed as body postures as these two represent the natural interactions with the smartphone. For the laboratory

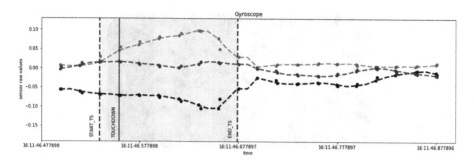

Fig. 2. Continuous gyroscope reading with the slicing window and corresponding times-tamps. The timestamp of the touchdown event (moment when the finger touches the screen for the first time) is used as an anchor point.

study, participants were asked to perform 6 consecutive trials in the TapSensing application, whereas one trail includes tapping all grid button four times in randomized order. It is important to note that each subject was not allowed to alter the body posture or input modality during a trial. After all laboratory trials were performed, participants were asked to continue with the field study. During the field study, participants performed one trial daily on 6 separate days. On each day push notifications were sent as a reminder to participate. Participants were free to decide which input modality or body posture to use.

3.5 Feature Extraction

Before features can be extracted from individual taps, the continuous sensor recording from each trial is sliced to obtain the portion of the recordings which is relevant for the tap. The process is illustrated in Fig. 2.

Since taps on different locations of the screen generate different sensor signatures, the features are designed to capture the properties of the tap. For this purpose, a total of 230 features have been extracted for each individual tap. The Table 1 below shows the complete list of both time domain and the frequency domain features.

3.6 Classification

After the features are extracted for all the tap data acquired, learning algorithms are applied in order to measure the classification accuracy. In this experiment, a SVM with radial basis kernel is used as well as a feedforward artifical neural network [9,21]. To evaluate the classifiers trained in the classification part of the experiment, a 10-fold cross-validation is used with a train/test split of 0.7. As the amount of taps are equal for each subject and grid cell, the amount of training examples for each class is balanced. The standard accuracy is used in this case since the amount of classes in the training data is balanced across all evaluated data sets:

$$A = \frac{TN + TP}{TN + FP + TP + FN},$$ (1)

where TN is the number of true negative cases, FP is the number of false positive cases, FN is the number of false negative cases and TP is the number of true positive cases.

Table 1. Table of features extracted from every tap.

Name	Description
peak	Amount of peaks
zero_crossing	Amount of zero crossings
energy	Energy of the signal
entropy	Entropy measure
mad	Median absolute deviation
ir	Interquartile range
rms	Root mean square
mean	Mean
std	Standard deviation
min	Minimum
median	Median
max	Maximum
var	Variance
skew	Skewness
kurtosis	Kurtosis
sem	Standard error
moment	Moments
spline	Spline interpolation
fft	Fast fourier transform
cos_angle	Cosine angles
pears_cor	Pearson correlations
fro_norm	Frobenius matrix norm
inf_norm	Infinity matrix norm
l2_norm	L2 matrix norm

4   Results

4.1   Laboratory vs. Field Environment

Table 2, shows that the inference accuracies measures range from 0.35 to 0.43 for the laboratory and 0.28 to 0.32 for the field data, respectively. The results show

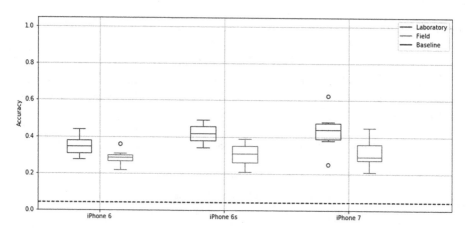

Fig. 3. Boxplot of the accuracy measures for the comparison between the laboratory (blue) and field (red) environment. Results show that all inference accuracies are above the baseline of $\frac{1}{20} = 5\%$ for this classification problem (dashed line). (Color figure online)

that across all devices the mean inference accuracies for estimators trained with field taps were lower compared to the classifiers trained with laboratory taps. The iPhone 7 shows highest mean accuracy scores of 0.43 for the data collected in the laboratory. A boxplot of the results is shown in Fig. 3.

Furthermore, the Wilcoxon signed-rank test shows that the classification results for both environments alter significantly. The fold accuracies in the laboratory were significantly higher than the fold accuracies in the field environment $(Z = 12, p < 0.05)$.

4.2   Input Modalities Comparison

As for the comparison between controlled and uncontrolled environments, the same classification experiment was performed to detect differences in the predictive models between the two input modalities: Index finger and thumb. As the participants were free to decide which input modality to use during the field study, the sample size has been adjusted in order to train each classifier with balanced classes.

As illustrated in Table 3, the results show that across all devices the mean inference accuracies for estimators trained with the thumb taps were lower compared to the classifiers trained with data containing index finger taps. For the iPhone 7, the estimator yields a mean accuracy of 0.54 for index finger samples compared to 0.38 for data representing the thumb as input modality. A boxplot is illustrated in Fig. 4.

A Wilcoxon signed-rank test shows that the classification results for both input modalities differ significantly. The fold accuracies on thumb data were statistically lower than the fold accuracies on index finger data $(Z = 29, p < 0.05)$.

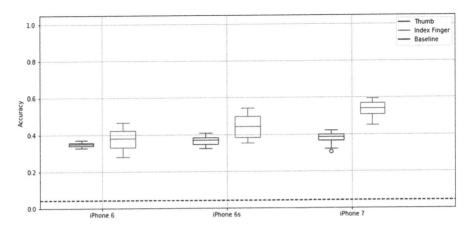

Fig. 4. Boxplot of the accuracy measures for the comparison between and the thumb (blue) and the index finger (red). Results show that all inference accuracies are above the baseline of $\frac{1}{20} = 5\%$ for this classification problem (dashed line). (Color figure online)

Table 2. Classification results for the comparison between laboratory and field environment for the 20-cell grid based on the iPhone type and environment.

iPhone	Env.	Accuracy				Cls.
		Mean	Min	Max	Std	
6	Lab	0.35	0.28	0.44	0.05	ANN
	Field	0.28	0.22	0.36	0.04	ANN
6s	Lab	0.42	0.34	0.49	0.05	SVM
	Field	0.31	0.21	0.39	0.06	ANN
7	Lab	0.43	0.25	0.62	0.09	SVM
	Field	0.32	0.21	0.45	0.08	SVM

4.3 Body Posture Comparison

For the comparison between the two body postures (sitting and standing) the overall training material was filtered based on the device and body posture the user had while tapping. As for the comparison of input modalities, the amount of training material was balanced.

As shown in Table 4, the results show that across all devices the mean inference accuracies for estimators trained with the sitting taps were higher compared to the classifiers trained with standing taps. Only the better performing classifier is shown in the table. For the iPhone 7, the estimator yields a mean accuracy of 0.58 for sitting samples compared to 0.43 for data representing standing as input modality. A boxplot is illustrated in Fig. 5. This is also indicated in a Wilcoxon signed-rank test showing that the classification results for both factors differed significantly ($Z = 31, p > 0.05$).

Table 3. Classification results for the comparison between index finger and thumb for the 20-cell grid based on the iPhone type and input modality.

iPhone	Modality	Accuracy				
		Mean	Min	Max	Std	Cls.
6	Index	0.38	0.28	0.47	0.06	ANN
	Thumb	0.35	0.33	0.37	0.01	ANN
6s	Index	0.44	0.35	0.54	0.06	SVM
	Thumb	0.37	0.33	0.41	0.02	ANN
7	Thumb	0.38	0.30	0.42	0.04	ANN
	Index	0.54	0.45	0.59	0.04	SVM

Table 4. Classification results for the comparison between sitting and standing for the 20-cell grid based on the iPhone type and the body posture.

iPhone	Posture	Accuracy				
		Mean	Min	Max	Std	Cls.
6	Standing	0.30	0.19	0.45	0.08	SVM
	Sitting	0.35	0.29	0.41	0.03	ANN
6s	Standing	0.37	0.34	0.42	0.03	SVM
	Sitting	0.47	0.34	0.61	0.08	SVM
7	Sitting	0.58	0.44	0.82	0.11	SVM
	Standing	0.43	0.35	0.52	0.05	ANN

5 Discussion

For the hypothesis tests, the assumptions made in the methods section will be either rejected or approved based on the results observed.

> **H.1** The environment of recorded sensory data has an effect on the prediction accuracy.
> **H1.1:** The prediction accuracy for a classifier trained with the data in the laboratory environment will score higher than one trained with data collected in the field.

As illustrated in Fig. 3, the results shows that the accuracies measured for the laboratory environment were higher when compared to the field environment. Furthermore, as the Wilcoxon signed-rank tests showed a significant difference between the performance measures of both estimators, both hypothesis can be approved. Aligning with these results, it can be stated that the environment of the recorded sensor data has an influence on the prediction performance of the tap location inference.

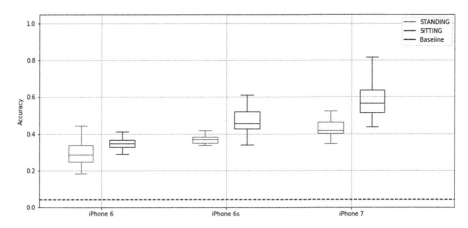

Fig. 5. Boxplot of the accuracy measures for the comparison between the standing (blue) and sitting (red) body postures. Results show that all inference accuracies are above the baseline of $\frac{1}{20} = 5\%$ for this classification problem (dashed line).

Since device motion sensors are capable of capturing the slightest device vibrations, a vibrant environment or activity, one to which subjects where exposed during the field acquisition, is presumably prone to polluting the sensor signals with increased noise. This noise can distort the tap information encoded in the sensor signals aggravating clear predictions of the tap locations. Consequently, as subjects were free to perform tap generation trails where and how they wanted, this freedom is reflected in the recorded data sets with increased variability negatively impacting the classification accuracies.

Moreover, in Table 2 it has been shown that the tap location inference is reasonably possible for both environments with accuracy drops of approximately 20% to be measured for the field environment. When comparing the measured accuracies with previously proposed systems, the system presented in this work yields lower prediction accuracies than, for instance, *TapPrints* [15]. However, as the scope of this work is to highlight the difference between both environments and not to display an upper bound to what is feasible, by interpreting the results, it is indicated that the tap inference in the field is considerably more difficult.

H2: The input modality has an effect on the prediction accuracy.
H2.1: The prediction accuracy for a classifier trained with index finger tap data will score higher than one trained with thumb tap data.

The analysis shows that classification results of the computed models, when comparing the input modalities, differed significantly, as illustrated in Fig. 4. As the index finger taps could be predicted at higher measures compared to the thumb taps, both hypothesis can be approved. It has therefore been shown that the input modality of a tap has an effect on the prediction accuracy.

This outcome can be explained by comparing the motion of the individual input modalities. When a user taps the device with the index finger, the striking force of the finger hits the smartphone screen causing a shift towards the z-axis. When the other hand is used as a support, the applied force is partially resisted stopping the device from tilting. In contrast, when a user taps with the thumb, the striking force causes the device to rotate as the device is held in the same hand. This rotation causes a higher variance in the recorded data which results in an inferior predictability.

H3: The body posture has an effect on the prediction accuracy.
H3.1: The prediction accuracy for a classifier trained with taps where a user sat will score higher than one trained with taps where a user stood.

In Fig. 4, it is shown that classification measures for both body postures, sitting and standing, also differed significantly. The classification for sitting data yielded higher accuracies when compared to the standing data sets. Due to this finding, both hypothesis can be approved. As shown for the input modalities, the body posture also has an effect on the prediction accuracy. This indicates that the body posture poses an important influence factor on the variability in the motion data collected. This result can be explained based on two assumptions. Firstly, it is likely that subjects used their device while walking during the field study which poses a source for increased noise. Secondly, during the data acquisition in the laboratory environment, it is known that subject did not walk while tapping the device. As this data was also contained in the training examples, it is assumed that standing on the spot also enables the user to make slight body movements which can effect the variability of the recorded samples.

With the overall findings in this work, it has been shown that the performance of a tap inference system is strongly influenced by various sources of data variability. Consequently, if an inference system was to be deployed for a side-channel attack, it would have to overcome the user switching input modalities, changing body postures and a potential increase in environmental noise from the user's current location in the field. However, we believe that the performance gap between the field and laboratory environment could be bridged with appropriate filtering techniques or the design of more resilient features, the possibility of inferring tap locations with the help of motion sensor emanation is yet prevalent.

6   Conclusion

In this paper, *TapSensing* was presented, a data acquisition system that collects touchscreen tap event information with corresponding accelerometer and gyroscope readings. Having performed a data acquisition study with 27 subjects and 3 different iPhone models, a total of 25,000 labeled taps could be acquired from a laboratory and the field environment. After a feature extraction on the acquired sensor recordings, classifiers have been trained and compared in order to firstly, determine if tap location inference is feasible for the field environment and secondly, to identify the sources of variability in the collected data. The overall findings have shown that tap location inference is generally possible for data acquired in the field, however, with a performance reduction of approximately 20% when comparing both environments. Moreover, it has been shown that the body posture and input modality pose sources for an increased variability in the motion data. As the tap inference has been shown for a more realistic data set, this work shows that the tap location inference could be used as a side-channel attack to harm the user's privacy. For future studies, it could be investigated if applying appropriate filtering on the sensor data could mitigate the "field effect" found in this work. A second option would be to design more resilient features that are capable to overcome background noise on the sensor recordings. However, as hand-crafting such features requires high domain knowledge, convolution neural networks could be used to automatically extract features instead. Convolution neural networks have shown to achieve high accuracies solving the Human Activity Recognition (HAR) problem [26] in which accelerometer signals are used to predict which activity the smartphone user currently has. As the gyroscope and accelerometer signals could be encoded as a single matrix, the convolution network is able to apply convolution filters on the input to automate the feature extraction process. This approach could not only be resilient against environmental noise but could also achieve higher accuracies than the currently proposed methods.

References

1. Asonov, D., Agrawal, R.: Keyboard acoustic emanations. In: Proceedings of IEEE Symposium on Security and Privacy, pp. 3–11, May 2004. https://doi.org/10.1109/SECPRI.2004.1301311
2. Backes, M., Chen, T., Duermuth, M., Lensch, H.P.A., Welk, M.: Tempest in a teapot: compromising reflections revisited. In: 2009 30th IEEE Symposium on Security and Privacy, pp. 315–327, May 2009. https://doi.org/10.1109/SP.2009.20
3. Backes, M., Dürmuth, M., Unruh, D.: Compromising reflections-or-how to read LCD monitors around the corner. In: 2008 IEEE Symposium on Security and Privacy (SP 2008), pp. 158–169, May 2008. https://doi.org/10.1109/SP.2008.25
4. Backes, M., Dürmuth, M., Gerling, S., Pinkal, M., Sporleder, C.: Acoustic side-channel attacks on printers. In: Proceedings of the 19th USENIX Conference on Security, USENIX Security 2010, p. 20. USENIX Association, Berkeley (2010). http://dl.acm.org/citation.cfm?id=1929820.1929847
5. Cai, L., Chen, H.: Touchlogger: inferring keystrokes on touch screen from smartphone motion. In: Proceedings of the 6th USENIX Conference on Hot Topics in Security, HotSec 2011, p. 9. USENIX Association, Berkeley (2011). http://dl.acm.org/citation.cfm?id=2028040.2028049
6. Case, M.A., Burwick, H.A., Volpp, K.G., Patel, M.S.: Accuracy of smartphone applications and wearable devices for tracking physical activity data. JAMA 313(6), 625–626 (2015)
7. van Eck, W.: Electromagnetic radiation from video display units: an eavesdropping risk? Comput. Secur. 4(4), 269–286 (1985). https://doi.org/10.1016/0167-4048(85)90046-X

8. Feijoo, C., Gómez-Barroso, J.L., Aguado, J.M., Ramos, S.: Mobile gaming: industry challenges and policy implications. Telecommun. Policy **36**(3), 212–221 (2012)
9. James, G., Witten, D., Hastie, T., Tibshirani, R.: An Introduction to Statistical Learning: With Applications in R. Springer, New York (2014). https://doi.org/10.1007/978-1-4614-7138-7
10. Kuhn, M.G.: Optical time-domain eavesdropping risks of CRT displays. In: Proceedings 2002 IEEE Symposium on Security and Privacy, pp. 3–18 (2002). https://doi.org/10.1109/SECPRI.2002.1004358
11. Kuhn, M.G.: Electromagnetic eavesdropping risks of flat-panel displays. In: Martin, D., Serjantov, A. (eds.) PET 2004. LNCS, vol. 3424, pp. 88–107. Springer, Heidelberg (2005). https://doi.org/10.1007/11423409_7
12. Lane, N.D., Miluzzo, E., Lu, H., Peebles, D., Choudhury, T., Campbell, A.T.: A survey of mobile phone sensing. IEEE Commun. Mag. **48**(9), 140–150 (2010). https://doi.org/10.1109/MCOM.2010.5560598
13. Link, J.A.B., Smith, P., Viol, N., Wehrle, K.: Footpath: accurate map-based indoor navigation using smartphones. In: 2011 International Conference on Indoor Positioning and Indoor Navigation (IPIN), pp. 1–8. IEEE (2011)
14. Marquardt, P., Verma, A., Carter, H., Traynor, P.: (sp)iphone: decoding vibrations from nearby keyboards using mobile phone accelerometers. In: Proceedings of the 18th ACM Conference on Computer and Communications Security, CCS 2011, pp. 551–562. ACM, New York (2011). https://doi.org/10.1145/2046707.2046771. http://doi.acm.org/10.1145/2046707.2046771
15. Miluzzo, E., Varshavsky, A., Balakrishnan, S., Choudhury, R.R.: Tapprints: your finger taps have fingerprints. In: Proceedings of the 10th International Conference on Mobile Systems, Applications, and Services, MobiSys 2012, pp. 323–336. ACM, New York (2012). https://doi.org/10.1145/2307636.2307666. http://doi.acm.org/10.1145/2307636.2307666
16. Nalty, B.C.: The war against trucks aerial interdiction in southern laos 1968–1972. Technical report, Office of Air Force History Washington DC (2005)
17. NATO: Tempest equipment selection process. http://www.ia.nato.int/niapc/tempest/certification-scheme
18. Nowosielski, L., Wnuk, M.: Compromising emanations from USB 2 interface. In: PIERS Proceedings (2014)
19. NSA: Tempest: a signal problem (2007). https://www.nsa.gov/news-features/declassified-documents/cryptologic-spectrum/assets/files/tempest.pdf
20. Owusu, E., Han, J., Das, S., Perrig, A., Zhang, J.: Accessory: password inference using accelerometers on smartphones. In: Proceedings of the Twelfth Workshop on Mobile Computing Systems & #38; Applications, HotMobile 2012, pp. 9:1–9:6. ACM, New York (2012). https://doi.org/10.1145/2162081.2162095. http://doi.acm.org/10.1145/2162081.2162095
21. Pedregosa, F., et al.: Scikit-learn: machine learning in python. J. Mach. Learn. Res. **12**, 2825–2830 (2011). http://dl.acm.org/citation.cfm?id=1953048.2078195
22. Przesmycki, R.: Measurement and analysis of compromising emanation for laser printer. In: PIERS Proceedings, pp. 2661–2665 (2014)
23. Quisquater, J.-J., Samyde, D.: ElectroMagnetic analysis (EMA): measures and counter-measures for smart cards. In: Attali, I., Jensen, T. (eds.) E-smart 2001. LNCS, vol. 2140, pp. 200–210. Springer, Heidelberg (2001). https://doi.org/10.1007/3-540-45418-7_17. http://dl.acm.org/citation.cfm?id=646803.705980
24. Smulders, P.: The threat of information theft by reception of electromagnetic radiation from RS232 cables. Comput. Secur. **9**, 53–58 (1990)

25. Vuagnoux, M., Pasini, S.: Compromising electromagnetic emanations of wired and wireless keyboards. In: Proceedings of the 18th Conference on USENIX Security Symposium, SSYM 2009, pp. 1–16. USENIX Association, Berkeley (2009). http://dl.acm.org/citation.cfm?id=1855768.1855769

26. Zeng, M., et al.: Convolutional neural networks for human activity recognition using mobile sensors. In: 2014 6th International Conference on Mobile Computing, Applications and Services (MobiCASE), pp. 197–205. IEEE (2014)

27. Zhuang, L., Zhou, F., Tygar, J.D.: Keyboard acoustic emanations revisited. ACM Trans. Inf. Syst. Secur. **13**(1), 3:1–3:26 (2009). https://doi.org/10.1145/1609956.1609959. http://doi.acm.org/10.1145/1609956.1609959

Private Cloud Storage: Client-Side Encryption and Usable Secure Utility Functions

Akihiro Tachikawa and Akira Kanaoka[✉]

Toho University, Miyama 2-2-1, Funabashi, Chiba 274-8510, Japan
akira.kanaoka@is.sci.toho-u.ac.jp

Abstract. With the development of cloud environments and smart-phones, and increasing awareness of security and privacy, client-side encryption, represented by end-to-end encryption (E2E Encryption), has made rapid progress over the last 10 years. When client-side encryption is adopted, a wide variety of utility functions such as search and sorting provided by the cloud side, utilization on multiple terminals, and data sharing with other users are restricted. To solve this problem, there has been a great deal of interest in technologies such as searchable encryption and order preserving encryption, which allow data to be processed while being encrypted. However, there are few examples in which the effectiveness was discussed by applying these actually to the application. In particular, these technologies were rarely discussed from the viewpoint of usability. Therefore, we focus on cloud storage and propose an application that combines multiple encryption technologies on the client side to realize secure and usable cloud storage that can be closely linked with existing cloud storage services. The proposed application is then evaluated to demonstrate its usability. The application we proposed provides file encryption on the client side, secure retrieval, sorting, and folder sharing with other users. As a result of the user study, it was shown that the usability of the prototype application did not differ from that of the unencrypted application developed for comparison, and the usability of the proposed application was high. Furthermore, implementation and user experiments have revealed a number of new challenges in securely implementing utility functions while providing client-side encryption for contents, and have newly demonstrated the need for applied research in this field.

Keywords: Usable security · Encrypted search · Secure file sharing

1 Introduction

Users have data in the cloud, and it is becoming common for users to browse and process data on handheld devices such as smartphones. Messaging such as LINE and Facebook messenger and cloud storage such as Dropbox and Google Drive are representative examples.

© Springer Nature Switzerland AG 2020
A. Moallem (Ed.): HCII 2020, LNCS 12210, pp. 652–670, 2020.
https://doi.org/10.1007/978-3-030-50309-3_44

As the cloud service became convenient, the importance of that security has become the focus. As a result, the communication path was protected by TLS/SSL with many services, so that third parties other than the end user and the service provider side cannot view the data. Furthermore, as the importance of privacy has also increased, the viewpoint that information should be protected against service providers has been made. Client-side encryption, typified by end-to-end encryption (E2E encryption), has rapidly advanced in the past decade. Primary messaging tools now use E2E encryption from the initial setup.

Cryptographic technology has been widely deployed to society from basic theory through applied research and implementation. As a result, a new perspective of discussion began with cryptographic techniques that everyone can use like E2E encryption. That is usability. Although the cryptographic technique fulfills the security of user data, if the usability is low, the user abandons continuing to use the cryptographic technique, and as a result, the safe state is not maintained. Research on encryption and usability was developed by Whitten and Tygar et al. [36], and became a new research field as usable security and privacy.

The primary function in the cloud service is data transmission, and its security is the protection of transmitted data. Encryption is a fundamental technology to protect its data. On the other hand, the cloud service provides various utility functions other than data transmission in order to handle data more flexible. A typical function would be search. Also, sort multiple data and sharing data with multiple users will be significant utility functions. It also has the function of detecting malware and phishing sites and judging inappropriate advertisement as a security function. When client-side encryption is adopted, it becomes difficult to use various utility functions provided by the cloud side.

As a method for solving the problem, attention is being paid to technologies capable of processing data while encrypting data such as Searchable Encryption and Order Preserving Encryption. However, there are a few cases where they are applied to applications to discuss their effectiveness. In particular, these technologies were rarely discussed at the viewpoint of usability [27].

Therefore, we focused on cloud storage that has abundant utility functions and put the research questions as follows.

RQ1: Is it technically possible to simultaneously realize client-side encryption and secure utility functions in cloud storage services?
RQ2: If the above is possible, is the application or service usable?

In order to respond to these research questions, this paper proposes applications that realize secure and usable cloud storage that can combine multiple cryptographic technologies on the client side and can closely cooperate with existing cloud storage services. Then we make prototypes and evaluate the proposed application and show its usefulness.

The proposed application achieved file encryption on the client side, secure search and sort and folder sharing with other users (Fig. 1). As a result of a user study, it was shown that there was no difference in usability between the prototype application and the non-encrypted application developed for comparison,

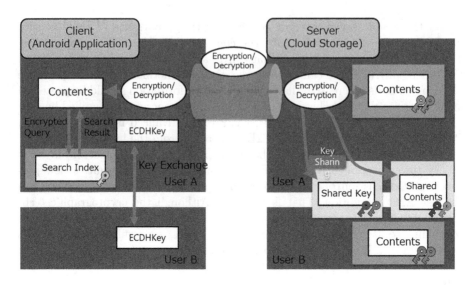

Fig. 1. An organization of proposed application: secure contents encryption and utility functions on the client side without changing the server side function of cloud storage service

indicating that the usability of the proposed application is high. In addition to answering the Research Question by the above, Multiple tasks for safely achieving utility functions while applying client-side encryption are newly revealed from the result of developing prototype application and user studies, and it is possible to show the new necessity to applied research in this field did it.

The contributions of the paper are as follows.

1. Proposal for safe and usable cloud storage application mechanism applicable to existing cloud storage service and application realization
2. A presentation that the proposed application by subject experiment is high in terms of usability
3. Discovering multiple tasks for achieving usability at a higher level of safe utility functions

2   Related Works

Whitten and Tygar made rich discussions on security and usability for the first time. Whitten and Tygar made a fulfilling discussion about security and usability for the first time [36]. Their research investigated whether the technology is safe and usable for encryption technology PGP (Pretty Good Privacy) applied to e-mail. Research on encryption and usability was subsequently studied further by Garfinkel et al. [21–24]. Many types of research have been done, such as applying Facebook messenger by Fhal et al. [20], and compatibility of security and usability of email by Sheng et al. [35].

Encryption and usability in e-mail have been further advanced, such as Ruoti et al. propose automatical e-mail encryption on the client side to reduce the burden on users in 2013 [32–34]. The system Pwm they proposed was expressed as "transparent" to automate the encryption process completely. Although it was expected to realize high usability according to its automation, although its height was shown, another interesting fact was also observed. Some subjects understand that randomized messages are displayed on the screen as ciphertext when encrypted, confusing in Pwm which is transparently encrypted without display of them, Activities such as cancellation of encryption were observed. It was also observed by Fahl et al. that displaying a random character string plays a part in securing usability [20].

Many studies on encryption and usability centering on e-mails and messaging are done, but we will pay attention to cloud storage which occupies another important position among cloud-based services. Kamara et al. academically held the approach of applying cryptographic techniques to cloud storage services and making them safe [27]. After that, various papers were announced towards the realization of secure cloud storage with an academic approach, and the technology came to the height [16,18,37]. On the other hand, commercial services considering security and privacy such as protection of communication paths and use of encryption in data protection on the cloud side have been widely spread. Protection of communication via TLS/SSL is adopted in representative services such as Dropbox, Google Drive, Microsoft Onedrive and others. Besides, there are cases where the server side encrypts the stored data in order to protect the information stored on the server side. Dropbox encrypts with AES using a key of 128 bits or more [2], and Google says that Google also encrypts the stored data [7].

Encryption related to cloud storage is used for protection of the communication path and data protection on the server side, and it does not hide the user's data on the server side. The server side can see the information of the user. This point became a big argument when Evernote announced the change of privacy policy in 2016. According to the new policy announced by Evernote, it was clearly stated that the Evernote side confirms the user's information as necessary for developing new functions. Although it was revised the next day after announcing many criticisms, it became an important trigger that attention was paid to the privacy when depositing data on the cloud side [6].

In order to protect the privacy of user data in cloud storage as well as e-mail and messaging, encryption on the client side is the basic strategy. Client side encryption has already been done with multiple commercial services [3–5,8]. In this way, it is technically difficult to perform encryption on the client side itself. The problem is key management and usability. Fahl et al. proposed Confidentiality as a Service (CaaS) as a framework focusing on usability [19], as far as the authors knew, few studies discussed this point with academic approaches. CaaS is a third party service responsible for data protection and is a model that reduces the burden on both the client side and the cloud storage provider side.

On the other hand, there are not many studies discussing constraints on encryption on the client side. Midorikawa et al. pointed out that the function of the original Web service is restricted when encrypting the e-mail on the client side in the Web service like Pwm and CaaS. They focused on the search function on Webmail service and showed that search could be achieved safely and usable by adopting searchable encryption technology [28].

Many techniques are being studied that can provide utility functions for encrypted data. In searchable ciphers mentioned above, symmetric searchable encryption (Searchable Symmetric Encryption) using common key encryption and searchable encryption using public key encryption (Public Key Encryption with Keyword Search) have been proposed [15,31]. SSE has been studied various applications mainly by the method of Curtmola et al. [17] Its performance is becoming practical [26,30]. PEKS has been developed from the method of Boneh et al. [13,14] Many methods with various functions are proposed [16,37]. In addition to searching, there are also methods that can check the order-preserving encryption (Order Preserving Encryption) [10,12] and the presence or absence of data retention [18], and furthermore general arithmetic operations can be performed by using Fully-homomorphic Encryption [9,25]. Studies on techniques for safely implementing utility functions also proceed, and it is conceivable to consider usability as a next stage further.

3   Client Side Encryption and Secure Utility Function Realization

3.1   Threat Model in Cloud Storage Service

In this research, we examine the threat of cloud storage service focusing on information leakage not intended by users.

In the cloud storage service, it is possible to assume three players, a service provider and a user, and a third party not related to the service. Then, as the occurrence of information leakage unintended by the user, the following two threats can be cited.

– Information leakage to a third party (including intentional information acquisition by a third party)
– Information leakage to service provider (including intentional information acquisition by service provider)

As information leakage to a third party, it is possible to deal with two kinds of protection of information in the communication path between the service provider and the user, and data protection by the service provider side.

Regarding the leakage of information to the service provider, it is not possible to cope with data protection by the service provider side, and the user must implement the protection function.

In order to use the cloud storage service securely, it is necessary to deal with the above two threats.

3.2 Utility Function Required for Cloud Storage and Its Implementation Method

In order to prevent information leakage to the service provider information protection on the client side is required.

When uploading data to the service provider side, the file name including the extension and the file data are encrypted then transmitted. When downloading, the encrypted file name and file data are downloaded and decrypted by the client side application and displayed. Here, encryption of file name and file contents is collectively called "content encryption."

When content encryption merely is performed, contents such as file/folder name and file contents cannot be viewed from the service provider side. Therefore, when content encryption is performed on the user side, some functions provided must be improved to functions that take into account encrypted data and implemented on the user side.

The primary functions provided by the cloud storage service include search, sort, and data sharing functions. We examine how to implement each function corresponding to contents encryption. The sharing features include file sharing, folder sharing, link sharing, and several methods. We focused on folder sharing in this research.

Secure Search Function. The search method is roughly divided into a sequential search in which the entire text is searched for a character string when the user requests a search and an index type search in which information held in the contents are prepared in advance for searching. A sequential search is more accessible to install, but search speed is not high. Search index type has search terms and results prepared beforehand. It is efficient, but if the index information is created without protection, the information leaks from the index. In Apache Lucene, which is a representative example of an open source search engine, the specification of the data format of the index is disclosed [1], the keywords and their search results are kept in plain text, and the contents can be analogized from the index information. In this research, Symmetric Searchable Encryption (SSE) which can realize index protection and has high search efficiency is adopted. In SSE, an encryption index is created in advance, an encrypted query (trapdoor) is generated at the time of searching, and a search result is obtained from the encryption index using an encrypted query. The encryption index may be placed on either the server side or the client side, but this time we decided to place it on the client side to be able to work tightly with the existing cloud storage service.

Secure Sort. There are two methods of sorting, sorting on the server side and returning the result to the client, and sorting on the client side after downloading the data on the server side. The former cannot be realized when client-side encryption is used because sorting is performed on the server side. Therefore, it is possible to apply Order Preserving Encryption (OPE) as a method of being able to rearrange while encrypting it. Since OPE is a cryptosystem that maintains the order of cryptograms, sorting on the server side is possible by encrypting sort objects such as file names and date and time with OPE. The processing performance of the sort depends on the performance of the OPE. In the latter case, it is necessary to download data necessary for a sort on the server side and perform sort after decrypting on the user side, so the performance depends on the amount of data.

Since it is difficult to think that the number of files users can put in one folder will be several thousand or tens of thousands in consideration of efficiency at the time of use, The latter method is adopted in this research considering the performance when it is incorporated in the application.

Secure Folder Sharing. In order to achieve folder sharing with client-side encryption, we need to consider security problems such as leakage of an encryption key. Therefore, the encryption key for the shared folder must be prepared separately from the other keys for file encryption. The shared folder is then re-encrypted with the shared key.

The encryption key for the shared folder (SharedKey) is shared using the key exchange algorithm using the public key cryptography. Sharing of encrypted SharedKey responds by creating a key exchange folder that shares one-to-one with a sharer on the cloud storage, uploading and sharing the encrypted Shared-Key. The folder owner can decrypt and display the shared folder by decrypting the encrypted SharedKey using the key exchange algorithm.

3.3 Prototype Application and Service

Application Overview. We tried to make a client-side Android application that achieves the function proposed in Sect. 3.2. Dropbox is selected for a cloud storage service. Communication between applications and dropboxes is done via Dropbox API. The prototype application has functions of content encryption and decryption on the client side, data communication with the dropbox, sorting by file name and update date and time, search using SSE, generation and sharing of SharedKey.

AES for file encryption, SimpleSSE [30] for SSE, and elliptic curve Diffie-Hellman key exchange (ECDH) for key exchange for shared folders are selected.

A dedicated server independent of Dropbox is prepared for the ECDH public key repository, and a public key is stored together with a list of Dropbox accounts corresponding to the prototype application.

Operation of the Prototype Application. The basic operation of the prototype application is explained here. When the prototype application is activated, a list of file names and folder names, a search window, a sort button, and a home button are displayed. A folder sharing button is displayed on the display portion of the folder, unlike a file.

The file contents, file name, last update date and time are encrypted and stored on the Dropbox. When the application displays the file name, the encrypted file name is downloaded and decrypted. The application encrypts the file and uploads it to Dropbox, and the new folder encrypts the folder name on the terminal side and creates it on Dropbox. When an application user taps on an icon from the list of files, the corresponding encrypted file is downloaded from Dropbox. The file has since been decrypted. Then, an action corresponding to the file is executed.

The search is executed by entering a keyword in the search window and pressing the search button. When a search keyword is input, and the search button is pressed, SSE encrypted query (trapdoor) is created, and the search is performed using the encrypted index stored in the application. Then, decrypts the encrypted file name obtained from the search result and displays the search result.

The sorting can be carried out with file name and last modified date. Sorting is supported for both ascending and descending order. A list of encrypted file names in the folder is downloaded and decrypted. It is then sorted in plain text on the client side.

Sharing can be done on folders. Prepare a share button at the display position of each folder and start sharing setting by pressing the share button. A shared button is placed in the display field of each folder. A dialog opens when the share button is pressed. The user enters a sharer on the dialog. The application then performs an ECDH key exchange with the incoming peer.

Next, the application downloads the data of the sharing target folder from the drop box and decrypts it. Then generate SharedKey, encrypt and upload all the folder data with SharedKey. If a folder for key exchange has already been generated between sharing users, SharedKey is encrypted with the recipient's ECDH public key and uploaded. If it is not created, a newly created folder is created, and the shared setting is made using Dropbox API Upload SharedKey encrypted later by ECDH. Also, share settings encrypted with SharedKey using the Dropbox API. The shared folder for key exchange is not displayed on the application screen.

4   User Study

In considering the usability of the proposed application which realized various utility functions using encryption, we made one hypothesis.

Hypothesis: Due to the development of Android hardware and encryption technology, the performance of various types of encryption does not affect usability.

An user study were conducted to verify the hypothesis.

4.1   Study Overview

A user study is conducted centering on semi-structured interviews using a total of two Android applications. In order to observe the relationship between the required time for the study and the usability, the participants were asked to measure the required time for each item of tasks. An another android application with different functions were created as a comparison target for the usability evaluation of the client-side encrypted cloud storage service.

The behavior in the study is video-captured and qualitative analysis is performed using the text from the interview content and the video content.

4.2 Ethical Considerations

In the user study, we received approval from the relevant internal review board (IRB) within the university. We obtained informed consent from all participants to take part in the study and to have the interviews video recorded.

4.3 Study Procedure

The user study was conducted after explaining the purpose of the study and the task. Then participants are interviewed and related questions after complete tasks.

In order to analyze the usability of multiple utility functions, multiple tasks were prepared. Also, some tasks were performed under the direction of the experimenter.

i) Confirmation of file contents: Opening a file and contents confirmation of the file instructed by the experimenter
ii) Sort of files in a folder: Sort by date and time of the last update of folder instructed by experimenter and answer of the latest file name
iii) Search by keyword: Search is performed using the keyword specified by the experimenter, and the number of search results is answered.
iv) Folder sharing 1: The experimenter performs folder sharing with the participant, and the participant confirms the shared folder contents
v) Folder sharing 2: The participant performs folder sharing to the folder specified by the experimenter, and the experimenter confirms the shared folder contents

The participants themselves measured the time required for each task using another Android device.

In the interview, firstly basic questions about application usability are made. Also about actual feeling and factors of stress in using the application, efficiency as the application of online storage, awareness of security in using online service, and execution time when using experimental application, are asked.

The files used in the experiment were copyright-free English text files and were used in such a way that they could be understood as files for subjects and experimenters.

Table 1. Pariticipants information of the user study

Participant ID	Department	Gender	App
P1	Information Science	Female	CryptApp
P2	Information Science	Male	CryptApp
P3	Information Science	Male	CryptApp
P4	Information Science	Male	CryptApp
P5	Information Science	Female	CryptApp
P6	Information Science	Male	CryptApp
P7	Information Science	Male	PlainApp
P8	Information Science	Female	PlainApp
P9	Information Science	Male	PlainApp
P10	Information Science	Female	PLainApp
P11	Information Science	Male	PlainApp

4.4   Applications for the Study

In the user study, two applications were developed. One is an Android application "CryptApp" that applies encryption technology to the three utility functions of search, sort, and folder sharing in addition to client-side encryption of content. The other is an application "PlainApp" that uses the same utility function without applying encryption technology. The look & feel of the two applications are identical so that there is no difference in usability due to the UI.

CryptApp is an application that supports search, sort, and folder sharing functions with client-side encryption. The search function is implemented using SimpleSSE [30], and the search index is stored in the local storage of the device. The sort function decrypts the file name list after downloading it from Dropbox, and sorts and displays it on the terminal side. The folder sharing function is realized by encrypting the shared folder with SharedKey, exchanging the SharedKey using ECDH, and passing the encryption key for the shared folder.

4.5   Recruitment of Participants

Recruitment of participants was conducted from 17th December 2018 to 25th January 2019 according to the university registration system and the internal bulletin board. The participants' information is shown in Table 1. Rewards were considered as 500 yen book cards after reviewing from multiple viewpoints.

5   Study Results and Discussion

5.1   Time Required for Tasks

The average time of each task in the user study is summarized in Table 2.

Table 2. The average time of each task in the user study

Task ID	Task	PlainApp (s)	CryptApp (s)
i	File contents confirmation	10.338	10.178
ii	Sort	18.687	21.708
iii	Search	11.826	12.837
iv	Folder sharing 1	33.027	53.813
v	Folder sharing 2	24.599	49.474

When comparing the difference in the average time of each task between the CryptApp and PlainApp, the task with the most significant difference was the folder sharing tasks (Task iv and v). From the table, it can be confirmed that the time taken for folder sharing of CryptApp takes 20 s or more as compared with PlainApp. The reason why the difference between the two types of applications is more than 20 s is mainly due to the download and upload processes performed during the sharing process of the encrypted application, not the encryption process. When sharing a folder with an encrypted application, once the shared file is downloaded from Dropbox and decrypted. After that, processing is performed such as uploading after encryption with the shared key. Other than this download and upload process, CryptApp is using Dropbox API in the same way as PlainApp, so it seems unlikely to make a big difference.

5.2   Consideration of Categories Classified from Coding

To analyze text obtained from interview, we followed a standard coding process. Based on the 154 responses obtained in the questions about the study, the coding process was performed. As a result, 9 categories are obtained in total. We show the result of analyzing the characteristic thing in each concept.

Function Understanding. The answers included in this category can be broadly divided into two types: "understand how to operate the application" and "understand prior knowledge before operating the application." The answer regarding the understanding of the operation method is further divided into two types of opinion. The first is the opinion that the operation method is simple and anyone can use it immediately, as follows.

> *"Since it's simple, you can see it with a glance" (P4, CryptApp)*
> *"The operation is similar to other applications. How to use comes in." (P10, PlainApp)*

Next is the opinion that support may be needed depending on the experience of using PC and smartphone, as follows.

"If you have used this kind of app, I don't think you need support." (P6, CryptApp)
"I think that the elderly people need to explain about the operation after tapping and the function such as login." (P7, PlainApp)

The majority of participants answered that they did not need prior knowledge before operating the application. Some participants thought that they needed to learn about folder and cloud functions.

"I thought that there was no problem except in English" (P1, CryptApp)
"I don't need to learn much, but I need to learn more about folders and other concepts." (P7, PlainApp)

Only one participant answered that knowledge about encryption was necessary. The participant also worried that the folder sharing function would make the encryption function unavailable.

"Some peripheral knowledge of encryption and sharing may be necessary. Knowledge such as disabling encryption with the share function may be better." (P4, CryptApp)

Efficiency. This category classified answers on cloud storage efficiency. Many of the answers included in this category were positive.

Although the negative opinion that the efficiency was not good or bad was not confirmed from either application users, some participants answered that it could not be compared because of insufficient comparison materials, as follows.

"I do not know whether it is efficient because I do not know the regular." (P5, CryptApp)
"I did not know only in this study because I did not install this app myself." (P10, PlainApp)

Processing Time. In this category, answers about the execution time of the application used in the study are classified. Among the answers from 6 participants using CryptApp, there are some responses felt that the processing time for folder sharing was slow.

"I felt that the folder sharing was somewhat slow. I did not feel anything else except that." (P3, CryptApp)
"The processing is long compared to the normal application. Specifically, the share function was a bit slow. The other part did not feel particularly long waiting time." (P4, CryptApp)

On the other hand, some participants answered that they did not feel anything about the processing time. A point common to all CryptApp users is that they do not particularly feel anything other than the processing of the folder sharing part.

As for the answers of 5 participants using PlainApp, there were multiple participants who felt that processing of folder sharing was slow as well as CryptApp. There were also participants who mentioned "speed of opening file" that did not appear from participants using CryptApp.

"I felt that the part of folder sharing took so long. The only part I bothered was folder sharing." (P8, PlainApp)

Stress. This category classifies the answers regarding the stress felt when using the applications. Most of the classified answers were "the stress was not felt," but there was a participant who answered that he/she felt the stress greatly because the application UI and the file name/file contents were written in English.

"I can not understand where I should press, because it's all in English. I could not use English parts." (P8, PlainApp)

There were no participants who answered that they felt stressed except in English, which indicates that there were no participants who felt stress in the function of the application.

Security Awareness and Encryption. This category classifies answers about security awareness and encryption. Concerning security awareness, most of the participants had not been aware of cloud storage security before conducting the study. Few participants were aware of the threat viewed by the service provider.

"What should I do if I download a suspicious file?" (P1, CryptApp)
"I have thought that it is safe when I download it. The user side has never thought that this information would leak." (P11, PlainApp)

The only participant who answered that he/she was aware of the threat that the service provider view data, had thought that the possibility but not as a threat.

"I've noticed a little bit. I wonder if the data uploaded on the Internet is really not completely seen by other people. I wondered if there is something seen by the service provider side. I do not feel the threat."(P2, CryptApp)

For the encryption function, most of the participants wanted to use it. It has been confirmed that many participants want to use encrypted applications if the functional aspect is the same as an existing application.

"I thought that encryption is necessary because the content can be viewed with simple security." (P2, CryptApp)
"I have used Dropbox. The application I used is the same as Dropbox, so I want to use it if it is highly secure." (P3, CryptApp)

General Usability. This category classifies answers regarding the usability of the application. Most of the answers classified into this category are positive opinions to the application, and both application users have said that they were "easy to use", "simple" and "easy to understand".

Function Usability. This category classifies answers regarding usability of application with emphasis on functionality. The answer to the function were both pros and cons. Most of the negative opinions about the function were about the app UI. There was no particular mention of cloud storage functionality. On the contrary, there were positive opinions that could be used in the same way as the existing Dropbox application. The participant who answered that the cloud storage functions are inconvenient was not confirmed.

> *"I thought that sorting, moving folders and decryption were well integrated." (P4, CryptApp)*
> *"All the necessary functions such as sorting and searching are available." (P8, PlainApp)*

Contradiction. The participants did not feel any contradiction in the function or behavior of the application, as both application users have stated that "I did not feel any contradiction in particular" and "there was nothing that I thought was contradictory."

5.3 Consideration on User Study Results

From the analysis results of each category, there was no big denial of usability from the viewpoint of the encryption technology applied utility functions and client encryption. As the negative aspects were also mentioned for PlainApps that did not use encryption, they were not due to the functionality of the proposed application, but relying on the essential aspects of cloud storage and its utility functionality.

6 Findings and Future Issues

At the time of prototyping of the proposed application, at the time of user study, and at the time of analysis, some issues which are different from the research purpose but thought to be solved in future research have become clear. We will organize them in this chapter.

6.1 Problems Related to Cryptographic Techniques for Utility Functions

We summarized the issues to be solved when implementing cryptographic techniques in utility functions. In the future, it is considered that the solution is a vital issue as this field advances.

Index Update at File Movement. In a system using a search index, when the user moves the file location, it is necessary to change the file path information of the search result. When performing a search using an index on the client side when data is not at hand like cloud storage, it is necessary to continually monitor the movement of data on online storage and reflect it in the local index in real time. It may be a burden on the client side.

Index Update at Sharing and Releasing Sharing. Sharing files and folders on cloud storage allow users who have granted to view data of other users. Therefore, it is necessary to add shared files and folders to the search index as well as adding files and folders by themselves. The addition to the index can be performed in the same way as when adding data itself, but it is difficult to achieve with a simple mechanism at the time of sharing cancellation. If sharing is canceled by the other user who has set sharing, the information of the corresponding file or folder should be deleted from the index, but it is difficult to judge it from the index itself and delete the index appropriately. For example, it is conceivable to monitor data on online storage in real time, but it is also an issue whether it is possible to appropriately delete only information related to deleted files and folders from index data.

Presentation of Data Information at Approval Timing of Sharing. Generally, the sharing function of the cloud storage service sends a sharing request to a user who wants to share. The user who received the request performs sharing after confirming the data to be shared. For example, Dropbox shows a folder or a file name to a user who received a request to share.

In the model of this research, because sharing of the SharedKey is not complete at the start of sharing, the file or folder name cannot be decrypted. Since the sharer can decrypt and view the file or folder name only after allowing the sharing request, the sharer must permit the sharing request while the file or folder name is unclear.

As a solution method, it is conceivable to encrypt and decrypt only the file or folder name by another mechanism and to present it to the other party before allowing to share. Since the presentation of shared data information at the approval timing is partial information leakage. Therefore, the issue of how much information leakage is tolerable comes out.

Key Management for Shared Keys. In the application implemented in this study, one shared key is created for each folder sharing, so the number of shared keys increases while using it. The burden of key management becomes high. Key management is considered to be important, as it is necessary to manage correspondence tables between shared folders and shared keys.

6.2   Problems Related to Cloud Storage Service Specification

Several issues specific to cloud storage services have become apparent. We will explain the issues that became apparent while using Dropbox used in this prototype application.

Specification of Sharing Cancellation. In the Dropbox API specification, different internal processes are performed on the host side (sharing setting side) and the guest side when sharing is canceled.

When the host side cancels sharing, the specified folder is returned from the shared folder to the regular folder, and all the members sharing the folder are unshared. On the other hand, when the guest side cancels the sharing, the process is finished only by releasing the sharing from the specified folder (the access is disabled), and the remaining members are not affected. When the host and the guest share one-to-one, and sharing is canceled on the guest side, although only the host can access, the folder is still a shared folder. In this case, the host has a folder encrypted with a key different from the host's own key although there is no other shared member. The complexity of key management is expected to increase. Therefore, we think that different consideration is necessary on the host side and the guest side when using encryption.

Process When Adding Files to Shared Folder. When a file is added to a shared folder, Dropbox does not explicitly notify the client side of the event occurrence, so the application side needs its own event handler.

6.3   Limitations

There are some limitations in the application proposed in this paper and the user study. Here, we aim to clarify the contribution of this research by arranging them.

Number of Participants. There were 11 participants in the user study, of which 5 were using PlainApp and 6 were using CryptApp. It is a study that can not be said that the number of participants is large. According to Nielsen et al., It has been analyzed that 85% of usability problems can be found by conducting a user study with 5 participants [29]. It is not always consistent with the results of Nielsen et al. because the studies conducted in this paper are related to security and are studies using Android as a platform, though, we do not think that there are not enough participants in the studies.

Enabling Multi-devices. One of the big advantages of cloud storage is that one user can view and edit the same data in multiple environments. Similar benefits are expected for client-side encrypted cloud storage, but in that case, a mechanism is needed to distribute the user's keys to multiple environments securely. In the application model proposed in this paper, consideration of secure key distribution to multiple environments is not considered.

As a solution, it is possible to adopt the Key Registration model that was surveyed in the study by Bai et al. [11]. For example, we can have in mind a method of preparing a folder for storing a user's key in cloud storage and accessing the folder first to obtain a user's key when accessing from each environment. In this case, simply uploading the key to cloud storage does not keep the key secure, so it is necessary to protect the key. As the protection mechanism, use of a password derivation function that generates an encryption key using a password, use of biometric authentication as in the FIDO standard, and use of authentication by a hardware token can be considered.

7   Conclusion

In this paper, focusing on client-side data protection in cloud storage service, we propose an application for client-side encryption and secure utility function. The proposed application is applicable directly to existing cloud storage services and can achieve not only content encryption but also search, sort and sharing safely. In the user study using the prototype of the proposed application, it was shown that the usability degradation due to the performance degradation by applying the cryptographic technology was not seen, and it was shown that the proposed application could achieve a safe and usable cloud storage environment.

References

1. Apache lucene - index file formats. https://lucene.apache.org/core/3_0_3/fileformats.html
2. Architecture - dropbox business. https://www.dropbox.com/business/trust/security/architecture
3. Cryptomator: free cloud encryption for dropbox & others. https://cryptomator.org/
4. Encryption software to secure cloud files — boxcryptor. https://www.boxcryptor.com/en/
5. End-to-end encrypted cloud storage for businesses — tresorit. https://tresorit.com/
6. Evernote revisits privacy policy change — evernote — evernote blog. https://evernote.com/blog/evernote-revisits-privacy-policy-change/
7. Security - google cloud help. https://support.google.com/googlecloud/answer/6056693?hl=en
8. Spideroak secure software — spideroak. https://spideroak.com/
9. Acar, A., Aksu, H., Uluagac, A.S., Conti, M.: A survey on homomorphic encryption schemes: theory and implementation. ACM Comput. Surv. **51**(4), 79:1–79:35 (2018). https://doi.org/10.1145/3214303. http://doi.acm.org/10.1145/3214303
10. Agrawal, R., Kiernan, J., Srikant, R., Xu, Y.: Order preserving encryption for numeric data. In: Proceedings of the 2004 ACM SIGMOD International Conference on Management of Data, SIGMOD 2004, pp. 563–574. ACM, New York (2004). https://doi.org/10.1145/1007568.1007632. http://doi.acm.org/10.1145/1007568.1007632
11. Bai, W., Namara, M., Qian, Y., Kelley, P.G., Mazurek, M.L., Kim, D.: An inconvenient trust: user attitudes toward security and usability tradeoffs for key-directory encryption systems. In: Twelfth Symposium on Usable Privacy and Security (SOUPS 2016), pp. 113–130. USENIX Association, Denver (2016). https://www.usenix.org/conference/soups2016/technical-sessions/presentation/bai
12. Boldyreva, A., Chenette, N., Lee, Y., O'Neill, A.: Order-preserving symmetric encryption. In: Joux, A. (ed.) EUROCRYPT 2009. LNCS, vol. 5479, pp. 224–241. Springer, Heidelberg (2009). https://doi.org/10.1007/978-3-642-01001-9_13
13. Boneh, D., Di Crescenzo, G., Ostrovsky, R., Persiano, G.: Public key encryption with keyword search. In: Cachin, C., Camenisch, J.L. (eds.) EUROCRYPT 2004. LNCS, vol. 3027, pp. 506–522. Springer, Heidelberg (2004). https://doi.org/10.1007/978-3-540-24676-3_30

14. Boneh, D., Franklin, M.: Identity-based encryption from the weil pairing. In: Kilian, J. (ed.) CRYPTO 2001. LNCS, vol. 2139, pp. 213–229. Springer, Heidelberg (2001). https://doi.org/10.1007/3-540-44647-8_13
15. Bösch, C., Hartel, P., Jonker, W., Peter, A.: A survey of provably secure searchable encryption. ACM Comput. Surv. **47**(2), 18:1–18:51 (2014). https://doi.org/10.1145/2636328. http://doi.acm.org/10.1145/2636328
16. Cao, N., Wang, C., Li, M., Ren, K., Lou, W.: Privacy-preserving multi-keyword ranked search over encrypted cloud data. IEEE Trans. Parallel Distrib. Syst. **25**(1), 222–233 (2014). https://doi.org/10.1109/TPDS.2013.45
17. Curtmola, R., Garay, J., Kamara, S., Ostrovsky, R.: Searchable symmetric encryption: improved definitions and efficient constructions. In: Proceedings of the 13th ACM Conference on Computer and Communications Security, CCS 2006, pp. 79–88. ACM, New York (2006). https://doi.org/10.1145/1180405.1180417. http://doi.acm.org/10.1145/1180405.1180417
18. Erway, C.C., Küpçü, A., Papamanthou, C., Tamassia, R.: Dynamic provable data possession. ACM Trans. Inf. Syst. Secur. **17**(4), 15:1–15:29 (2015). https://doi.org/10.1145/2699909. http://doi.acm.org/10.1145/2699909
19. Fahl, S., Harbach, M., Muders, T., Smith, M.: Confidentiality as a service - usable security for the cloud. In: 2012 IEEE 11th International Conference on Trust, Security and Privacy in Computing and Communications, pp. 153–162, June 2012. https://doi.org/10.1109/TrustCom.2012.112
20. Fahl, S., Harbach, M., Muders, T., Smith, M., Sander, U.: Helping Johnny 2.0 to encrypt his Facebook conversations. In: Proceedings of the Eighth Symposium on Usable Privacy and Security, SOUPS 2012, pp. 11:1–11:17. ACM, New York (2012). https://doi.org/10.1145/2335356.2335371. http://doi.acm.org/10.1145/2335356.2335371
21. Garfinkel, S.L.: Enabling email confidentiality through the use of opportunistic encryption. In: Proceedings of the 2003 Annual National Conference on Digital Government Research, dg.o 2003, pp. 1–4. Digital Government Society of North America (2003). http://dl.acm.org/citation.cfm?id=1123196.1123245
22. Garfinkel, S.L., Margrave, D., Schiller, J.I., Nordlander, E., Miller, R.C.: How to make secure email easier to use. In: Proceedings of the SIGCHI Conference on Human Factors in Computing Systems, CHI 2005, pp. 701–710. ACM, New York (2005). https://doi.org/10.1145/1054972.1055069. http://doi.acm.org/10.1145/1054972.1055069
23. Garfinkel, S.L., Miller, R.C.: Johnny 2: a user test of key continuity management with s/mime and outlook express. In: Proceedings of the 2005 Symposium on Usable Privacy and Security, SOUPS 2005, pp. 13–24. ACM, New York (2005). https://doi.org/10.1145/1073001.1073003. http://doi.acm.org/10.1145/1073001.1073003
24. Garfinkel, S.L., Schiller, J.I., Nordlander, E., Margrave, D., Miller, R.C.: Views, reactions and impact of digitally-signed mail in e-commerce. In: Patrick, A.S., Yung, M. (eds.) FC 2005. LNCS, vol. 3570, pp. 188–202. Springer, Heidelberg (2005). https://doi.org/10.1007/11507840_18
25. Gentry, C.: Fully homomorphic encryption using ideal lattices. In: Proceedings of the Forty-first Annual ACM Symposium on Theory of Computing, STOC 2009, pp. 169–178. ACM, New York (2009). https://doi.org/10.1145/1536414.1536440. http://doi.acm.org/10.1145/1536414.1536440
26. Han, F., Qin, J., Hu, J.: Secure searches in the cloud: a survey. Future Gener. Comput. Syst. **62**, 66–75 (2016). https://doi.org/10.1016/j.future.2016.01.007. http://www.sciencedirect.com/science/article/pii/S0167739X16000091

27. Kamara, S., Lauter, K.: Cryptographic cloud storage. In: Sion, R., et al. (eds.) FC 2010. LNCS, vol. 6054, pp. 136–149. Springer, Heidelberg (2010). https://doi.org/10.1007/978-3-642-14992-4_13

28. Midorikawa, T., Tachikawa, A., Kanaoka, A.: Helping johnny to search: encrypted search on webmail system. In: 2018 13th Asia Joint Conference on Information Security (AsiaJCIS), pp. 47–53, August 2018. https://doi.org/10.1109/AsiaJCIS.2018.00017. http://doi.ieeecomputersociety.org/10.1109/AsiaJCIS.2018.00017

29. Nielsen, J., Landauer, T.K.: A mathematical model of the finding of usability problems. In: Proceedings of the INTERACT 1993 and CHI 1993 Conference on Human Factors in Computing Systems, CHI 1993, pp. 206–213. ACM, New York (1993). https://doi.org/10.1145/169059.169166. http://doi.acm.org/10.1145/169059.169166

30. Ogata, W., Koiwa, K., Kanaoka, A., Matsuo, S.: Toward practical searchable symmetric encryption. In: Sakiyama, K., Terada, M. (eds.) IWSEC 2013. LNCS, vol. 8231, pp. 151–167. Springer, Heidelberg (2013). https://doi.org/10.1007/978-3-642-41383-4_10

31. Poh, G.S., Chin, J.J., Yau, W.C., Choo, K.K.R., Mohamad, M.S.: Searchable symmetric encryption: designs and challenges. ACM Comput. Surv. **50**(3), 40:1–40:37 (2017). https://doi.org/10.1145/3064005. http://doi.acm.org/10.1145/3064005

32. Ruoti, S., et al.: "we're on the same page": a usability study of secure email using pairs of novice users. In: Proceedings of the 2016 CHI Conference on Human Factors in Computing Systems, CHI 2016, pp. 4298–4308. ACM, New York (2016). https://doi.org/10.1145/2858036.2858400. http://doi.acm.org/10.1145/2858036.2858400

33. Ruoti, S., Andersen, J., Hendershot, T., Zappala, D., Seamons, K.: Private webmail 2.0: simple and easy-to-use secure email. In: Proceedings of the 29th Annual Symposium on User Interface Software and Technology, UIST 2016, pp. 461–472. ACM, New York (2016). https://doi.org/10.1145/2984511.2984580. http://doi.acm.org/10.1145/2984511.2984580

34. Ruoti, S., Kim, N., Burgon, B., van der Horst, T., Seamons, K.: Confused johnny: when automatic encryption leads to confusion and mistakes. In: Proceedings of the Ninth Symposium on Usable Privacy and Security, SOUPS 2013, pp. 5:1–5:12. ACM, New York (2013). https://doi.org/10.1145/2501604.2501609. http://doi.acm.org/10.1145/2501604.2501609

35. Sheng, S., Broderick, L., Koranda, C.A., Hyland, J.J.: Why johnny still can't encrypt: evaluating the usability of email encryption software. In: Symposium On Usable Privacy and Security, pp. 3–4 (2006)

36. Whitten, A., Tygar, J.D.: Why johnny can't encrypt: a usability evaluation of PGP 5.0. In: Proceedings of the 8th Conference on USENIX Security Symposium - Volume 8, SSYM 1999, p. 14. USENIX Association, Berkeley (1999). http://dl.acm.org/citation.cfm?id=1251421.1251435

37. Xia, Z., Wang, X., Sun, X., Wang, Q.: A secure and dynamic multi-keyword ranked search scheme over encrypted cloud data. IEEE Trans. Parallel Distrib. Syst. **27**(2), 340–352 (2016). https://doi.org/10.1109/TPDS.2015.2401003

Time-Lapse Detection for Evolution of Trustworthy Network User Operation Behavior Using Bayesian Network

Yuhan Wang[1], Qian Yi[2(✉)], Shuping Yi[1], Jiajia Li[1], and Shiquan Xiong[1]

[1] Department of Industrial Engineering, Chongqing University, Chongqing 400044, China
{wangyuhan,yshuping,lijiajia,xiongshiquan}@cqu.edu.cn
[2] Department of Mechanical Engineering, Chongqing University, Chongqing 400044, China
yiqian@cqu.edu.cn

Abstract. In the environment of human-computer interaction of information systems, people are paying more attention to user identity authentication based on operation behaviors. Behavior science research shows that each user has a his/her own behavioral pattern that reflects the unique habits, and maintains stability over a period. As known, most of the previous research have explored the user's behavior using static authentication models. However, the user's behavior is evolutionary, even the same user will develop different behavioral tendencies under various times and conditions (job position change or promotion, business content change, increase in age, etc.), causing the difficulty of user authentication under the evolution of user's behavior. This paper proposes a method named time-lapse detection attempting to establish the authentication model based on the evolution of user's behavior. We obtained the log data of several years period of the information system of a publishing house. Firstly, we extracted the data of employees' early operation behaviors and the Bayesian network is used to identify a detection model. Next, the behavior data are divided into multiple test sets according to the time series, and multiple authentication models are carried out to observe the change of authentication accuracy over time. The result shows that, for employees with stable positions and business content, the characteristics of their behavior patterns will change when the number of interactions increases. Moreover, the consequences of the initial detection model fluctuate to different degrees, reducing the accuracy of authentication. Therefore, in future we need to grasp the rules of user behavior and continue to optimize the existing authentication methods of information systems.

Keywords: Time-lapse detection · Information system · Identity authentication · Operation behavior · Bayesian network

1 Introduction and Literature Review

With the rapid development of information age, computer networks have played a massive role in promoting social progress by improving the efficiency of business operations,

A. Moallem (Ed.): HCII 2020, LNCS 12210, pp. 671–682, 2020.
https://doi.org/10.1007/978-3-030-50309-3_45

improving management and decision-making, and enhancing corporate competitiveness. At the same time, people face many network securities issues in the process of using information systems, such as data theft, confidential information leakage, and network fraud. Although researchers have developed a variety of protection technologies and products, such as firewalls, intrusion detection, intrusion prevention, and isolation gatekeepers, user authentication is still a challenge for human computer interaction [1].

The abnormal behaviors of users, which can influence the regular operation of information systems, are significant threats to information systems [2, 3]. Therefore, scholars have carried out a lot of study on identity authentication based on user behaviors of information systems. Multiple studies show that users have unique and stable behavioral patterns that can be utilized to authenticate users in a certain period. However, the same person in different time and conditions will lead to distinct behavioral tendencies, and his behavior will evolve, these changes may affect the effectiveness of authentication.

1.1 Research on Network User Behaviors

The massive interactive behavior data generated by network users have the characteristics of substantial volume, fast speed and variety, and the traditional data analysis and processing methods are no longer applicable under the big data environment. From a macro perspective, the studies of network user behaviors are closely related to psychology, sociology, social psychology, anthropology and other disciplines. These studies mainly focus on the regularity of network user behaviors, to predict the behavior of users and realize the service purposes of economy and culture [4].

Researches on network user behavior are about the composition, characteristics and rules of network user behaviors. Network user behaviors are generated in the virtual space and have their own characteristics. The first is concealment. Information on the Internet exists in digital form, so users can modify the content and form of the information without leaving any traces during the data transmission process. The second characteristic is a more initiative and extensive involvement, which can fully reflect users' personality and subjective volition. Besides, the network behavior can be considered as a complex cyberspace, determining that the nature of network behavior is of diversity and can be regarded an accurate mirror of real-world behavior.

In the research of network user behavior, the user behavior of information systems is both the focus of the academic and industrial circles. In information systems, users can perform various file operations, network data transmission, and resource management. Researchers have carried out various analyses and researches and proposed user behavior analysis models represented by rational behavior theory [5], planned behavior theory [6], technology acceptance model [7], technology adoption and utilization integration theory [8], etc. Some researchers were inspired by behavioral and social psychology and proposed that human behaviors are not entirely rational, and users could be affected by irrational factors such as personal emotions, attitudes, and psychological perceptions during people's continued use of information systems. Burton-Jones proposed that the user operation behaviors of information systems are motivated by the work tasks assigned by the organization, which is compulsory and related to the scope of users' rights and responsibilities. These behaviors adapt dynamically at the organizational and individual levels. Furthermore, they could constitute a habit in the long-term use process [9].

1.2 Trusted Identity Detection

In the field of network security, users' behaviors can be divided into normal behaviors and abnormal behaviors (not necessarily intrusive behavior), or be divided into kindness behaviors and malicious behaviors. The analysis of network user behavior is generally based on network log mining, including the application of conventional models in certain aspects or the improvement of a specific algorithm [10]. Network user behavior is usually expressed in a vector manner. For an individual behavior with n attributes, it can be expressed as <attribute 1, attribute 2, ..., attribute n>, where n attributes represent n samples of the behavior point.

Generally, the detection process consists of two parts. The first is the training process, which trains historical information about legal user behaviors and establishes a regular behavior model of legitimate user. The second is the detection process. Current operational behavior is compared with regular operation behaviors to determine whether the user's behavior is illegal. If the current behavior deviates from the customary behavior, the current behavior can be considered illegal [11].

The conventional detection methods are based on time series, which record the ordered data generated by the phenomenon over time [12]. Time series contains a large amount of data, from which effective information and knowledge can be obtained. For example, Hosseini used time series records of user behaviors to measure the credibility of behaviors to identify abnormal users and protect the security of information systems [13]. Lane proposed a method based on the hidden Markov model to detect the user's abnormal operation. The advantages of these methods are high detection accuracy, low detection efficiency, and a large amount of calculation in training and detection [14].

Li Jiajia and Yi Shuping [15, 16], members of our research group, analyzed user behavioral differences in browsing and operation, used decision trees and random forests to implement user authentication, and discussed and analyzed the credibility of each interactive behavioral feature. Besides, Xu Mengyao proposed a user untrusted interaction behavior recognition method based on the Markov chain [17].

Researchers usually use the detection rate and false detection rate as the leading indicators to measure the performance of a detection method. The current authentication methods based on user behavior usually detect user behavior in a short period. It can't ensure the accuracy of the authentication for a long period.

1.3 Bayesian Network Detection and Applications

Anomaly detection based on user behavior is the main research direction in intrusion detection [18]. The user's operation sequence can reflect the characteristic attributes. Anomaly detection based on behavior sequence is the principal direction of user behavior abnormality detection.

The Bayesian network was first proposed by Judea Pearl in 1985. It is also called belief network or directed acyclic graph model. It is a means of applying probability statistics to complex areas for uncertainty reasoning and data analysis. It aims to simulate the uncertainty treatment of causality in human thinking. The foremost advantage is to guarantee the correctness of the reasoning results [19].

In the Bayesian network, let $G = (I, E)$ represent a directed acyclic graph (DAG), where I represents a set of all nodes in the graph, and E represents a set of directed connected line segments. Let $X = (Xi)(i \in I)$, be the random variable represented by a node i in the directed acyclic graph. The joint probability assignment of node X can be expressed as:

$$p(x) = \prod_{i \in I} p(x_i | x_{pa(i)})$$ (1)

The X is a Bayesian network relative to the directed acyclic graph G, where $pa\ (i)$ is the "parent" of node i. In addition, for any random variable, the joint probability can be obtained by multiplying the respective local conditional probability distributions:

$$p(x_1, \ldots, x_K) = p(x_K | x_1, \ldots, x_{K-1}) \ldots p(x_2 | x_1) p(x_1)$$ (2)

As shown below, here is a simple Bayesian network. Then, we have $p\ (a, b, c) = p\ (c\ |\ a, b)\ p\ (b\ |\ a)\ p\ (a)$ (Fig. 1).

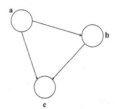

Fig. 1. The diagram of Bayesian network

Building a complete Bayesian network needs to accomplish two tasks, namely structure learning and parameter learning. The Bayesian network structure is achieved by structure learning, and the conditional probability table of nodes is obtained through parameter learning. The Bayesian network functions to perform inference, get the posterior probability of the variable to be queried and update the probability parameter of the network.

At present, Bayesian network, as a type of the machine learning technologies, is widely applied in various aspects. Inference algorithms are commonly used in Bayesian networks mainly include variable elimination, cluster tree propagation, etc. [20]. Researchers have established Bayesian network anomaly detection models in various fields and achieved great results in experiments [21].

Therefore, the purpose of this paper is to explore the impact of the evolution of user behavior on authentication. This study proposes a method named time-lapse detection, which tackles the issue of evolution of user's behavior in current trusted identity verification. From the comparison of authentication accuracy, we can explore whether the user's operating behavior has changed significantly in a long time.

The remainder of this paper is organized as follows: The method and procedure for how to establish a time-lapse detection in Sect. 2. The results is given in Sect. 3. Finally, the concluding remarks are addressed in Sect. 5.

2 Method and Procedure

This paper proposed a method named time-lapse detection by using the Bayesian network. In this study, we conducted a field survey of a publishing company in China and obtained the logs of user operations. Then, all data were divided into two parts by random sample extraction: training set (70%) and test set (30%). The Bayesian network was constructed to realize the identification based on users' behaviors. Here, we selected user A with complete log information, stable position and business content, and use his early operation behavior data to establish an identification model. We divided the subsequent operation behavior data into multiple test sets according to time-split, which was substituted into the original detection model to analyze and observe the change of identification accuracy over time. Subsequently, we randomly extracted the behavior data of user A in a few early years, established a new hybrid detection model, and put the following behavior data of user A into the model to observe the change in authentication accuracy. In order to secure the validity of our time-lapse detection, we performed repeated experiments on the data of other employees to avoid the influence of unforeseen factors. Lastly, we reveal whether the user's operation behavior changes from the results and discuss the impact of the evolution of trustworthy network user operation behavior on user detection.

2.1 Participants and Data Collection

The publishing house selected in this paper introduced an information system in 2008 and put it into use. The average number of working years of the subjects was 12.3 years, with an average of 7 hours of work per day. They worked an average of 7 hours a day and had spent more than ten years on average using the system. This paper is mainly for the staff of the logistics department of the publishing house, and all participants expressed their informed consent.

All the data in this article come from the log of the publishing house's system. These log data recorded the operating behaviors of all the employees in the information system at the time the system was put into use in 2008 to December 2017. Users' behaviors were recorded in a time series in the log record. During the period from 2008 to 2011, the information system was debugged several times, and the employees were also adapting to the operation. This article selects the system logs from 2012 to 2017 for research. The relevant original record table displayed in Chinese is shown below (Fig. 2).

2.2 Characteristic Extraction

According to the log record, these system log data include four types of characteristics related to bills, operations, time, and operators in users' operations. The specific characteristics and classifications are shown in the following table (Table 1).

During the feature analysis and selection process, this article found that there is a corresponding relationship between *Bill type* and *Enter function*. There is a corresponding relationship between *Clog code ID* and *Login time*, so we choose *Bill type* and the *Login time*. In addition, in the original log records, *Login time* and *Logout time* are reflected

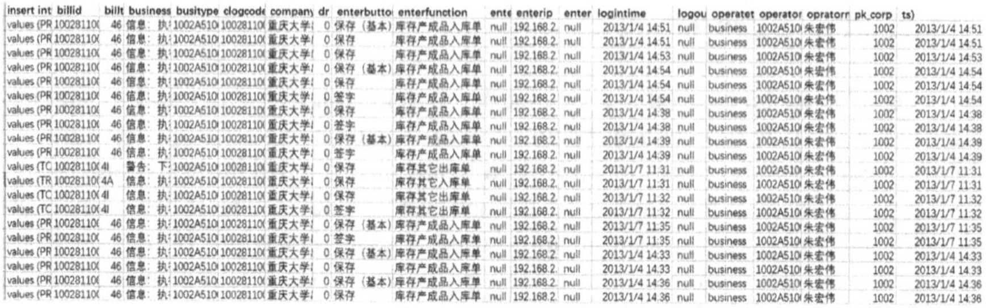

insert int	billid	billt	business	busitype	clogcode	company	dr	enterbutto	enterfunction	ente	enterip	enter	logintime	logou	operatet	operator	opratorr	pk_corp	ts)
values (PR	10028110(	46	信息：执	1002A510	10028110(	重庆大学	0	保存（基本）	库存产成品入库单	null	192.168.2.	null	2013/1/4 14:51	null	business	1002A510	朱宏伟	1002	2013/1/4 14:51
values (PR	10028110(	46	信息：执	1002A510	10028110(	重庆大学	0	保存	库存产成品入库单	null	192.168.2.	null	2013/1/4 14:51	null	business	1002A510	朱宏伟	1002	2013/1/4 14:51
values (PR	10028110(	46	信息：执	1002A510	10028110(	重庆大学	0	保存	库存产成品入库单	null	192.168.2.	null	2013/1/4 14:53	null	business	1002A510	朱宏伟	1002	2013/1/4 14:53
values (PR	10028110(	46	信息：执	1002A510	10028110(	重庆大学	0	保存（基本）	库存产成品入库单	null	192.168.2.	null	2013/1/4 14:54	null	business	1002A510	朱宏伟	1002	2013/1/4 14:54
values (PR	10028110(	46	信息：执	1002A510	10028110(	重庆大学	0	保存	库存产成品入库单	null	192.168.2.	null	2013/1/4 14:54	null	business	1002A510	朱宏伟	1002	2013/1/4 14:54
values (PR	10028110(	46	信息：执	1002A510	10028110(	重庆大学	0	签字	库存产成品入库单	null	192.168.2.	null	2013/1/4 14:54	null	business	1002A510	朱宏伟	1002	2013/1/4 14:54
values (PR	10028110(	46	信息：执	1002A510	10028110(	重庆大学	0	保存	库存产成品入库单	null	192.168.2.	null	2013/1/4 14:38	null	business	1002A510	朱宏伟	1002	2013/1/4 14:38
values (PR	10028110(	46	信息：执	1002A510	10028110(	重庆大学	0	签字	库存产成品入库单	null	192.168.2.	null	2013/1/4 14:38	null	business	1002A510	朱宏伟	1002	2013/1/4 14:38
values (PR	10028110(	46	信息：执	1002A510	10028110(	重庆大学	0	保存（基本）	库存产成品入库单	null	192.168.2.	null	2013/1/4 14:39	null	business	1002A510	朱宏伟	1002	2013/1/4 14:39
values (PR	10028110(	46	信息：执	1002A510	10028110(	重庆大学	0	签字	库存产成品入库单	null	192.168.2.	null	2013/1/4 14:39	null	business	1002A510	朱宏伟	1002	2013/1/4 14:39
values (TC	10028110(	4I	警告：下	1002A510	10028110(	重庆大学	0	保存	库存其它出库单	null	192.168.2.	null	2013/1/7 11:31	null	business	1002A510	朱宏伟	1002	2013/1/7 11:31
values (TR	10028110(	4A	信息：执	1002A510	10028110(	重庆大学	0	保存	库存其它入库单	null	192.168.2.	null	2013/1/7 11:31	null	business	1002A510	朱宏伟	1002	2013/1/7 11:31
values (TC	10028110(	4I	信息：执	1002A510	10028110(	重庆大学	0	保存	库存其它出库单	null	192.168.2.	null	2013/1/7 11:32	null	business	1002A510	朱宏伟	1002	2013/1/7 11:32
values (TC	10028110(	4I	信息：执	1002A510	10028110(	重庆大学	0	签字	库存其它出库单	null	192.168.2.	null	2013/1/7 11:32	null	business	1002A510	朱宏伟	1002	2013/1/7 11:32
values (PR	10028110(	46	信息：执	1002A510	10028110(	重庆大学	0	保存（基本）	库存产成品入库单	null	192.168.2.	null	2013/1/7 11:35	null	business	1002A510	朱宏伟	1002	2013/1/7 11:35
values (PR	10028110(	46	信息：执	1002A510	10028110(	重庆大学	0	签字	库存产成品入库单	null	192.168.2.	null	2013/1/7 11:35	null	business	1002A510	朱宏伟	1002	2013/1/7 11:35
values (PR	10028110(	46	信息：执	1002A510	10028110(	重庆大学	0	保存（基本）	库存产成品入库单	null	192.168.2.	null	2013/1/4 14:33	null	business	1002A510	朱宏伟	1002	2013/1/4 14:33
values (PR	10028110(	46	信息：执	1002A510	10028110(	重庆大学	0	保存	库存产成品入库单	null	192.168.2.	null	2013/1/4 14:33	null	business	1002A510	朱宏伟	1002	2013/1/4 14:33
values (PR	10028110(	46	信息：执	1002A510	10028110(	重庆大学	0	保存（基本）	库存产成品入库单	null	192.168.2.	null	2013/1/4 14:36	null	business	1002A510	朱宏伟	1002	2013/1/4 14:36
values (PR	10028110(	46	信息：执	1002A510	10028110(	重庆大学	0	保存	库存产成品入库单	null	192.168.2.	null	2013/1/4 14:36	null	business	1002A510	朱宏伟	1002	2013/1/4 14:36

Fig. 2. The relevant original Chinese record

Table 1. The characteristics of the log record

Company-related characteristics	Operation-related characteristics	Time-related characteristics	Individual basic characteristics
Bill code	Dr (delete or not)	Login time	Enter IP
Bill ID	Enter button	Logout time	Enter system
Bill type	Enter function	Ts	Operate type
Business log	Enter function code		Operate ID
Business type			Operator name
Company name			

in the form of "year-month-day-hour-minute-second". The information is very concentrated, and it is challenging to retain the complete information by directly assigning it. Therefore, this paper derives features from it and obtains features such as *Month, Day, Hour, Login S, and Logout S*. The feature selection used to build the model in this article is presented in the following table (Table 2).

Table 2. Selected characteristics

Characteristics	Instructions
Bill type	There are seven types of tickets, encoding them
Business type	There are 17 types of business operation, encoding them
Month	Encode the 12 months in turn
Day	Encode each day of the month
Nth day	It represents the days of the year, and there are 365 types
Hour	Dividing a day into 24 time periods, and encode each time period
Delta S	It represents the sum of all user operations on a ticket
Next bill type	Type of next ticket

An example serves to illustrate the significance of these characteristics. The operation record is (136,1,2,12,1,335,1,10,3), it indicates that the user operates the document with serial number 136, and the ticket type is 1 and the operation type is 2. This operation occurred on December 1st, the 335th day of the year, and the operation time was in the range of 8:00–9:00. The operation on the note continued for a total of about 150 s, the type of for the next set of operations is 3.

2.3 Detection Model Based on Bayesian Network

In machine learning, training models require a large amount of data, about 70% of the training set of the model is usually randomly selected from the experimental data, and the remaining 30% is used as the model's validation set.

This paper chooses to use a Bayesian network structure to build the model. It is necessary to determine the nodes and their dependencies. The five characteristics of *Bill type, Business type, Hour, Month,* and *Next Bill* were selected as the nodes of the Bayesian network to establish the Bayesian network structure. Because the range of the remaining time features is too small to calculate the probability distribution, or there is duplicate information, they are only used as the basis for ranking time series (Fig. 3).

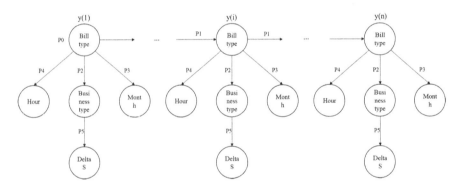

Fig. 3. The Bayesian network structure constructed by these characteristics

After the construction of the Bayesian network, the randomly extracted training set data is substituted into the calculation, and the detection model of user A is established to verify the test set data of user A and other users' data. The specific approach is to input the test set into the anomaly detection model and output the behavior probability (BP) of the test set. The threshold value in the test phase is the same as that in the test phase. When the test set's behavior probability BP $(n) \geq \lambda$, the abnormal detection model considers the behavior reasonable and does not respond. When BP$(n) < \lambda$, the user's behavior is deemed to be abnormal, and the exception is immediately reported.

2.4 Time-Lapse Detection

Among the staff of the logistics department of the publishing house, the user A is utilized the most frequently, and his position is stable for many years, and the business content is relatively stable. Therefore, this article selects the operation record of user A for modelling and testing. This article uses *Enter function* and *Enter button* to count the type and frequency of user A's business operations, as shown in the following figure (Figs. 4 and 5).

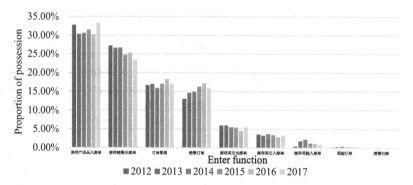

Fig. 4. Statistics on the business types (*Enter function*) of user A from 2012 to 2017

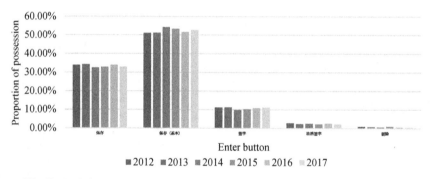

Fig. 5. Statistics on the business types (*Enter button*) of user A from 2012 to 2017

Then, establish a detection model for user A, and observe the validity of the detection model based on Bayesian network. This paper proposes a method named time-lapse detection. It establishes a detection model by selecting early user behavior data, to observe whether long-term user behavior data can be applied to the detection model and ensure the security of the information system for a long time. According to the time series, subsequent operation data are divided into multiple test sets, and identity authentication is performed one by one. Observe the change of accuracy over time, and compare the detection results to explore whether the user operation behavior has changed significantly.

We divided the log data of user A from 2013 to 2017 into monthly time-lapse test units. Then, the test sets were used for the built identification model. Next, we observe the changes in identification accuracy. Subsequently, operation data of user A in 2012 and 2013 were randomly extracted to establish a new hybrid detection model, and the operation data from 2014 to 2017 was substituted into the detection and observation the change in authentication accuracy. Finally, this study repeated experiments with other employees of the publishing house to rule out the influence of unforeseen factors.

3   Results

The results show that, when modeling with the user's operation data and setting the threshold (logarithmic probability) to −90, the average accuracy of authentication was 98.25%, and the recall rate was 99.65%. So, the model is effective for the detection (Figs. 6 and 7).

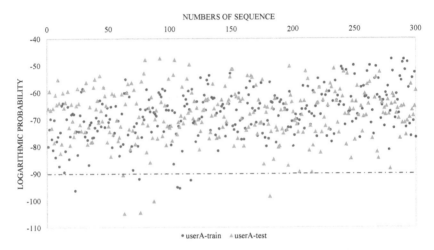

Fig. 6. Observation sequence probability set of training data

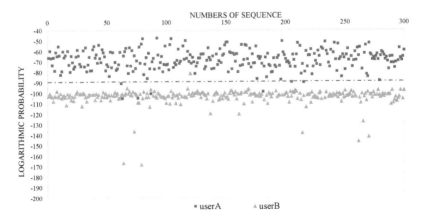

Fig. 7. Comparison of observation sequence probabilities between users A and B

When putting data of later years into the detection model with time-lapse, the lowest identification accuracy was only 68.57%, and the average identification accuracy was 87.96%. For the hybrid detection model with time-lapse, the average identification accuracy increased to 95.46%. Finally, repeated detection with data of other employees showed that the results were similar, and the accuracy of authentication fluctuated to different degrees (Figs. 8 and 9).

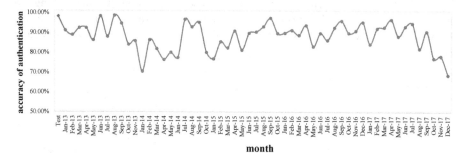

Fig. 8. Changes in accuracy of authentication under the first detection model

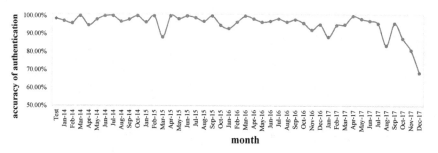

Fig. 9. Changes in accuracy of authentication under the second detection model

It can be observed that users have unique behavior patterns, which are relatively stable in a short period. However, expanding the time horizon for authentication, the operation behaviors of network users are evolutionary under the premise of stable business content. With the increase of the number of trusted interactions, some changes may take place in the physical, psychological, and social attributes of network users over time. This study shows that these changes will cause corresponding changes in the behavior characteristics of network users, which may affect the effects of detection models.

4   Discussion and Conclusion

Many pieces of research on authentication based on user behavior can guarantee accuracy and effectiveness, which is enough to ensure the security of information systems at a certain time. However, these studies did not consider that due to users' various subjective and objective reasons, there will be some gradual changes in the process of using the information system. These behaviors do not represent intrusion behaviors or abnormal behaviors. If the detection system misidentifies these behaviors as abnormal and issues warnings, it will affect the regular operation of the information system. Similarly, there will be some changes in the behavior of abnormal users. The detection system needs to be able to detect various real abnormal and intrusive behaviors to ensure the security and normal operation of the information system.

This paper proposes a method to maintain the long-term effectiveness of user behavior detection methods. First, the effects and potential problems of the current detection methods are discussed. Secondly, we use the Bayesian network to establish a detection model, verify the validity of the model, and then use the user's operation data from subsequent years to substitute the model for detection. The results show that the accuracy of authentication fluctuates to different degrees. Besides, this method is based on the division of periods, and it has a wide application range, which is not limited to any detection method and the detection object.

In future research, we will further consider the evolutionary mechanism of user behaviors from physiological, psychological, social identity, and other dimensions. We will also use more samples to prove the universality of the conclusion. Besides, we will attempt to optimize the detection model based on the rules of behavior evolution during the detection of trustworthy network user interactions.

Acknowledgment. This work was supported by the National Natural Science Foundation of China under Grant No. 71671020.

References

1. Zhao, G., Gong, Y.S., Wang, D.L.: Information security risk analysis model considering costs and factors relevance. J. Shenyang Univ. Technol. **37**(1), 69–74 (2015)
2. Pierrot, D., Harbi, N., Darmont, J.: Hybrid intrusion detection in information systems. In: International Conference on Information Science & Security. IEEE (2017)
3. Cheng, Y., Miao, Y.C., Tan, P.F., et al.: Research on mining and detection method of abnormal learning behavior. In: International Conference on Information System and Artificial Intelligence (ISAI). IEEE (2016)
4. Chen, L., Zhou, Y., Chiu, D.M.: A study of user behavior in online VoD services. Comput. Commun. **46**, 66–75 (2016)
5. Ajzen, I., Fishbein, M.: Attitude-behavior relations: a theoretical analysis and review of empirical research. Psychol. Bull. **84**(5), 888 (1977)
6. Ajzen, I.: The theory of planned behavior. Organ. Behav. Hum. Decis. Process. **50**(2), 179–211 (1991)
7. Davis, F.D.: Perceived usefulness, perceived ease of use, and user acceptance of information technology. MIS Q. **13**(3), 319–340 (1989)
8. Venkatesh, V., Morris, M.G., Davis, G.B., et al.: User acceptance of information technology: toward a unified view. MIS Q. 425–478 (2003)
9. Bhattacherjee, A.: Understanding information systems continuance: an expectation-confirmation mode. MIS Q. **25**(3), 351–370 (2001)
10. Amirkhanyan, A., Sapegin, A., Cheng F., et al.: Simulation user behavior on a security testbed using user behavior states graph. In: 8th International Conference on Security of Information and Networks (SIN 2015). ACM (2015)

11. Chandola, V., Banerjee, A., Kumar, V.: Anomaly detection: a survey. ACM Comput. Surv. **41**(3), 1–58 (2009)

12. Zhu, Z.: Change detection using landsat time series: a review of frequencies, preprocessing, algorithms, and applications. ISPRS J. Photogramm. Remote Sens. **130**, 370–384 (2017)

13. Hosseini, S.B., Shojaee, A., Agheli, N.: A new method for evaluating cloud computing user behavior trust. In: Information & Knowledge Technology. IEEE (2015)

14. Lane, T., Brodley, C.E.: An empirical study of two approaches to sequence learning for anomaly detection. Mach. Learn. **51**(1), 73–107 (2003)

15. Li, J.J., Yi, Q., Yi, S.P.: A user verification method based on differences of individual behavior via using random forest algorithm. In: 48th International Conference on Computers and Industrial Engineering (2018)

16. Yi, S.P., Li, J.J., Yi, Q.: Trustworthy interaction detection method in view of user behavior flow diagram. Control Decis. (2019). https://doi.org/10.13195/j.kzyjc.2018.1618

17. Xu, M., Yi, Q., Yi, S., Xiong, S.: An identification method of untrusted interactive behavior in ERP system based on Markov chain. In: Moallem, A. (ed.) HCII 2019. LNCS, vol. 11594, pp. 204–214. Springer, Cham (2019). https://doi.org/10.1007/978-3-030-22351-9_14

18. Burton-Jones, A., Detmar, W., Straub, J.: Reconceptualizing system usage: an approach and empirical test. Inf. Syst. Res. **17**(3), 228–247 (2007)

19. Tsamardinos, I.: The max-min hill-climbing Bayesian network structure learning algorithm. Mach. Learn. **65**, 31–78 (2006). https://doi.org/10.1007/s10994-006-6889-7

20. Bayar, N., Darmoul, S., Hajri-Gabouj, S.: Fault detection, diagnosis and recovery using artificial immune systems: a review. Eng. Appl. Artif. Intell. **46**, 43–57 (2015)

21. Lane, T.D.: Machine Learning Techniques for the Computer Security Domain of Anomaly Detection. Purdue University (2000)

Author Index